SPORTS MARKETING

Fourth
Edition

SPORTS MARKETING

A Strategic Perspective

Matthew D. Shank, Ph.D.

*Dean, School of Business Administration
and Professor of Marketing
University of Dayton*

PEARSON
Prentice
Hall

UPPER SADDLE RIVER, NEW JERSEY 07458

Library of Congress Cataloging-in-Publication Data

Shank, Matthew D.
  Sports marketing: a strategic perspective / Matthew D. Shank.
    p. cm.
  Includes bibliographical references and index.
  ISBN-13: 978-0-13-228535-3 (hardcover: alk. paper)
  ISBN-10: 0-13-228535-5 (hardcover: alk. paper)
  1. Sports—United States—Marketing. 2. Sports—Economic aspects—United States. I. Title.
GV716.S42 2009
796.06'98—dc22

2008005328

Editorial Director: Sally Yagan
AVP/Executive Editor: Melissa Sabella
Product Development Manager: Ashley Santora
Marketing Manager: Anne Howard
Marketing Assistant: Susan Osterlitz
Senior Managing Editor: Judy Leale
Associate Managing Editor: Suzanne DeWorken
Permissions Project Manager: Charles Morris
Senior Operations Specialist: Arnold Vila
Operations Specialist: Carol O'Rourke
Cover Design: Maureen Eide
Cover Illustration: Getty Images

Director, Image Resource Center: Melinda Patelli
Manager, Rights and Permissions: Zina Arabia
Manager, Visual Research: Beth Brenzel
Manager, Cover Visual Research & Permissions:
  Karen Sanatar
Image Permission Coordinator: Joanne Dippel
Composition: Integra Software Services Pvt. Ltd
Full-Service Project Management: Thistle Hill Publishing
  Services, LLC
Printer/Binder: Hamilton
Typeface: 10/12 TimesTen Roman

Credits and acknowledgments borrowed from other sources and reproduced, with permission, in this textbook appear on appropriate page within the text.

Microsoft® and Windows® are registered trademarks of the Microsoft Corporation in the U.S.A. and other countries. Screen shots and icons reprinted with permission from the Microsoft Corporation. This book is not sponsored or endorsed by or affiliated with the Microsoft Corporation.

Pearson Education LTD.
Pearson Education Singapore, Pte. Ltd
Pearson Education, Canada, Ltd
Pearson Education–Japan

Pearson Education Australia PTY, Limited
Pearson Education North Asia Ltd
Pearson Educación de Mexico, S.A. de C.V.
Pearson Education Malaysia, Pte. Ltd.

10 9 8 7
ISBN-13: 978-0-13-228535-3
ISBN-10:   0-13-228535-5

To my twins Grace and Olivia, Sports Stars in the Making

Brief Contents

Contents

Preface

OVERVIEW

One of the greatest challenges for sports marketers is trying to keep pace with the ever-changing, fast-paced environment of the sports world. Since the first edition of this text was published in 1999, amazing changes have taken place and challenges to sports marketers emerge daily. First, costs have been rising quickly. Athletes' salaries continue to escalate; for example, Alex Rodriguez recently renegotiated his contract and now earns an unprecedented $27.5 million per year over a ten-year contract, adding to the Yankees payroll, which was nearly $200 million in 2007. To pay for this, new stadiums and arenas have been built at a rapid pace. For instance, industry experts estimate that more than $2.1 billion is committed to various college football stadium construction projects from 2007 through 2010.

Each ticketholder will also pay more to attend the games in these plush new facilities. Ticket prices continue to increase and to drive the common fan out of the sport arena. For instance, the average seat price at an NBA game more than doubled from $22.52 in 1991 to $46 in 2006. But this may not be the largest problem in sports, as scandals emerge daily. For example, Barry Bonds, the Home Run King, has been indicted on perjury and obstruction of justice charges, Michael Vick has pled guilty to charges stemming from dogfighting, NBA referee Tim Donaghy allegedly bet on NBA games, including contests that he officiated, and the list goes on and on.

The one constant in this sea of change is the incredible appetite of consumers for sports. We get sports information on the Web, watch sports in high definition on network and cable TV, read about sports in the newspaper and sports magazines, talk to friends about sports, purchase sports merchandise, participate in sports (both fantasy and real), and attend sporting events in record numbers. The sports industry has experienced tremendous growth and is currently estimated to be a $350 billion industry in the United States. Moreover, the sports industry is flourishing around the globe. The expansion of the sports industry has triggered a number of important outcomes: More sports-related jobs are being created and more students are interested in careers in the sports industry. As student interest grows, demand for programs in sports administration and classes in sports marketing has also heightened.

In this book, we will discover the complex and diverse nature of sports marketing. Moreover, a framework will be presented to help explain and organize the strategic sports marketing process. Even if you are not a sports enthusiast, you should become excited about the unique application of marketing principles and processes to the sports industry.

WHY THIS BOOK?

Programs and courses in sports marketing are emerging at universities across the country. Surprisingly, few sports marketing textbooks exist and none is written from a strategic marketing perspective. In the first edition of this book, I sought to fill this void. The second edition represented an effort to improve the first edition and capitalize on its strengths. The third edition attempted to continuously improve the content and focus on the current relevant issues in sport marketing. My goals for the fourth edition are to provide:

- *A framework or conceptual model of the strategic marketing process that can be applied to the sports industry.* The contingency framework is presented as a tool for organizing the many elements that influence the strategic sports marketing process and recognizes the unpredictable nature of the sports industry. In addition, the contingency framework allows us to explore complex relationships between the elements of sports marketing.

- *A more concise and focused approached to understanding strategic sports marketing.* After several editions and many comments from faculty, the length of the text has been significantly reduced. Using the "less is more" philosophy, several chapters have been eliminated without damaging the spirit of the text. This will allow faculty and students to spend more time on the most relevant and key issues.

- *An appreciation for the growing emphasis on the globalization of sport.* As such, international sport topics are integrated throughout the text, and are also highlighted in chapters in the "Spotlight on International Sports Marketing" boxes.

- *An examination of current research in the area of sports marketing.* The study of sports marketing is still in its relative infancy and academic research of interest to sports marketers (e.g., sports sponsorships, using athletes as endorsers, and segmenting the sports market) has grown exponentially since the first edition of this text. It is important that students learn how academic research is applied to the "real world" of sports marketing.

- *An awareness of the many job opportunities available in the sports industry.* The one common denominator for all sports business students is the desire to secure their first job after graduation and start their careers. In this edition, we focus on several successful sports marketers who provide perspective about how and why they got started in the industry. Also, this edition retains an appendix devoted to careers in sports marketing.

- *A balanced treatment of all aspects of sports marketing at all levels.* This book attempts to capture the diverse and rich nature of sporting marketing by covering the marketing of athletes, teams, leagues, and special events. Although it is tempting to discuss only "major league" sports because of their intense media coverage, the book explores different sports (e.g., cricket and women's football) and different levels of competition (e.g., collegiate and recreational). Moreover, the book discusses the activities involved in marketing to participants of sports—another area of interest to sports marketers.

- *An introduction of the concepts and theories unique to sports marketing and a review of the basic principles of marketing in the context of sports.* Even though many of the terms and core concepts are repetitive, they often take on different meanings in the context of sports marketing. Consider the term *sports involvement*. Although you probably recognize the term *product involvement* from your principles of marketing and/or consumer behavior class, what is sports involvement? Is involvement with sports based on participation or watching sports? Is involvement with sports deeper and more enduring than it is for other products that we consume? How can sports marketers apply sports involvement to develop a strategic marketing plan? As you can see, the core marketing concept of involvement in the context of sports presents a whole new set of interesting questions and a more comprehensive understanding of sports marketing.

- *Comprehensive coverage of the functions of sports marketing.* While some texts focus on specialized activities in sports marketing, such as sports media, this book seeks to cover all the relevant issues in designing an integrated marketing strategy. Extensive treatment is given to understanding consumers as spectators and participants. In addition to planning the sports marketing mix (product, price, promotion, and place), we will examine the execution and evaluation of the planning process.

GROUND RULES

This text is organized into four distinct but interrelated parts. Each part represents an important component in the strategic sports marketing process.

Part I: Contingency Framework for Strategic Sports Marketing

In Chapter 1, we introduce sports marketing and illustrate the breadth of the field. In addition, we will take a look at the unique nature of sports products and the sports marketing mix. Chapter 2 presents the contingency framework for strategic sports marketing. This chapter also highlights the impact of the internal and external contingencies on the strategic sports marketing process. Internal contingencies such as the sports organization's mission and organizational culture are considered, as are external contingencies like competition, the economy, and technology.

Part II: Planning for Market Selection Decisions

Chapter 3 presents an overview of the tools used to understand sports consumers—both participants and spectators. Each step in the marketing research process is discussed, illustrating how information can be gathered to aid in strategic decision making. In Chapters 4 and 5, respectively, participants and consumers of sport are studied. Chapter 4 examines the psychological and sociological factors that influence our participation in sport, while Chapter 5 looks at spectator issues such as fan motivation. In addition, we will discuss the relationship between the participant and spectator markets. Chapter 6 explores the market selection decisions of segmentation, targeting, and positioning in the context of sport.

Part III: Planning the Sports Marketing Mix

Chapters 7 through 12 explain the sports marketing mix, the core of the strategic marketing process. Chapters 7 and 8 cover sports product issues such as brand loyalty, licensing, and the new product development process. Chapter 9 introduces the basic promotion concepts, and Chapter 10 gives a detailed description of the promotion mix elements of advertising, public relations, personal selling, and sales promotions. Chapter 11, the final chapter on promotion, is devoted to designing a sports sponsorship program. Chapter 12 tackles the basic concepts of pricing.

Part IV: Implementing and Controlling the Strategic Sports Marketing Process

While the previous sections have focused on the planning efforts of the strategic marketing process, Part IV focuses on the implementation and control phases of the strategic marketing process. Chapter 13 begins with a discussion of how sports organizations implement their marketing plans. In this chapter, we see how factors such as communication, motivation, and budgeting all play a role in executing the strategic plan. We also examine how sports marketers monitor and evaluate the strategic plans after they have been implemented. Specifically, three forms of control (process, planning assumption, and contingency) are considered.

PEDAGOGICAL ADVANTAGES OF *SPORTS MARKETING*

To help students learn about sports marketing and make this book more enjoyable to read, the following features have been retained from previous editions of *Sports Marketing: A Strategic Perspective.*

- Text organized and written around the contingency framework for strategic sports marketing
- Chapters incorporating global issues in sport and how they affect sports marketing
- Sports Marketing Hall of Fame boxes featuring pioneers in the field integrated throughout the text
- Text incorporates up-to-date research in the field of sports marketing
- Internet exercises at the end of each chapter
- Experiential exercises at the end of each chapter that ask you to apply the basic sports marketing concepts and perform mini-research projects
- Vignettes throughout the text to illustrate core concepts and make the material come to life
- Detailed glossary of sports marketing terms
- Use of ads, Internet screen captures, and photos to illustrate core concepts of sports marketing
- Appendix describing careers in sports marketing
- Appendix presenting Internet addresses of interest to sports marketers

ENHANCEMENTS TO THE FOURTH EDITION

While I have attempted to retain the strengths of the previous editions of *Sports Marketing: A Strategic Perspective*, I also hoped to improve the fourth edition based on the comments of reviewers, faculty who adopted the text, and most importantly, students who have used the book. New additions include the following features:

- Up-to-date examples illustrate the core sports marketing concepts in the text. As mentioned previously, the sports industry is rapidly changing and nearly 80 percent of the examples introduced in the third edition are now obsolete. It was my goal to find new, relevant examples to illustrate key points in every chapter of the text. These new examples are meant to keep the book fresh and the students engaged.
- New advertisements and illustrations have been incorporated into each chapter to highlight key sports marketing concepts and make the material more relevant for students. These ads and photos are examples of sports marketing principles that have been put into practice and bring the material in the text "to life."
- New spotlights on careers in sports marketing introduce students to successful sports marketers and their jobs.
- The spotlights on international sports marketing have been revised and updated for the fourth edition to highlight this key area of growth in the sports industry.

- New screen captures of relevant Web sites illustrate key concepts. Because the Internet is now playing such a large role in sports marketing, screen captures from various Web sites have been incorporated throughout the text to bring the material to life for students. In addition, Internet exercises appear at the end of each chapter, and discussions of the Internet as an emerging tool for sports marketers appear throughout.
- Since the writing of the third edition, the number of Web sites devoted to sports business has grown substantially. The fourth edition includes the latest Web sites of interest to sports marketers and the sites that have withstood the test of "Web" time.
- New spotlights on ethical issues are integrated throughout the text. Hopefully, this will generate lively discussion in the classroom and make students more aware of the ethical issues that they will confront in the workplace.
- The number of chapters has been significantly reduced, from 16 to 13 chapters. This reduction in length should add focus for faculty and students, allowing more time to learn and discuss the most significant concepts and their applications.

INSTRUCTIONAL SUPPORT

Various teaching supplements are available to accompany this textbook. They consist of an Instructor's Manual, Test Item File, and PowerPoint presentation. These items may be found online only at www.pearsonhighered.com, the home page for Prentice Hall's online Instructor's Resource Center (IRC). In order to access these materials, please follow the instructions below:

- Go to www.pearsonhighered.com
- Click on Educators
- Use the "Search our Catalog" field across the top of the page to search for this textbook
- Once you locate the book's catalog page, locate the Resources tab and click on it.
- Click on any download link. You will then be taken to a login page. Follow the instructions to register if you have not already done so. Once your status as an instructor has been validated (allow 24–48 hours), you will receive an e-mail message confirming your username and password. You only need to register once to access any Prentice Hall instructor resource.

COURSESMART

CourseSmart is an exciting new *choice* for students looking to save money. As an alternative to purchasing the print textbook, students can purchase an electronic version of the same content and save money off the suggested list price of the print text. With a CourseSmart etextbook, students can search the text, make notes online, print out reading assignments that incorporate lecture notes, and bookmark important passages for later review. For more information, or to purchase access to the CourseSmart eTextbook, visit www.coursesmart.com.

ACKNOWLEDGMENTS

The new edition of any textbook is a challenge. In fact, much more of a challenge than people think. Typically colleagues joke that a new edition just means changing dates and examples. Nothing could be farther from the truth, and the fourth edition posed significant professional and personal hurdles and opportunities. On the professional side, the fourth edition of *Sports Marketing: A Strategic Perspective* is the most significant revision of the text since its inception. Chapters have been eliminated and difficult decisions were made on what material would make the grade. On the personal side, my twin daughters, Grace and Olivia, were born in the midst of the revision, adding new and welcome meaning to the term *time management*. Before going any further, I have to thank my wife Lynne for her patience and support.

Even though this is a sole authored textbook, the project could never have been completed without the expertise and encouragement of many others. Although there are countless people to thank, I was greatly assisted by the thoughtful reviews that undoubtedly improved the fourth edition of the text. These reviewers include:

Ronald Borrieci, *University of Central Florida*
James Cannon, *University of South Alabama*
Renee Florsheim, *Loyola Marymount University*
Patricia Kennedy, *University of Nebraska, Lincoln*
Stephen McKelvey, J.D., *University of Massachusetts, Amherst*
Michael Smucker, *Texas Tech University*

I also wish to thank the reviewers who reviewed and helped shape the first three editions. These colleagues include:

Ketra Armstrong, *The Ohio State University*
Chris Cakebread, *Boston University*
Joseph Cronin, *Florida State University*
Pat Gavin, *New Mexico State University*
Lynn Kahle, *University of Oregon*
Jerry Lee Goen, *Oklahoma Baptist University*
Deborah Lester, *Kennesaw State University*
Ann Mayo, *Seton Hall University*
David Moore, *University of Michigan*
Gregory Pickett, *Clemson University*
Joseph Terrian, *Marquette University*
Lou Turley, *Western Kentucky University*
Kathleen Davis, *Florida Atlantic University*
Robert E. Baker, *Ashland University*
Susan Logan Nelson, *University of North Dakota*
Mark McDonald, *University of Massachusetts, Amherst*
Eddie Easley, *Wake Forest University*

In addition to these formal reviews, I am especially grateful to the informal comments that I received from many of you who adopted the first three editions and provided me with feedback. I have tried to incorporate all of your suggestions and comments.

I am very grateful to many of my colleagues at Northern Kentucky University (NKU) who have supported me throughout this process. In addition to my colleagues at NKU, thanks go to all of my students at NKU who have helped fuel my interest in sports marketing. I'd like to thank all of those sports business students who have used the book at NKU (and other universities) and pointed out their likes and dislikes. A special thanks to Kim Patterson for her assistance with securing permissions for the text.

A number of organizations have been very helpful in providing permission to use ads and articles throughout the text. Thanks goes out to all the individuals within these organizations who have made this book more meaningful and readable for students.

Finally, I am indebted to the Prentice Hall team for their encouragement and making the fourth edition a reality. Special thanks go to Ashley Santora and Suzanne DeWorken of Prentice Hall. Last, but certainly not least, thank you to Renata Butera of Thistle Hill Publishing for her superb project management.

PART

I

CONTINGENCY FRAMEWORK FOR STRATEGIC SPORTS MARKETING

1

EMERGENCE OF SPORTS MARKETING

After completing this chapter, you should be able to:

■ Define sports marketing and discuss how the sports industry is related to the entertainment industry.

■ Describe a marketing orientation and how the sports industry can use a marketing orientation.

■ Examine the growth of the sports industry.

■ Discuss the simplified model of the consumer–supplier relationship in the sports industry.

■ Explain the different types of sports consumers.

■ Define sports products and discuss the various types of sports products.

■ Understand the different producers and intermediaries in the simplified model of the consumer–supplier relationship in the sports industry.

■ Discuss the elements in the sports marketing mix.

■ Explain the exchange process and why it is important to sports marketers.

■ Outline the elements of the strategic sports marketing process.

Mary is a typical "soccer mom." At the moment, she is trying to determine how to persuade the local dry cleaner to provide uniforms for her daughter's Catholic Youth Organization soccer team.

George is the president of the local Chamber of Commerce. The 10-year plan for the metropolitan area calls for developing four new sporting events that will draw local support while providing national visibility for this growing metropolitan area.

Sam is an events coordinator for the local 10K road race, which is an annual fund raiser for fighting lung disease. He is faced with the difficult task of trying to determine how much to charge for the event to maximize participation and proceeds for charity.

Ramiz is the athletic director for State U. In recent years, the men's basketball team has done well in postseason play; therefore, ESPN has offered to broadcast several games this season. Unfortunately, three of the games will have to be played at 10 P.M. local time to accommodate the broadcaster's schedule. Ramiz is concerned about the effect this will have on season ticket holders

Spaulding's New Offical NBA Game Ball is just one example of Sports Marketing.
Source: Spaulding

because two of the games are on weeknights. He knows that the last athletic director was fired because the local fans and boosters believed that he was not sensitive to their concerns.

WHAT IS SPORTS MARKETING?

Many people mistakenly think of sports marketing as promotions or sports agents saying, "Show me the money." As the previous examples show, sports marketing is more complex and dynamic. **Sports marketing** is "the specific application of marketing principles and processes to sports products and to the marketing of nonsports products through association with sport."

Mary, the soccer mom, is trying to secure a sponsorship; that is, she needs to convince the local dry cleaner that they will enjoy a benefit by associating their service (dry cleaning) with a children's soccer team.

As president of the Chamber of Commerce, George needs to determine which sports products will best satisfy his local customers' needs for sports entertainment while marketing the city to a larger and remote audience.

In marketing terms, Sam is trying to decide on the best pricing strategy for his sporting event.

Finally, Ramiz is faced with the challenge of balancing the needs of two market segments for his team's products. As you can see, each marketing challenge is complex and requires careful planning.

To succeed in sports marketing one needs to understand both the sports industry and the specific application of marketing principles and processes to sports contexts. In the next section, we introduce you to the sports industry. Throughout this book, we continue to elaborate on ways in which the unique characteristics of this industry complicate strategic marketing decisions. After discussing the sports industry, we review basic marketing principles and processes with an emphasis on how these principles and processes must be adapted to the sports context.

UNDERSTANDING THE SPORTS INDUSTRY

Sport as Entertainment

Webster's defines **sport** as "a source of diversion or a physical activity engaged in for pleasure." Sport takes us away from our daily routine and gives us pleasure. Interestingly, "entertainment" is also defined as something diverting or engaging. Regardless of whether we are watching a new movie, listening to a concert, or attending an equally stirring performance by Dwayne Wade, we are being entertained.

Most consumers view movies, plays, theatre, opera, or concerts as closely related forms of entertainment. Yet, for many of us, sport is different. One important way in which sport differs from other common entertainment forms is that sport is spontaneous. A play has a script and a concert has a program, but the action that entertains us in sport is spontaneous and uncontrolled by those who participate in the event. When we go to a comedic movie, we expect to laugh, and when we go to a horror movie, we expect to be scared even before we pay our money. But the emotions we may feel when watching a sporting event are hard to determine. If it is a close contest and our team wins, we may feel excitement and joy. But if it is a boring event and our team loses, the entertainment *benefit* we receive is quite different. Because of its spontaneous nature, sport producers face a host of challenges that are different from those faced by most entertainment providers.

Nonetheless, successful sport organizations realize the threat of competition from other forms of entertainment. They have broadened the scope of their businesses, seeing themselves as providing "entertainment." The emphasis on promotional events and stadium attractions that surround athletic events is evidence of this emerging entertainment orientation. Consider the NBA All-Star Game. What used to be a simple competition between the best players of the Western Conference and the best players of the Eastern Conference has turned into an entertainment extravaganza. The event (not just a game any more) lasts four days and includes slam-dunk contests, a rookie game, concerts, a 3-point shooting competition, and plenty of other events designed to promote the NBA.[1] In 1982, the league created a separate division, NBA Entertainment, to focus on NBA-centered TV and movie programming. NBA TV has created original programming featuring shows like *NBA Player Nation, Real Playoffs, Insiders, Virtual GM,* and *Hardwood Classics*. As Alan Brew, a corporate identity specialist at Addison, a branding and communication firm, states, "The line between sport and entertainment has become nearly nonexistent."[2]

Of course, one of the most highly visible examples of "sporttainment" is the WWE or World Wrestling Entertainment. For the past two decades, the WWE has managed to build a billion-dollar empire and posted revenue of $400 million in fiscal year 2006, a nearly 11 percent gain after a recent history of fluctuating sales. Live and televised entertainment accounted for 73 percent of those sales, followed by consumer products (22 percent), digital media (5 percent), and a new brand extension called WWE Films. Vince McMahon, the founder and chairman, has been called the P. T. Barnum of our time.

Another exciting new development in the sports/entertainment industry is the Ultimate Sports Resort. The resort, being built in the entertainment capital of

SPOTLIGHT ON INTERNATIONAL SPORTS MARKETING

NFL Comes to Big Screen in Mexico

Fans clutched beer, hot dogs and tickets for stadium-style seats. They were moments away from a clash between the Carolina Panthers and the Tampa Bay Buccaneers—all that was missing were the teams. Thanks to broadcaster ESPN, they would be along in a second—on a giant 26-foot by 65-foot projection screen.

The recent Monday Night Football game, shown live in a movie theater here, was as close as it gets to sitting in a stadium without actually being there. It came as part of a new push by the National Football League to promote itself in Latin America, where football is considered an up-and-coming sport but lags behind the other fútbol, Spanish for soccer. Last year, more than 103,467 people packed Mexico City's Aztec Stadium to watch the Arizona Cardinals and the San Francisco 49ers. The crowd was the biggest ever to witness a regular season game, according to the NFL, leaving little doubt of the potential for football in Mexico.

The theater shows here have proven to be a way to fill hundreds of seats that, on notoriously slow Monday nights, likely would have been empty for the evening. NFL and ESPN banners hang from the walls. Below the screen, stands are set up for selling food, drinks and team clothing, such as caps and shirts. There's even a booth to apply for a credit card.

"I have loved the NFL for years," said Héctor Jácome, a 19-year-old student. You can't compare watching the game at home or in a bar to seeing it at the theater, he said. "The sound is better, the screen is bigger—it is the intensity," Jácome said. There were no commercials. Downtime was filled with clips from classic football games or bloopers. There were cheers and laughs, especially for fumbles and a report on Tampa Bay quarterback Bruce Gradkowski's ritual of vomiting before taking the field.

Many fans seemed to be indifferent about who won, but they enjoyed watching the play, even if the commentator noted the teams were "equally inept." Halfway through the season, officials with Grupo Cinemex said they had sold more than 10,000 tickets among the five Mexico City theaters where the Monday night games are shown.

"This is the first time we have had a live event in a movie theater," said Claudio Sánchez, marketing director for Cinemex, the nation's largest chain of theaters. The theaters have been at least 90 percent full for the games, and extra salons have had to be opened up to accommodate the audiences for longtime Mexico favorites, such as the Dallas Cowboys, he said. "It has been a success so far," said Geraldine González Soberanes of NFL Mexico. González said the Mexico City showings are a pilot program and that they could spread. For right now, they are limited to Mexico City and only Monday Night Football.

Source: Dane Schiller, http://www.mysanantonio.com/news/mexico/stories/MYSA120706.17A.NFLMexico. 2d71d41.html.

the world, Las Vegas, is estimated to cost more than $5 billion. The 17 million sq. ft. complex is devoted to everything that is sports and will include 10 sports venues featuring a 26,000-seat main arena, a casino, and a 5,000+ room hotel.[3]

The sports entertainment phenomenon is also sweeping the globe, as the accompanying article suggests.

Organizations that have not recognized how sport and entertainment relate are said to suffer from marketing myopia. Coined by Theodore Levitt, **marketing myopia** is described as the practice of defining a business in terms of goods and services rather than in terms of the benefits sought by customers. Sports organizations can eliminate marketing myopia by focusing on meeting the needs of consumers rather than on producing and selling sports products.

A Marketing Orientation

The emphasis on satisfying consumers' wants and needs is everywhere in today's marketplace. Most successful organizations concentrate on understanding the consumer and providing a sports product that meets consumers' needs while achieving the organization's objectives. This way of doing business is called a **marketing orientation.**

Marketing-oriented organizations practice the marketing concept that organizational goals and objectives will be reached if customer needs are satisfied. Organizations employing a marketing orientation focus on understanding customer preferences and meeting these preferences through the coordinated use of marketing. An organization is marketing oriented when it engages in the following activities.[4]

- *Intelligence generation*—analyzing and anticipating consumer demand, monitoring the external environment, and coordinating the data collected
- *Intelligence dissemination*—sharing the information gathered in the intelligence stage
- *Responsiveness*—acting on the information gathered to make market decisions such as designing new products and services and developing promotions that appeal to consumers

Using the previous criteria (intelligence generation, intelligence dissemination, and responsiveness), one study examined the marketing orientation of minor league baseball franchises.[5] Results of the study indicate that minor league baseball franchises do not have a marketing orientation and that they need to become more consumer focused. Although the study suggests that minor league baseball franchises have not moved toward a marketing orientation, more and more organizations are seeing the virtue of this philosophy, as the accompanying article suggests.

Fan Friendly Minor League Ballparks a Fun Destination

Sitting at picnic table above the ballpark's left field wall, Susan Schaffer munched on sweet corn and a chocolate chip cookie. Her five boys stood along the fence hoping to catch a home run ball and cheering on the minor league's Toledo Mud Hens. "The seats are cheap enough that it's one of the few activities we can do as a family without going broke," said Schaffer, of Toledo. "It's just a good time."

A building boom over the last decade has turned drab minor league ballparks into showplaces of America's pastime. Combining brick facades and architecture that blends the ballparks into their urban settings, they are a far cry from their concrete and steel predecessors. Many have the same fan-friendly features found in the major leagues without the high prices. And combined with nearby attractions, a trip to the ballpark can be part of a perfect getaway.

Oklahoma City's ballpark is the anchor of the town's entertainment district. Louisville Slugger Field in Kentucky is a short trolley ride from the bat maker's museum. And Brooklyn's KeySpan Park is steps from New York's famed Coney Island boardwalk. "When it's done right, you can make a weekend out of it," said Charlie O'Reilly, of Rutherford, N.J., a baseball fan who has visited more than 300 ballparks.

Tickets at minor league parks average about $9 although food and drink prices are sometimes more in line with those at most major league games. A number of new parks have playgrounds or grassy areas where the kids can play if they get antsy. Movies such as *Bull Durham* and the season-ending major league baseball strike in 1994 have helped renew interest in the minors, O'Reilly said.

So have the new urban ballparks. Among the best are those nestled into downtowns and close to other attractions. Auto Zone Park in Memphis, Tenn., is steps from the renowned Peabody Hotel and two blocks from the music clubs on Beale Street. The ballpark serves up barbecue nachos with pulled pork from a nearby rib joint. The smell of grilling ribs sometimes makes it way into the seats, said Kyle Parkinson, a spokesman for the Memphis Redbirds.

AT&T Bricktown Ballpark, home of the Oklahoma Redhawks, sits next to a canal where visitors can ride a water taxi. There's also plenty of shopping, outdoor dining, and nightclubs. "The whole neighborhood has become a destination," O'Reilly said. Louisville Slugger Field is close to not only the baseball bat museum but also the Fourth Street Live entertainment district, featuring a comedy club, music clubs, and a Hard Rock Cafe.

(Continued)

(*Continued*)

"People just pour over there after the game," said Louisville Bats spokesman Svend Jansen. "Most of the people who come here aren't coming to see the players. It's the attractions, the promotions."

Toledo's Fifth Third Field has picnic tables beyond the outfield and a view of the downtown skyline from most seats. The view surprises most out-of-towners, who don't expect to see skyscrapers in a midsize city, said Joe Napoli, general manager of the Mud Hens. Next to the stadium is a new Tony Packo's restaurant that serves up Hungarian hot dogs made famous by Toledo native Jamie Farr on television's *M-A-S-H*. The baseball-themed eatery has ballpark seats in its lobby. Jeff Parthum, of Detroit, plans a two-day trip with his family to Toledo for a day at the ballpark and the zoo in late July. "My son is an absolute baseball nut," he said.

Two years ago, the team surveyed fans and found it had visitors from every state except Hawaii.

"You would be surprised at how many people actually do plan to see different ballparks on a driving vacation. I hear from them all year round," said Joe Mock, who runs a Web site called http://www.baseballparks.com and has traveled to 42 parks just this year. Among his favorites are The Dell Diamond in Round Rock, Texas; FirstEnergy Stadium in Reading, Pa.; Isotopes Park in Albuquerque, N.M.

He also was impressed with West End Field in Greenville, S.C., which opened this season. The ballpark is a mini-version of Boston's Fenway Park and is an anchor of the revitalized neighborhood now filled with art galleries and restaurants. "It's just fantastic how this ballpark is integrated into the area," Mock said.

Some ballparks are worth visiting for the view alone. All three minor league parks in Utah's Salt Lake City, Ogden, and Orem have stunning views of the Wasatch Mountains. The Richmond County Bank Ballpark, home of the Staten Island Yankees, overlooks New York harbor, the Statue of Liberty, and lower Manhattan. Getting there can be half the fun as it's near the Staten Island ferry.

The Atlantic Ocean and Coney Island are the backdrop at Brooklyn Cyclones games. Fans making a trip to the game can add a stop at Nathan's Famous for a hot dog or a ride on the Cyclone roller coaster. There's also the beach and the New York Aquarium. "A lot of people make a full day of it," said Dave Campanaro, a spokesman for the team. "Everything is within walking distance." Plus, the $14 seats behind home plate for weekend games are still cheaper than upper deck tickets at Yankee Stadium. Outfield bleacher seats are $7. "It's such an inexpensive way to have a great time even if you don't love baseball," Campanaro said.

Source: John Seewer, "Fan Friendly Minor League Ballparks a Fun Destination," Associated Press, July 11, 2006. All rights reserved.

Growth of the Sports Industry

Sport has become one of the most important and universal institutions in our society. It is estimated that the sports industry generates over $200 billion dollars a year. This total is based on a number of diverse areas within the industry including gambling, advertising, sponsorships, and so on. As ESPN founder Bill Rasmussen points out, "The games are better, and, well, the athletes are just amazing and it all happens 24 hours a day. America's sports fans are insatiable."[6] For better or worse, sports are everywhere. The size of sport and the sports industry can be measured in different ways. Let us look at the industry in terms of attendance, media coverage, employment, and the global market.

Attendance

Not only does sport spawn legions of "soccer moms and dads" who faithfully attend youth sport events, but also for the past several years, fans have been flocking to major league sports in record numbers. The NFL experienced another record-setting year in paid attendance in 2006 with over 22 million fans, an increase of more than 400,000 (407,616) over the previous record total in 2005. It marked the first time in NFL history that the 22-million paid attendance mark was reached.[7] "We once again thank the most passionate fans in sports for their tremendous support this year and every year," said NFL commissioner Roger Goodell. "Our clubs and players are very appreciative of the large and enthusiastic crowds that make NFL games so special."

The number of tickets sold represents paid attendance at more than 90 percent of stadium capacity, and local TV blackouts were lifted due to sold-out games in a record 97.3 percent of games in 2006. Out of 256 games, there were seven local blackouts on the season.

The NBA finished the 2006–07 regular season with the highest average attendance in history and the highest total attendance, surpassing the previous records established in each of the last three years. The NBA total attendance was 21,841,480 with an average attendance of 17,757 spectators a game. Overall, in the 2006–2007 season NBA arenas were filled to 92.3 percent capacity with a total of 600 sellout games.[8]

Even with steroid scandals in the works, major league Baseball announced that the 2007 regular season closed with a record attendance total of 79,502,524, breaking the overall single-season record for the fourth consecutive year. This season's average attendance of 32,785 was the highest in baseball history. "The immensity of this record is staggering, and it serves as a perfect illustration of the passion and excitement for the game that exists across the entire major league Baseball landscape," Baseball Commissioner Allan H. (Bud) Selig said.[9]

Despite the lockout that suspended play in the National Hockey League in 2005 and a soft economy, NHL fans turned out in record numbers for the 2006–07 regular season, with total attendance of 20,861,787 and a per-game average of 16,961 surpassing the marks set in 2005–06. In all, NHL teams played to 97 percent of capacity.[10]

Media Coverage

Although millions of Americans attend sporting events each year, even more of us watch sports on network and cable television or listen to sports on the radio. For example, the 2008 Super Bowl with the Giants upset victory over the then-unbeaten New England Patriots was seen by 97.5 million viewers, behind only the 1982 *M-A-S-H* finale and the 1996 Super Bowl between Dallas and Pittsburgh as the most-watched TV broadcast of all time.[11]

During the 2004 Summer Olympics from Athens, Greece, more than 300 television channels provided a total of 35,000 hours of dedicated coverage, and 3.9 billion viewers in 220 countries and territories each watched an average of more than 12 hours of coverage.[12] By contrast, the Winter Olympic torch seemed snuffed, as the 17-night contest from Torino, Italy, marked the least-watched Winter Olympics since at least 1988. The Games averaged only 20.2 million viewers in prime time on NBC, according to Nielsen Media Research.[13]

ESPN, the original sports-only network launched in 1979, reaches 89 million homes with 5,100 hours of live, original sports programming, and ESPN2 is the fastest network to reach the 90 million households mark. Additionally, ESPN Classic can now be found in over 56 million homes.[14]

Traditional networks are trying to keep pace with the demand for sports programming. The four major networks devote in excess of 2,000 hours to sports programming annually, and a family with cable has access to 86,000 hours of sports TV. NBC spent a record $2.3 billion to secure the broadcast and cable rights for the Olympic Games in 2004, 2006, and 2008. In addition, NBC paid $1.27 billion to televise the Olympics in 2000 and 2002. NBC extended its stronghold on the Olympics by winning the broadcast rights to the 2010 and 2012 Games for $2.2 billion. Add to this the four-year deal worth $2.64 billion paid by NBC and Turner Sports to televise NBA contests or the $18 billion paid by the networks to the NFL, and you can see the value of sports to the league and the networks.[15] These numbers show no signs of slowing down in the future.

The growth of sports information on the Web.

Source: Materials courtesy of ESPN Enterprises, Inc.

The huge demand for sports broadcasting has led to the introduction of more sport-specific channels. New sports networks such as the College Sports Television (www.cstv.com), Blackbelt TV, the Tennis Channel, and the NFL Network are emerging because of consumer demand. This practice of "narrowcasting," reaching very specific audiences, seems to be the future of sports media.

In addition to traditional sports media, pay-per-view cable television is growing in popularity. Satellite stations, such as DirecTV, allow spectators to subscribe to a series of sporting events and play a more active role in customizing the programming they want to see. For example, DirecTV offers the NHL Center Ice package where subscribers can choose from 40 out-of-market (i.e., not local) regular season NHL games per week.

Employment

Another way to explore the size of the sports industry is to look at the number of people the industry employs. *The Sports Market Place Registry,* an industry directory, has more than 24,000 listings for sports people and organizations.[16] A *USA Today* report estimates that there are upward of 4.5 million sports-related jobs in marketing, entrepreneurship, administration, representation, and media.[17] Some estimates range as high as 6 million jobs. In addition to the United States, the United Kingdom employs some 400,000 people in their $6 billion a year sports industry.[18] Consider all the jobs that are created because of sports-related activities such as building and staffing a new stadium. The Sports Business Directory lists 13 career areas in sport. These include event suppliers, event management and marketing, sports media, sports sponsorship, athlete services, sports commissions, sports lawyers, manufacturers and distribution, facilities and facility suppliers, teams, leagues, college athletics, and finance.

The number of people working directly and indirectly in sports will continue to grow as sports marketing grows. Sports marketing creates a diverse workforce from the players who create the competition, to the photographers who shoot the competition (see Appendix A for a discussion of careers in sports marketing).

INTERNATIONAL SPORTS MARKETING

Chinese Basketball Fans: "I Love This Game"

A team of NBA stars making up Team USA blew out a Yao-Ming-less Chinese national team 119–73 in Guangzhou, China. Despite the loss, the Chinese are loving basketball, which could mean major money for the NBA and its league partners looking to enter the vast marketplace.

How do you open China's door? Marketers of every large company are asking that question. But those associated with a big, orange, round ball already have the key. With 1.3 billion people, China is the emerging market that many multinational companies are salivating to embrace. And while it's not exactly getting the foot in the door, sports marketers are discovering that using basketball certainly helps.

"When you go to China and you drive around and you see basketball courts everywhere, they don't play five on five, they'll play 15 on 15, they'll get as many kids on the court as they can," said Team Yao's marketing agent, Bill Sanders. Interest in basketball has always been high in China, but the sport reached a fever pitch when native Yao Ming was selected as the first overall pick in the 2002 NBA draft.

"When Yao is around Chinese people, the reaction is completely different. It reminds me of the old clips I used to see of the Beatles or Elvis. It's on that level where these people are so thrilled to see them they have trouble containing themselves," said Sanders.

With an estimated three hundred million people playing basketball in China, the NBA is riding the wave. Twenty percent of all traffic to NBA.com comes from China and they signed eight new China marketing partners last year—including a deal with Haier, one of China's largest appliance manufacturers. "As you get closer to the Olympics, there will be a huge crescendo of all sports marketing, but what the NBA can offer is real stars that are identifiable to a Chinese audience," said *China, Inc.* author Ted Fishman.

Despite Yao's popularity, the league's latest release of jersey sales shocked many. Yao was the third most popular jersey, his Houston Rockets teammate Tracy McGrady in the top spot. "He's got the talent, but he's also got the laid back personality which the Chinese sort of relate to. They call him 'Old Sleepy Eyes'," said Lawrence Norman, VP of Global Basketball for Adidas.

Using McGrady, Adidas has taken China by storm, where store openings are a daily occurrence. "We have 2,000, but we are opening two every day and this is going to continue all the way through the Olympics and probably beyond. When you see all the Starbucks opening here, it's kind of similar to that. They're just down the street from each other, but Adidas is such a strong brand, we can do this," said Norman.

Marketers say that China's growth potential is vast, though understanding the culture and the healthy counterfeiting business is a must for those hoping to cash in.

Source: Darren Rovell, "Chinese Basketball Fans: 'I Love This Game' " CNBC, http://www.msnbc.msn.com/id/14245395/.

Global Markets

Not only is the sports industry growing in the United States, but it is also growing globally. As the spotlight on international sports marketing discusses, the NBA is a premier example of a powerful global sports organization that continues to grow in emerging markets.

The Structure of the Sports Industry

There are many ways to discuss the structure of the sports industry. We can look at the industry from an organizational perspective. In other words, we can understand some things about the sports industry by studying the different types of organizations that populate the sports industry such as local recreation commissions, national youth sports leagues, intercollegiate athletic programs, professional teams, and sanctioning bodies. These organizations use sports marketing to help them achieve their various organizational goals. For example, agencies such as the United States Olympic Committee (USOC) use marketing to secure the funding necessary to train and enter American athletes into the Olympic Games and Pan American Games.

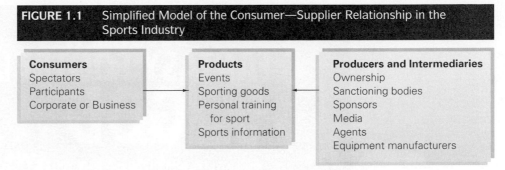

FIGURE 1.1 Simplified Model of the Consumer—Supplier Relationship in the Sports Industry

Consumers
Spectators
Participants
Corporate or Business

Products
Events
Sporting goods
Personal training
    for sport
Sports information

Producers and Intermediaries
Ownership
Sanctioning bodies
Sponsors
Media
Agents
Equipment manufacturers

The traditional organizational perspective, however, is not as helpful to potential sports marketers as a consumer perspective. When we examine the structure of the sports industry from a consumer perspective, the complexity of this industry and challenge to sports marketers becomes obvious. Figure 1.1 shows a **simplified model of the consumer–supplier relationship.** The sports industry consists of three major elements: consumers of sport, the sports products that they consume, and the suppliers of the sports product. In the next sections, we explore each of these elements in greater detail.

The Consumers of Sport

The sports industry exists to satisfy the needs of three distinct types of consumers: spectators, participants, and sponsors.

The Spectator as Consumer

If the sporting event is the heart of the sports industry, then the spectator is the blood that keeps it pumping. **Spectators** are consumers who derive their benefit from the observation of the event. The sports industry, as we know it, would not exist without spectators. Spectators observe the sporting event in two broad ways: They attend the event, or they experience the event via one of several sports broadcast media.

Spectator consumers are also of two types. Some are individuals, whereas others are corporations. As shown in Figure 1.2, there are two broad types of consumers: individual consumers and corporate consumers. Similarly, there are two broad ways in which consumers can become spectators: in person or via the media. This creates four distinct consumer groups. Individuals can attend events in person by purchasing single event tickets or series (season) tickets. Not only do individuals attend sporting events, but so too do corporations. Today, stadium luxury boxes and conference rooms are

Sports marketing fills the stands.

Fantasy sports blurring the line between spectator and participant.
Source: Sporting News

designed specifically with the corporate consumer in mind. Many corporate consumers can purchase special blocks of tickets to sporting events. At times, there may be a tension between corporate consumers' and individual consumers' needs. Many believe that corporate consumers, able to pay large sums of money for their tickets, are pushing out the individual consumer and raising ticket prices.

Both individual spectators and corporations can also watch the event via a media source. The corporate consumer in this case is not purchasing the event for its own viewing, but, rather, acting as an intermediary to bring the spectacle to the end user groups or audience. For example, CBS (the corporate consumer) purchases the right to televise the Masters Golf Tournament. CBS then controls how and when the event is experienced by millions of individual spectators who comprise the television audience.

Historically, the focus of the sports industry and sports marketers was on the spectator attending the event. The needs of the consumer at the event were catered to first, with

FIGURE 1.2 Classification of Spectators

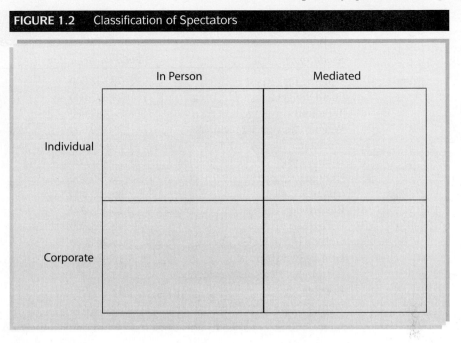

little emphasis on the viewing or listening audience. Due to the power of the corporate consumer, the focus has changed to pleasing the media broadcasting the sporting event to spectators in remote locations. Many season ticket holders are dismayed each year when they discover that the starting time for events has been altered to fit the ESPN schedule. Because high ratings for broadcasted sporting events translates into breathtaking deals for the rights to collegiate and professional sports, those who present sporting events are increasingly willing to accommodate the needs of the media at the expense of the on-site fan. The money associated with satisfying the needs of the media is unprecedented. For example, in 1997, the NFL signed a contract with a major television network for nearly $18 billion.[19] That number is continuing to grow as seen in Table 1.1. Identifying and understanding the different types of spectator consumption is a key consideration for sports marketers when designing a marketing strategy.

The Participant as Consumer

In addition to watching sports, more people are becoming active **participants** in a variety of sports at a variety of competitive levels. Table 1.2 shows "core" participation in sports and fitness activities. As the number of participants grows, the need for sports marketing expertise in these areas also increases.

As you can see, there are two broad classifications of sports participants: those that participate in unorganized sports and those that participate in organized sports.

TABLE 1.1 NFL Media Rights

Network	Years Covered	AVG. Annual Cost	Total Cost
CBS (AFC)	2006–2011	$622.5M	$3.73B
DirecTV (Sunday Ticket)	2006–2010	$700M	$3.5B
ESPN (Monday Night)	2006–2013	$1.1B	$8.8B
FOX (NFC)	2006–2011	$712.5M	$4.27B
NBC (Sunday Night)	2006–2011	$600M	$3.6B
Total	**2006–2010/11/13**	**$3.734B**	**$23.9B**

TABLE 1.2	Most Popular Sports and Fitness Activities Based on Core Participation (age 6 and above; U.S. residents)	
Rank/Sport	**2006 Participation**	**Core Level of Frequency**
Walking for Fitness	70,342,000	50+ Days a Year
Hand Weights	29,333,000	50+ Days a Year
Treadmill	28,489,000	50+ Days a Year
Weight/Resistance Machines	26,210,000	50+ Days a Year
Stretching	24,900,000	50+ Days a Year
Dumbbells	22,481,000	50+ Days a Year
Running/Jogging	22,120,000	50+ Days a Year
Billiards/Pool	19,663,000	13+ Days a Year
Basketball	18,761,000	13+ Days a Year
Barbells	18,595,000	50+ Days a Year
Golf on a 9/18 Hole Course	17,285,000	8+ Days a Year
Home Gym Exercise	15,424,000	50+ Days a Year
Abdominal Machine/Device	14,007,000	50+ Days a Year
Bowling	13,979,000	13+ Days a Year
Stationary Cycling (Upright)	13,312,000	50+ Days a Year

Source: http://www.sgma.com/displayindustryarticle.cfm?articlenbr=33686

Unorganized Sport Participants/Organized Sport Participants

Amateur
    Youth recreational instructional
    Youth recreational elite
    Schools
    Intercollegiate
Professional
    Minor/Secondary
    Major

Unorganized sports are the sporting activities people engage in that are not sanctioned or controlled by some external authority. Kids playing a pickup game of basketball, teenagers skateboarding, or people playing street roller hockey, as well as fitness runners, joggers, and walkers are only a few of the types of sporting activities that millions of people participate in each day. The number of people who participate in unorganized sports is difficult to estimate. We can see how large this market is by looking at the unorganized sport of home fitness. In 2007, Americans spent over $5.4 billion on exercise equipment.[20]

We can see that the size of the market for unorganized sports is huge, and there are many opportunities for sports marketers to serve the needs of these consumers.

Organized sporting events refer to sporting competitions that are sanctioned and controlled by an authority such as a league, association, or sanctioning body. There are two types of participants in organized events: amateur and professional.

Amateur sporting events refer to sporting competitions for athletes who do not receive compensation for playing the sport. Amateur competitions include recreational youth sports at the instructional and elite (also known as "select") levels, high school sports controlled at the state level through leagues, intercollegiate sports (NCAA Division 1–3, NAIA, and NJCAA), and adult community-based recreational sports. **Professional sports** are also commonly classified by minor league or major league status.

Sponsors as Consumer

Other equally important consumers in sports marketing are the many business organizations that choose to sponsor sports. In **sports sponsorship,** the consumer (in most cases, a business) is exchanging money or product for the right to associate its name or product with a sporting event. The decision to sponsor a sport is complex. The sponsor must not only decide on what sport(s) to sponsor, but must also consider what level of competition (recreational through professional) to sponsor. They must choose whether to sponsor events, teams, leagues, or individual athletes.

Although sponsorship decisions are difficult, sponsorship is growing in popularity for a variety of reasons. As Pope discusses in his excellent review of current sponsorship thought and practices,[21] sponsorship can help achieve corporate objectives (e.g., public awareness, corporate image building, and community involvement), marketing objectives (e.g., reaching target markets, brand positioning, and increasing sales), media objectives (e.g., generate awareness, enhance ad campaign, and generate

Multiple sponsors of the Country Music Marathon.
Source: Elite Racing

publicity), and personal objectives (management interest). Continuing a pattern begun in postrecession 2003, sponsorship spending will continue to grow. Spending by North American companies should rise 11.7 percent in 2007, reaching $14.93 billion, according to IEG SR's 22nd annual industry forecast.[22]

The Sports Product

Perhaps the most difficult conceptual issue for sports marketers is trying to understand the nature of the sports product. Just what is the sports product that participants, spectators, and sponsors consume? A **sports product** is a good, a service, or any combination of the two that is designed to provide benefits to a sports spectator, participant, or sponsor.

Goods and Services

Goods are defined as tangible, physical products that offer benefits to consumers. Sporting goods include equipment, apparel, and shoes. We expect sporting goods retailers to sell tangible products such as tennis balls, racquets, hockey equipment, exercise equipment, and so on. By contrast, **services** are defined as intangible, nonphysical products. A competitive sporting event (i.e., the game itself) and an ice-skating lesson are examples of sport services.

Sports marketers sell their products based on the **benefits** the products offer to consumers. In fact, products can be described as "bundles of benefits." Whether as participants, spectators, or sponsors, sports products are purchased based on the benefits consumers derive. Ski Industry America, a trade association interested in marketing the sport of snowshoeing, understands the benefit idea and suggests that the benefits offered to sports participants by this sports product include great exercise, little athletic skill, and low cost (compared with skiing). It is no wonder snowshoeing has recently emerged as one of the nation's fastest growing winter sports.[23]

Spectators are also purchasing benefits when they attend or watch sporting events. For example, the 2006 World Cup stands as one of the most watched event in television history garnering an estimated 26.29 billion non-unique viewers, compiled over the course of the tournament. The final attracted an estimated audience of 715.1 million people and provided consumers with benefits such as entertainment, ability to socialize, and feelings of identification with their countries' teams and athletes.[24]

Moreover, organizations such as Federal Express, which paid $205 million over 27 years for the naming rights to the Washington Redskins sports complex that opened in 1999, believe the association with sports and the subsequent benefits will be worth far more than the investment.[25] The benefits that organizations receive from naming rights include enhanced image, increased awareness, and increased sales of their products.

Different Types of Sports Products

Sports products can be classified into four categories. These include sporting events, sporting goods, sports training, and sports information. Let us take a more in-depth look at each of these sports products.

Sporting Events

The primary product of the sports industry is the **sporting event**. By primary product we are referring to the competition, which is needed to produce all the related products in the sports industry. Without the game there would be no licensed merchandise, collectibles, stadium concessions, and so on. You may have thought of sports marketing as being important only for professional sporting events, but the marketing of collegiate sporting events and even high school sporting events is becoming more common. For example, *High School Hoops* is a new mainstream glossy preview magazine

CAREER SPOTLIGHT

Dean Bonham, CEO the Bonham Group

Career Questions

1. How did you get started in the sports industry? What was your first sports industry job?

   In 1986, after owning and operating several entrepreneurial ventures, I presented Sidney Shlenker, the owner of the Denver Nuggets, with a proposal to hire me as president of the franchise. I had previously been active at the Denver Athletic Club and heavily involved in Denver's pursuit of major league baseball, but this was my first formal industry job.

2. Can you describe the type of work you are doing right now? What are your job responsibilities? What are the greatest challenges?

   As chairman and CEO of The Bonham Group, I'm the spokesman and public face for the company. I'm also actively involved in developing new business, making presentations, and cultivating new strategic opportunities, such as our entrée into the European, Asian, and South American markets. I'm frequently the lead negotiator for our clients in complex naming rights agreements. Because I travel so much, it's sometimes difficult to interact with employees as much as I'd like.

3. Do you foresee any changes in demand in this field in the future? If so, what or how?

   The field of sports marketing has exploded since I entered 20 years ago. New sports, new media, and new fans have transformed the landscape dramatically. I expect the growth and changes to continue as new markets are exposed to the opportunities that have been pioneered in the United States.

4. Who or what has influenced you the most in your sports business career?

   As a teenager, I was out on my own and struggling to make a living. I was exposed to the writings of Dale Carnegie *(How to Win Friends and Influence People)* and Napoleon Hill *(Think and Grow Rich)*. I was impressed with how these books wove together discipline, positive habits and psychology to guide people on the path to improvement. I was motivated to succeed and they gave me the tools I needed. Later, I met and became close with the late John Burton Tigrett, the Memphis entrepreneur who was the driving force behind the construction of The Pyramid. With Tigrett's encouragement and financial backing, I formed The Bonham Group.

5. What advice would you offer students who are considering a career in sports marketing?

   It's a competitive field! To succeed you must be willing to do what others won't. That often means working longer hours for less money than you might make in another industry. An internship is just about essential these days. It also helps to focus on how your assets and skills can help your employer fill a need or solve a problem.

produced by the *Sporting News*. The first-of-its-kind magazine is devoted solely to the coverage of nationwide prep basketball.

Historically, a large distinction was made between amateur and professional sporting events. Today, that line is becoming more blurred. For example, the Olympic Games, once considered the bastion of amateur sports, is now allowing professional athletes to participate for their countries. Most notably, the rosters of the Dream Teams of USA Basketball fame and the USA Hockey team are almost exclusively professional athletes. This has been met with some criticism. Critics say that they would rather give the true amateur athletes their chance to "go for the gold."

Athletes Athletes are participants who engage in organized training to develop skills in particular sports. Athletes who perform in competition or exhibitions can also be thought of as sports products. David Beckham, Chamique Holdsclaw, and Lance Armstrong are thought of as "bundles of benefits" that can satisfy consumers of sport both on and off the court.

One athlete to achieve this "superproduct" status is the multimillion-dollar phenomenon named Eldrick "Tiger" Woods. Tiger seems to have it all. He is handsome, charming, young, multiethnic, and most important—talented. Tiger's sponsors certainly think he is worth the money. Nike, Buick, NetJets, and American Express have all purchased a piece of Tiger for millions in sponsorship fees. The terms of the new Nike contract are undisclosed but the contract is worth more than his current five-year, $100 million deal. Tiger will even have his own sports drink called Gatorade Tiger.

Sports marketers must realize that the "bundle of benefits" that accompany an athlete varies from person to person. The benefits associated with Allen Iverson are different from those associated with Kevin Garnett or golfer Natalie Gulbis. Regardless of the nature of the benefits, today's athletes are not thinking of themselves as athletes but as entertainers. Of course, sometimes athletes such as Chad Johnson of the Cincinnati Bengals can draw criticism from fans and media for being more showman than player.

Arena   A final sports product that is associated with the sporting event is the site of the event—typically an arena or stadium. Today, the stadium is much more than a place to go watch the game. It is an entertainment complex that may include restaurants, bars, picnic areas, and luxury boxes. In fact, stadium seating is becoming a "product" of its own. For example, ChoiceSeat was introduced at Super Bowl XXXII and promises to be the stadium seat of the future. The ChoiceSeat is a Pentium-powered touch screen that allows individuals to access real-time camera views from a variety of camera angles, replays, player and game statistics, and merchandising information. With this new technology, the seat within the stadium becomes an attractive product to market.[26] In another example, Angel Stadium of Anaheim is utilizing Epson Mobilink(TM) wireless POS printers and Symbol PPT8800 mobile computers to deliver seat-side concession service to baseball fans. Up and running since July 2006, the mobile POS installation allows fans to order, receive, and pay for concessions seat-side, boosting sales and enhancing customer service. In addition, concession staff workers using the mobile POS benefit from increased tips and less running, which helps reduce staff turnover.[27]

Sporting Goods

Sporting goods represent tangible products that are manufactured, distributed, and marketed within the sports industry. The sporting goods and recreation industry, consisting of three segments, was nearly a $57.6 billion industry in 2006. The three segments and their relative contribution to the industry sales figure include sports equipment ($19 billion), sports apparel ($26.6 billion), and athletic footwear ($12 billion). Sports equipment sales were relatively flat in 2006 with a very slight increase from the previous year. The largest product category, in terms of sales, was exercise equipment ($4.2 billion), followed by golf equipment ($2.9 billion), firearms and hunting ($2.1 billion), camping ($1.6 billion), and fishing ($1.1 billion).[28] Although sporting goods are usually thought of as sports equipment, apparel, and shoes, there are a number of other goods that exist for consumers of sport. Sporting goods also include licensed merchandise, collectibles, and memorabilia.

Licensed Merchandise   Another type of sporting good that is growing in sales is licensed merchandise. **Licensing** is a practice whereby a sports marketer contracts with other companies to use a brand name, logo, symbol, or characters. In this case, the brand name may be a professional sports franchise, college sports franchise, or a sporting event. Licensed sports products usually are some form of apparel such as team hats, jackets, or jerseys. Licensed sports apparel accounts for 60 percent of all sales. Other licensed sports products such as novelties, sports memorabilia, trading cards, and even home goods are also popular.

The Licensing Magazine reports that sales of all licensed sports products reached $19.3 billion in 2006, a 3 percent increase over the previous year's retail sales. This growth is expected to continue, according to research from the National Sporting Goods Manufacturers Association. U.S. retail sales of licensed products for the four major professional sports leagues (NBA, NFL, MLB, and NHL) and colleges and universities have grown exponentially from $5.35 billion in 1990 to $12.4 billion in 2006.[29]

Through this period, the various major professional sports leagues developed a sprawling network of licensing arrangements with more than 600 companies. Another 2,000 companies have arrangements with the various college and university licensing groups. As far as the retail distribution of product, a network of "fan shops" grew to over 450 in number and licensed products found their way into sporting goods stores, department stores, and eventually, the mass merchants. To compete, most of the major sporting goods chains and many department stores developed separate areas devoted exclusively to licensed goods. Sales of licensed sports products will continue to grow as other "big league" sports gain popularity. For example, NASCAR has seen the sale of licensed goods increase from $ $500 million in 1994 and to $2.1 billion in 2006.

Collectibles and Memorabilia   One of the earliest examples of sports marketing can be traced to the 1880s when baseball cards were introduced. Consider life before the automobile and the television. For most baseball fans, the player's picture on the card may have been the only chance to see that player. Interestingly, the cards were featured as a promotion in cigarette packages rather than bubble gum. Can you imagine the ethical backlash that this practice would produce today?

Although the sports trading card industry reached $1.2 billion in 1991, industry-wide yearly sales plummeted to $700 million in 1995 and are now stable at between $400 and $500 million. What caused this collapse? One answer is too much competition. David Leibowitz, an industry analyst, commented that "With the channel of distribution backed up and with too much inventory, it was hard to sustain prices, let alone have them continue to rise." From the beginning of the 1980s there were only a few major card companies (Topps, Donruss, and Fleer) and by the early '90s there were more sets of cards produced by six different companies, more in the market than ever before. This flooded market and the cartoon fad cards have hurt the sports trading card industry. Other problems include labor problems in sports, escalating card prices, and kids with competing interests. Industry sales have fallen 15 percent per year from 2000 to 2005.

There is, however, some evidence that the industry will rebound. In 2006, only two companies were in the baseball sport card market. Citing a glut in the marketplace and the desire to regain some control over the baseball card industry, major league Baseball declined to renew Donruss' license, leaving Topps and Upper Deck as the only producers.[30]

Perhaps the biggest boost will be selling and trading cards on the Internet.[31] The first major company in this market was the industry leader, Topps. Each week on etopps.com the company promotes six new limited edition cards or IPOs (Initial Player Offerings). The buyer can then purchase the card and takes physical possession, sells

The sports collectors dream—the Baseball Hall of Fame.

the card in an auction, or holds the card until it appreciates in value. The new product has been a huge success for Topps and could be the future of the card industry.

Personal Training for Sports

Another growing category of sports is referred to as **personal training.** These products are produced to benefit participants in sports at all levels and include fitness centers, health services, sports camps, and instruction.

Fitness Centers and Health Services   When the New York Athletic Club was opened in 1886, it became the first facility opened specifically for athletic training. From its humble beginning in New York, the fitness industry has seen an incredible boom. "Pumping iron" was a common phrase in the 1970s and early 1980s. Moreover, the 1970s aerobics craze started by Dr. Ken Cooper added to the growth of health clubs across the United States.

It is no secret that a physically fit body is becoming more important to society. The growth of the fitness industry follows a national trend for people to care more about their health. In 1993, there were 11,655 clubs in the United States billed as "health and fitness" centers. In 2005, this number had grown to a record high of 26,831 clubs. Moreover, health club membership climbed to a record high 41.3 million people and is expected to double by 2010.[32] Why are people joining health clubs in record numbers? According to a study conducted by the International Health, Racquet, and Sportsclub

Association, the factors that will continue to support the growth of health club membership in the United States include the following:

1. The growing number of health clubs that make it more convenient for consumers.
2. The continued and increased promotion of the benefits of exercise by organizations like the U.S. Surgeon General.
3. More Americans are concerned about the adverse effects of poor exercise and eating habits.[33]

Sports Camps and Instruction Sports camps are organized training sessions designed to provide instruction in a specific sport (e.g., basketball or soccer). Camps are usually associated with instructing children; however, the "fantasy sports camp" for aging athletes has received considerable attention in the past few years. Fantasy sports camps typically feature current or ex-professional athletes, and the focus is more on having fun than actual instruction. Nearly every major league baseball team now offers some type of fantasy camp for adults. For example, Chicago Fantasy Baseball Camp allows you (if you're over 30 years old) to be a major leaguer for a week. The experience consists of social activities, games, and instruction with former major league players, but this does not come cheap. The price for participating is roughly $3,000 per person.

Along with camps, another lucrative sports service is providing personal or group instruction in sports. The difference between instruction and camps is the ongoing nature of the instruction versus the finite period and intense experience of the camp. For example, taking golf or tennis lessons from a professional typically involves a series of half-hour lessons over the course of months or sometimes years. Contrast this with the camp that provides intense instruction over a week-long period.

Ski.com provides information for ski enthusiasts.
Source: NBA (from ESPN) Nell Devane

Sports Information

The final type of sports product that we discuss is sports information. **Sports information** products provide consumers with news, statistics, schedules, and stories about sports. In addition, sports information can provide participants with instructional materials. Sports-specific newspapers (e.g., *The Sporting News*), magazines (e.g., *Sports Illustrated*), Internet sites (e.g., cnnsi.com), television (e.g., The Golf Channel), and radio (e.g., WFAN) can all be considered sports information products. All these forms of media are experiencing growth in terms of both products and audience. Consider the following examples of new sports information media. ESPN launched its new magazine in March 1998 to compete with *Sports Illustrated,* which leads all sports magazines with a circulation of over 3.2 million. The current circulation for *ESPN The Magazine* is 1.9 million, but all indications are that there is room at the top for two sports magazine powerhouses.[34]

The fastest growing source of sports information is on the World Wide Web. The ESPN Chilton Sports Poll estimates that 34 percent of all computer owners and people with access to computers get sports information online and use the computer for that purpose an average of 2.4 times per week. Due to the tremendous amount of information that sports fans desire (e.g., team stats, player stats, and league stats) and the ability of Web sites to supply such information, Web sites and sports marketing make a perfect fit. One example of the success of providing sports information via the World Wide Web is www.ESPN.com (ESPN's Web site). A look at the top 10 sports Web sites is shown in Table 1.3.

The Multidimensional Nature of the Sports Product

As you can see from our previous discussion, there are a wide variety of sports products. Our earlier definition of the sports product incorporated the distinction between goods and services. Although this is a traditional approach to categorizing consumer products, the complexity of the sports product makes the goods–services classification inadequate. Consider the rich diversity of the sports products that we have just considered. Everything from a hockey puck to the NCAA championship game of the Final Four in basketball is included in our definition. Because of this diversity and complexity, we have added an additional dimension to the sports product known as the body–mind continuum. The body–mind continuum is based on the notion that some sports products benefit consumers' minds, while other products act on consumers' bodies. Figure 1.3 illustrates

TABLE 1.3	Top 10 Sports Web Sites (September 2006; Total U.S. Home, Work and University Internet Users)		
	August 2006 (000)	*September 2006 (000)*	*Percentage Change*
Total Internet : Total Audience	*173,407*	*173,428*	*0%*
ESPN	17,850	20,385	14
Yahoo! Sports	13,763	17,472	27
FOX Sports on MSN	13,133	16,471	25
NFL Internet Group	13,355	16,401	23
MLB.com	10,896	9,122	–16
AOL Sports	6,629	8,049	21
CSTV: College Sports TV	5,797	7,083	22
CBS SportsLine	5,851	7,024	20
SI.com	5,115	5,785	13
NASCAR.com	3,888	4,137	6

Source: comScore Media Metrix.

FIGURE 1.3 The Sports Product Map

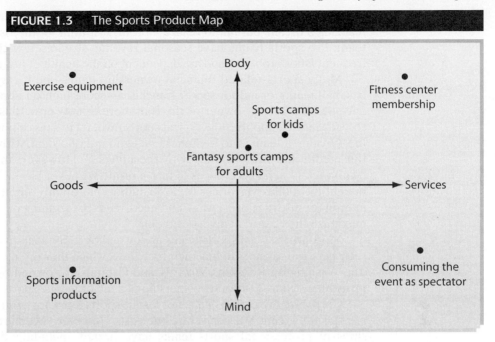

the multidimensional nature of sports products using two dimensions: goods–services and body–mind. These dimensions make up the **sports product map.**

As you can see, we have positioned some sports products on this map. Exercise equipment is shown as a good that works on the body of the consumer. At the other end of the map, attending or watching a sporting event is considered a service that acts on the mind of consumers. Perhaps we can best describe the differences based on the mind–body and goods–services dimension by exploring sports camps. Sports camps for children are primarily instructional in nature. The primary product being sold is the opportunity for kids to practice their physical skills. However, the fantasy camp targeting adults is a product that acts more on the mind than body. The adults are purchasing the "fantasy" of interacting with professional athletes rather than the physical training.

Understanding where sports products fall on this map is critical for sports marketers. Marketers must understand how they want their sports product to be perceived by consumers so they can understand what benefits to stress. For example, the marketers of a sporting event may want to sell the intangible excitement or the tangible features of the arena. This strategic decision is based on a number of factors that will be considered in detail throughout this text.

Producers and Intermediaries

Producers and intermediaries represent the manufacturers of sports products or the organizations that perform some function in the marketing of sports products. Organizations or individuals that perform the function of producer or intermediary include team owners, sanctioning bodies, agents, corporate sponsors, media, and sporting goods manufacturers. In the following paragraphs, we take a look at each of these producers and intermediaries as they relate to the various sports products.

Sports Labor   Owners of professional sports franchises, partnerships that own sporting events, and universities that "own" their athletic teams all represent producers of sporting events. One of the unique aspects of the sports industry is that often businesspeople purchase a team because they always dreamed of becoming involved in sports. Typically, sports owners are entrepreneurs who have made their riches in other businesses before deciding to get involved in the business of sports. All too often these owners may be realizing a dream, but fail to realize a profit. Just think of the risks in owning your own team. Pro sports teams have seasonal revenue streams, few chances to expand, and frequent labor problems, and are dependent on the health of just a select few employees.

Many sports-related financial ownership deals—be it racehorses, minor league baseball teams, or indoor soccer franchises—score high on appeal and low on profits. J. W. Stealey, former owner of the Baltimore Spirit (now Blast) professional indoor soccer team, exemplifies the typical sports owner. He says, "Sports has always been my life. Owning a team is, to be honest, an ego kind of a deal, with all the attention from the media and involvement with the players." However, there is just one catch. "Although I keep expecting us to turn a profit, we never have."[35] As Mark Cuban, who bought the Dallas Mavericks for $280 million, has openly admitted, "Having paid $200 million for my franchise, I want, and need, the NBA running on all cylinders in order to maximize the return on my investment."[36]

Most professional sports teams are owned by individual investors who have staked their personal fortunes to buy their franchises, which they often operate as a public trust. The Washington Redskins, Wizards, and Capitals are owned by individuals and their investment teams. Corporate ownership of a major league sports team is rare, but exists.

Corporate ownership of a major league sports team, for example, the Atlanta Braves are owned by Time Warner, is rare but exists. However, several recent corporate ownerships of professional sports teams have fizzled, including the Disney Company's ownership of the then-Anaheim Angels and the Mighty Ducks. The Los Angeles Dodgers were owned for several years by News Corp., before the company sold the team to an investor group from Boston. Most recently, the Chicago Cubs were sold by the Tribune Company. Interestingly, the NFL forbids corporate ownership of franchises.

Sanctioning Bodies   Sanctioning bodies are organizations that not only market sports products, but also, more importantly, delineate and enforce rules and regulations,

NCAA: One of the most powerful sanctioning bodies.
Source: NCAA

determine the time and place of sporting events, and provide athletes with the structure necessary to compete. Examples of sanctioning bodies include the NCAA, NFL, NHL, IOC (International Olympic Committee), and MLB. Sanctioning bodies can be powerful forces in the sports industry by regulating the rules and organizing the structure of the leagues and sporting events.

The PGA (Professional Golf Association) of America is one of the largest sanctioning bodies in the world. It is comprised of more than 22,000 members that promote the game of golf to "everyone, everywhere." In addition to marketing the game of golf, the PGA organizes tournaments for amateurs and professional golfers, holds instructional clinics, and hosts trade shows.[37] Although the PGA has a long history of advancing golf, other sport sanctioning bodies are surrounded by controversy. Kevin Iole of the *Las Vegas Review Journal* describes boxing's woes as follows. "Imagine convicted mob boss John Gotti at the helm of the Internal Revenue Service and you have a sense of what it's like in boxing with the WBA, WBC, WBO, and IBF controlling world titles. A surgeon general's warning should be slapped on the side of every one of their title belts: Sanctioning bodies are hazardous to boxing's health."[38]

NASCAR is another of the most influential and powerful sanctioning bodies in sport. Ever since NASCAR began sanctioning stock car races, there have been cries of foul play and that NASCAR has somehow influenced the outcome of a race. One of NASCAR's roles is the car inspection process prior to races, and this has always raised questions. Allegations of wrongdoing go all the way back to the early days of the sport. For example, there was legendary Junior Johnson's so-called banana car in 1966, a Ford that NASCAR said was legal but others say was given a free pass through inspection because the series was trying to bring the manufacturer back into racing. On the track, skeptics say NASCAR deliberately uses yellow flags to close up the field for a tight finish. True or false, there is no doubt of the clout of NASCAR.

Sponsors Sponsors represent a sport intermediary. As we discussed, corporations can serve as a consumer of sport. However, corporations also supply sporting events with products or money in exchange for association with the event. The relationship between the event, the audience, and the sponsor is referred to as the *event triangle*.[39] The basis of the event triangle is that the event, the audience, and the sponsor are all interdependent or depend on each other to be successful. All three groups work in concert to maximize the sport's exposure. The events showcase talented athletes and attract the audience, who watch the event in person or through some medium. The audience, in turn, attracts the sponsor, who pays the event to provide them with access to the audience. In addition, the sponsor promotes the event to the audience, which helps the event reach its attendance goals. It is safe to say that sponsors represent an important intermediary or link between the event and the final consumers of sports—the audience.

Media Earlier in this chapter, we commented on the growth of media in bringing sporting events to consumers. In fact, the media, which is considered an intermediary, may be the most powerful force in sports today and is getting stronger. The primary revenue generator for networks is selling prime advertising time. As the price of advertising time rises, so does the cost of securing broadcast rights; however, the networks are willing to pay.

Sports organizations cannot survive without the mass exposure of the media, and the media needs sports to satisfy the growing consumer demand for this type of entertainment. As the demand for sports programming increases, innovations in media will emerge. For example, fans are able to watch English Premier League highlights, catch ESPN, or view a major league Baseball game on cell phones, iPods, and computers.

Agents Another important intermediary in bringing the athlete to the consumer is the sports **agent.** From a sports marketing perspective, sports agents are intermediaries whose primary responsibility is leveraging athletes' worth or determining their bargaining power. The first "super-agent" in sports was Mark McCormack (see box, Sports Marketing Hall of Fame). Prior to his emergence, agents had never received the exposure and recognition that they enjoy today. Interestingly, it is not the agents themselves who have provoked their current rise to prominence, but rather the increased bargaining power of their clients.

The bargaining power of the athletes can be traced to two factors. First, the formation of new leagues in the 1970s, such as the American Basketball Association (ABA) and the World Hockey Association (WHA), resulted in increased competition to sign the best athletes. This competition drove the salaries to higher levels than ever before and made agents more critical. Second, free agency and arbitration have given players a chance to shop their talents on the open market and question the final offer of owners. In addition, owners are now able to pay players the higher salaries because of the multimillion-dollar national television contracts and cable television revenues.

Although most people associate agents with contract negotiations, agents do much more. Here are some of the other responsibilities of the agent:[40]

- Determines the value of the player's services
- Convinces a club to pay the player the aforementioned value
- Develops the package of compensation to suit the player's needs
- Protects the player's rights under contract (and within the guidelines set by the collective bargaining agreement)
- Counsels the player about postcareer security, both financial and occupational
- Finds a new club upon the player's free agency
- Assists the player in earning extra income from endorsements, speeches, appearances, and commercials
- Advises athletes on the effect of their personal conduct on their career

SPORTS MARKETING HALL OF FAME

Mark McCormack

Many people trace the beginnings of modern sports marketing to one man—Mark McCormack. In 1960, Mark McCormack, a Cleveland lawyer, signed an agreement to represent Arnold Palmer. With this star client in hand, McCormack began the International Management Group, better known as IMG. Today, IMG is a multinational sports marketing organization that employs over 3,000 people, has sales of over $1 billion, and represents some of the finest professional athletes in the world.

In addition to his contribution to sports marketing in the United States, McCormack has globalized sports marketing. He opened an Asian office of IMG in Tokyo in 1969, led in the sponsorship of events in Europe, and continues to expand into the Middle Eastern markets. One example of McCormack's enormous reach into international markets is IMG's Trans World International. TWI is the largest independent producer of sports programming in the world. One of its shows, *Trans World Sports*, is viewed in more than 325 million homes in over 76 countries. Along with representing athletes and producing sports programming, IMG runs several sports academies that serve as training facilities for elite athletes. Additionally, IMG manages and creates sporting events such as the Skins Game, Superstars Competition, and CART races. Unfortunately for the sports world, Mr. McCormack died in May 2003 at the age of 72.

Source: Susan Vinella, "Sports Marketing Pioneer Dead at 72"; "IMG's McCormack Hailed as Visionary," *Plain Dealer,* May 17, 2003, a1; Eric Fisher, "IMG Founder McCormack Spiced Up the Sports World," *The Washington Times,* May 18, 2003, c3.

Sports Equipment Manufacturers

Sports equipment manufacturers are responsible for producing and sometimes marketing sports equipment used by consumers who are participating in sports at all different levels of competition. Some sporting equipment manufacturers are still associated with a single product line, whereas others carry a multitude of sports products. For example, Platypus Sporting Goods only manufactures cricket balls. However, Wilson manufactures football, volleyball, basketball, golf, tennis, baseball, softball, racquetball or squash, and youth sports equipment.

Although it is obvious that equipment manufacturers are necessary to supply the equipment needed to produce the competition, they also play an important role in sports sponsorship. Sports equipment manufacturers become sponsors because of the natural relationship they have with sports. For instance, Rawlings, one of the best known baseball glove manufacturers, sponsors the American and National League Golden Glove Award, which is given to the best defensive players in their position. Molten sponsors the NCAA Volleyball Championship by supplying the official game balls. In addition, Spalding is the official game ball of the WNBA.

BASIC MARKETING PRINCIPLES AND PROCESSES APPLIED TO SPORT

The Sports Marketing Mix

Sports marketing is commonly associated with promotional activities such as advertising, sponsorships, public relations, and personal selling. Although this is true, sports marketers are also involved in product and service strategies, pricing decisions, and distribution issues. These activities are referred to as the **sports marketing mix,** which is defined as the coordinated set of elements that sports organizations use to meet their marketing objectives and satisfy consumers' needs.

The basic marketing mix elements are the sports product, price, promotion, and distribution. When coordinated and integrated, the combination of the basic marketing mix elements is known as the *marketing program*. The marketing mix or program elements are controllable factors because sports marketing managers have control over each element. In the following sections, we take a closer look at the four marketing mix elements as they apply to the sports industry.

Product Strategies

One of the basic sports marketing activities is developing product and service strategies. In designing product strategies, decisions regarding licensing, merchandising, branding, and packaging are addressed. In addition, sports marketing managers are responsible for new product development, maintaining existing products, and eliminating weak products. For instance, the Anaheim Ducks recently changed their name from the Mighty Ducks and also will sport new uniforms with different colors and a redesigned logo.[41] This product decision is a result of cutting the ties with former owner The Walt Disney Co. The team kept Ducks in its nickname after a poll of season ticket holders. "A brand image is so hard to build," new owner Henry Samueli said. "If you have to change the name, then you're wiping out 13 years of brand history, not only in Orange County but in the whole country." Toronto's new major league Soccer expansion team deciding on "Toronto FC" (football club) for its nickname, and Callaway introducing a new driver are also product issues of interest to sports marketers.

Because so much of sports marketing is based on services rather than goods, understanding the nature of services marketing is critical for the sports marketing manager. Services planning entails pricing of services, managing demand for services, and evaluating the quality of services. For instance, sports marketing managers want to know fans' perceptions of ticket ushers, concessions, parking, and stadium comfort. These service issues are especially important in today's sports marketing environment because fans equate value with high levels of customer service.

Distribution Strategies

Traditionally, the role of distribution is finding the most efficient and effective way to get the products into the hands of the consumers. Issues such as inventory management, transportation, warehousing, wholesaling, and retailing are all under the control of distribution managers. Selling sporting goods at superstores such as Dick's Sporting Goods or the Sports Authority, offering sports memorabilia on the Home Shopping Network, and marketing sports products on the Internet (e.g., finishline.com) are examples of the traditional distribution function at work. Sports marketing managers are also concerned with how to deliver sports to spectators in the most effective and efficient way. Questions such as where to build a new stadium, where to locate a recreational softball complex, or how to distribute tickets most effectively are potential distribution issues facing sports marketers.

Pricing Strategies

One of the most critical and sensitive issues facing sports marketing managers today is pricing. Pricing strategies include setting pricing objectives, choosing a pricing technique, and making adjustments to prices over time.

The price of tickets for sporting events; fees for personal seat licenses, pay-per-view, and television sports programming; and the rising costs of participating in recreational sports such as golf are all examples of how the pricing function affects sports marketing.

Promotion Strategies

Just ask someone what comes to mind when they think of sports marketing, and the likely response is advertising. They may think of athletes such as Maria Sharapova or Tom Brady endorsing a product or service. Although advertising is an element of promotion, it is by no means the only one. In addition to advertising, promotional elements include communicating with the various sports publics through sponsorships, public relations, personal selling, or sales promotions. Together these promotional elements are called the *promotion mix*. When designing promotional strategies, sports marketers must consider integrating their promotions and using all aspects of the promotion mix.

The Exchange Process

Understanding the exchange process is central to any successful marketing strategy. As generally defined, an **exchange** is a marketing transaction in which the buyer gives something of value to the seller in return for goods and services. For an exchange to occur, several conditions must be satisfied:

- There must be at least two parties.
- Each party must have something of value to offer the other.
- There must be a means for communication between the two or more parties.
- Each party must be free to accept or decline the offer.
- Each party must believe it is desirable to deal with the other(s).

Traditionally, a marketing exchange consists of consumers giving money to receive a product or service that meets their needs. Other exchanges, not involving money, are also possible. For example, trading a Pedro Martinez rookie baseball card for a Derek Jeter card represents a marketing exchange between two collectors.

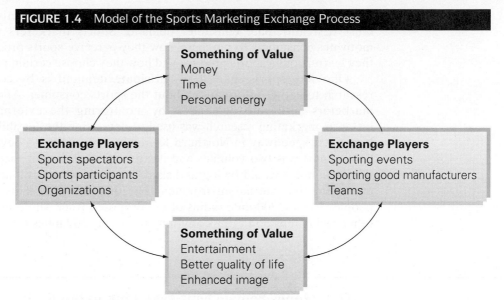

FIGURE 1.4   Model of the Sports Marketing Exchange Process

Examples of elements that make up other exchanges appear in Figure 1.4. The two parties in the exchange process are called *exchange players*. These two participants are consumers of sport (e.g., spectators, participants, or sponsors) or producers and intermediaries of sport. Sports spectators exchange their time, money, and personal energy with sports teams in exchange for the entertainment and enjoyment of watching the contest. Sports participants exchange their time, energy, and money for the joy of sport and the better quality of life that participating in sports brings. In sponsorships, organizations exchange money or products for the right to associate with a sporting event, player, team, or other sports entity.

Although these are rather elementary examples of the exchange process, one of the things that makes sports marketing so unique is the complex nature of the exchange process. Within one sporting event, multiple exchanges will occur. Consider a Sprint Cup NASCAR event. There are exchanges between spectators and the track ownership (i.e., money for entertainment); spectators and product vendors who are licensed by NASCAR (i.e., money for goods associated with racing); the track owner and the NASCAR sanctioning body (i.e., money for organizing the event and providing other event services); media and NASCAR (i.e., event broadcast coverage for money); product sponsors and the driving team owner (i.e., promotional benefits for money); and the track owner and the driving team owner (i.e., producer of the competition for money). As you may imagine, trying to sort out all these exchanges, much less determine the various marketing strategies involved in each exchange, is a complicated puzzle that can only be solved by having a full understanding of the industry within each sport. Although the nature of each sporting event and industry is slightly different, designing a marketing strategy incorporates some fundamental processes that span the sports industry.

The Strategic Sports Marketing Process

Sports marketers manage the complex and unique exchange processes in the sports industry by using the strategic sports marketing process. The **strategic sports marketing process** is the process of planning, implementing, and controlling marketing efforts to meet organizational goals and satisfy consumers' needs.

To meet these organizational goals and marketing objectives, sports marketers must first anticipate consumer demand. Sports marketers want to know what motivates consumers to purchase, how they perceive sports products or services, how they learn about a sports product, and how they choose certain products over others.

One way sports marketers anticipate demand is by conducting marketing research to gather information about the sports consumer. Another way that sports marketers anticipate demand is by monitoring the external environment. For instance, marketing research was used to determine the feasibility of locating a new NASCAR speedway in Northern Kentucky. According to developer Jerry Carroll, "The report was two volumes and it not only said a major racetrack would work in this area, but it would be a grand slam." In addition, Carroll anticipated demand by examining the external environment. He found out that there are about 51 million people within a 300-mile radius of the proposed track and that "NASCAR fans and other racing fans don't think anything of driving 300 miles for a race."[42] Thus far, the

---

NHL Hopes Female Fans Take Pink to the Rink

There will be a rose-coloured haze in the stands next hockey season. The NHL is producing team jerseys in bubble-gum pink. "It allows women to be fashionable and still support their teams," said Jenny Lyons Cohane, a spokeswoman for Reebok, which manufactures official NHL team jerseys.

Both the NBA and the NFL have produced pink jerseys for two years and many NHL teams already offer T-shirts and other apparel in feminine cuts and pastel hues. But this is the first time pink jerseys are to be offered by all the teams in the league. "What's happened in the licensed category is a significant increase in items that are not necessarily athletic, but a fashion item," said Ross McCracken, director of league partnerships at Reebok's Montreal office.

Oddly enough, hockey's new pastel tinge is because the NHL is getting more aggressive about marketing. (The jerseys will also be available in pale blue.) About 40 percent of hockey fans are women. Women's clothing is one of the fastest growing segments of the licensed sports apparel market, about as hot as the vintage look was two or three years ago.

Reebok's pink jerseys, like the official version, will feature the NHL's shield and tags. Available starting Oct. 1, the pink jerseys will retail for about $70 compared to $110 for the licensed men's jersey. The women's product is made of a softer polyester and it features a screen print of the team crest instead of the embroidered crest and shoulder patches. The idea has been received with derision in some quarters by both men and women.

"Let's fast forward to the not-too-distant future," noted one male blogger after a sample pink Leafs jersey appeared in *Women's Wear Daily*. "The 'Pinkies' have become official team third or fourth jerseys, complete with alternate pink helmets. I believe stats will show that fighting in games where one of the teams are wearing its pink jerseys will be nonexistent. It would be like punching your Mom."

Female fans are divided on the issue. Ottawa hockey fan Christine Blouin said she likes the lines of the new jersey. She won't buy a regular jersey because they're designed to wear hockey equipment under them. But pink? "It's not right. It's just not the right colour," she said. "It would still be very nice in red."

Heidi Haraldsson said she loves pink, but this would be too trendy. "Everyone would think you're just trying to be cutesy." Erik Marsh, son of former NHLer Brad Marsh, said he has seen pink apparel for women at a Philadelphia game. "As much as you're saying, 'It's not a team colour,' it's a fashion trend. It's nice to see team spirit no matter where it's coming from," he said.

In order to thrive, the NHL has to be risk innovative and appeal to a younger, more hip audience, said Frank Pons, an assistant professor of marketing at the University of San Diego who specializes in sports marketing. "The NHL is trying to tap into what other sports are doing," said Pons, a Canadian who avidly follows hockey marketing.

So far, the NHL has not lost as much fan support as the league feared it would. But it hasn't gained anyone, either. "What's worse, they haven't attracted anyone who wasn't interested in hockey before," said Pons. "Pink jerseys are not necessarily the answer. But they are one of the answers."

Source: Joanne Laucius, CanWest News Service, July 27, 2006.

research has proven to be true. The Kentucky Speedway has been a huge success since opening its doors for the 2000 season.

Next, sports marketers examine different groups of consumers, choose the group of consumers in which to direct the organization's marketing efforts, and then determine how to position the product or service to that group of consumers. These market selection decisions are referred to as *segmentation, targeting,* and *position.* The final aspect of the planning phase is to offer products that are promoted, priced, and distributed in ways that appeal to the targeted consumers. The accompanying article illustrates the NHL's attempt to target women and design a product that will appeal to female hockey fans.

Summary

The sports industry is experiencing tremendous growth, and sports marketing is playing an important role in this emerging industry. Chapter 1 provided a basic understanding of sports marketing and the sports industry. Sports marketing is "the specific application of marketing principles and processes to sports product and to the marketing of nonsports products through association with sport." The study and practice of sports marketing is complex and interesting because of the unique nature of the sports industry.

Today sports organizations define their businesses as entertainment providers. In addition, sports organizations know that to be successful in the competitive environment of sports, they must practice a marketing orientation. An organization with a marketing orientation concentrates on understanding consumers and providing sports products that satisfy consumers' needs.

Sports marketing will continue to grow in importance as sports become more pervasive in the U.S. culture and around the globe. This phenomenal growth of the sports industry can be seen and measured in a number of ways. We can identify growth by looking at the increasing numbers of sport spectators, the growth of media coverage, the increase in sports participation, rising employment opportunities, and the growth in sports internationally. To better understand this growing and complex industry, a simplified model of the consumer–supplier relationship was presented.

The simplified model of the consumer–supplier relationship in the sports industry consists of three major elements: consumers of sport, sports products, and producers and intermediaries. Three distinct types of sports consumers are identified in the model. These consumers of sport include spectators who observe sporting events, participants who take part in sporting events, and sponsors who exchange money or product for the right to be associated with a sporting event. The spectators, participants, and sponsors use sports products.

A sports product is a good, service, or any combination of the two that is designed to provide benefits to a sports consumer. The primary sports product consumed by sponsors and spectators is the sporting event. Products related to the event are athletes such as Derek Jeter and arenas such as the Staples Center, which both provide their own unique benefits. Other categories of sports products common to the sports industry include sporting goods (e.g., equipment, apparel and shoes, licensed merchandise, collectibles, and memorabilia), personal training services for sports (e.g., fitness centers and sports camps), and sports information (e.g., news and magazines). Because there is a variety of sports products, it is useful to categorize these products using the sports product map.

Producers and intermediaries represent the third element of the simplified model of the consumer–supplier relationship in the sports industry. Producers include those organizations or individuals that help "manufacture" the sporting event, such as owners, sanctioning bodies, and sports equipment manufacturers. Intermediaries are also critical to the sports industry because they bring the sport to the end user of the sports product. Sponsors, the media, and agents are the three intermediaries presented in this chapter.

Although sports marketers must have a thorough understanding of the sports industry to be successful, the tool of their trade is the sports marketing mix. The sports marketing mix is defined as the coordinated set of elements that sports organizations use to meet their marketing mix objectives and satisfy consumers' needs. The elements of the marketing mix are sports products, distribution or place, pricing, and promotion.

In addition to the marketing mix, another central element of marketing is the exchange process. The exchange process is defined as a marketing transaction in which the buyer gives something of value to the seller in return for goods and services. One of the things that makes the sports industry so unique is the complex nature of the exchange process and the many exchanges that take place within a single sporting event.

To manage the complexities of the sports industry and achieve organizational objectives, sports marketers use the strategic sports marketing process. The strategic sports marketing process consists of three major parts: planning, implementation, and control. The planning process begins by understanding consumers' needs, selecting a group of consumers with similar needs, and positioning the sports product within this group of consumers. The final step of the planning phase is to develop a marketing mix that will appeal to the targeted group of consumers and carry out the desired positioning. The second major part of the strategic sports marketing process is putting the plans into action or implementation. Finally, the plans are evaluated to determine whether organizational objectives and marketing goals are being met. This third, and final, part of the strategic sports marketing process is called control.

Key Terms

- agent, p. 25
- amateur sporting event, p. 14
- benefits, p. 16
- exchange, p. 28
- goods, p. 16
- licensing, p. 18
- marketing myopia, p. 5
- marketing orientation, p. 6
- organized sporting events, p. 14
- participants, p. 13
- personal training, p. 20
- professional sports, p. 14
- producers and intermediaries, p. 23
- services, p. 16
- simplified model of the consumer–supplier relationship, p. 11
- spectators, p. 11
- sport, p. 4
- sporting event, p. 16
- sporting goods, p. 18
- sports equipment manufacturers, p. 27
- sports information, p. 21
- sports marketing, p. 3
- sports marketing mix, p. 27
- sports product, p. 16
- sports product map, p. 22
- sports sponsorship, p. 15
- strategic sports marketing process, p. 29
- unorganized sports, p. 14

Review Questions

1. Define sports marketing and discuss how sports are related to entertainment.
2. What is a marketing orientation, and how do sports organizations practice a marketing orientation?
3. Discuss some of the ways that the sports marketing industry is growing.
4. Outline the simplified model of the consumer–supplier relationship in the sports industry.
5. What are the three distinct types of sports consumers? What are the different types of spectators? How are sports participants categorized?
6. Define sports products. What are the different types of sports products discussed in the simplified model of the consumer–supplier relationship in the sports industry?
7. Describe the different producers and intermediaries in the simplified model of the consumer–supplier relationship in the sports industry.
8. What are the basic elements of the sports marketing mix?
9. What is the marketing exchange process, and why is the exchange process critical for sports marketers?
10. Define the strategic sports marketing process, and discuss the various elements in the strategic sports marketing process.

Exercises

1. Provide five recent examples of sports marketing that have been in the news and describe how each relates to our definition of sports marketing.
2. How does sport differ from other forms of entertainment?
3. Provide an example of a sports organization that suffers from marketing myopia and another sports organization that defines its business as entertainment. Justify your choices.
4. Attend a high school, college, and professional sporting event and comment on the marketing orientation of the event at each level of competition.
5. Provide three examples of how you would *measure growth* in the sports marketing industry. What evidence do you have that the number of people participating in sports is growing?
6. Discuss the disadvantages and advantages of attending sporting events versus consuming a sporting event through the media (e.g., television or radio).
7. Develop a list of all the sports products produced by your college or university. Which are goods and which are services? Identify ways in which the marketing of the goods differs from the marketing of the services.
8. Choose any professional sports team and describe how it puts the basic sports marketing functions into practice.

Internet Exercises

1. Using Internet sites, support the growth of the sporting goods industry.

2. Compare and contrast the Internet sites of three professional sports teams. Which site has the strongest marketing orientation? Why?

Endnotes

1   John Mossman, "Denver to Host 2005 NBA All-Star Game," The Associated Press (June 16, 2003).

2. David Barboza, "Michael Jordan Movie Is Sports Marketing in New and Thinner Air," *The New York Times* (May 1, 2000), C16.

3. Ultimate Sports Resort, http://www.ultimatesportsresort.com/summary.html.

4. A. K. Kohli and B. J. Jaworski, "Marketing Orientation: The Construct, Research Propositions, and Managerial Implications," *Journal of Marketing* 54 (2): 1–18.

5. Jeffery D. Derrick, "Marketing Orientation in Minor League Baseball," www.cjsm.com/Vol1/derrick.html.

6. Michele Himmelberg, "The Sporting Life; Long Hours, Low Pay, Starting at the Bottom, What Fun!" *Orange County Register* (June 14, 1999), c1; Don Walker, "Money Game: Sports Becoming Big Business," *Journal Sentinel,* www.jsonline.com/news/gen/jan00/csports23012200.asp.

7. "NFL Sets All-Time Paid Attendance Record Fifth Straight Year; Surpasses 22 Million in Total Attendance for First Time," http://io.stlouisrams.com/MediaContent/2007/03/26/06/NFLPaidAttendance_60929.pdf

8. "NBA Sets All-Time Attendance Records," April 20, 2006, http://www.nba.com/news/attendancerecords_060420.html?rss=true.

9. "MLB Shatters Attendance Record. Fourth Consecutive Record Year for Baseball; Total Surpasses 79.5 million,"http://pressbox.mlb.com/news/press_releases/press_release.jsp?ymd=20071002&content_id=2245590&vkey=pr_mlb&fext=.jsp&c_id=mlb.

10. "NHL Sets Records for Total, Average Attendance," NHL.com, April 9, 2007, http://www.nhl.com/nhl/app?articleid=298726&page=NewsPage&service=page.

11. "2008 Super Bowl is the Second Most-Watched TV Show Ever," http://philly.com/dailynews/local/20082004_2008_Super_Bowl_is_the_second_most-watched_TV_show_ever.html.

12. http://multimedia.olympic.org/pdf/en_report_344.pdf.

13. "Olympics Flame Out in Ratings," http://www.usatoday.com/life/television/news/2006–02–27-olympics-ratings_x.htm.

14. http://www.espncms.com/index.aspx?s1=57&id=34.

15. "NBC Shells Out $2.2 Billion for Olympic Broadcast Rights,"Jun 16, 2003. http://broadcastengineering.com/news/broadcasting_nbc_shells_billion/.

16. Stedman Graham, Joe Jeff Goldblatt, and Lisa Delphy, *The Ultimate Guide to Sport Event Management and Marketing* (Chicago: Irwin, 1995), 6.

17. Michele Himmelberg, "The Sporting Life; Long Hours, Low Pay, Starting at the Bottom, What Fun!" *Orange County Register* (June 14, 1999), c1; Don Walker, "Money Game: Sports Becoming Big Business," *Journal Sentinel,* www.jsonline.com/news/gen/jan00/csports23012200.asp.

18. Nick Pandya, "Sporting a New Career," *The Guardian* (February 27, 1999), 2.

19. Vito Stellino, "Big NFL Figures Disguise Modest Corporate Reality; Financially, Few Teams Play major-league Ball," *The Baltimore Sun* (July 27, 1999), 1C; Larry Weisman, "TV Cash Expands NFL Millionaires Club," *USA Today* (June 16, 1999), 1C.

20. 2006 Consumer Equipment Purchases by Sport http://www.sgma.com/associations/5119/files/%Market%20Rec%20Report%202006.pdf

21. Nigel Pope, "Overview of Current Sponsorship Thought," www.cjsm.com/Vol2/pope21.htm.

22. "Sponsorship Fees Near $15 Billion: IEG," http://promomagazine.com/research/other/sponsorship_fees_15_billion_012407/.

23. Geoffrey Smith, "Sports: Walk, Don't Schuss," *Business Week,* www.businessweek.com/1997/49/b3556153.htm.

24. "The FIFA World Cup TV Viewing Figures,"http://www.fifa.com/mm/document/fifafacts/ffprojects/ip-401_05a_tvstats_9299.pdf.

25. Skip Rozin, "Welcome to U.S. Widget Stadium," *Business Week* (September 11, 2000), 125–126.

26. "Venue Media Teams with Williams to Provide Choice Seat Interactive Network at Super Bowl XXXII," *Yahoo!—The Williams Companies Inc. Company News,* www.biz.yahoo.com/bw/980123/venue_medi_1. html.

27. PR Newswire, "U.S. Mobile Technologies from Epson and Symbol Provide Seat-Side Concessions at Angel Stadium of Anaheim; Mobile POS Boosts Sales, Keeps Fans and Concession Staff Happy," November 6, 2006.

28. SGMA Recreation Market Report—2006 Edition,http://www.sgma.com/associations/5119/files/Market%20Rec%20Report%202006.pdf.

29. Industry Report, http://www.licensemag.com/licensemag/data/articlestandard//licensemag/412007/463807/article.pdf, October 2007.

30. Erik Spanberg, "An Industry Reshuffles to Recapture Its Youth," http://www.csmonitor.com/2005/0801/p11s01-alsp.html.

31. Thomas Corwin, "Sports-Card Dealers Strike Out; Web Traders Hurting Bricks-and-Mortar Stores, Owners Say," *The Plain Dealer* (November 4, 2000), 1C.

32. Survey of International Health, Racquet and Sportsclub Association members, 2005, http://fitnessbusinesspro.com/statistics/.

33. "Health and Fitness Industry Applauds Colorado and Denver for Leading the Nation in Health Club Memberships," http://cms.ihrsa.org/IHRSA/viewPage.cfm?pageId=3101.

34. *ESPN Magazine* Circulation, http://www.espncms.com/index.aspx?id=125.

35. Jill Andresky Frasier, "Root, Root, Root for Your Own Team," *Inc.* (July 1997), 111.

36. Angelo Bruscus, "Cuban Swears by the Bottom Line," *Seattle Post-Intelligencer Reporter,* June 20, 2007.

37. "The Role of the PGA in America," www.pga.com/FAQ/pga_role.html.

38. Kevin Iole, "Sanctioning Bodies Endanger Boxing," *Las Vegas Review-Journal,* April 29, 2006.

39. Phil Schaaf, *Sports Marketing: It's Not Just a Game Anymore* (Amherst, MA: Prometheus Books, 1995), 46–75.

40. "Frequently Asked Questions," Sim-Gratton, Inc., www.home.istar.ca/~simagent/faq.html.

41. Associated Press, "Mighty No More: Ducks Change Name, Uniforms, Logo," National Hockey League Newswire. (June 22, 2006).

42. Andrea Tortora, "NASCAR Track City's Future?" *The Enquirer* (November 16, 1997).

2

CONTINGENCY FRAMEWORK FOR STRATEGIC SPORTS MARKETING

After completing this chapter, you should be able to:

- Understand the contingency framework for strategic sports marketing.
- Describe the strategic sports marketing process.
- Describe the major internal contingencies and explain how they affect the strategic sports marketing process.
- Describe external contingencies and explain how they affect the strategic sports marketing process.
- Discuss the importance of monitoring external contingencies and environmental scanning.
- Explain and conduct a SWOT analysis.

The foundation of any effective sports organization is a sound, yet flexible, strategic framework. The process should be systematic and well organized, but must be readily adaptable to changes in the environment. In fact, as the next article illustrates, the league may even shut down for a season. Each strategic marketing process may have unique characteristics, but the fundamentals are all the same. To help make sense of the complex and rapidly changing sports industry, we use a contingency framework to guide the strategic sports marketing process. For the remainder of this chapter, let us look at an overview of this process.

CONTINGENCY FRAMEWORK FOR STRATEGIC SPORTS MARKETING

Sports marketing managers must be prepared to face a continually changing environment. As Burton and Howard pointed out, "marketers considering careers or already employed in sports marketing must be prepared for unexpected, often negative actions that jeopardize a sports organization's brand equity."[1] Think about what can happen over the course of an event or a season. The team that was supposed to win the championship cannot seem to win a game or the likely cellar dwellers end up contending for titles. Take, for example, the Detroit Tigers. They lost 406 games from 2002 through 2005 and their last winning season was 1993. Suddenly they win the American League

After the Lockout, NHL Is Still Thriving

The truth today in all professional sports is that schedules might end—but leagues never shut down. Just about three and a half months after the National Hockey League Commissioner, Gary Bettman, handed the Stanley Cup to Carolina Hurricanes captain Rod Brind'Amour, and 27 months after many predicted doom and gloom for the NHL because of an owner's lockout, the 30 NHL franchises are back at work. Franchises have to sell luxury boxes, club seats, and season subscriptions and tickets to the regular folks who want to see a few games here and there.

On the league level, there are sponsorships and marketing agreements that need to be sold. The NHL, which has a revenue-sharing agreement with NBC (television networks typically pay upfront for American broadcast rights), has the additional task of finding national sponsors for network broadcasts. On the local level, NHL teams are charged with acquiring sponsors and marketing partners and, in some cases, have to find sponsors for games aired on regional sports cable channels. Canadian television, various satellite and cable TV packages, along with international broadcast arrangements, radio, the Internet, and all the other technically advanced gadgets like iPods, cellular downloads, and video games also require attention.

So just how is the NHL doing two years after the lockout that wiped out the 2004–05 season?

It's too early to gauge by ticket sales, but NBC has added a number of games to its hockey package and the Peacock may shortly announce that it will extend its broadcast agreement with the league beyond 2007. The NHL's cable partner, Versus, now reaches 70 million homes in America. So the league figures to increase its national exposure in America. Versus is not at ESPN subscriber levels, but a cable TV network—even one that is as branded as the self-described "World Wide Leader" ESPN—is not the sole source of hockey or sports on TV, the Internet, video on-demand, or other technology. A number of Versus cablecasts will be shown on Yahoo! Sports on a weekly basis, and the NHL will be given prominent space on the new NBCSports Web site when the network begins its 2007 broadcast package.

The NHL also begins the second year of a 10-year $100 million deal with XM, which has a dedicated hockey channel. The league will enjoy some presence on Sirius this year and in 2007–08, XM will become the exclusive satellite radio partner. The XM deal followed the deal with Versus and came just weeks after the end of the lockout. The lockout seemed to have little effect on NHL corporate partnerships.

At some point during the next two years, when TV rights come up for renegotiation, the league is going to hit

a financial jackpot in Canada. A Canadian senate committee would like to see the state-run Canadian Broadcast Corporation get out of the sports business. The CBC holds the rights to the biggest TV sporting franchise in Canada, "Hockey Night in Canada," and the program is a big revenue and audience producer for the CBC. There is nothing better for Bettman and the 30 NHL owners than to see a major bidding war between the CBC and the CTV-TSN combination. TSN is partly owned by the Walt Disney Company (which owns ESPN) and it seems highly unlikely ESPN will be carrying NHL games in America anytime soon—for a variety of reasons—even though the NHL-Versus deal could end after the 2006–07 season.

Comcast, which owns the Philadelphia Flyers and 76ers, created Versus (previously the Outdoor Life Network, then OLN) and is partnered in various cable TV deals with the Boston Bruins, Madison Square Garden, the Washington Capitals, and the Chicago Blackhawks ownership groups. ESPN does not have any partnerships with NHL ownership at the moment. Comcast is also creating an American hockey channel.

On the sponsorship side, the 2004–05 lockout and its aftermath has not scared off companies from signing marketing deals with the league. Pepsi is in, and Coke is out, as the official beverage of the NHL. The Pepsi-owned Gatorade will become the "official sports drink" of the NHL. The deal was signed last June, just days after Pepsi-QTG Canada and Frito Lay Canada signed a three-year

(Continued)

(Continued)

marketing agreement with the Pittsburgh Penguins center, Sidney Crosby.

Exactly where Crosby will be playing after this season is a major concern for the NHL. The Penguins aren't trading Crosby but the franchise is being sold to a Hartford businessman, Sam Fingold, who may move the team to Kansas City if Pittsburgh does not commit to building a new arena soon.

Mario Lemieux and his partners have decided they don't want the franchise anymore. This leaves the NHL and Fingold to deal with a possible franchise shift. Lemieux and his partners did work out a deal with a Mississippi-based company, the Isle of Capri Casinos, to help fund a new Pittsburgh arena with some of the proceeds from a slot machine parlor license, should Harrisburg, Penn., state gaming officials award the casino company a slot license. If another group gets the slots license, there is no guarantee that Pittsburgh will receive funding for a new building.

Kansas City and Houston, along with Las Vegas, Hamilton, Winnipeg, Quebec City, and Hartford—three cities that once had NHL franchises—seem to be most interested in landing an NHL team.

There seems to be potential for problems to arise in certain cities: The ownership groups in Edmonton and Calgary want to replace existing arenas, while San Jose's ownership has informed the city that its 13- year-old arena needs sprucing up. It has asked San Jose officials to look into having the arena re-fitted so the Sharks' ownership can go after a National Basketball Association franchise.

It also appears that Newark Mayor Cory Booker is not going to stop construction of an arena in the city as he had threatened shortly before he assumed office in July. The arena, which will be home to the New Jersey Devils, is scheduled to open in about a year. Booker thought the monies allocated for arena construction would be better spent on other projects in Newark.

On Long Island, Islanders owner Charles Wang will oversee the renovation of Nassau Coliseum; apparently, he is serious about staying on the Island as he demonstrated in signing goaltender Rick DiPietro to be the face of the organization through 2021.

When NHL owners and players ended sports' longest work stoppage 14 months ago, there were questions about the league's future. The questions were way off base. The sports business is very sophisticated and all leagues have business plans—something that was virtually unheard of 40 years ago.

Sports fans come in two varieties: ticket-buyers and those who never set foot in arenas or stadiums. Owners cater to the ticket-buyers and hope that sports fans that watch the games on TV or call in to sports radio talk shows produce revenue by buying T-shirts and other team paraphernalia.

The NHL still maintains a loyal following from both these types of fans. And that's why the league was able to get back to doing business with no problems. Their customers have no problems with the way the NHL goes about doing its business.

Source: Evan Weiner, *New York Sun,* http://www.nysun.com/article/40978, October 5, 2006.

Championship in 2006 and play for the World Series. The New Orleans Saints also provide a great example of a team who faced tremendous odds after suffering displacement from Hurricane Katrina and went on to unexpectedly make the 2006 NFL playoffs. In fact, Hurricane Katrina and its impact on the city of New Orleans and the Saints ranks as one of the most compelling examples of the changing environment that marketers cannot plan for.

Other unexpected events become commonplace in the sports marketing landscape. The star player gets injured halfway through the season. Attendance at the sporting event is affected by poor weather conditions. Leagues are shut down by lockouts. Team owners threaten to move the franchise, build new stadiums, and change personnel. All this affects the sports marketing process.

At the collegiate level, a different set of situations may alter the strategic marketing process. For example, players may be declared ineligible because of grades, star players may leave school early to join the professional ranks, programs may be suspended for violation of NCAA regulations, or conferences may be realigned.

Sports marketers need to be prepared for either positive or negative changes in the environment. These factors are out of the sports marketer's control, but they must be acknowledged and managed. Sports marketers must be prepared to cope with these rapid changes. One model that provides a system for understanding and managing the complexities of the sports marketing environment is called the **contingency framework for strategic sports marketing.**

Contingency Approaches

Contingency models were originally developed for managers who wanted to be responsive to the complexities of their organization and the changing environments in which they operate.[2] Several elements of the contingency framework make it especially useful for sport marketers. First, sports marketers operate in unpredictable and rapidly changing environments. They can neither predict team or player success nor control scheduling or trades. A quote by former New York Mets Marketing Vice President Michael Aronin, who spent 13 years with Clairol, captures the essence of this idea: "Before, I had control of the product, I could design it the way I wanted it to be. Here the product changes every day and you've got to adapt quickly to these changes".[3]

Second, the contingency approach suggests that no one marketing strategy is more effective than another. However, one particular strategy may be more appropriate than another for a specific sports organization in a particular environment. For example, sports marketers for the Boston Red Sox have years of tradition on their side that influence their strategic planning. This marketing strategy, however, will not necessarily meet the needs of the relatively new teams such as the Houston Dynamo of MLS. Likewise, strategies for an NCAA Division I program are not always appropriate for a Division II program. The contingency framework can provide the means for developing an effective marketing strategy in all these situations.

Third, a contingency model uses a systems perspective, one that assumes an organization does not operate in isolation but interacts with other systems. In other words, although an organization is dependent on its environment to exist and be successful, it can also play a role in shaping events outside the firm. Think about the Chicago Black Hawks and all the resources required from the environment to produce the core product—entertainment. These resources include professional athletes, owners, management and support personnel, and minor league franchises to supply talent, facilities, other competitors, and fans. The different environments that the Chicago Black Hawks actively interact with and influence include the community, the NHL, sponsors, employees and their families, and the sport itself. Understanding the relationship between the organization and its many environments is fundamental to grasping the nature of the contingency approach. In fact, the complex relationship that sports organizations have with their many publics (e.g., fans, government, businesses, and other teams) is one of the things that makes sports marketing so complicated and so unique.

One way of thinking about the environments that affect sports organizations is to separate them on the basis of internal versus external contingencies. The external contingencies are factors outside the organization's control; the internal are considered controllable from the organization's perspective. It is important to realize that both the internal and external factors are perceived to be beyond the control, though not the influence, of the sports marketer.

The essence of contingency approaches is trying to predict and strategically align the strategic marketing process with the internal and external contingencies. This alignment is typically referred to as strategic fit or just "fit." Let us look at the contingency approach shown in Figure 2.1 in greater detail.

The focus of the contingency framework for sports marketing, and the emphasis of this book, is the strategic sports marketing process. The three primary components of this process are planning, implementation, and control. The planning phase begins with understanding the consumers of sports. As previously discussed, these consumers may

FIGURE 2.1   Contingency Framework for Strategic Sports Marketing

be participants, spectators, or perhaps both. Once information regarding the potential consumers is gathered and analyzed, **market selection decisions** can be made. These decisions are used to segment markets, choose the targeted consumers, and position the sports product against the competition. The final step of the planning phase is to develop the sports marketing mix that will most efficiently and effectively reach the target market.

Effective planning is merely the first step in a successful strategic sports marketing program. The best-laid plans are useless without a method for carrying them out and monitoring them. The process of executing the marketing program, or mix, is referred to as implementation. The evaluation of these plans is known as the control phase of the strategic marketing plan. These two phases, implementation and control, are the second and third steps of the strategic sports marketing process.

As you can see from the model, a contingency framework calls for alignment, or fit, between the strategic marketing process (e.g., planning, implementation, and control) and external and internal contingencies. Fit is based on determining the internal strengths and weaknesses of the sports organizations, as well as examining the external opportunities and threats that exist. **External contingencies** are defined as all influences outside the organization that can affect the organization's strategic marketing process. These external contingencies include factors such as competition, regulatory and political issues, demographic trends, technology, culture and values, and the physical environment. **Internal contingencies** are all the influences within the organization that can affect the strategic marketing process. These internal contingencies usually include the **vision** and mission of the organization, organizational goals and strategies for reaching those goals, and the organizational structure and systems.

The **strategic sports marketing process** was defined in Chapter 1 as the process of planning, implementing, and controlling marketing efforts to meet organizational goals and satisfy consumers' needs (see also Figure 2.2) and is the heart of the contingency

FIGURE 2.2 Strategic Sports Marketing Process

PLANNING PHASE

Step 1: Understanding Consumers' Needs
    A. Marketing research
    B. Consumers as participants
    C. Consumers as spectators

Step 2: Market Selection Decisions
    A. Marketing segmentation
    B. Target markets
    C. Positioning

Step 3: Marketing Mix Decisions
    A. Sports products
    B. Pricing
    C. Promotion
    D. Place

IMPLEMENTATION PHASE

CONTROL PHASE

framework. The **planning phase,** which is the most critical, begins with understanding the consumers of sport through marketing research and identifying consumer wants and needs. Next, market selection decisions are made, keeping the external and internal contingencies in mind. Finally, the **marketing mix,** also known as *the four Ps,* is developed and *integrated* to meet the identified sport consumer needs.

Once the planning phase is completed, plans are executed in the **implementation phase.** In this second phase of the strategic sports marketing process, decisions such as who will carry out the plans, when the plans will be executed, and how the plans will be executed are addressed. After implementing the plans, the third phase is to evaluate the response to the plans to determine their effectiveness. This is called the **control phase.** The strategic sports marketing process and its three phases will be described in detail in the remainder of the book. Let's turn to a discussion of the internal and external contingencies for the rest of this chapter.

INTERNAL AND EXTERNAL CONTINGENCIES

A complex relationship exists between internal contingencies and the strategic marketing process. Sports marketers must ensure that the marketing strategies are aligned with the broader organizational purpose. Factors controlled by the organization such as its vision and mission, organizational objectives, and **organizational culture** must be considered carefully. Additionally, this organizational strategy is often based on changes that occur in the environment. It is at this point that external and internal contingencies must complement one another. Let's take a further look at the various factors that make up the internal and external contingencies and gain an appreciation for just how much they can influence the strategic marketing process.

INTERNAL CONTINGENCIES

Internal contingencies are all influences within and under the control of the sports organization that can affect the strategic sports marketing process. Typically, the internal or controllable factors, such as designing the vision and mission, are the function of top management. In other words, these organizational decisions are usually made by top management rather than sports marketing managers. The more marketing-oriented the organization, the more the marketing function becomes involved in the initial development and refinement of decisions regarding the internal contingencies. Irrespective of their involvement, sports marketers should have an understanding of internal contingencies and how they influence the strategic marketing process Let us describe some of the internal contingencies that sports marketers must consider within the contingency framework.

Vision and Mission

One of the first steps in developing a strategic direction for an organization is shaping a vision. The **vision** has been described as a long-term road map of where the organization is headed. It creates organizational purpose and identity. A well-written vision should be a prerequisite for effective strategic leadership in an organization. The vision should address the following:

- Where does the organization plan to go from here?
- What business do we want to be in?
- What customer needs do we want to satisfy?
- What capabilities are required for the future?

As you can see, the organizational questions addressed in the vision are all oriented toward the future. The mission, however, is a written statement about the organization's present situation. The purpose of a written mission statement is to inform various stakeholders (e.g., consumers, employees, general public, and suppliers) about the direction of the organization. It is particularly useful for motivating employees internally and for communicating with consumers outside the organization. Here are examples of mission statements constructed by New Balance athletic footwear company[4] and the University of Texas at Austin Athletics Departments.[5]

Mission of New Balance
To be the world's leading manufacturer of high performance athletic and active lifestyle products while operating in a socially responsible manner.

Mission of the University of Texas at Austin Athletics Departments
The Athletics Departments at The University of Texas at Austin are committed to The University's mission of achieving excellence in education, research, and public service. Specifically, our mission is focused on three interrelated communities:

Student-Athletes
To provide opportunities and support for University student-athletes to achieve academically and compete athletically at the highest level, and provide programming and resources that help prepare them with skills for life.

University Community
To operate with quality and integrity in our role as a focal point for school identity and spirit, while complementing the academic, cultural, and social facets of University life for the general student body, faculty, staff, and alumni.

Citizens of the State of Texas
To support the community through public service and to be a source of pride and entertainment by representing the state of Texas with internationally successful sport programs and thereby benefit the state economy.

These mission statements address several key questions:

- What business are we currently in?
- Who are our current customers?
- What is the scope of our market?
- How do we currently meet the needs of our customers?

In addition to addressing these four key questions, the mission statements for New Balance and the UT at Austin Athletic Departments also contain statements about the core values of the organization. In fact, these core values are fundamental to carrying out the vision and mission of the organization.

How do mission and vision influence the strategic sports marketing process? Both vision and mission define the consumers of sport in broad terms. For example, New Balance sees its customers from a global perspective, whereas the University of Texas uses the term *communities* to represent its consumers. Also, vision and mission define the products and services that are being marketed to consumers. New Balance, in stating its core offering is high-performance athletic and active lifestyle products, takes a somewhat broad view in defining its products and services; in fact, much broader than its previous mission where the sole focus was on athletic footwear. The vision and mission also help to identify the needs of consumers and ultimately guide the marketing process in meeting these needs.

Nike provides an excellent illustration of the dependent relationship among vision, mission, and the strategic marketing process. Originally, the product was aimed toward the serious track athlete who wanted a low-priced, high-quality performance shoe for competition. By 1969, Nike had begun to build a strong brand reputation as the shoe for competitive athletes. Over time, however, Nike redefined and broadened its vision and mission. In 1978, footwear represented 97 percent of Nike's total sales. Today, this percentage has decreased to roughly 67 percent as Nike produces footwear and apparel to meet the needs of almost every consumer in global markets. Nike's strategic decision to sell more than just high-performance footwear aimed only to serious athletes has changed the entire marketing mix. Now, more Nike products are being sold at more places than ever before. In fact, Nike's mission is "to bring inspiration and innovation to every athlete in the world."[6]

Organizational Objectives and Marketing Goals

Organizational Objectives

The **objectives** of the organization stem from vision and mission. They convert the vision and mission into performance targets to be achieved within a specified timeframe. Objectives can be thought of as signposts along the road that help an organization focus on its purpose as stated in the mission statement. More specifically, an objective is a long-range purpose that is not quantified or limited to a time period.

Organizational objectives are needed to define both financial and strategic direction. Organizational leaders typically develop two types of objectives: financial objectives and strategic objectives. Financial objectives specify the performance that an organization wants to achieve in terms of revenues and profits. Achieving these financial performance objectives is critical to the long-term survival of the organization. Some examples of financial objectives include the following:

- growth in revenues,
- increase in profit margins, and
- improved return on investment (ROI).

Strategic objectives are related to the performance and direction of the organization. Achieving strategic objectives is critical to the long-term market position and competitiveness of an organization. Whereas strategic objectives may not have a direct link to the bottom line of an organization, they ultimately have an impact on its financial performance. Here are a few examples of general strategic objectives:

- increased market share,
- enhanced community relations efforts, and
- superior customer service.

Marketing Goals

Marketing goals guide the strategic marketing process and are based on organizational objectives. A **goal** is a short-term purpose that is measurable and challenging, yet attainable and time specific.

Here is a sampling of common marketing goals:

- Increase ticket sales by 5 percent over the next year.
- Introduce a new product or service each year.
- Generate 500 new season ticket holders prior to the next season.
- Over the next six months, increase awareness levels from 10 to 25 percent for women between the ages of 18 and 34 regarding a new sports product.

Although multiple goals are acceptable, goals in some areas (e.g., marketing and finance) may conflict, and care must be taken to reduce any potential conflict. After developing marketing goals, the organization may want to examine them based on the following criteria:

- *Suitability*—The marketing goals must follow the direction of the organization and support the organization's business vision and mission.
- *Measurability*—The marketing goals must be evaluated over a specific timeframe (such as the examples just discussed).
- *Feasibility*—The marketing goals should be within the scope of what the organization can accomplish, given its resources.
- *Acceptability*—The marketing goals must be agreed upon by all levels within the organization. Top management must feel that the goals are moving the organization in the desired direction; middle managers and first-line supervisors must feel the goals are achievable within the specified timeframe.
- *Flexibility*—The marketing goals must not be too rigid, given uncontrollable or temporary situational factors. This is especially true when adopting the contingency framework.
- *Motivating*—The marketing goals must be reachable but challenging. If the goals are too easy or too hard, then they will not direct behavior toward their fulfillment.

- *Understandability*—The marketing goals should be stated in terms that are clear and simple. If any ambiguities arise, people may inadvertently work against the goals.
- *Commitment*—Employees within the sports marketing organization should feel that it is their responsibility to ensure goals are achieved. As such, managers must empower employees so everyone in the organization is committed and will act to achieve goals.
- *People Participation*—As with commitment, all employees in the organization should be allowed to participate in the development of marketing goals. Greater employee involvement in setting goals will foster greater commitment to goal attainment.
- *Linkage*—As discussed earlier, marketing goals must be developed with an eye toward achieving the broader organizational objectives. Marketing goals incongruent with organizational direction are ineffective.

Organizational Strategies

Organizational strategies are the means by which the organization achieves its organizational objectives and marketing goals. Whereas the organizational vision, mission, objectives, and goals are the "what," the organizational strategy is the "how." It is, in essence, the game plan for the sports organization. Just as football teams adopt different game plans for different competitors, sports organizations must be able to readily adapt to changing environmental conditions. Remember, flexibility and responsiveness are the cornerstones of the contingency framework.

In general, there are four levels of strategy development within organizations: corporate strategy, business strategy, functional strategy, and operational strategy. The relationship among these strategy levels is pictured in Figure 2.3. Notice that there must be a good fit among the levels, vertically and horizontally, for the firm to succeed.

Corporate-level strategies represent the overall game plan for organizations that compete in more than one industry. Business-level strategies define how a business unit gains advantage over competitors within the relevant industry. Functional-level strategies are those developed by each functional area within a business unit. For example, the strategic sports marketing process is the functional-level strategy developed by sports marketing managers, just as financial strategy is the purview of their finance manager counterparts. The operational-level strategies are more

FIGURE 2.3 Relationship Between Levels of Strategy

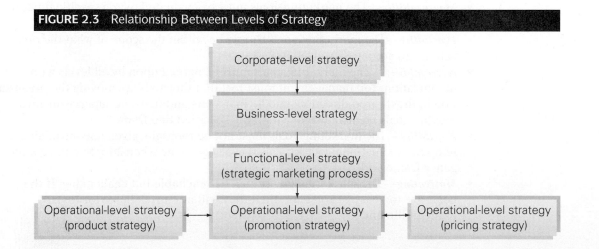

narrow in scope. Their primary goal is to support the functional-level strategies. Let us take a look at the relationship among the four levels of strategy at the Maloof Companies to see how a good fit among strategies can lead to overall organizational effectiveness.

The Maloof Companies[7] are a diversified group of business ventures including entertainment, sports, hotels, casinos, banking, food and beverage, and transportation headquartered in Albuquerque, New Mexico, and operated in New Mexico, Colorado, and Nevada. The Maloof family owns the Palms, a $285 million hotel casino just off the Las Vegas strip with a 42-story tower and 447 guestrooms. In addition to their gaming business, the Maloofs have exclusive proprietorship rights to the distribution of Coors beer throughout New Mexico. The Maloof Companies also are the largest single shareholder in Wells Fargo Bank, which operates banks and branches in 23 states throughout the Western United States with over $200 billion in assets and 15 million customers. The Maloofs are in the process of expanding their business in the entertainment industry with the development of Maloof Productions and Maloof Music. Maloof Productions is committed to developing and producing quality television and motion picture entertainment. Also of interest is that the Maloof Companies are best known for being the owners of the Sacramento Kings of the National Basketball Association (NBA) and the Sacramento Monarchs of the Women's National Basketball Association (WNBA).

The corporate strategy for the Maloof Companies is based on competing in all of these industries. The corporate strategy should allow the Maloof Companies to obtain the broader organizational goals and pursue its vision and mission.

At the business level, Maloof management specifies strategies for each business unit within each of the industry segments. For example, the Kings and the Monarchs would each have a unique business-level strategy, even though they are in the same industry sector—sports. These strategies are aimed at gaining competitive advantage within each relevant industry. However, each business-level strategy must support the corporate-level strategy, goals, vision, and mission.

At Maloof Corporation, there are numerous functional areas within the organization. For example, the Kings functional areas may include finance and administration, general management and operations, business affairs, civic affairs, sales, and marketing. Leadership within each of these functional areas would be responsible for designing their own strategies to meet their respective business-level strategies.

Finally, within the functional areas such as sales and marketing, operational-level strategies are developed. Promotion, ticket sales, product, and pricing strategies must all be designed and coordinated to attain the sales and marketing objectives set forth in the functional-level strategy. As you can see, sports marketing managers responsible for each operational unit must be concerned with satisfying not only their own goals, but also the objectives of the broader organization.

Corporate Level

Most professional sports franchises are owned by individuals or corporations that have many business interests. Sometimes these businesses are related, and sometimes the professional sports franchise is nothing more than a hobby of a wealthy owner. Today, the latter is becoming far less common as corporations include sports franchises in their portfolio. Even more rare is the sports franchise owned and operated as the primary, if not sole, source of owner income (e.g., the Mike Brown family and the Cincinnati Bengals).

There are typically two types of diversified companies—those that pursue related diversification and those that pursue unrelated diversification. In related diversification, the corporation will choose to pursue markets in which it can achieve synergy in marketing, operations, or management. In other words, the corporation looks for markets that are similar to its existing products and markets. The underlying principle in related diversification is that a company that is successful in existing markets is more likely to achieve success in similar markets. Unrelated diversification, however, refers to competing in markets that are dissimilar to existing markets. The primary criteria for choosing markets are based on spreading financial risk over different markets.

Professional sports franchises can be owned privately by one or more individuals, publicly owned corporations, or some combination of both. Corporate ownership of a major league sports team is becoming more rare. Most teams are owned by individual investors who have staked their personal fortunes to buy their franchises, which they often operate as a public trust.

On the corporate side, most organizations have discovered the problems inherent with running a sports organization. Fewer and fewer corporations are dabbling into the business of owning sports teams. And that trend does not appear likely to shift in the coming years.

Developing Corporate-Level Strategy   Corporate-level strategies must make three types of decisions. First, top managers must determine in which markets they want to compete. Sports organizations have a core product and service, plus they also compete in ancillary markets. The core product has been defined as the game itself and the entertainment provided to consumers, whereas secondary markets include sale of licensed merchandise, fantasy sports camps, sports magazines, sports art, and so on. The leaders of a sports organization must also attempt to identify ways of capitalizing on the similarities in markets. For instance, fans for the core product often represent a natural target market for additional products and services. The Comcast Corporation owns a share of the Philadelphia Flyers and 76ers. It also owns Comcast SportsNet (CSN) Philadelphia, a regional sports network that appeals to the same fan base. CSN Philadelphia broadcasts the Comcast76ers and Flyers, along with the Philadelphia Phillies. In addition, CSN-Philadelphia also carries some games of the AHL's Philadelphia Phantoms (also owned by Comcast), indoor soccer of the Philadelphia Kixx, indoor lacrosse of the Philadelphia Wings, and local college sports games, particularly of the Philadelphia Big Five, the Atlantic 10, and the Colonial Athletic Association.

The second type of decision deals with enhancing the performance within each of the chosen markets. Top managers constantly need to monitor the mix of markets in which the organization competes. This evaluation might lead to decisions that involve pursuing growth in some markets or leaving others. These decisions are based on the performance of the market and the ability of the organization to compete successfully within each market.

The third type of decision involves establishing investment priorities and placing organizational resources into the most attractive markets. For a sports organization, this could involve decisions regarding stadium renovation, player contracts, or investing more heavily in merchandising. Corporate decisions within a sports organization must constantly recognize that the core product, the competition itself, is necessary to compete in related markets.

Business-Level Strategy

The next level of strategic decision-making is referred to as business-level, or competitive, strategies. Business-level strategies are based on managing one business interest within the larger corporation. The ultimate goal of business-level strategy decisions is to gain advantage over competitors. In the sports industry, these competitors may be other sports organizations in the area or simply defined as entertainment, in general.

One strategic model for competing at the business level contains four approaches to gaining the competitive advantage. These approaches include low-cost leadership, differentiation, market niche based on lower cost, and market niche based on differentiation. Choices of which of the four strategies to pursue are based on two issues: strategic market target and strategic advantage.

Strategic market targets can include a broader market segment or a narrow, more specialized market niche. Strategic advantage can be gained through becoming a low-cost provider or creating a real or perceived differential advantage.

The focus of low-cost leadership is to serve a broad customer base at the lowest cost to any provider in the industry. Although there may be a number of competitors pursuing this strategy, there will be only one low-cost leader. Many minor league teams compete as low-cost leaders due to the lower operating costs relative to their major league counterparts. Differentiation strategies attempt to compete on the basis of their ability to offer a unique position to a variety of consumers. Typically, companies differentiate themselves through products, services, or promotions. With differentiation strategies, companies can charge a premium for the perceived value of the sports product. Professional sports franchises attempt to differentiate themselves from competitors by providing a high-quality product on and off the field. This is done through a unique blend of sports promotion, community relations, stadium atmosphere, and a winning team.

Although low-cost leadership and differentiation strategies have mass-market appeal, the market niche strategies are concerned with capturing a smaller market segment. These market segments may be based on consumer demographics, geographic location, lifestyle, or a number of other consumer characteristics. Within the market niche chosen, sports organizations can gain strategic advantage through a focus on low cost or differentiation. Two examples of the low-cost market niche strategy include the

Myrtle Beach Pelicans using a low-cost market niche strategy.
Source: Ryan Ibbotson

Association of Volleyball Professionals (AVP), whose tournaments have free general admission, and the Pro Rodeo Cowboys Association (PRCA), whose events are priced inexpensively between $10 and $15.

Functional-Level Strategy

Each functional area of the organization (e.g., marketing, personnel, and operations) must also develop a game plan that supports the business-level and corporate-level initiatives. Again, the contingency framework calls for "fit" between each level of strategy within the organization. It is also important to coordinate among each functional area. For example, the marketing strategies should dovetail with personnel and operations strategies. The strategic marketing process discussed earlier provides the functional-level strategy for the organization's marketing efforts.

Operational-Level Strategy

Within the strategic sports marketing process, several narrower strategies must be considered. Plans must be designed, implemented, and evaluated in areas such as promotion, new product and service development, pricing, sponsorship, and ticket distribution. For example, the Los Angeles Dodgers have unveiled a new operational-level promotion strategy to increase attendance by offering fans an "all you can eat" ticket. The right-field pavilion at Dodger Stadium will be converted into the special section, giving around 3,000 fans as many hot dogs, peanuts, popcorn, nachos, and sodas as they want. Tickets will sell for $35 in advance and $40 on game day.[8] Other major league teams are taking note and testing this idea.

Each strategy at the operational level must also fit the broader strategic marketing process, as well as be integrated across the marketing function.

Organizational Culture

Culture is described as the shared values, beliefs, language, symbols, and tradition that are passed on from generation to generation by members of a society. Culture can affect the importance placed on sports by a region or nation, whether we participate in sports, and even the types of sports we enjoy playing or watching. A similar concept applied to organizations is called organizational culture. **Organizational culture** is the shared values and assumptions of organizational members that shape an identity and establish preferred behaviors in an organization.

As one of the internal contingencies, organizational culture influences the sports marketer in a number of ways. First, the organizational culture of a sports organization dictates the value placed on marketing. For instance, just look at the numbers of people employed and the titles of front office personnel at a variety of sports organizations. These are just two important indicators of the marketing orientation of the organization and the importance of the marketing function.

Second, organizational culture is important because it is linked with organizational effectiveness. In a study of campus recreation programs, organizational culture was found to be positively associated with organizational effectiveness. That is, a positive culture is associated with an effective organization. A positive culture rewards employees for their performance, has open communication, has strong leadership, encourages risk taking, and is adaptive. The ability to adapt to change is one of the most important dimensions from the contingency framework perspective.

Third, the organizational culture of professional sports organizations and college athletic programs not only has an impact on the effectiveness of the organization, but also can influence consumers' perceptions of the organization. For example, the Oakland Raiders, under owner Al Davis, have an organizational culture that values risk taking and doing anything necessary to get the job done. This organizational culture translated to the team's successful and ruthless performance on the field. Subsequently, the fans began to adopt this outlaw image. Ultimately, the black and silver bad boys of football have attracted a fan following that has come to expect this rebel image.

University athletic departments and their programs are also defined by the organizational culture. Athletic programs are known to either value education or attempt to win at all costs and be marred in scandal. The University of Miami, a prestigious, private university known for high-quality academics, has had its image tarnished by athletics, most notably its football program. The University of Miami program has been characterized by its outlaw image since 1986 when several football players were given cars provided by a sports agent to the latest bench-clearing brawl with Florida International University. In this case, the athletic programs have influenced consumers' perceptions of the university at large and may ultimately influence the broader university culture.

EXTERNAL CONTINGENCIES

External contingencies are all influences outside the organization that might affect the strategic sports marketing process. External contingencies include competition; technology; cultural and social trends; physical environment; the political, legal, and regulatory environment; demographics; and the economy. Let us take a brief look at each of these factors and how they might affect sports marketing strategy.

Competition

Assessing the competitive forces in the **marketing environment** is one of the most critical components in the strategic sports marketing process. **Competition** is the attempt all organizations make to serve similar customers.

Sellers realize that, to successfully reach their objectives, they must know who the competition is—both today and tomorrow. In addition, sellers must understand the strengths and weaknesses of their competitors and how competitors' strategies will affect their own planning. An example of many "sellers" attempting to fill the same customer need can be found in college sports broadcasting.

Two digital cable networks, ESPNU and College Sports Television (CSTV), are battling for college sports fans like two prizefighters going toe to toe. The key to victory may be a multimedia strategy. CSTV, started in 2005, is available in more than 20 million homes, although many have access only through a digital pay tier of sports networks. To expand its reach, CSTV gets its biggest Internet showcase yet—the opportunity to broadcast the NCAA men's basketball tournament. ESPN recently launched its own network dedicated to college **sports,** ESPNU. In its first year, ESPNU broadcast about 300 live events ranging from Division I football to volleyball to lacrosse.[9] Table 2.1 illustrates the relative market share of the three primary players.

TABLE 2.1 College Sports TV: The Main Players	
Channel	*Subscribers (millions)*
CSTV	15
ESPNU	8
Fox College Sports	4

The Nature of Competition

Sports marketers most often categorize their competition as product related. There are three types of product-related competition. The first of these is termed **direct competition,** the competition between sellers producing similar products and services. High school football games on a Friday night in a large metropolitan area pose direct competition in that the "product" being offered is very similar. One interesting example of direct competition is found in the game schedule of the NBA Indiana Pacers. High school basketball is so popular in Indiana that the Pacers rarely play a home game on Friday or Saturday night because of the competition posed by high school games.

Another type of product competition is between marketers of substitute products and services, the competition between a product and a similar substitute product. For example, when several professional sports teams have scheduled games that overlap, a consumer may have to choose to attend the Philadelphia 76ers (NBA), the Philadelphia Phillies (MLB), or the Philadelphia Eagles (NFL). Another example of substitute products is when spectators choose to watch a sporting event on television or listen to a radio or Web broadcast rather than attend the event.

The third type of product-related competition, called **indirect competition,** is more general in nature and may be the most critical of all for sports marketers. Marketers of sporting events at any level realize their true competition is other forms of entertainment. Professional, collegiate, and high school sporting events compete with restaurants, concerts, plays, movies, and all other forms of entertainment for the consumer dollar. In fact, a recent study was conducted to examine how closely other forms of entertainment are related to sports. Preliminary findings suggest that respondents' most preferred entertainment activities are going out to dinner, attending parties, playing sports, watching movies, attending sporting events, attending live music or theatre, watching TV, shopping for pleasure, watching sports on TV, dancing, and gambling. In addition, video games seem to be competing in the same "entertainment space" as watching sports on TV. Obviously, the toy industry has capitalized on this notion by creating a multitude of sports-related video games. Some people fear that today's interactive, virtual reality video games may replace watching "real games" on TV. Similarly, playing sports and gambling are perceived to be in the same perceptual space. Sport marketers may want to better understand the excitement and risks associated with gambling and add these attributes when marketing sports participation.

Indirect competition is present when even the popular USC and UCLA football games fail to sell out their respective home stadiums (the L.A. Memorial Coliseum and the Rose Bowl). There is simply too much entertainment competition in Southern California compared to Ann Arbor, Michigan (University of Michigan) or South Bend, Indiana (Notre Dame).

Technology

Technology represents the most rapidly changing environmental influence. New technologies affect the field of sports marketing daily. Some advances in technology have a direct impact on how sports marketers perform their basic marketing functions, whereas others aid in the development of new sports products. For example, new technologies are emerging in advertising, stadium signage, and distributing the sports product. Internet sites remain one of the fastest growing technologies to affect sports marketing (see Appendix B for examples of Internet sites of interest to sports marketers). Internet sites have been developed to provide information on sports (e.g., www.nascar.com), sites of sporting events (e.g., www.daytona500.com), teams (e.g., www.penske.com), and individuals (e.g., www.rustywallace.com). Nascar.com is one of the fastest growing major sports sites and is tenth on the list of the most visited sport Web sites with 205,834,000 visitors in 2006. And, of course, ESPN.com is still the

SkiNet.com providing sports information via the Internet.
Source: Skinet.com

king of sports information on the Internet and part of sports fans' daily routines with 1,244,550,000 visits in 2006.

In addition, the Internet has emerged as another popular way to broadcast live events to fans. Beginning in 1995 AudioNet, Inc. (www.Audionet.com) was one of the pioneers of live game broadcasts via the Internet. Today each of the major leagues offers its fans opportunities to follow games online. Major league Baseball's premium package allows fans to watch up to six games live and includes a "Player Tracker" that alerts the subscriber when his or her favorite player steps to the plate. Season-long access is a reasonable $119.95.

The University of Nebraska game against San Jose State on September 2, 2000, was the first ever intercollegiate football game to be video webcast. The webcast resulted in more than 200,000 video streams around the world. Nebraska Athletic Director Bill Byrne summed it up nicely by stating that "we believe the Internet brings us one step closer to our fans, particularly those who are miles from home and have limited access to our normal radio and TV broadcasts."[10] The NCAA 2007 Men's Basketball Championship is an example of how far things have come in a few years. March Madness® on Demand allowed fans to watch live game broadcasts of CBS Sports television coverage of the NCAA Championship on their computer for free.

In addition to providing information and game coverage to consumers, the Internet has emerged as a popular alternative to purchasing tickets at a box office. MLB Advanced Media, LP (MLBAM), the interactive media and Internet company of major league Baseball, said that in 2006, it sold, on behalf of the league's 30 clubs, a record 20 million tickets online at MLB.com, the official league Web site, and all 30 individual club sites. This represented the first time MLBAM reached the 20 million tickets sold milestone and the company's sixth consecutive annual record.[11]

The accompanying article presents an excellent look at some technologies that have, or will, dramatically altered the way spectators consume sport.

Media Technology: Technologies That Are Changing the Way People Consume Sports

Video on Demand

On its face, video on demand is antithetical to sports, as live viewing is at the center of the sports experience. But that hasn't stopped most sports programmers from pursuing the VOD market with gusto, and they appear to have found the "killer app"—the shortened game. A step up from straight highlights packages, 10- to 15-minute versions of games have become a new way for fans to quickly get the flavor of an event and experience its most dramatic moments.

Optical Tracking Systems

Optical tracking systems are methods of tracking a moving object with a camera, the technology behind features such as the K-Zone on ESPN's Sunday Night Baseball or the ShotSpot animation that marks the exact spot a tennis ball lands.

The gadget: Three sensors are placed on at least two cameras measuring the pan, tilt, and zoom. That data is then combined with algorithms that recognize certain pixel configurations as representing a particular object, such as a moving ball. The data can be analyzed to figure out the trajectory or location of a ball, and then be represented graphically on a screen.

The leaders: Sportvision, which markets the 1st & Ten line for football and many other television enhancement products, has a patent on tracking a moving object in three dimensions and then highlighting it or enhancing it on a field of video. It's the original patent used for the infamous glowing hockey puck, and is the foundation of K-Zone and other Sportvision products that now do not require any sensor being placed in the moving object. Another is Pass Track, which shows the height and speed of a football as it's thrown through the air.

3G

Shorthand for "Third Generation," 3G describes new mobile communications technology that will support robust content including video and high-speed Internet. Already the norm in Europe, 3G will become standard for most new phones sold in the United States by the end of the year, making video highlight and game packages available through most mobile phone carriers.

High Definition

Virtually all major sporting events are now televised in high definition, but the transition on the consumer end is slow. Estimates of the number of homes getting true high definition are in the 4 million to 5 million range. DirecTV, Comcast, and Time Warner Cable have about 2.6 million high-definition customers between them. There are many more sets on the market, but a surprising number of people use them only to watch DVDs or don't have the correct cable box or service.

The gadgets: The most popular models come in two varieties, rear-projection "LCD" sets and flat-paneled plasma televisions. Prices on all HD sets can range from less than $1,000 all the way up to $10,000.

On the production end, new miniature HD cameras have come on the market just in the last 18 months. Sony also has introduced the first multiformat camera that works for both 1080i and 720p, standards used by broadcasters, as well as the ultra-high-definition 1080p format, which has 1080 lines of pixels on the screen at all times (1080i means "interlacing," so only 540 appear at any given moment).

IPTV

Internet Protocol Television is the technology that delivers high-quality television signals to the home using the

(Continued)

(*Continued*)

same technologies as the Internet, but on a closed network managed by a service provider. Not only does it offer a few consumer-friendly advantages, like instant switching between channels, but it promises to make true convergence between television and home computers a reality. Some potential applications include allowing a viewer to input the names of players on his or her fantasy team, and automatically receive updates on those players, or even have the channel switch automatically whenever one of those players is on the screen.

Satellite Radio

The impact of satellite radio has already been felt. Just ask the accountants at major league Baseball. The league kicked off a $650 million, 11-year deal with XM this year, the richest non-television deal in the history of sports. Rival Sirius doled out $107.5 million to steal NASCAR from XM, and committed $220 million to the NFL over seven years, the first of the mega sports rights packages in the satellite space. (Howard Stern's five-year, $100-million-a-year deal dwarfs them all.)

Source: Andy Bernstein,*Sports Business Journal,*August 8, 2005, http://www.sportsbusinessjournal.com/index.cfm?fuseaction=search.show_article&articleId=46458&keyword=regional,%20sport,%20networks.

Teams and leagues have has also formed partnerships with high-tech companies. For example, the NBA has teamed up with StratBridge to utilize the StratTix inventory management tool to further enhance ticket sales efforts. Throughout the year, NBA teams will be able to utilize the latest technology for managing ticket inventory, including access to graphical representations of sold and available in-arena seating, complete analysis of ticket sales and individual seating information for every game, and use of StratTix Premium service to access up-to-the-minute sales information at any time. Interestingly, many owners have emerging from high-tech companies who are using their technology experience and strength to benefit their sports franchises. Examples of high-tech owners include Charles Wang of the New York Islanders and chairman of Computer Associates International; Paul Allen of the Seattle Seahawks and Portland Trailblazers, and cofounder of Microsoft; Ted Leonsis of the Washington Capitals, Washington Wizards, and America Online; Daniel Snyder of the Washington Redskins and Web marketer; and Mark Cuban of the Dallas Mavericks and founder of broadcast.com.

So far, our discussion of technology is based more on how technology influences spectators and the distribution of sport. How do technologically advanced products affect sports participants and their performance? Although most sporting goods have experienced major technological improvements since the early 1990s, two sports that live and die by technology are golf and tennis. In the golf industry, one company that positions itself based on cutting-edge technology is E21. E21 holds the exclusive right to manufacture golf products using proprietary E21 Scandium metal alloys. Through a sophisticated multi-technology production path, E21 manufactures shafts, drivers, and other clubs with marked improvements in distance, accuracy, and feel over competing products. In recent months a number of high-profile golf professionals have switched to or began testing E21's Eagle One shafts. E21 Scandium products are 55 percent lighter and offer 25 percent strength to weight advantage over titanium alloys, the current standard in the golf equipment industry. The advanced dynamics of E21 alloys and the material economics offer a performance-enhanced alternative to manufacturing driver clubs with titanium, the largest segment of the annual $5.5 billion U.S. golf equipment marketplace.[12]

Technology is even becoming a unique way to differentiate in the highly competitive sports apparel market. For example, Textronics, Inc., a pioneer in the field of electronic textiles, has produced NuMetrex, a brand of clothes that monitor the body. The NuMetrex Heart Sensing Sports Bra was named 2006 Sports Product of the Year by the Sporting Goods Manufacturers Association. The garment features electronic sensing technology that is actually integrated right into the knit of the fabric, which

Prince showing its latest advances in tennis technology.
Source: Prince Tennis

picks up the heart's electrical pulse and radios it to a wristwatch via a tiny transmitter in the bra. It offers a new level of comfort and convenience for women wishing to monitor their heart rate while they exercise.[13]

In another recent development linking technology and sport, global brands Nike and Apple Computer are introducing their collaborative Nike+iPod Sport Kit, a shoe/MP3 player/personal trainer that could bring runners around the world together—virtually—enabling them to train on a level beyond the asphalt. The product consists of a shoe equipped with sensors under the sole insert and a tricked-out iPod nano. The sensors will transfer dynamic workout information to the arm-strapped MP3 player. Data, such as time, distance, pace, and calories burned, determined by a person's physiological makeup and the amount of steps the sensor picks up, are stored for later retrieval on the iPod. Immediate audible retrieval is also available through headphones, should a person choose to keep track of statistics during the run.[14]

Although some marketers have a hard time grasping the special language of technology, they still agree that a whole new culture of technology has emerged. Cisco Field, proposed home of the Oakland A's, is yet another example of the latest in the high-tech stadium experience. Cisco President and CEO John Chambers states, "Technology is changing every aspect of our life experiences and for Cisco, this is an opportunity to harness the power of our own innovative technologies to create a truly unique experience that transcends sports, connects communities, and takes the fan experience to a whole new level."[15]

The stadium project underscores the A's commitment to creating a new standard for sports venues. As the official technology partner of the A's, Cisco will provide networking and communication products and services to transform the way that the A's team and ballpark operations will be managed. Cisco Field, when completed, will be a state-of-the-art technology showcase featuring an integrated IP network built on Cisco technology and will be the platform for a multitude of applications that will take the fans' experience to the next level. For example, digital signs could ensure "smart" traffic flow; fans could

Cobra stresses an improved performance based on their technological product improvements.

Source: Cobra

purchase merchandise or concessions while in their seat by ordering from a mobile device; onsite ticket kiosks could enable fans to upgrade seats in real-time. Luxury suites will have the opportunity to include multimedia amenities for premium video content, and Cisco TelePresence technology may even enable new forms of player-to-fan communications.

In another stadium technology advancement, 12 MLB ballparks began accepting MasterCard® PayPass™, a new "contactless" payment option giving fans the chance to pay for their purchases under $25 with a simple tap of their PayPass-enabled card or device on specially equipped merchant terminals. With MasterCard PayPass, sports fans spend less time standing in line or fumbling for cash at concession stands, and more time catching the on-field action.[16]

Computer-driven video sport is another area of technological impact. Douglas Lowenstein, president of Entertainment Software Association, believes "The video game industry is entering a new era, an era where technology and creativity will fuse to produce some of the most stunning entertainment of the 21st century. Decades from now, cultural historians will look back at this time and say it is when the definition of entertainment changed forever."[17]

Video sports games, a subset of the video gaming industry, are called simulations because of their lifelike approximation of real sporting events. In fact, the danger for franchises lies in fans caring more about these games and simulations than they do the "real" sports. Nearly 28% percent of video games sold are sports or racing related. Stated differently, sports games account for $1 billion of the $5.5–$6 billion spent in 2005 on games for systems like PlayStation, Xbox, and GameCube. The leading interactive sports software brand in the world is Electronic Arts (EA) Sports (www.easports.com), with games including FIFA Soccer, John Madden Football, NHL Hockey, Knockout Kings, NBA Live Basketball, Tiger Woods PGA Tour, Triple Play Baseball, and NASCAR Thunder (see Table 2.2 for the top ten video game titles). Its latest product set to hit the market is SSX3, which pits you and your snowboard "against the mountain." Paul Allen, cofounder of Microsoft and owner of the Portland Trail Blazers, believes "the only thing holding back sports simulation products is the level of reality that can be achieved."

Video sports participation is not just limited to the coach potato or kids in the living room. Pro gaming leagues are now becoming the rage and viable sports entities of their own. CPL, or the Cyberathlete Professional League, which has been around since 1997, has awarded more than $3 million in prize money. Television deals are even being struck. For instance, major league Gaming has signed a deal with the USA Network to televise seven one-hour episodes featuring the events and its participants. There is even hope of bringing video gaming to the Olympics in 2008 as an exhibition sport![18]

Cultural and Social Trends

Perhaps the most important aspects of any culture are the shared and learned values. **Cultural values** are widely held beliefs that affirm what is desirable by members of a society. Several of the core American values of interest to sports marketers include individualism, youthfulness, achievement and success, and family.

Sports are symbolic of many core American values. In fact, what could be more American than baseball, our national pastime? ESPN used this rich tradition in a series of television advertisements promoting its major league Baseball coverage. These advertisements claim "It's baseball—you're American—watch it."

All these core values are directly or indirectly relevant to sports marketing. For instance, certain sports or sporting events stress individualism. Individualism is based

TABLE 2.2	Top 10 Sports Video Game Titles				
Ranked by total U.S. units sold, Jan.–Nov. 2006					
Rank	*Title*	*Platform*	*Publisher*	*Release date*	*U.S. units sold*
1	Madden NFL '07	PS2	EA Sports	August	1,800,000
2	NCAA Football '07	PS2	EA Sports	July	850,000
3	Madden NFL '07	Xbox 360	EA Sports	August	825,000
4	Fight Night Round 3	Xbox 360	EA Sports	February	625,000
5	MLB '06: The Show	PS2	Sony	March	620,000
6	Madden NFL '07	Xbox	EA Sports	August	560,000
7	Fight Night Round 3	PS2	EA Sports	February	485,000
8 (tie)	MVP '06 NCAA Baseball	PS2	EA Sports	January	460,000
9 (tie)	NCAA Football '07	Xbox 360	EA Sports	July	460,000
10	FIFA World Cup '06	PS2	EA Sports	April	390,000

on nonconformance or the need to be unique. Nothing could be more directly linked to individualism than the X Games featuring sports such as skateboarding and street luge.

The central or underlying values inherent in all sports are achievement and success. Virtually every sports marketing theme is either directly or indirectly linked to the achievement and success of an individual athlete or a team.

Youthfulness is another core American value that is continually stressed by sports marketers. People participate in sports and watch sports to feel young and have fun. Those in the mature market are making strides at staying in shape; they are also watching their own age cohorts still participating in sports at a professional level via any number of senior tours (men's and women's golf, tennis, and bowling). In addition, products like Just for Men are endorsed by sports legends Keith Hernandez, Walt "Clyde" Frazier, and Michael Waltrip, who all use the product to "stay looking great."

Another core American value is family and the need to feel a sense of belonging. According to a recent study, team sports, which foster the sense of "group identity," continue to play an important role in the lives of American children. Team sports duplicated their 2004 performance in 2005, with six of seven sports showing increases. Tackle football, which had slipped by 5.3 percent in 2004, bounced back with a 15.5 percent increase in 2005 to 9.9 million participants. Other double-digit increases came in softball (+12.7 percent to 14.1 million) and volleyball (+11.9 percent to 13.2 million). Basketball was the highest-ranking team sport at No. 12 with 29.9 million participants (+7.3 percent). Soccer (14.1 million) increased 6.4 percent. Ice hockey showed a 0.4 percent increase to 2.4 million. The only team sport to show a decline was baseball, down 7.7 percent to 14.6 million[19]

Physical Environment

The **physical environment** refers to natural resources and other characteristics of the natural world that have a tremendous impact on sports marketing. For instance, the climate of a region dictates the types of sports that are watched and played in that area.

The mature market: staying young and having fun in record numbers.

In fact, various sports were developed because of the physical characteristics of a region. Skiing and hockey in the north and surfing on the coasts are obvious examples.

Sports marketers attempt to control the physical environment for both spectators and sports participants. For example, the Australian Open (tennis) was hit by a heat wave that affected both players and spectators. Tournament officials closed the roof over the center court and artificially controlled the physical environment. Many players, however, wanted their matches rescheduled, and others argued that they had trained for the heat. This attempt to artificially control Mother Nature seems to have backfired, or at least come under scrutiny.

Artificial turf replaced natural grass surfaces in stadiums in the late 1960s. In the new millennium, all new stadiums being built have switched back to natural grass. Grass not only seems to be easier on the athletes in terms of avoiding potential injuries, but fans also seem to appreciate the "natural" look of grass. Likewise, domed stadiums seem to have run their (un)natural course. The newer stadiums are all open-air venues, which have greater appeal for spectators. An interesting example of state-of-the-art stadium technology designed to control the physical environment is the new Cardinals Stadium in Arizona with the first roll-out playing surface. At the touch of a button, the grass field slides in and out of the stadium along 13 steel rails. The purpose of the sliding field is threefold: It eliminates indoor watering and related humidity problems; allows the field to soak up direct sunlight; and leaves behind 152,000 square feet of unobstructed floor space for things such as concerts, conventions, and expos.[20]

In addition to the climate, the physical environment of sports marketing is concerned with conservation and preserving natural resources. This trend toward conservation is most often referred to as "green marketing." Marketing ecologically responsible products and being conscious about the effects of sports on the physical environment is one of the concerns of green marketing. For instance, many golf course management groups have come under attack from environmentalists concerned about the effect of phosphate-based chemicals used in keeping golf courses green. Other groups have criticized the sport of fishing as cruel and unusual punishment for the fish.

Political, Legal, and Regulatory Environment

Sports marketers are continually faced with **political, legal,** and **regulatory environments** that affect their strategic decisions. Politics have always played a major role in sports and are becoming an increasingly important part of the sports landscape. In professional sports, politicians are involved in promoting or discouraging passage of stadium tax issues. Since 1953, most stadiums have been owned by city governments. The question is, "How far does one go in sacrificing taxpayers' wealth to promote civic pride?" Additional evidence of the relationship between government and sports marketing is the growing number of sports commissions. Since 1980, the number of sports commissions, designed to attract sporting events to cities, states, or regions, has increased from 10 to roughly 150.

The legal environment of sports has certainly taken on a life of its own in the new millennium. Sports officials (i.e., league commissioners, judges, sports arbitrators, coaches, and athletic directors) are continually confronted with legal challenges that arise on and off the playing field. These officials must be adept at interpreting the language of collective bargaining, recruiting student-athletes, understanding Title IX, avoiding antitrust issues, licensing team logos, and handling other sports law issues.

One of the most famous pieces of legislation, passed in 1972 under President Richard Nixon, was Title IX. Simply, Title IX states that "no person in the United States shall, on the basis of sex, be excluded from participation in, be denied the benefits of, or be subjected to discrimination under any education program or activity receiving Federal financial assistance." Interestingly, the law that has had the most dramatic impact on the growth of women's sports participation does not even mention the word "sports." Perhaps the most famous Title IX decision was a 1997 ruling by the U.S. Supreme Court in the *Brown University v. Cohen* case. The courts ruled that Brown University did not meet any part of the three-step Title IX compliance.

This three-part test includes the following:

1. Are opportunities for female and male athletes proportionate to their enrollment?
2. Does the school have a history of expanding athletic opportunities for the underrepresented sex?
3. Has the school demonstrated success in meeting the needs of those students?

Unfortunately, Title IX implementation has led to reduction in men's sports programs. Rather than adding women's sports programs, universities have chosen to cut men's sports such as baseball and wrestling to address the problem of proportionality.

As mentioned earlier, sports legal issues involve much more than Title IX and antitrust issues. Recent examples of sports legal issues in the news include cases of breach of contract, player-on-player/coach/fan violence, and trademark infringement. Recently, NBA commissioner David Stern handed down a total of $1 million in fines and 47 games in suspensions for the fight between the Knicks and the Denver Nuggets. To most, it was reminiscent of a brawl that not only involved players, but fans. In arguably the most violent fight in NBA history, the Indiana Pacers scuffled with the Detroit Piston players and ultimately rushed the stands, involving some drunken Detroit Pistons fans. In both these violent acts, the sanctioning body (NBA) and law enforcement became involved.

Due to the billions of dollars of sports-licensed merchandise sold each year, a more common form of legal issues in sport is a trademark violation. In one example, American Media, Inc. (parent company of the *National Enquirer* and *Globe*) was sued by the U.S. Olympic Committee (USOC) for using images of Olympic athletes without their consent and using the word "Olympics" in a publication entitled *Olympics USA*. Similarly, the IOC has filed a lawsuit against 1,800 Internet sites abusing the Olympic name. In yet another example, Callaway Golf recently stopped the sale of counterfeit clubs on eBay.com.

A regulatory body or agency is responsible for enacting laws or setting guidelines for sports and sports marketers. Regulatory agencies can be controlled by either governmental or nongovernmental agencies. One example of a nongovernmental regulatory body that has tremendous control over sports and sports marketing practices is the Federation Internationale de Football Association (FIFA). FIFA is the international federation for the world's most popular sport, soccer. FIFA, which was formed in 1904, promotes soccer through development programs for youth and supervises international competition to ensure the rules and regulations of the game are being followed. In addition, FIFA is responsible for maintaining the unified set of rules for soccer called the *Laws of the Game*.

Although FIFA is concerned with regulating the game itself, it also controls many facets outside the game that have an impact on sports marketing. For example, FIFA is committed to improving stadiums for the fans and protecting them against the rising costs of attendance. Another example of FIFA's control over sports marketing is that virtual advertising—superimposing marketing messages on the field during televised broadcasts—is forbidden.

In addition, FIFA works with ISL Marketing to secure sponsors for major soccer events, such as the World Cup. As a regulatory agency, FIFA attempts to make sure that the sponsors do not intrude in any way on the integrity of the game. FIFA General Secretary Joseph Blatter describes the delicate but beneficial relationship between FIFA and its sponsors as follows: "It's important for the sponsors not to influence—or even try to influence—the game itself, any more than it is FIFA's role or intention to influence how these companies do their own business."[21]

As the accompanying article illustrates, the sanctioning body can even have an impact on what athletes wear in competition and can dictate what manufacturers produce.

Demographics

Assessing the **demographic environment** entails observing and monitoring population trends. These trends are observable aspects of the population such as the total number of consumers and their composition (i.e., age or ethnic background) or the geographic dispersion of consumers. Let us look at several aspects of the demographic profile of the United States, including size of the opulation, age of the population, shifts in ethnic groups, and population shifts among geographic regions.

Tennis Bodies' Rulings Force Adidas to Change Its Stripes

Tennis's governing bodies, following the lead of the Olympics, banned Adidas' iconic three-stripe brand as it now appears on the company's apparel.

With endorsers ranging from Marat Safin to Tim Henman wearing its shirts and shorts, Adidas will now have to go back to the drawing board to comply with the sport's regulations.

However, tennis split in one key regard: While the four Grand Slams will not allow the stripes—or any other logo—unless they are between two and three square inches, the ATP and WTA Tours will allow apparel logos of 12 square inches. The Grand Slam size would be far too small for the stylish three stripes, but the tours' size might allow a smaller version of the design.

"We think this significantly curtails what Adidas is currently allowed to do . . . with the three-stripe branding," said Sophie Goldschmidt, marketing vice president at the Sony Ericsson WTA Tour.

While the new regulation applies to all apparel makers, companies in the business are referring to it as the "Adidas rule."

Adidas' head of tennis, Jim Latham, declined to comment.

The brouhaha started in May when the International Olympic Committee ruled the three stripes, first introduced in 1949, were not a design, as Adidas claimed, but a logo that is subject to the organization's apparel regulations.

Meanwhile, Nike, in protest over Adidas-sponsored tennis players continuing to wear the stripes even though all of the sport's governing bodies limited logos to between two and four square inches, sent star endorser Rafael Nadal into a prestigious May tournament with a super-sized swoosh.

That quickly led tennis's disparate organizations to confer over the last few months, with the unanimous decisions made at last month's Wimbledon that Adidas' stripes are a logo subject to regulation. Had the stripes been deemed a design, the issue would have been moot.

The Grand Slams and Davis Cup kept their current logo rules, while the two tours significantly increased the allowable logo size as a concession to Adidas.

"It is an eye to try to keep Adidas involved in the sport, and at the same time be fair to the other manufacturers," said Richard Davies, chief executive of ATP Properties, the commercial arm of the men's tennis circuit.

Adidas is understood to be developing a stripe design to fit in a 12-square-inch space.

"If the style is changed for one company, that shows a lack of respect," charged Martin Mulligan, a tennis scout with Fila, who said most of the shirt makers in tennis were content with the current logo sizes mandated by the tours. "Why didn't the IOC cave in like the WTA and ATP?"

"It's unfortunate the tours felt that they had to increase the manufacturers' identification six times from their current size," said Bill Babcock, executive administrator of the Grand Slam committee, which represents the slams. "Before, the logo size difference . . . was a square inch here or there."

Source: Daniel Kaplan, http://www.sportsbusinessjournal.com/index.cfm?fuseaction=article.printArticle& articleId=45977 *Sports Business Journal.*

Size of the Population

Currently, the U.S. population stands at over 300 million consumers and is growing at a rapid pace. It is estimated that by the year 2020, the U.S. population will increase to as much as 336 million. As with the U.S. population, the world population is also expanding at an alarming rate. The present world population is over 6.6 billion and is growing at a rate of roughly 76 million per year.[22] This is of special interest to marketers of sports entities who are considering expansion into international markets.

Age

Age is one of the most common variables used in segmenting and targeting groups of consumers. As such, sports marketers must continually monitor demographic shifts in the age of U.S. consumers. The "graying of America" has and will continue to exert a huge influence. The older adult population (defined as 65 and older) is expected to grow to a rate of 17 percent of the total U.S. population by 2030, whereas the U.S. population as a whole is projected to increase at a rate of 19 percent. This trend is a function of the baby boom generation growing older.

Studies show that by the year 2015, mature adults will make up almost 25 percent of the entire population; this number will grow even larger to comprise one-third of the population by the year 2050. This means that in about 50 years, one out of every three Americans will be 55 years of age or older. Apparently, with new technological advances bringing about breakthroughs in medicine, a lower mortality rate, and preventive approaches to health, Americans are living longer.

Moreover, the 76-million-strong baby boom generation is already entering midlife and will soon age. Four out of every 10 adults in the United States are baby boomers; in the year 2000, they were between 35 to 50 years old. Also of significance is the baby bust generation (children of baby boomers) that follows in the wake of its parental tidal wave. In 2000, there were an estimated 19 million children under five years of age, compared with the 16 million in 1980.

Shifts in Ethnic Groups

The United States has been called a melting pot because of its diversity and multiethnic population. The number of white Americans is diminishing, while roughly 33 percent of the U.S. population is represented by some minority group. By 2050, non- Hispanic whites will account for only 54 percent of the U.S. population. In terms of sheer size, nearly 98 million people represent either the African American, Asian, or Hispanic ethnic groups. All three of these ethnic groups have rising income levels, which translate into more purchasing power.[23] Although all minority groups are growing, the fastest-growing segment are Hispanics with buying power just over $860 billion in 2007, an 8 percent increase from 2006.[24] This group reached over 40 million of the total U.S. population. The next fastest-growing minority are Asian Americans, who represent 14.4 million people. African Americans remain the second largest minority group, with nearly 40 million people and $572 billion in annual buying power.

These ethnic groups are important subcultures that share a portion of the larger (white) American culture, but also have unique consumption characteristics. There are a number of benefits in developing a marketing mix that appeals to specific ethnic groups. The accompanying article describes how major league Baseball has recognized the value of ethnic marketing tactics.

Population Shifts

Through 2020, the greatest population shift will be evident in the South and West. Between the 2000 census and 2005 the population in the western states grew by nearly 8 percent and grew by 7 percent in the South, compared to lower rates of growth in the Midwest and Northeast (2 percent and 1.5 percent, respectively). The states with the

Ethnic Studies: How to Create Ethnic Promotional Nights That Grow Ticket Sales

Ethnic theme nights have represented as much as a 9,000-seat bump in ticket sales for a major league Baseball team.

While it is unlikely to expect this level of success with every event like a "Hispanic Night" and "Italian Heritage Night," there are some essential lessons that every team marketer should understand before scheduling their own culturally themed promotional nights.

The aim of this report is to showcase the variables that led to success and failures of ethnic-based promotional nights.

Think Long-Term

The New York Mets began their ethnic promotions during the 1996 season and have watched it grow every year since. The promotion, which originally began as "International Weekend," has grown into a full-week of promotional nights dedicated to celebrating the heritage of different cultures living in New York during each of the team's seven home games during the week.

"It's only natural that if you stay committed to something and are consistent with it that it will grow," said Tina Bucciarelli, director of marketing for the Mets. "People have so much pride with their heritage that if you put out a good event that the people will naturally spread it virally."

The Mets, like most teams, started out the promotion as a group sales initiative. While group tickets still drive the promotional staple, it has spawned incremental revenue streams through sponsorships and concessions.

For the Mets, a typical ethnic promotional night includes culturally themed pre-game entertainment, food, on-field recognition, and music.

Bucciarelli said planning these elements is the easy part. The primary challenge, according to Bucciarelli, is to ensure that the scheduling is convenient for the group and not just the team.

For example, the team rotated out Greek Day and replaced it with Black Heritage Day because of a poorly attended Greek Day last year.

The reason for the low attendance was not a lack of interest among Greek fans. The depleted numbers were more a sign of the game being scheduled in August, which is annually known as the time of year that most traditional Greeks return to Greece for a vacation.

Recognizing this, the Mets pulled Greek Night out of the International Week festivities and planned Greek Night in June and the group sales numbers increased.

"We've learned it's wrong to just say 'Italian Night' will be Monday, August 30th,' " Bucciarelli said.

She said it is important to seek feedback from organizations entrenched in the specific communities you are trying to celebrate.

"It's always been better to listen first before acting," Bucciarelli said. "If not, you run the risk of not only having a poor sales night but potentially alienating a key group of your fanbase."

By listening to the community, the Mets have watched some of their promotional nights grow to account for an increase of as many as 9,000 ticket sales.

While this number, Bucciarelli admits, is well above the team's ethnic promotional night goal of moving an extra 5,000 tickets, intangible goals are equally important as quantifiable results.

"Our underlying goal for these theme nights is to get new audiences in to the park and show them a good time, to want them to come out whether it is a theme night or not," Bucciarelli said. "To do this, it takes time and momentum and a commitment from ownership to stay with it."

Language Lessons

When the Tampa Bay Devil Rays made Hispanic Heritage night a staple of their promotional roster since year one the team hoped it had a promotion that could move the ticket sales needle by 10 to 20 percent.

While the promotion, and other culturally inspired initiatives, have helped net double-digit ticket sales increases, the Devil Rays have discovered that these promotions can attract mainstream sponsors that would otherwise have not spent money with the team.

The team has tried unsuccessfully to secure Kellogg's as a sponsor in the past but the Battle Creek, Mich.-based company had a different response when approached with an opportunity to sponsor the team's Hispanic Heritage night on September 4th.

While terms of the deal were not disclosed, Devil Rays Vice President of Marketing John Browne said the package allowed Kellogg's to be involved in delivering a ticket discount to Hispanic consumers. Working with an area grocery store chain, the offer gave fans a $5 discount on tickets to the Hispanic game with a Kellogg's purchase listed on the receipt.

"Kellogg's wanted to position this singular event as if they were bringing this offer to the Hispanic marketplace," Browne said.

The key to securing this deal, according to Browne, was time.

"Both from a sponsorship and group sales perspective, the more time you have in advance, the greater your revenue potential will be," Browne said. "Sponsors and community ethnic groups both start to button up their plans in the fourth quarter of the previous year and the more you understand their perspective the better your prospects for success will be."

(Continued)

(*Continued*)

Start Slow

The San Francisco Giants must have talked to the Mets to follow their lead of moving slowly with ethnic-themed promotions.

The Giants added two separate ethnic nights celebrating Irish and Italian heritages and marketed the two events almost exclusively through the team's Internet site.

The grass roots marketing strategy allowed the team a low-cost and minimal labor outlet to launch ethnic-based promotions.

To help entice online sales the team purchased Irish- and Italian-themed Giants hats at a cost of $6.00 per hat.

The Irish hat is green with the Giants logo on the front and an Irish flag stitched on the back. The Italian hat is black with the Giants logo on the front and an Italian flag stitched on the back.

The team sold 1,200 tickets to the Irish night and only 200 for the Italian night.

Giants Special Events Manager Todd Lindenbaum attributes the difference to the uniqueness of the giveaway.

"The green hats were extremely unique and addressed the Irish culture more than the black Italian hats addressed their culture," Lindenbaum said.

Source: Reprinted by permission of the Migala Report. Dan Migala, http://www.migalareport.com/stats9000.cfm.

highest growth in absolute number of people are California, Texas, and New York. The least populated states in 2005 were Wyoming (509,300), Vermont (623,100), and North Dakota (636,700). In terms of percentage growth, Nevada led the way with an enormous 21 percent increase in population between 2000 and 2005. The next fastest growing states include Arizona (16 percent), and Florida (11 percent).

There is no definitive explanation for this shift, although some believe it is due to the previously discussed aging of America or the growth of employment opportunities in these areas. Keep in mind that, until 1957 when the Brooklyn Dodgers moved to Los Angeles, there were no major league Baseball teams west of St. Louis.

Along with exploring population shifts by state, sports marketers must assess the dispersion of people within an area. Are people moving back to urban areas, or is the "flight to the suburbs" still occurring? The 2000 census showed the greatest growth to be in suburban areas. There are still fewer people living in or moving back to the central city. These measures of population dispersion are having an impact on where new professional teams are locating and where new stadiums are being built.

The Economy

The economic environment is another important but uncontrollable factor for sports marketers to consider. Economic factors that affect sports organizations can be described as either macroeconomic or microeconomic elements. A brief explanation of each follows.

Macroeconomic Elements

Economic activity is the flow of goods and services between producers and consumers. The size of this flow and the principal measure of all economic activity is called the gross national product (GNP). The business cycle, which closely follows the GNP, is one of the broadest macroeconomic elements. The four stages of the business cycle are as follows:

Prosperity—the phase in which the economy is operating at or near full employment, and both consumer spending and business output are high

Recession—the downward phase, in which consumer spending, business output, and employment are decreasing

Depression—the low phase of the business cycle, in which unemployment is highest, consumer spending is low, and business output has declined drastically

Recovery—the upward phase when employment, consumer spending, and business output are rising

Each cyclical phase influences economic variables, such as unemployment, inflation, and consumers' willingness to spend. Decisions about the strategic sports marketing process are affected by these fluctuations in the economy. Ticket sales may boom during times of economic growth. In addition, the growth period may have an even greater impact on corporate demand for luxury boxes and season tickets. If the country is in either a recession or a depression, consumers may be reluctant to purchase nonessential goods and services such as sporting goods or tickets to sporting events. Mistakenly, the sports industry sometimes seems to operate under the "ignorance is bliss" philosophy when it comes to the economy. As Steve Wilstein points out, "salaries for athletes kept rising, TV deals soared, and ticket prices spiraled ever upward as if the leagues were living in their own fantasyland, immune to economic cycles."[25] Although Wilstein believes the sports that are hardest hit by the economy are those already on the periphery (e.g., the Women's Professional Bowling Tour), even the major sports are hit hard by a poor economy.

Although the relationship between the purchase of sporting goods and tickets to sporting events is likely to be associated with good economic times, this may not always be the case. During a recession or depression, sports may serve as a rallying point for people. Consumers can still feel good about their teams, even in times of economic hardship. This is one of the important, but sometimes neglected, societal roles of sport.

Microeconomic Elements

Whereas **macroeconomic elements** examine the big picture, or the national income, **microeconomic elements** are those smaller elements that make up the big picture. One of the microelements of concern to sports marketers is consumer income level. As economist Paul Samuelson points out, "Mere billions of dollars would be meaningless if they did not correspond to the thousand and one useful goods and services that people really need and want."[26] Likewise, having sports products would be meaningless if consumers could not afford to purchase them. A primary determinant of a consumer's ability to purchase is income level.

Consumer income levels are specified in terms of gross income, disposable income, or discretionary income. Of these types of income, discretionary is of greatest interest to sports marketers. This is the portion of income that the consumer retains after paying taxes and purchasing necessities. Sports purchases are considered a nonnecessity and, therefore, are related to a consumer's or family's discretionary income. According to a new analysis by The Conference Board, slightly more than half (51 percent) of American households have some discretionary income they can spend on nonnecessities. In addition, the number of families with discretionary income is expected to rise slightly over the next decade.

Sports advocates argue that new stadia and consumer spending on sports support local economic growth. The local economic benefits from a major professional sports team are typically derived from four major sources of spending: (1) attendance (tickets and parking) at the games, (2) concession items sold at the games such as food and merchandise, (3) spending before and after the events for other consumption items such as meals, and (4) taxes paid to local government on spending for the previous three categories. Others argue that spending on sport has little impact and that professional sport is an economic drain. The following quote summarizes this notion.

> People have a limited amount of discretionary income. They may use it on attendance at professional sporting events. In the absence of pro sports, they will spend the money elsewhere—lower-level sporting events, the movies, etc. The same is true for large corporations. If they don't buy sky boxes, they will

entertain their clients elsewhere (i.e., restaurants). Sports facilities generate very few jobs. For a local economy, player management (and that may come from outside) and low-level game day employment (vendors, etc. . . .). A modest factory, or a small research facility has far more impact.[27]

Monitoring the External Contingencies

As discussed, external contingencies are dynamic, and sports marketers must keep abreast of these continually changing influences. A systematic analysis of these external factors is the first step taken by sports marketers using the contingency framework. In addition, as the sports industry becomes more competitive, one of the keys to success will be identifying new market opportunities and direction through assessing the external contingencies. The method used to monitor the external contingencies is known as environmental scanning.

Environmental Scanning

An outward-looking, environmental focus has long been viewed as a central component of strategic planning. In fact, it has been argued that the primary focus of strategic planning is "to look continuously outward" and to keep the organization in step with the anticipated changes in the external environment. This process of monitoring external contingencies is called environmental scanning. More formally, **environmental scanning** is a firm's attempt to continually acquire information on events occurring outside the organization so it can identify and interpret potential trends.[28]

A sports organization can do several things to enhance its environmental scanning efforts. First, the organization can identify who will be responsible for environmental scanning. The only way to move beyond the pressures of daily business activities is to include environmental scanning responsibilities in the job description of key members of the organization.

Second, the organization can provide individuals conducting the environmental scan with plenty of information on the three Cs: customers, competition, and company. Your scanners cannot correctly monitor the environment without having a solid base of information about the following: customer expectations and needs; the strengths, weaknesses, distinctive competencies, and relative market positioning of the competition; and the strengths, weaknesses, distinctive competencies, and relative market positioning of your own company—as well as the major developmental opportunities that await exploitation.

Third, the organization can ensure integration of scanned information through structured interactions and communication. All too often, information needed to recognize new market opportunities is identified but never gets disseminated among the various functional areas. That is, marketing, finance, and operations may all have some information, or pieces to the puzzle, but unless these individuals share the information, it becomes meaningless. Organizations with the most effective environmental scanning systems schedule frequent interactions among their designated scanners.

Fourth, the organization can conduct a thorough analysis of ongoing efforts to improve the effectiveness of environmental scanning activities. This systematic study consists of evaluating the types of scanning data that are relevant and available to managers. This focus on previous environmental scanning efforts can often lead to the identification of new market opportunities.

Fifth, the organization can create a culture that values a "spirit of inquiry." When an organization develops such a spirit, it is understood that the environmental scanning process is necessary for success. In addition, it is understood that environmental scanning is an ongoing activity that is valued by the organization.

Environmental scanning is an essential task for recognizing the external contingencies and understanding how they might affect marketing efforts. However, there are two reasons why environmental scanning practices may fail to identify market opportunities or threats. First, the primary difficulty in effectively scanning the environment lies in the nature of the task itself. As scanning implies, sports marketers must look into the future and predict what will likely take place. To make matters even more difficult, these predictions are based on the interaction of the complex variables previously mentioned, such as the economy, demographics, technology, and so on. Second, predictions about the environment are based on data. Sports marketers are exposed to enormous amounts of data and only with experience can individuals selectively choose and correctly interpret the "right data" from the overwhelming mass of information available to them.

ASSESSING THE INTERNAL AND EXTERNAL CONTINGENCIES: SWOT ANALYSIS

To this point, we have looked at both the external and internal contingencies. To guide the strategic sports marketing process, an organization conducts a SWOT analysis. SWOT is an acronym for strengths, weaknesses, opportunities, and threats. The strengths and weaknesses are controllable factors within the organization. In other words, a firm must evaluate its strengths and weaknesses based on the internal contingencies. The opportunities and threats are assessed as a result of the external contingencies found in the marketing environment. These elements may be beyond the control of the sports organization.

The strategic sports marketing process must first examine its own internal contingencies. These internal strengths and weaknesses include human resources, financial resources, and whether organizational objectives and marketing goals are being met with the current marketing mix. Products and services, promotional efforts, pricing structure, and methods of distribution are also characterized as either strengths or weaknesses.

After assessing the organizational strengths and weaknesses, the firm identifies external opportunities and threats found in the marketing environment. As discussed earlier in the chapter, sports marketing managers must monitor the competition; demographic shifts; the economy; political, legal, and regulatory issues; and technological advances. Each of these external factors may affect the direction of the strategic marketing process.

The intent of conducting a SWOT analysis is to help sports marketers recognize or develop areas of strength capable of exploiting environmental opportunities. When sports marketers observe opportunities that match a particular strength, a strategic window is opened. More formally, **strategic windows** are limited periods of time during which the characteristics of a market and the distinctive competencies of a firm fit together well and reduce the risks of seizing a particular market opportunity. For example, IMG, a leading sports and entertainment marketing company, has created "IMG X Sports" to capitalize on the growing popularity in extreme and lifestyle sports. In addition to capitalizing on strengths, sports marketers develop strategies that eliminate or minimize organizational weaknesses.

At this stage, you should have a broad understanding of how each of the external contingencies may affect your marketing plan. Table 2.3 provides a common list of questions to consider when developing the opportunities and threats (OT) portion of your SWOT analysis.

NCAA capitalizes on the new opportunities based on the growth in women's sports.
Source: NCAA

TABLE 2.3	Assessing External Contingencies

1. **Social**—What major social and lifestyle trends will have an impact on the sports participants or spectators? What action has the firm been taking in response to these trends?

2. **Demographics**—What impact will forecast trends in size, age, profile, and distribution of population have on the firm? How will the changing nature of the family, the increase in the proportion of women in the workforce, and changes in ethnic composition of the population affect the firm? What action has the firm taken in response to these developments and trends? Has the firm reevaluated its traditional sports products and expanded the range of specialized offerings to respond to these changes?

3. **Economic**—What major trends in taxation and in income sources will have an impact on the firm? What action has the firm taken in response to these trends?

4. **Political, Legal, and Regulatory**—What laws are now being proposed at federal, state, and local levels that could affect the strategic marketing process? What recent changes in regulations and court decisions have affected the sports industry? What action has the firm taken in response to these legal and political changes?

5. **Competition**—Which organizations are competing with us directly by offering a similar product? Which organizations are competing with us indirectly by securing our customers' time, money, energy, or commitment? What new competitive trends seem likely to emerge? How effective is the competition? What benefits do our competitors offer that we do not?

6. **Technological**—What major technological changes are occurring that affect the sports organization and sports industry?

Summary

Chapter 2 provides an overview of the contingency framework for the strategic sports marketing process. Although there are many ways to think about constructing a sports marketing plan, it is best to lay a foundation that is prepared for the unexpected. The contingency framework is especially useful for sports marketers because of the complex and uncertain conditions in which the sports organization operates. The unexpected changes that occur over the course of a season or event may be positive or negative. The changes that occur may be either controllable or uncontrollable events that affect the sports organization. The contingency framework includes three major components: the internal contingencies, the external contingencies, and the strategic sports marketing process. Uncontrollable occurrences are typically in the marketing environment and are referred to as external contingencies, whereas internal contingencies are within the control of the organization (sometimes beyond the scope of the marketing function). The heart of the contingency framework is the strategic sports marketing process, which is defined as the process of planning, implementing, and controlling marketing efforts to meet organizational goals and satisfy consumers' needs.

Internal contingencies, thought of as managerial, controllable issues, include the vision and mission of the sports organization, organizational objectives and marketing goals, organizational strategies, and organizational culture. The vision and mission of the sports organization guide the strategic sports marketing process by addressing questions such as: What business are we in? Who are our current customers? What is the scope of our market? How do we currently meet the needs of our customers? The organizational objectives and marketing goals stem from the vision and mission of the sports organization. The objectives of the organization are long term and sometimes unquantifiable. Alternatively, marketing goals are short term, measurable, and time specific. It is extremely important to remember that the marketing goals are directly linked to decisions made in the strategic sports marketing process. Another internal contingency that influences the strategic sports marketing process is organizational strategy. The organizational strategy is how the sports organization plans on carrying out its vision, mission, objectives, and goals. There are four different levels of strategy development within the organization. These include corporate-level strategies, business-level strategies, functional-level strategies, and operational-level strategies. Marketing is described as a functional-level strategy. The operational-level strategies such as pricing and promotion must fit the broader strategic sports marketing process. A final internal contingency is the organizational culture or the shared values and assumptions of organizational members that shape an identity and establish preferred behaviors in an organization.

The external contingencies that affect the strategic sports marketing process include competition; technology; cultural and social trends; physical environment; political, legal, and regulatory environment; demographic trends; and the economy. As with any industry, understanding competitive threats that exist is critical to the success of all sports organizations. Competition for sporting events and sports organizations comes in many forms. Typically, we think of competition as being any other sporting event. However, other forms of entertainment are also considered competitive threats for sports organizations. Technological forces represent another external contingency. Advances in technology are changing the way that consumers watch sports, play sports, and receive their sports information. Cultural and social trends must also be carefully monitored. Core values, such as individualism, youthfulness, and the need for belonging, can have an impact on the target markets chosen and how sports products are positioned to spectators and participants. The physical environment, such as the climate and weather conditions, is another external contingency that can have a tremendous influence on the success or failure of sporting events. Another of the uncontrollable factors is the political, legal, and regulatory environment. Proposed legislation, such as the banning of all tobacco advertising and sponsorship at sporting events, could have a tremendous impact on the motor sports industry. Demographic trends are another critical external contingency that must be monitored by sports marketers. For instance, the graying of America will bring about changes in the levels of participation in sports and the types of sports in which the "mature market" will participate. Finally, economic conditions should be considered by sports marketers. Sports marketers must monitor the macroeconomic elements, such as the national economy, as well as microeconomic issues, such as the discretionary income of consumers in the target market.

Because the marketing environment is so complex and dynamic, sports marketers use a method for monitoring external contingencies called environmental scanning. Environmental scanning is the sports organization's attempt to acquire information continually on events occurring outside the organization and to identify and interpret potential trends. Sports marketers must continually monitor the environment to look for opportunities and threats that may affect the organization.

External and internal contingencies are systematically considered prior to the development of the strategic marketing process. The process that many organizations use to analyze internal and external contingencies is called a SWOT analysis. SWOT is an acronym for strengths, weaknesses, opportunities, and threats. The strengths and weakness are internal, controllable factors within the organization that may influence the direction of the strategic sports marketing process. For example, human resources within the organization may represent strengths or weaknesses within any organization. However, the opportunities and threats are uncontrollable aspects of the marketing environment (e.g., competition and the economy). The purpose of conducting a SWOT analysis is to help sports marketers recognize how the strengths of their organization can be paired with opportunities that exist in the marketing environment. Conversely, the organization may conduct a SWOT analysis to identify weaknesses in relation to competitors.

Key Terms

- competition, p. 49
- contingency framework for strategic sports marketing, p. 38
- control phase, p. 40
- cultural values, p. 56
- culture, p. 48
- demographic environment, p. 60
- direct competition, p. 50
- economic activity, p. 63
- environmental scanning, p. 65
- external contingencies, p. 39

- goal, p. 43
- implementation phase, p. 40
- indirect competition, p. 50
- internal contingencies, p. 39
- macroeconomic elements, p. 64
- market selection decisions, p. 39
- marketing environment, p. 49
- marketing mix, p. 40
- microeconomic elements, p. 64
- objectives, p. 42
- organizational culture, p. 40

- organizational strategies, p. 44
- physical environment, p. 57
- planning phase, p. 40
- political, legal, and regulatory environment, p. 58
- strategic sports marketing process, p. 39
- strategic windows, p. 66
- technology, p. 50
- vision, p. 39

Review Questions

1. Describe the contingency framework for strategic sports marketing. Why is the contingency approach especially useful to sports marketers?
2. Outline the strategic marketing process, and comment on how it is related to the external and internal contingencies.
3. Define the marketing environment. Are all elements of the marketing environment considered uncontrollable? Why or why not?
4. What is environmental scanning? Why is environmental scanning so important? Who conducts the environmental scan, and how is one conducted?
5. Define competition. What are the different types of competition?
6. How has technology influenced the sports marketing industry? Discuss how "out-of-market" technology benefits sports spectators.
7. Identify several cultural and social trends in our society and describe their impact on sport and sports marketing.

8. What are the core American values, and why are they important to sports marketers?
9. How does the physical environment play a role in sports marketing? How can sports marketers manipulate or change the physical environment?
10. Define the political and regulatory environment. Cite several examples of how this can influence or dictate sports marketing practices.
11. Describe the different demographic trends of interest to sports marketers. How will these demographic trends influence the strategic marketing process?
12. Differentiate between macro- and microeconomic elements. Which (macro- or microelements) do you feel plays an important role in sports marketing? Why?
13. How can sports marketers assess the external environment? What are some sources of secondary data that may assist in understanding the current and future external environment?

Exercises

1. Interview the marketing manager of a local college or professional sports organization and develop a list of the uncontrollable factors that were unexpected throughout the last season.
2. Interview the marketing manager of a sporting goods retailer or sports organization about the company's strategic sports marketing process. Ask how the external and internal contingencies affect planning.
3. Find two sports organizations that, in your opinion, have effective mission and vision statements. How do they promote these statements and how are they reflected in the organization?
4. Describe all the ways the changing marketing environment will have an impact on NASCAR racing. How should NASCAR prepare for the future?
5. Your university's athletic program has a number of competitors. List all potential competitors and categorize what type of competition each represents.
6. Find examples of how technology has influenced the sporting goods industry, a professional sports franchise, and the way spectators watch a sporting event. For each example, indicate the technology that was used prior to the new technology.
7. Develop advertisements for athletic shoes that reflect each of the core American values discussed in this chapter.
8. Interview five international students and discuss the core values used by sports marketers in their culture. Do these values differ from the core American values? For example, do the British value individualism more or less than Americans? What evidence do the students have to support their claims?
9. How does the physical environment of your geographic area or location play a role in sports marketing?
10. Describe how changing demographic trends have led to the development of new sports leagues, the shifting of professional sports franchises, and new sports products. Provide three specific examples of each.

Internet Exercises

1. Experience a portion of any sporting event via Internet broadcast. What did you enjoy the most about this experience, and what could be done to improve this technology?
2. Find three sports products on the Internet that stress technological innovation. Do the companies communicate their technological advantages differently?
3. Search the Internet for articles or sites that discuss the pros and cons of the banning of tobacco advertisements at sporting events.
4. Go to the Internet and find census data to support what sports fans in 2020 might look like from a demographic perspective.

Endnotes

1. Rick Burton and Dennis Howard, "Recovery Strategies for Sports Marketers: The Marketing of Sports Involves Unscripted Moments Delivered by Unpredictable Individuals and Uncontrollable Events," *Marketing Management,* vol. 9, no. 1 (Spring 2000), 43.
2. W. Richard Scott, *Organizations: Rational, Natural, and Open Systems* (Upper Saddle River, NJ: Prentice Hall, 1987), 87–89.
3. Bernard J. Mullin, Stephan Hardy, and William Sutton, *Sport Marketing* (Champaign, IL: Human Kinetics Publishers, 1993), 16.
4. New Balance Mission Statement, http://www.newbalance.com/cms-service/stream/pdf/?pdf_id=6901874.
5. University of Texas Mission Statement, http://www.texassports.com/this-is-texas/article.aspx?id=12408.
6. Nike Mission Statement, http://www.nike.com/nikebiz/nikebiz.jhtml?page=4.
7. Maloof Family Information, http://www.arcoarena.com/default.asp?lnopt=4&pnopt=0.
8. "Food for Thought: Dodgers Offer All-You-Can-Eat Seats," The Associated Press State & Local Wire, January 12, 2007.
9. Ken Kerschbaumer, "Battle for College Sports Fans," *Broadcasting & Cable,* March 14, 2005, p. 23; "First and Ten for a TV Upstart," *Business Week,* December 18, 2006, p. 48.
10. K. Kerschbaumer, "Cornhusker Fans Surf for Tackles," *Broadcasting and Cable* (August 28, 2000).
11. "MLB.com Sets Online Ticketing Record for Sixth Straight Year Passing the 20 Million Tickets Sold Mark for First Time," PR Newswire US, August 21, 2006.
12. "Golf Company Featured on the Golf Channel," Market Wire, November 21, 2006 , E21. "Textronics Expands into UK with NuMetrex Clothes That Monitor the Body," Business Wire, September 12, 2006.

13. "Textronics Expands into UK with NuMetrex Clothes That Monitor the Body," **Business Wire,** September 12, 2006.

14. Wesley Cropp, "Shoes Going Very High Tech," *The Daily Iowan,* July 19, 2006.

15. "Cisco and Athletics Announce Cisco Field; State-of-the-Art Technology to Take Fan Experience to New Level," November 14, 2006, http://newsroom.cisco.com/dlls/2006/corp_111406.html?CMP=ILC-001&POSITION=SEM&COUNTRY_SITE=us&CAMPAIGN=HN&CREATIVE=STADIUM&REFERRING_SITE=GOOGLE&KEYWORD=null.

16. "Twelve Baseball Parks to Use MasterCard PayPass Technology This Season," http://www.finextra.com/fullpr.asp?id=11531, September 27, 2006.

17. "Essential Facts about the Computer and Video Game Industry," Entertainment Software Association, http://www.theesa.com/archives/files/Essential%20Facts%202006.pdf.

18. Brian D. Crecente, "The Highest Level; Video Gaming Pros Take Next Big Step: To Televised League and Tournament Play," *Rocky Mountain News,* December 8, 2006, p. 16d.

19. "Team Sports Participation," http://www.nsga.org/public/pages/index.cfm?pageid=1418.

20. Scott Wong, "New-Age Stadium Is on a High-Tech Roll," *The Arizona Republic,* August 10, 2006.

21. "For the Good of the Game," http://www.fifa.com/aboutfifa/federation/mission.html, 1996.

22. http://www.census.gov/population/pop-profile/dynamic/PopDistribution.pdf.

23. "Minorities Getting Closer to the Majority," May 11, 2006, http://www.cnn.com/2006/US/05/10/hispanics/index.html.

24. "Hispanic Entrepreneurship, Buying Power on the Rise," http://www.cnn.com/2007/US/10/01/hispanics.economy/index.html.

25. Steve Wilstein, "Think the NBA Can't Go Belly Up? Think Again," Associated Press (September 26, 2003), http://news.mysanantonio.com

26. Paul A. Samuelson, *Economics,* 10th ed. (New York: McGraw Hill, 1976).

27. Brian Reich, "Baseball and the American City," http://www.stadiummouse.com/stadium/economic.html, April 30, 2001.

28. Matthew D. Shank and Robert A. Snyder, "Temporary Solutions: Uncovering New Market Opportunities in the Temporary Employment Industry," *Journal of Professional Services Marketing,* vol. 12, no. 1 (1995), 5–17.

PART

II

PLANNING FOR MARKET SELECTION DECISIONS

CHAPTER

3

RESEARCH TOOLS FOR UNDERSTANDING SPORTS CONSUMERS

After completing this chapter, you should be able to:

■ Discuss the importance of marketing research to sports marketers.

■ Explain the fundamental process for conducting sports marketing research.

■ Identify the various research design types.

■ Describe the process for questionnaire development.

■ Understand how to prepare an effective research report.

As the accompanying River Rats example illustrates, marketing research is a fundamental tool for understanding and ultimately satisfying customers' needs. As described in Chapter 1, one way of demonstrating a marketing orientation is to gather information used for decision making. Another way of establishing a marketing orientation is to disseminate information and share the marketing information with those responsible for making decisions. Marketing research is viewed as an essential element in marketing-oriented organizations.

The information gathered through marketing research can be as basic as where consumers live, how much money they make, and how old they are. Research also provides information for decision makers in identifying marketing opportunities and threats, segmenting markets, choosing and understanding the characteristics of target markets, evaluating the current market positioning, and making marketing mix decisions.

More specifically, marketing research may provide answers to questions such as the following:

• What new products or services would be of interest to consumers of sport?
• What do present and potential consumers think about our new ad campaign?
• How does the advertising and promotion mix affect purchase decisions?
• What are the latest changes or trends in the sport marketplace?
• How are consumers receiving sports information and programming?
• What are sports fans spending, and what are they buying?
• Who are the biggest sponsors of professional sports leagues or college sports?
• How interested are fans in my team, my players, and in the sport itself?

- How do consumers perceive my team, league, or event relative to competitors?
- What is the best way to promote my sports product or service?
- Who participates in sports, and in what sports are they are participating? Also, where are they participating, and how often?
- Are current consumers satisfied with my sports products and services? What are the major determinants of customer satisfaction?
- What price are consumers willing to pay for my sports product or service?
- What image does the team, player, or event hold with current consumers and potential consumers?

These are just a few of the questions that may be addressed through marketing research. **Marketing research** or **sports marketing research** is the systematic process of collecting, analyzing, and reporting information to enhance decision making throughout the strategic sports marketing process.

Three key issues emerge from this definition. First, marketing research must be systematic in its approach. Systematic research is both well organized and unbiased. The well-organized nature of good research depends on adherence to the marketing research process, which is discussed later in this chapter. Researchers must also be careful not to make up their minds about the results of a study prior to conducting it; therefore, researchers must conduct the study in an unbiased manner.

Second, the marketing research process involves much more than collecting data and then reporting it back to decision makers. The challenge of research lies in taking the data collected, analyzing it, and then making sense of the data. Marketing researchers who can collect data, dump it in the computer, and spit out reports are a dime a dozen. The most valuable marketing researcher is the person who has the

---

Marketing Research in Action: The Albany River Rats

The Albany River Rats of the American Hockey League conducted a detailed study to gather information that would guide the planning phase of their strategic marketing process. Garen Szablewski, River Rats' president and CEO, stated that "We're absolutely committed to providing the best family entertainment experience in the region. . . . these surveys will let our fans sound off about what they like, what they don't, and what they'd like to see."

The research objectives were to examine media usage, consumption behavior, and intentions (e.g., number of games attended and likelihood of attending again), and to explore the demographic characteristics of River Rat fans (e.g., age and gender). In addition, the study was designed to look at how survey responses differed according to fan demographics. For instance, are males more likely than females to attend a River Rats game in the future?

All fans attending the game and completing a survey received one complimentary ticket to a future River Rats' game. Some of the survey questions included:

- How many River Rats games have you attended?
- Would you come to a River Rats game again?
- What are the best two nights of the week to attend a River Rats game?
- To what radio stations do you listen?
- On what radio stations have you heard River Rats commercials?
- What newspapers do you read?
- What are your favorite television stations?
- Do you find the promotions and entertainment between periods fun?
- Demographic information (age, gender, occupation, and hometown)

Analysis of the overall fan base helped to guide the strategic marketing process for the River Rats. More specifically, the survey helped to target their advertising efforts more efficiently.

Source: http://www.albanyriverrats.com/news/?id=4313.

ability to examine the data and then make recommendations about how the information should be used (or not used) in the strategic marketing process.

Third, the importance of marketing research is found in its ability to allow managers to make informed decisions. Without the information gathered in research, management decision making would be based on guessing and luck. As Woody Hayes, Ohio State's legendary football coach, once said about the forward pass, "Three things can happen and two of them are bad!"

Finally, the definition states that marketing research is useful throughout the entire strategic sports marketing process. Traditionally, the focus of marketing research has been on how the information can be used in better understanding consumers during the planning phase of the strategic sports marketing process. It is also important to realize that marketing research is relevant at the implementation and control phases of the strategic marketing process. For example, research is used in the control phase to determine whether marketing goals are being met.

THE MARKETING RESEARCH PROCESS

As previously mentioned, marketing research is conducted using a systematic process, or the series of interrelated steps shown in Figure 3.1. Before we discuss each step in the research process in greater detail, two points should be kept in mind. First, the basic framework or process for conducting marketing research does not change, although every marketing research problem will be different. For example, the Detroit Red Wings may engage in research to understand fan satisfaction or the effectiveness of a between-period promotion. Each of these research questions is different. However, the basic marketing research process used to address each question is the same.

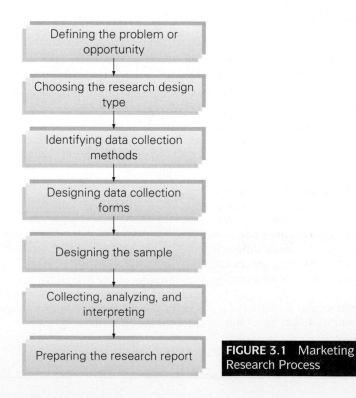

FIGURE 3.1 Marketing Research Process

Second, you should understand that the steps of the research process are interdependent. In other words, defining the problem in a certain way will affect the choice of research design. Likewise, selecting a certain type of research design will influence the selection of data collection tools. Let us now examine each of the steps in the research process.

Defining the Problem or Opportunity

The first and most important step of the marketing research process for sports marketers is to define the problem or opportunity. **Problem definition** requires the researcher to specify what information is needed to assist in either solving problems or identifying opportunities by developing a **research problem statement**. If the research addresses the correct problem or opportunity and seeks to properly define the problem or opportunity, then the project could be successful. However, the data collected may be useless if it is not the information needed by the sports marketing manager.

How does the researcher identify problems or opportunities that confront the sports organization? Initially, information is gathered at a meeting between the researcher and his or her client. In this meeting, the researcher should attempt to collect as much information as possible to better understand the need for research. Table 3.1 shows a list of the typical questions or issues addressed at the first information-gathering meeting.

Research Objectives

Based on this initial meeting, the researcher should have collected the proper information to develop a set of research objectives. **Research objectives** describe the various types of information needed to address the problem or opportunity. Each specific objective will provide direction or focus for the rest of the study.

Here is an example of the research objectives developed for the NASCAR Sponsorship Study conducted by Sponsorship Research and Strategy (SRS).[1] The purpose of the study was to provide information that would assist NASCAR sponsors in planning, evaluating, and justifying their NASCAR sponsorships. More specifically, the research objectives were as follows:

- Identify the benefits associated with NASCAR sponsorships.
- Record fan preferences for sales promotions.
- Identify lucrative market segments among NASCAR fans.
- Develop an extensive profile of NASCAR fans.
- Examine fan attitudes toward NASCAR and NASCAR sponsors.
- Analyze sponsorship effectiveness for different types of NASCAR sponsorships (e.g., car vs. league).
- Provide a comparative basis for sponsorship performance among NASCAR Nextel Cup drivers.
- Provide a comparative basis for sponsorship performance among official NASCAR sponsors in selected product categories.

TABLE 3.1   Issues Addressed at Initial Research Meeting

- A brief background or history of the organization or individual(s) requesting the research
- A brief background of the types of research the organization has done in the past, if any
- The information the organization wants and why (i.e., what they plan to do with the information once it is obtained)
- The targeted population of interest for this research
- The expectations in terms of the timeframe for the research and costs of conducting the study

How would NASCAR or any sports entity go about measuring whether these objectives have been reached? The accompanying article describes the evaluation of one specific and growing concern about measuring sponsorship ROI.

Measuring Return on Sports Marketing Investment

You won't find a sports marketer who says the industry's skill in measuring return on investment hasn't improved in the past five years. But you also won't find a sports marketer who says the industry has really figured it out.

And sports marketers aren't alone. A survey done this year by three broad-based marketing advocacy and research groups found that 60 percent of marketers think it's important to define, measure and act on return on investment (ROI). But only 20 percent said they're satisfied with their efforts.

The reasons are many. For starters, some marketing realities are hard to quantify, such as how brand awareness or good will translates to financial return. Or how a good hospitality experience affects the bottom line in subsequent weeks or months.

But even that's getting ahead of things. The challenge of ROI begins with what ROI is. "You have to determine exactly what you're measuring, and a methodology for measuring and tracking," said Jay Kenney, senior vice president for IMG Consulting. "You also have to set a benchmark for what success is. And most importantly, you have to have an internal alignment in senior management sign off on all of the above."

Indeed, it's easy for a company to get off the track during the process—at almost any stage. ROI measurement problems can start with a poorly conceived purchase.

"You hear stories about a company that gets into sponsorship and takes the elements and then says, 'How do we develop the activation program?'" said Steve Lauletta, president of Omnicom's Radiate group of sports marketing agencies. "We say, develop that [activation strategy] up front and then just go buy [the appropriate] elements. It's hard work, but the industry is getting better at this."

Initial purchases are made harder by the fact that, historically, sports properties don't do a great deal of sophisticated research into their fan demographics, nor do they have incentive to help in the analysis after a deal, in case results are lackluster.

"There is a greater demand at the moment on the owners of sports properties to provide good quality data on their demographics," said Michael Stirling, an attorney specializing in sports rights negotiations with London law firm Field Fisher Waterhouse, whose clients include Fortune 500 companies and leading Champions League soccer teams. "But we audit the data and we are often very worried about the quality that the rightsholders come up with."

The ideal is a sharing of good data between sponsor and property. But sponsors also fail to keep the bargain sometimes. "There's that fear, if [the property] knows how successful we are at driving the bottom line, it could affect fees in the future, so there's a little bit of hesitancy to share," said Rob Vogel, president and chief operating officer of The Bonham Group.

Oh, and there's the issue of how to interpret the ROI numbers themselves. "Most people who I see making sponsorship decisions are not necessarily trained in market research and statistical analysis," said Katie Delahaye Paine, CEO of the analytics firm KDPaine & Partners and publisher of The Measurement Standard newsletter. "You have all these fabulous tools, and most people say, 'Um, I don't know how to deal with the numbers.'"

This creates an opportunity for agencies with the right expertise. Analysts see agencies continuing to lead clients through the ROI process, and the agencies see themselves making new investments in ROI measurement technology.

"It will become a lot closer to, if not a daily, then a weekly or monthly management tool," said Jim Nail, principal analyst at Forrester Research. "And what that will mean is . . . less and less the agency doing their thing and saying, 'Put your money here' and more and more about 'Here's where the model says you should put your money.'"

IMG's Kenney said his firm is looking into developing a suite of online-based ROI tools. "We would also consider buying a company; we're sort of thinking about developing an alliance or a purchase," he said. "There's a future for it as more companies go online with [their analytics]. As a business model it makes sense." The Bonham Group already has the tools in development, Vogel said.

Indeed, there's a strong feeling that some of the perplexing facts of ROI measurement can be sorted out by computer-based analytical systems—of course, when they're accompanied by good planning, wholehearted execution and informed number-crunching.

In this article, we look at some of the strides being made by agencies to develop and improve these systems.

Up-Front Analysis

As marketers have noted, to maximize return on investment, it helps to make the right investment in the first place. One of the tools now employed on the front end of the sponsorship process is SponsorAid, developed three years ago by the Chicago-based company of the same

(Continued)

(Continued)

name, in collaboration with Miller Brewing, which now uses the system to analyze more than 1,000 sponsorship proposals annually. More precisely, Miller lets the system pre-analyze the proposal based on extensive data provided by the property online, at sponsoraid.com.

The property enters the proposal inventory—things such as signs, activation tools, promotional tools in and out of venue, print, TV, radio—and SponsorAid vets the program for overall conformity to Miller's goals and assigns a dollar value to each of the components listed above, and more.

There are other pre-analysis products available to sponsors—such as SponsorWise, SponsorDirect and Sponsorium—but SponsorAid president Chris Thompson says SponsorAid is the only product that puts a dollar valuation on each component. And he has a patent application pending to back up the claim.

Rick Hall, vice president at Omnicom's GMR Marketing, Miller's sports agency of record, said SponsorAid "gives us a line of sight into the true market value of what Miller's buying."

He points to one example when SponsorAid assigned a higher value to the use of a team's logo rights than Miller would have. "It allowed us to see that there were multiple factors going into the value of the trademark, in terms of the franchise value, its performance on the field, its attendance," Hall said. "It showed we could really take that trademark to retail and identify with it as a marketing tool."

Another indication of SporsorAid's influence on Miller: Former Miller sports marketing boss Steve Lauletta is using SponsorAid as the front end of a two-prong system he's developing at Radiate. The second prong is a post-sponsorship analysis tool that serves the cause of "being more disciplined about going back and looking at what you said you were going to do," Lauletta said.

While Miller takes sponsorship assets to market, Thompson is taking SponsorAid to market, as well. He has been angling for single deep partners in each of the remaining seven or eight top sponsorship categories—soft drink, fast food, etc.—but so far hasn't landed one. "I guess I've been spoiled with Miller," he said with a laugh. "But I'm not out to just sell site licenses to a bunch of companies."

So he's putting new energy into developing agency relationships and is adding to SponsorAid the capability to do "one-time applications," basically a sponsorship valuation snapshot with a one-day turnaround at a cost of between $500 and $1,000. A deeper, Miller-style relationship would run in the mid-five figures, Thompson said.

In the meantime, Thompson has made improvements to SponsorAid, such as adding a user-friendly version for smaller properties. "I had to make it easier for the less-seasoned, say a Saturday night dirt-track racer," Thompson said.

But even big properties benefit from SponsorAid, he said. "The quicker both sides see what each thinks something is worth, the quicker they can start to talk productively."

Up-Front . . . and Beyond

SponsorDirect is one of many companies offering online sponsorship pre-analysis tools, and it has recently rolled out version 2.0 of its SponsorPort tool, aiming to facilitate the ROI evaluation on a company's full portfolio of deals.

Bank of America, Nokia, Dodge and Panasonic are some of the companies that have used earlier versions of SponsorPort.

For Bank of America, there's immediate ROI. Before automating the pre-analysis, Bank of America had roughly three dozen regional marketers spending up to 18 hours a week vetting proposals. The man-hours have been cut in half, according to Joe Goode, corporate spokesman for Bank of America's sponsorship group.

In the last few months, SponsorDirect has been introducing 2.0 to clients, and Bank of America and Chevron are two that will be using the new portfolio management and ROI-measurement tools. Goode said it's too early to comment on the performance, and Chevron marketer Trisha Roche said company policy prevents her from talking about vendors' products.

But here's what 2.0 offers users, according to Ken Brenner, president of SponsorDirect: a listing of all the costs that go into a sponsorship; objectives described numerically or qualitatively; the sponsor's metrics for measuring projected value vs. the actual value derived; and external metrics, such as sales figures and performance.

"We can build algorithms behind the scenes based on a company's methodology, and we think this is the first time the industry is offering infrastructure for companies to arrive at this kind of measurement and ROI in a centralized platform," Brenner said.

There's a flip side to the high claims SponsorDirect is making for the functionality of 2.0. It's the absolute need for participation by all sponsor employees involved in the marketing process. From executives throwing their weight behind the system to field marketers inputting sales results and updates on execution elements, the system needs extensive data to process.

"Buy-in is so critically important," said SponsorDirect CEO Mark Rockefeller. "Across an organization you can't have certain brand managers excited about it and some not."

Where Rubber Hits Road

Increasingly, marketing agencies are offering field research tools that a sponsor can use to measure the impact of their execution as it's happening.

(Continued)

(Continued)

DaimlerChrysler has used Event Metrics Co. and Turnkey Sports recently for this. In the latter case, Turnkey stationed roughly a dozen questioners at Historically Black College and Universities football games last season and captured information on their car-buying habits and their likelihood of purchasing DaimlerChrysler products.

The auditors didn't ask questions about perceptions of DaimlerChrysler's sponsorship itself. The time was spent in determining whether the fan was a good sales prospect. Immediately after the event, the information—originally collected on PDAs—was uploaded to the company's data-collection system, administered by agency BBDO.

Soon, dealers had the information on top prospects, and BBDO continued to track sales efficacy at the 30-, 60- and 90-day marks. Melissa Killinger, senior vice president, director of integrated strategic marketing at GlobalHue, Daimler Chrysler's multicultural marketing agency of record, would not describe the sales results of the data, but she had no qualms about Turnkey's execution of the program or of the quality of the data.

"Turnkey was well organized, and they did a great job in working with BBDO," she said. "They had set up systems, and Turnkey followed them."

Experts say in-event audience polls can be flawed if they're angling for a true cross-section of fans and their true feelings.

"Some fan sections are not going to feel comfortable doing such a survey, or a high-tech survey in the first place," said Whitney Wagner, adjunct instructor of marketing at the Warsaw Sports Marketing Center at the University of Oregon, who spent seven years at the NFL in the marketing department. "And then you have the same problem: What does 'I'm satisfied with this' mean? How reliable is the question, 'Would you be willing to pay five dollars more for the experience?' Just because it comes in real time doesn't get to the heart of the issue."

But Turnkey and Chrysler believe they narrowed the criteria enough to get reliable results. "Part of the direction was that they make sure the person is actually educated on the product and then asked politely if they are interested in more information—and if they were in-market, if they could give us their contact information," said Killinger.

"This was not just lead generation, but a more in-depth profile of the people at the event, so they can tweak their approach, or the whole package, after the event," said Len Perna, president of Turnkey Sports. "In terms of ROI, you can really figure out where the rubber hits the road: 'Are they considering us?'"

After the Party

Once an agency has a system developed to pre-analyze or manage a sponsorship portfolio, it's natural for it to try to build on new functionalities, such as SponsorDirect has.

SportsMark's SportsManager has proved itself as a dependable hospitality-management tool, tracking the myriad administrative details that go into hosting hundreds of guests at a major event, such as the Olympics. But the company is also pushing its post-event analysis tools, which build off the same system. Where SportsManager helped ROI by making hospitality more efficient, the new functionalities aim to make ROI measurement itself more exact.

It starts with a few questions asked of guests before the event, about their perceptions of the brand doing the hosting. After the event, guests are asked via e-mail to answer a few questions about the brand and its event, such as "What did you see at this event and how did the brand come across?" and "Is the brand in tune with contemporary lifestyles?"

The Hartford used SportsManager around its NCAA corporate partnership during last year's Final Four, including the post-event analysis, married with survey work done by The Hartford.

"The Hartford wanted to increase its corporate customers' sense that it is a leadership brand in tune with its consumers' contemporary lifestyles," said Keith Bruce, CMO of SportsMark. Thanks to the NCAA relationship, and thanks to the hospitality program, as measured by SportsManager, "The Hartford realized a significant growth in its customers' perceptions of the company as a more contemporary leadership brand."

And as with some of the other systems profiled here, SportsManager can help a company track eventual sales made with those guests.

Where perception is concerned, Bruce said companies are careful about how they approach guests after the event, and they're careful with the questions. But he said after a good hospitality experience—SportsMark has also administered Olympics hospitality for Xerox, among its relationships—guests are usually willing to answer a few questions.

On the other hand, how does SportsManager assure that the guests don't feel obligated to give positive answers? Or are afraid to give negative ones? "There's always a risk, but there are plenty of different strategies [for encouraging honest responses], depending on the question content," Bruce said. "Many times, the guests are assured their responses will be anonymous."

SportsMark is an event-management company that has been tracking hospitality activity online for several years. But more agencies and clients are getting into the act. Paragon Marketing Group rolled out an extensive ticket-management program, called TAP, for its client Continental Airlines this summer, in connection with Web developer American Eagle. The product is now available to corporations for a roughly $30,000 up-front fee, plus maintenance. The Bonham Group has developed its own system.

(Continued)

(Continued)

"The ticket allocation piece, people see it as a necessary evil, but frankly it's a difficult thing to manage, it's a nasty beast," said Robert Madrigal, professor of sports marketing at Oregon's Warsaw Sports Marketing Center. "And, again, it's a difficult thing to really analyze what makes the use of a particular piece of hospitality effective."

Sharpening the Picture

Event signage is as much (or more) for television as it is for the fans at the event, but television isn't always kind to the signs. Partial or obstructed views of logos vex brand marketers, including when they try to measure the value of those exposures.

Joyce Julius & Associates and TNS Sport are two companies that are trying to make the measurement process more exact—Julius with its new Image Identification Technology and TNS Sport with Sportsi, which it rolled out more than a year ago.

Joyce Julius & Associates has developed a huge client roster for its television brand-exposure analysis work, yet you still hear the industry complain of a methodological weakness in how the firm handles partial exposures of a logo. The firm might have solved that perception problem with its Image Identification Technology, powerful software that calculates logo exposure and makes fine distinctions in the quality of that exposure.

"I would use the analogy of watching a baseball game and knowing that the last pitch was a fastball," said Eric Wright, vice president of research and development for the company. "Then putting a radar gun on the next pitch and seeing it was a 91 mph fastball."

The technology, developed by UK-based OmniPerception and contracted for on a non-exclusive basis by Joyce Julius, does what the company's human analysts have always done, but with a pixel-by-pixel exactitude. The technology was developed from forensic tools that searched for face patterns in security videos.

"In basic terms, we can tell the amount of space occupied by a logo, the amount of logo on screen per frame, the percentage of blockage, say by someone standing in front of it, and where on the screen the logo appeared," Wright said.

It also offers speed. Six weeks worth of human work was recently done so quickly that the company released its U.S. Open tennis results five days after the event.

With the computer to supplement work being done by humans, "Now we can say, 'Here's why you received 10, not 15, minutes [worth of exposure], and for those five minutes, look at your clarity rating. We could have done it before, but it would have been labeled subjective," Wright said. "We believe strongly in our researchers, but now we have percentages and images to back up the concepts that we would have tried to relay."

TNS' Sportsi is now being used by some leagues and individual sponsors, and recently gained traction with agencies, said Mark Davis, director of business development. The technology can measure partial and obscured logos, and it produces a numeric score based on how close to perfect the logo is.

Sponsors are demanding a closer accounting of on-screen logos, Davis said. "Since there are so many more opportunities for companies to buy into sports from a media standpoint—so many different sports and ways to be integrated into action—there's more call to measure it. People are not just looking at the commercial strategy but the whole media strategy."

Radio's Reach

Marketers like to say that ROI measurement has evolved beyond calculating the television cost-per-thousand equivalent of various kinds of brand exposure. But in the radio world, you haven't always been able to get a dependable cost per thousand to start with.

Arbitron is the first to admit this—especially now that it's starting an audience measurement system for radio based on next-day phone surveys rather than the traditional 12-week paper diaries.

The new service—called the Custom Sports Survey—is a steppingstone to Arbitron's "personal people meter" service, which will roll out over two years starting next year and employ pager-sized devices that track listener habits simply by picking up codes in radio signals.

When pre-testing of the PPM suggested that Arbitron's diaries had seriously undercounted listenership, the company felt it would be profitable to offer the phone service in the meantime. The product rolled out this summer; the Los Angeles Angels are its first client. A 20-game unaided-recall study done this season produced a cumulative rating of 1.6 over a wide range of days and times—twice what the diary had logged for the same male 25–54 audience.

"We've always felt that audiences were bigger than the diaries showed, and this was borne out," said Bob Koontz, station manager at ESPN-owned KSPN-AM in Los Angeles.

The next stage is getting agencies to respect the results, Koontz said. Sales for Arbitron-audited stations have been a loose negotiation in which agencies drove down prices because of the flaws inherent in the diary system, which was generally adequate for broad-stroke ratings over three months but were wildly inaccurate—in both directions—for discrete time slots such as a three-hour Sunday-night baseball game.

"We can't just ask double our former rates now," Koontz said. "This still has to prove itself. But we've made good inroads in the past few weeks and we haven't had a bad response from an agency yet."

(Continued)

(Continued)

The service costs between $50,000 and $65,000 per study, which involves between 1,000 and 1,500 calls. Demographic questions can also be a part of the phone call thanks to Arbitron's relationship with Scarborough Research, according to John Snyder, vice president of national group services for Arbitron.

Considering that sports teams typically spend less on market research than other consumer businesses of their size, Arbitron is hoping the ability to do radio and demographic research in one fell swoop will prove tempting to teams and their radio partners.

Source: Noah Liberman, "Agencies Roll Out New Measurement Tools as Sponsors Seek to Justify Their Investments Measuring ROI," *Sports Business Journal,* September 26, 2005, p. 23; http://www.sportsbusinessjournal.com/index.cfm?fuseaction=search.show_article&articleId=47131& keyword=Measuring%20Return%20on%20Sports%20Marketing%20Investment.

Writing a Marketing Research Proposal

To ensure agreement between the researcher and the client on the direction of the research, a research proposal is developed. A **research proposal** is a written blueprint that describes all the information necessary to conduct and control the study. The elements of the research proposal include background for the study, research objectives based on the need for the research, research methodology, timeframe, and cost estimates. An outline for developing a research proposal is shown in Table 3.2.

Choosing the Research Design Type

Once the researcher is certain that the problem is correctly defined, the research design type is considered. The **research design** is the framework for a study that collects and analyzes data. Although every study is unique and requires a slightly different plan to reach the desired goals and objectives, three research design types have emerged: exploratory, descriptive, and causal designs. Whatever research design or designs are ultimately chosen, it is important to remember the crucial principle in research is that the design of the research should stem from the problem.[2]

Exploratory Designs

Exploratory designs are useful when research problems are not well defined. For instance, the general manager for the River Rats may say that ticket sales are down, but he is unsure why. In this case, an exploratory research design would be appropriate

---

TABLE 3.2   Marketing Research Proposal Outline

Background and History

Defining the Problem or Opportunity

Research Objectives

Research Methodology
    a. Sample
    b. Procedures
    c. Topical areas

Time Estimate
    a. Design of instrument
    b. Data collection
    c. Data entry
    d. Data analysis
    e. Final report preparation

Cost Estimate

because there is no clear-cut direction for the research. The research is conducted to generate insight into the problem or to gain a better understanding of the problem at hand. For example, the researcher may recommend examining AHL attendance trends or conducting one-on-one interviews with team management to determine their ideas about the lack of attendance. Because exploratory research design types address vague problems, a number of data collection techniques are possible. These data collection techniques will be addressed during the next phase of the research process.

Descriptive Designs

If the research problem is more clearly defined, then a descriptive design is used. A descriptive design type describes the characteristics of a targeted group by answering questions such as who, what, where, when, and how often. The targeted group or population of interest to the decision maker might be current season ticket holders, people in the geographic region who have not attended any games, or a random group of people in the United States.

The River Rats study used a descriptive research design. The targeted group in this case was fans attending River Rat home games. Characteristics of the group of interest in the study included where the fans were coming from (geographic area), how often they attended games, when they were most likely to attend games (weekends, weekdays, day, or evening), and demographics (age and gender).

In addition to describing the characteristics of a targeted group, descriptive designs show the extent to which two variables differ or correlate. For example, a researcher may want to examine the relationship between game attendance and merchandising sales. Using the River Rats example, researchers wanted to understand the relationship between age of the fans and likelihood of attending games in the future. A descriptive research design type would allow us to examine the relationship or correlation between these two variables (age and future attendance).

If a positive relationship were found between age and likelihood of attending games in the future, then the older you get, the more likely you would be to attend future River Rat games. That is, as the age of the fan increases, the likelihood of going to future games also increases (see Figure 3.2a). However, a negative relationship means that as age increases, the likelihood of going to games decreases (see Figure 3.2b). Knowing the shape of this relationship will help the River Rats marketers make decisions on whom to target and how to develop the appropriate marketing mix for this group. What do you think the relationship between age and attendance would look like?

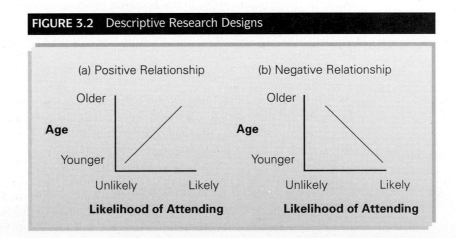

FIGURE 3.2   Descriptive Research Designs

Causal Designs

Using a descriptive design, we can explore the relationship between two variables, such as age and likelihood of attending games in the future. However, what this does not tell us is that age *causes* the likelihood of attending to either increase or decrease. This can only be determined through a causal design.

Causal designs are useful when problems are very clearly defined. More specifically, causal designs examine whether changing the level of one variable causes the level of another variable to change. This is more commonly called a cause-and-effect relationship.

In an example of a causal design, the River Rats could conduct a study to determine whether varying the level of advertising on a local radio station has any effect on attendance. In this case, level of advertising is the independent variable and attendance is the dependent variable. The **dependent variable** is the variable to be explained, predicted, or measured (i.e., attendance). The **independent variable** is the variable that can be manipulated or altered in some way (i.e., level of advertising or perhaps whether to advertise at all).

To show cause-and-effect relationships, three criteria must be satisfied. The first criterion for causality is that the occurrence of the causal event must precede or be simultaneous to the effect it is producing. Using our example, advertising must precede or occur at the same time as the increase in attendance to demonstrate a cause-and-effect relationship.

The second criterion for causality involves the extent to which the cause and the effect vary together. This is called **concomitant variation.** If advertising expenditures are increased, then season ticket sales should also increase at the same rate. Likewise, when advertising spending is decreased, season ticket sales should also decline. Keep in mind, however, that concomitant variation does not prove a cause-and-effect relationship, but it is a necessary condition for it.

A third criterion used to show causal relationships requires the elimination of other causal factors. This means that another variable or variables may produce changes in the independent variable. This possibility is called a spurious association or spurious correlation. In the dynamic sports marketing environment, it could be difficult to isolate and eliminate all possible causal factors. For instance, an increase in attendance may be due to the success of the team, ticket prices, and addition of other promotions (e.g., Puck Night) rather than increased advertising. A researcher must attempt to eliminate these other potential factors, hold them constant, or adjust the results to remove the effects of any other factors.

Identifying Data Collection Techniques

As with the previous steps in the research process, decisions regarding data collection techniques are very much a function of problem definition and research design type. If the research problem is loosely defined and requires an exploratory research design, then there are more alternatives for collecting that information. However, for well-specified problems using a causal design, the choice of data collection techniques decreases dramatically.

Data collection techniques can be broadly categorized as secondary or primary. **Secondary data** refers to data that were collected earlier but are still related to the research question. This data may come from within the sports organization or from outside the organization. For example, useful internal secondary data might include a history of team merchandise sales figures, event attendance figures, or fan satisfaction studies that were conducted previously. External secondary data, or data from outside the organization, may come from any number of the sources presented later in this chapter.

Although a researcher should always try to use existing data before conducting his or her own inquiries, it is sometimes impossible to find data relevant to the problem at hand. In that case, research must turn to the other data collection alternative, primary data. **Primary data** is information gathered for the specific research question at hand.

Before turning our discussion to the various types of primary and secondary data, it is important to note that both types of data are useful in understanding consumers. For example, sports marketers from the Phoenix Cardinals may want to look at trends in merchandising sales for each NFL team before undertaking a study to determine why their sales have decreased. In this case, secondary data is a useful supplement to the primary data they would also need to collect.

Secondary Data

As just mentioned, secondary data may be found within the sports marketing organization (internal secondary data) or from outside sources (external secondary data). External secondary data can be further divided into the following categories:[3]

- Government reports and documents
- Standardized sports marketing information studies
- Trade and industry associations
- Books, journals, and periodicals

Government Reports and Documents

As we discussed in Chapter 2, environmental scanning is an essential task for monitoring the external contingencies. Government reports and documents are excellent sources of data for sports marketers exploring the marketing environment. Government sources of data can provide demographic, economic, social, and political information at the national, state, and local levels. This information is generally abundant and can be obtained at no cost. There are thousands of government sources that are useful for environmental scanning. In fact, many are now published on the Internet. Let us look at a few of the most useful sources of government data.

Bureau of the Census of the U.S. Department of Commerce (www.census.gov) The Bureau of the Census is one of the most comprehensive sources of secondary data that is readily available via the Internet. Here are some of the census documents that may be of interest: Census of Population, Census of Retail Trade, Census of Service Industries, and Census of Manufacturing Industries.

The Statistical Abstract of the United States (www.census.gov/stat_abstract) The *Statistical Abstract of the United States*, which is published each year by the Bureau of the Census, is an excellent place to begin a search for secondary data. In addition to more general statistical information on the population and economy, the *Statistical Abstract* has a section entitled "Parks, Recreation and Travel." Within this section, statistics can be found on both participants and spectators.

Chambers of Commerce Usually, Chambers of Commerce have multiple sources of demographic information about a specific geographic area, including education, income, and businesses (size and sales volume). This type of information can be helpful to sports marketers conducting research on teams or events within a metropolitan area.

Small Business Administration (SBA) SBA-sponsored studies can be a valuable source for the environmental scan. The sources include statistics, maps, national market analyses, national directories, library references, and site selection.

Standardized Sports Marketing Information Studies

Although government sources of secondary data are plentiful, they are generally more useful for looking at national or global trends in the marketing environment. Standardized sports marketing information studies, such as the ESPN Sports Poll

The growing number of women's sports participants is being monitored through secondary marketing research.

(www.sportspoll.com) or the Sports Business Research Network (www.sbrnet.com), focus more specifically on sports consumers and markets. In fact, these sources of secondary data can provide extremely specialized information on consumers of a specific sport (e.g., golf) at a specific level of competition or interest (avid golfers). Table 3.3 shows the table of contents for a standardized study available for better understanding the golf market in North America.

These studies are called standardized because the procedures used to collect the information and the type of data collected are uniform. Once the information is collected, it is then sold to organizations that may find the data useful. Although the data collected are more specific than other sources of secondary data, the data may still not directly address the research question. Table 3.4 shows a sampling of the standardized sources of secondary data that may be useful to sports marketers.

TABLE 3.3   North American Golf Report Table of Contents

Executive Summary
Golf Supply
  Golf Supply by Country
  Population per 18 Holes
  Courses by State
Golf Development
  Golf Development by Country
  Golf Course Openings
  Recent Golf Course Openings
  New Openings by State
Golfer Participation
  Golfer Participation by Country
  Golfer Participation by State
  Number of Golfers by State
Regional Breakdown of Supply, Growth, and Participation
Trade in Golf-Related Goods
  Imports and Exports by Country

Source: http://www.golf-research-group.com/reports/report/22/content. html. Used by permission of the Golf Research Group. All rights reserved.

TABLE 3.4	Standardized Sports Marketing Information Studies

Team Marketing Report's Sports Sponsor Factbook
Team Marketing Report's Stadium Signage Report
Team Marketing Report's Inside the Ownership of Professional Sports Team
IEG's Sponsorship Report
IEG's Intelligence Reports
Sports & Media Challenges Sports Sponsorship Survey
National Sporting Goods Manufacturers' Sports Media Index
National Sporting Goods Manufacturers' Country Market Research Studies
American Sports Data's American Sport Analysis Reports
National Golf Foundation's Golf Business Publications
Gallup Poll's Sports Participation Trends
Simmons Market Research Bureau's Study of Media and Market, Sports and Leisure
ESPN Chilton Sports Poll
Yankelovich Monitor Sports Enthusiast Profile

Trade and Industry Associations

There are hundreds of associations that can be helpful in the quest for information. Sports associations range from the very broad in focus (e.g., NCAA) to the more specific (e.g., National Skating Suppliers Association). For example, the Women's Sport Foundation (www.womenssportsfoundation.org), established in 1974 by Billie Jean King, works to improve public understanding of the benefits of sports and fitness for females of all ages. To support this educational objective, the foundation has a number of publications and research reports that serve as excellent sources of secondary data. In fact, the Women's Sport Foundation now has a cyberlibrary that contains 33 years of information gathered on topics and issues such as business, coaching, ethics, gender equity, history, homophobia, leadership and employment, media, medical, participation, sexual harassment, special needs, and training and fitness. Here is just a small sampling of trade and sport associations:

North American Society for Sport Management
European Association for Sport Management
Institute of Sport and Recreation Management
National Association of Sports Commissions
Sport Management Association of Australia and New Zealand Sport
    Marketing Association
Sporting Goods Manufacturers Association
National Collegiate Athletic Association
Sport Marketing Association

Books and Journals

A comprehensive list of journals related to sport follows the books listed here.

Books

IEG's Complete Guide to Sponsorship
Sport Marketing (Mullins, Hardy, & Sutton)
Sport Marketing (Pitts and Stotlar)
Team Marketing Report's Newsletter
Cases in Sport Marketing (McDonald and Milne)
Case Studies in Sport Marketing (Pitts)
Developing Successful Sports Marketing Plans (Stotlar)
Sports Marketing: Global Marketing Perspectives (Schlossberg)

Sports Marketing: It's Not Just a Game Anymore (Schaaf)
Sports Marketing: Famous People Sell Famous Products (Pemberton)
Sports Marketing: The Money Side of Sports (Pemberton)
Sports Marketing/Team Concept (Leonardi)
The Elusive Fan: Reinventing Sports in a Crowded Marketplace (Rein, Kotler, and Shields)
Marketing of Sport (Chadwick and Beech)
Team Sports Marketing (Wakefield)
Keeping Score: An Inside Look at Sports Marketing (Carter)
Ultimate Guide to Sport Marketing (Graham, Neirotti, and Goldblatt)
Sports Marketing: Managing the Exchange Process (Milne and McDonald)

Academic Journals of Interest to Sports Marketers

Sports Marketing Quarterly
Journal of Sport Behavior
Journal of Sport and Social Issues
Journal of Sport Management
Journal of Services Marketing
International Journal of Sports Marketing and Sponsorship
Sport Management Review

Primary Data

Data collected specifically to answer your research questions are called primary data. There are a wide variety of primary data collection techniques. Again, remember that your method of collecting primary data depends on your earlier choice of research design. Let us look briefly at some of the primary data collection methods and their pros and cons.

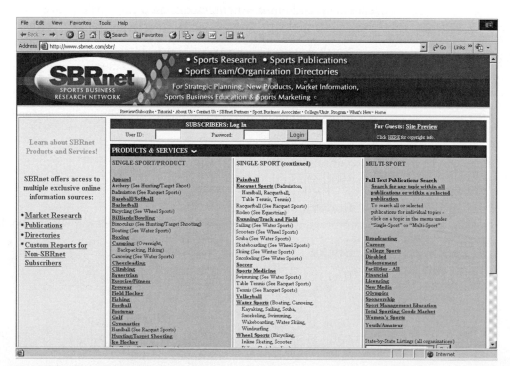

Sports Business Research is an excellent source of primary and secondary data.
Source: www.sbrnet.com. Sports Business Research Network.

Depth Interviews

Depth interviews are a popular data collection technique for exploratory research. Sometimes called "one-on-ones," depth interviews are usually conducted as highly unstructured conversations that last about an hour. *Unstructured* means that the researcher has a list of topics that need to be addressed during the interview, but the conversation can take its natural course. As the respondent begins to respond, new questions may then emerge that require further discussion.

The primary advantage of depth interviews is that they gather detailed information on the research question. Researchers may also prefer depth interviews to other primary methods when it is difficult to coordinate any interface with the target population. Just think of the difficulty in trying to organize research using professional athletes as the target population. For instance, a sports marketing researcher may want to determine what characteristics a successful athlete-endorser requires. To address this research question, depth interviews may be conducted with professional athletes who have been successful endorsers, athletes who have never endorsed a product, brand managers of products being endorsed, or any other individuals who may provide insight into the research question. The responses given in these interviews then would be used to determine the characteristics of a successful endorser.

Depth interviews may also be appropriate when studying complex decision making. For example, researchers may want to find out how others influence your decision to attend a sporting event. The information gathered in the depth interviews at the initial phase of this research may then be used in the development of a survey or some other type of primary research. In yet another example, depth interviews were used in a study to understand the decision-making process used by corporate sponsors.[4]

Focus Groups

Another popular exploratory research tool is the focus group. A **focus group** is a moderately structured discussion session held with eight to 10 people. The discussion focuses on a series of predetermined topics and is led by an objective, unbiased moderator. Much like depth interviews, focus groups are a qualitative research tool used to gain a better understanding of the research problem at hand. For instance, focus groups may be useful in establishing a team name or logo design, deciding what food to offer for sale in the concession areas, determining how best to reposition an existing sporting goods retailer, or learning what kinds of things would attract children to a collegiate sporting event. Let us look at two examples of sports organizations that have used focus groups.

Focus group and observers.

Louisiana State University's athletic department used focus group, among a number of other research techniques, to better understand reactions to possibly raising season ticket prices.[5] The results and discussion from these groups provided the direction for the strategic sports marketing process at LSU. In another example, the Ottawa Lynx, the Triple A affiliate of the Baltimore Orioles, used focus group information to help understand how to draw more fans. Through these focus groups, the Lynx assessed what people think of the team and why the community was not supporting the team. Findings included putting more emphasis on marketing to kids and getting the team more involved in the local community, so fans would identify with the players.[6]

Conducting focus groups, like those in the LSU and Ottawa examples, requires careful planning. Table 3.5 provides questions and answers that must be considered when planning and implementing focus groups.

TABLE 3.5   Planning and Implementing Focus Groups

Q. How many people should be in a focus group?
A. Traditionally, focus groups are composed of 8 to 10 people. However, there is a current trend toward having minigroups of 5 to 6 people. Minigroups are easier to recruit and allow for better and more interaction among focus group participants.

Q. How many people should I recruit, if I want 8 people in my group?
A. The general rule of thumb is to recruit 25 percent more people than the number needed. For example, if you are planning on holding minigroups with 6 people, you should recruit 8. Unfortunately, some respondents will not show up for the group, even if there is an incentive for participation.

Q. What is a good incentive for participants?
A. Naturally, a good incentive depends largely on the type of individual you want to attract to your group. For example, if your group wants to target runners who might be participating in a local 10K race, $35 to $50 may be the norm, including dinner or light snacks. However, if your group requires lawyers to discuss the impact of Title IX on the NCAA, an incentive of $75 to $100 may be more appropriate. In addition to or instead of cash, noncash incentives could also serve. For example, free tickets or merchandise may work better than cash for some groups.

Q. Where should the focus groups be conducted?
A. The best place to conduct focus groups is at a marketing research company that has up-to-date focus group facilities. The facility is usually equipped with a one-way mirror, videotape, microphones connected to an audio system, and an observation room for clients. In addition, more modern facilities have viewing rooms that allow the client to interact with the moderator via transmitter while the group is being conducted.

Q. How should I choose a moderator?
A. There is no rule of thumb, but research has identified a set of characteristics that seem to be consistent among good moderators. These characteristics include the following: quick learner, friendly leader, knowledgeable but not all-knowing, excellent memory, good listener, a facilitator—not a performer, flexible, empathic, a "big-picture" thinker, and a good writer. In addition, a good moderator should have a high degree of sports industry knowledge or product knowledge.[7]

Q. How many groups should be conducted?
A. The number of groups interviewed depends on the number of different characteristics that are being examined in the research. For example, Notre Dame may want to determine whether regional preferences exist for different types of merchandise. If so, two groups may be conducted in the North, two groups in the South, and so on. Using the previous example, if lawyers were the participants in a focus group, two or three total groups may suffice. Any more than this and the information would become redundant and the groups would become inefficient.

Q. What about the composition of the groups?
A. A general rule of thumb is that focus group participants should be homogenous. In other words, people within the group should be as similar as possible. We would not want satisfied, loyal fans in the same group as dissatisfied fans. Similarly, we would not want a group to be composed of both upper-level managers and the employees that report to them. In the latter case, lower-level employees may be reluctant to voice their true feelings.

Projective Techniques

Another source of data collection is through the use of projective techniques. **Projective techniques** refer to any of a variety of methods that allow respondents to project their feelings, beliefs, or motivations onto a relatively neutral stimulus. Projective techniques were developed by psychologists to uncover motivations or to understand personality. The most famous projective technique is the Rorschach test, which asks respondents to assign meaning to a neutral inkblot. Although the Rorschach may not have value for sports marketing researchers, other projective techniques are useful. For instance, sentence completion, word association, picture association, and cartoon tests could be employed as data collection techniques. Figure 3.3 demonstrates the use of sentence completion to gain insight into consumer attitudes toward Fila. The responses to these sentences could be analyzed to determine consumer perceptions of the target market for Fila (question 1), the brand image of Fila (question 2), and product usage (question 3).

Surveys

Data collection techniques are more narrowly defined for descriptive research design types. As stated earlier, a descriptive study describes who, where, how much, how often, and why people are engaging in certain consumption behaviors. To capture this information, the researcher would choose to conduct a survey. Surveys allow sports marketing researchers to collect primary data such as awareness, attitudes, behaviors, demographics, lifestyle, and other variables of interest. For example, the Cleveland Indians handed out roughly 30,000 surveys over 14 games to understand fans' perceptions of the team's on-the-field winning prospects, the quality of the team's management and commitment to winning, and pricing issues. Glenn Goodstein, director of J. D. Power's newly formed sports division, points out that "10 years ago, if the teams won, that was all that mattered—who cared what fans thought. But that is changing. Soon, about 75 percent of more than 100 professional sports teams in the country will be doing (this kind of research)."[8]

Surveys that are considered "snapshots" and describe the characteristics of a sample at one point in time are called **cross-sectional studies.** For example, if a high school athletics program wanted to measure fan satisfaction with its half-time promotions at a basketball game, a cross-sectional design would be used. However, if a researcher wanted to investigate an issue and examine responses over a longer period of time, a **longitudinal study** would be used. In this case, fan satisfaction would be measured, improvements would be made to the half-time promotions based on survey responses, and then fan satisfaction would be measured again at a later time. Although longitudinal studies are generally considered more effective, they are not widely used due to time and cost constraints.

Experiments

For well-defined problems, causal research is appropriate. As stated earlier, cause-and-effect relationships are difficult to confirm. **Experimentation** is research in which one

---

FIGURE 3.3 Sentence Completion Test

1. People who wear Fila footwear are _____ .

2. When I think of Fila, I _____ .

3. I would be most likely to buy Fila shoes for _____ .

SPOTLIGHT ON INTERNATIONAL SPORTS MARKETING

Survey Uncovers Canadian Fan Passion Drivers

A new research study conducted by Octagon quantifies for the first time the key factors that ignite the passion Canadian fans have for ice hockey, golf, and the Winter Olympics. Octagon's unique Passion Drivers(TM) research provides sports marketers and rights-holders quantifiable data that explains for the first time "why fans are fans." These insights better enable marketers to create more compelling, targeted, and cost-effective leveraging programs supporting their sports sponsorships.

At the Sponsorship Marketing Council of Canada conference in Toronto, Rick Dudley, president and CEO of Octagon Worldwide, and Kim Smither, managing director of Octagon Canada, announced the findings of the study conducted earlier this year among more than 1,200 Canadian sports fans.

"For years, we have quantified the 'who, what, where, and when' about sports fans. Now, we can quantify and know the 'why'," said Dudley. "Passion Drivers(TM) analysis fills a significant void in the sports marketing industry. Our proprietary analysis combined with existing demographic and psychographic data provide marketers a more full dimensional portrait of consumers as sports fans."

In the past year, Octagon, one of the world's leading sports and entertainment marketing companies, has conducted Passion Drivers(TM) studies in the U.S., U.K., France, South Africa, China, and Australia encompassing 20,000 fans in 26 sports. "At a time when rights fees are escalating and sports sponsorship as a first-tier marketing strategy requires greater accountability, it's imperative for marketers to have a tool that can truly help them harness the power of sponsorship to differentiate their brands, grow sales, and engage consumers in meaningful ways," Dudley said.

"Broad sponsorship activation programs can give way to tailored initiatives that appeal directly to a fan's emotional connection to their favorite sport," said Smither. "It's important for marketers to know how hockey, golf, and Olympics fans differ in the ways they relate to these sports. It's also just as important for them to understand the different types of fans within the fan base of each sport," she explained.

The Passion Drivers(TM) research produces profiles of fan types based on 12 Passion Drivers(TM) factors. These factors contribute to the passion a fan has for a sport. For marketers in Canada, the research reveals important local insights and for multinational marketers comparisons with fans of the same sports in other countries.

Hockey

Above everything else, Canadian hockey fans are driven by devotion to their teams. Hockey as an opportunity to talk and socialize with family and friends and strong feelings of nostalgia associated with either the history of the sport or fans having played the sport in the past are key motivating factors. "Love of the game" also emerged as a key factor, meaning many fans enjoy the competition and excitement associated with the sport regardless of the teams playing or the outcome of the game.

Hockey fans in the U.S. share Canadian fans' team devotion. The opportunity to talk and socialize around the sport is also essential though U.S. fans don't possess Canadian fans' passion for the game's history or overall love of the game. In the U.S., these feelings are the domain of baseball.

Winter Olympics

Canadian fans of the Winter Olympics are driven by three primary factors led by an interest in the lives of the Olympians away from the competition (Athlete Affinity). "Olympic athletes aren't in the public eye nearly as much as their professional team sports counterparts," said Smither. "As the Games get closer, fans want to know as much about these athletes as possible. One of the reasons may be because most of these athletes don't make a living playing sport. They are more like us, and we can more readily relate to them," she said.

This Athlete Affinity factor is followed closely by National Team Devotion and Active Appreciation for the Olympic sports. "Canada's performance in Torino certainly enhanced National Team Devotion, and this factor will be more powerful as Canada assumes the role of host country in 2010," said Smither. Active Appreciation means that fan passion stems from participating in the sport. "In this instance, Canadian and American Olympic fans differ significantly. Fans in the U.S. love the Olympic Games, but their passion doesn't come from having played these sports now or in the past," she said.

Golf

Despite the relatively short season, Active Appreciation is the key motivator for Canada's golf fans. This is similar to golf fans in the U.K., Australia, and the U.S. Unlike golf fans in these countries, Canadians rely more on a factor identified as "TV Preference," watching events on television to help satisfy their passion for the sport. Player Excitement,

(Continued)

(*Continued*)

an appreciation for the skills exhibited by the game's top players, is also a powerful motivator for Canadian golf fans.

"Sponsorship leveraging in golf really starts at giving fans an opportunity to play and improve their games," said Smither. "This can happen in different kinds of venues. Sponsors who put on clinics or pro-am events and support opportunities for fans to see top touring professionals will find a very responsive audience," she said.

One of the Passion Drivers(TM) factors conspicuous by its absence among the vast majority of Canadian sports fans, at least among the sports surveyed, is Gloating. "We refer to gloating as the 'darker side of sports,'" said Smither. "In our Canada study, we only saw this factor in a small subset of hockey fans comprised of younger people for whom hockey is their life and gloating is the primary Passion Drivers(TM) factor," she said.

"Octagon is passionate about knowing 'why fans are fans' and the implications this knowledge has for sponsors and rights holders," said Dudley. Octagon is expanding the survey to other sports in countries where Passion Drivers(TM) fan profiles have already been developed in addition to developing research on fans of different forms of entertainment.

Source: "New Study Examines Canadian Fans' Sports Passion," *Canadian Corporate Newswire*, APRIL 27, 2006.

or more variables are manipulated while others are held constant; the results are then measured. The variables being manipulated are called independent variables, whereas those being measured are called dependent variables.

An experiment is designed to assess causality and can be conducted in either a laboratory or a field setting. A laboratory, or artificial setting, offers the researcher greater degrees of control in the study. For example, major league Baseball may want to test the design of a new logo for licensing purposes. Targeted groups could be asked to evaluate the overall appeal of the logo while viewing it on a computer. The researchers could then easily manipulate the color and size of the logo (independent variables) while measuring the appeal to fans (dependent variable). All other variation in the design would be eliminated, which offers a high degree of control.

Unfortunately, a trade-off must be made between experimental control and the researchers' ability to apply the results to the "real purchase situation." In other words, what we find in the lab might not be what we find in the store. Field studies, therefore, are conducted to maximize the generalizability of the findings to real shopping experiences. For example, MLB could test the different colors and sizes of logos by offering them in three different cities of similar demographic composition. Then, MLB could evaluate the consumer response to variations in the product by measuring sales. This common approach to experimentation used by sports marketers is called test marketing.

Test marketing is traditionally defined as introducing a new product or service in one or more limited geographic areas. Through test marketing, sports marketers can collect many valuable pieces of information related to sales, competitive reaction, and market share. Information regarding the characteristics of those purchasing the new products or services could also be obtained. First Union Bank ran a two-week test market to determine consumer preference for two debit cards. One of the debit cards featured NASCAR driver Wally Dallenbach and the other was an Atlanta Braves card. The test showed that consumers preferred the NASCAR card—1,800 people chose the Dallenbach version compared with only 300 that chose the Braves' card.[9] Another test market recently occurred in Columbus, Ohio, for the National Lacrosse League. Columbus, known as a good test market city because of its demographic composition, featured a star-studded demonstration match. If the game drew more than 5,000 spectators, the league was likely to consider Columbus as a strong possibility for a new franchise.[10] Columbus did not enter the league, but the NLL is now 13 teams strong (www.nll.com).

Although test marketer information is invaluable to a sports marketer wanting to roll out a new product, it is not without its disadvantages. One of the primary disadvantages of test marketing is cost and time. Products must be produced, promotions or ads developed, and distribution channels secured—all of which cost money. In addition, the results of the test market must be monitored and evaluated at an additional cost. Another problem related to test marketing is associated with competitive activity. Often, competitors will offer consumers unusually high discounts on their products or services to skew the results of a test market. In addition, competitors may be able to quickly produce a "me-too" imitation product or service by the time the test market is ready for a national rollout.

The problems of cost, time, and competitive reaction may be alleviated by means of a more nontraditional test market approach called a **simulated test market.** Typically, respondents in a simulated test market participate in a series of activities, such as (1) receiving exposure to a new product or service concept, (2) having the opportunity to purchase the product or service in a laboratory environment, (3) assessing attitudes toward the new product or service after trial, and (4) assessing repeat purchase behavior.

DESIGNING DATA COLLECTION INSTRUMENTS

Once the data collection method is chosen, the next step in the marketing research process is designing the data collection instrument. Data collection instruments are required for nearly all types of data collection methods. Guides are necessary for depth interviews and focus groups. Data collection forms are needed for projective techniques. Even experiments require data collection instruments.

One of the most widely used data collection instruments in sports marketing is the questionnaire or survey. All forms of survey research require the construction of a questionnaire. The process of designing a questionnaire is shown in Figure 3.4.

Specify Information Requirements

As the first step of **questionnaire design,** the information requirements must be specified. In other words, the researcher asks what information needs to be gathered via the questionnaire. This should be addressed in the initial step of the research process if the problem is carefully defined. Remember, in the first step of the marketing research process, research objectives are developed based on the specified information requirements. The research objectives are a useful starting point in questionnaire design because they indicate what broad topic will be addressed in the study.

Decide Method of Administration

The method of administration is the next consideration in questionnaire design. The most common methods of administration are via mail, phone, e-mail, Web sites, or personal interview. Each method has its own unique advantages and disadvantages that must be considered (see Table 3.6). For example, if a short questionnaire is designed to measure fan attitudes toward the new promotion, then a phone survey may be appropriate. However, if the research is being conducted to determine preference for a new logo, then mail or personal interviews would be necessary.

Determine Content of Questions

The content of individual questions is largely governed by the method of administration. However, several other factors must be kept in mind. First, does the question address at least one research objective? Second, are several questions necessary to

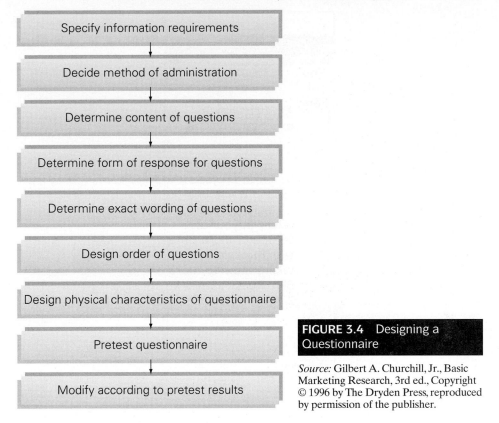

FIGURE 3.4   Designing a Questionnaire

Source: Gilbert A. Churchill, Jr., Basic Marketing Research, 3rd ed., Copyright © 1996 by The Dryden Press, reproduced by permission of the publisher.

answer an objective? Contrary to popular belief, more is not always better. Third, does the respondent have the information necessary to answer the question? For example, respondents may not be able to answer questions regarding personal seat licenses (PSLs) if they do not have a full understanding or description of what is meant by a PSL. Finally, will the respondent answer the question?

Sometimes respondents possess the necessary information, but they elect not to respond. For instance, questionnaires may sometimes ask sensitive questions (e.g., about income levels) that respondents will not answer.

TABLE 3.6   Comparison of Methods of Administration

	Methods of Administration			
Issues	*Mail*	*Telephone*	*Stadium and Event Interviews*	*Internet*
Costs	Inexpensive	Moderately expensive	Most expensive because of time	Inexpensive
Ability to use complex survey	Little, because self-administered	Same	Greatest because interviewer is present	Little, because self-administered
Opportunity for interviewer bias	None	Same	Greatest because interviewer is present	None
Response rate	Lowest	Moderate	Greatest	Low
Speed of data collection	Slowest	High	Medium to high	High

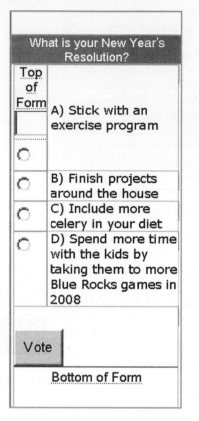

Web surveys are continuing to grow in popularity.

Source: Adapted from www.bluerocks.com

Determine Form of Response

After deciding on the content of the questions, the form of response should be considered. The form of the response is dependent on the degree of structure in the question. Unstructured questionnaires use a high number of open-ended questions. These types of questions allow respondents to provide their own responses rather than having to choose from a set of response categories provided by the researcher. The following are examples of open-ended questions:

- How do you feel about personal seat licenses?
- How many years have you been a season ticket holder?
- How will the personal seat license affect your attitude toward the team?

Determine Exact Wording of Questions

One of the most rigorous aspects of questionnaire design is deciding on the exact wording of questions. When constructing questions, the following pitfalls should be avoided:

- ***Questions should not be too lengthy***—Lengthy, run-on questions are difficult to interpret and have a higher likelihood of being skipped by the respondent.
- ***Questions should not be ambiguous***—Clarity is the key to good survey design. For instance, "Do you like sports?" may be interpreted in two very different ways. One respondent may answer based on participation, whereas another may answer from a spectator's viewpoint. In addition, there may be ambiguity in how the respondent defines sports. Some respondents would call billiards a sport, whereas others may define it as a game.

- ***Questions should not be double barreled or contain two questions in one***—For example, "Do you enjoy collecting and selling baseball cards?" represents a double-barreled question. This should be divided into two separate questions: "Do you enjoy collecting baseball cards?" and "Do you enjoy selling baseball cards?"
- ***Questions should not lack specificity***—In other words, clearly define the questions. "Do you watch sports on a regular basis?" is a poorly written question in that the respondent does not know the researcher's definition of *regular*. Does the researcher mean once per week or once per day?
- ***Questions should not be technical in nature***—Avoid asking respondents a question that will be difficult for them to answer. For instance, "What type of swing weight do you prefer in your driver?" may be too technical for the average golfer to answer in a meaningful fashion.

Determine Question Sequence

Now that the question wording has been determined, the researcher must determine the proper sequence of the questions. First, a good questionnaire starts with broad, interesting questions that hook the respondents and capture their attention. Similarly, questions that are more narrow in focus, such as demographic information, should appear at the end of the questionnaire. Second, questions that focus on similar topical areas should be grouped together. For example, a fan satisfaction questionnaire may include sections on satisfaction with concessions, stadium personnel, or game promotions.

Finally, proper question sequencing must consider branching questions and skip patterns. Branching questions direct respondents to questions based on answers to previous questions. For example, the first question on a questionnaire may be, "Have you ever been to a River Rats game?" If the respondents answer "yes," they might continue with a series of questions concerning customer satisfaction. If the respondents answer "no," then they might be asked to skip forward to a series of questions regarding media preferences. Because branching questions and skip patterns are sometimes confusing to respondents, these types of questions should be avoided if at all possible.

Design Physical Characteristics of Questionnaire

One of the final steps in the questionnaire development process is to consider carefully the physical appearance of the questionnaire. If the questionnaire is cluttered and looks unprofessional, respondents will be less likely to cooperate and complete the instrument. Other questionnaire design issues include the following:

- Questionnaire should look simple and easy to fill out.
- Questionnaire should have subheadings for the various sections.
- Questionnaire should provide simple and easy-to-understand instructions.
- Questionnaire should leave sufficient room to answer open-ended questions.

Pretest

After the questionnaire has been finalized and approved by the client, the next step in the questionnaire design process is to pretest the instrument. A **pretest** can be thought of as a "trial run" for the questionnaire to determine if there are any problems in interpreting the questions. In addition to detecting problems in interpreting questions, the pretest may uncover problems with the way the questions are sequenced.

An initial pretest should be conducted with both the researcher and respondent present. By conducting the pretest through a personal interview, the researcher can discuss any design flaws or points of confusion with the respondent. Next, the pretest should be conducted using the planned method of administration. In other words, if the survey is being conducted over the phone, the pretest should be conducted over the phone.

The number and nature of the respondents should also be considered when conducting a pretest. The sample for the pretest should mirror the target population for the study, although it may be useful to have other experienced researchers examine the questionnaire before full-scale data collection takes place. The number of people to pretest depends on time and cost considerations. Although pretests slow down the research process, they are invaluable in discovering problems that would otherwise make the data collected meaningless.

Designing the Sample

After the data collection instrument has been designed, the research process turns to selecting an appropriate sample. A **sample** is a subset of the population of interest from which data is gathered that will estimate some characteristic of the population. Securing a quality sample for sports marketing research is critical. Researchers rarely have the time or money to communicate with everyone in the population of interest. As such, developing a sample that is representative of this larger group of consumers is required.

To design an effective and efficient sample, a variety of sampling techniques are available. Sampling techniques are commonly divided into two categories: **nonprobability sampling** and **probability sampling.** The primary characteristic of nonprobability sampling techniques is that the sample units are chosen subjectively by the researcher. As such, there is no way of ensuring whether the sample is representative of the population of interest. Probability sampling techniques are objective procedures in which sample units have a known and nonzero chance of being selected for the study. Generally, probability sampling techniques are considered stronger because the accuracy of the sample results can be estimated with respect to the population.

Nonprobability Sampling

The three nonprobability sampling techniques commonly used are convenience, judgment, and quota sampling. **Convenience sampling techniques** are also called accidental sampling because the sample units are chosen based on the "convenience" of the researcher. For example, a research project could be conducted to assess fans' attitudes toward high school soccer in a large metropolitan area. Questionnaires could be handed out to fans attending Friday night games at three different high schools. These individuals are easy to reach but may not be representative of the population of interest (i.e., high school fans in the area).

Other researchers may approach the same problem with a different data collection method. For example, three focus groups might be conducted to gain a better understanding of the fans' attitudes toward high school soccer. Using this scenario, long-time, loyal soccer fans might be chosen as participants in the three focus groups. These participants represent a **judgment sample** because they are chosen subjectively and, based on the judgment of the researcher, they best serve the purpose of the study.

A quota sampling technique may also be used to address the research problem. In **quota sampling,** units are chosen on the basis of some control characteristic or characteristics of interest to the researcher. For instance, control characteristics such as gender and year in school may be appropriate for the soccer study. In this case, the researcher may believe there may be important distinctions between male and female fans and between freshmen and seniors. The sample would then be chosen to capture the desired number of consumers based on these characteristics. Often, the numbers are chosen so that the percentage of each sample subgroup (e.g., females and juniors) reflects the population percentages.

Probability Sampling

As stated earlier, the stronger sampling techniques are known as probability sampling. In probability sampling, the sample is chosen from a list of elements called a sampling frame. For example, if students at a high school define the population of interest, the sampling frame might be the student directory. The sample would then be chosen objectively from this list of elements.

Although there are many types, a simple random sample is the most widely used probability sampling technique. Using this technique, every unit in the sampling frame has a known and equal chance of being chosen for the sample. For example, Harris Interactive (http://www.harrisinteractive.com/) e-mails a random and representative sample of the U.S. population drawn from a database of more than 6.5 million respondents who have agreed to cooperate. Respondents who agree to participate are directed to the appropriate URL for each survey. The Internet-based methodology allows Harris to randomly sample a minimum of 10,000 people each month on various topics of interest to decision makers in the sports and entertainment industry. A probability sampling technique, such as simple random sampling, allows the researcher to calculate the degree of sampling error, so the researcher knows how precisely the sample reflects the true population.

Sample Size

Another question that must be addressed when choosing a sample is the number of units to include in it, or the sample size. Practically speaking, sample sizes are determined largely on the basis of time and money. The more precise and confident the researchers want to be in their findings, the greater the necessary sample size.

Another important determinant in sample size is the homogeneity of the population of interest. In other words, how different or similar are the respondents? To illustrate the effect of homogeneity on sample size, suppose the River Rats are interested in determining the average income of their season ticket holders. If the population of interest includes all the season ticket holders and each person has an income of $50,000, then how many people would we need to have a representative sample? The answer, because of this totally homogeneous population, is one. Any one person that would be in our sample would give us the true income of River Rats' season ticket holders.

As you can see from this brief discussion, sample size determination is a complex process based on confidence, precision, the nature of the population of interest, time, and money. Larger samples tend to be more accurate than smaller ones, but researchers must treat every research project as a unique case that has an optimal sample size based on the purpose of the study.

Data Analysis

After the data is collected from the population of interest, data analysis takes place. Before any analytical work occurs, the data must be carefully scrutinized to ensure its quality. Researchers call this the editing process. During this process, the data is examined for impossible responses, missing responses, or any other abnormalities that would render the data useless.

Once the quality of the data is ensured, coding begins. Coding refers to assigning numerical values or codes to represent a specific response to a specific question. Consider the following question:

How likely are you to attend River Rats' games in the future?

1. Extremely unlikely
2. Unlikely
3. Neither unlikely nor likely
4. Likely
5. Extremely likely

The response of *extremely unlikely* is assigned a code of 1, *unlikely* a code of 2, and so on. Each question in the survey must be coded to facilitate data analysis.

After editing and coding are completed, you are ready to begin analyzing the data. Although there are many sophisticated statistical techniques (and software programs) to choose from to analyze the data, researchers usually like to start by "looking at the big picture." In other words, researchers want to describe and summarize the data before they begin to look for more complex relationships between questions.

Often, the first step in data analysis is to examine two of the most basic informational components of the data—central tendency and dispersion. Measures of central tendency (also known as the mean, median, and mode) tell us about the typical response, whereas measures of dispersion (range, variance, and standard deviation) refer to the similarity of responses to any given question.

To give us a good feel for the typical responses and variation in responses, frequency distributions are often constructed. A frequency distribution, such as the one shown in Table 3.7, provides the distribution of data pertaining to categories of a single variable. In other words, frequency distributions or one-way tables show us the number (or frequency) of cases from the entire sample that fall into each response category. Normally, these frequencies or counts are also converted into percentages.

After one-way tables or frequency distributions are constructed, the next step in data analysis involves examining relationships between two variables. A cross-tabulation allows us to look at the responses to one question in relation to the responses to another question. Two-way tables provide a preliminary look at the association between two questions. For example, the two-way table shown in Table 3.8 explores the relationship between the likelihood of going to River Rats' games and gender. Upon examination, the two-way table clearly shows that females are less likely to attend River Rats' games in the future than males. Implications of this finding may include the need to conduct future research to better understand why females are less likely to attend River Rats' games than males and the design of a marketing mix that appeals to females.

TABLE 3.7   Frequency Distribution or One-Way Table

How likely are you to attend River Rats games in the future?

	Respondents	
	Number	*Percent*
1. Extremely unlikely	20	13.3
2. Unlikely	30	20.0
3. Neither unlikely or likely	25	16.7
4. Likely	45	30.0
5. Extremely likely	30	20.0
Total	**150**	**100%**

TABLE 3.8	Two-Way Table or Cross-Tabulation	

How likely are you to attend River Rats' games in the future?

	Gender	
	Male	*Female*
1. Extremely unlikely	5	15
2. Unlikely	5	25
3. Neither unlikely or likely	10	15
4. Likely	30	15
5. Extremely likely	25	5
Total	75	75

PREPARING A FINAL REPORT

The last step in the marketing research process is preparing a final report. Typically, the report is intended for top management of the sports organization, who can either put the research findings into action or shelve the project. Unfortunately, the greatest research project in the world will be viewed as a failure if the results are not clearly communicated to the target audience.

How can you prepare a final report that will assist in making decisions throughout the strategic marketing process? Here are some simple guidelines for preparing an actionable report:

- *Know your audience*—Before preparing the oral or written report, determine your audience. Typically, the users of research will be upper management, who do not possess a great deal of statistical knowledge or marketing research expertise. Therefore, it is important to construct the report so it is easily understood by the audience who will use the report, not by other researchers. One of the greatest challenges in preparing a research report is presenting technical information in a way that is easily understood by all users.

- *Be thorough, not overwhelming*—By the time they are completed, some written research reports resemble volumes of the *Encyclopedia Britannica*. Likewise, oral presentations can drag on for so long that any meaningful information is lost. Researchers should be sensitive to the amount of information they convey in an oral research report. Oral presentations should show only the most critical findings, rather than every small detail. Generally, written reports should include a brief description of the background and objectives of the study, how the study was conducted (methodology), key findings, and marketing recommendations. Voluminous tables should be located in an appendix.

- *Carefully interpret the findings*—The results of the study and how it was conducted are important, but nothing is as critical as drawing conclusions from the data. Managers who use the research findings often have limited time and no inclination to carefully analyze and interpret the findings. In addition, managers are not only interested in the findings alone, but they also want to know what marketing actions can be taken based on the findings. Be sure you do not neglect the implications of the research when preparing both oral and written reports.

Summary

Chapter 3 focuses on the tools used to gather information to make intelligent decisions throughout the strategic sports marketing process. More specifically, the chapter describes the marketing research process in detail. Marketing research is defined as the systematic process of collecting, analyzing, and reporting information to enhance decision making throughout the strategic sports marketing process.

The marketing research process consists of seven interrelated steps. These steps include defining the problem; choosing the research design type; identifying data collection methods; designing data collection forms; designing the sample; collecting, analyzing, and interpreting data; and preparing the research report. The first step is defining the problem and determining what information will be needed to make strategic marketing decisions. The tangible outcome of problem definition is to develop a set of research objectives that will serve as a guide for the rest of the research process.

The next step in the marketing research process is to determine the appropriate research design type(s). The research design is the plan that directs data collection and analysis. The three common research design types are exploratory, descriptive, and causal. The choice of one (or more) of these design types for any study is based on the clarity of the problem. Exploratory designs are more appropriate for ill-defined problems, whereas causal designs are employed for well-defined research problems.

After the research design type is chosen, the data collection method(s) is selected. Once again, decisions regarding data collection are contingent upon the choice of research design. Data collection consists of two types—secondary and primary. Secondary data refers to data that was collected earlier, either within or outside the sports organization, but still provides useful information to the researcher. Typically, sources of secondary data include government reports and documents; trade and industry associations; standardized sports marketing information studies; and books, journals, and periodicals. Primary data is information that is collected specifically for the research question at hand. Common types of primary data collection techniques include, but are not limited to, in-depth interviews, focus groups, surveys, and experiments.

The fourth step in the research process is to design the data collection instrument. Regardless of whether you are collecting data by in-depth interviews, focus groups, or surveys, data collection instruments are necessary. The most widely used data collection technique in sports marketing research is the questionnaire. As such, it is important that sports marketing researchers understand how to construct a questionnaire properly. The steps for questionnaire design include specifying information requirements, deciding the method of administration (i.e., mail, phone, and stadium interview), determining the content of questions, determining the form of response for questions, deciding on the exact wording of the questions, designing the order of the questions, designing the physical characteristics of the questionnaire, pretesting the questionnaire, and modifying it according to pretest results.

Once the data collection forms are constructed, the next step in the research process is choosing a sampling strategy. Rarely, if ever, can we take a census where we communicate with or observe everyone of interest to us in a research study. As such, a subset of those individuals is chosen to represent the larger group of interest. Sampling strategy identifies how we will choose these individuals and how many people we will choose to participate in our study.

Data analysis is the next step in the marketing research process. Before the data can be analyzed, however, it must be edited and coded. The editing process ensures the data being used for analysis is of high quality. In other words, it makes sure that there are no problems, such as large amounts of missing data or errors in data entry. Next, coding takes place. Coding refers to assigning numerical values to represent specific responses to specific questions. Once the data are edited and coded, data analysis is conducted. The method of data analysis depends on a variety of factors, such as how to address the research objectives. The last step in the marketing research process is to prepare a final report. Oral and written reports typically discuss the objectives of the study, how the study was conducted, and the findings and recommendation for decision makers.

Key Terms

- concomitant variation, p. 84
- convenience sampling techniques, p. 88
- cross-sectional studies, p. 91
- data collection techniques, p. 84
- dependent variable, p. 84
- experimentation, p. 91
- focus group, p. 89
- independent variable, p. 84
- judgment sample, p. 98

- longitudinal study, p. 91
- marketing research, p. 3
- methodology, p. 101
- nonprobability sampling, p. 98
- pretest, p. 97
- primary data, p. 85
- probability sampling, p. 98
- problem definition, p. 77
- projective techniques, p. 97
- questionnaire design, p. 94

- quota sampling, p. 98
- research design, p. 83
- research objectives, p. 77
- research problem statement, p. 77
- research proposal, p. 83
- sample, p. 98
- secondary data, p. 84
- simulated test market, p. 94
- sports marketing research, p. 3
- test marketing, p. 93

Review Questions

1. Define sports marketing research. Describe the relationship between sports marketing research and the strategic marketing process.
2. What are the various steps in the marketing research process?
3. Define problem and opportunity definition and explain why this step of the research process is considered to be the most critical.
4. What are some of the basic issues that should be addressed at a research request meeting?
5. Outline the steps in developing a research proposal.
6. Define a research design. What are the three types of research designs that can be used in research? How does the choice of research design stem from the problem definition? Can a researcher choose multiple designs within a single study?
7. Describe some of the common data collection techniques used in sports marketing research. How does

the choice of data collection technique stem from the research design type?
8. What are some of the central issues that must be considered when conducting focus groups?
9. What are the pros and cons of laboratory studies versus field studies?
10. Outline the nine steps in questionnaire design. What are some of the most common errors in the wording of questions?
11. Define nonprobability sampling and probability sampling techniques. What are three types of nonprobability sampling?
12. What is a sampling frame? How do researchers decide on the appropriate sample size for a study?
13. What are some of the guidelines for preparing oral and written research reports?

Exercises

You are interested in purchasing a new minor league baseball franchise. The franchise will be located in your area. To reduce the risk in your decision making, you have requested that a sports marketing firm submit a detailed research proposal. The following questions pertain to this issue:

1. What is the broad problem/opportunity facing you in this decision? Write the research objectives based on the problem formulation.
2. What type of research design type do you recommend?
3. The sports marketing firm has submitted the following preliminary questionnaire. Please provide a detailed critique of their work.

   Age: _____   Gender: _____

   Are you likely to go to a baseball game at the new stadium?

   Yes _____   No _____

How many minor league games did you go to last year?

0–3 _____   4–6 _____   6–9 _____
10+ _____

What types of promos would you like to see?

Beer Night _____   Straight-A Night _____
Polka Night _____

4. Now that you have looked at their survey, create a questionnaire of your own. Would any other data collection techniques be appropriate, given the research problem?
5. What sampling technique(s) do you recommend? How is the correct sample size determined, given your choice of sampling technique?

Internet Exercises

1. Using secondary data sources on the Internet, find the following and indicate the appropriate URL (Internet address):
   a. Number of women who participated in high school basketball last year
   b. Attendance at NFL games last year
   c. Sponsors for the New York City Marathon
   d. Universities that offer graduate programs in sports marketing
2. Using the Internet, find at least five articles that relate to the marketing of NASCAR.
3. Using the Internet, locate three companies that conduct sports marketing research. What types of products and services do the companies offer?

Endnotes

1. NASCAR Sponsorship Study, Sponsorship Research and Strategies, http://sponsorstrategy.com/_wsn/page9.html.
2. Gilbert Churchill, *Basic Marketing Research,* 3rd ed. (Ft. Worth: Dryden Press, 1996).
3. Ibid.
4. Kristie McCook, Douglas Turco, and Roger Riley, "A Look at the Corporate Sponsorship Decision Making Process," *Cyber Journal of Sport Marketing,* vol. 1, no. 2 (1997), www.cad.gu.edu.au/market/cy...rnal_of_sport_marketing/mcook.html.
5. "Mike Triplett, "Tigers' Bertman is ready to make pitch," *Times-Picayune* (August 21, 2003), 1.
6. Dave Gross, "Lynx Reach Out and Ask Fans for Input," *The Ottawa Sun* (December 12, 2002), 81.
7. Gilbert Churchill, *Basic Marketing Research,* 3rd ed. (Fort Worth: Dryden Press, 1996).
8. "Cleveland Indians Look to Long-Term Viability Through Market Research," *Akron Beacon Journal* (April 16, 1999).
9. "IEG Network: Assertions," www.sponsorship.com/forum/assertions.html.
10. Craig Mertz, "Pro Lacrosse League to Test Local Support," *The Columbus Dispatch* (July 7, 2000), 5D.

4

UNDERSTANDING PARTICIPANTS AS CONSUMERS

After completing this chapter, you should be able to:

■ Define participant consumption behavior.

■ Explain the simplified model of participant consumption behavior.

■ Describe the psychological factors that affect participant decision making.

■ Identify the various external factors influencing participant decision making.

■ Describe the participant decision-making process.

■ Understand the different types of consumer decision making.

■ Discuss the situational factors that influence participant decision making.

Think about the sports and recreational activities in which you participated during the past month. Maybe you played golf or tennis, lifted weights, or even went hiking. According to data from the National Sporting Goods Association (NSGA) provided in Table 4.1, millions of Americans participate in a variety of physical activities each year.

At this point you may be asking yourself, "Why are sports marketers concerned with consumers who participate in sports?" Recall from our discussion of sports marketing in Chapter 1 that one of the basic sports marketing activities was encouraging participation in sports. Sports marketers are responsible for organizing events such as the Boston Marathon, the Iron Man Triathlon, or the Gus Macker 3-on–3 Basketball Tournament in which thousands of consumers participate in sports. Moreover, sports marketers are involved in marketing the equipment and apparel necessary for participation in sports. As you might imagine, sports participants constitute a large and growing market both in the United States and internationally.

To successfully compete in the expanding sports participant market, sports organizations must develop a thorough understanding of participant consumption behavior and what affects it. **Participant consumption behavior** is defined as actions performed when searching for, participating in, and evaluating the sports activities that consumers believe will satisfy their needs. You may have noticed this definition relates to the previous discussion of the marketing concept and consumer satisfaction. Sports marketers must understand why consumers choose to participate in certain sports and what the benefits of participation are for consumers. For instance, do we play indoor soccer for exercise, for social contact, to feel like part of a team, or

TABLE 4.1	Top 30 Participation Activities in the United States
Activities and Sports	**Number of Participants (in millions)**
Exercise walking	86.0
Swimming	58.0
Exercising with equipment	54.2
Camping (vacation/overnight)	46.0
Bowling	45.4
Fishing	43.3
Bicycle riding	43.1
Billiards/pool	37.3
Weightlifting	35.5
Workout at club	34.7
Aerobic exercising	33.7
Basketball	29.9
Hiking	29.8
Running/jogging	29.2
Boating, motor/power	27.5
Golf	24.7
Target shooting	21.9
Hunting with firearms	19.4
Baseball	14.6
Soccer	14.1
Softball	14.1
Backpack/wilderness camping	13.3
Volleyball	13.2
In-line roller skating	13.1
Skateboarding	12.0
Tennis	11.1
Scooter riding	10.4
Football (tackle)	9.9
Mountain biking (off road)	9.2
Paintball games	8.0
Kayaking/rafting	7.6
Skiing (alpine)	6.9
Archery (target)	6.8
Water skiing	6.7
Target shooting—airgun	6.7
Hunting w/bow and arrow	6.6
Snowboarding	6.0
Muzzleloading	4.1
Cheerleading	3.3
Hockey (ice)	2.4
Skiing (cross country)	1.9

Source: Reprinted by permission of the National Sporting Goods Association, Mt. Prospect, IL 60056. This information is based on participants ages six and up in 2006.

to enhance our image? Also, the study of participant consumer behavior attempts to understand when, where, and how often consumers participate in sports. By understanding consumers of sports, marketers will be in a better position to satisfy their needs.

Three lifelong sports participants in training.

The definition of participant consumption behavior also incorporates the elements of the participant decision-making process. The **decision-making process** is the foundation of our model of participant consumption. It is a five-step process that consumers use when deciding to participate in a specific sport or activity. Before turning to our model of participant consumption behavior, it must be stressed that the primary reason for understanding the participant decision-making process is to guide the rest of the strategic sports marketing process. Without a better understanding of sports participants, marketers would simply be guessing about how to satisfy their needs.

MODEL OF PARTICIPANT CONSUMPTION BEHAVIOR

To help organize all this complex information about sports participants, we have developed a model of participant consumption behavior that will serve as a framework for the rest of our discussion (see Figure 4.1). At the center of our model is the participant decision-making process, which is influenced by three components: (1) internal or psychological processes such as motivation, perception, learning and memory, and attitudes; (2) external or sociocultural factors, such as culture, reference groups, and family; and (3) situational factors that act on the participant decision-making process.

Participant Decision-Making Process

Every time you lace up your running shoes, grab your tennis racquet, or dive into a pool, you have made a decision about participating in sports. Sometimes these decisions are nearly automatic because, for example, you might jog nearly every day. Other decisions, such as playing in a golf league, require more careful consideration because of the time and cost involved. The foundation of our **model of participant consumption behavior** is trying to understand how consumers arrive at their decisions.

Participant decision making is a complex, cognitive process that brings together memory, thinking, information processing, and making evaluative judgments. The five steps that make up the process used to explain participant decision making are shown in Figure 4.1. It is important to remember that every individual consumer arrives at

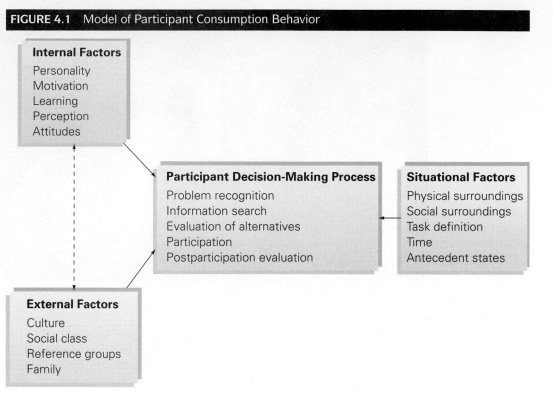

FIGURE 4.1   Model of Participant Consumption Behavior

Internal Factors
Personality
Motivation
Learning
Perception
Attitudes

Participant Decision-Making Process
Problem recognition
Information search
Evaluation of alternatives
Participation
Postparticipation evaluation

Situational Factors
Physical surroundings
Social surroundings
Task definition
Time
Antecedent states

External Factors
Culture
Social class
Reference groups
Family

decisions in a slightly different manner because of his or her own psychological makeup and environment. However, the five-step participant decision-making process, moving from problem recognition through postparticipation evaluation, is relatively consistent among consumers and must be understood by sports marketers to develop strategies that fit with consumers' needs.

As we progress through the participant decision-making process, let us consider the case of Jack, a 33-year-old male who just moved from Los Angeles to Cincinnati. Jack has always been active in sports and would like to participate in an organized sports league. Because of work and family commitments, Jack only has the time to participate in one league. He is unsure about what sport to participate in, although he does have a few requirements. Because he is a newcomer to the city, Jack would like to participate in a team sport to meet new people. Also, he wants the league to be moderately competitive so as to keep his competitive juices flowing. Finally, he would like to remain injury free, so the sport needs to be non- or limited-contact. Let us see how Jack arrives at this important decision by using the participant decision-making process.

Problem Recognition

The first step in the participant decision-making process is problem recognition. During problem recognition, consumers realize they have a need that is not presently being met. **Problem recognition** is the result of a discrepancy between a desired state and an actual state large enough and important enough to activate the entire decision-making process.[1] Stated simply, the desired state reflects the "ideal" of the participant. In other words, what is the absolute best sport for Jack to participate in, given his unique needs? If there is a difference between ideal and actual levels of participation, then the decision-making process begins.

The desire to resolve a problem and to reach goals, once recognized by consumers, is dependent on two factors: (1) the magnitude or size of the discrepancy and (2) the relative

Many consumers see a discrepancy between the "ideal" and "actual" body.

importance of the problem. Let us look at how these two factors would affect problem recognition. Jack currently jogs on a daily basis and wants to participate in a competitive, organized, and aggressive team sport. Is the discrepancy between actual state (individual, recreational, and nonaggressive) and desired state (team play, competitive, and aggressive) large enough to activate the decision-making process? Let's assume that it is and consider the second condition of problem recognition, the importance of the problem.

The second condition that must be met for problem recognition to occur is that the goal must be important enough to Jack. Some consumers may recognize the difference between participating in recreational sports versus an organized league. Would the benefits of participating in the new organized league (hopefully making some friends and being more competitive) outweigh the time, expense, and energy required to play? If the problem is important enough to Jack, then he moves on to the next stage of the decision-making process—information search.

What strategic implication does problem recognition hold for sports marketers? Generally, we would first identify the actual and desired states of sports participants or potential participants. Once these states have been determined, sports marketers can offer activities and events that will fill these needs and eliminate "problems." In addition, sports marketers can attempt to alter the perceived ideal state of consumers. For example, it is common for health clubs to show the "ideal" body that can be achieved by purchasing a membership and working out.

Information Search

After problem recognition occurs, the next step in the participant decision-making process is information search. **Information search** occurs when a participant seeks relevant information that will help resolve the problem. The sources of information sought by consumers can be broken down into two types: internal and external sources.

Internal sources of information are recalled from our own memories and are based on previous exposure to sports and activities. The internal information activated from memory can provide us with a wealth of data that may affect the decision-making process. Jack has spent most of his life participating in sports and recreational activities so information based on past experience is readily available. For instance, because Jack has played in an organized league in the past, he would use internal information to recall his experiences. Did he enjoy the competition of organized sport? Why did he stop participating in the sport?

External sources of information are environmentally based and can occur in three different ways. First, Jack might ask **personal sources,** such as friends or family, to provide him with information about possible organized team sports in which to participate. Friends and family are important information sources that can have a great deal of influence on our participation choices. Second, **marketing sources,** such as advertisements, sales personnel, brochures, and Web sites on the Internet are all important information sources. In fact, sports marketers have direct control over this source of information, so it is perhaps the most critical from the perspective of the sports organization. The third type of external information source is called an **experiential source.** Jack may watch games in several different sports leagues to gather information. His decision is influenced by watching the level of competition.

Some participants may require a great deal of information before making a decision, whereas others require little to no information. The amount of information and the number of sources used is a function of several factors, such as the amount of time available, the importance of the decision, the amount of past experience, and the demographics and psychographics of the participants.

The extent of the information search also depends on the **perceived risk** of the decision. Perceived risk stems from the uncertainty associated with decision making and is concerned with the potential threats inherent in making the wrong decision. For individual sports participants, perceived risk surfaces in many different forms. Perceived risk may be the embarrassment of not having the skill necessary to participate in a competitive league (social risks) or being concerned about the money needed to participate (economic risks). Also, an important perceived risk for many adult participants is health and safety (safety risks).

Online information source.

Source: Copyright © 2000–2004. Kayak Online. All rights reserved. http://www.kayakonline.com/

At this stage of the participant decision-making process, sports marketers must understand as much as they can about the information sources used by consumers. For instance, marketers for the Cincinnati Recreational Commission want to know the information sources for teams, what is the most effective way to provide teams with information, how much information is desired, and to whom they should provide this information. Moreover, sports marketers want to understand the perceived risks for potential participants such as Jack. This information is essential for developing an effective promotional strategy that targets both teams and individual participants.

Evaluation of Alternatives

Now that the information search has yielded all the available participation alternatives that have some of the basic characteristics that appeal to Jack, he must begin to evaluate the alternatives. Jack thinks about all the organized team sports in which he might participate and chooses a subset to which he will give further consideration. The few sports given the greatest consideration are called the **evoked set** of alternatives. Jack's evoked set might consist of four sports: softball, basketball, bowling, and indoor soccer.

After consumers develop their evoked set, which is comprised of acceptable alternatives, they must evaluate each sport based on the important features and characteristics. These features and characteristics that potential consumers are looking for in a sport are called **evaluative criteria.** The evaluative criteria used by Jack include team sport, organized or league play, moderate level of competition, and moderately aggressive sport. It is important to realize that each of the four evaluative criteria carries a different weight in Jack's overall decision-making process. To continue with our example, let us say that Jack attaches the greatest importance to participating in a team sport. Next, Jack is concerned with participating in a league or organized sport. The level of aggression is the next most important criterion to Jack. Finally, the least important factor in choosing from among the four sports is the level of competition.

In complex decision making, Jack would evaluate each of the sports against each of the evaluative criteria. He would base his final decision regarding participation on which sport measures best against the various factors he deems important. The two most important criteria—team sport and league play—are satisfied for each of the four sports in the evoked set. In other words, all the sports that Jack is evaluating are team sports, and all have league play. Therefore, Jack moves on to his next criteria, level of aggression. Ideally, Jack wants to remain injury free, so he eliminates indoor soccer and basketball from further consideration. Bowling seems to be a clear winner in satisfying these criteria, and Jack is aware of several competitive bowling leagues in the area. Therefore, Jack decides to participate in a bowling league.

The **evaluation of alternatives** has two important implications for sports marketers. First, sports marketers must ensure their sports are included in the evoked set of potential consumers. To accomplish this objective, consumers must first become aware of the alternative. Second, sports marketers must understand what evaluative criteria are used by potential consumers and then develop strategies to meet consumers' needs based on these criteria. For example, marketers of bowling have determined that there are two different participant bowling markets: league or organized and recreational bowlers.

Recreational bowlers are growing in numbers and care most about the facilities at which they bowl and the related services provided. The evaluative criteria used by recreational bowlers might include the type of food served, other entertainment offered (e.g., arcade games and billiards), and the atmosphere of the bowling alley. League bowlers, however, constitute a diminishing market. This segment of bowlers cares most about the location of the bowling center and the condition of the lanes.[2]

Participation

The evaluation of alternatives has led us to what marketers consider the most important outcome of the decision-making process—the participation decision. The participation stage of the decision-making process might seem to be the most straightforward, but many things need to be considered other than actually deciding what sport to play. For instance, the consumer's needs may shift to the equipment and apparel needed to participate. Jack may decide that he needs a new bowling ball, shoes, and equipment bag to look the part of bowler for his new team. Thus, marketers working for equipment manufacturers are interested in Jack's participant consumption behavior. In addition, Jack may have to decide which bowling alley offers the best alternative for his needs. He may choose a location close to home, one that offers the best price, or the alley that has the best atmosphere. Again, these criteria must be carefully considered by sports marketers, because participants make choices regarding not only what sports they want to participate in, but also where they want to participate.

Other things might occur that alter the intended decision to participate in a given sport. At the last minute, Jack's coworkers may talk him out of playing in a competitive men's league in lieu of a co-rec, work league. There might be a problem finding an opening on a roster, which would also change Jack's decision-making process at the last moment. Perhaps the bowling team that Jack wanted to join is scheduled to play during a trip that he had planned. All these "unexpected pleasures" may occur at the participation stage of the decision-making process.

Postparticipation Evaluation

You might think that the decision-making process comes to an abrupt halt after the participation decision, but there is one more very important step—**postparticipation evaluation.** The first activity that may occur after consumers have made an important participation decision is **cognitive dissonance.** This dissonance occurs because consumers experience doubts or anxiety about the wisdom of their decision. In other words, people question their own judgment. Let us suppose Jack begins participating in a competitive bowling league, and the first time he bowls, he is embarrassed. His poor level of play is far worse than that of everyone else on the team. Immediately, he begins to question his decision to participate.

Whether dissonance occurs is a function of the importance of the decision, the difficulty of the choice, the degree of commitment to the decision, and the individual's tendency to experience anxiety.[3] Jack does not know his teammates well and only paid $50 to join the league, so he may decide to quit the team. However, he does not want to let his team down and ruin his chance of making new friends, so high levels of dissonance may cause him to continue with the team. In either case, the level of dissonance that Jack feels is largely based on his own personality and tendency to experience anxiety.

Another important activity that occurs after participation begins is evaluation. First, the participant develops expectations about what it will be like to play in this competitive bowling league. Jack's expectations may range from thinking about how much physical pain the sport will cause to thinking about how many new friends he will make as a result of participating. Next, Jack evaluates his actual experience after several games. If expectations are met or exceeded, then satisfaction occurs. However, if the experience or performance is poorer than expected, then dissatisfaction results. The level of satisfaction Jack experiences will obviously have a tremendous impact on his future participation and word-of-mouth communication about the sport.

Types of Consumer Decisions

We have just completed our discussion of Jack's decision-making process and have failed to mention one very important thing: Not all decisions are alike. Some are extremely important and, therefore, take a great deal of time and thought. Because we are creatures of habit, some decisions require little or no effort. We simply do what we have always done in the past. The variety of decisions that we make about participation in sport can be categorized into three different types of participation decision processes. The decision processes, also known as levels of problem solving, are habitual problem solving, limited problem solving, and extensive problem solving.

Habitual Problem Solving

One type of decision process that is used is called **habitual problem solving (or routinized problem solving).** In habitual problem solving, problem recognition occurs, followed by limited internal information search. As we just learned, internal search comes from experiences with sports stored in memory. Therefore, when Jack is looking for information on sports next year, he simply remembers his previous experience and satisfaction with bowling. The evaluation of alternatives is eliminated for habitual decisions because no alternatives are considered. Jack participates in bowling again, but this time there is no dissonance and limited evaluation occurs. In a sense, Jack's decision to participate in bowling becomes a habit or routine each year.

Limited Problem Solving

The next type of consumer decision process is called **limited problem solving.** Limited problem solving begins with problem recognition and includes internal search and sometimes limited external search. A small number of alternatives are evaluated using a few evaluative criteria. In fact, in limited problem solving, the alternatives being evaluated are often other forms of entertainment (e.g., movies or concerts). After purchase, dissonance is rare and a limited evaluation of the product occurs. Participation in special sporting events, such as a neighborhood 10K run or charity golf outing, are examples of sporting events that lend themselves to limited problem solving.

Extensive Problem Solving

The last type of decision process is called **extensive problem solving (or extended problem solving)** because of the exhaustive nature of the decision. As with any type of decision, problem recognition must occur for the decision-making process to be initiated. Heavy information search (both internal and external) is followed by the evaluation of many alternatives on many attributes. Postpurchase dissonance and postpurchase evaluation are at their highest levels with extensive decisions. Jack's initial decision to participate in the bowling league was an extensive decision due to his high levels of information search, the many sports alternatives he considered, and the comprehensive nature of his evaluation of bowling.

For many people who are highly involved in sports, participation decisions are more extensive in nature, especially in the initial stages of participating in and evaluating various sports. Over time, what was once an extensive decision becomes routine. Participants choose sports that meet their needs, and the decision to participate becomes automatic. It is important for marketers to understand the type of problem solving used by participants so the most effective marketing strategy can be formulated and implemented.

PSYCHOLOGICAL OR INTERNAL FACTORS

Now that we have looked at the participant decision-making process, let us turn our focus to the internal, or psychological, factors. Personality, motivation, learning, and perception are some of the basic **psychological or internal factors** that will be unique to each individual and guide sports participation decisions.

Personality

One of the psychological factors that may have a tremendous impact on whether we participate in sports, the sports in which we participate, and the amount of participation, is personality. Psychologists have defined **personality** as a set of consistent responses an individual makes to the environment.

Although there are different ways to describe personality, one common method used by marketers is based on specific, identifiable personality traits. For example, individuals can be thought of as aggressive, orderly, dominant, or nurturing.[4] Consider the potential association between an individual's personality profile and the likelihood of participating in a particular sport. The self-assured, outgoing, assertive individual may be more likely than the apprehensive, reserved, and humble person to participate in any sport. Moreover, the self-sufficient individual may participate in more individual sports (e.g., figure skating, golf, or tennis) than the group-dependent individual.

In one study, Generation X-ers were found to be more interested in fast-paced, high-risk activities, such as rock climbing and mountain biking.[5] As such, action sports may be a good choice for the happy-go-lucky, venturesome personality type of the Generation X-ers. Action or extreme sports are defined as the pantheon of aggressive, nonteam sports, including snowboarding, in-line skating, super modified shovel racing, wakeboarding, ice and rock climbing, mountain biking, and snow mountain biking.[6] Another example of the relationship between sports participation and personality traits can be seen in Table 4.2. As illustrated, golfers most often described themselves as responsible, family-oriented, self-confident, and intelligent. The poorest descriptors for golfers were *bitter, sick a lot, extravagant,* and *risk-averse.* Interestingly, golfers described themselves as team players, although they participate in this highly individual sport.

Although personality and participation may be linked, take care not to assume a causal relationship between personality and sports participation. Some researchers believe sports participation might shape various personality traits (i.e., sports is a character builder). Other researchers believe we participate in sports because of our

A growing number of consumers participate in high-risk sports.

TABLE 4.2	Golfers' Self-Reported Traits and Personality Characteristics		
Best Descriptors	%	*Poorest Descriptors*	%
Responsible	80%	Bitter	3%
Family-oriented	75	Sick a lot	3
Self-confident	70	Extravagant	6
Intelligent	66	Risk-averse	6
Fun-loving	64	Virgin	6
Team player	63	Fun-loving	8
Sensitive	62	Lonely	8
Ambitious	61	Outside the mainstream	14
Competent	61	Sexy	15
Practical	60	Born again	16

Source: Yankelovich Partners, "How Golfers Are Likely to Describe Themselves."
Yankelovich Monitor Sports Enthusiast Profile.

particular personality type. To date, little research supports the causal direction of the relationship between personality and participation in sport.

Not only does personality dictate whether someone participates in sports, but it may also be linked with participation in particular types of sports. The violent, aggressive personality type may be drawn to sports such as football, boxing, or hockey. The shy, introverted personality type may be more likely to participate in individual sports, such as tennis and running. Knowing the relationship between participation and personality profiles can help sports marketers set up the strategic sports marketing process so it will appeal to the appropriate personality segment. In addition, sports marketers of large participant sporting events use personality profiles to attract potential corporate sponsors who may want to appeal to the same personality segment.

Motivation

Why do people participate in sports? What benefits are people looking for from participating in sport, and what needs do participating in sport satisfy? McDonald, Milne, and Hong,[7] drawing on Maslow's human needs hierarchy, present evidence illustrating that consumers possess multiple and unique motivations—including achievement, competition, social facilitation, physical fitness, skill mastery, physical risk, affiliation, aesthetics, aggression, value development, self-esteem, self-actualization, and stress release—for participating in particular sport activities. Other studies suggest there are three basic reasons for participation in sport (see Table 4.3). Finally, studies have

TABLE 4.3	Why People Participate in Sports

Personal Improvement
Release of tension or relaxation, sense of accomplishment, skill mastery, improved health and fitness, other people's respect for one's athletic skill, release of aggression, enjoyment of risk taking, personal growth, development of positive values, and sense of personal pride

Sport Appreciation
Enjoyment of the game, sport competition, and thrill of victory

Social Facilitation
Time spent with close friends or family and sense of being part of a group

Source: George Milne, William Sutton, and Mark McDonald, "Niche Analysis: A Strategic Measurement Tool for Managers," *Sport Marketing Quarterly,* vol. 5, no. 3 (1996), 17–21.

TABLE 4.4	Segmentation of Runners by Motives

Healthy Joggers

"I find running to be both relaxing and is the primary way along with a good diet that I keep up my plan for good health and fitness."—Female, 50+ years old, runs 18 miles/week, 4 days per week

"Running is very important because I use running to relieve stress and to think about what is bothering me. I use running to clear my head. Running is important to maintain fitness and to counteract my poor diet of late."—Male, < 25 years old, no mileage reported

Social Competitors

"Running is one of the greatest joys of life. Keeps the body, mind, and spirit soaring. Running with friends is special. Competition pushes me to new levels. Can travel to races and see new places. I can share stories with runners from all over the world."—Female, 25–39 years old, runs 40 miles per week, 5 days/week

"I just recently started running 3 years ago. I used to weigh 317 lbs; I'm now down to 245. Before I leave work I change and go directly to a half-mile track located on the way home. My running is very important; it relieves a lot of stress and is something that is within my control. I have made many acquaintances at the track. We all motivate each other. If someone misses one day, everybody is aware and concerned. That alone motivates you to keep going. Besides, I am trying to get down to 199 lbs."—Male, 40–49, runs 24 miles/week, 6 days/week

Actualized Athletes

"I quit smoking at age 33, in 1978, and took up running, and I will never stop running. I bike and kayak but running is my first love. It makes me feel good about myself and it gave me a lot of confidence. I've run many marathons in my past years and many races and you cannot describe the feeling of accomplishment at the end. It gave me the confidence to go back to school at the age of 40 and get a degree in nursing."—Female, 50+ years old, runs 30 miles, 6 days/week

"I love to run. I've always been athletic and enjoyed team sports. But running is different. It's a solitary sport. It pits me against me. I'm 42 years old and I know I've yet to reach my potential as a runner. My best years are behind me and I know I'll never be world class, but I still have room to improve and I'll keep trying, training, testing. It makes me fit, it makes me happy. I love to run."—Male, 40–49 years old, runs 35 miles/week, 5 days/week

Devotees

"It is a big part of my life. It's like brushing your teeth—it's a gift I give myself every day or almost every day. It is who I am and I never want not to run. It's the most wonderful total feeling in life. It has made me grow in so many ways and also appreciate life so much more. You can do it anywhere at any time—no expense."—Male, 50+ years old, runs 38 miles/week, 6 days/week

"It's part of who I am. Running is the most important free time activity I have besides spending time with my kids. I'm a happier person when I get my running."—Female, 25–39, runs 20 miles/week, 4 days/week

*Source: **Sport Marketing Quarterly,** 2006, **15,** 29–39, © 2006 West Virginia University*
A Mixed-Method Approach for Developing Market Segmentation Typologies in the Sports Industry Andrew J. Rohm, George R. Milne, and Mark A. McDonald

looked at understanding the motives for participation in a specific sport. For example, Rohm, Milne, and McDonald[8] recently explored the motives of runners (see Table 4.4 for segmentation of runners by motives).

The study of human motivation helps to better understand the underlying need to participate in sports. **Motivation** is an internal force that directs behavior toward the fulfillment of needs. In our earlier discussion of the participant decision-making process, problem recognition resulted from having needs that are not currently being met. As the definition indicates, motivation is discussed in terms of fulfilling unmet needs. Although there is no argument that all humans have needs, there is disagreement about the number of needs and the nature of them.

FIGURE 4.2 Maslow's Hierarchy of Needs

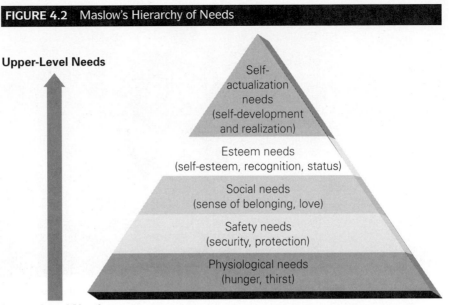

Upper-Level Needs

Self-actualization needs (self-development and realization)

Esteem needs (self-esteem, recognition, status)

Social needs (sense of belonging, love)

Safety needs (security, protection)

Physiological needs (hunger, thirst)

Lower-Level Needs

Source: A. H. Maslow, *Motivation and Personality,* 2nd ed. (New York: Harper and Row, 1970).

One popular theory of human motivation based on classification of needs is called **Maslow's hierarchy of needs** (see Figure 4.2). Maslow's hierarchy of needs consists of five levels. According to Maslow, the most basic, primitive needs must be fulfilled before the individual can progress to the next level of need. Once this higher level of need is satisfied, the individual is then motivated to fulfill the next higher level of need. Let us look at the hierarchy of needs as it relates to participation in sports.

The first and most basic level of needs in Maslow's hierarchy is called **physiological needs.** These are the biological needs that people have—to eat, drink, and meet other physiological needs. For some individuals, there may be a physiological need to exercise and have some level of activity. Once this lower order need is met, safety needs are addressed.

Safety needs are concerned with physical safety, as well as the need to remain healthy. Sports equipment manufacturers address the need participants have for physical safety. With respect to the need for health, many participants cite that the primary reason for joining health clubs is to maintain or improve their health.

The next need level is based on **love and belonging.** Many people choose to participate in sport because of the social aspects involved. One of the early need theories of motivation includes "play" as a primary social need.[9] For some individuals, sports participation is their only outlet for being part of a group and interacting with others. The need to be part of a team and to be respected by teammates has been demonstrated in a number of studies.

As these social needs are satisfied, **esteem** needs of recognition and status must be addressed. Certainly, sport plays a major role in enhancing self-esteem and the impact of sport participation on enhanced self-esteem has been well documented. Bungee jumping provides an excellent illustration of how sport influences esteem. The president of the U.S. Bungee Association (USBA), Casey Dale, describes the motives of people who use risky activities as a self-image booster. "People are less satisfied than they used to be with being pigeonholed by what they do, so they want to change their self-image. A quick fix is to become this extreme, risk-taking individual. All of a sudden, Bill the accountant goes bungee jumping off a 20-story bridge, and all of his coworkers see him in a new light."[10]

Sports participants fulfilling the need for self-actualization.

Finally, the highest order need, **self-actualization,** should be met. This refers to the individual's need to "be all that you can be" and is usually fulfilled through participation in mountain climbing, triathlons, or any sport that pushes an individual to the utmost of his or her physical and mental capacities. For example, ultramarathons in which runners compete in 100K road races certainly test the will of all participants. Another example of self-actualization can be found in the amateur athlete who trains his or her whole life for the Olympic Games.

As a sports marketer, you may be able to enhance strategies for increasing participation if you identify and understand the needs of consumers. In some instances, participation might fill more than one need level. Consumers may satisfy physiological needs, safety needs, social needs, esteem needs, or possibly self-actualization needs. For instance, marketing a health club membership might appeal to consumers wanting to fulfill any of the need levels in the hierarchy. The members' physiological needs are being met through exercise. Safety needs might be met by explaining that the club has state-of-the-art exercise equipment that is designed to be safe for all ages and fitness levels. Social needs are addressed by describing the club as a "home away from home" for many members. The need for esteem for health club members might be easily satisfied by depicting how good they will look and feel after working out. Finally, self-actualization needs may be fulfilled by working out to achieve the ideal body.

The needs that have just been presented can be described in two ways: motive direction and motive strength. Motive direction is the way that a consumer attempts to reduce tension by either moving toward a positive goal or moving away from a negative outcome. In the case of sports participation, an individual wants to get in good physical condition and may move toward this goal by running, biking, lifting weights, and so on. Likewise, this same individual may want to move away from eating fatty foods and drinking alcohol.

Of particular interest to sports marketers is the strength of the sports participation motive. Motivational strength is the degree to which an individual chooses to actively pursue one goal over another. In sports marketing, the strength of a motive is characterized in terms of **sports involvement.** Sports involvement is the perceived interest in and personal importance of sports to an individual participating in a sport.[11]

Triathletes are an excellent example of an extreme level of sports involvement because of the importance placed on training for events. In their study, Hill and Robinson demonstrated that extreme involvement in a sport affects many aspects of the athletes' lives.[12] Participation could have positive effects, such as increased self-esteem, improved moods, and a better sense of overall wellness. Conversely, high involvement in a sport (e.g., triathlon) may produce neglected responsibilities of work, home, or family, and feelings of guilt, stress, and anxiety. Said simply, extremely involved individuals frequently have a difficult time balancing their lives.

Sports marketers are interested in involvement because it has been shown to be a relatively good predictor of sports-related behaviors. For example, a study found that level of involvement was positively related to the number of hours people participate in sports, the likelihood of planning their day around a sporting event, and the use of sports-related media (e.g., television, newspaper, or magazines).[13] Knowledge of sports involvement can help sports marketers develop strategies for both low- and high-involvement groups of potential participants.

Perception

Think for a moment about the image you have of the following sports: soccer, hockey, and tennis. You might think of soccer as a sport that requires a great deal of stamina and skill, hockey as a violent and aggressive sport, and tennis as a sport

Your performance is our passion–the high involvement cyclist.
Source: R&A Cycles

for people who belong to country clubs. Ask two friends about their images of these same sports, and you are likely to get two different responses. That is because each of us has our own views of the world based on past experience, needs, wants, and expectations.

Your image of sport results from being exposed to a lifetime of information. You talk to friends and family about sports, you watch sports on television, and you listen to sports on the radio. In addition, you may have participated in a variety of sports over the course of your life. We selectively filter sports information based on our own view of the world. Consumers process this information and use it in making decisions about participation.

The process by which consumers gather information and then interpret that information based on their own past experience is described as perception. **Perception** is defined as the complex process of selecting, organizing, and interpreting stimuli such as sports.[14] Ultimately, our perception of the world around us influences participant consumer behavior. The images that we hold of various sports and of ourselves dictate, to some extent, what sports we participate in. One of the primary goals of sports marketing is to shape your image of sports and sports products.

Before sports marketers can influence your perceptions, they must get your attention. **Selective attention** describes a consumer's focus on a specific marketing stimulus based on personal needs and attitudes. For example, you are much more likely to pay attention to advertisements for new golf clubs if you are thinking about purchasing a set.

Sports marketers fight with other sports and nonsports marketing stimuli for the limited capacity that consumers have for processing information. One job of the sports marketer is to capture the attention of the potential participant. But how is this done? Typically, sports marketers capture our attention through the use of novel promotions, using large and colorful promotional materials, and developing unique ways of communicating with consumers.

While sports marketers attempt to influence our perceptions, each participant brings a unique set of experiences, attitudes, and needs that affect the perceptual process. Generally speaking, consumers perceive things in ways that are consistent with their existing attitudes and values. This process is known as **selective interpretation.** For example, those who have played hockey all their life may not see it as a dangerous and violent sport, whereas others hold a different interpretation.

Finally, **selective retention,** or the tendency to remember only certain information, is another of the influences on the perceptual process. Selective retention is remembering just the things we want to remember. The hockey player does not remember the injuries, the training, or the fights—only the victories.

Although sports marketers cannot control consumers' perceptions, they can and do influence our perceptions of sports through their marketing efforts. For example, a sports marketer trying to increase volleyball participation in boys ages 8 to 12 must first attempt to understand their perception of volleyball. Then the sports marketer tries to find ways of capturing the attention of this group of consumers, who have many competing sports and entertainment alternatives. Once they have the attention of this group of potential participants, a marketing mix is designed to either reinforce their perception of volleyball or change the existing image.

In addition to understanding these consumers' images of volleyball, sports marketers are also interested in other aspects of perception. For instance, how do potential participants perceive advertisements and promotional materials about the sport? What are the parents' perceptions of volleyball? Do the parents perceive volleyball to be costly? The answer to all these questions depends on our own unique view of the world, which sports marketers attempt to understand and shape.

Learning

Another psychological factor that affects our participation decisions is learning. **Learning** is a relatively permanent change in response tendency due to the effects of experience. These response tendencies can be either changes in behavior (participation) or in how we perceive a particular sport. Consumers learn about and gather information regarding participation in various sports in any number of ways. **Behavioral learning** is concerned with how various stimuli (information about sports) elicit certain responses (feelings or behaviors) within an individual. **Cognitive learning,** however, is based on our ability to solve problems and use observation as a form of learning. Finally, **social learning** is based on watching others and learning from their actions. Let us look briefly at these three theories of learning as they apply to sports participation.

Behavioral Learning

One behavioral learning theory of importance to sports marketers is operant conditioning. Conditioning teaches people to associate certain behaviors with certain consequences of those behaviors. A simplified model of operant conditioning is illustrated in Figure 4.3.

Let us illustrate the model of operant conditioning using participation in snow skiing. We may decide to try snow skiing (specific behavior) as a new sport. Next and unfortunately, our behavior is punished as we continually fall down, suffer social embarrassment, and feel uncomfortably cold. Finally, the likelihood of our engaging in this behavior in the future is decreased because of the negative consequences of our earlier attempts at skiing. However, if we are rewarded through the enjoyment of the sport and being with others, then we will continue to ski more and more.

The theory of operant conditioning lies at the heart of loyalty to a sport. In other words, if the sports we participate in meet our needs and reinforce them, then we will continue to participate in those sports. The objective of the sports marketer is to try to heighten the rewards associated with participating in any given sport and diminish any negative consequences.

Cognitive Learning

Although much of what we learn is based on our past experience, learning also takes place through reasoning and thought processes. This approach to learning is known as cognitive learning. Cognitive learning is best known as learning through problem solving or insight, as shown in Figure 4.4.

Consider a goal that concerns some of us—weight loss. Once this goal is established, consumers search for activities that allow them to achieve the goal. The activities necessary to achieve weight loss might include dieting, participating in aerobics, weight training, playing basketball, or jogging. When consumers finally realize what specific activities they feel are necessary to achieve the desired goal, insight occurs. Finally, and hopefully, the goal of weight loss is achieved.

By using the concept of cognitive learning, the first focus of sports marketers is to understand the goals of potential consumers or participants. In addition, marketers must make potential participants aware of how the sport or sports product will help participants achieve their goals.

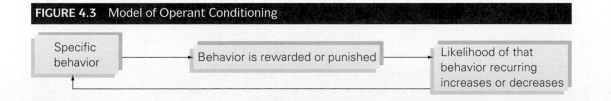

FIGURE 4.3   Model of Operant Conditioning

Specific behavior → Behavior is rewarded or punished → Likelihood of that behavior recurring increases or decreases

America's greatest car designer, Harley Earl. The world's greatest golfer, Tiger Woods.

The one car company where they both hang their hats.

BUICK
THE SPIRIT OF AMERICAN STYLE

The innovative 2003 Rendezvous at buick.com. ©2003 GM Corp. All rights reserved.

The Nike golf hat elicits a learned response of a famous golfer.

Source: © 2004 GM Corporation. All rights reserved.

Social Learning

Much of our learning takes place by watching how others are rewarded or punished for their actions. This way of learning is called social learning. As children, we watched our friends, family members, and our heroes participate in various sports. To a large extent, this early observation and learning dictates the sports in which we choose to participate later in life. In social learning, we not only see someone benefiting from sport, but we also learn how to participate in the sport ourselves.

Those individuals we choose to observe and the process of observation are called models and modeling, respectively. The job of the sports marketer is to present positive models and present sports in a positive light, so others will perceive the benefits of sports participation. For example, Venus and Serena Williams may be seen as role models for young African American athletes thinking about participating in tennis, or Peyton Manning may be a model for young men interested in football.

Attitudes

Because of the learning and perceptual processes, consumers develop attitudes toward participating in sports. **Attitudes** are learned thoughts, feelings, and behaviors toward some given object. What is your attitude toward participation in bowling? One positive aspect of bowling is the chance to interact socially with other participants. However,

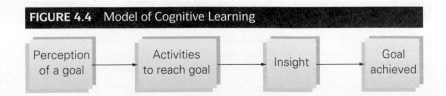

FIGURE 4.4   Model of Cognitive Learning

Perception of a goal → Activities to reach goal → Insight → Goal achieved

FIGURE 4.5 Model of Attitude Formation

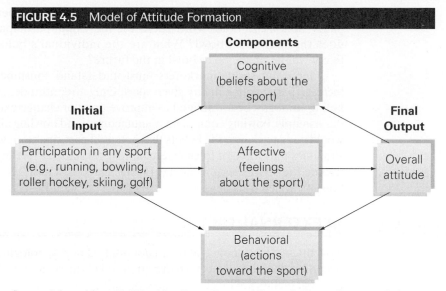

Source: Adapted from Del Hawkins, Roger Best, and Kenneth Coney, *Consumer Behavior: Building Marketing Strategy,* 7th ed. (New York: McGraw-Hill, 1998). Reproduced with permission of the McGraw-Hill Companies.

bowling does not burn a lot of calories and may be seen as expensive. Your overall attitude toward bowling is made up of these positive and negative aspects of the sport.

Attitudes represent one of the most important components of the overall model of sports participation because they ultimately guide the decision-making process. Our attitudes are formed on the basis of an interaction between past experience and the environment in which we live. A simple model of attitude formation or how attitudes are developed is shown in Figure 4.5.

As the model of attitude formation suggests, an attitude is based on our thinking, feeling, and actions toward a sport. These three components interact to form an overall attitude. Let us look briefly at its three components: cognitive, affective, and behavioral.

The **cognitive component** of attitude holds the beliefs that people have toward the object. Beliefs can be either a statement of knowledge regarding bowling or thoughts someone has toward bowling. They are neither right nor wrong and vary from individual to individual. For example, here are some beliefs about participation in bowling that consumers might hold:

- Bowling is expensive.
- Bowling is time consuming.
- Very few women bowl.
- Bowling is for old people. (*Note:* The largest participant group for bowling is 18- to 34-year-olds.)

The **affective component** of attitude is based on feelings or emotional reactions to the initial stimulus. Most beliefs, such as the ones shown for cognitive attitude, have a related affective evaluation. More recently, affects, or feelings, have taken a more central role in explaining attitudes than beliefs or behaviors. In other words, some people equate attitudes with feelings that are held toward an object.[15]

Here are some potential affective statements:

- I hate bowling.
- Bowling is a boring sport.

The final component is called the **behavioral component** and is based on participants' actions. In other words, does the individual participate in bowling? How often does the individual bowl? What are the individual's behavioral intentions, or how likely will he or she be to bowl in the future?

Generally, sports marketers must understand consumer attitudes to maintain or increase participation in any given sport. Only after attitudes are assessed can sports marketing strategies be formulated to improve upon or change existing attitudes. In our previous example, bowling equipment manufacturers and bowling alley management companies would need to change the beliefs that potential participants have about bowling. Additional strategies may attempt to change potential participants' feelings about bowling by repositioning the sport's current image. Finally, marketers may get potential participants to try bowling, which could lead to possible changes in their beliefs and feelings about the sport.

SOCIOLOGICAL OR EXTERNAL FACTORS

Now that we have looked at the major internal or psychological factors that influence participation decisions, let us turn our attention to the sociological factors. The **sociological or external factors** are those influences outside the individual participant that affect the decision-making process. The external factors are also referred to as sociological because they include all aspects of society and interacting with others. The external factors discussed in this chapter include culture, social class, reference groups, and family.

Culture

Participating in sports and games is one of the most long-standing traditions of civilization. Since the time of the ancient Greeks, participation in sports was expected and highly valued.[16] In the United States, sports are criticized for playing too important a role in our society. Many detractors frown at public monies being spent to finance private stadiums for professional athletics or institutions of higher education spending more on a new coach than on a new president for the university. As the accompanying article illustrates, other cultures are trying to emulate sports participation patterns in the United States.

SPOTLIGHT ON INTERNATIONAL SPORTS MARKETING

China Wants Its People Fighting Fit for 2008

While most ordinary Chinese are more concerned about Yao Ming's injury and comeback than the state of their own fitness, authorities are hoping to persuade more people to give exercise a sporting chance. With the Beijing 2008 Olympic Games fast approaching, senior officials of China's governing body of sport admit that there is a misbalance between interest in sport and participation, a crucial part of the Olympic spirit.

"Chinese people still lack awareness of how to get fit by getting involved in different sports," said Feng Jianzhong, deputy director of the State General Administration of Sport (SGAS). "The media coverage is unbalanced. There are so many reports about how Chinese athletes compete for gold medals, but not so much exposure for community sports activities.

"The participation of all the people is a significant part of preparing to host a successful Olympic Games. We have to take the chance to show how Chinese athletes have reached a global level, as well as show how passionate ordinary people are about fitness." Ten years ago, the government issued a document called "An Outline of the National Fitness Program," which was a milestone in the history of mass sports. Also 10 years ago the government promulgated the Law on Physical Culture and Sports, which consolidated and upgraded the legal status of the national fitness undertaking. By enhancing health awareness and providing convenient places to exercise, it has helped people improve their fitness level.

Reports say that thanks in part to the program, China's average life expectancy has risen to 71.8 years,

(Continued)

(*Continued*)

and about 37 percent of people regularly participate in sports activities. The country has also invested heavily in building sports facilities. The sports participation rate does not stack up well against developed countries, where it can often reach 80 or 90 percent.

In the last year before the 2008 extravaganza officials are urging local governments to organize activities to stir interest in sport. According to Liu Peng, director of the SGAS, more than 60 national and international activities concerning fitness and Olympic promotion will be launched around the country next year. "A People's Olympics is a core part of the Beijing Olympic concept. We should make extra efforts to have more and more people take part in the scheduled activities." Early in 2006, China began to organize a series of campaigns with a theme of "National Fitness and Move with the Olympics," which set a solid base for a further spread of the 2007 program.

"We have done a lot of work to popularize community sports and raise awareness in 2006. We are also trying to combine the Olympic spirit with national fitness. In 2007, we will continue the concept of the Olympics being closely linked to all activities." Obesity battle Apart from the inspiration of the Olympics, emerging health problems are also encouraging more people to exercise.

According to a national survey last September, more men are obese and an increasing number of students have poor eyesight. About one in 10 (9.3 percent) male adults between 20 and 59 suffers from obesity, up 22 percent from 2000 when the country released its first National Physical Fitness Report. In the 40–59 age group, the rate stands at 11.7 percent. For male adults, 33.2 percent are overweight, up 1.3 percent. In contrast, women in the same age bracket have seen little change from 2000.

The obesity rate among students has also increased by at least 1 percent, while strength and stamina are on the decline, according to the report. The report also indicates that urban Chinese are more physically fit than people in rural areas. Geographically speaking, residents of Shanghai, Jiangsu, Shandong, Guangxi, and Beijing have the highest fitness levels, while those in Xinjiang, Guizhou, Qinghai, and Tibet have the lowest. Authorities are acting to deal with the lack of sporting facilities in rural areas. The country aims to ensure each village has one cement-paved basketball court equipped with a pair of standard hoops and two outdoor ping-pong tables. The SGAS has promised to launch a number of important new projects next year.

"We will put the priority on the implementation of major projects like 'Billions of People Fitness Campaign,' 'National Fitness Week,' 'Community Action,' and the 'Rural Residents' Fitness Project," Liu said. Apart from increasing investment in sports facilities, China also plans to introduce some traditional sports to make 2007 more interesting.

These include a wide range of activities, deeply rooted in the nation's culture, that encourage people to exercise to improve their health. Apart from the fun element, people can enjoy the same benefits as other more demanding sports, officials said. The list includes Taiqi, a Chinese martial art with a history dating back thousands of years, roller-skating, dragon boat racing, kicking shuttlecocks, tug-of-war, and yangko dancing, a traditional street activity in northeast China. "Competitive sports like soccer and basketball are just a small part of the series of activities. We have asked local associations to organize different sports according to local culture and tradition," said Liu.

Source: Times Information Limited—Asia Intelligence Wire, Chinadaily.com.cn, February 16, 2007.

Culture is the set of learned values, beliefs, language, traditions, and symbols shared by a people and passed down from generation to generation. One of the most important aspects of this definition of culture includes the learning component. **Socialization** occurs when we learn about the skills, knowledge, and attitudes necessary for participating in sports. Sports marketers are interested in better understanding how the **consumer socialization** process takes place and how they might influence this process.

A model of sports socialization is presented in Figure 4.6, which provides a framework for understanding how children learn about sports. Although the sports socialization process begins at increasingly younger ages, it extends throughout the life of the individual. Sports marketers are interested in learning how the socialization process differs on the basis of gender, income, family lifestyle, and the number of children in the family.

Socializing agents also have a tremendous impact on the process. These factors represent the direct and indirect influences on the children. Sports marketers are also interested in understanding the relative impact of each socializing agent on a child's interest in participating in sports. For instance, is watching parents or professional athletes a better predictor of sports participation among children? One study

FIGURE 4.6   Model of Consumer Socialization

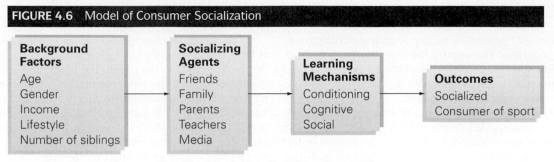

Source: John Mowen, *Consumer Behavior,* 3rd ed. (New York: Macmillan, 1993).

has shown that children look to parents first, but if they are unacceptable or unwilling role models, children turn to other people.[17]

The learning mechanisms of observation and reinforcement are just two ways that facilitate the socialization process. As discussed earlier, observation refers to looking to others as models for sports participation. For example, older siblings may serve as models for sports participation at earlier ages, whereas friends may become a more important learning mechanism as children age. Reinforcement may occur as children receive praise for participation in sport from parents, coaches, and friends.

The final element in the socialization model is the emergence of a socialized sports participant. Here, the child becomes actively engaged in sports participation. From the sports marketer's perspective, when children participate in sports at an early age, they may have better potential to become lifelong participants. Certainly, sporting goods manufacturers are interested in having children associate their brands with the enjoyment of sport at the earliest possible age.

Aside from the learning that takes place during the socialization process, values represent another important aspect of any culture. **Values** are widely held beliefs that affirm what is desirable in a culture. Several of the core values that reflect U.S. culture are shown in Table 4.5.

Some of the core American values listed in Table 4.5 have intimate ties to sports participation in the United States. Obviously, the last value mentioned, fitness and health, relates directly to our preoccupation with participating in sports. The activity value has a direct impact on the way Americans spend their leisure time, including

TABLE 4.5   Core American Values

Core American Value	Descriptor
Achievement and success	Sense of accomplishment
Activity	Being active or involved
Efficiency and practicality	Saves time and effort; solves problems
Progress	Continuous improvement
Material comfort	Money; status
Individualism	Being themselves
Freedom	Democratic beliefs
External conformity	Adaptation to society
Humanitarianism	Overcoming adversity; supporting
Charity	Giving to others
Youthfulness	Looking and acting young
Fitness and health	Exercise and diet

Source: Reprinted by permission of The Sporting Goods Marketing Association. Leon Shiffman and Leslie Kanuk, *Consumer Behavior,* 5th ed. (Upper Saddle River, NJ: Prentice Hall, 1994).

sports participation. Likewise, achievement and success are a theme that is continually underscored as consumers participate in sports.

Although they are not directly related, other core U.S. values may tangentially affect sports participation. For example, the value of individualism and being oneself may manifest itself in the types of sports or activities in which we choose to participate. Many sports, such as surfing, hang-gliding, climbing, and hiking, allow a consumer to express his or her own personality. Youthfulness is also expressed through participation in sport as consumers keep "young at heart" by staying active. Consumers may also participate in sporting events to help raise money for charities.

Social Class

Throughout history, people within various cultural systems have been grouped together based on social class. Whether it is the "haves" versus the "have nots" or the "upper class" versus the "lower class," social class distinctions have always been present. **Social class** is defined as the homogeneous division of people in a society sharing similar values, lifestyles, and behaviors that can be hierarchically categorized.

Important to this definition is the idea that individuals are divided into homogeneous classes, or strata. Typically, social strata are described in terms of a hierarchy ranging from lower to upper class. Consumers are grouped into the various social classes based on the interaction of a number of factors. Occupation, income, and education are usually considered the three primary determinants of social class. In addition, possessions (e.g., home and car) and affiliations (e.g., club membership, professional organizations, and community organizations) are also believed to be important factors.

Although researchers agree that there are distinct social strata, there is little agreement on how many categories there are in the hierarchy. For instance, some researchers believe a seven-tiered structure (as illustrated in Figure 4.7) explains

FIGURE 4.7   The Structure of Social Class

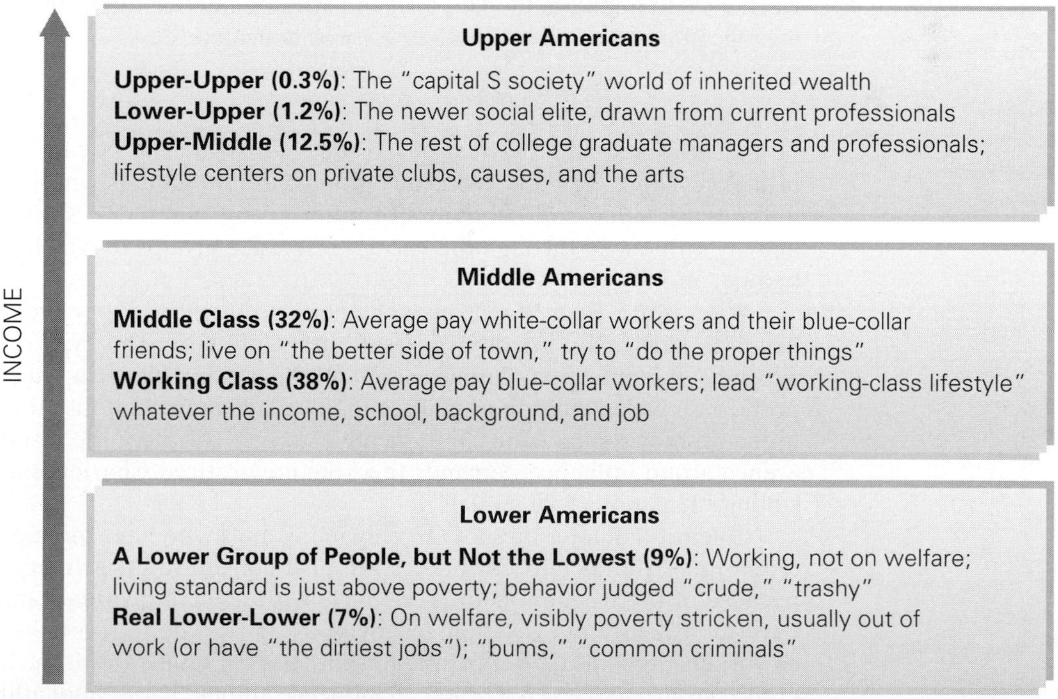

Upper Americans

Upper-Upper (0.3%): The "capital S society" world of inherited wealth
Lower-Upper (1.2%): The newer social elite, drawn from current professionals
Upper-Middle (12.5%): The rest of college graduate managers and professionals; lifestyle centers on private clubs, causes, and the arts

Middle Americans

Middle Class (32%): Average pay white-collar workers and their blue-collar friends; live on "the better side of town," try to "do the proper things"
Working Class (38%): Average pay blue-collar workers; lead "working-class lifestyle" whatever the income, school, background, and job

Lower Americans

A Lower Group of People, but Not the Lowest (9%): Working, not on welfare; living standard is just above poverty; behavior judged "crude," "trashy"
Real Lower-Lower (7%): On welfare, visibly poverty stricken, usually out of work (or have "the dirtiest jobs"); "bums," "common criminals"

INCOME

Source: Richard P. Coleman, "The Continuing Significance of Social Class to Marketing," *Journal of Consumer Research*, vol. 10 (December 1983), 265–280.

TABLE 4.6	Household Income for Select Sports and Activities		
Activity	*Household Income (in thousands)*	*Activity*	*Household Income (in thousands)*
Basketball	$58	Roller hockey	$73
Bowling	$60	Running/jogging	$63
BMX bicycling	$49	Sailing	$82
Day hiking	$66	Saltwater fishing	$64
Downhill skiing	$83	Snorkeling	$83
Fitness bicycling	$71	Snowboarding	$63
Fitness swimming	$69	Soccer	$59
Fitness walking	$66	Surfing	$74
Football (tackle)	$54	Tennis	$68
Golf	$80	Tent camping	$58
Horseback riding	$65	Yoga/tai chi	$68

Source: Sporting Goods Manufacturers Association, http://www.sportsbusinessdaily.com.

social class in the United States. Others, however, believe in a simple two-tiered system (i.e., upper and lower).

Regardless of the class structure, sports marketers are interested in social class as a predictor of whether consumers will participate in sports and, if they do participate, the types of sports in which consumers might participate. Table 4.6 shows the relationship between average household income and participation in 22 selected sports activities.

Other research has shown that more than one in four Americans would like to have more time for leisure activities such as bowling and softball. A disproportionate number of those people who want more leisure time are lower income, blue-collar workers.[18] In addition, the U.S. Fish and Wildlife Service found that anglers are above average in income and are moderately well educated.[19]

Reference Groups

"Be Like Mike" and "I Am Tiger Woods" illustrate the power of reference group influence. More formally, **reference groups** are individuals who influence the information, attitudes, and behaviors of other group members. Sports participation is heavily influenced through the various reference groups to which an individual may belong.

Witness the Tiger Woods phenomenon and the hordes of children who have now begun to participate in golf as a result of his influence. This type of reference group, which has an impact on our participation in sports as well as on our purchase of sports products, is called an aspirational group. Although many famous athletes recognize the influence they can have on children, others refuse to accept the responsibility that reference group influence demands (e.g., the now-retired Charles Barkley of the NBA stating, "I am not a role model").

Celebrity athletes are not the only individuals who have an impact on sports participation. Friends and coworkers are also considered a **primary reference group** because of the frequent contact we have with these individuals and the power they have to influence our decisions. Many of us participate in sports because friends and coworkers urged us to join their team, play a set of tennis, or hit the links. Primary reference groups may exert a powerful influence among high-school athletes as participation continues to grow at this level.

SPORTS MARKETING HALL OF FAME

The Babe: Babe Didrikson Zaharias

Mildred "Babe" Didrikson Zaharias was known by sports fans all over as the "best at everything." Her early success as an all-around athlete began as she played on basketball, softball, and track and field teams, named the Golden Cyclones, sponsored by the Employers Casualty Insurance Company. Babe represented the Golden Cyclones by herself in the 1932 Olympic track and field qualifying trials and entered eight of the 10 events. She ended up winning six of the events, and her legend was born.

As an amateur, Babe won two gold medals and one silver in track and field events at the 1932 Olympics. She began a professional career that included stints in basketball, baseball, boxing, football, and hockey. Didrikson's most impressive sport of all, however, was golf. Returning to amateur status in golf, Babe ran up an unprecedented 17 straight wins, including a victory in the 1947 British Women's Amateur—never before won by an American. In 1949, she was one of the founding members of the LPGA.

In addition to her impressive athletic achievements, Babe was the consummate sports promoter and marketer. For example, she participated in publicity stunts such as harness racing and pitched against New York Yankee Joe DiMaggio. She published a book of golfing tips, had her own line of golf clubs through Spalding Sporting Goods, and appeared in movies such as the classic *Pat and Mike*. Through her example and performance, Babe Didrikson Zaharias legitimized women's sports. Her excellence in so many sports made her a marketer's dream. Just imagine her today.

Source: Elizabeth Lynn, *Babe Didrikson Zaharias: Champion Athlete* (New York: Chelsea House, 1989).

Family

Another primary reference group that has one of the greatest influences on sports participation is the family. As you might guess, family plays a considerable role because sports marketers target families as spectators. But how does **family influence** affect participation in sport? Consider families of friends or your own family. It is common for family members to exert a great deal of influence on one another with respect to decisions about sports participation and activities. For example, children may either directly or indirectly get parents involved in a sport (e.g., in-line skating, soccer, or biking) so the entire family can participate together. Conversely, parents may urge their kids to get off the couch and get involved in sports.

Traditionally, fathers have had the greatest impact on their children's (mostly their sons') sports participation. Dad might have encouraged junior to play organized football because he did or go fishing because his father took him fishing. Of course, these scenarios are vanishing, as is the traditional family structure.

Long gone are the days of the mom, dad, two kids, and a dog. Long gone is the *Leave It to Beaver* mentality where fathers are breadwinners and mothers are homemakers. Today's modern family structure typically includes dual-income families with no kids (DINKS), divorced parents, single parents, or parents who are dually employed with kids (DEWKS).

Each of these modern family structures may influence participation in sports for both adults and children. For instance, dual-income families with no kids may have the time and the money to participate in a variety of "country club" sports. However, single or divorced parents may face time and financial constraints. Sports products such as the "10-minute workout" and 30-minute aerobic classes are targeted to working moms on the move. In addition, the tremendous increase in sales of home exercise equipment may be traced back to the constraints of the modern family structure.

Girls' sport participation is eroding traditional gender roles.

Children's ability to participate in organized sport may also be hampered by the single-parent family, although women are increasingly taking on the traditional male sex role of coach, sports participant, and sports enthusiast. Also, fathers are increasingly encouraging daughters to participate in sport, another sign of changing sex roles.

Situational Factors

Now that we have looked at how the psychological and sociological factors influence the participant decision-making process, let us turn to the situational factors. Unlike the

---

High School Sports Participation Climbs

Based on figures from the 50 state high school athletic/activity associations, plus the District of Columbia, that are members of the NFHS, participation for the 2006–07 school year rose by 183,006 students to 7,342,910, according to the High School Athletics Participation Survey conducted by the NFHS.

For the 18th consecutive year, the number of student participants in high school athletics increased in 2006–07, according to the National Federation of State High School Associations (NFHS). Through the survey, it was also determined that 54.2 percent of students enrolled in high schools participate in athletics.

For years, the NFHS has been the source of official playing rules, training programs for coaches and officials, and coordination and communications among individual state high school associations. In addition to the growth in numbers, girls' participation cracked the 3 million barrier for the first time.

Robert Kanaby, Executive Director of the NFHS, stated that "the girls' participation figure is particularly exciting since this year is the 35th anniversary of Title IX. We are pleased that more and more girls' are taking part in the opportunity to participate in high school sports."

"In addition to the overall numbers, as stated earlier, the girls' participation total of 3,021,807 set an all-time record. The boys' total also increased, reaching 4,321,103, the highest participation in the past 28 years. This year's

(Continued)

(Continued)

boys' participation figure is second only to the record 4,367,442 in 1977–78.

Soccer gained the most female participants in 2006–07 with 16,077, followed by volleyball with 15,798, and cross country with 7422. Eleven-player football gained the most participants among boys' sports in 2006–07 with 32,773, followed by soccer with 19,064, outdoor track and field with 10,195, and basketball with 9934.

Basketball remained the most popular sport for girls with 456,967 participants, followed by outdoor track and field (444,181), volleyball (405,832), fast pitch softball (373,448), soccer (337,632), cross country (183,376), tennis (176,969), swimming and diving (143,639), competitive spirit squads (95,177), and golf (66,283).

In boys' sports, 11-player football once again topped the list with 1,104,548 participants, followed by basketball (556,269), outdoor track and field (544,180), baseball (477,430), soccer (377,999), wrestling (257,246), cross country (216,085), golf (159,747), tennis (156,944), and swimming and diving (106,738).

Source: **"High School Sports Participation Increases Again,"** National Federation of State High School Associations, http://www.nfhs.org/web/2006/09/participation_in_high_school_sports_increases_again_confirms_nf.aspx.

psychological and sociological factors that are relatively permanent in nature, the situational factors are temporary aspects that affect participation. For instance, the culture in which we make our participation decision is considered a long-term environmental factor. Likewise, personality is a set of consistent responses that we make to our environment. However, **situational factors** are those temporary factors within a particular time or place that influence the participation decision-making process.[20]

Consider the following examples of situational influences on participant behavior. Your best friend is in town and, although you do not normally enjoy golfing, you do so anyway to spend time with your friend. You typically run five miles per day, but an unexpected ice storm puts a halt to your daily exercise routine. You have to study for final exams, so you settle for a 30-minute workout versus your normal 75 minutes. Each of these examples represents a different type of situational influence on participant decision making.

Consumer researchers have identified five situational influences that affect decision making. The five primary types of situational influences include physical surroundings; social surroundings; time; reason for participation, or task definition; and antecedent states. Let us briefly look at each in the context of participant decision making.

Physical Surroundings

The location, weather, and physical aspects of the participation environment comprise the **physical surroundings.** In sports participation, the physical surroundings play an extremely important role in decision making. When the weather outside is good, people who might not participate in sports normally do so. Likewise, the weather can have a situational influence on where we choose to participate. The runner described in the earlier example may decide to jog indoors rather than skip the workout. In addition to the weather, location might influence our decision to participate. For example, nonskiers may be tempted to try skiing if they are attending a sales conference in Vail or Aspen. Other aspects of the physical environment, such as a perfectly groomed championship golf course or scenic biking trail, can also influence our participation decisions in a positive manner. From the perspective of the sports marketer, any attempt to increase participation must carefully consider the physical surroundings. Even the worst athletes in the world enjoy playing in nice facilities.

Social Surroundings

The effect of other people on a participant during participation in a sport is another situational influence, called **social surroundings.** In other words, who we are with may have a positive or negative impact on participation decisions. The earlier golf example presented a case where the presence of a friend caused the person to participate. Likewise, golfing in the presence of unfamiliar coworkers at a corporate outing can be an unpleasant and intimidating experience. In this case, participation might be avoided altogether.

Crowds represent another social situation that is usually avoided. For example, if the tennis courts or golf courses are full, you might decide to participate in another sport that day. Biking and hiking represent two other activities where crowds are usually perceived to have a negative impact on participation. In other words, people generally do not like to bike or hike in large crowds. However, some people may take pleasure when participating among large crowds. Consider, for example, runners who feel motivated when participating in events with thousands of other runners.

Time

The effect of the presence or absence of **time** is the third type of situational influence. In today's society, there are increasing time pressures on all of us. Changes in family structure, giving rise to dual-income families and single parents, have made time for participation in sports even scarcer. Slightly more than half of all U.S. residents under the age of 50 complain of a lack of leisure time, and this percentage is even higher for dual-income families. How many times have you heard someone say, "I don't have the time to work out today"?

Because of time constraints, sports marketers are concentrating on ways to make our participation activities more enjoyable and more time effective. For example, few of us can afford to take five hours out of our day to enjoy 18 holes of golf. As such,

Social surroundings may have a negative or positive influence on participation.

golfing associations are always communicating ways to speed up play. Similarly, few of us feel that we have the time to drive to the gym each day. The marketers' response to this was the development of the shorter, higher intensity workout (see accompanying article) and the enormous home health equipment industry.

Reason for Participation or Task Definition

Another situational influence, **task definition,** refers to the reasons that occasion the need for consumers to participate in a sport. In other words, the reason the consumer participates affects the decision-making process. Some participants may use jet skis or scuba dive once a year while they are on vacation. Other consumers may participate in a fantasy baseball camp once in a lifetime.

These examples represent special occasions or situational reasons for participating. Moreover, the participation occasion may dictate the sports apparel and equipment we choose. For example, a consumer participating in a competitive softball league might wear cleats, long softball pants, and batting gloves. However, the recreational participant playing softball at the company picnic would only bring a glove.

Antecedent States

Temporary physiological and mood states that a consumer brings to the participant situation are **antecedent states.** In certain situations, people may feel worn out and lack

---

Workout Combos for the Time-Starved

Halfway through a lunch-hour "boot camp" at Goodson Recreation Center, fitness instructor Ann Lantz steers her charges off the indoor running track and back into the aerobics room for a second round of interval training. The 11 women and two men in the class, panting after half a lap of skipping, align themselves next to floor mats, step benches, and jump ropes and prepare to sweat a little more.

As techno music throbs from a boom box in the background, Lantz fingers the whistle her mother used to carry at recess as an elementary-school teacher in the 1960s. "Ready, set, off you go!" she exults, and with a quick blast she propels them into yet another series of flexes, stretches and bends, to be capped by still more running and a final spasm of three 45-second sets of crunches—all accompanied by shouts of encouragement and exhortations to push harder.

As the 45-minute session comes to an end, Rosanne Juergens, one of several rec center employees who regularly take part, sums up its multifaceted appeal: "This is really high intensity. It kicks your butt, but I love it." The "boot camp" at Goodson, part of a constantly changing repertoire of workouts called "Noon Express," illustrates a growing movement toward more varied offerings in the world of group exercise.

"Traditionally, you think of group classes as step or high-low (aerobics). The current trend is centered more around the concept of personal training in a group setting," says Daren Parks, athletic director at the Cherry Creek Athletic Club. "The classes are more military in style, incorporating three or four activities in one session, and the choreography is relatively simple, so that people of any age or experience level can step in and participate."

Thus, health clubs and community recreation centers are offering classes that combine weight training with treadmill running, fitness balls with barbells, kick-boxing with dancing, yoga with Pilates. "I think what people are looking for is variety, so they gain strength in all the different systems of the body," Parks says. "That leads to greater prevention of injury and more cardiovascular strength, so they can participate in a lot of different activities."

Tiffany Ulatowski, assistant director of the Coors Fitness Center at the University of Denver's Ritchie Center, says all-in-one workouts are especially appealing to busy students and professionals. "People are so strapped for time they're looking for classes that will meet all their needs in just one hour," she says.

In addition to offering more varied exercises, many health clubs and rec centers are changing group classes by shortening sessions to 30 or 45 minutes rather than the traditional hour. "We do a lot of a la carte programs," says Shannon Griffiths-Fable. "People can create their own workouts by running on a treadmill for 30 minutes and then doing 30 minutes of strength training (in a group), instead of being stuck in a class for 60 minutes, which is longer than most of us ever do on our own."

Source: Jack Cox, *Denver Post,* October 25, 2006.

energy. This physiological state may motivate some people to work out and become reenergized at the end of a long day of work. However, feeling tired can elicit another response in others, such as "I'm too tired to do anything today."

Certainly, other situational mood states, such as being "stressed out," can activate the need to participate in sports or exercise. Yet feeling tired or hungry can cause us to decide against participation. At the very least, our mood can influence our decision to ride or walk 18 holes of golf.

It is important to remember that antecedent means "prior to" or "before." Therefore, the mood or physiological condition influences our decision making. For example, people who are experiencing bad moods may turn to sports to lift their spirits. Contrast this with those who feel great because they have just participated in a sporting event.

Summary

The focus of Chapter 4 is on understanding the sports participant as a consumer of sports. Sports marketers are not only concerned with consumers who watch sporting events, but also with the millions of consumers who participate in a variety of sports. To successfully market to sports participants, sports marketers must understand everything they can about these consumers and their consumption behaviors. Participant consumption behavior is defined as the actions performed when searching for, participating in, and evaluating the sports activities that consumers believe will satisfy their needs.

To simplify the complex nature of participant consumption behavior, a model was developed. The model of participant consumption behavior consists of four major components: the participant decision-making process, internal or psychological factors, external or sociological factors, and situational variables. The participant decision-making process is the central focus of the model of participant consumption behavior. It explains how consumers make decisions about whether to participate in sports and in which sports to participate. The decision-making process is slightly different for each of us and is influenced by a host of factors. However, the basis of the decision-making process is a five-step procedure that consumers progress through as they make decisions. These five steps include problem recognition, information search, evaluation of alternatives, participation, and postparticipation evaluation. The complexity of this process is highly dependent on how important the decision is to participants and how much experience consumers have had making similar decisions.

The internal or psychological factors are those things that influence our decision-making process. These psychological factors include personality, motivation, perception, learning, and attitudes. Personality is a set of consistent responses we make to our environment. Our personality can play a role in which sports we choose to participate in or whether we participate in any sports. For example, an aggressive personality type may be most likely to participate in boxing or hockey. Motivation is the reason we participate in sports. Some of the more common reasons we participate in sports are for personal improvement, appreciation of sport, or social facilitation. The strength of our motives to participate in sports is referred to as sport involvement. Another important psychological factor that influences our participation decisions is perception. Perception influences our image of the various sports and their participants as well as shaping our attitudes toward sports participation. Learning also affects our participant behavior. We learn whether to participate in sports because we are rewarded or punished by our participation (behavioral theories), because we perceive sports as a way to achieve our goals (cognitive theories), and because we watch others participating (social theories). A final internal or psychological factor that directly influences our sports participation decisions is attitudes. Attitudes are defined as learned thoughts, feelings, and behaviors toward some given object (in this case, sports participation). Our feelings (affective component of attitude) and beliefs (cognitive component) about sports participation certainly play a major role in determining our participation (behavioral component).

The external or sociological factors also influence the participant decision-making process. These factors include culture, social class, reference groups, and family. Culture is defined as the learned values, beliefs, language, traditions, and symbols shared by people and passed down from generation to generation. The values held by people within a society are a most important determinant of culture. Some of the core American values that influence participation in sports include achievement and success, activity, individualism, youthfulness, and fitness and health. Social class is another important determinant of participant decision making. Most people erroneously associate social class only with income. Our social class is also determined by occupation, education, and affiliations. Another important sociological factor is the influence of reference groups. Reference groups are individuals who influence the information, attitudes, and behaviors of other group members. For example, our friends may affect our decision to participate in a variety of recreational sports and activities. One reference group that has a great deal of influence over our attitudes and participation behavior is our family.

The final component of the model of participant behavior is situational factors. Every decision that we make to participate in a given activity has a situational component. In other words, we are always making a decision in the context of some unique situation. Five major situational influences that affect participant decision making include physical surroundings (physical environment), social surroundings (interaction with others), time (presence or absence of time), task definition (reason or occasion for participation), and antecedent states (physiological condition or mood prior to participation).

Key Terms

- affective component, p. 123
- antecedent states, p. 133
- attitudes, p. 122
- behavioral component, p. 123
- behavioral learning, p. 121
- cognitive component, p. 123
- cognitive dissonance, p. 112
- cognitive learning, p. 121
- consumer socialization, p. 124
- culture, p. 124
- decision-making process, p. 107
- esteem, p. 117
- evaluation of alternatives, p. 111
- evaluative criteria, p. 111
- evoked set, p. 111
- experiential source, p 110
- extensive problem solving (or extended problem solving), p. 113
- external sources, p. 110
- family influence, p. 129
- habitual problem solving (or routinized problem solving), p. 113

- information search, p. 109
- internal sources, p. 109
- learning, p. 121
- limited problem solving, p. 113
- love and belonging, p. 117
- marketing sources, p. 110
- Maslow's hierarchy of needs, p. 117
- model of participant consumption behavior, p. 107
- motivation, p. 116
- participant consumption behavior, p. 105
- perceived risk, p. 110
- perception, p. 120
- personality, p. 114
- personal sources, p. 110
- physical surroundings, p. 131
- physiological needs, p. 117
- postparticipation evaluation, p. 112
- primary reference group, p. 128
- problem recognition, p. 108

- psychological or internal factors, p. 113
- reference groups, p. 128
- safety needs, p. 117
- selective attention, p. 120
- selective interpretation, p. 120
- selective retention, p. 120
- self-actualization, p. 118
- situational factors, p. 131
- social class, p. 127
- socialization, p. 124
- social learning, p. 121
- socializing agents, p. 124
- social surroundings, p. 131
- sociological or external factors, p. 124
- sports involvement, p. 118
- task definition, p. 133
- time, p. 132
- values, p. 126

Review Questions

1. Define participant consumption behavior. What questions does this address with respect to consumers of sport? From a marketing strategy perspective, why is it critical to understand consumer behavior?
2. Outline the components of the simplified model of participant consumer behavior.
3. Outline the steps in the decision-making process for sports participation. What are the three types/levels of consumer decision making? How do the steps in the decision-making process differ for routine decisions versus extensive decisions?
4. Define personality. Why is it considered one of the internal factors of consumption behavior? Do you think personality is related to the decision to participate in sports? Do you think personality is linked to the specific sports we choose to play?
5. Describe Maslow's hierarchy of needs. How is Maslow's theory linked to sports marketing?
6. What is meant by the term *sports involvement* from the perspective of sports participants? How is sports involvement measured and used in the development of the strategic marketing process?

7. Define perception and provide three examples of how the perceptual processes apply to sports marketing.
8. Describe the three major learning theories. Which learning theory do you believe best explains the sports in which we choose to participate? Why is learning theory important to sports marketers?
9. Describe the three components of attitude. How do these components work together? Why must attitudes be measured to increase sports participation?
10. Define culture and explain the process of sports socialization. Describe the core American values.

11. Define social class and explain the characteristics of individuals at each level of the seven-tiered structure.
12. Explain how reference groups play a role in sports participation.
13. Discuss the traditional family structure and then the nontraditional family structures. How do today's nontraditional families influence sports participation? Is this for the better or the worse?
14. Explain each of the five situational factors that influence the participant decision-making process.

Exercises

1. Trace the simplified model of participant behavior for a consumer thinking about joining a health club. Briefly comment on each element of the model.
2. Ask three males and three females about the benefits they seek when participating in sports. What conclusions can you draw regarding motivation? Are there large gender differences in the benefits sought?
3. Interview five adult sports participants and ask them to describe the sports socialization process as it relates to their personal experience. Attempt to interview people with different sports interests to determine whether the socialization process differs according to the specific sports.
4. Watch three advertisements for any sporting goods on television. Briefly describe the advertisement and then suggest which core

American value(s) are reflected in the theme of the advertisement.
5. Develop a survey instrument to measure attitudes toward jogging. Have 10 people complete the survey and then report your findings. How could these findings be used by your local running club to increase membership (suggest specific strategies)? Are attitudes and behaviors related?
6. Interview five children (between the ages of eight and 12) to determine what role the family and other reference group influences have had on their decision to participate in sports. Suggest promotions for children based on your findings.
7. Prepare a report that describes how time pressures are influencing sports participation in the United States. How are sports marketers responding to increasing time pressures?

Internet Exercises

1. Using the World Wide Web, prepare a report that examines sport participation in Australia. What are the similarities and differences in the sports culture of Australia versus that of the United States?
2. Find and describe two sports Web sites that specifically appeal to children. How does this

information relate to the process of consumer socialization?
3. Find and describe a Web site for a health club. How does the information relate to the consumer decision-making process to join the club?

Endnotes

1. Del Hawkins, Roger Best, and Kenneth Coney, *Consumer Behavior: Building Marketing Strategy,* 7th ed. (New York: McGraw-Hill, 1998).
2. Ian P. Murphy, "Bowling Industry Rolls Out Unified Marketing Plan," *Marketing News* (January 20, 1997), 2.
3. Del Hawkins, Roger Best, and Kenneth Coney, *Consumer Behavior: Building Marketing Strategy,* 7th ed. (New York: McGraw-Hill, 1998).
4. R. B. Cattell, H. W. Eber, and M. M. Tasuoka, *Handbook for the Sixteen Personality Factors Questionnaire* (Champaign, IL: Institute for Personality and Ability Testing, 1970).
5. Douglas M. Turco, "The X Factor: Marketing Sport to Generation X," *Sport Marketing Quarterly,* vol. 5, no. 1: 21–23.
6. Terry Lefton and Bernhard Warner, "Alt Sportspeak: A Flatliner's Guide," *Brandweek* (January 27, 1997), 25–27.
7. M. A. McDonald, G. R. Milne, and J. Hong, "Motivational Factors for Evaluating Sport Spectator and Participant Markets," *Sport Marketing Quarterly* vol. 11 (2002), 100–113.
8. Andrew J. Rohm, George R. Milne, and Mark A. McDonald, "A Mixed-Method Approach for

Developing Market Segmentation Typologies in the Sports Industry," *Sport Marketing Quarterly* (2006, West Virginia University), 15, 29–39.

9. H. Murray, *Exploration in Personality: A Clinical and Experimental Study of Fifty Men of College Age* (New York: Oxford University Press, 1938).

10. "You Can Buy a Thrill: Chasing the Ultimate Rush," www.demographics.com/publications/ad/97_ad/9706_ad/ad970631.htm.

11. Fred M. Beasley and Matthew D. Shank, "Fan or Fanatic: Refining a Measure of Sports Involvement," *Journal of Sport Behavior,* vol. 21, no. 4 (1998), 435–443.

12. Ronald Paul Hill and Harold Robinson, "Fanatic Consumer Behavior: Athletics as a Consumption Experience," *Psychology & Marketing*, vol. 8, no. 2 (1991), 79–99.

13. Fred M. Beasley and Matthew D. Shank, "Fan or Fanatic: Refining a Measure of Sports Involvement," *Journal of Sport Behavior*, vol. 21, no. 4 (1998), 435–443.

14. Robert Sekular and Randolph Blake, *Perception*, 2nd ed. (New York: McGraw-Hill, 1990).

15. John Kim, Jeen-Su Lim, and Mukesh Bhargava, "The Role of Affect in Attitude Formation: A Classical Conditioning Approach," *Journal of the Academy of Marketing Science,* vol. 26, no. 2 (1998), 143–152.

16. Harry Edwards, *The Sociology of Sport* (Homewood, IL: Dorsey Press, 1973).

17. Elizabeth Moore-Shay and Britts Berchmans, "The Role of the Family Environment in the Development of Shared Consumption Values: An Intergenerational Study," *Advances in Consumer Research,* vol. 2. Kim Corfman and John G. Lunch, Jr., eds. (Provo, UT: Association for Consumer Research, 1996), 484–490.

18. "Something to Wish for: Time to Relax," *US News and World Report* (November 11, 1996), 17.

19. Diane Crispell. "Targeting Hunters" *American Demographics,* www.demographics.com/ publications/ad/94_ad/9401_ad/ad508.htm.

20. Russel Belk, "Situational Variables and Consumer Behavior," *Journal of Consumer Research* (December 1975): 157–163.

5

UNDERSTANDING SPECTATORS AS CONSUMERS

After completing this chapter, you should be able to:

■ Understand the similarities and differences between spectator and participant markets.

■ Describe the eight basic fan motivation factors.

■ Explain how game attractiveness, economic factors, and competitive factors relate to game attendance.

■ Describe the demographic profile of spectators and explain the changing role of women as spectators.

■ Understand the relationship between stadium factors and game attendance.

■ Discuss the components of the sportscape model.

■ Describe the multiple values of sport to the community.

■ Explain sport involvement from a spectator's perspective.

■ Discuss the model of fan identification.

In Chapter 4, we examined participants as consumers. This chapter examines another group of consumers of great importance to sports marketers—spectators. Before we turn to our discussion of spectator consumption, two key points need to be addressed. First, the model of participant consumption behavior discussed in Chapter 4 can also be applied to spectator consumption. Think for a moment about your decision to attend sporting events. Certainly, there are sociological factors that influence your decision. For instance, reference groups such as friends and family may play a major role in influencing your decision to attend sporting events. Psychological factors, such as personality, perception, and attitudes, also affect your decision to attend sporting events or which sporting events to attend. For example, the more ambitious and aspiring you are, the more likely you may be to attend sporting events. In addition, situational factors can affect your decision to attend sporting events. Maybe you were given tickets to the game as a birthday gift (e.g., task definition).

As you can see, the factors that influence participant decision making are also applicable to spectator decisions. However, the focus of this chapter is to understand why people attend sporting events and to examine what additional factors relate to game attendance. Rather than using the framework for participant consumption behavior, however, we

Some of the most enthusiastic spectators in the world are soccer fans.

concentrate on the wants and needs of spectators. Understanding the consumer's needs and wants, in turn, is important when developing an effective marketing mix for spectators.

The second key point addresses the basis for considering spectators and participants as two separate markets. Many people who watch and attend sporting events also participate in sports and vice versa. For example, you may watch March Madness and also play basketball on a recreational basis. Research has shown, however, that two different consumer segments exist.[1] In fact, marketing to "either participants or spectators would miss a large proportion of the other group." Let us look at Figure 5.1 to illustrate the differences between spectators and participants.

FIGURE 5.1 Relationship Between Spectator and Participant Markets

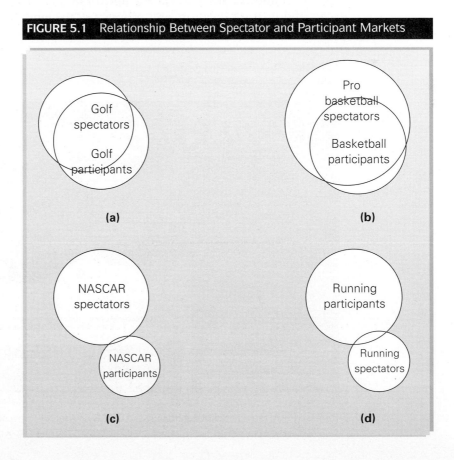

Each diagram in Figure 5.1 depicts the potential relationship between spectator and consumer markets for golf, basketball, NASCAR, and running. Golf (see Figure 5.1a) represents a sport in which there is a large crossover between participants and spectators. A study conducted by Milne, Sutton, and McDonald supports this notion, finding that 84 percent of the golf participant market overlaps the golf spectator market.[2] In another study, it was found that 87.3 percent of the spectators in attendance at an LPGA event also participated in golf.[3]

A similar pattern is shown for basketball (see Figure 5.1b). The results of the study indicated an 81 percent overlap between basketball participation and watching pro basketball. Surprisingly, this same relationship did not exist for college basketball spectators. In that case, the overlap in the participation market and the college basketball spectator market was only 43 percent. The study also found that there was only a 36 percent overlap between spectators of professional basketball and spectators of college basketball—evidence that there are not only differences in spectators and participants, but also among spectators at different levels of the same sport.[4]

The other two sports shown in Figure 5.1, NASCAR racing and running, demonstrate more extreme differences in the spectator and participant markets. There is virtually no overlap between the spectators and participants of NASCAR (see Figure 5.1c). Obviously, the NASCAR participant market is virtually nonexistent. However, new "fantasy camps" are springing up across the United States for spectators who want to try racing. For example, participants can enroll in classes at the Richard Petty Driving Experience. The "Rookie Experience" is designed for the "layperson who has a strong desire to experience the thrill of driving a Sprint Cup race car." For prices starting at $399, racing enthusiasts can begin to experience driving around the track at speeds up to 145 mph. Top speeds vary according to driver ability, track location, and program. Race fans can also experience a heart-pounding ride around one of the tracks with a professional instructor. Prices for the

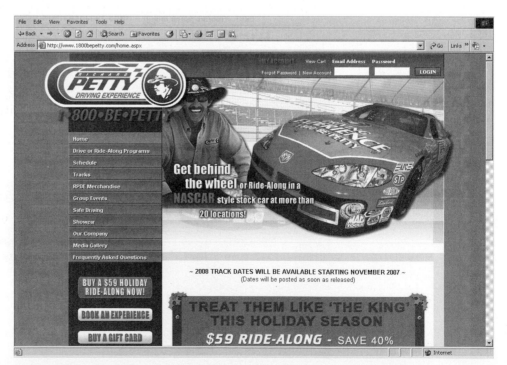

Richard Petty Driving School: Allowing NASCAR spectators to become participants.
Source: Richard Petty Driving Experience™ Copyright © 2004 RPDE. All rights reserved.

There is no overlap in the spectator and participant market for bull fighting.

ride start at $99.00 and speeds will reach up to 165 mph. There are very few requirements, and participants soon will feel like their favorite racecar driver.[5]

Figure 5.1d depicts the potential participant and spectator markets for running. As opposed to the previous examples, the participant running market is much larger than the spectator running market. In addition to the size of the markets, there are also differences in motivations for spectators and participants. Participants, for instance, may be motivated to run for reasons of personal improvement. However, spectators are likely to watch to provide support to a family member or friend.

In addition to looking at the overlap (or lack thereof) between participants and spectators on a sport-by-sport basis, other research has explored the differences between these two groups for sports in general. Table 5.1 summarizes the findings of a study conducted by Burnett, Menon, and Smart, which examined spectator and participant socioeconomic characteristics and media habits. Based on the results of this and other studies, sports participants and sports spectators seem to represent two distinct markets that should be examined separately by sports marketers.

Before we explore spectators in greater detail, it is important to note that this market can be differentiated into two groups on the basis of consumer behavior. The first group consists of spectators who attend the sporting event. The second group of spectators consumes the sporting event through some medium (e.g., television, radio, or Internet). This chapter is primarily concerned with understanding why consumers

---

TABLE 5.1   Differences Between Spectators and Participants

- Spectator and participant markets differ from each other with respect to socioeconomic characteristics and media habits.
- Consumers categorized as heavy participants were more likely to be male, better educated, white-collar workers, minorities, and young, compared with the heavy spectator group.
- Consumers categorized as heavy participants also differ from heavy spectators with respect to media usage. Heavy participants are more likely to use business news-reporting media. In addition, heavy participants are more likely to watch intellectually appealing programming.
- Compared with male participants, male spectators exhibit an interest in a wider variety of media, especially television.
- Heavy participants and heavy spectators are different with respect to how they can be reached by advertising and how they perceive advertising.

Source: Adapted from John Burnett, Anil Menon, and Denise T. Smart, "Sports Marketing: A New Ball Game with New Rules," *Journal of Advertising Research* (September–October 1993), 21–33.

attend sporting events and what factors influence attendance. Let us begin by looking at some of the major factors that influence the decision to attend sporting events rather than watch them from the comfort of home.

FACTORS INFLUENCING ATTENDANCE

It is opening day in Cleveland and the hometown Indians are set to take on the New York Yankees. Fred has gone to the traditional opening day parade and then attended the ball game for the past five years. The game promises to be a great one because the Indians are returning from last year's winning season and playing the rival Yankees. Fred will be joined at the game by his eight-year-old son and a potential business client.

As this hypothetical scenario illustrates, there are a variety of factors influencing Fred's decision to attend the season opener. He wants to experience the new stadium and watch the team that he has identified with since his childhood. As a businessman, Fred views the game as an opportunity to build a relationship with a potential client. As a father, Fred views the game as a way to bond with his son. In addition to these factors, Fred is prone to gambling and has placed a $50 bet on the home team. Finally, Fred thinks of opening day as an entertaining event that brings the whole community together and, as a lifelong resident, he wants to feel that sense of belonging.

Certainly, the interaction of the factors mentioned affected Fred's decision to attend the game. Sports marketers must attempt to understand all the influences on game attendance to market effectively to Fred and other fans like him.

A variety of studies have examined some of the major issues related to game attendance. A study conducted by Ferreira and Armstrong[6] found that eight distinct factors influence game attendance. Factor 1 included items related to the overall popularity of sport and were collectively labeled *popularity of sport.* Factor 2 outlined items related to overall *game attractiveness,* including opposing team quality, home team quality, strategy displayed, athleticism, and skill displayed. The third factor was based on *free offerings and promotions,* such as offerings of free T-shirts, prizes, free tickets, and promotions on concessions (e.g., dime-a-dog). Factor 4 denoted *pregame and in-game entertainment* items such as band, music, and pregame activities. Factor 5, labeled *physical contact,* conveyed the degree of physical contact displayed. Factor 6 included items that related to *convenience and accessibility,* such as seating arrangement, seats location/sightlines, location convenience, and parking. Factor 7, *facility,* signified items of facility newness and niceness. Finally, Factor 8 was labeled *cost* and referenced items related to ticket prices.

Other research has shown that weather and parking,[7,8,9] ticket cost,[10,11] promotional events,[12,13] team success,[14,15] attributions for team success,[16,17] and the presence of star players[18,19] all play a role in sport consumption decisions.

Let's delve deeper into some of these critical drivers of game attendance, such as fan motivation factors, game attractiveness, economic factors, competitive factors, demographic factors, stadium factors, value of sport to the community, sports involvement, and fan identification.

Fan Motivation Factors

The foundation of any strategic sports marketing process is understanding why spectators attend sporting events, or **fan motivation factors.** Based on an extensive literature review, Trail[20] proposed that nine different motives explain why individuals consume sport or are sport fans. Most of these motives are based on social and psychological needs: vicarious achievement, acquisition of knowledge, aesthetics, social interaction, drama/excitement, escape (relation), family, physical attractiveness of participants, and quality of physical skill of the participants. Trail and his colleagues also suggested that spectators attend games due to one or a combination of these motives.

Additional research by Wann has found eight basic motives for watching sport. The motives are categorized as **self-esteem enhancement, diversion from everyday life, entertainment value, eustress,** economic value, **aesthetic value,** need for affiliation, and **family ties.** It is important to note that these fundamental motives represent the most basic needs of fans. Because of this, the eight motives are often related to other factors, such as sports involvement and fan identification, which are discussed later in the chapter. Let us now examine the eight underlying motives of fans identified in a study conducted by Wann.[21]

- *Self-Esteem Enhancement*—Fans are rewarded with feelings of accomplishment when their favorite players or teams are winning. These fans more commonly are called "fair weather fans"; their association with the team is likely to increase when the team is winning and decrease when the team is doing poorly.

  The phenomenon of enhancing or maintaining self-esteem through associating with winning teams has been called BIRGing, or basking in reflected glory.[22] When BIRGing, spectators are motivated by a desire to associate with a winner and, thus, present themselves in a positive light and enhance their self-esteem. Madrigal developed a model to explain why BIRGing might occur. He found that the three antecedent conditions that are related to BIRGing are expectancy disconfirmation, team identification, and quality of the opponent. In other words, BIRGing increases when the team does much better than expected, when the fan has high levels of association with the team, and when the team upsets stronger opponents.[23]

  Spectators who dissociate themselves from losing teams because that negatively affects self-esteem accomplish this through CORFing, or cutting off reflected failure. The BIRGing and CORFing behaviors even have a high-tech influence on fans. A recent study found that fans are more likely to visit their team's Web site after a victory and less likely to visit the site after a defeat.[24]

  A new construct has been posited to explain why some fans, although it may sound crazy, don't want to associate themselves with a winner. In this instance, although a team might have a winning record, fans may actually dissociate themselves from the team.

  Reasons for such behavior, know as CORSing (cutting off reflected success), may include rebelliousness, loyalty (to an earlier era, a previous style of play, prior coaching/management, etc.), a need for individuality (informally seen as a need to stand apart from the crowd), and possibly a fear of success (e.g., to ascend to new heights implies a chance for a greater fall). The CORSing fans do not want to be associated with the new era of winning; rather, they prefer to stay linked to the past. By CORSing the fans are managing their self-image through an expression of individualism.[25]

- *Diversion from Everyday Life*—Watching sports is seen as a means of getting away from it all. Most people think of sports as a novel diversion from the normal routines of everyday life. In a recent article, the University of Nebraska Cornhusker fans were cited as having intense emotional ties to the team, and it was stated that football served as a diversion from everyday life in Nebraska. "For several hours on a Saturday afternoon the struggling farmers of rural Nebraska—the inspiration for the school's nickname—can put aside their own problems and focus on someone else's."[26]

  In another example, there was great debate about whether and when major league Baseball and other sports would resume their schedules after the events of September 11. Ultimately, it was decided that play should go on to serve as diversion and to ensure that the American way of life was not disrupted.

- *Entertainment Value*—Entertainment is closely related to the previous motive for attendance. Sports serve as a form of entertainment to millions of people. As discussed in previous chapters, sports marketers are keenly aware of the heightened entertainment value of sports. In fact, one of the unique aspects of attending a sporting event is the uncertainty associated with the outcome. The drama associated with this uncertainty adds to the entertainment value of sports. Among spectators, the entertainment value of sports is believed to be the most highly motivating of all factors. In fact, Harris Interactive Company states that "contrary to popular belief, lowering ticket prices is not the best way—or even the most profitable way—to get people into seats. Creating an entertainment experience with flexible season tickets, VIP perks, etc., is a far better alternative. In short, people want to have fun, and for an increasing number of sports attendees this may have very little to do with the actual competition."[27]

A number of sports are attempting to find interesting and innovative ways to increase their entertainment value for the fans on the field of play by changing the rules of the game. College football officials felt they needed to do something to keep fans involved and entertained because five of the six major conferences averaged game times of more than 3.5 hours. Here's what the conferences have done to speed up the pace of play.[28]

First, the clock will start on kickoffs when the ball is kicked instead of when the receiving team touches the ball. This is not a big change and should have very little impact on the outcome of the game. But coaches will have to adjust, and this could shave around three or four plays off each contest.

Second, on changes of possession, the clock will start when the referee starts the 25-second play clock. This will have more of an impact on the games since 25 seconds will be able to run off the clock and teams will have to utilize their timeouts in a different fashion. Essentially, a team will be able to run the time off the clock four times during a set of downs instead of three. With teams being given only three timeouts each half, there will be one occasion when they will not be able to stop the clock.

Others feel that college football should consider adopting NFL rules to shorten game times. This includes shortening halftime to 15 minutes and not stopping the clock on first downs, which is too much of an advantage for the offensive team and allows them numerous built-in timeouts.

The NHL has also taken strides to improve the entertainment of the game through rule changes.[29] For starters, the dimensions of goaltender equipment will be reduced by more than 10 percent. In addition to a one-inch reduction (to 11 inches) in the width of leg pads, the blocking glove, upper-body protector, pants, and jersey will also be reduced. This should increase scoring and therefore increase fan entertainment.

Rink dimension will also be altered to increase offensive firepower. The neutral-zone edges of the blue lines will be positioned 64 feet from the attacking goal line and 75 feet from the end boards in the attacking zone. The addition of four feet in each of the offensive zones is intended to encourage more offensive play, particularly on power plays. The goal lines will be positioned 11 feet from the end boards, two feet closer to the end boards than before. The size of the neutral zone will be reduced to 50 feet from 54.

As the accompanying article indicates, sometimes having a solid product on the field of play or court still doesn't translate into game attendance.

- *Eustress*—Sports provide fans with positive levels of arousal. In other words, sports are enjoyable because they stimulate fans and are exciting to the senses. For example, imagine the excitement felt by Indy fans when the announcer says,

WNBA Has the Game, Not Fans

At 7:30 on a Friday night, you wouldn't expect to find the head of a major professional sports league hanging around her downtown Manhattan office taking phone calls from the media. But that is precisely what WNBA president Donna Orender was doing last week, working the clock in overdrive to help her 10-year-old league score more points.

Of course, her efforts parallel those of the WNBA itself at the halfway point of the 2006 season, as it prepares for tonight's All-Star Game at 7:30 in Madison Square Garden on ESPN. The league is riding a wave of heightened attention in the wake of several rules changes this year, chief among them a shortened shot clock that has significantly quickened the pace of the games and sent scoring to an all-time high.

Gone is the 30-second clock, replaced by the more prevalent 24-second clock, which has forced players to speed up their game and play offense with more abandon. In addition, the WNBA ditched the collegiate style of two halves in favor of the NBA's four quarters, enhancing the pro feel of the women's brand of basketball.

Orender was in attendance when the Minnesota Lynx set a league record for most points in a game, beating the Los Angeles Sparks 114–71—also tying the league mark for most 3-pointers in a game with 15. "It was awesome," she said. "The timing for these changes has been great: our 10th anniversary, with a chance to recognize the talent of these players and let them showcase what they've got, which they've been doing."

The numbers support that. Teams have been averaging seven points more than the league mark of 70 in 1998 and nearly 10 points more than last season. Furthermore, six teams are ahead of Houston's record of 77.3 points per game established in 2000.

"We've had more 70-point games, more 80, more 90," said Orender, in her second year on the job. "We have more shot attempts. I mean the whole thing has been elevated. And actually, as the game has gotten faster, the quality's even gotten better."

One offshoot of the speedier brand of ball is that coaches have had to rethink how they use their players, often working in 10 instead of eight per contest to give starters a chance to catch their breath. And more rookies are seeing increased action, with a chance to establish connections with fans as Phoenix's Cappie Poindexter has done. Poindexter set the league's rookie scoring record last week with 35 in a 91–76 victory over Detroit.

Still, getting fans into the stands remains a challenge for Orender, appointed to the job in 2005 by NBA commissioner David Stern after four years as the senior vice president of the PGA Tour. Despite the increase in the excitement quotient, attendance during the 2006 season has been around 7,100, lagging behind last year's average of 8,173.

"We want more people in the arenas, without a doubt," Orender said. "The reaction is that once people see it, they're very much taken by it and want to come back and experience more as they become connected to it. And so our job is to continue to create easy access ways for people to sample the great experience that it is."

Source: Dave Scheiber, *St. Petersburg Times,* July 12, 2006, http://www.sptimes.com/2006/07/12/Sports/WNBA_has_the_game_no.shtml.

"Gentlemen, start your engines" or the anticipation surrounding the opening kickoff for fans at the Super Bowl.

- *Economic Value*—A subset of sports fans are motivated by the potential economic gains associated with gambling on sporting events. Their enjoyment stems from having a vested interest in the games as they watch. Because this motive is only present for a small group of spectators, the economic factor is the least motivating of all factors. However, the number of spectators who gamble on sports continues to rise, especially among college students. Keith Whyte, executive director for the National Council on Problem Gambling, says, "college campuses bring together a lot of Internet access, a propensity for sports wagering, and most students have credit cards. We are seeing signs that it is becoming a problem."

Here are some staggering facts and figures[30] about the sports gambling market:

- Seven of 10 U.S. adults placed some sort of wager in the last year.
- According to the NCAA, 35 percent of male college students bet on sports.

SPORTS MARKETING HALL OF FAME

David Stern

David Stern, the commissioner of the NBA since 1984, has earned his place in sports marketing history. Stern is currently called the best commissioner in sport, the best in NBA history, and perhaps the best of any sport, ever. Prior to Stern, the NBA had a shaky network reputation, plummeting attendance figures, and no television contract.

During his tenure as commissioner, Stern took a floundering NBA and turned it "into an entity that is the envy of professional sports—an innovative, multifaceted, billion-dollar global marketing and entertainment company whose future literally knows no bounds." Stern has redefined the NBA and focused his marketing efforts on licensing, special events, and home entertainment. The league has gone from the arena business to radio, television, concessions, licensing, real estate, and home video—all under Stern's leadership. When the NBA was experiencing a public relations nightmare because of the number of players believed to be on drugs, it was again Stern who cleaned up the mess.

The All-Star Weekend, the made-for-television NBA lottery, making basketball the most popular sport in America with kids, and marketing the NBA across the world are all part of the sports marketing legacy that is David Stern.

Source: Adapted from E. M. Swift, "Corned Beef to Caviar," *Sports Illustrated* (June 3, 1991), 74–87.

- The online gambling industry generated $12 billion in revenue in 2005.
- Online sports betting is estimated to be five times bigger than Las Vegas sports betting. Illegal sports betting (barroom bookies) is estimated to be 35 times bigger than legalized sports gaming in the state of Nevada.
- The biggest sports betting company has a market value of almost $3 billion.
- The biggest sportsbooks employ over 2,000 people during football season.

To curb this trend, a bill was introduced in February 2000 by Senator Sam Brownback to make betting on college and amateur sports illegal anywhere in the United State.[31] In 2006, the House of Representatives passed a bill that made it illegal for Americans to use credit cards or checks for online gambling. Advocates of the ban say that these online games have left too many Americans crippled by addiction and debt. If they cannot access the games, they are less likely to blow the rent check on virtual craps. One bill that is being floated would remove the ban on Internet gambling and would put protections in place against underage gamblers, compulsive gamblers, fraud, and money laundering. Advocates of this proposed legislation say that it is not the government's job to monitor how and when consumers spend their time and money and point to the economic benefits of the industry.

- *Aesthetic Value*—Sports are seen by many as a pure art form. Basketball games have been compared with ballets, and many fans derive great pleasure from the beauty of athletic performances (e.g., gymnastics and figure skating).
- *Need for Affiliation*—The need for belonging is satisfied by being a fan. Research has shown that reference groups, such as friends, family, and the community, influence game attendance. The more an individual's reference group favors going to a game, the more likely the person will attend games in the future. Additionally, individuals who become fans of a team later in life (adolescence and adulthood) are more likely to be influenced by friends in forming an attachment with a particular team.[32]

In addition to influencing game attendance, one study found that reference groups can also affect other game-related experiences, such as perceived quality of the stadium, perceived quality of the food service, overall satisfaction with the stadium, and perceived ticket value. For instance, individuals who perceive their reference group as opposing going to games will also have less satisfaction with the stadium environment.

- *Family Ties*—Some sports spectators believe attending sporting events is a means for fostering family togetherness. The entire family can spend time together and lines of communication may be opened through sports. Interestingly, women are more motivated than men to attend sporting events to promote family togetherness.[33] Research has also shown that "fathers" are the persons who have the greatest influence in becoming a fan of a specific team. This is especially true for individuals who became fans early in life (preteen years). This finding has important implications for sports marketers in creating opportunities for fathers to interact with children in team-related activities.[34]

Game Attractiveness

Another factor related to game attendance is the perceived attractiveness of each game. **Game attractiveness** is a situational factor that varies from game to game and week to week. The perceived quality of a single game or event is based on the skill level of the individuals participating in the contest (i.e., the presence of any star athletes), team records, and league standings. In addition to these game-attraction variables, if the game is a special event (opening day, bowl game, or all-star game), game attractiveness is heightened. The more attractive the game, the more likely attendance will increase.

Economic Factors

Both the controllable and uncontrollable **economic factors** can affect game attendance. The controllable economic factors include aspects of the sports marketing environment that can be altered by sports marketers, such as the price of tickets and the perceived value of the sports product. The uncontrollable economic factors are things such as the average income of the population and the economic health of the country.

Generally, the greater the perceived value of the game and the greater the income of the population, the greater the game attendance. Surprisingly, one study found that attendance has no relationship to increased ticket prices.[35] In other words, raising ticket prices does not negatively affect game attendance. Other researchers, however, have found just the opposite.[36]

Competitive Factors

As discussed in Chapter 2, competition for sporting event attendance can be thought of as either direct (other sports) or indirect (other forms of entertainment). Ordinarily, the lesser the competition for spectators' time and money, the more likely they will be to attend your sporting event.

One form of direct competition of interest to sports marketers is the televised game. Sports marketers need to understand spectators' media habits and motivations to appeal to this growing segment. In addition, sports marketers want to learn whether to treat the viewing audience as a separate segment or whether it overlaps with spectators who attend games.

Some of these issues were addressed in a series of studies conducted to understand consumers' motivations for watching televised sports. Overall, the excitement, enthusiasm, and entertainment value associated with the telecasts are the primary motivating factors[37] Interestingly, the need for watching televised sports differed by gender. Women indicated they were more motivated to watch sports for the social value and the fact that friends and family were already doing so. Men, however, were motivated to watch sports on television because they enjoy the telecasts and find them entertaining.

With respect to their viewing behavior, men are more interested in watching sports on television, want more sports coverage, watch more sports coverage, and follow it up by watching news reports of the action more frequently than do their female counterparts. In short, men appear more highly involved in televised sports.

How does consuming the game via some alternative media such as radio, webcast, or television affect game attendance? One study examined the influence of television and radio broadcasting on the attendance at NBA games. The results indicated that television broadcasts of home games would have a negative impact on attendance, with over 60 percent of the fans indicating they would watch the game on television rather than attend. However, watching televised sports can also have a positive impact on home game attendance. For instance, the more one watches away games on television, the more one attends home games. In addition, the more one listens to the radio (for both home and away games), the greater the likelihood of attending home games.[38]

Demographic Factors

Demographic factors or variables, such as population, age, gender, education, occupation, and ethnic background, are also found to be related to game attendance. Although the number of women attending sporting events is greater than ever before, males are still more likely to be in attendance. The sports that possess the male fan base include the NFL, college football, and major league Baseball. The most avid female fans flock to figure skating, the NFL, and major league Baseball.

In addition, male sport fans tend to be younger, more educated, and have higher incomes than that of the general population. With the exception of baseball, the majority of ticket holders at sporting events now have annual income levels of $80,000 or more. According to the most recent census data, only 15 percent of American households reach this level of income, a relatively small market segment.[39] Interestingly, the National Hockey League, PGA Tour, and ATP (tennis) have the greatest percentage of fans with household incomes over $50,000.[40]

As you might imagine, it is very difficult to come up with the profile of the typical sports fan because of the varying nature of sport. However, it is important not to generalize and run the risk of neglecting a potentially huge market.[41]

Table 5.2 presents the demographic profile of Americans who consider themselves sports fans.

Stadium Factors

New stadiums are being built across the United States. Moreover, team owners who cannot justify or afford new stadiums are moving to cities that will build a new facility or attempt to renovate the existing stadium. Obviously, these stadium improvements are believed to affect the bottom line for team owners or for university presidents.

Stadium factors refer to variables such as the newness of the stadium, stadium access, aesthetics or beauty of the stadium, seat comfort, and cleanliness of the stadium. One study found that all these factors are positively related to game attendance. That is, the more favorable the fans' attitude toward the stadium, the higher the attendance.[42]

TABLE 5.2   Who's a Sports Fan?

Percentage of Americans who follow sports news "very" or "somewhat" closely

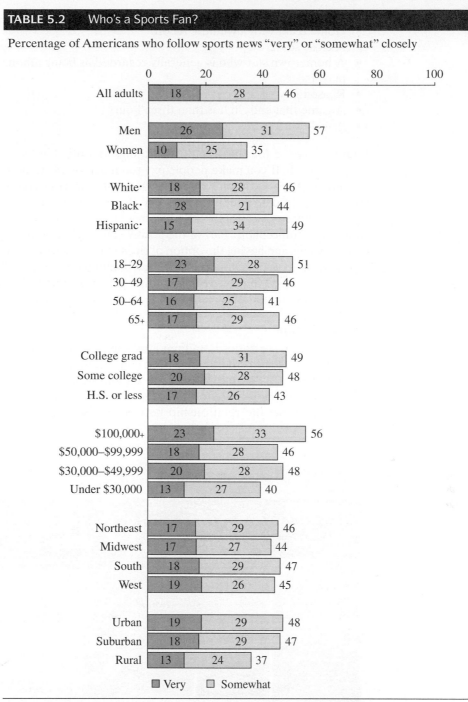

Source: Pew Research Center, pewresearch.org/social/chart.php?ChartID=135.

Similar results were found in a study conducted for *Money* magazine by IRC Survey Research Group.[43] This study looked at what 1,000 sports fans value when attending professional sporting events. The major findings, in order of importance, are:

- Parking that costs less than $8 and tickets under $25 each
- Adequate parking or convenient public transportation
- A safe, comfortable seat that you can buy just a week before the game

- Reasonably priced snack foods, such as a hot dog for $2 or less
- Home team with a winning record
- A close score
- A hometown star who is generally regarded as being among the sport's 10 best players
- Reasonably priced souvenirs
- A game that ends in less than three hours
- A wide variety of snack foods

Interestingly, the four most important things identified in the study were unrelated to the game itself. If you make people pay too much or work too hard, they would rather stay home. Apparently, only after you are seated in your comfortable chair with your inexpensive food do you begin to worry about rooting for the home team.

In addition, spectators were concerned about having a clean, comfortable stadium with a good atmosphere. Part of the positive atmosphere is having strict controls placed on rowdy fans and having the option of sitting in a nonalcohol section of the stadium. An emerging area of some importance to new stadium design, as well as to stadium rehabilitation, is the need to provide more and larger restrooms. Because stadium atmosphere seems to be so important to fans, let us examine it in greater detail.

Sportscape

As you might have noticed, stadium atmosphere appears to be a critical issue in game attendance. Recently, studies have been conducted in the area of stadium environment or "sportscape."[44] **Sportscape** refers to the physical surroundings of the stadium that affect the spectator's desire to stay at the stadium and ultimately return to the stadium. Figure 5.2 shows the relationship between these sportscape factors and spectator behavior.

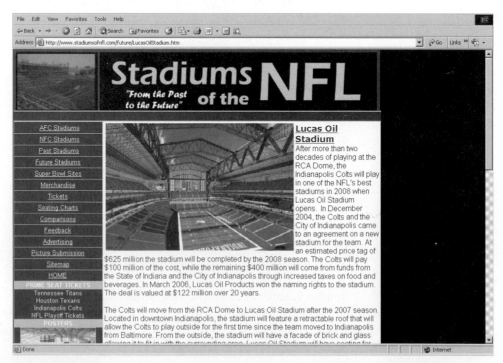

New sports facilities, such as the Lucas Oil Stadium in Indianapolis, influence attendance.
Source: Indianapolis Colts and Stadiums of the NFL.

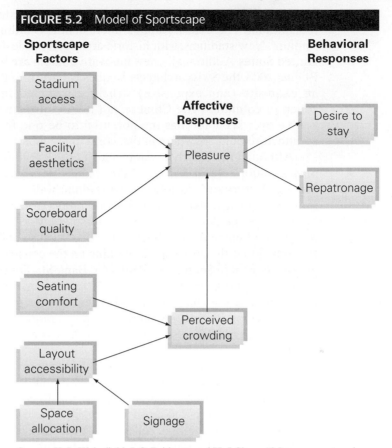

FIGURE 5.2 Model of Sportscape

Source: K. L. Wakefield, J. G. Bridgett, and H. J. Sloan, "Measurement and Management of the Sportscape," *Journal of Sport Management,* vol. 10, no. 6 (1996), 16. Reprinted by permission.

As shown in Figure 5.2, sportscape factors include stadium access, facility aesthetics, scoreboard quality, seating comfort, and layout accessibility. Each sportscape factor serves as input to the spectator's affective response or judgment of pleasure or displeasure with the stadium. The affective response, as we learned in Chapter 4, is the "feeling" component of attitudes. Similarly, the affective response with the sportscape is the feeling of perceived pleasure or displeasure the spectator has with the stadium. The perceptions of the stadium sportscape are linked to behavioral responses or actions of the spectator. In this case, the two behavioral responses are the desire to stay in the stadium and repatronage, or returning to the stadium for future events. Let us further examine the sportscape factors and their impact on spectators' pleasure.

Stadium Accessibility   Many of us have left sporting events early to avoid traffic hassles or walked long distances to get to a game because of limited parking. For example, I recently attended a game at Wrigley Field in Chicago and, because of limited parking spaces, had to walk over three miles to get to the game. By the time I reached my seat, it was the third inning! This experience certainly resulted in displeasure with the entire game experience.

Stadium access includes issues such as availability of parking, the ease of entering and exiting the parking areas, and the location of the parking relative to the stadium. From the spectator's perspective, anything that can make it easier to get in and out of the stadium quicker will positively affect a return for future games.

Facility Aesthetics   Facility aesthetics refers to the exterior and interior appearance of the stadium. The exterior appearance includes stadium architecture and age of the stadium. New stadiums, with historic architectural designs, are springing up across the United States. Additionally, new innovative stadia are being built around the word. For Beijing 2008, the Swiss architects Jacques Herzog and Pierre de Meuron have designed an exquisite (and expensive) structure wrapped in a delicate-looking tangle of concrete columns. (The Chinese call it "the bird's nest.") It looks like no stadium you've ever seen and has the potential to be one of the most significant pieces of architecture built anywhere in the world in the next five years.

Although the external beauty adds to the stadium aesthetics, the interior can also play a major role in fan satisfaction and attendance. The interior of the stadium includes factors such as color of the stadium walls, facades, and seats; the presence of sponsors' signage; and the presence of symbols from the team's past. For example, The Metrodome, the domed home of University of Minnesota football, has been rated the poorest stadium in the Big Ten Conference because of its sterile game day atmosphere. It's so bad that the university is working on the construction of a new stadium on campus set to open in September 2009. TCF Bank Stadium will feature 36 suites, 1,000 outdoor club seats, 300 indoor club seats, 59 loge boxes, a club lounge, a 20,000-square-foot facility for the marching band, and several locker rooms. Compare this with Fenway Park in Boston, one of the oldest and most unique stadiums in the United States. As former pitcher Bill Lee stated, "Fenway Park is a religious shrine. People go there to worship."

Obviously, professional sports franchises are not the only ones who care about facility aesthetics. University marketers and athletic departments are equally concerned with their venues. In a recent article, the top 10 college football venues were ranked based on atmosphere and aesthetics, tradition, and how well the team plays at home. The number one stadium in college sport was Ben Hill Griffin Stadium, also known as the "Swamp," at the University of Florida. The rest of the best in college facilities include the following: (2) Notre Dame Stadium—University of Notre Dame, (3) Husky Stadium—University of Washington, (4) Neyland Stadium—University of Tennessee, (5) Kyle Stadium—Texas A&M University, (6) Ohio Stadium—Ohio State University, (7) Tiger Stadium—Louisiana State University, (8) Memorial Stadium—University of Nebraska, (9) Michigan Stadium—University of Michigan, and (10) LaVell Edwards Stadium—Brigham Young University.[45]

Scoreboard Quality   One of the specific interior design considerations that represents a separate dimension of sportscape is **scoreboard quality.** In fact, the scoreboard in some stadiums is seen as the focal point of the interior. Throughout the game, fans continually monitor the stadium scoreboard for updates on scoring, player statistics, and other forms of entertainment, such as trivia contests, cartoon animation, and music videos. Examples of scoreboard quality range from the traditional scoreboard at Fenway Park, which is manually operated, to the NFL's biggest scoreboard at Heinz Field in Pittsburgh.

The scoreboard at Heinz measures 27 feet tall by 96 feet wide and is designed to create pure entertainment. Most of the entertainment will be produced like a TV show and feature in-stand giveaways, trivia contests, features on players, and facts and figures about the field. Rick Fairbend, the executive producer/broadcast manager for the Steelers, said that "[the fans] will be amazed at the whole entertainment package from now on."

Not to be outdone, the newest improvement to San Francisco's AT&T Park is an AVL-OD10 with a 20 mm physical pixel-pitch, 32-by-9 aspect ratio, and peak power consumption of 271 kW. In layman's terms, the Giants and AT&T introduced a 3,200-square-foot, high-definition Mitsubishi Electric Diamond Vision scoreboard—loaded with those above-mentioned technical features—in the 2007 season, along with 100 percent color LED information boards on the ballpark's Club Level.

Even smaller colleges like Coastal Carolina University are enjoying the benefits of custom scoreboards. Underscoring the importance of the scoreboard is Warren Koegel, athletic director at Coastal Carolina University, who believes that fans are used to high-definition TV and large-screen displays, so they made the decision to invest in top-of-the-line equipment.

Perceived Crowding   As shown in Figure 5.2, seating comfort and layout accessibility are the two factors that were found to be determinants of spectators' perceptions of crowding. Perceived crowding, in turn, is believed to have a negative influence on the spectator's pleasure. In other words, spectator pleasure decreases as perceived crowding increases.

Perceived crowding not only has an impact on pleasure but also on spectator safety. For example, English football grounds are moving away from terraces (standing areas renowned for hooliganism and violence) and toward a requirement of all-seater facilities. There has been a great deal of debate about reintroducing terracing. However, based on a report that identified all-seating as the factor that contributes the most to spectator safety, the British government has no plans to bring back terraces at English football grounds.[46]

Seating Comfort   **Seating comfort** refers to the perceived comfort of the seating and the spacing of seats relative to each other. Anyone who has been forced to sit among the more than 100,000 fans at a University of Michigan football game can understand the influence of seating on the game experience. Likewise, those who have been fortunate enough to view a game from a luxury box also know the impact of seating on enjoyment of the game. The latest seating innovation in new stadia is the "club seat." These seats typically offer the padded seat luxuries of a private box without the privacy. Club level seats commonly include climate-controlled lounges, multiple TV sets, buffets, parking benefits, concierge service, and more space between rows of seats.

Chris Bigelow, president of a facility management company, contends that more seating capacity in our stadiums will not guarantee financial success in the future. Less capacity with a higher level of comfort may be a much more profitable route to attracting fans. The trend should not be for more seats in a venue but for better seating. Bigelow states, "Our culture is willing to pay for comfort."

Layout Accessibility   **Layout accessibility** refers to whether spectators can move freely about the stadium. More specifically, does the layout of the stadium make it easy for spectators to get in and out of their seats and reach the concession areas, restrooms, and so on? To facilitate access to these destinations, there must be proper **signage** to direct spectators and there must be adequate **space allocation.** Inadequate space and signage cause spectators to feel confused and crowded, leading to negative feelings about the game experience.

As stated previously, all the sportscape factors affect spectators' feelings about the game experience. These positive or negative feelings experienced by spectators ultimately affect their desire to stay in the stadium and return for other games. Although all the sportscape factors are important, research has shown that perceived crowding is the most significant predictor of spectators having a pleasurable game experience. In addition, the aesthetic quality of the stadium was found to have a major impact on spectators' pleasure with the game.[47]

The findings of the sportscape research present several implications for sports marketers and stadium or facilities managers. First, stadium management should consider reallocating or redesigning space to improve perceived crowding. This might include enlarging the seating areas, walkways, and the space in and around concession waiting areas. Second, before spending the money to do major renovations or even building a new stadium to improve aesthetic quality, focus on more inexpensive alternatives. For instance, painting and cleaning alone might significantly improve the aesthetic value of an aging stadium.

UCLA has moved the Pauley Pavilion renovation process forward and will expand and improve the building that has been a campus landmark for more than 40 years and the home court of 38 NCAA championship teams. The goal is to dedicate the restored Pauley Pavilion on October 14, 2010, to honor Coach John Wooden on his 100th birthday. Among the many enhancements being considered are a new retractable seating system to bring spectators closer to the court and new concession areas, restrooms, and modern arena technology to enhance fan experience; new and expanded locker rooms, medical treatment and media rooms, and dedicated practice facilities; and a main lobby that would serve as a central entrance and celebrate UCLA's illustrious athletic tradition. These types of changes have provided downtown Cincinnati with a first-class facility that spectators feel good about, at a cost much lower than for new construction.[48]

Based on the studies conducted by Wakefield and his colleagues, there seems to be no doubt that the stadium atmosphere, or sportscape, plays a pivotal role in spectator satisfaction and attendance. Moreover, the pleasure derived from the sportscape causes people to stay in the stadium for longer periods of time. Certainly, having spectators stay in the stadium is a plus for the team, who will profit from increased concession and merchandise sales. In describing the importance of the sportscape, Wakefield states, "Effective facility management may enable team owners to effectively compete for consumers' entertainment dollars even when they may be unable to compete on the field."[49]

Value of Sport to the Community

Values, as you will recall, are widely held beliefs that affirm what is desirable. In this case, values refer to the beliefs about the impact of sport on the community. Based on the results of a recent study, spectators' perceptions of the impact of professional sport on a community can be grouped into eight value dimensions (see Table 5.3 for a brief description of values).

As you might expect, each value is related to spectators' game attendance and intentions to attend future games. For instance, spectators who believe sports enhance community solidarity are more likely to attend sporting events. Sport marketers should carefully consider these values and promote positive values when developing marketing strategy.

TABLE 5.3   Eight Value Dimensions of Sport to the Community

- *Community Solidarity*—Sport enhances the image of the community, enhances community harmony, generates a sense of belonging, and helps people to feel proud.
- *Public Behavior*—Sport encourages sportsmanship, reinforces positive citizenship, encourages obedience to authority, and nurtures positive morality.
- *Pastime Ecstasy*—Sport provides entertainment and brings excitement.
- *Excellence Pursuit*—Sport encourages achievement and success, hard work, and risk taking.
- *Social Equity*—Sport increases racial and class equality and promotes gender equity.
- *Health Awareness*—Sport eliminates drug abuse, encourages exercise, and promotes an active lifestyle.
- *Individual Quality*—Sport promotes character building and encourages competitive traits.
- *Business Opportunity*—Sport increases community commercial activities, attracts tourists, and helps community economic development.

Source: James J. Zhang, Dale G. Pease, and Sai C. Hui, "Value Dimensions of Professional Sport as Viewed by Spectators," Sports and Social Issues (February 21, 1996), 78–94. Reprinted by permission of Sage Publications, Inc.

CAREER SPOTLIGHT

Dan Mason, General Manager Rochester Red Wings, Triple A Affiliate of the Minnesota Twins

Career Questions

1. How did you get started in the sports industry? What was your first sports industry job?

    Started in January 1990 as an unpaid intern for the Rochester Red Wings. Doing an internship is paramount in getting started in this industry. I was very lucky when the team had an opening just before Opening Day that season and they hired me as the group sales director. I was responsible for selling tickets to corporate groups, Little Leagues, Scouts, churches, schools, and so on.

2. Can you describe the type of work you are doing right now? What are your job responsibilities? What are the greatest challenges?

    My job as general manager is to run the business side of our operation, including advertising sales, ticket sales, marketing, Web site, radio/TV broadcast, promotions, media/public relations, mascots, community relations, HR, accounting, and grounds crew. I also serve as the main contact with our major league affiliate. As a minor league GM, I don't make any player personnel decisions. Our major league affiliate (Minnesota Twins) supplies us with all of our players, manager, coaching staff, and trainer. The bottom line is that it's up to my staff and myself to make sure you have a great time when you come out to the ballpark.

    My staff and I are judged on our attendance and the two biggest factors that drive our attendance are the weather and the play of the team, neither of which we have any control over. So it can definitely be a challenge if you run into a bad stretch of weather or if the team has a lousy record. The other challenges that we face are that many people have less time available for entertainment or less money for entertainment these days.

    Our forms of competition are not just other sporting events but really any type of family entertainment options. . . . movies, cable TV, amusement parks, cottages/lakes, minigolf/golf.

3. Do you foresee any changes in demand in this field in the future? If so, what or how?

    The advent of so many new facilities and so many new leagues/teams over the last 10–15 years has created many more jobs in the sports management industry. There's a good chance that trend will continue for some time. In addition, many teams have decided to bring some jobs in-house rather than outsourcing certain responsibilities. For example, some major league teams have their own television networks now, with hours of programming dedicated to those teams. Also, food service at ballparks and arenas has become so much more sophisticated in the last decade with the advent of suites/club seats, and many teams have decided to manage their own concessions operation rather than subcontracting it out. And as attendance continues to soar in the majors and minors more staff is necessary to make sure the fan experience is as good as it can be.

4. Who or what has influenced you the most in your sports business career?

    Joe Altobelli is somebody I consider to be a mentor. Joe managed the Orioles to a World Championship in 1983 and was a player, coach, and manager for over 40 years. In 1992 he returned to his adopted hometown to become the Red Wings GM. I was the assistant GM at the time and what Joe taught me was immeasurable. He taught me how to treat people, how to manage, and how to get the most out of our staff. He also taught me how to speak in public and how to deal with the media, two important skills for any GM. Although he had no front office training, I couldn't have asked for a better teacher and I would never be where I am today without him. The other person that has influenced me the most is our chairman of the board and

    (Continued)

(Continued)

COO, Naomi Silver. Her father saved our team in the '50s and she had basically been raised at the ballpark and had been around this game her entire life. She decided that she wanted to follow in her dad's footsteps and learned every aspect of the operation from the ground up. She is one of the few female high-ranking officials in baseball and cares so much about our staff, our fans, and our community. She hired me as GM and I'll never be able to thank her enough for giving me that chance and for all the support she has given myself and our staff over the years. She leads by example and encourages all to strive for excellence. You'd be hard pressed to find somebody better to work for than Naomi.

5. What advice would you offer students who are considering a career in sports marketing?

My best suggestions are . . .

1. *Do an internship!* Be it at your school in the athletic department, your school newspaper, a local team, in almost any case you are going to have to do an internship before you get hired full time in this industry. It's the best way to try out a variety of jobs in this industry to see where you might want to focus your future in sports management.

2. Get some sales experience . . . almost every entry-level job in the minors will involve some type of sales no matter what your job title is. Most people will sell tickets, advertising, or food or a combination of the three. Especially in Minor League Baseball, GMs are looking for people who can sell.

3. Take a public speaking class. Fan interaction is essential, whether you're speaking one on one to a season seatholder or to two hundred members of your local Rotary club. Every member of our staff is a spokesperson for our team at some point.

4. Take some writing courses. Writing is a vital skill in many jobs in our industry.

5. You must be willing to work hard and put in some long hours. It takes a ton of effort to put on an event like a game. You must be willing to make sacrifices.

6. *Smile and have fun.* People come to our ballparks to have fun. If we don't act like we're happy to be there, how can we expect the fans to be? Fun is infectious . . . spread it around. I love what I do and I can't imagine doing anything else.

Sports Involvement

In Chapter 4, involvement was examined in the context of sports participation. Measures of sports involvement have also been used to understand spectator behavior. From the spectator's perspective, **sport involvement** is the perceived interest in and personal importance of sports to an individual attending sporting events or consuming sport through some other medium. What sports are people most interested in? Just 4 percent of adults in this country rate soccer as their favorite sport to watch, compared with 34 percent who say this about football, 14 percent about basketball, and 13 percent about baseball, according to a Pew Research Center study.

Fan interest and involvement in the remaining sports can be seen in Table 5.4.

Detailed studies have looked at the involvement levels of golf spectators, baseball spectators, Division I women's basketball spectators, and sports spectators in general.[50] In addition, a study has examined the cross-cultural differences in sport involvement (see Spotlight on International Sports Marketing). Generally, these studies have shown that higher levels of spectator involvement are related to the number of games attended, the likelihood of attending games in the future, and the likelihood of consuming sport through media, such as newspapers, television, and magazines. Also of importance, high-involvement spectators were more likely to correctly identify the sponsors of sporting events.

Fan Identification

Sports involvement was previously defined as the level of interest in and importance of sport to consumers. A concept that extends this idea to a sports organization is fan identification. Two contrasting examples of fan identification were seen with the movement of NFL franchises. When the Cleveland Browns moved to Baltimore,

TABLE 5.4 What's Your Favorite Sport?
Favorite sport to watch by interest in sports news

| | All Adults | Follow Sports | |
		Very/Some-What closely	Not very/Not at all closely
	%	%	%
Football	34	45	26
Basketball	14	18	11
Baseball	13	14	12
Soccer	4	6	2
Auto racing	4	4	4
Ice skating	3	1	5
Ice hockey	3	3	3
Golf	2	2	3
Tennis	2	2	2
Boxing	2	1	2
Wrestling	1	1	1
Other	5	2	8
None	12	1	20
Don't know	1	*	1
	100	100	100
Number of respondents	2,250	1,029	1,216

Source: http://pewresearch.org/pubs/?ChartID=140.

Browns fans became irate, holding protests and filing lawsuits to try to stop the team's move.[51] However, when the Houston Oilers moved to Nashville, relatively little fan resistance was observed, indicating low levels of fan identification.

Sports marketers are interested in building and maintaining high levels of fan identification for organizations and their players. If high levels of identification are developed, a number of benefits can be realized by the sports organization. Before examining the benefits of fan identification, let us take a closer look at what it is. **Fan identification** is defined as the personal commitment and emotional involvement customers have with a sports organization.[52] A conceptual framework was developed by Sutton, McDonald, Milne, and Cimperman for understanding the antecedents and outcomes of fan identification.[53] The model is shown in Figure 5.3.

Managerial correlates are those things such as team characteristics, organizational characteristics, affiliation characteristics, and activity characteristics that directly contribute to the level of fan involvement. Team characteristics include, most notably, the success of the team. Typically, the more successful the team, the higher the level of fan identification—because people want to associate themselves with a winner (BIRGing). However, some fans see loyalty to the team to be more important than team success. For instance, the Chicago Cubs continue to have high levels of fan identification even though they have not won the World Series since early in the twentieth century.

Organizational characteristics also lead to varying levels of fan identification. In contrast to team characteristics, which pertain to athletic performance, organizational characteristics relate to "off-the-field" successes and failures. Is the team trying to build a winning franchise or just reduce the payroll? Is the team involved in the community

FIGURE 5.3   Model for Fan Identification

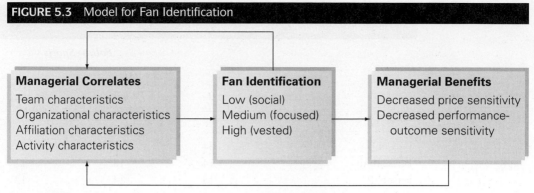

Source: William A. Sutton. *Sports Marketing Quarterly.* Reproduced with permission of Fitness Information Technology, Inc., in the format Textbook via Copyright Clearance Center.

and community relations? Is the team owner threatening to move to another city if a new stadium is not built with taxpayers' monies? An example of the impact of team and organizational characteristics on fan identification was provided by the Florida Marlins. As soon as the team won the 1997 World Series (team characteristic that should foster high fan identification), the owner talked about selling the team, and the organization traded several of its star players (organizational characteristic that will diminish fan identification).

Affiliation characteristics refer to the sense of community that a fan builds as a result of a team. According to Sutton et al., "The community affiliation component is . . . defined as kinship, bond, or connection the fan has to a team. Community affiliation is derived from common symbols, shared goals, history, and a fan's need to

A Web page for high identification fans.
Source: Used by permission of Kristen Cornette, webmaster. All rights reserved.

SPOTLIGHT ON INTERNATIONAL SPORTS MARKETING

A Comparative Analysis of Spectator Involvement: United States vs. United Kingdom

As the field of sports marketing expands into international markets, the success of U.S. sports entities will depend on understanding the core consumer abroad—the international sports fan. Recently, a study was conducted to better understand the domestic and U.K. sports fan by measuring sports involvement and by exploring the relationship between sports involvement and sports-related behaviors.

The findings indicated that there are two dimensions of sports involvement that are consistent across the U.S. and U.K. sample. The cognitive dimension refers to the way that consumers think about sports, and the affective dimension is the way that consumers feel about sports. Both the cognitive and affective factors were positively related to viewing sports on television, reading about sports in magazines and newspapers, attending sporting events, and participating in sports. That is, higher levels of involvement are related to more viewing, reading about, and attending sporting events.

There were some differences in the responses of people from the United States and the United Kingdom. People from the United Kingdom spent less time each week watching sports on television; however, they were more likely to read the sports section of the newspaper on a daily basis. Compared with the U.S. sample, people from the United Kingdom were less interested in local sports teams as opposed to national teams. Finally, the British respondents were more likely than their American counterparts to perceive sports as necessary, relevant, and important.

There were no significant differences in the responses of people from the two countries concerning (1) the likelihood of planning your day around watching a sporting event, (2) hours spent reading sports-related magazines, and (3) participation in sports-related activities.

Source: Adapted from Matthew Shank and Fred Beasley, "A Comparative Analysis of Sports Involvement: U.S. vs. U.K.," Advertising and Consumer Psychology Conference, Portland, OR, May 1998.

belong."[54] As discussed in the study on the impact of sports on the community, the sports team provides fans with a way to feel connected to the community and fulfill the **need for affiliation.** In addition, the more a fan's reference group (friends and family) favors going to games, the more the individual identifies with the team.[55]

Activity characteristics represent another antecedent to fan identification. In this case, activity refers to attending sporting events or being exposed to events via the media. As technology continues to advance, sports fans are afforded more opportunities to watch their favorite team via cable or pay-per-view, listen to games via radio, or link to broadcasts from anywhere via the Internet. With increased exposure, fan identification should be enhanced.

The interaction of the four preceding factors will influence the level of fan identification. An individual's level of identification with a team or player can range from no identification to extremely high identification. However, for simplicity, Sutton et al. describe three distinct categories of fan identification.[56]

Low Identification

Fans who attend sporting events primarily for social interaction or for the entertainment benefit of the event characterize low-level identification. These "social fans" are attracted by the atmosphere of the game, promotions or events occurring during the competition, and the feelings of camaraderie that the game creates. Although this is the lowest level of fan identification, if fans are reinforced by the entertainment benefits of the game, then they may become more involved.

Medium Identification

The next higher classification of fan involvement is called medium identification, or focused fans. The major distinguishing characteristic of these fans is that they identify with the team or player, but only for the short term. In other words, they may associate with the team, or player, if it is having an especially good year. However, when the team starts to slump or the player is traded, "focused" identification will fade. As with low-level identification, a fan that experiences medium levels of identification may move to higher levels.

High Identification

The highest classification of fan involvement is based on a long-term commitment to the sport, team, or player. These vested fans often recruit other fans, follow the team loyally, and view the team as a vital part of the community. Fans classified as high involvement exhibit a number of concrete behavioral characteristics. Most important, high-identification fans are the most likely to return to sporting events. Moreover, high-involvement fans are more likely to attend home and away games, have been fans for a greater number of years, and invest more financially in being a fan.

Managerial Benefits

The final portion of the fan identification model put forth by Sutton et al. describes the outcomes of creating and fostering vested fans. One outcome is that high-identification fans have decreased price sensitivity. Price sensitivity refers to the notion that small increases in ticket prices may produce great fluctuations in demand for tickets. Fans that stick with the team for the long run are more likely to be season ticket holders or purchase personal seat licenses to get the right to purchase permanent seats. Fans that exhibit low levels of identification may decide not to purchase tickets, even for small increases in ticket prices.

Another outcome of high levels of fan identification is decreased performance-outcome sensitivity. Stated simply, fans that are vested will be more tolerant of poor seasons or in-season slumps. Fans will be more likely to stick with the team and not give up prime ticket locations that may have taken generations to acquire.

Summary

In this chapter, we explored the spectator as a consumer of sport. Although there are many people who both participate in and observe sports, research suggests that there are two distinct segments of consumers. For instance, participants tend to be male, better educated, and younger than spectators.

There are a variety of factors that influence our decision to attend sporting events. These factors include fan motivation, game attractiveness, economic factors, competitive factors, demographic factors, stadium factors, value of sport to the community, sports involvement, and fan identification. Fan motivation factors are those underlying reasons or needs that are met by attending a sporting event. Researchers believe that some of the primary reasons fans attend sporting events are enhancement of self-esteem, diversion from everyday life, entertainment value, eustress (feelings of excitement), economic value (gambling on events), aesthetic value, need for affiliation, and time with family members.

Another factor that influences our decision to attend sporting events is game attractiveness. Game attractiveness refers to the perceived value and importance of the individual game based on what teams or athletes are playing (e.g., Is it the crosstown rival or is Ken Griffey, Jr. in town?), the significance of the event to the league standings, whether the event is postseason versus regular season competition, or whether the event is perceived to be of championship caliber (e.g., the four majors in golf or the NCAA Final Four). In general, the greater the perceived attractiveness of the game, the more likely we will want to attend.

Economic factors also play a role in our decision to attend sporting events. As we discussed briefly in

Chapter 2, the economic factors that may affect game attendance can be at the microeconomic level (e.g., personal income) or macroeconomic level (e.g., state of the nation's economy). Although these are uncontrollable factors, the sports organization can attempt to control the rising cost of ticket prices to make it easier for fans to attend sporting events.

Competition is another important factor that influences our decision to attend sporting events or observe them through another medium. Today, sports marketers must define the competition in broad terms—as other entertainment choices such as movies, plays, and theater compete with sporting events. Interestingly, sports organizations sometimes compete with themselves for fans. For example, one study found that televising home basketball games had a negative impact on game attendance.

Demographic factors such as age, ethnic background, and income are also related to spectator behavior. There is no such thing as a profile of the typical spectator. However, spectators are more likely to be male, young, more educated, and have higher incomes than that of the general population.

Perhaps the most important factor that influences attendance is the consumer's perception of the stadium. Stadium atmosphere appears to be a critical issue in attracting fans. The stadium atmosphere, or environment, has been referred to as the sportscape. The sportscape is the physical surroundings of the stadium that affect spectators' desire to stay at the stadium and ultimately return to the stadium. The multiple dimensions of sportscape include stadium access, facility aesthetics, scoreboard quality, seating comfort, and layout accessibility.

Another factor influencing game attendance and the likelihood of attending sporting events in the future is the perceived value of sport to the community. A study found that the more value attributed to sport, the more likely people were to attend. The value dimensions of sport to the community include community solidarity (bringing the community together), public behavior, pastime ecstasy (entertainment), pursuit of excellence, social equity, health awareness, individual quality (builds character), and business opportunities.

As discussed in Chapter 4, sports involvement refers to the consumer's perceived interest in and importance of participating in sport. Sports involvement has a related definition for those observing sporting events. High-involvement spectators are more likely to attend sporting events, read sports magazines, and plan their entire day around attending a sporting event.

A final factor related to spectator behavior is fan identification. Fan identification is the personal commitment and emotional involvement customers have with the sports organization. The characteristics of the team, the characteristics of the organization, the affiliation characteristics (sense of community), and the activity characteristics (exposures to the team) all interact to influence the level of fan identification. The higher the level of fan identification, the more likely fans are to attend events.

Key Terms

- aesthetic value p. 143
- demographic factors, p. 148
- diversion from everyday life, p. 143
- economic factors, p. 147
- economic value, p. 145
- entertainment value, p. 143
- eustress, p. 143
- facility aesthetics, p. 152
- family ties, p. 143
- fan identification, p. 157
- fan motivation factors, p. 142
- game attractiveness, p. 147
- layout accessibility, p. 153
- need for affiliation, p. 159
- scoreboard quality, p. 152
- seating comfort, p. 153
- self-esteem enhancement, p. 163
- signage, p. 153
- space allocation, p. 153
- sport involvement, p. 156
- sportscape, p. 150
- stadium access, p. 151
- stadium factors, p. 148

Review Questions

1. Describe the differences and similarities between spectators and participants of sport.
2. Discuss the spectators' eight basic motives for attending sporting events. Which of these are similar to the motives for participating in sports?
3. Provide two examples of how game attractiveness influences attendance.
4. What are the economic factors that influence game attendance? Differentiate between the controllable and uncontrollable economic factors.
5. Describe the typical profile of spectators of women's sporting events. How would a sports marketer use this information in the strategic sports marketing process?

6. Discuss, in detail, the sportscape model and how the sportscape factors affect game attendance.
7. What are the value dimensions of professional sport to the community? How would sports marketers use these values in planning the strategic sports marketing process?
8. Define sports involvement from the spectator perspective. Why is it important to understand the levels of involvement among spectators?

9. Discuss, in detail, the model of fan identification and its implications for sports marketers.
10. Explain the relationship among the eight basic fan motivation factors and the other factors that influence game attendance (i.e., game attractiveness, economic factors, competitive factors, demographic factors, stadium factors, value to the community, sports involvement, and fan identification).

Exercises

1. Go to a high school sporting event, college sporting event, and professional sporting event. At each event, interview five spectators and ask them why they are attending the events and what benefits they are looking for from the event. Compare the different levels of competition. Do the motives for attending differ by level (i.e., high school, college, and professional)? Are there gender differences or age differences among respondents?
2. Go to a sports bar and interview five people watching a televised sporting event. Determine their primary motivation for watching the sporting event. Describe other situations in which motives for watching sporting events vary.
3. Attend a women's sporting event and record the demographic profile of the spectators. What are your observations? Use these observations and suggest how you might segment, target, and position (market selection decisions) if you were to market the sport.
4. Attend a collegiate or professional sporting event. Record and describe all the elements of sportscape. How do these affect your experience as a spectator?
5. Ask 10 consumers about the value they believe a professional sports team would (or does) bring to the community. Then ask the same people about the value of college athletics to the community. Comment on how these values differ by level of competition.
6. How will marketing play a role in revitalizing the following sports: baseball, tennis, and cricket? How has marketing played a role in the increased popularity in the following sports: golf, basketball, and soccer?

Internet Exercises

1. Find examples via the Internet of how sports marketers have attempted to make it easier for fans to attend sporting events.
2. Locate two Web sites for the same sport—one for women and one for men (e.g., women's basketball and men's basketball). Comment on differences, if any, in how these sites market to spectators of the sport.
3. Locate two Web sites for the same sport—one American and one international (e.g., major league Soccer and British Premier League). Comment on differences, if any, in how these sites market to spectators of the sport.

Endnotes

1. John Burnett, Anil Menon, and Denise T. Smart, "Sports Marketing: A New Ball Game with New Rules," *Journal of Advertising Research* (September–October 1993), 21–33.
2. George R. Milne, William A. Sutton, and Mark A. McDonald, "Niche Analysis: A Strategic Measurement Tool for Managers," *Sport Marketing Quarterly,* vol. 5, no. 3 (1996), 17–22.
3. Ibid.
4. Ibid.
5. *Richard Petty Driving Experience,* http://www. 1800bepetty.com/experience/Ride.aspx.
6. Mauricio Ferreira and Ketra L. Armstrong, "An Exploratory Examination of Attributes Influencing Students' Decisions to Attend College Sport Events," *Sport Marketing Quarterly*, vol. 13 (1994), 194–208.
7. R. D. Hay and C. P. Rao, "Factors Affecting Attendance at Football Games," in M. Etzel & J. Gaski (Eds.), *Applying Marketing Technology to Spectator Sports* (South Bend, IN: University of Notre Dame Press, 1982), 65–76.
8. R. G. Noll, "Attendance and Price Setting." In R. G. Noll (Ed.). *Government and the Sports Business* (Washington, DC: The Brookings Institute, 1974), 115–157.
9. D. H. Rivers and T. D. DeSchiver, "Star Players, Payroll Distribution, and major league Baseball Attendance," *Sport Marketing Quarterly,* vol. 1 (2002),164–173.

10. H. Hansen and R. Gauthier, "Factors Affecting Attendance at Professional Sport Events", *Journal of Sport Management,* vol. 3, (1989), 15–32.

11. J. J. Zhang, D. G. Pease, S. C. Hui, and T. J. Michaud, "Variables Affecting the Spectator Decision to Attend NBA Games," *Sport Marketing Quarterly,* vol. 4, no. 4 (1995), 29–39.

12. J. R. Hill, J. Madura, and R. A. Zuber, "The Short Run Demand for major league Baseball," *Atlantic Economic Journal,* vol. 10 (1982), 31–35.

13. M. McDonald and D. Rascher, "Does Bat Day Make Sense? The Effect of Promotions on the Demand for major league Baseball," *Journal of Sport Management,* vol. 14 (2000), 8–27.

14. R. A. Baade and L. J. Tiehen, "An Analysis of major league Baseball Attendance, 1969–1987," *Journal of Sport & Social Issues,* vol. 14, no. 1 (1990), 14–32.

15. J. A. Schofield, "Performance and Attendance at Professional Team Sports," *Journal of Sport Behavior,* vol. 6 (1983), 196–206.

16. S. E. Iso-Ahola, "Attributional Determinants of Decisions to Attend Football Games," *Scandinavian Journal of Sports Sciences,* vol. 2 (1980), 39–46.

17. D. L. Wann, A. Roberts, and J. Tindall, "The Role of Team Performance, Team Identification, and Self-Esteem in Sport Spectators' Game Preferences," *Perceptual and Motor Skills,* vol. 89 (1999), 945–950.

18. R. G. Noll, "Attendance and Price Setting," in R. G. Noll (Ed.), *Government and the Sports Business* (Washington, DC: The Brookings Institute, 1974), 115–157.

19. J. M. Schwartz, "Causes and Effects of Spectator Sports," *International Review of Sport Sociology,* vol. 8 (1973), 25–45.

20. G. Trail, D. F. Anderson, and J. Fink, "A Theoretical Model of Sport Spectator Consumption Behavior," *International Journal of Sport Management,* vol. 1 (2000), 154–180.

21. Daniel L. Wann, "Preliminary Validation of the Sport Fan Motivation Scale," *Journal of Sport & Social Issues* (November 1995), 337–396.

22. R. B. Cialdini, R. J. Borden, A. Thorne, M. R. Walker, S. Freeman, and L. R. Sloan, "Basking in Reflected Glory: Three (Football) Field Studies," *Journal of Personality and Social Psychology,* vol. 34 (1976), 366–375.

23. Robert Madrigal, "Cognitive and Affective Determinants of Fan Satisfaction with Sporting Events," *Journal of Leisure Research,* vol. 27 (Summer 1995), 205–228.

24. Flip Boen, N. Vanbeselaere, and J. Feys, "Behavioral Consequences of Fluctuating Group Success: An Internet Study of Soccer-Team Fans," *The Journal of Social Psychology,* vol. 142 (2002), 769–782.

25. Richard M. Campbell, Jr., Damon Aiken, and Aubrey Ken, "Beyond BIRGing and CORFing: Continuing the Exploration of Fan Behavior," *Sport Marketing Quarterly,* vol. 13 (2004), 151–157, © 2004 West Virginia University.

26. Malcolm Moran, "For Nebraska, Football Is Personal," *USA Today* (October 27, 2000).

27. "Get Them Out to the Ballpark—and Off of the Couch," Harris Interactive, *Sporttainment News,* vol. 1, no. 3 (June 12, 2001).

28. "Rule Changes in College Football," http://www.phoenixsports.com/list_articles.php?cappers_article_id123=459&show=articles.

29. "ESPN.com—NHL—Rules: Changes Are Widespread," sports.espn.go.com/nhl/news/story?id = 2114523.

30. http://sportsgambling.about.com/od/legalfacts/a/Betting_Facts.htm.

31. Rick Alm, "Brownback Aims to Ban All Betting on Colleges," *The Kansas City Star* (February 2, 2000), A1.

32. Richard Kolbe and Jeffrey James, "An Identification and Examination of Influences That Shape the Creation of Professional Team Fan," *International Journal of Sports Marketing and Sponsorship,* vol. 2 (2000), 23–38.

33. Daniel L. Wann, "Preliminary Validation of the Sport Fan Motivation Scale," *Journal of Sport & Social Issues* (November 1995), 337–396.

34. Richard Kolbe and Jeffrey James, "An Identification and Examination of Influences That Shape the Creation of Professional Team Fan," *International Journal of Sports Marketing and Sponsorship,* vol. 2 (2000), 23–38.

35. R. A. Baade and L. J. Tiechen, "An Analysis of major league Baseball Attendance, 1969–1987," *Journal of Sport & Social Issues,* vol. 14 (1990), 14–32.

36. Brad Edmondson, "When Athletes Turn Traitor," *American Demographics* (September 1997). www.demographics.com/publications/ad/97_ad/9709_ad/ad970916.htm.

37. Walter Gantz, "An Exploration of Viewing Motives and Behaviors Associated with Televised Sports," *Journal of Broadcasting* (1981), 263–275.

38. James Zhang and Dennis Smith, "Impact of Broadcasting on the Attendance of Professional Basketball Games," *Sport Marketing Quarterly,* vol. 6, no. 1 (1997), 23–32.

39. Noel Paul, "High Cost of Pro-Sports Fandom May Ease Attendance at Most Major Events Drop—and Ticket Prices Are Expected to Follow," *Christian Science Monitor* (November 19, 2001), p. 16.

40. "2003 ESPN Sports Fan Poll Is Now Available," Sporting Goods Manufacturers Association, www.sgma.com/press/2003.

41. Donna Lopiano, "Marketing Trends in Women's Sports and Fitness," *Women's Sports Foundation.* www.lifetimetv.com/sports/index.html.

42. Kirk L. Wakefield and Hugh J. Sloan, "The Effects of Team Loyalty and Selected Stadium Factors on Spectator Attendance," *Journal of Sport Management* (1995), 153–172.

43. Jillian Kasky, "The Best Ticket Buys for Sports Fans Today," *Money,* vol. 24, no. 10 (October 1995), 146.

44. Kirk L. Wakefield, Jeffrey G. Blodgett, and Hugh J. Sloan, "Measurement and Management of the Sportscape," *Journal of Sport Management* (1996), 15–31.

45. Kevin Acee, "States of Grace; College Football's Finest Venues Are Almost Shrines to the Game," *The San Diego Union Tribune* (October 20, 2001), D2.

46. "British Sports Minister Says 'The Terraces Are History.' " (October 1997), www.nando.net/newsroom/spor.../feat/archive/102297/ssoc45127.html.

47. Kirk L. Wakefield, Jeffrey G. Blodgett, and Hugh J. Sloan, "Measurement and Management of the Sportscape," *Journal of Sport Management* (1996), 15–31.

48. Andy Hemmer, "Gardens Gets Skyboxes in Makeover," *Cincinnati Business Courier Inc.,* vol. 11, no. 48 (April 10, 1995), 1.

49. Kirk L. Wakefield, Jeffrey G. Blodgett, and Hugh J. Sloan, "Measurement and Management of the Sportscape," *Journal of Sport Management* (1996), 15–31.

50. Deborah L. Kerstetter and Georgia M. Kovich, "An Involvement Profile of Division I Women's Basketball Spectators," *Journal of Sport Management,* vol. 11 (1997), 234–249; Dana-Nicoleta Lascu, Thomas D. Giese, Cathy Toolan, Brian Guehring, and James Mercer, "Sport Involvement: A Relevant Individual Difference Factor in Spectator Sports," *Sport Marketing Quarterly,* vol. 4, no. 4 (1995), 41–46.

51. Geoff Hobson, "Just Another Sunday," *The Cincinnati Enquirer* (December 7, 1996).

52. William A. Sutton, Mark A. McDonald, George R. Milne, and John Cimperman, "Creating and Fostering Fan Identification in Professional Sports," *Sport Marketing Quarterly,* vol. 6, no. 1 (1997), 15–22.

53. Ibid.

54. William A. Sutton, Mark A. McDonald, George R. Milne, and John Cimperman, "Creating and Fostering Fan Identification in Professional Sports," *Sport Marketing Quarterly,* vol. 6, no. 1 (1997), 15–22.

55. Ibid.

56. Ibid.

6

SEGMENTATION, TARGETING, AND POSITIONING

After completing this chapter, you should be able to:

■ Discuss the importance of market selection decisions.

■ Compare the various bases for marketing segmentation.

■ Understand target marketing and the requirements of successful target marketing.

■ Describe positioning and its importance in the market selection decisions.

■ Construct a perceptual map to depict any sports entity's position in the marketplace.

Market selection decisions are the most critical elements of the strategic sports marketing process. In this portion of the planning phase, decisions are made that will dictate the direction of the marketing mix. These decisions include how to group consumers together based on common needs, whom to direct your marketing efforts toward, and how you want your sports product to be perceived in the marketplace. These important market selection decisions are referred to as segmenting, targeting, and positioning (STP). In this chapter, we examine these concepts in the context of our strategic sports marketing process. Let us begin by exploring market segmentation, the first of the market selection decisions.

SEGMENTATION

Not all sports fans are alike. You would not market the X Games to members of the American Association of Retired People (AARP). Likewise, you would not market the PGA's Champions Tour to Generation Xers. The notion of mass marketing and treating all consumers the same has given way to understanding the unique needs of groups of consumers. This concept, which is the first market selection decision, is referred to as market segmentation. More specifically, **market segmentation** is defined as identifying groups of consumers based on their common needs.

Market segmentation is recognized as a more efficient and effective way to market than mass marketing, which treats all consumers the same. By carefully exploring and understanding different segments through marketing research, sports marketers determine which groups of consumers offer the greatest sales opportunities for the organization.

If the first market selection decision is segmentation, then how do sports marketers group consumers based on common needs? Traditionally, there are six common bases for market segmentation. These include demographics, socioeconomic group, psychographic profile, geographic region, behavioral style, and benefits. Let us take a closer look at how sports marketers use and choose from among these six bases for segmentation.

Bases for Segmentation

The bases for segmentation refer to the ways that consumers with common needs can be grouped together. Six bases for segmenting consumer markets are shown in Table 6.1.

Demographic Segmentation

One of the most widely used techniques for segmenting consumer markets is **demographic segmentation**. Demographics include such variables as age, gender, ethnic background, and family life cycle. As the accompanying article illustrates, sports fans may even be segmented by their religious affiliation.

Segmenting markets based on demographics is widespread for three reasons. First, these characteristics are easy for sports marketers to identify and measure. Second, information about the demographic characteristics of a market is readily available from a variety of sources, such as the government census data described in Chapter 3. Third, demographic variables are closely related to attitudes and sport behaviors, such as attending games, buying sports merchandise, or watching sports on television.

Age   Age is one of the most simplistic, yet effective demographic variables used to segment markets. Not only is age easy to measure, but it also is usually related to consumer needs. In addition, age of the consumer is commonly associated with other demographic characteristics, such as income, education, and stage of the family life cycle. A number of broad age segments exist such as the children's market, the teen market, and the mature market. Care must be taken, however, not to stereotype consumers when using age segmentation. How many 10-year-olds do you know who think they are 20, and how many 75-year-olds think they are 45?

Children.   There has always been a natural association between children and sports. However, sports marketers are no longer taking the huge children's market for granted—and with good reason. Children have tremendous influence on purchasing decisions within the family and are increasingly purchasing more and more on their own.[1]

TABLE 6.1	Sports League Interest		
	Total (%)	*Male (%)*	*Female (%)*
NFL (National Football League)	52	**67**	36
NBA (National Basketball Association)	40	**50**	30
MLB (Major League Baseball)	37	**46**	28
NCAA Football (College Football)	32	**45**	19
NCAA Men's Basketball (College Basketball)	30	**41**	19
WWE (World Wrestling Entertainment)	24	**32**	15
NASCAR (stock-car Racing)	23	**30**	16
UFC/Pride (Ultimate Fighting Championship)	19	**29**	9
MLS (Major League Soccer)	18	**23**	14
NLL (National Lacrosse League)	7	**8**	5

Bolding *denotes significant difference*
Source: The TRU Study 2008.

Our Father Who Art at Home Plate

A U.S. Christian marketing company that organizes "faith nights" at sporting arenas is in negotiations to bring its events to Canada, talking to franchises with both the NHL and CFL. Brent High, president of Third Coast Sports, a Nashville-based company that has helped bring Christian fans out to cheer teams ranging from the Odessa Jackelopes to the Atlanta Braves, says he has spoken to several Canadian sports teams about potential partnerships.

Third Coast Sports signs on with individual teams to draw Christian fans to games in exchange for a cut of ticket sales or a percentage of sponsorship deals. In the southern U.S., faith nights are as common at minor league ball games as hot dogs and beer, and usually involve a Christian rock band and revival meeting held on site—but off the field—before or after the game.

The idea of bringing together church and home plate has recently caught on in major league sports, with team executives hoping Third Coast can boost attendance the same way the Evangelical community has been credited with making Mel Gibson's *Passion of the Christ* a success and ensuring George W. Bush's presidential reelection. This year, Mr. High's company is organizing more than 70 events in 44 markets, and word of faith nights' success has spread north of the border and overseas.

"The problem we work against in the summertime is that you've got mission trips, Bible school, family vacation, church camp—all this stuff happens in the summer and takes away from the baseball events," he said. "During the winter, they're all kind of in pocket. We think we'll have even better success."

After Third Coast signs on with a team, it contacts leaders within the market's Christian community, from priests to youth pastors to Sunday school teachers.

Those individuals promote the event within their networks, and Third Coast supplements their efforts with phone calls, direct mail campaigns, and the lure of Bible Bobbleheads, figurines shaped like Moses and other Christian figures and given away at faith night events. "People line up hours before the gates even open to make sure they get one," Mr. High said.

"Sports execs are all about trying to reach out to people, and if religion can be one of those things without causing controversy or division or alienating in nature, they're going to continue to respond to it," he said. There are some cities where the nights have not been overly successful, but Mr. High said those failures had more to do with organizers than interest levels.

One Third Coast arena football event held in Las Vegas drew an additional 2,000 fans, he noted, the highest Sunday game attendance in team history. "This will work anywhere," he said. "There are Christian people everywhere."

But the concept of bringing a religious message into a sporting event is not without controversy. This month, the Associated Press reported that the Atlanta Braves has barred Focus on the Family from participating in faith nights organized by Third Coast. The controversial conservative group founded by James Dobson was barred from the arena after sponsoring an event in July, reportedly because of comments made at the game comparing homosexuality to a disease or addiction.

Source: Siri Agrell, *National Post* (f/k/a *The Financial Post*) (Canada), August 28, 2006, p. A3.

Kids influence the sale of $200 billion of all products and services sold per year. In the United States, kids aged three to 11 comprise a population subgroup of 36 million that had a collective $18 billion in purchasing power last year, according to estimates in *The Kids' Market in the U.S.* The report projects that the kids' market will see significant growth over the next four years, reaching $21.4 billion in "disposable income" by 2010.[2]

Approximately 8 percent of all sports equipment is purchased by children, and 10 percent of all sports equipment purchases are influenced by children.[3] Children are participating in sports and are identifying with teams, players, and brands at younger ages each year. Thus, sports marketers have recognized the power of the kids' market. They realize children will become the fans and the season ticket holders of the future. As such, they have segmented markets accordingly.

Examples of sports marketers reaching the kids' market are plentiful. For instance, Fisher-Price, the toy company, is in the final stages of negotiations to acquire a NASCAR license to produce battery-operated race cars for children. The mini-vehicles

American Youth Football targets youth football and cheering.
Source: American Football Inc.

with engine sound effects will normally feature two gears to achieve speeds of 2.5 or 5 mph, plus reverse, and will sell for around $220.

The Houston Astros and Minute Maid unveiled the redesigned Squeeze Play interactive entertainment center at Minute Maid Park designed for fans ages 12 and under. Sponsored by Minute Maid, Squeeze Play features a new virtual reality hitting game and pitching cage and a new, multistory climbing structure where kids can climb through a replica of Minute Maid Park, complete with its own train.

In 1998, the NFL and the NFL Players Association formed the NFL Youth Football Fund (YFF), a 501(c)3 nonprofit foundation that supports the game at the youth level and promotes positive youth development.

The NFL conducts six youth football clinics for more than 600 elementary school students on Oahu during Pro Bowl Week. Similarly, the NHL has a learn-to-skate program. Since the program's inception in 1996, more than 40,000 youngsters, starting at the age of six, have attended. There currently are 39 programs in 15 states, three Canadian provinces, and the District of Columbia.

The children's segment is also growing in importance to those organizations marketing to kids via the Internet. For example, ToysRUs.com recently introduced a new sporting goods site called SportsRUs.com with a "just for kids" area designed to help parents select sports equipment for kids ages five to 12. In another example, the President's Council on Physical Fitness and Activity has launched a Web site (www.presidentschallenge.org) to help motivate kids and families become more physically active. The NFL is also trying to promote fitness for children through its youth clinics. The "NFL Fitness Through Football Youth Clinics" incorporate physical education activities with a football emphasis, including agility drills, throwing, catching, and relay races.

Teens.   The number of teens is also expected to rise exponentially, because the U.S. Census Bureau projects that by 2010 there will be 30.81 million teens in the United

Professional sports are realizing the importance of the kid's market to their long-term success.

States.[4] With an estimated spending power of $153 billion in 2006,[5] teenagers present a vast marketing opportunity that is multifaceted and touches on many products and services. One key to reaching this teen market is to involve them in the marketing process and engage them in the brand. What brands (or leagues, in this case) are hot with teens? Figure 6.1 shows the pro sports of interest to the teen market, including differences among males and females.

Although teens represent a sizable and important market, sports marketers must better understand this group, or it will be lost. For instance, American teens are not tuning in to major sporting events in large numbers, at least not compared with the general population. None of the traditional championships attract a television audience that is higher than 7.3 percent of teens ages 12–17. For the Daytona 500 and the World Series, only about one in 30 television viewers are teens. The one championship that can claim more than 10 percent of its audience is teenagers is the X Games, but even that finds the overwhelming majority its viewers from outside the teen ranks.

What can sport marketers do to better reach teens? As the accompanying article illustrates, thinking "outside the norm" may be the answer.

The Mature Market. Another market that is expected to increase at a staggering pace is the age 55 and older, mature market. **Mature adults, age 55-plus** number some 59 million or roughly 21 percent of the U.S. population. Their staggering numbers equal the entire populations of New York and California, Washington State, and the District of Columbia, or New York, California, and Massachusetts combined. Additionally, people age 65-plus comprise 12.4 percent of the population, and this number is expected to double to 70.3 million by 2030.[6]

Stereotypically, the elderly are perceived to be inactive and thrifty. Nothing could be further from the truth. The mature market is living longer and becoming more physically active. In addition, income per capita of the mature market is 26 percent higher than the national average, and this segment spends more than one trillion dollars on goods and services. As a result, sports marketers are capitalizing on this growing market in a variety of ways.

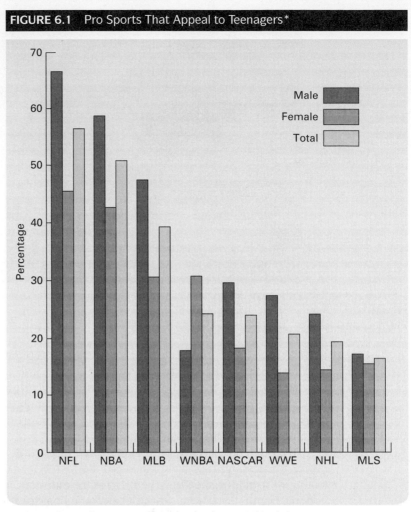

FIGURE 6.1   Pro Sports That Appeal to Teenagers*

* Youth who say they are very or somewhat interested in the sport.
Source: Teen Research Unlimited.

Traditionally, senior citizen discounts have been promoted in Major League Baseball. For example, the Milwaukee Brewers created the 60+ fan club, providing tickets, merchandise, and other special promotional offers to seniors. Promotions such as the "World's Oldest Tailgate Party" are designed to strengthen the relationship between the Brewers and the teams' senior fans.[7]

Reaching Youthful Audience Demands Break from the Norm

With an average attendance of more than 46,000 over five events in its inaugural 2005 season, the Dew Action Sports Tour topped the average attendance of every team in the NBA, NHL, and MLB with the exception of the New York Yankees.

How did an action sports tour, long regarded as a niche market, outdraw some of the most storied sports institutions in the United States?

By clearly identifying and doing everything possible to connect to its target market—in this case, extreme sports fans in Generation Y.

From the beginning, officials discussed with that demographic (the 60 million young adults born between 1979 and 1994) how to make the Dew Tour a success. The team designing the logos for the tour hung out at skate parks and surf shops, talking to the

(Continued)

(*Continued*)

event's core audience and involving them in the creative process.

This tactic is especially useful when marketing to Generation Y, who are a central part of virtually every sports organization's target market. Not only does the technique ensure that an organization's marketing strategy, visual design, and branding appeal to its target demographic, but it also begins the process of creating a community around the product.

Studies have shown that Generation Y, which has grown up being bombarded daily by advertisements, is much more influenced by the opinions of friends and others with similar interests than by traditional advertising.

How, then, can a sports organization cultivate and create a community of fans and supporters?

Many marketers try to dazzle this audience with slick graphics and flashy Web sites. A much more effective strategy is to stick to principles that will keep a marketing plan focused on meeting the needs, and therefore gaining the loyalty, of Generation Y.

A Few Guidelines

- *Understand your audience:* Generation Y is a complex, diverse, and often poorly understood demographic. There is no such thing as a unified Generation Y point of view.

  You must identify and understand a specific target segment of the population. Make sure that your research includes your target market's favorite methods of communication (often cell phone or Internet-based) and entertainment activities.
- *Talk to the consumer:* The only way to be sure that your research is on the mark is to confirm it in face-to-face interactions. Don't send the intern.

  Have the decision makers and those in charge of the product talk to the people who will be consuming it.
- *Be honest:* Generation Y is skeptical when it comes to marketing and will tend to disbelieve any claim you make unless and until it has been independently verified.

  This means that (a) you shouldn't make any claims that you can't support, and (b) you should work to become a trusted informational resource on your product and your industry.
- *Use new tools:* Generation Y sees billboards, television and print ads, and Internet banners as annoying clutter. To get your message across, you will have to find new ways to communicate your message.

  Branded events, interactive Internet campaigns, and sponsoring consumer-generated media have all been successfully employed to connect to a Generation Y market. The trick is to make sure that a clear and beneficial connection exists among your product, your target market, and your campaign.
- *Stay focused:* Sometimes the process of creating and executing a marketing strategy can defeat the strategy itself. A great idea gets bogged down in the bureaucratic process, an executive wants to change the plan because it doesn't suit his or her personal taste, or too many compromises result in a mixed message that confuses and alienates consumers.

  Generation Y responds to short, focused, relevant messages (think of the popularity of text messaging), so keep your strategy focused on a small number of key points that will resonate with your audience.

The Dew Action Sports Tour connected to teens because it developed a strategy that encompassed the simple guidelines above. Instead of relying on the popular perception that teens are naturally attracted to anything having to do with action sports, the tour took the time to understand its audience, even using it to check its own designs and plans.

The Dew Tour sought out new ways to communicate with the consumer and never lost sight of the fact that the Tour shouldn't be designed for boardroom executives. It should be designed for the consumers who will ultimately decide its success or failure.

Using this model will help any company to connect with its target audience. The advantage is particularly significant if that target audience includes Generation Y.

Keys to Connecting with Generation Y

Do's	Don'ts
- Identify your audience.	- Homogenize your message.
- Become a trusted resource.	- Make claims you can't back up.
- Know how they communicate.	- Rely on the usual clutter.
- Keep the message relevant.	- Get bogged down in bureaucracy.

Source: Sports Business Journal, October 2, 2006, p. 21, http://www.sportsbusinessjournal.com /index.cfm? fuseaction=search.show_article&articleId=52109&keyword=Reaching%20youthful%20audience %20demands%20break%20from%20the%20norm.

Other examples of sports markets being segmented by age can be seen in the growing number of "senior" sporting tours and events. The Champions Tour of the PGA has nearly the following of the regular tour events. Although not as successful as the golf tour, other professional senior tours include tennis and bowling.

Seniors are also becoming more active as sports participants. The fastest-growing participation sports for seniors, classified as age 55 and older, include exercising to music and running or walking on the treadmill. Table 6.2 shows some of the most popular sports for the mature market.

Worldwide sports participation is also growing in the senior segment. The Israeli Senior Olympic Games have grown into an annual event drawing around 350 senior athletes from around the country. The games, officially known as SABA—the Hebrew word for grandfather and the Israeli acronym for Sport, Health, Quality of Life—were created to highlight the positive side of aging and to challenge older adults to maintain an active lifestyle long after they retire. With more than 11 percent of all Israelis over the age of 65, it is no wonder that the SABA games are so well received. Professor Yitzhak Brick, one of SABA's organizers, states, "These competitions show just how much older people can achieve in sport. This demonstration of excellence is important in motivating other seniors to start participating in physical activity."[8] This example of the senior athletes in Israel is representative of the mature market worldwide and demonstrates what a vibrant, independent, and viable segment this is for sport marketers.

Gender The number of women who now indicate that they are interested in sports is approaching 50 percent, according to a recent ESPN poll. The NBA and Major League Baseball were tied with 46 percent of women indicating that they were interested in the league, followed by the NFL at 44 percent, the NHL (42 percent), and NASCAR (41 percent).

TABLE 6.2	Most Popular Sports/Athletic/Fitness Activities U.S. Population, Age 55+, Based on Total Participation	
Rank	*Athletic Activity*	*Participants*
1.	Fitness walking	10.3 million
2.	Treadmill exercise	8.8 million
3.	Stretching	8.2 million
4.	Hand weights	5.3 million
5.	Golf	4.9 million
6.	Freshwater fishing	4.6 million
7.	Day hiking	3.7 million
8.	Weight/resistance machines	3.6 million
9.	Stationary cycling (upright bike)	3.4 million
10.	Bowling	3.3 million
11.	Recreational vehicle camping	2.8 million
12.	Saltwater fishing	2.7 million
13.	Other exercise to music	2.6 million
14.	Dumbbells	2.5 million
15.	Stationary cycling (recumbent bike)	2.4 million

Source: From *SGMA's Superstudy of Sports Participation.* http://www.sgma.com/displayindustryarticle.cfm?articlenbr=31547&startrec=21SENIORSENSATIONSOFSPORTS&FITNESS-SGMAStudyShowsSeniorsStrivetoBeFit

Hodgeman is capitalizing on the growing mature market.
Source: Hodgeman.

The NFL has realized the importance of women fans and is developing a strategic plan to attract them and keep them interested in a traditionally male-oriented sport. Based on research conducted by the NFL, women fans do not want to be treated differently than men. NFL Commissioner Roger Goddell stated, "(Women) fans want to be treated as real fans because they love the game, understand the game, and want to have the opportunity to experience the game just as anyone else does."

The NBA has also developed a strategic approach to targeting a growing female fan base, as the accompanying article indicates.

Despite the obvious male overtones of the increasingly popular mixed martial arts scene—as exhibited by the success of the Ultimate Fighting Championship—fans of the female persuasion are also flocking to the newest sporting trend to hit the pay-per-view circuit.

In fact, for a sport that used to be known as little more than a glorified bar brawl, mixed martial arts fights have been branded and stamped with a marketable seal of approval by sponsors and UFC stakeholders alike.

These widely publicized fights between experts in various martial arts are becoming a hit with women both in and out of the ring. Historically, sports enthusiasts have been male. However, stereotypes are eroding quickly as women are becoming more involved in every facet of sport. More women are participating in sports, and more women are watching sports. Moreover, every attempt is being made to make women's sports equitable with their male counterparts.

One example of females participating in a historically male sport is football. Nationwide, 1,173 girls played on high school tackle football teams in 2006, according to a survey by the National Federation of State High School Associations.

NBA Also Is Female Fan-Tastic

Basketballs sold in team stores now come in a pink-and-white motif. Advertisements are placed in *US Weekly*, and a line of purses might not be far off. It's official. It's a Bibbylicious world after all.

Actually, it's "Bibbylic10us," a merged tribute to Mike Bibby's name and uniform number, and it's right there across the front of shirts being sold to women in the Kings store at Arco Arena. Just like the beachwear the NBA expects to launch with Ocean Pacific this season and the joint venture with Adidas for female jerseys, complete with their own fit and fabric, and the NBA-themed jewelry now on sale.

In the latest attempt to find new fans and develop revenue streams, the league is undertaking a push with female-specific marketing and female-specific products, because the money projected to come in return is not gender specific. So much money, said Lisa Piken, the senior director of the NBA global merchandising group, that women could represent $100 million in sales this year.

Indeed, a line of nba4her was launched in 2002. But a new push began late last season, most noticeably with magazine ads touting the playoffs, and eventually the finals, in uncommon spots such as *In Touch Weekly, People Magazine,* www.MySpace.com, *US Weekly.*

Into this brave new world went promotions for professional basketball, sort of, with an approach geared to the human side of the participants rather than actual showdowns or the storylines for the hardcore fans.

"What we saw around the playoffs," said Carol Albert, the vice president of advertising, marketing development, and integration for the NBA, "was that our ratings were up 33 percent with women."

Hoping to build on that interest in 2006–07, the NBA began working with individual teams to organize clinics in hopes of offering a basic knowledge of the game that would become the first step to more women becoming serious fans. It moved forward with design, production, and sales of clothes and accessories for women, from bathing suits to dresses to pajamas to jewelry and, maybe one day, purses. To "Bibbylic10us" shirts in Sacramento.

The emergence of the WNBA 10 years ago was an additional draw, and potential, if not likely, transition into the NBA is an obvious benefit. It's a connection no other league can match at this level. When the season opened last month, the league said 46 percent of its backers were female and, citing a 2005 ESPN poll, that women make up a larger portion of the fan base than in any other professional league.

And that 33 percent increase in playoff viewership from the year before?

TNT, the cable network that has remained a constant for coverage, reports a combined jump of 42 percent for regular season and postseason broadcasts since the 2000–01 season. Finals ratings among women 18 to 49, a critical demographic for advertisers, climbed 41 percent from 2003 to 2006.

The league does not release team-by-team data. But Danette Leighton, the vice president of marketing and branding for the Kings, said the female fan base here consistently has been strong because of the franchise's unparalleled standing in Sacramento, growing into part of the civic landscape.

The success of the Monarchs—champions in 2005, finalists last summer—has been a bridge to deliver whatever fans might have originally become interested in professional basketball because of the WNBA. The Kings have tried to build on that, adding the hip-hop dancers formed for Monarchs games to the lineup of in-game entertainment at the NBA events, among other things.

Hoops Women: A Glance at Female Fans of the NBA

They're Buying
- More than $100 million in sales of consumer products for women is expected this year.
- The NBA was the first league to have a full line of apparel designed for women: nba4her.
- Product line includes jerseys, jewelry, swim gear, and watches.

They're Watching
- Since the 2000–01 season, women watching games on TNT, the one constant for NBA coverage, has increased by 42 percent.
- The 2003 NBA Finals drew a 2.7 rating for women ages 18 to 49. For the 2006 Finals, the rating increased to 3.8.

They're Fans
- 44 percent of women 12 and older in the U.S. say they are interested in the NBA (estimated 55 million female fans).
- 72 percent of girls 12–17 are NBA fans—higher than the NFL (71 percent), MLB (55 percent), NASCAR (43 percent), and NHL (31 percent).

Source: Scott Howard, "NBA Also Is Female Fan-Tastic; The League Seeks to Cash In on the Rising Interest of Women," *Sacramento Bee,* December 14, 2006, p. C1.

Getting a Handle on Women's Professional Football

The Women's Professional Football League, formed in 1999, is the only woman's league to go head-to-head with the men's college and pro seasons in the fall. The WPFL bills itself as the most accurate replica of the men's game and as the league with the highest standards—enforcing minimum roster requirements, and ensuring that owners have the financial wherewithal to keep a team playing, even if ticket sales flounder. The WPFL fields some of the strongest women's teams in the country, including the Dallas Diamonds, which maintains a 52-week training schedule and regularly draws some 3,000 fans. But the league has lost teams in recent years, pushing up travel costs for the remaining 13 teams scattered across the country.

A rival league, established in 2000, became the National Women's Football Association. Although the NWFA is growing, several teams have defected to join the upstart Independent Women's Football League in the past two years.

The IWFL, a nonprofit that started with four exhibition teams in 2001, now has 31 teams, including one in Montreal.

"Since our focus is providing an opportunity for women to play the sport, we kind of measure our success in terms of how many women we have registered to play," says IWFL CEO Laurie Frederick. "There were 1,281 last year, up from 60 women at first. We define that as pretty successful."

Source: Kari Huus, "Are You Ready for Some (Women's) Football?" MSNBC, February 2, 2007.

Some 80 professional women's football teams in three leagues exist across the country. The three leagues all play the same game, with minor deviations from NFL rules, but they approach the business in very different ways.

Ethnic Background   Segmenting markets by **ethnic background** is based on grouping consumers of a common race, religion, and nationality. Ethnic groups, such as African Americans (12.3 percent of the U.S. population), Hispanic Americans (12.5 percent of the U.S. population), and Asian Americans (3.6 percent of the U.S. population) are increasingly important to sports marketers as their numbers continue to grow. With segmenting based on ethnic background, marketers must be careful not to think of stereotypical profiles but to understand the unique consumption behaviors of each group through marketing research.

Major League Soccer (MSL) has long espoused the philosophy of having an ethnic fan base. Commissioner Don Garber believes the MSL is "perfectly suited to capitalize on what's going on in this country. We are a nation of increasing ethnic diversity. We are a nation that's finding itself in an increasingly growing global community. And that global community is linked by one language, a language that is shared by all, and that's the sport of soccer." Garber has also helped league officials and marketing folks understand that there are increasing numbers of immigrants—particularly in Hispanic communities—to whom soccer is a cultural necessity. Garber said, "Capturing the ethnic fan" is essential in making that approach work. "It requires careful considerations. It means realizing that fans bang drums and stand throughout the game. It means courting Spanish-language media, Caribbean media, and other foreign-language interests."[9] As Commissioner Garber and others point out in the accompanying article, understanding any subculture goes well beyond the language.

Another example of marketing to ethnic groups includes the introduction of *Deportes Hoy,* the premier Spanish-language sports daily. The sports information product will be circulated in Los Angeles, Orange, and San Diego counties (California) and will be targeted to reach everyone from the occasional to the most highly involved sports enthusiasts.[10] Similarly, SportsYA.com, which translates as "sports now," is the leading Internet brand among Hispanic users seeking sports information. ESPN began to publish

Learning the Hispanic Market

Not long after she took the newly created job of director of market development for the New York Mets last March, Sandra Van Meek, born in Colombia and raised in Miami, found herself correcting friends and colleagues who saw an unfamiliar culture at Mets games and equated it with another sport. "It's like soccer," many of them would say when the crowd at Shea Stadium broke into jubilant chants of "Jo-se, Jose, Jose, Jose" in salute to Dominican-born shortstop Jose Reyes. "No, it's like baseball," Van Meek would respond, shaking her head grimly. "But Spanish."

Venture to the baseball parks of Spanish-speaking countries in the Caribbean—to Puerto Rico or the Dominican Republic or Cuba; or in much of Central and South America—to Mexico or Venezuela; and you will find the stands filled with fans chanting, singing and dancing, rattling cowbells, tooting whistles and blowing horns.

These days, baseball in Queens—where the roster includes Reyes and iconic Pedro Martinez from the Dominican Republic and the Carloses, Beltran and Delgado, from Puerto Rico—has ignited interest across a city that includes about 4 million Hispanics.

The distinctions here are not of sport—eminently global soccer vs. the American pastime, baseball—but of culture. The Mets start off by eliminating language as a barrier, with ads that run in Spanish-language newspapers, on Spanish radio and TV, and on the back of city buses. Their Web site allows fans to buy tickets on pages written in Spanish, rather than bouncing them to an English page. In the ballpark, Spanish-speaking ushers and other staff wear "Hablo Español" buttons that make them easy to find.

But then the Mets go beyond language to address culture. They host Fiesta Latina—formerly known as the less aptly named "Hispanic Heritage Night"—which features music popular in the Puerto Rican community. And, separately, they host La Noche de Merengue, geared toward Dominicans. "It starts with the language," said Dave Howard, the Mets' executive vice president of business operations, "but you have to go beyond that and understand what is culturally relevant. We're sensitive to the preferences and interests of a diverse fan base."

For many, understanding Hispanic culture requires heavy lifting. And understanding the Hispanic market, which includes not only varied cultures that trace back to different nations of origin, but also different levels of proficiency in English and corresponding levels of assimilation, can be daunting. Yet the payoff is obvious. Hispanics number nearly 43 million, making them the largest minority group in the United States, at 14 percent. Beginning this year, they also will wield the most buying power of any minority group, $863 billion, according to the Selig Center for Economic Growth. That's four times what it was in 1990.

Hispanics are also the fastest-growing segment of the country, accounting for about one of every two people added to the population each day, according to the U.S. Census Bureau. Projections have the Hispanic population reaching 102 million by 2050, at which point one in four U.S. residents will be Hispanic. That the growth going forward will be fueled more by new births than immigration will create a bilingual, bicultural dynamic that may complicate matters even more for those trying to reach them. Still, most who specialize in Hispanic marketing see opportunities that far outweigh the effort.

"I think the biggest pitfall [in marketing to Hispanics] is that some people forget that marketing is marketing, and there are marketing principles that you have got to apply across whatever consumer segment you are going after," said Paul Mendieta, marketing director, U.S. Hispanic and Latin America, for Coors Brewing Co. "When you are not very familiar with someone, what you see are the differences. But when you are trained as a marketer, you are looking for the common denominator."

"Clearly, language is important in our view. We transmit in Spanish," said Lino Garcia, general manager of ESPN Deportes, the Spanish-language channel on which the sports uber network is placing increased emphasis. "We're able to serve the English-speaking Latino with ESPN and ESPN2. We serve the Spanish-speaking group with Deportes in Spanish, with content they can't get anywhere else."

Others stress that it is important not to oversimplify the connection between a large segment of Hispanics—those of Mexican heritage—and the overall market. "The key is to understand that because we all speak the same language, that does not mean we all like the same things," said Dario Brignole, director of sports marketing agency IMG's Hispanic, Latin American, and soccer divisions. "In the United States, you have Canadians, Australians, and British, and also you have Americans from the South, the Northeast, and the West. All speak English, but they're all different."

"You need to segment," David Sternberg said. "You can't just assume they're all the same, and you're making a mistake as a marketer if you approach it that way. There's a critical mass that still is Spanish dominant. There is a critical mass of Mexican Americans. If you need to place bets, that's still a place to go. But you need to understand that it's fragmented, like the overall market."

Source: Bill King, *Sports Business Journal*, January 22, 2007, p. 15, http://www.sportsbusinessjournal.com/index.cfm?fuseaction=search.show_article&articleId=53677&keyword=.

a monthly Spanish-language edition of *ESPN The Magazine* beginning in 2007, demonstrating their ongoing commitment to Hispanic sports fans in the United States.

The Hispanic market is not the only ethnic segment of interest to sport marketers. Here in the United States, according to the 2000 census, families of Asian descent have the nation's largest average income among all ethnic groups, as well as the highest graduation rates at the high school and college levels. Moreover, they are the nation's fastest growing ethnic group, with large population centers in major cities that are home to multiple pro sports franchises. When it comes to putting fans in the stands and merchandise in their homes and offices, Asian Americans should be a sports marketer's dream.[11] Whether it's the Hispanic market, Asian market, or any other ethnic market, sport organizations are realizing the critical nature of understanding and catering to these growing segments for all sports products and services.

Family Life Cycle   The **family life cycle** was a concept developed in the 1960s to describe how individuals progress through various "life stages," or phases of their life. A traditional life cycle begins with an individual starting in the young, single "life stage." Next, an individual would progress through stages such as young, married with no children; young, married with children; to, finally, older with no spouse. As you can see, the traditional stages of the family life cycle are based on demographic characteristics such as age, marital status, and the presence or absence of children.

Today, the traditional family life cycle is no longer relevant. In 2006, 3.6 per 1,000 people in the United States are divorced, compared with 7.5 per 1,000 people that are married, and the number of single-parent households is on the rise. Changes in family structure such as these have led marketers to a more modern view of the family life cycle, shown in Figure 6.2.

FIGURE 6.2   Modern Family Life Cycle

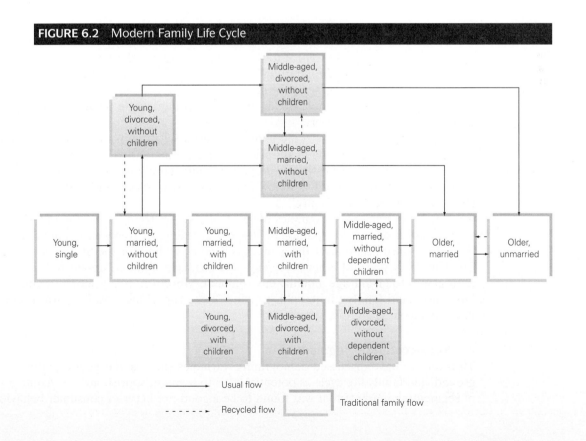

Pygmy is segmenting on the basis on the family life cycle.
Source: Pygmy.

Sports marketers segmenting on the basis of family life cycle have a number of options. Do they want to appeal to the young and single, the elderly couple with no kids living at home, or the family with young children? Sports that are growing in popularity, such as biking, segment markets based on a stage of the family life cycle. Just imagine the incompatible biking needs of a young, single person versus a young, married couple with children.

Professional sports has come under increased scrutiny in the past decade for its lack of family values. Rising ticket prices, drunken fans, and late games have all been cited as examples of professional sports becoming "family unfriendly." Realizing this, sports marketers have tried to renew family interest in sports and make going to the game "fun for the entire family."

There are numerous examples of sports marketers trying to become more family friendly. For instance, the addition of Homer's Landing, an area where families can picnic before, during, and after the game, has become a "hit" for the St. Louis Cardinals. The Chicago Cubs and other professional teams have initiated no-alcohol sections at their games to encourage a family environment. Moreover, many sports organizations have instituted family nights, which include tickets, parking, and food for a reduced price to encourage family attendance.

Socioeconomic Segmentation

Thus far, we have discussed demographic variables such as age, gender, ethnic background, and family life cycle as potential ways to segment sports markets. Another way of segmenting markets that was found to be a good predictor of consumer behavior is

Polo is a sport that has typically appealed to the upper class.

through **socioeconomic segmentation.** As previously defined, **social class** is a division of members of a society into a hierarchy of distinct status classes, so that members of each class have relatively the same status and members of all other classes have either more or less status.

Although most people immediately equate social class with income, income alone can be a poor predictor of social class. Other factors such as educational level and occupation also determine social standing. Usually, income, education, and occupation are highly interrelated. In other words, individuals with higher levels of education typically have higher income and more prestigious occupations. Based on these factors (income, education, and occupation), members of a society are artificially said to belong to one of the social class categories. The traditional social class categories are upper-, middle-, and lower-class Americans. Participation in certain sports has been associated with the various social strata. For instance, golf and tennis are called "country club" sports. Polo is a sport of the "rich and famous." Bowling is usually thought of as the "blue-collar" sport of the working class.

As with sex roles, the relationship between social class and sport is now shifting. Golf is now being enjoyed by people of all income levels. Attending a professional basketball or football game, once affordable for the whole family, can now only be enjoyed by wealthy corporate season ticket holders. In addition, NASCAR fans are stereotypically "good ol' boys" with "blue-collar" values. However, NASCAR has turned into a multibillion-dollar-a-year industry and a marketing success story. During this tremendous growth, the sport is moving beyond its "good-ol'-boy" mentality and reaching a new market in yuppie America. Just consider the demographics of the NASCAR fan. Approximately 43 percent of NASCAR fans earn $50,000 or more per year—the same figure as for the U.S. population. At the other end of the wage scale, 34 percent of the U.S. population earn under $30,000, compared to 33 percent of NASCAR fans.[12]

Psychographic Segmentation

Psychographic segmentation is described as grouping consumers on the basis of a common lifestyle preference and personality. Because personality alone is very difficult to measure and has not been linked to sports behavior, few sports marketing practitioners find it useful alone. The results of one recent study suggest that individuals who are most likely to identify with a team are those who are most likely to seek out and enjoy social exchanges. The researchers suggest that marketing plans should be designed to emphasize communal aspects of events and that individuals rated high

TABLE 6.3	AIO Dimensions	
Activities	**Interests**	**Opinions**
Work	Family	Themselves
Hobbies	Home	Social issues
Social events	Job	Politics
Vacation	Community	Business
Entertainment	Recreation	Economics
Club membership	Fashion	Education
Community	Food	Products
Shopping	Media	Future
Sports	Achievements	Culture

Source: William Wells and Douglas J. Tigert, "Activities, Interests, and Opinions," *Journal of Advertising Research,* vol. 11 (August 1971), 127–135. Courtesy of the *Journal of Advertising Research,* The Advertising Research Foundation.

on extraversion, agreeability, and materialism may be more responsive to such promotions. Psychographics, however, looks more toward lifestyle preferences and less toward specific personality measures.

Psychographic segments are believed to be more comprehensive than other types of segmentation, such as demographics, behavioral, or geodemographic. As consumer behavior researcher Michael Solomon points out, "Demographics allow us to describe *who* buys, but psychographics allows us to understand *why* they do."[13] For this reason, many sports marketers have chosen to segment their markets on the basis of psychographics. To gain a better understanding of consumers' lifestyles, marketers assess consumers' **AIO dimensions,** or statements describing activities, interests, and opinions (AIO). The three AIO dimensions are shown in Table 6.3.

Typically marketers quantify AIOs by asking consumers to agree or disagree with a series of statements reflecting their lifestyle. These statements can range from measures of general interest in sports to measures focusing on a specific sport. As seen in Table 6.3, many of these AIO dimensions relate indirectly or directly to sports. For example, sports, social events, recreation, and products may have a direct link to sports, whereas club memberships, fashion, community, and economics may be indirectly linked.

An example of psychographic segmentation in the golf market can be seen in Table 6.4. This table illustrates a golfer's lifestyle based on research from *SRDS: The Lifestyle Market Analyst/National Demographic and Lifestyle.* This type of information examines activities and interests of golfers to determine what products and services might be successfully marketed to this group. For example, many professional golf tournaments are sponsored by large investment companies to capitalize on this popular activity of golfers.

Geographic Segmentation

Geographics is a simple, but powerful, segmentation basis. Certainly, this is critical for sports marketers and as long-standing as "rooting for the home team." All sports teams use **geographic segmentation;** however, it is not always as straightforward as it may initially seem. For instance, the Dallas Cowboys, Chicago Bulls, Atlanta Braves, and the Fighting Irish are all known as "America's Team."

Geographic segmentation can be useful in making broad distinctions among local, regional, national, and international market segments. International or multinational

TABLE 6.4   Golfer's Lifestyles Ranked by Index

Snow Skiing Frequently	229	Watching Sports on TV	168
Tennis Frequently	218	Real Estate Investments	167
Wines	177	Frequent Flyer	161
Stock/Bond Investments	172	Bicycling Frequently	158
Boating/Sailing	170	Running/Jogging	157

Home Life	Households	%	Index	Sports, Fitness & Health	Households	%	Index
Avid Book Reading	9,010,127	45.6	123	Bicycling Frequently	6,480,968	32.8	158
Bible/Devotional Reading	4,900,244	24.8	104	Dieting/Weight Control	6,619,282	33.5	122
Flower Gardening	8,417,355	42.6	120	Health/Natural Foods	5,552,293	28.1	117
Grandchildren	6,401,932	32.4	111	Improving Your Health	5,690,606	28.8	119
Home Furnishing/Decorating	8,259,283	41.8	111	Physical Fitness/Exercise	11,144,104	56.4	147
Home Office	1,995,664	10.1	120	Running/Jogging	4,188,919	21.2	157
Own a Cat	5,433,739	27.5	99	Snow Skiing Frequently	3,260,243	16.5	229
Own a Dog	8,535,910	43.2	112	Tennis Frequently	2,805,785	14.2	218
Shop by Catalog/Mail	10,590,851	53.6	118	Walking for Health	8,338,319	42.2	123
Vegetable Gardening	5,394,221	27.3	112	Watching Sports on TV	12,349,406	62.5	168

Good Life

Great Outdoors

Good Life				Great Outdoors			
Attend Cultural/Arts Events	4,445,786	22.5	133	Boating/Sailing	3,596,147	18.2	170
Cruise Ship Vacations	4,999,040	25.3	155	Camping/Hiking	6,461,209	32.7	128
Fashion Clothing	4,070,364	20.6	122	Fishing Frequently	8,041,933	40.7	141
Fine Art/Antiques	3,042,894	15.4	122	Horseback Riding	1,086,748	5.5	122
Foreign Travel	4,939,763	25.0	156	Hunting/Shooting	4,979,281	25.2	147
Frequent Flyer	7,706,030	39.0	161	Recreational Vehicles	2,825,544	14.3	138
Gourmet Cooking/Fine Foods	5,907,956	29.9	141	Wildlife/Environmental	3,675,183	18.6	121
Travel in USA	10,333,983	52.3	149	**High Tech Activities**			
Wines	6,718,077	34.0	177	Electronics	4,742,172	24.0	130

Hobbies & Interests							
Hobbies & Interests				Listen to Records/Tapes/CDs	11,163,863	56.5	117
Automotive Work	3,319,520	16.8	116	Own a Blackberry	1,699,278	8.6	156
Buy Pre-Recorded Videos	5,809,161	29.4	117	Own a CD Player	15,570,131	78.8	117
Coin/Stamp Collecting	2,351,327	11.9	123	Own a CD Rom	13,673,263	69.2	119
Collectibles/Collections	3,615,906	18.3	116	Own a Cellular Phone	16,973,024	85.9	115
Crafts	5,749,884	29.1	108	Own a Digital Camera	12,981,696	65.7	116
Current Affairs/Politics	3,675,183	18.6	133	Own a Digital Video Recorder	5,631,329	28.5	126
Donate to Charitable Causes	12,211,093	61.8	132	Own a DVD Player	16,103,626	81.5	106
Home Workshop	7,152,776	36.2	131	Own a GPS Locator	2,450,122	12.4	144
Needlework/Knitting	3,141,689	15.9	106	Own a HDTV	4,228,437	21.4	146
Our Nation's Heritage	1,877,110	9.5	140	Own an Apple/Macintosh PC	1,600,483	8.1	117
Self-Improvement	5,572,052	28.2	121	Own an IBM Compatible PC	12,902,660	65.3	120
Sewing	3,457,834	17.5	104	Own a Satellite Dish	4,445,786	22.5	115
				Own a Smart Cellular	3,339,279	16.9	129
Investing & Money				Photography	6,342,655	32.1	126
Casino Gambling	4,682,895	23.7	153	Science Fiction	2,213,014	11.2	112
Entering Sweepstakes	2,845,303	14.4	113	Science/New Technology	2,608,195	13.2	125
Moneymaking Opportunities	2,983,617	15.1	132	Subscribe to Online Service	14,839,047	75.1	116
Real Estate Investments	3,299,761	16.7	167	Use a Wireless Internet	6,639,041	33.6	126
Stock/Bond Investments	6,935,427	35.1	172	VCR Recording	3,655,424	18.5	127

Base Index US = 100

Source: Reprinted from the 2007 edition of The Lifestyle Market Analysis,® published by SRDS with data supplied by Equifax Marketing Services.

marketing is a topic of growing interest for sports marketers. For example, Major League Baseball has held regular-season games in Japan, Mexico, and Puerto Rico, and the NBA games are televised in 215 countries in 41 languages. The NFL is discussing expansion into international markets. As the Spotlight on International Sports Marketing indicates, the leagues are realizing that the key to growth is going global.

The physical climate also plays a role in segmenting markets geographically. Classic examples include greater demand for snow skiing equipment in Colorado and surfboards in Florida. However, Colorado ski resorts have the greatest number of sports tourists who come from Florida, hardly thought of as a snow ski mecca. Therefore, segments of sports consumers may exist in unlikely geographic markets. In this example, the psychographics of the sports consumer may be more important in predicting behavior than geographic location.

SPOTLIGHT ON INTERNATIONAL SPORTS MARKETING

Sports' Next Expansion: Going Global

About 13 months ago, General Electric's chairman of the board and chief executive officer, Jeffrey Immelt, addressed National Football League owners in Orlando, Florida, urging them to really think about expanding their business. Immelt, whose GE National Broadcast Company's sports division partners with the NFL, was discussing the need of the league to get into China and start marketing the NFL brand in the Asian country.

Immelt did not really have to do much in the way of getting the NFL owners to think his way. The NFL promptly announced that a 2007 preseason game would be held in Beijing. The NFL pulled the plug on that game recently and will instead devote its global marketing to the New York Giants–Miami Dolphins game that will be held in London in late October. The NFL really gave no reason for canceling the Beijing contest and the league is hoping to get back into the China market in 2009.

This is the new expansion by North American sports. Exporting baseball, basketball, football, and hockey while North America imports soccer and cricket. Don't expect to see any new North American Major League Baseball teams, don't expect to see any new North American National Football League teams, nor should you expect to see any new National Basketball Association or National Hockey League teams in either the United States or Canada. The major leagues have stopped adding teams. The NFL was forced to expand to 32 after Art Modell moved his Cleveland Browns to Baltimore in late 1995 to get Cleveland and Ohio officials off the league's collective back. It's the only reason

Cleveland got an expansion franchise in 1999, and Houston was added because the league wanted 32 teams and the owners could split up about $700 million in expansion fees.

The NBA went from 23 teams to 30 with expansions in the late 1980s, mid 1990s, and the recent addition of Charlotte. The NHL grew from 21 in the early 1990s to 30 by the end of the decade. Major League Baseball added four teams in the 1990s. The NFL added four teams in the 1990s, two planned, Charlotte (Carolina) and Jacksonville, and two forced on them.

The only way any of those leagues will expand in the near future is because of United States Congressional threats of ending Major League Baseball's antitrust exemption (the 1991 addition of the Florida Marlins and Colorado Rockies was due to that), or antitrust lawsuits against an established league (the 1976 expansion to Seattle by Major League Baseball was the result of King County, Washington's planned antitrust suit against Major League Baseball over the relocation of the Seattle Pilots to Milwaukee in 1970), or the establishment of a new league to rival the established leagues (nine American Football League teams joined the National Football League in 1966, four American Basketball Association franchises joined the National Basketball Association in 1976, and four World Hockey Association franchises were admitted to the National Hockey League in 1979).

The leagues, which can and do act as monopolies, also need to hold open cities like Los Angeles in football, Kansas City, Las Vegas, and Winnipeg in hockey, and

(Continued)

(Continued)

Oklahoma City in basketball in the event an owner needs leverage in getting a new stadium and play city against city to get the best possible stadium or arena deal. There could be some teams moving in the future.

With the leagues set at 30 or 32 teams, there will be no more North American growth, but the leagues need more and more revenues and new markets. Europe and Asia will be the new targets for North American sports owners and the way the leagues plan to capture euros, yen, and the yuan is simple. Have some teams conduct training camps or play regular season games in countries and then sell sports packages through satellite, cellular, or Internet services. All the major Northern American sports leagues have TV deals in place globally, a good number of games are available on the computer, and as technology gets better, more and more people will watch games on their computer.

The National Hockey League's Anaheim Ducks and Los Angeles Kings will play two regular season games in London next fall to open the season. Coincidentally, the games will be played at the London arena that Kings owner Phil Anschutz helped build.

The National Basketball Association is sending teams to train in both Europe and China this fall and will play a variety of preseason games in China and Europe. The National Basketball Association has a marketing footprint in China because of Yao Ming and don't think the other leagues have not noticed that.

Major League Baseball invited China to play in the 2006 World Baseball Classic, not because China has a good baseball team, but because China is the world's largest market. New York Islanders owner Charles Wang, who was born in China, has led National Hockey League cultural exchange efforts in trying to build a fan base. The New York Yankees organization has jumped feet first into China with a deal that calls for the Yankees not only to hold clinics in the country but to also help build baseball fields and stadiums. Baseball teams regularly tour Japan.

The National Football League has fumbled away an opportunity by pulling out of China in 2007. The NFL has no real international presence other than in Canada and Mexico and that is a big problem for the league. London is a big promotion for the league.

Meanwhile, Anschutz (who once owned most of Major League Soccer's teams) has signed David Beckham to a deal with his MLS Los Angeles Galaxy. Beckham is not necessarily in the United States to play soccer and just be a soccer player. Beckham brings glamour and a buzz, as he is a worldwide celebrity who married a Spice Girl, Victoria Adams, who was known professionally as Posh Spice in the 1990s singing group. Anschutz's hope is that Beckham will be the celebrity draw that he and his wife are in Europe and drum up interest in the game because he is David Beckham and his wife was a Spice Girl and they make a marketable couple. Both will also be offered other entertainment opportunities in the U.S. because they are the Becks.

Every sport now is all about marketing and developing revenue streams globally. One-time Major League Baseball Commissioner Peter Ueberroth once said that a team's most valuable asset wasn't its players but its logo and selling the logo was important. Ueberroth was so right when he made that statement two decades ago. The NBA, Major League Baseball, and the NHL are well ahead of the NFL in the global marketing race; soccer or football is making inroads in the United States and Canada. The NFL likes to tout the Super Bowl as the tour de force when it comes to big events, but the TV numbers globally show that World Cup Soccer and international cricket championships have more pull and viewers.

The sports industry is changing with the help of major technological advances on the Internet and cellular applications, and that means global expansion, not league expansion, is the next big thing for North American sports owners.

Source: Evan Walker, *New York Sun*, April 8, 2007.

Although the climate plays an important role in sports, marketers have attempted to tame this uncontrollable factor. For instance, tons of sand were shipped to Atlanta, creating beach-like conditions, for the first ever Olympic beach volleyball competition. Domed stadiums, since the opening (and now closing) of the Astrodome in Houston, have also allowed sports marketers to tout the perfect conditions in which fans can watch football in the middle of a blizzard in Minnesota.

Behavioral Segmentation

For sports marketers engaged in the strategic sports marketing process, two common goals are attracting more fans and keeping them. Behavioral segmentation lies at the heart of these two objectives. **Behavioral segmentation** groups consumers based on how much they purchase, how often they purchase, and how loyal they are to a product or service.

Interestingly, in today's professional sports environment, loyalty is an increasingly important topic. Many professional sports teams have held their fans and cities hostage, and cities are doing everything they can to keep their beloved teams. Taxpayers nationwide paid more than $14 billion for stadiums and arenas during the past 20 years. This new construction and renovation was done largely to keep team owners satisfied and curb any threat of moving. For 2009 and 2010 combined, the value of major league arenas and stadiums opening will top $7 billion. Add collegiate and minor league facility construction, and the number increases beyond $9 billion.

Franchises and players within each team move so rapidly that fan loyalty becomes a difficult phenomenon to capture. The day of the lifelong fan is over. Because of this, fans may identify more with individual players or even coaches (e.g., Derek Jeter and the Yankees, Shaquille O'Neal and the Heat, or Joe Paterno and Penn State football) than they do with teams. According to some sports marketing experts, next to wins, fans like to see famous faces on the field.[14] This is true even in team-dominated sports, such as football.

Fans may be more concerned with the individual performance of Albert Pujols than they are with the St. Louis Cardinals. Certainly, sports marketers have to monitor this trend of diminishing loyalty to a team. However, some sports fans show extreme loyalty by purchasing personal seat licenses (PSLs). PSLs require fans to pay a leasing fee for their seats. This fee would guarantee the consumer his or her seat for several years. The PSL, of course, demonstrates the extreme devotion of a group of fans.

Sports marketers have recently taken a lesson in loyalty marketing from other industries and are creating loyalty marketing programs. A study by Pritchard and Negro[15] found that these programs are effective when they build on the genuine affinity fans have for their teams, rather than rewarding attendance alone. Increasing fan interaction with players, coaches, and the entire organization through direct access or personal communication was shown to be much more important to the success of loyalty programs than rewarding attendance.

Along with behavioral segmentation based on loyalty to a team or sports product, consumers are frequently grouped on the basis of other attendance or purchasing behaviors. For instance, lifelong season ticket holders represent one end of the usage continuum, whereas those who have never attended sporting events represent the other end. A unique marketing mix must be designed to appeal to each of these two groups of consumers.

Benefits Segmentation

The focus of **benefits segmentation** is the appeal of a product or service to a group of consumers. Stated differently, benefits segments describe why consumers purchase a product or service or what problem the product solves for the consumer. In a sense, benefits segmentation is the underlying factor in all types of marketing segmentation in that every purchase is made to satisfy a need. Benefits segmentation is also consistent with the marketing concept (discussed in Chapter 1) that states that organizations strive to meet customers' needs.

Major shoe manufacturers, such as Nike, focus on "benefits sought" to segment markets. Some consumers desire a high-performance cross-training shoe, whereas others want a shoe that is more of a fashion statement. In fact, one study asked consumers what is important to them when purchasing athletic footwear. Consumers stated that comfort is the primary influence on their athletic footwear purchases. Price and "a fashionable look" placed second and third as purchase influencers.[16]

Golf ball manufacturers also try to design products that will appeal to the specific benefits sought by different groups of golfers. Pro V1 has enhanced aerodynamics with slightly higher flight for longer distance, soft feel, and Drop-And-Stop control. DT SoLo gives the ultimate combination of distance with soft feel and guaranteed cut-proof durability. NXT Tour has long distance off the driver and improved control with long irons. The Titleist DT Spin offers a combination of long tee-to-green distance, wound-ball spin, improved feel, and guaranteed cut-proof durability, whereas the Titleist DT Distance offers golfers longer and straighter two-piece distance with cut-proof durability. Sports marketers really hit a home run when they design products that satisfy multiple needs (i.e., distance, feel, accuracy, durability) of consumers.

Choosing More Than One Segment

Although each of the previously mentioned bases for segmentation identifies groups of consumers with similar needs, it is common practice to combine segmentation variables. An example of combining segmentation approaches is found in a study of the golf participant market.[17] A survey was conducted to determine playing ability, purchase behavior, and the demographic characteristics of public and private course golfers. The resulting profile produced five distinct market segments that combine some of the various bases for segmentation discussed earlier in the chapter. These five segments are shown in Table 6.5.

Geodemographic Segmentation

One of the most widely used multiple segment approaches in sports is **geodemographic segmentation.** Although geographic segmentation and demographic segmentation are useful tools for sports marketers, combining geographic and demographic characteristics seems to be even more effective in certain situations. For instance, many direct marketing campaigns apply the principles of geodemographic segmentation.

TABLE 6.5   Five Market Segments for Golf Participants

Competitors (18.6 percent)
- Have a handicap of less than 10
- Indicate love of game
- Play for competitive edge
- Practice most often
- Most likely to play in league
- Own most golf clothing
- Are early adopters (e.g., third wedge)
- Buy most golf balls

Players (25.7 percent)
- Have handicap between 10 and 14
- Use custom club makers
- Practice a lot
- Like competition
- Exercise and companionship are important
- Most likely to take out-of-state golf vacation

Sociables (17.8 percent)
- Have handicap between 15 and 18
- Often play with family
- Purchase from off-price retailers
- Play for sociability
- Most likely to take winter vacation to warm destination

(Continued)

(*Continued*)

Aspirers (18.4 percent)
- Have handicap between 19 and 25
- Love to play; hate to practice
- Most inclined to use golf for business purposes
- Golf shows are important as source of information
- Competition and sociability are unimportant reason to play

Casual (19.5 percent)
- Have handicap of 26 or more
- Do not practice
- More women in this segment
- Play less frequently than other segments
- Own the least golf clothing
- Purchase the fewest golf balls
- Recreation is most important factor for play
- Exercise and companionship are moderately important
- Least likely to take a golf vacation
- Most likely to shop in course pro shop

Source: Sam Fullerton and H. Robert Dodge, "An Application of Market Segmentation in a Sports Marketing Arena: We All Can't Be Greg Norman," *Sport Marketing Quarterly,* vol. 4, no. 3 (1995), 43–47. Reprinted with permission of Fitness Information Technology, Inc., Publishers.

The basis for geodemographic segmentation is that people living in close proximity are also likely to share the same lifestyle and demographic composition. Because lifestyle of the consumer is included in this type of segmentation, it is also known as geolifestyle. Geodemographics allows marketers to describe the characteristics of broad segments such as standard metropolitan statistical areas (SMSAs) all the way down to census blocks (consisting of roughly 340 houses). The most common unit of segmentation for geodemography is the zip code. Claritas, Inc., a marketing firm leading the charge in geodemographics, established the PRIZM system in the 1970s. PRIZM is used to identify potential markets for products. Each unit of geography is classified as one of the 62 PRIZM clusters, which have been given names that best characterize those populations. Some examples of the PRIZM cluster categories are shown in Table 6.6.

TABLE 6.6   Sample PRIZM Cluster Categories and Descriptions

Kids and Cul-de-Sacs—Ranked number 1 of all 62 clusters in married couples with children and large (4 plus) families. As this characteristic governs every aspect of their lives and activities, one rightly pictures these neighborhoods as a noisy medley of bikes, dogs, rock music, and sports.

God's Country—Populated by educated, upscale professionals, married executives who choose to raise their children in the far exurbs of major metropolitan areas. Their affluence is often supported by dual incomes. Lifestyles are family and outdoor centered.

Towns and Gowns—Describes most of our nation's college towns and university campus neighborhoods. With a typical mix of half locals (towns) and half students (gowns), it is totally unique. Thousands of penniless 18- to 24-year-old kids, plus highly educated professionals with a taste for prestige products beyond their means.

Winner's Circle—Second in American affluence and typified by new money, living in expensive new mansions in the suburbs of the nation's major metros. These are well-educated, mobile executives and professionals with teenage families. Big producers, prolific spenders, and global travelers.

Source: How to Use PRIZM (Alexandria, VA: Claritas, 1996). Courtesy of Claritas, Inc., of Arlington, VA.

TARGET MARKETS

After segmenting the market based on one or a combination of the variables discussed in the previous section, target markets are chosen. **Target marketing** is choosing the segment(s) that will allow an organization to most efficiently and effectively attain its marketing goals.

Sports marketers must make a systematic decision when choosing groups of consumers they want to target. To make these decisions, each potential target market is evaluated on the basis of whether it is sizable, reachable, and measurable, and whether it exhibits behavioral variation. Let us look at how to judge the worth of potential target markets in greater detail.

Evaluation of Target Markets

Sizable

One of the first factors to consider when evaluating and choosing a potential target market is the size of the market. In addition to the current size of the market, sports marketers must also analyze the estimated growth of the market. The market growth would be predicted, in part, through environmental scanning, already discussed in Chapter 2.

Sports marketers must be careful to choose a target market that has neither too many nor too few consumers. If the target market becomes too large, then it essentially becomes a mass, or undifferentiated market. For example, we would not want to choose all basketball fans as a target market because of the huge variations in social class, lifestyles, and consumption behaviors.

However, sports marketers must guard against a target market that is too small and narrowly defined. We would not choose a target market that consisted of all left-handed female basketball fans between the ages of 30 and 33 who live in San Antonio and have income levels between $40,000 and $50,000. This market is too narrowly defined and would not prove to be a good return on our marketing investment.

One common trap that marketers fall into with respect to the size of the potential market is known as the majority fallacy. The **majority fallacy** assumes that the largest group of consumers should always be selected as the target market. Although in some instances the biggest market may be the best choice, usually the competition is the fiercest for this group of consumers; therefore, smaller and more differentiated targets should be chosen.

These smaller, distinct groups of core customers that an organization focuses on are sometimes referred to as a market niche. **Niche marketing** is the process of carving out a relatively tiny part of a market that has a very special need not currently being filled. By definition, a **market niche** is initially much smaller than a segment and consists of a very homogeneous group of consumers, as reflected by their unique need. The differences between market segments and niches are highlighted in Table 6.7. Milne and McDonald provide support for the use of niche markets in the sports industry by pointing out the proliferation of specialist magazines (e.g., *Triathlete, Cross Country*

TABLE 6.7 Market Segments vs. Market Niches	
Segment	*Niche*
Small mass market	Very small market
Less specialized	Very specific needs
Top down (go from large market into smaller pieces)	Bottom up (cater to the smaller pieces of the market)

Skier, Skydiving Magazine); the TV coverage of new, niche sports on major broadcast network channels, and cable niche channels such as the Xtreme Sports Channel; and the continued interest of sponsors, such as Novell, Pepsi, and Van's Shoes, in affiliating with niche sports.[18]

One specific example of a niche market is individuals (as opposed to corporations) who have financially invested in the sports franchise through the purchase of season tickets for many seasons. In addition to their financial investment, these loyal fans have a high emotional investment in the team. To retain these valuable consumers, sports marketers must develop a specialized marketing mix to reinforce and reward the loyalty that these fans have shown to the organization.

Reachable

In addition to exploring the size of the potential target market, its ability to be reached should also be evaluated. Reach refers to the accessibility of the target market. Does the sports marketer have a means of communicating with the desired target market? If the answer to this question is no, then the potential target market should not be pursued.

Traditional means of reaching the sports fan include mass media, such as magazines, newspapers, and television. In today's marketing environment, it is possible to reach a very specific target market with technology such as the Internet. For instance, fans of women's soccer can interact on the "Women's Soccer World" at www.womensoccer.com. In addition to the Internet, satellite technology products, such as DirecTV, are allowing sports fans across the United States access to their favorite teams. This, of course, opens new geographic segments for sports marketers to consider.

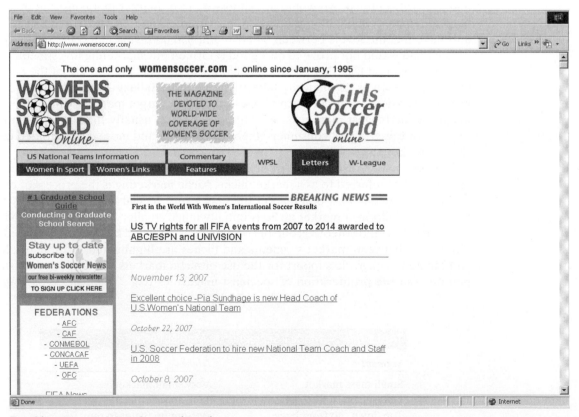

Reaching women's soccer fans on the web.

Source: Used by permission www.womensoccer.com.

Measurable

The ability to measure the size, accessibility, and purchasing power of the potential target market(s) is another factor that needs to be considered. One of the reasons demographic segmentation is so widespread is the ease with which characteristics such as age, gender, income level, and occupation can be assessed or measured. Psychographic segments are perhaps the most difficult to measure because of the complex interaction of personality and lifestyle.

Behavioral Variation

Finally, if the target market is sizable, reachable, and measurable, sports marketers must examine behavioral variation. We want consumers within the target market to exhibit similar behaviors, attitudes, lifestyles, and so on. In addition, marketers want these characteristics to be unique within a target market. This component is the underlying factor in choosing any target market.

An example of behavioral variation among market segments is the corporate season ticket holder versus the individual season ticket holder. Although both corporate season ticket holders and individual season ticket holders may be fans at some level, their motivation for attending games and attitudes toward the team may be quite different. These variations would prompt different approaches to marketing to each segment.

How Many Target Markets?

Now that we have evaluated potential target markets, do we have to choose just one? The answer depends largely on the organization's marketing objectives and its resources. If the firm has the financial and other resources to pursue more than one target market, it does so by prioritizing the potential target markets.

The market distinguished as the most critical to attaining the firm's objectives is deemed the primary target market. Other, less critical markets of interest are called secondary, tertiary, and so on. Again, a unique marketing mix may need to be developed for each target market, so the costs associated with choosing multiple targets are sometimes prohibitive.

POSITIONING

Segmentation has been considered and specific target markets have been chosen. Next, sport marketers must decide on the positioning of their sporting events, athletes, teams, and so on. **Positioning** is defined as fixing your sports entity in the minds of consumers in the target market.

Before discussing positioning, three important points should be stressed. First, positioning is dependent on the target market(s) identified in the previous phase of the market selection decisions. In fact, the *same* sport may be positioned differently to distinct target markets. As the spotlight demonstrated earlier in the chapter, the positioning of the NBA and other professional sports is changing with the opening of a new target market—women.

Second, positioning is based solely on the perceptions of the target market and how its members think and feel about the sports entity. Sometimes positioning is mistakenly linked with where the product appears on the retailer's shelf or where the product is placed in an advertisement. Nothing could be further from the truth. Position is all about how the consumer perceives your sports product relative to competitive offerings.

Third, the definition of positioning reflects its importance to all sports products. It should also be noted that sports leagues (Arena Football versus NFL), sports teams (e.g., Dallas Cowboys as "America's Team"), and individual athletes (e.g., Tiger Woods as the youthful, hip golfer, or the NBA's perennial bad boy, Allen Iverson) all must be positioned by sports marketers.

How does the sports marketer attempt to fix the sports entity in the minds of consumers? The first step rests in understanding the target market's perception of the relevant attributes of the sports entity. The relevant attributes are those features and characteristics desired in the sports entity by the target market. These attributes may be intangible, such as a fun atmosphere at the stadium, or tangible, such as having cushioned seating. Golf manufacturers such as Slazenger have positioned their equipment as the "standard of excellence" and having "impeccable quality."

In another example, consider the possible product attributes for in-line skates. Pricing, status of the brand name, durability, quality of the wheels, and weight of the skate may all be considered product attributes. If serious, competitive skaters are chosen as the primary target market, then the in-line skates may be positioned on the basis of quality of the wheels and weight of the skate. However, if first-time, recreational skaters are considered the primary target market, then relevant product attributes may be price and durability. Marketers attempt to understand all the potential attributes and then which ones are most important to their target markets through marketing research.

Perceptual Maps

Through various advanced marketing research techniques, perceptual maps are created to examine positioning. **Perceptual maps** provide marketers with three types of information. First, perceptual maps indicate the dimensions or attributes that

New Era Cap positions itself as the Authentic Cap of Major League Baseball.

Source: Authentic Collection.

FIGURE 6.3   One-Dimensional Perceptual Map of Sports

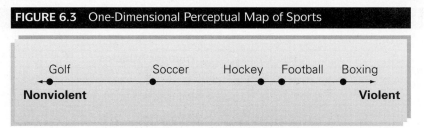

consumers use when thinking about a sports product or service. Second, perceptual maps tell sports marketers where different sports products or services are located on those dimensions. The third type of information provided by perceptual maps is how your product is perceived relative to the competition.

Perceptual maps can be constructed in any number of dimensions, based on the number of product attributes being considered. Figure 6.3 demonstrates a one-dimensional perceptual map, which explores the positioning of various spectator sports based on the level of perceived aggression or violence associated with the sports. This hypothetical example can be interpreted as follows: Boxing is seen as the most violent or aggressive sport, followed by football, hockey, and soccer. However, golf is the least aggressive sport. These results would vary, of course, based on who participated in the research, how aggression or violence is defined by the researchers, and what level of competition is being considered (i.e., professional, high school, or youth leagues).

Although it is easy to conceptualize one-dimensional perceptual maps, the number of dimensions is contingent upon the number of attributes relevant to consumers. For example, Converse positions its shoes for multiple uses like action sports, basketball, cheerleading, or cross-training. New Balance, however, positions its shoes solely on the basis of running.

A study using perceptual mapping techniques found that consumers identify six-dimensions of sport (shown in Table 6.8). Although it is possible to create a six-dimensional perceptual map, it is nearly impossible to interpret. Therefore, two-dimensional perceptual maps were constructed that compared 10 sports on the six dimensions identified by consumers.

Figure 6.4 shows a two-dimensional perceptual map using Dimension 4 (skill developed primarily with others versus skill developed alone) and Dimension 5 (younger athletes versus broad age ranges of participants). Interpreting this perceptual map, we see that football is considered a sport whose participants are younger athletes and skill is developed primarily with others. Compared with football, golf is seen as a

TABLE 6.8	Six Dimensions or Attributes of Sports
Dimension 1	Strength, speed, and endurance vs. methodical and precise movements
Dimension 2	Athletes only as participants vs. athletes plus recreational participants
Dimension 3	Skill emphasis on impact with object vs. skill emphasis on body movement
Dimension 4	Skill development and practice primarily alone vs. primarily with others
Dimension 5	A younger participant in the sport vs. participant ages from young to older
Dimension 6	Less masculine vs. more masculine

Source: James H. Martin, "Using a Perceptual Map of the Consumer's Sport Schema to Help Make Sponsorship Decisions," *Sport Marketing Quarterly,* vol. 3, no. 3 (1994), 27–33.

FIGURE 6.4   Two-Dimensional Perceptual Map for Sports

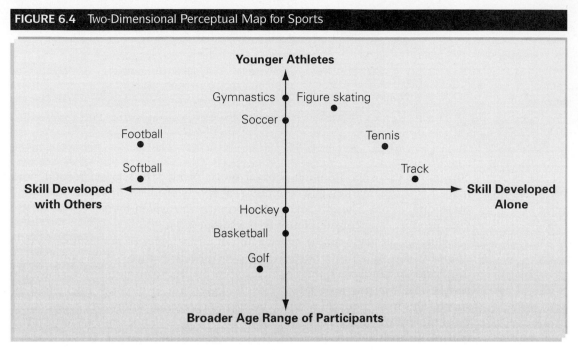

sport for a broader range of participants with skills developed more on your own. Using these results, sports marketers can better understand the image of their sport from the perspective of various target markets and decide whether this image needs to be changed or maintained.

Repositioning

As suggested, sport marketers may use the results of positioning studies to change the image of their sport. For instance, professional cycling, one of the most popular sports in the world, has been marred by doping scandals in recent years. Cycling took a big hit when the "Operation Puerto" case alleged that a number of riders had accepted illegal doping substances, and that scandal was followed by the Tour de France, which was tainted by the revelation that U.S. rider and Tour winner Floyd Landis had failed both of his drug tests. Obviously this is not the image the cycling federations and the cyclists themselves wish to project. Thus, the sport of cycling is trying to **reposition** itself or change the image or perception of the sports entity in the minds of consumers in the target market.

In response to those drug allegations, and in hopes of cleaning up the reputation of the sport, Team Slipstream took a proactive response. Team Slipstream is a professional cycling team based in the United States, consisting of 23 riders who have subjected themselves to weekly drug testing instead of just waiting until race day to be tested.

"It's ensuring [to] the public, the fans, and ourselves that our riders are clean," said team director Jonathan Vaughters, who retired from competitive racing in 2003. "It's enormously important as far as sponsors go to know that their team is not getting caught up in a scandal, and it's setting an example for young athletes."[19]

Cycling is not the only sports entity attempting to reposition itself. Following a series of scandals with coaches and athletes, the NCAA is also experiencing image problems. And let's not forget baseball players such as slugger Barry Bonds, who has some problems of his own. One professional sport team, albeit a temporary tenant, can even serve to reposition an entire city, as discussed in the accompanying article.

Hornets' Stay Helped Create a Pro Sports Image for City

Serving as the Hornets' temporary home didn't necessarily improve Oklahoma City's sports profile. It's impossible to improve on something you don't have. The Hornets' experience instead resulted in something much more significant for Oklahoma City.

"I think it actually created a profile for us," mayor Mick Cornett said. "I don't think we had much of a sports profile before the Hornets. We've held events in the past, but this is the first time we've had a team that has carried our name that wasn't a minor-league team. I think it's created a profile and an image for us, especially with the amount of (national) media coverage last season."

In the history of the NBA, no city has shown what Oklahoma City showed the past 20 months after welcoming the displaced Hornets. Then again, no other city has been given that opportunity. There has only been one Hurricane Katrina, thank goodness. It took a catastrophe for Oklahoma City to strut its stuff. "You're trying to compare this to some other experience, and there really has been no other experience like this anywhere," Cornett said.

"No city has ever had a team on a temporary basis anywhere under these circumstances. And there is no track record for what happens from here on out, just like there'd be no track record if you moved a franchise for a couple years. We're on uncharted water and just trying to steer the ship as best we can." Because of its locale near New Orleans and having an available arena that offered an NBA-type capacity, Oklahoma City was given a once-in-a-lifetime tryout to prove itself as a pro town.

Success in the venture was not a slam dunk, but that certainly was the end result. "I think the impact of the Hornets on Oklahoma City has been extraordinary, most obviously by showing the nation that this is a tremendous sports city that can easily support and sustain an NBA franchise," Governor Brad Henry said. "The Hornets brought some terrific hoops action to Oklahoma, but it's also worth noting that Oklahoma City has left a lasting impression on the Hornets. In the wake of the Hurricane Katrina tragedy, Oklahomans embraced the Hornets with great enthusiasm and hospitality. It truly was a win-win for both the team and basketball fans."

This area's passion toward collegiate sports never has been in question, but questions did surround its capability to embrace pro sports. "To me, I just felt there was a void that wasn't being filled by OU and OSU for Oklahoma City sports," Cornett said. "I didn't really have a way to prove that, until this (the Hornets). What you saw is that it was something for everybody to rally around. It wasn't bedlam. It was the most inclusive thing we've ever had."

Media market size often is used as a barometer in rating pro sports cities. According to Nielsen Media Research, Oklahoma City is tied for 45th (with Albuquerque) nationally and would rank last out of the 30 NBA markets, one spot behind Memphis.

When the Hornets return to New Orleans next season, they'll be going to a smaller market. New Orleans has dropped 12 spots in the rankings since Hurricane Katrina, falling to No. 54.

Source: John Rohde, *Daily Oklahoman*, April 13, 2007.

Summary

Chapter 6 focuses on the critical market selection decisions, also referred to as segmentation, targeting, and positioning. Segmentation, the first market selection decision, is identifying consumers with common needs. Typically, the bases for segmentation of consumer markets include demographics, socioeconomics, psychographics, behaviors, and benefits. Marketers using demographic segmentation choose groups of consumers based on common ages, gender, ethnic background, and stage of the family life cycle. Geographic segmentation groups people who live in similar areas such as cities, states, regions of the country, or even countries (e.g., the United States versus international markets). Socioeconomic segmentation groups consumers on the basis of similar income levels, educational levels, and occupations. Psychographic segments are especially useful to sports marketers; they are based on consumers' lifestyles, activities, interests, and opinions. Behavioral segments are groups of consumers that are similar on the basis of consumer actions, such as how often they purchase sports products or how loyal they are when purchasing a sports product. Finally, benefits segmentation are groups of consumers attempting to satisfy similar needs by consuming the sports product together. Sports marketers may choose to segment their markets using one of the previously mentioned segmentation variables (e.g., demographics) or combine several of the bases for segmentation (e.g., geodemographic).

Once market segments have been chosen, the next market selection decision is picking a target market. Target marketing is choosing the segment or segments that will allow the organization to most effectively and efficiently achieve its marketing goals. When evaluating potential target markets, care should be taken to ensure the markets are the right size (neither too large nor too small), reachable (accessible), measurable (i.e., size, purchasing power, and characteristics of the segments can be measured), and demonstrate behavioral variation (i.e., consumers share common characteristics within the target market).

The final market selection decision is positioning. After the target market has been chosen, sports marketers want to position their products or fix them in the minds of the target markets. Positioning is based on the perception or image that sports marketers want to develop or maintain for the sports product. For example, a minor league baseball team may want to position itself as an inexpensive, family entertainment alternative. To understand how a sports product is positioned relative to its competition, perceptual maps are developed through marketing research techniques. By looking at perceptual maps, sports marketers can identify whether they have achieved their desired image or whether they need to reposition their sports product in the minds of the target market.

Key Terms

- AIO dimensions, p. 180
- behavioral segmentation, p. 183
- benefits segmentation, p. 165
- demographic segmentation, p. 166
- ethnic background, p. 175
- family life cycle, p. 187
- geodemographic segmentation, p. 185

- geographic segmentation, p. 180
- market niche, p. 187
- majority fallacy, p. 187
- market segmentation, p. 165
- market selection decisions, p. 165
- mature adults, age 55-plus, p. 169
- niche marketing, p. 187

- perceptual maps, p. 190
- positioning, p. 189
- psychographic segmentation, p. 179
- reposition, p. 192
- social class, p. 179
- socioeconomic segmentation, p. 179
- target marketing, p. 187

Review Questions

1. Describe the key components of market selection decisions and indicate how market selection decisions are incorporated into the larger strategic marketing process.
2. What is market segmentation? Provide some examples of how sports marketers segment the sports participant market (those who play) and the sports spectator market (those that watch).
3. Discuss the various ways to segment the sports market based on demographics. Which of the demographic bases are the most effective when segmenting the sports market and why?
4. Describe, in detail, the family life cycle and how it is used as a strategic tool when segmenting sports markets. What stage of the family life cycle are you currently in? How does this affect your sports participation and spectator behavior?
5. Provide examples of sports you believe would appeal to each of the six social class categories (upper-upper through lower-lower). What sports appeal to all social class segments?

6. What are AIOs? Why is psychographic segmentation so difficult to practice?
7. Provide several examples of the growth of international sports marketing.
8. What is behavioral segmentation? What are some of the common behaviors that sports marketers would use for segmentation purposes?
9. Define benefits segmentation and discuss why benefits segmentation is considered to be at the core of all segmentation. What benefits do you look for when attending a sporting event? Does your answer vary from event to event?
10. Define a target market. What are the requirements for successful target markets (i.e., how should each target be evaluated)? Provide examples of sports products or services that target two or more distinct markets.
11. How many target markets should a sports marketer consider for a single product?
12. Describe positioning and discuss how perceptual mapping techniques are used by sports marketers. What is repositioning?

Exercises

1. Find two advertisements for sports products that compete directly with one another. For example, you may want to compare Nike running shoes with Reebok running shoes or King Cobra golf clubs with Taylormade golf clubs. How is each product segmented, targeted, and positioned? Are there more

differences or similarities in these market selection decisions?
2. How is the health and fitness industry segmented in general? Describe the segmentation, targets, and positioning of health and fitness clubs in your area.

3. You are hired as the director of sports marketing for a new minor league hockey franchise in Chicago, a city that already has an NHL team. Describe how you would segment, target, and position your new franchise.

4. Describe the primary target market for the following: NASCAR, the Kentucky Derby, "The Rhino" bowling ball, and the WNBA. Next, define a potential secondary target market for each of these sports products.

5. Interview five consumers who have recently attended a high school sporting event, five consumers who have recently attended a college sporting event, and five who have recently attended any professional sporting event. Ask them to identify why they attended this event and what benefits they were looking for. Were their needs met?

6. Develop a list of all the possible product attributes that may be considered when purchasing the following sports products: a tennis racquet, a basketball, and a mountain bike. After you have developed the list of attributes, ask five people which attributes they consider to be the most important for each product. Do all consumers agree? Are there some attributes that you may have omitted? Why are these attributes important in positioning?

7. How do you think the following races are positioned: Boston Marathon, "Run Like Hell" 5K Halloween Race, and the Bowling Green 10K Classic? Draw a two-dimensional perceptual map to illustrate the positioning of each race.

8. Provide examples of individual athletes, teams, and sports (leagues) that have had to develop repositioning strategies.

Internet Exercises

1. Using the Internet, find the demographic profile for fans attending the LPGA (women's tour) versus the PGA (men's tour). Are there differences? Use this information to comment on the market selection decisions for the LPGA.

2. Find two Internet sites that target children interested in sports and two Internet sites that target the mature market. Note any similarities and differences between the sites.

3. Find two Internet sites for soccer. One site should focus on U.S. soccer, whereas the other focus should be international. Comment on the relative positioning of soccer in the United States versus abroad based on information found on the Internet.

Endnotes

1. James U. McNeal, "Tapping the Three Kids' Markets," *American Demographics* (April 1998); "Kids in 2010," *American Demographics* (September 1999).

2. "Kids Wield $18 Billion in Spending Power: Study," May 15, 2006, http://promomagazine.com/research/kidsspending/.

3. "Young Consumers, Perils and Power," *The New York Times* (February 11, 1990).

4. Laura Zinn, "Teens: Here Comes the Biggest Wave Yet," *Business Week* (April 11, 1994), 76.

5. Spending Power of the Teen Consumer in the United States," September 2006, http://www.researchand markets.com/reports/c44645.

6. http://www.suddenlysenior.com/maturemarket statsmore.html.

7. "Brew Crew Creates Senior Club," *Sports Business News,* www.sportsbusinessnews.com (February 26, 2003).

8. "Israel: Senior Olympics Promote Physical Activity," http://www.aarp.org/international/agingadvances/ communityprograms/Articles/3_06_israel_SABA.html.

9. David Boyce, "Commissioner Plans for Growth," *The Kansas City Star* (July 29, 2000), D11.

10. "Group Seven Communications, Inc. Launches 'Deportes Hoy,' The Premier Spanish-Language Sports Daily," www.guide-p.infoseek.com (January 22, 1998).

11. Richard Lapchick, "Promise to Prominence for Asian Athletes," May 18, 2006, http://sports.espn.go.com/ espn/news/story?id=2449595&lpos=spotlight&lid= tab4pos3.

12. John Sturbin, "NASCAR's Fan Figures Have Got You Covered," *Fort Worth Star Telegram,* March 15, 2007.

13. Michael Solomon, *Consumer Behavior,* 3rd ed. (Upper Saddle River, NJ: Prentice Hall, 1996).

14. Jon Morgan, "Oriole Makeover Likely to Put Sales in Foul Territory," *The Baltimore Sun* (August 2, 2000), 1A.

15. M. Pritchard and C. Negro, "Sport Loyalty Programs and Their Influence on Fan Relationships," *International Journal of Sports Marketing and Sponsorship,* vol. 3 (2001), 317–338.

16. "NPD Sees Fashion Focus Driving Athletic Footwear Sales," March 14, 2007.

17. Sam Fullerton and H. Robert Dodge, "An Application of Market Segmentation in a Sports Marketing Arena: We All Can't Be Greg Norman," *Sport Marketing Quarterly,* vol. 4, no. 3 (1995), 42–47.

18. George Milne and Mark McDonald, *Sports Marketing: Managing the Exchange Process* (Sudbury, MA: Jones and Bartlett, 1999).

19. Juliet Macur, "Welcoming the Testing Needle, Team Battles Cycling's Image," *The New York Times,* February 13, 2007, A1.

PLANNING THE SPORTS MARKETING MIX

CHAPTER

7 | SPORTS PRODUCT CONCEPTS

After completing this chapter, you should be able to:

- Define sports products and differentiate between goods and services.

- Explain how sports products and services are categorized.

- Define branding and discuss the guidelines for choosing an effective brand name.

- Discuss the branding process in detail.

- Examine the advantages and disadvantages of licensing from the perspective of the licensee and licensor.

- Identify the dimensions of service quality and goods quality.

- Define product design and explain how product design is related to product quality.

*T*hink about attending a Major League Baseball game at Wrigley Field in Chicago. Inside the stadium you find vendors selling game programs, scorecards, Major League Baseball–licensed merchandise, and plenty of food and drink. An usher escorts you to your seat to enjoy the entertainment. During the game, you are exposed to more product choices.

Every game experience presents us with a number of opportunities to purchase and consume sports products. Some of the products, such as the scorecards, represent a pure good, whereas others, such as the game itself, represent a pure service. Each sports product represents a business challenge with incredible upward and downward potential. In this chapter, we explore the multidimensional nature of sports products.

DEFINING SPORTS PRODUCTS

A **sports product** is a good, a service, or any combination of the two that is designed to provide benefits to a sports spectator, participant, or sponsor. Within this definition, the marketing concept discussed in Chapter 1 is reintroduced. As you recall, the marketing concept states that sports organizations are in the business of satisfying consumers' needs. To do this, products must be developed that anticipate and satisfy consumers' needs. Sports marketers sell products based on the benefits they offer consumers. These benefits are so critical to marketers that sometimes products are defined as "bundles of benefits." For example, the sport of snowshoeing has recently emerged as one of the nation's fastest-growing winter sports. Ski Industry America, a trade association interested in marketing the sport of snowshoeing, suggests that the bundle of benefits this sports product offers include great exercise, little athletic skill required

This baseball, glove, and bat represent pure goods.

This competition represents
a pure service. (Rim Light
Getty Images, Inc./PhotoDisc)

to participate, and much less expense than skiing. The sport is easy to learn, virtually inexpensive (compared to other winter sports), poses little risk of injury, and is a great way to exert energy during the cold winter months. According to research provided by Snowsports Industries America (SIA), 40.8 percent of snowshoers are women (a number that is increasing rapidly), 9.4 percent of snowshoers are children (ages 7–11), and 44.2 percent of snowshoers are ages 25–44.[1]

In addition to sports and sporting goods, athletes can also be thought of as sports products that possess multiple benefits. For example, NBA teams are currently seeking players who can perform multiple roles on the court rather than those who have more specialized skills. The player who can rebound, is great defensively, dribbles well, and can play the post is invaluable to the franchise. The classic example of the "hybrid" player with multiple skills was Magic Johnson, who played center and guard in the 1980 NBA Finals. Today's NBA stars, such as Kevin Garnett, Lebron James, and Dwayne Wade, exemplify the versatile player who offers many benefits to the team.

A number of athletes offer a unique bundle of benefits both on and off the court. Consider Miami Heat's star center, Shaquille O'Neal. The Shaq is clearly a top performer, helping the Lakers earn a three-peat championship and one of three players in NBA history to be selected to the NBA All-Star Game for 14 consecutive seasons. In addition, Shaq has made and appeared in several movies and raps, written his autobiography, and owns his own sportswear company. The 7-foot-1-inch center has been aligned with numerous endorsement contracts, from Taco Bell to Payless Shoes, and has helped a number of nonprofit organizations. All of these activities contribute to the "product" we know as Shaq.[2]

Goods and Services as Sports Products

Our definition of products includes goods and services. It is important to understand the differences in these two types of products to plan and implement the strategic sports marketing process. Because services such as watching a game are being produced (by the players) and consumed (by the spectators) simultaneously, there is no formal channel of distribution. However, when you purchase a pure good, such as a pair of hockey skates, they must be produced by a manufacturer (e.g., Nike Bauer Supreme), sent to a retailer (e.g., Sports Authority), and then sold to you. This formal channel of distribution requires careful planning and managing. Let us explore some of the other differences between goods and services.

Goods are defined as tangible, physical products that offer benefits to consumers. Obviously, sporting goods stores sell tangible products such as tennis balls and racquets, hockey equipment, exercise equipment, and so on. By contrast, **services** are usually described as intangible, nonphysical products. For instance, the competitive aspect of any sporting event (i.e., the game itself) or an experience such as receiving an ice-skating lesson reflects pure services.

It is easy to see why soccer balls and exercise equipment are classified as pure goods and why the intangible nature of the game constitutes a pure service, but what about other sports products? For example, sporting events typically offer a variety of pure goods (such as food, beverages, and merchandise). However, even these goods have a customer service component. The responsiveness, courtesy, and friendliness of the service provider are intangible components of the service encounter.

Most sports products do not fall so neatly into two distinct categories, but possess characteristics of both goods and services. Figure 7.1 shows the goods–services continuum. On one end, we have sporting goods. At the other end of the continuum, we have, almost exclusively, sports services. For example, a sports service that has received considerable attention in the past few years is the fantasy sports camp. Sports camps from a variety of team and individual sports have sprung up to appeal to the aging athlete.

FIGURE 7.1   The Goods–Services Continuum

Pure goods		Pure services
← (tennis balls, hockey equipment)		(game itself) →

CAREER SPOTLIGHT

J. Jonathan Hayes, Managing Director, U.S. Bank Professional Sports Division

Career Questions

1. How did you get started in the sports industry? What was your first sports industry job?

I started with U.S. Bank (fka Star Bank) in 1989 in the Private Banking Group, and almost immediately started doing banking work with some of the local pro athletes. As a former college athlete, my managers thought it would be a good fit to have me working with guys that were also roughly my same age. Once we identified how poorly managed and advised athletes were relative to their finances, we made the decision in 1995 to start a separate line of business, our Professional Sports Division, dedicated to assisting and advising pro athletes globally on wealth management. This was my first sports industry job.

2. Can you describe the type of work you are doing right now? What are your job responsibilities? What are the greatest challenges?

I manage the Pro Sports Division for U.S. Bank, the sixth largest bank in the country and tenth largest in the world. We manage pro athletes in all aspects of their financial lives, both during their careers as well as into retirement, including managing their assets, advising on contract structures, budgeting, estate planning, and retirement planning. Our greatest challenge is getting clients to accept and embrace financial discipline, so that they truly can be financially secure for life, and hopefully be able to create a financial legacy for their heirs and beneficiaries.

3. Do you foresee any changes in demand in this field, in the future? If so, what or how?

There are, unfortunately, few in this field that truly operate with the client's best interests in mind. So on one hand there is no shortage of financial advisors to athletes and therefore the supply of practitioners meets, if not exceeds, the demand. But on the other hand, recognizing the first statement, the demand exists for those that can and will provide real value and expert advice, in such a way that is primarily and foremost beneficial to the athlete.

4. Who or what has influenced you the most in your sports business career?

There are many biblical references that influence my thinking and the advice I try to pass on to my clients. In my efforts to get clients to live and act with financial prudence, the tenth commandment ("Thou shalt not covet thy neighbor's house . . . or anything that belongs to your neighbor," Exodus 20:17) provides a powerful doctrine of how we should be content and not try to "keep up with the Joneses." Likewise, the teachings of Solomon in Ecclesiastes, especially 5:8–20, show that the pursuit of goods and riches will only result in folly, as you will never be satisfied and will always be wanting more, like "chasing the wind." If the new car you purchased was one you had to have, why then will you want next year's model when it comes out? Because you weren't satisfied with the original and will find that you're not satisfied with the newer model either.

5. What advice would you offer students who are considering a career in sports marketing?

Be prepared to be discouraged early on; the sports industry is a difficult one in which to gain entry, and many find that it is not as glamourous, once in, as it's perceived to be. As with almost every career, the road to success is a difficult one, and you must work hard, and look and be prepared for opportunities when they present themselves. Once you realize and come to terms with this, however, that a job is still a job and that you have to continue to work very hard, the perks and ancillary benefits are enjoyable. If you enjoy sports, and work hard enough and are lucky enough to get a job in sports, you will likely find it a lot of fun, on a comparative basis. Plus, you get to read ESPN.com all day and your boss can't get mad at you.

For instance, the L.A. Dodgers' Adult Baseball Camp offers lifelong memories and mementos for $4,395. During the week, campers receive the following tangible goods: two L.A. Dodger uniforms (home and road) with name and number, L.A. Dodger cap, baseball autographed by an instructor, 50 baseball cards with the camper's picture and camp stats, videotaped highlights of the week at camp, L.A. Dodger T-shirt, team photo, camp certificate, and camp pin.

Thus far, the distinction between goods and services has been based on the tangible aspects of the sports product. In addition to the degree of tangibility, goods and services are differentiated on the basis of perishability, separability, and standardization. These distinctions are important because they form the foundation of product planning in the strategic sports marketing process. Because of their importance, let us take a look at each dimension.

Tangibility

Tangibility refers to the ability to see, feel, and touch the product. Interestingly, the strategy for pure goods often involves stressing the intangible benefits of the product. For example, advertisements for Nike's F.I.T. performance apparel highlight not only the comfort of the product, but also the way the clothing will make you "ready to take on the challenges of wild and wicked workouts." Similarly, Formula 1 racing is paired with TAG Heuer watches in a sponsorship agreement and product line that leverages the benefits of both brands by asking "What are you made of?" By pairing with Formula 1 racing, TAG Heuer hopes to capitalize on the intangible attributes of excitement, danger, excellence, and pushing yourself to be the best.

However, the strategy for intangible services is to "tangibilize them."[3] For example, a major league team may wish to highlight the tangible comforts of its new facility rather than promote the game itself. Sportscape dimensions, or the tangible aspects of the stadium such as the stadium design, seating, and aesthetics, should be stressed, especially when the team is performing poorly.

Standardization and Consistency

Another characteristic that distinguishes goods from services is the degree of **standardization.** This refers to receiving the same level of quality over repeat purchases. Because sporting goods are tangible, the physical design of a golf ball is manufactured with very little variability. This is even truer today, as many organizations focus on how to continuously improve their manufacturing processes and enhance their product quality.

Pure services, however, reflect the other end of the standardization and consistency continuum. For example, think about the consistency associated with different individual and team athletic performances. How many times have you heard an announcer state before a game, "Which team (or player) will show up today?" Meaning, will the team play well or poorly on that given day?

The Duke University men's basketball team, under the leadership of Mike Krzyzewski, has been one of the most consistent teams in college sports over the past 25 seasons. This, however, does not guarantee they will win the night you attend the game. Even the regular season, high-performing Buffalo Bills had the embarrassing distinction of being the only team ever to lose four consecutive Super Bowls.

Consider another example of the lack of consistency within a sporting event. You may attend a doubleheader and see your favorite team lose the first game 14 to 5 and win the second game of the day by a score of 1 to 0. One of the risks associated with using individual athletes or teams to endorse products is the high degree of variability associated with their performance from day to day and year to year. Because sports marketers have no control over the consistency of the sports product, they must focus on those things that can be controlled, such as promotions, stadium atmosphere, and, to some extent, pricing.

Perishability

Perishability refers to the ability to store or inventory "pure goods," whereby services are lost if not consumed. Goods may be inventoried or stored if they are not purchased immediately, although there are many costs associated with handling this inventory. If a tennis professional is offering lessons, but no students enroll between the hours of 10:00 A.M. and noon, this time (and money) is lost. This "down time" in which the service provider is available but there is no demand is called **idle product capacity.** Idle product capacity results in decreased profitability. In the case of the tennis pro, there is a moderate inventory cost associated with the professional's salary.

Another example with much higher inventory costs is a professional hockey team that is not filling the stands. Consider the St. Louis Blues, the NHL team with the poorest average attendance and lowest percentage of attendance to capacity (~60%) in the 2006 to 2007 season. The costs of producing one professional game include everything from the "astronomical" salaries of the players to the basic costs of lighting and heating the arena. If paying fans are not in the seats, the performance or service will perish, never to be recouped. As a general rule, the most perishable products in business are airline seats, hotel rooms, and athletic event tickets.

In an effort to reduce the problem of idle product capacity, sports marketers attempt to stimulate demand in off-peak periods by manipulating the other marketing mix variables. For example, if tennis lessons are not in demand from 10:00 A.M. to noon, the racquet club may offer reduced fees for enrolling during these times.

Separability

Another factor that distinguishes goods from services is **separability.** If a consumer is purchasing a new pair of running shoes at a major shoe store chain, such as The Athlete's Foot, the quality of the good (the Reebok shoes) can be separated from the quality of the service (delivered by The Athlete's Foot sales associate). Although it is possible to separate the good from the person providing the service, these often overlap. What this suggests is that manufacturers will selectively choose the retailers that will best represent their goods. In addition, manufacturers and retailers often provide detailed training to ensure salespeople are knowledgeable about the numerous brands that are inventoried.

As we move along the goods–services continuum from pure goods toward pure services, there is less separability. In other words, it becomes more difficult to separate the service received from the service provider. In the case of an athletic event, there is no separation between the athlete, the entertainment, and the fan. The competition is being produced and consumed simultaneously. As such, sport marketers can capitalize on a team or athlete when they are performing well. When things are going poorly, they may have to rely on other aspects of the game (food, fun, and promotions) to satisfy fans. The Dallas Cowboys have sold the history and tradition of the team to the fans. Despite several losing seasons the team has had a streak of 160 sold-out regular and postseason games that began in 1990, and included 79 straight sellouts at Texas Stadium and 81 straight sellouts on the road.

Classifying Sports Products

In addition to categorizing products based on where they fall on the goods–services continuum, a number of other classification schemes exist. For sports organizations that have a variety of products, the concepts of product line and product mix become important strategic considerations. Let us look at these two concepts in the context of a goods-oriented sports organization and a services-oriented sports organization.

A **product line** is a group of products that are closely related because they satisfy a class of needs, are used together, are sold to the same customer groups, are distributed through the same type of outlets, or fall within a given price range. Wilson Sporting Goods sells many related product lines such as shoes, bats, gloves, softballs, golf clubs, and tennis racquets. The total assortment of product lines that a sports organization sells is the **product mix**. Table 7.1 illustrates the relationship between the product lines and product mix for Wilson Sporting Goods. The number of different product lines the organization offers is referred to as the breadth of the product mix. If these product lines are closely related in terms of the goods and services offered to consumers, then there is a high degree of product consistency.

Nike recently increased the breadth of its product mix by adding new brands and product lines. The company acquired Converse and its famous Chuck Taylor All-Star shoes, as well as Hurley International, a surf- and skateboard apparel brand. Other new acquisitions include Cole Haan dress shoes and Bauer hockey equipment. The strategic advantage of this related diversification is the use of Nike's established marketing muscle.[4] Synergy in distribution and promotion, as well as strong brand identification, should make Nike's launch into new markets a successful venture. Joycelyn Hayward, the manager of a sporting goods store that carries Nike, summed it up best by saying, "Nike's ability to churn out innovative products and marketing plans has kept it ahead of rivals.[5]"

TABLE 7.1   Wilson Sporting Goods Product Mix

Baseball	*Basketball*	*Football*	*Golf*	*Racquetball*	*Soccer*
Gloves	Accessories	Footballs	Irons	Racquets	Soccer balls
Bats	Basketballs	Tees/accessories	Woods	Gloves	Protective gear
Baseballs	Uniforms	Youth protective uniforms	Wedges	Eyewear	Bags
Protective gear		NFL accessories	Putters	Racquetballs	
Bags			Complete sets	Footwear	
Accessories			Balls	Bags	
Uniforms			Bags	String	
			Gloves	Accessories	
			Accessories	Apparel	
			Retired models		

Volleyball	*Softball Fastpitch*	*Softball Slowpitch*	*Squash*	*Tennis*	*Badminton*
Outdoor balls	Gloves	Gloves	Racquets	Balls	Racquets
Indoor balls	Bats	Bats	Bags	Footwear	Shuttlecocks
Uniforms	Balls	Balls	String	Legacy footwear	String
Ball carts	Protective gear	Accessories	Grips	Accessories	
Bags	Accessories			Platform tennis	
				Court equipment	
				Retired models	
				Racquets	
				Bags	
				String	
				Grips	

Source: Wilson Sporting Goods, www.wilsonsports.com.

Today, Nike is focusing on increasing their talent pool of athletes and expanding their growing product lines in new sports. For example, LeBron James joined the Phil Knight stable in 2003 for a $90 million, multiyear endorsement contract prior to playing a college or professional game. Nike certainly pinned its hopes on James to invigorate sales in the high-end market. In addition, Nike, under the leadership of Knight, is quickly moving into international markets. However their race in the athletic footwear marketing ends, Knight will always be remembered as the man who realized the true marketing power of sports celebrities.

The depth of the product lines describes the number of individual products that comprise that line. The greater the number of variations in the product line, the deeper the line. For example, the Wilson basketball product line currently features over 60 different basketballs, 4 of which are indoor and 56 of which are indoor/outdoor. Now, think about how the product concepts might relate to a more service-oriented sports organization, such as a professional sports franchise. All these organizations have gone beyond selling the core product, the game itself, and moved into other profitable areas, such as the sale of licensed merchandise, memorabilia, and fantasy camps. In essence, sports organizations have expanded their product lines or broadened their product mix.

Understanding the depth, breadth, and consistency of the product offerings is important from a strategic perspective. Sports organizations might consider adding product lines, and, therefore, widen the product mix. For example, Nike is using this strategy and capitalizing on its strong brand name. Alternatively, the sports organization can eliminate weak product lines and focus on its established strengths. In addition, the product lines it adds may be related to existing lines (product line consistency) or may be unrelated to existing lines (product line diversification).

Another strategic decision may be to maintain the number of product lines, but add new versions to make the line deeper. For instance, the MLS, which has 12 teams

TaylorMade-adidas golf extends their product line with adidas golf footwear and apparel.

Source: Courtesy of TaylorMade-adidas Company

divided into Eastern and Western conferences, added a thirteenth team, Toronto FC, in 2007. All of these product planning strategies require examining the overarching marketing goals and the organizational objectives, as well as carefully considering consumers' needs.

PRODUCT CHARACTERISTICS

Products are sometimes described as "bundles of benefits" designed to satisfy consumers' needs.[6] These "bundles" consist of numerous important attributes or characteristics that, when taken together, create the total product. These **product characteristics,** which include branding, quality, and design, are illustrated in Figure 7.2. It is important to note that each of the product characteristics interacts with the others to produce the total product. Branding is dependent on product quality, product quality is contingent on product design, and so on. Although these product features (i.e., branding, quality, and design) are interdependent, we examine each independently in the following sections.

Branding

What first comes to mind when you hear University of Notre Dame, Green Bay, or adidas? It is likely that the Fighting Irish name, along with the Lucky Leprechaun ready to battle, comes to mind for Notre Dame. The Packers are synonymous with Green Bay, Wisconsin, and the symbolic three stripes are synonymous with adidas. All these characteristics are important elements of branding.

Branding is a name, design, symbol, or any combination that a sports organization (or individual athlete as is the case with David Beckham) uses to help differentiate its products from the competition. Three important branding concepts are brand name, brand marks, and trademarks. A **brand name** refers to the element of the brand that can be vocalized, such as the Nike Air Jordan, the Minnesota Wild, and the Vanderbilt University Commodores. When selecting a brand name for sporting goods or a team name, considerable marketing effort is required to ensure the name symbolizes strength and confidence. Because choosing a name is such a critical decision, sports marketers sometimes use the following guidelines for selecting brand names:

- The name should be positive, distinctive, generate positive feelings and associations, be easy to remember and to pronounce. For team names, the positive associations include those linked with a city or geographic area.
- The name should be translatable into a dynamite attitude-oriented logo. As an example of a successful logo choice, consider Binghamton University, who recently changed their name from the Colonials to the Bearcats. Athletic Director Joel Thirer called the move a huge success based on the number of fans who now sport the Bearcat logo.[7]

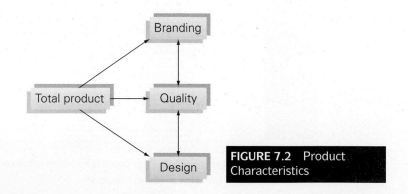

FIGURE 7.2 Product Characteristics

SPOTLIGHT ON INTERNATIONAL SPORTS MARKETING

Brand Beckham

David Beckham and Major League Soccer seem to be a match made in marketing heaven. Sometime soon, perhaps in a year or two, maybe three or four, soccer's most famous current star likely will be coming to America, injecting glamour and glitz into MLS and following the path created by Pele and Franz Beckenbauer three decades ago. "I want to play at the highest level for a few more years yet. I've got that planned out," Beckham said Thursday at England's World Cup training camp. "Going to America is one of the ideas that I've thought of in the future." Beckham exited the World Cup on Saturday, injured in the second half of England's loss to Portugal in a penalty-kick shootout. Beckham buried his face in his hands on the bench, and appeared to be in tears. He later sat on the ground, stretching out his leg with towels covering it. Not exactly the picture of an entertainment personality who draws paparazzi like a movie star, regularly finding his way onto tabloid and magazine covers.

With snazzy clothes, rotating hair colors and styles, and a pop star wife, he is the epitome of the modern mix of celebrity and athlete. He's even had a movie named after him: *Bend It Like Beckham,* released three years ago. That he's a 31-year-old midfielder who plays for Real Madrid's "Galacticos" and the captain of England's national team is only part of the equation. He's David Beckham Inc., a multinational corporation with links to Pepsi, Gillette, Motorola, and adidas. "He's a cultural icon," said former U.S. soccer star Alexi Lalas, the president and general manager of the Los Angeles Galaxy. "I think that the people that don't know a tremendous amount about soccer know who Beckham is, whether it's the way he looks or who he's married to or what he's done in international soccer."

In January, 2007 Beckham signed with the LA Galaxy for $250 million over 5 years. The move to the U.S. is the missing piece in the global brand jigsaw—Beckham is big in Europe, big in Japan, but in the States, he has a limited brand presence. Moving to the LA Galaxy extends his football career, which remains important to him—he recently insured his body for $100 million, which indicates playing football is his key focus for the next three to four years.

Joining Galaxy, in particular, should deepen his appeal to the Hispanic population, which is a large market—20% of the U.S. population—for whom soccer is hugely important. Also, California will be a good base: it's the lifestyle and entertainment capital of the world and David and Victoria are very much a lifestyle brand. It gives them an ideal launch pad for media exposure.

The potential stumbling block, however, might be that the move from Real Madrid to the U.S. reduces his visibility in Europe and Asia. He could drop out of sight and out of mind to the audiences who are most familiar with him. Most importantly, for brand Beckham to take off in the U.S., David needs to have a sustained positive impact on Major League Soccer, in terms of awareness and audience figures.

Peter Walshe is global brand director at Millward Brown, which has researched perceptions of brand Beckham. Over the last few years, the affinity that people have with Beckham has been sliding and is now relatively low compared to that for other celebrities. This change is particularly noticeable in the UK where he had high "brand affinity" (in that he was someone people liked and identified with) compared to other celebrities. People that like him do so because of his style and physical attraction.

Beckham in 2007 is a brand going through a period of decline. He is seen by relatively more people as overexposed and less trustworthy and credible. Nonetheless, he is still a good fit for luxury brands who want a celebrity to help reinforce their brand messages of style and appearance. But he would be less help to a brand that needed to portray credibility or trust, such as cars, food, or finance.

He is an ambassador for football—his work setting up the Football Academy is one thing that contributes to brand recognition and loyalty. People in Europe and Asia will still be interested in him due to the global nature of football. His brand recognition and affinity is highly likely to grow, propelled by a small but core set of soccer fans who will leverage his popularity for the good of the sport. He could score a double whammy.

Source: "Beckham Likely to Give MLS Some Glamour and Glitz," http://sports.espn.go.com/espn/ wire?section=soccer&id=2506559; "Brand Beckham: Bigger Bucks for Beckham?" *Brand Strategy,* February 5, 2007, p. 12.

- The name should imply the benefits the sports product delivers. For example, the name communicates the product attributes the target market desires.
- The name should be consistent with the image of the rest of the product lines, organization, and city. Again, this is especially important for cities naming their sports franchises. One example of this concept in action is MLS's Columbus Crew.[8] The Crew was chosen to represent the Columbus community in a positive manner. The name suggests the hard work, do-not-quit attitude that people in the Columbus community value.
- The name should be legally and ethically permissible. That is, the name cannot violate another organization's trademarks or be seen as offensive to any group of people. For example, a great many team names with reference to (and perceived negative connotations of) Native Americans have been changed or are under scrutiny (e.g., Miami University of Ohio Redskins to RedHawks, Atlanta Braves, and Washington Redskins). The NCAA decided in 2005 to ban the use of American Indian mascots by sports teams during its postseason tournaments. Schools using American Indian mascots or nicknames would also be barred from hosting NCAA postseason tournaments.

  While choosing a team/brand name is critical to marketing success, some teams and leagues haven't fared so well in the name game. For example, the National Lacrosse League has had a history of poor team names.[9] The Columbus Land Sharks is a name that doesn't seem to make much sense. It's possible they added the "land" due to the inland nature of Ohio's state capital. Other teams in the league, such as the Chicago Shamrox and Portland Lumber Jax, use phonetic spelling, which is always a bad mix. The name Colorado Mammoth conjures up images such as big, slow, and extinct—not exactly a good fit for a professional athletic team.

A **brand mark,** also known as the **logo** or **logotype,** is the element of a brand that cannot be spoken. One of the most recognizable logos in the world is the Nike Swoosh. Interestingly, Carolyn Davidson was paid just $35 in 1971 to create the logo that now adorns Nike products as well as CEO Phil Knight's ankle in the form of a tattoo. It's important for sports marketers to realize that while the Nike logo was created for the paltry sum of $35, the cost of changing logos and nicknames can swell to $250,000. Some of the incidental costs of changing your brand include surveys of constituent groups, designing the logo, retaining a marketing firm, developing a new ad campaign to create awareness, repainting facilities, buying new stationery, replacing signage, creating new uniforms, and even developing a new mascot costume.[10]

A **trademark** identifies that a sports organization has legally registered its brand name or brand mark and thus prevents others from using it. Unfortunately, product counterfeiting or the production of low-cost copies of trademarked popular brands is reaching new heights. Product counterfeiting and trademark infringement are especially problematic at major sporting events, such as the Super Bowl or Olympic Games. For example, Collegiate Licensing Co., recently purchased by IMG, which represents about 200 collegiate properties, found some 3,000 counterfeit items at football bowl games and the NCAA basketball tournament.

The Branding Process

The broad purpose of branding a product is to allow an organization to distinguish and differentiate itself from all others in the marketplace. Building the brand will then ultimately affect consumer behaviors, such as increasing attendance, merchandising sales,

SPOTLIGHT ON SPORTS MARKETING ETHICS

Native American Mascots: Racial Slur or Cherished Tradition?

Native American mascots and nicknames can be seen everywhere in our society. People drive Jeep Cherokees, watch Atlanta Braves baseball fans do the tomahawk chop, and enjoy professional and college football teams such as the Kansas City Chiefs and the Florida State University Seminoles. Are the use of these symbols a tribute to the Native American peoples, or as some feel, a slap in the face to their honored traditions?

Across the country, according to the National Coalition on Race and Sports in Media, which is part of the American Indian Movement (AIM), there are more than 3,000 racist or offensive mascots used in high school, college, or professional sports teams. In New Jersey alone, there are dozens of schools that use Native American images and symbols such as braves, warriors, chiefs, or Indians for their sports teams.

In April 2001, the U.S. Commission on Civil Rights recommended that all non–Native American schools drop their Native American mascots or nicknames. The commission declared that "the stereotyping of any racial, ethnic, religious or other group, when promoted by our public educational institutions, teaches all students that stereotyping of minority groups is acceptable, which is a dangerous lesson in a diverse society." The commission also noted that these nicknames and mascots are "false portrayals that encourage biases and prejudices that have a negative effect on contemporary Indian people."

Harmless Fun?

For years, Native American organizations have opposed the use of such mascots, finding them offensive and a racial slur against their people. Supporters of the nicknames believe they honor Native Americans and focus on their bravery, courage, and fighting skills.

Karl Swanson, vice president of the Washington Redskins professional football team, declared in the magazine *Sports Illustrated* that his team's name "symbolizes courage, dignity, and leadership," and that the "Redskins symbolize the greatness and strength of a grand people."

In the Native American mascot controversy, the nickname "redskins" is particularly controversial and offensive. Historically, the term was used to refer to the scalps of dead Native Americans that were exchanged for money as bounties, or cash rewards. When it became too difficult to bring in the bodies of dead Indians to get the money (usually under a dollar per person), bounty hunters exchanged bloody scalps or "redskins" as evidence of the dead Indian.

In 1992 seven Native Americans filed a lawsuit against the Washington Redskins football club. Suzan Shown Harjo, one of the plaintiffs in the case, wrote in her essay, "Fighting Name-Calling: Challenging 'Redskins' in Court," which appeared in the book titled *Team Spirits—The Native American Mascots Controversy,* that they "petitioned the U.S. Patent and Trademark Office for cancellation of federal registrations for Redskins and Redskinettes...and associated names of the team in the nation's capital." In 1999, the Trademark Trial and Appeal Board "found that Redskins was an offensive term historically and remained so from the first trademark license in 1967, to the present." In a 145-page decision, the panel unanimously canceled the federal trademarks because they "may disparage Native Americans and may bring them into contempt or disrepute," Harjo reported. The Washington Redskins appealed the decision and the case is now pending in federal district court.

Demeaning or Entertaining?

Supporters contend that such nicknames are an entertaining part of a cherished tradition and were never intended to harm or make a mockery of any group. There is also a financial side to the issue. The sale of merchandise with team mascots and nicknames on items such as T-shirts, hats and jackets brings in millions of dollars to various schools and sports teams every year. A changeover would cost money and render much of the current merchandise obsolete, the teams contend.

Opponents of Native American mascots and nicknames are not concerned about the cost and use words such as disrespectful and hurtful, degrading and humiliating to describe what they believe is racial stereotyping. They regard the mascots as caricatures of real Indians that trivialize and demean native dances and sacred Indian rituals.

"It's the behavior that accompanies all of this that's offensive," Clyde Bellecourt told *USA Today*. Bellecourt, who is national director of AIM, said "The rubber tomahawks, the chicken feather headdresses, people wearing war paint and making these ridiculous war whoops with a tomahawk in one hand and a beer in the other—all of these have significant meaning for us. And the psychological impact it has, especially on our youth, is devastating."

What Is the Price of Entertainment?

What is at stake, opponents of Native American mascots argue, is the self-image and self-esteem of American Indian children.

(Continued)

(Continued)

"Their pride is being mocked," Matthew Beaudet, an attorney and president of the Illinois Native American Bar Association, explained in "More Than a Mascot," an article that appeared in the newsletter, *School Administrator*. "The Native American community is saying we know you're trying to flatter us, but we're not flattered, so stop."

Washington Post columnist Richard Cohen agrees. "It hardly enhances the self-esteem of an Indian youth to always see his people and himself represented as a cartoon character," Cohen wrote. "And, always, the caricature is suggestive of battle, of violence—of the Indian warrior, the brave, the chief, the warpath, the beating of tom-toms."

Survey Says

The mascot issue is most controversial at the local level. Although numerous schools have voluntarily taken action to cease using Native American symbols, many school boards have refused to do so. Supporters of Native American mascots and nicknames point to surveys, such as the one published by *Sports Illustrated* in March 2002, which found that although most Native American activists found Indian mascots and nicknames offensive, the majority of nonactivist American Indians were not disturbed by them.

American Indian activists explained the discrepancy in the *Sports Illustrated* article that accompanied the survey, saying, "Native Americans' self-esteem has fallen so low that they don't even know when they're being insulted."

Harjo, who is president of the Morning Star Institute, an Indian-rights organization in Washington, D.C., stated in her essay, "There are happy campers on every plantation." Harjo implied that although many slaves may have been content with their lives in bondage, the institution of slavery still needed to be abolished and the same reasoning holds true for Native American mascots.

According to the *Sports Illustrated* survey, 87 percent of American Indians who lived off Indian reservations did not object to Native American mascots or nicknames. Of the Indians who lived on reservations, 67 percent were not bothered by the nicknames, while 33 percent opposed them.

In addition to the survey, those who would like to keep the traditional Native American nicknames give examples of American Indian tribes that have openly embraced schools and teams using their names. At Arapahoe High School in Littleton, Colorado, for example, the Warriors' school gym is named for Anthony Sitting Eagle, an Arapaho leader. Every year on Arapaho Day, tribal members come from the reservation to visit with students and teach Arapaho history and traditions. Tribal leaders have also advised the Warriors on how to make their logo authentic, and even persuaded the school to remove a painting on the gym floor because it was offensive to have students walk over it. Similar close relationships exist between Florida State University and the Seminole tribe, Central Michigan University and the Chippewa tribe, and the Arcadia High School Apaches in California, who have a relationship with an American Indian tribe in Arizona.

Racial Slur or Cherished Tradition?

The Native American mascot issue has caused debate throughout the country between communities and school boards, students and Native American groups. Although the outcome of the debates has varied from state to state, with some communities refusing to change, the trend in recent years has been to eliminate offensive Native American mascots and nicknames at schools and colleges. Not a single professional sports team, however, has changed its name. Given the strong opinions on both sides and the pending Washington Redskins case, the controversy will no doubt rage on.

Source: Phyllis Raybin Emert, "Native American Mascots: Racial Slur or Cherished Tradition?" New Jersey State Bar Association, http://www.njsbf.com/njsbf/student/respect/winter03–1.cfm.

or participation in sports. However, before these behaviors are realized, several things must happen in the **branding process** shown in Figure 7.3.

First, **brand awareness** must be established. Brand awareness refers to making consumers in the desired target market recognize and remember the brand name. Only after awareness levels reach their desired objectives can brand image be addressed. After all, consumers must be aware of the product before they can understand the image the sports marketer is trying to project.

After brand awareness is established, marketing efforts turn to developing and managing a **brand image.** Brand image is described as the consumers' set of beliefs

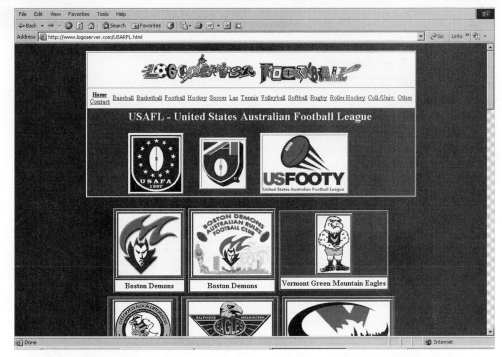

Sports logos gallery on the Web.
Source: Logo Server. Used by permission.

about a brand, which, in turn, shape attitudes. Brand image can also be thought of as the "personality" of the brand. Organizations that sponsor sporting events are especially interested in strengthening or maintaining the image of their products through association with a sports entity (athlete, team, or league) that reflects the desired image. For instance, the marketers of Mercedes-Benz automobiles have established sponsorships with tennis events to reinforce a brand image of power, grace, and control.

Sports marketers attempt to manage beliefs that we have about a particular brand through a number of "image drivers," or factors that influence the brand image. The image drivers controlled by sports marketing efforts include product features or characteristics, product performance or quality, price, brand name, customer service, packaging, advertising, promotion, and distribution channels. Each of these image drivers contributes to creating the overall brand image. After shaping a positive brand image, sports marketers can then ultimately hope to create high levels of brand equity.

Another link in the branding process is developing high levels of brand equity. **Brand equity** is the value that the brand contributes to a product in the marketplace. In economic terms, it is the difference in value between a branded product and its generic equivalent. Consumers who believe a sport product has a high level of brand equity are more likely to be satisfied with the brand. The satisfied consumers will, in turn, become brand-loyal or repeat purchasers. Gladden, Milne, and Sutton have developed a unique

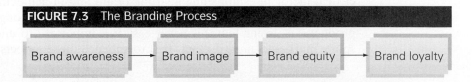

FIGURE 7.3 The Branding Process

Brand awareness → Brand image → Brand equity → Brand loyalty

FIGURE 7.4   Conceptual Model for Assessing Brand Equity

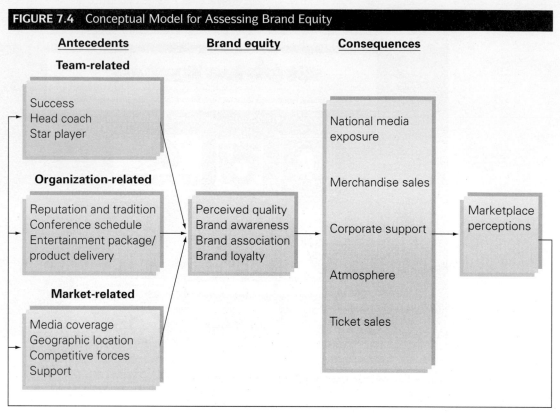

model of assessing brand equity for the sports industry. The components of the model can be seen in Figure 7.4. The authors explain brand equity by extending the previous work of Aaker (1991), who believes there are four major components of brand equity. These are perceived quality, brand awareness, brand associations, and brand loyalty. Gladden, Milne, and Sutton describe the perceived quality of sport as the consumers' perceptions of a team's success. Obviously, this could be extended beyond the notion of a team to other sport products. Brand awareness is defined as the consumers' familiarity with a particular team or sport product. Brand associations refer to the intangible attributes of a brand or, in the case of sport, the experiential and symbolic attributes offered by an athletic team. The final component, brand loyalty, is defined as the ability to attract and retain consumers. As the authors point out, this is sometimes difficult because of the inconsistent and intangible nature of the sports product.[11]

When describing the full model of brand equity for sport, Gladden and his colleagues also discuss the antecedents and consequences of brand equity for a sports product. These antecedent conditions are particularly important for marketing managers to understand because they will have an impact on the level of brand equity. The three broad categories of antecedents include team-related factors, organization-related factors, and market-related factors.

Team-related factors are further broken down into the success of the team, head coach, and star player(s). Previous research has shown that winning or success is still a critical factor in establishing a strong brand and in achieving the desired outcomes such as merchandise sales, media exposure, and so on. Although selling an inferior core product (i.e., losing team) is never easy, it is important to underscore the notion that sports marketers must do their best to enhance those aspects of the event experience

When Winning Isn't Everything

So why are fans coming? Even diehards like Steve MacGillivray of Hanover rationalized when asked why he paid hard-earned cash to spend his Friday night with his girlfriend watching a team that loses far more often than it wins. "I know they're bad, but they have a nucleus of young players and you know they're all trying," he said. "You can smell it coming slowly."

Celtics executives know it's been too long since the club was a contender. To sell tickets, they knew they needed something more than the team that lost a team record 18 consecutive games this season (2007). They needed: a dance team, free concerts by R&B singers and rock stars after the game, ticket packages aimed at corporate mavens during the week and at families on Sunday afternoons. A professional gymnast as a mascot, a swanky new club for courtside seat owners, and a new high-definition Jumbotron scoreboard. In short, the Celtics had to persuade fans that coming to see the game is about everything but. And it's working.

"They've created an environment that the game experience can be enjoyable regardless" of winning or losing, said Chip Tuttle, chief executive of sports marketing and advertising firm Conover Tuttle Pace. The Seattle game is a perfect example. The Celtics came back to win, but it might not have mattered to some fans because there was much else to pay attention to before and during the game. Two of the team's owners mingled with sponsors and fans in the new Lexus Courtside Club before tip-off. The Celtics Dancers, a troupe created this year for whom a Los Angeles choreographer was hired to lead, performed several times. Elementary school kids played on the court at halftime. A row of fans won Massachusetts Lottery scratch tickets and had their faces on the scoreboard. One fan even won a prize for answering a movie trivia question.

The Celtics may be benefiting from a resurgence in the NBA's popularity. Attendance waned after stars like Michael Jordan, Dennis Rodman, Magic Johnson, and Larry Bird retired in the 1990s, but the league predicts its fourth straight attendance record this year. Still, year-to-date attendance across the NBA is up only about 2 percent, so the league's rising popularity doesn't account for all of the Celtics' growth.

Some of the league's resurgence is owed to teams bringing in off-court entertainment at least a decade ago. The Celtics are Johnny-come-latelies to the trend. League officials and basketball specialists say the team has surpassed others in marketing because they've made a science of figuring out precisely not only who's coming to games, but who is not and how to get them there.

"They can tell you where their customers live, what kind of cars they drive, what country clubs they belong to," said Scott O'Neil, the NBA's senior vice president of team marketing and business operations. O'Neil monitors how NBA teams market themselves, then evangelizes on behalf of the best practices elsewhere. Lately, much of his gospel comes from the Book of Green and White.

The Celtics don't win much, but "they are the most analytically savvy team in the NBA," O'Neil said. But when the current owners took over four years ago, the team hardly knew anything about why fans bought tickets, said Rich Gotham, the Celtics' chief operating officer. Many, including O'Neil and Wycliffe Grousbeck, the Celtics' managing partner, credit Gotham, a former vice president of sales for Internet search firm Lycos, in large part for the move toward collecting fan data and using it to get people to buy tickets.

Under Gotham, the Celtics survey fans every chance they get, especially during games. They monitor how often season ticket holders show up, and if that falls below a certain level, the fan gets a call or e-mail from a team executive, asking why they're not showing up. George Matta, a 38-year-old Watertown fan who paid $3,800 for a package that includes two seats in section 19, row K, to half this season's games, said he got such an e-mail this season. He responded with his displeasure over what he considers unfair discounts offered to casual fans.

"They're selling my tickets at half-price," he said. "I'm paying full price for seats for a losing team," he complained, adding that he might not renew after three years as a season ticket holder. The team avoids discounting seats near season ticket holders, Gotham said, although they have offered tickets for $65 each in Matta's section to games against unpopular teams. Season ticket holders like Matta, whose seats cost $75 each, already get a discount off the face value of their tickets along with perks like first crack at playoff seats if the Celtics return to postseason play.

Gotham used an analogy from the airline industry—where one seat often has a drastically different price than the one next to it—to describe the Celtics' discount policy. "You don't want the plane to fly with any empty seats on it," he said. "The last 600 seats on a Wednesday night in February, we've got to figure out how to get people to say, 'yeah, I'm in.'"

If the Celtics are short that last 600 seats 48 hours before tip-off, they e-mail their best customers—season ticket owners, sponsors, and subscribers to their two e-mail newsletters—with a proposition. A $40 seat might go for $25, Gotham said, and come with other perks from a team sponsor. (Pepsi, for example, might offer free drinks.) That gives the Celtics another built-in edge:

(Continued)

(*Continued*)

Fans know that in order to be in line for a good deal, they need to buy season tickets or at least give up their e-mail addresses, which allows the team to gather its information.

The Celtics have inspired creativity, if not envy, from the other team that considers the Garden home. Charlie Jacobs, executive vice president for the Boston Bruins, said his team is trying to mimic the Celtics' success with tactics like a guerilla marketing campaign in which the team planted an ice sculpture at Faneuil Hall last summer, and the hiring of a liaison to youth hockey leagues. The Bruins have a better record than the Celtics and the team is still in contention for a playoff spot, but Bruins games at the Garden have averaged about 87 percent of capacity this season, Jacobs said.

Source: Keith Reed, "When Winning Isn't Everything: Battered Celtics Drawing Sellout Crowds with Deals, Dancers, and Rock and Roll," *The Boston Globe*, March 15, 2007, D1.

that they can control. As the accompanying article illustrates, the Boston Celtics are still selling out even after a series of losing seasons.

Although success is defined by wins and losses, it can also be thought of as the historical standard by which the team has been judged. Interestingly, the authors of the model also believe the head coach can be an important factor in establishing brand equity. The University of Minnesota received a tremendous boost when they hired basketball coach Tubby Smith, and the Chicago Cubs brand was bolstered with the hiring of former head coach Lou Piniella. Similarly, a star player or players can boost brand equity, especially in the sports of baseball and basketball. For example, the LeBron phenomenon has given the Cleveland Cavaliers a new image and chance to reposition their franchise. Even the already powerful Yankees enhanced their brand by trading for pitcher Andy Pettitte and re-signing (for the second time) Roger Clemens. The organization-related antecedents described in the model include reputation and tradition, conference and schedule, and entertainment package–product delivery. The reputation and tradition of the team off the field is believed to be a factor in building brand equity. An excellent example of problems in the front office influencing fan perceptions and brand equity is that of the hapless Arizona Cardinals. Owner Bill Bidwell has been scrutinized and criticized by the fans and media for years because of bad choices made on and off the field. The conference affiliation and schedule are also organizational factors influencing image. Gladden et al. believe college and professional teams who play in tougher conferences with long-standing rivals will create greater benefits for the team's equity in the long term. This must certainly hold some truth as college teams and conferences are constantly realigning. Louisville, Cincinnati, Marquette, DePaul, and South Florida have all left Conference USA for the Big East. In turn, Conference USA has lined up SMU, Tulsa, Marshall, and Rice as replacement schools. Additionally, the ACC has added Miami, Virginia Tech, and Boston College to their membership.[12] Finally, the entertainment aspect of sport created and managed by the organization will affect brand equity. As mentioned previously, this is one of the controllable elements of the largely uncontrollable sports industry.

The market-related antecedents are those things such as media coverage, geographic location, competitive forces, and support. Media coverage refers to the exposure the sport product receives in the media via multiple outlets such as radio, TV, newspaper, and the Internet. Obviously, the images portrayed in the media and amount of coverage can have a huge bearing on all aspects of brand equity. Geographic location is also related to equity in that certain areas of the United States are linked with certain types of sport. As described in Milne and McDonald,[13] "it may be easier to establish brand equity for a Division I men's basketball team in Indiana than it would be in Idaho." Competition must also be considered a market factor, and the authors of the model describe it as the most influential in creating equity. In some instances, competition can enhance the value of a brand, but more typically competitive forces vying for similar consumers will weaken equity and its outcomes. Fan support is the final market force influencing equity. Quite simply, the greater the number of loyal fans or supporters, the greater the brand equity.

Although the preceding discussion has focused on the antecedents of brand equity to a sports product, the model also describes the related outcomes or consequences of establishing a strong brand. More specifically, the authors believe higher levels of brand equity will lead to more national media exposure, greater sales of team merchandise, more support from corporate sponsors, enhanced stadium atmospherics, and increased ticket sales.

How can marketers assess the equity of a brand such as the Yankees or Nike? One popular technique to measure brand equity evaluates a brand's performance across seven dimensions. Brand equity is then calculated by applying a multiple, determined by the brand's performance on the seven dimensions, to the net brand-related profits. These dimensions include leadership or the ability of the brand to influence its market, stability or the ability of the brand to survive, market or the trading environment of the brand internationality or the ability of the brand to cross geographic and cultural borders, trend or the ongoing direction of the brand's importance to the industry, support or the effectiveness of the brand's communication, and protection of the owner's legal title.[14]

Although there are a number of ways to measure brand equity in consumer goods, there have been very few attempts to look at the equity of sports teams. One exception was a study that measured the brand equity of MLB franchises.[15] To measure brand equity, the researchers first calculated team revenues for each franchise. These revenues are based on gate receipts; media; licensing and merchandise; and stadium-oriented issues, such as concessions, advertising, and so on. The franchise value is then assigned a multiple based on growth projections for network television fees. Next, the total franchise value is subtracted from the value of a generic product to determine the brand equity. Because there is no such thing as a generic baseball team, the researchers used the $130 million fee paid by the two new expansion teams at the time of the study, Tampa Bay and Arizona. This $130 million fee represents the closest estimate to an unbranded team, because the new teams had yet to begin play.

Interestingly, only seven of the 30 MLB teams show any brand equity. Based on the research, the following teams have positive brand equity (in rank order): New York Yankees, Toronto Blue Jays and New York Mets, Boston Red Sox, Los Angeles Dodgers, Chicago White Sox, and Texas Rangers. The teams with the lowest brand equity include the Pittsburgh Pirates and Seattle Mariners. Given the fact that many of these "brands" have been around for decades, the brand equity for MLB franchises is surprisingly low.

Although the previous study used an economic basis for determining brand equity, other research has employed less precise, qualitative approaches. For example, a panel of sporting goods industry experts was asked to name the most powerful brands in sport. In this study of equity, sports brands were defined as those who directly manufacture sporting apparel, equipment, and shoes. Nike is in a league of its own when it comes to branding. Ever since the introduction of the Air Jordan basketball shoe, Nike has grown geometrically since the days when Phil Knight (CEO) sold shoes out of the trunk of his car.

Brand loyalty is one of the most important concepts to sports marketers, because it refers to a consistent preference or repeat purchase of one brand over all others in a product category. Marketers want their products to satisfy consumers, so decision making becomes a matter of habit rather than an extensive evaluation among competing brands.

SPORTS MARKETING HALL OF FAME

Phil Knight

A former University of Oregon track-and-field athlete and Stanford MBA, Knight is the founder and current CEO of Nike, Inc. By all accounts, Nike and Knight are still changing the face of sports marketing. Knight started his multibillion-dollar empire by selling his specialized running shoes out of the trunk of his car.

The ultimate driving force of Nike's success has been Knight's ability to attract top sports stars and build marketing campaigns around them. Nike's first celebrity athlete was the University of Oregon's track star, Steve Prefontaine. When Nike was surpassed by Reebok in the late 1980s, they landed their biggest success story to date—MJ, Michael Jordan. Quickly, Nike regained its position as market leader and has not relinquished it since. Most recently, Knight has added high school phenom LeBron James to the stable of Nike endorsers. He's been named the Most Powerful Man in Sports and Knight considers his job is to "wake up consumers."

Sources: Michael McCarthy, "Wake Up Consumers? Nike's Brash CEO Dares to Do It All," *USA Today*, June 16, 2003, 1B; Keith Elliot Greenberg, Bill Bowerman, and Phil Knight, *Building the Nike Empire* (Woodbridge, CT: Blackbird Press, 1994); David R. Collins and Philip H. Knight, *Running with Nike* (Ada, OK: Garrett Educational Corp., 1992).

In sports marketing, teams represent perhaps one of the most interesting examples of loyalty. It is common to hear us speak of people as being "loyal fans" or "fair-weather fans." The loyal fans endure all the team's successes and hardships. As the definition implies, they continue to prefer their team over others. Alternatively, the fair-weather fan will jump to and from the teams that are successful at the time.

What are the determinants of fan loyalty to a team? Psychologist Robert Passikoff believes the interaction of four factors creates fan loyalty.[16] The first factor is the *entertainment value* of athletics. As we discussed in Chapter 5, entertainment value is one of the underlying factors of fan motivation. In addition, entertainment was discussed as one of the perceived values of sports to the community. The second component of fan loyalty is *authenticity*. Passikoff defines authenticity as the "acceptance of the game as real and meaningful." *Fan bonding* is the third component of fan loyalty. *Bonding* refers to the degree to which fans identify with players and the team. The bonding component is similar to the concept of fan identification discussed in Chapter 5. The fourth and final component of fan loyalty is the *history and tradition* of the team. For example, the Cincinnati Reds are baseball's oldest team and, although they may be lacking in other dimensions of loyalty, they certainly have a long history and tradition with the fans in the greater Cincinnati area.

To measure fan loyalty, self-identified fans are asked to rate their hometown teams on each of the four dimensions. Interestingly, the fan loyalty measure does not specifically include a team performance component. Contrary to popular belief, Passikoff believes winning and loyalty do not always go hand in hand. Table 7.2 provides the 2006 Fan Loyalty Index for best and worst franchises in Major League Baseball.

Another way to operationalize the loyalty construct has been developed by researchers Dan Mahoney and his colleagues.[17] They believe that loyalty can be thought of as having two distinct components: attitudinal loyalty and behavioral loyalty. Attitudinal loyalty can be expressed as an individual's psychological commitment to the team (or PCT). To better understand how to measure PCT and what it means, Table 7.3 shows the scale developed by Mahoney.

In our society, loyalty to sports teams, at the high school, college, and professional levels, is perhaps higher than it is for any other goods and services we consume.

TABLE 7.2	Fan Loyalty Index for Major League Baseball: The Best and Worst

Major League Baseball

Top Five	*Bottom Five*
1. Boston Red Sox	16. Texas Rangers
2. Houston Astros	17. Kansas City Royals (tie)
3. New York Yankees	Florida Marlins (tie)
4. Cleveland Indians	18. Pittsburgh Pirates
5. Atlanta Braves (tie)	19. Colorado Rockies
St. Louis Cardinals (tie)	20. Baltimore Orioles (tie)
	Tampa Bay Devil Rays (tie)

Source: Adapted from Brand Keys, Inc. http://www.brandkeys.com/awards/sports06.cfm

Unfortunately, team loyalty at the professional level is beginning to erode because of the constant threat of uprooting the franchise and moving it to a new town. This is perhaps one reason for the increased popularity of amateur athletics. Colleges will not threaten to move for a better stadium deal, and athletes do not change teams for better contracts (although they do leave their universities early for professional contracts). To increase fan loyalty, many teams are establishing fan loyalty programs, pairing new technology with existing marketing principles. Scott Loft, vice president of ticket sales for the NHL's Nashville Predators, says that his team is using customer relationship management technology to collect detailed information about fan demographics and psychographics. Interestingly, Loft believes this is a shift for sports organizations. Loft estimates that "90 percent of sports teams either don't care or don't bother to find out any information about their fan base."

TABLE 7.3	Psychological Commitment to Team Scale

1. I might rethink my allegiance to my favorite team if this team consistently performs poorly.
2. I would watch a game featuring the [name of team] regardless of which team they are playing.
3. I would rethink my allegiance to the [name of team] if the best players left the team (i.e., transfer, graduate, etc.).
4. Being a fan of the [name of team] is important to me.
5. Nothing could change my allegiance to the [name of team].
6. I am a committed fan of the [name of team].
7. It would not affect my loyalty to the [name of team] if the athletic department hired a head coach that I disliked very much.
8. I could easily be persuaded to change my preference for the [name of team].
9. I have been a fan of the [name of team] since I began watching collegiate football.
10. I could never switch my loyalty from the [name of team] even if my close friends were fans of another team.
11. It would be unlikely for me to change my allegiance from the [name of team] to another team.
12. It would be difficult to change my beliefs about the [name of team].
13. You can tell a lot about a person by their willingness to stick with a team that is not performing well.
14. My commitment to the [name of team] would decrease if they were performing poorly and there appeared little chance their performance would change.

The loyalty programs are driven by a card that is swiped at kiosks when fans enter a stadium or event. The fans benefit by earning points that can be redeemed for rewards such as free tickets, merchandise, and concessions. The teams benefit by collecting valuable information on their fan base that can later be used to direct strategic marketing decisions. Major League Baseball seems to have taken the lead in fan loyalty efforts, with teams such as the Cardinals, Padres, and A's all successfully establishing programs.[18]

Nonsport organizations also seek to develop customer loyalty through sport. For example, Best Western Hotels wants consumers to stay at one of their properties every time they leave home for work or leisure travel, regardless of whether they have the most inexpensive rooms or competitive properties are being promoted. To establish loyal consumers, Best Western, the "Official Hotel of NASCAR," has developed a Speed Rewards loyalty program. Speed Rewards is Best Western's free frequent guest program tailored to the race enthusiast—and the first in the industry designed for a specific lifestyle demographic. As members, individuals can earn points that are redeemable for NASCAR-licensed merchandise such as jackets, caps, and race-related items including ProScan headsets and Richard Petty Driving Experience gift certificates.

From May to June, 2007 members of Speed Rewards earned an entry into the contest for each night they stayed at any Best Western hotels worldwide. A random drawing determined the grand prize winner, who received a VIP experience for two to the October 12 Busch Series race in Charlotte, N.C.

Licensing

The importance of having a strong brand is demonstrated when an organization considers product licensing. **Licensing** is a contractual agreement whereby a company may use another company's trademark in exchange for a royalty or fee. A branding strategy through licensing allows the organization to authorize the use of brand, brand name,

Future Redbirds in their St. Louis Cardinals licensed baby gear .

brand mark, trademark, or trade name in conjunction with a good, service, or promotion in return for royalties. According to Steve Sleight, "Licensing is a booming area of the sports business with players, teams, event names, and logos appearing on a vastly expanding range of products."[19] For example, the NFL has approximately 350 licensees selling more than 2,500 products such as apparel, sporting goods, basketball cards and collectibles, home furnishings, school supplies, home electronics, interactive games, home video, publishing, toys, games, gifts, and novelties.

Since the emergence of NFL Properties in 1963, licensing has become one of the most prevalent sports product strategies. In 2006, sales of licensed sport products reached an estimated $16.5 billion across Major League Baseball, the National Football League, National Basketball Association, collegiate products, and NASCAR. Additionally, the PGA and Major League Soccer are growing markets that together account for $1.5 billion in sales.[20]

Let's take a look at the top five properties and their plans for strategic growth.

1. **Major League Baseball, $4.7 billion**: MLB will continue to integrate the video game business with Take Two Interactive in conjunction with its 30 clubs and sponsors. Other initiatives: enhance and support the new baseball card model through a national marketing campaign; launch new MLB Authentic Collection performance-based products; market to fans through the Access to the Show marketing program; focus on the fast-growing women's and kids' apparel businesses.

2. **National Football League, $3.2 billion**: The video game category will drive the business with continued share growth of established titles and games reaching new segments. Steady growth of the core apparel business, particularly key segments such as performance, women's and children's, and international markets, will be important for 2007 as will lifestyle products such as games and toys, home goods, game day entertainment, the DVD business, and new properties.

3. **National Basketball Association, $3 billion**: A global partnership with adidas as official outfitter for the NBA, WNBA, and NBA D-League led to increased sales of apparel and footwear and to the activation of a record number of retail partner promotions and campaigns for 2006. The launch of the adidas Originals NBA Superstars Collection in December 2006 was the most successful footwear launch in the history of the NBA Store. Additionally, the fourth quarter was the strongest in the store's history. Categories of focus: video games, apparel, footwear, sporting goods, and trading cards. International business accounts for 25 percent of overall sales, with 50 percent growth expected in China in 2006. The NBAStore.com now offers a European-specific store and stores in Spanish, Chinese, and Japanese languages.

4. **The Collegiate Licensing Company, $3.5 billion (est.)**: CLC will launch the College Vault, an overriding vintage brand for colleges and universities featuring high-end vintage-inspired apparel penetrating bookstores, department stores, and new distribution channels such as clothing boutiques and Urban Outfitters. Officially licensed collegiate Crocs-branded footwear will launch in school colors in the near future. Spalding will launch high-end school-specific basketballs. "We will continue to work with nontraditional retailers to create collegiate sections within their stores," says Kit Walsh, senior vice president, marketing, CLC. "An example would be the home improvement channel such as Home Depot and Lowe's."

5. **NASCAR, $2.1 billion (est.)**: NASCAR's licensing division expected modest growth for 2007, due in large part to retail development that has opened many new doors for its licensees. From Bed, Bath and Beyond to Cracker Barrel and Target, NASCAR continues to expand into new channels of distribution.[21]

Licensed merchandise on the Web.
Source: Copyright © 2004 FansEdge, Inc. All rights reserved.

Indeed, licensing is everywhere and sports is the fastest growing segment of the licensed merchandise market, but just what are the benefits of merchandise licensing? First, let us look at the advantages and disadvantages for the licensee.

ADVANTAGES TO THE LICENSEE
- The licensee benefits from the positive association with the sports entity. In other words, the positive attributes of the player, team, league, or event are transferred to the licensed product or service.
- The licensee benefits from greater levels of brand awareness.
- The licensee benefits by saving the time and money normally required to build high levels of brand equity.
- The licensee may receive initial distribution with retailers and potentially receive expanded and improved shelf space for their products.
- The licensee may be able to charge higher prices for the licensed product or service.

DISADVANTAGES TO THE LICENSEE
- The athlete, team, league, or sport may fall into disfavor. For example, using an athlete such as Allen Iverson is risky given his past behavior, off the court as well as on the court.

In addition to the licensee, the licensor also experiences benefits and risks due to the nature of the licensing agreement.

ADVANTAGES TO THE LICENSOR
- The licensor is able to expand into new markets and penetrate existing markets more than ever before.
- The licensor is able to generate heightened awareness of the sports entity and potentially increase its equity if it is paired with the appropriate products and services.

DISADVANTAGES TO THE LICENSOR
- The licensor may lose some control over the elements of the marketing mix. For instance, product quality may be inferior, or price reductions may be offered frequently. This may lessen the perceived image of the licensor.

Based on all these considerations, care must be taken in choosing merchandising–licensing partnerships. Certainly, "the manufacturer of the licensed product should demonstrate an ability to meet and maintain quality control standards, possess financial stability, and offer an aggressive and well-planned marketing and promotional strategy."[22]

In addition to carefully choosing a partner, licensors and licensees must also be on the lookout for counterfeit merchandise. One estimate has it that $1 billion worth of counterfeit sports products hit the streets each year. For instance, the NFL typically confiscates $1 million worth of fake goods during Super Bowl week. The Beijing organizing committee was targeting income of $70 million from merchandising Olympic products for the 2008 Games and in previous games an estimated $17 million in bad goods were sold. In an attempt to stop or reduce counterfeit merchandise, Olympic officials have previously used a new DNA technology in which an official Olympic product has a special ink containing the DNA of an athlete. A handheld scanner determines whether the tag matches the DNA and whether the merchandise is legitimate.[23]

This problem has become so pervasive that the leagues now have their own logo cops who travel from city to city and event to event searching for violations. In addition to this form of enforcement, the Coalition to Advance the Protection of Sports Logos (CAPS; see http://www.capsinfo.com/) was formed in 1992 to investigate and control counterfeit products. CAPS has picked up millions of dollars' worth of counterfeit products and production equipment since 1992. In 2005, the coalition recovered nearly 300,000 pieces of counterfeit merchandise using the logos of professional and college sports teams. The items were valued at more than $60 million. How can consumers guard against fakes? CAPS offers the following suggestions to consumers who are purchasing sports products.[24]

- *Look for Quality*—Poor lettering, colors that are slightly different from the true team colors, and background colors bleeding through the top color overlay are all signs of poor product quality.
- *Verification*—Counterfeiters may try to fake the official logo. Official items will typically have holograms on the product or stickers with moving figures, and embroidered logos should be tightly woven.
- *Check Garment Tags*—Poor-quality merchandise is often designated by split garment tags. Rarely, if ever, will official licensed products use factory rejects or seconds.

Quality

Thus far, we have looked at some of the branding issues related to sports products. Another important aspect of the product considered by sports marketers that will influence brand equity is quality. Let us look at two different types of quality: service quality and product quality.

Quality of Services

As sports organizations develop a marketing orientation, the need to deliver a high level of service quality to consumers is becoming increasingly important. For instance, at NFL Properties (NFLP), service quality is taken to the highest levels. NFLP is highly committed to understanding the individualized needs of each of its sponsors. Every sponsor of the NFL receives the name of a primary contact at NFLP whom they can call at any time to discuss their marketing needs. They also recognize that each sponsor is in need of a unique sponsorship program, given their vastly different objectives and levels of financial commitment to the NFL.[25]

Although NFLP is an excellent example of an organization that values service quality, we have yet to define the concept. **Service quality** is a difficult concept to define, and as such, many definitions of service quality exist. Rather than define it, most researchers have resorted to explaining the dimensions or determinants of service quality. Unfortunately, there is also little agreement on what dimensions actually comprise service quality or how best to measure it.

Lehtinen and Lehtinen say service quality consists of physical, interactive, and corporate dimensions.[26] The physical quality component looks at the tangible aspect of the service. More specifically, physical quality refers to the appearance of the personnel or the physical facilities where the service is actually performed. For example, the physical appearance of the ushers at the game may affect the consumer's perceived level of service quality.

Interactive quality refers to the two-way flow of information that disseminates from both the service provider and the service recipient at the time of the service encounter. The importance of the two-way flow of information is why many researchers choose to examine service quality from a dyadic perspective. This suggests gathering the perceptions of service quality from stadium employees, as well as fans.

The image attributed to the service provider by its current and potential users is referred to as corporate quality. As just discussed, product performance and quality is one of the drivers of brand image. Moreover, Lehtinen and Lehtinen also cited customer service as one of the image drivers. This suggests a strong relationship between corporate quality, or image of the team, and consumers' perceptions of service quality.

Groonos describes service quality dimensions in a different manner.[27] He believes service quality has both a technical and functional component. Technical quality is described as "what is delivered." Functional quality refers to "how the service is delivered." For instance, "what is delivered" might include the final outcome of the game, the hot dogs that were consumed, or the merchandise that was purchased. "How the service is delivered" might represent the effort put forth by the team and its players, the friendliness of the hot dog vendor, or the quick service provided by the merchandise vendor. This is especially important in sports marketing, as "the total game experience" is evaluated using both the "what" and "how" components of quality.

The most widely adopted description of service quality is based on a series of studies by Parasuraman, Zeithaml, and Berry.[28] They isolated five distinct dimensions of service quality. These **dimensions of service quality** comprise some of its fundamental areas and consist of reliability, assurance, empathy, responsiveness, and tangibles. Because of their importance in service quality literature, a brief description of each follows.

Reliability refers to the ability to perform promised service dependably and accurately. **Assurance** is the knowledge and courtesy of employees and their ability to convey trust and confidence. **Empathy** is defined as the caring, individualized attention the firm provides its customers. **Responsiveness** refers to the willingness to help customers and provide prompt service. **Tangibles** are the physical facilities, equipment, and appearance of the service personnel.

To assess consumers' perceptions of service quality across each dimension, a 22-item survey instrument was developed by Parasuraman, Zeithaml, and Berry. The instrument, known as SERVQUAL, requires that the 22 items be administered twice. First, the respondents are asked to rate their expectations of service quality. Next, the respondents are asked to rate perceptions of service quality within the organization. For example, "Your dealings with XYZ are very pleasant" is a perception (performance) item, whereas the corresponding expectation item would be "Customers' dealing with these firms should be very pleasant."

From a manager's perspective, measuring expectations and perceptions of performance allows action plans to be developed to improve service quality. Organizational resources should be allocated to improving those service quality areas where consumer expectations are high and perceptions of quality are low.

The original SERVQUAL instrument has been tested across a wide variety of industries, including banking, telecommunications, health care, consulting, education, and retailing. Most important, McDonald, Sutton, and Milne adapted SERVQUAL and used it to evaluate spectators' perceptions of service quality for an NBA team. The researchers fittingly called their adapted SERVQUAL instrument **TEAMQUAL.**[29]

In addition to finding that the NBA team exceeded service quality expectations on all five dimensions, the researchers looked at the relative importance of each dimension of service quality. More specifically, fans were asked to allocate 100 points among the five dimensions based on how important each factor is when evaluating the quality of service of a professional team sport franchise. As the results show in Table 7.4, tangibles and reliability are considered the most important dimensions of service quality. Tangibles, as you will recall from Chapter 5, form the foundation of the sportscape, or stadium environment. This study provides additional evidence that the tangible factors, such as seating comfort, stadium aesthetics, and scoreboard quality, play an important role in satisfying fans. Understanding fans' perceptions of TEAMQUAL is critical for sports marketers in establishing long-term relationships with existing fans and trying to attract new fans. As McDonald, Sutton, and Milne point out, "Consumers who are dissatisfied and feel that they are not receiving quality service will not renew their relationship with the professional sport franchise."

On the sports participation side, an excellent study was conducted to explore the determinants of service quality in the sport recreation industry or recreation center. The researchers, Ko and Pastore,[30] suggest that service quality is multidimensional and consists of four primary factors. Factor one is program quality, which refers to the range of programs, such as the variety of recreation and fitness programs offered, operating time or whether programs start and finish on time, and whether participants can get up-to-date information on programs. Factor two, interaction quality, is the level of customer to employee interaction and also customer to customer relationships. Outcome quality is the third factor and is based on physical change, or does the participant realize the health benefit he or she wished to obtain; valence, which refers to postconsumption or whether the overall experience was a good or bad one; and sociability, or

TABLE 7.4	Importance Weights Allocated to the Five TEAMQUAL Dimensions	
Dimensions		*Allocation*
Reliability—ability to perform promised services dependably and accurately		23%
Assurance—knowledge and courtesy of employees and their ability to convey trust and confidence		16
Empathy—the caring, individualized attention provided by the professional sports franchise for its customers		18
Responsiveness—willingness to help customers and provide prompt service		19
Tangibles—appearance of equipment, personnel, materials, and venue		24

Source: Mark A. McDonald, William A. Sutton, and George R. Milne, "TEAMQUAL: Measuring Service Quality in Professional Team Sports," *Sport Marketing Quarterly*, vol. 4, no. 2 (1995), 9–15. Reprinted with permission of Fitness Information Technology, Inc., Publishers.

the social interaction, which motivates many participants to engage in physical activity. The final factor, environment quality, is the ambient condition, design, and equipment quality. All of these refer to the tangible, physical environment in which the consumption takes place.

Quality of Goods

The quality of sporting goods that are manufactured and marketed has two distinct dimensions. The first **quality dimension of goods** is based on how well the product conforms to specifications that were designed in the manufacturing process. From this standpoint, the quality of goods is driven by the organization and its management and employees. The other dimension of quality is measured subjectively from the perspective of consumers or end users of the goods. In other words, does the product perform its desired function? The degree to which the goods meet and exceed consumers' needs is a function of the organization's marketing orientation.

From the sports marketing perspective, the consumer's perception of **product quality** is of primary importance. Garvin found eight separate quality dimensions, which include performance, features, reliability, conformance, durability, serviceability, aesthetics, and perceived quality (see Table 7.5).

Whether it is enhancing goods or service quality, most sports organizations are attempting to increase the quality of their product offerings. In doing so, they can better

---

TABLE 7.5   Quality Dimensions of Goods

Quality Dimensions of Goods	*Description*
Performance	How well does the good perform its core function? (Does the tennis racquet feel good when striking the ball?)
Features	Does the good offer additional benefits? (Are the golf clubheads constructed with titanium?)
Conformity to specifications	What is the incidence of defects? (Does the baseball have the proper number of stitches or is there some variation?)
Reliability	Does the product perform with consistency? (Do the gauges of the exercise bike work properly every time?)
Durability	What is the life of the product? (How long will the golf clubs last?)
Serviceability	Is the service system efficient, competent, and convenient? (If you experience problems with the grips or loft of the club, can the manufacturer quickly address your needs?)
Aesthetic design	Does the product's design look and feel like a high-quality product? (Does the look and feel of the running shoe inspire you to greater performance?)

Source: Adapted from D. A. Garvin, "Competing on the Eight Dimensions of Quality," *Harvard Business Review* (November–December 1987), 101–109. Copyright © 1987 by the President and Fellows of Harvard College; all rights reserved. Reprinted by permission of Harvard Business School Press.

compete with other entertainment choices, more easily increase the prices of their products, influence the consumer's loyalty, and reach new market segments willing to pay more for a higher quality product.

Some sports franchises have been criticized for attempting to increase the quality of their overall products, while driving up the price of tickets. Unfortunately, it is becoming more costly for the "average fan" to purchase tickets to any professional sporting event. Sports marketers have targeted a new segment (corporations) and overlooked the traditional segments.

Other criticisms have been directed at the NCAA and professional sports for making it too easy for athletes to leave school and turn professional. The National Basketball Association announced that 83 players, including 58 players from U.S. colleges and institutions and 25 international players, have filed as early entry candidates for the 2007 NBA Draft. This exodus of stars may have detrimental effects on "product quality" at the high school and college levels. In the NFL, players whose high school class did not graduate three or more years before are not eligible for the draft and hence are not eligible to play. The most famous challenge to this ruling, in which the courts ultimately upheld the policies of the NFL, was former Ohio State standout Maurice Clarett. Clarett challenged the ruling of the NFL and entered the 2004 draft. Federal Judge Shira Scheindlin initially ruled that the NFL could not bar Clarett from participating in the 2004 NFL Draft. This decision was later overturned by the United States Court of Appeals for the Second Circuit, and Clarett's higher appeal was refused by the Supreme Court.

From a marketing standpoint, the fans are also suffering and may experience dissatisfaction when college players and high school players turn pro early. Teams no longer stay together long enough to get and capture the imagination of fans. Atlantic 10 Commissioner Linda Bruno stated, "It seems as soon as college basketball hooks on to a star, he's suddenly a part of the NBA. Athletes leaving early have definitely hurt the college game." Rick Pitino, whose opinion is widely respected, adds, "Quite frankly, I think college basketball is in serious trouble." Interestingly, the early departures that are making the college game less appealing are doing nothing to strengthen the quality of the NBA. The NBA is saturated with players whose games never had a chance to grow or, as former Stanford coach Mike Montgomery put it, "will have to be nurtured through [their] immaturity."[31]

A final product feature related to perceptions of product quality is product warranties. **Product warranties** are important to consumers when purchasing expensive sporting goods because they act to reduce the perceived risk and dissonance associated with cognitive dissonance. Traditional warranties are statements indicating the liability of the manufacturer for problems with the product. For example, Spalding's new basketball, called the Neverflat, has a product redesign with a new membrane, a redesigned valve, and the addition of NitroFlate, a substance added to the ball during inflation that forms a barrier preventing seepage. Spalding has produced a ball it says will not leak air for at least a year. It is backing that claim with a money-back guarantee.

Interestingly, warranties are also being developed by sports organizations. The New Jersey Nets offered their season ticket holders a money-back guarantee if they were dissatisfied with the Nets' performance. With the price of tickets skyrocketing for professional sporting events, perhaps these service guarantees will be the wave of the future. The Indiana Ice of the U.S. Hockey League offered their fans a similar deal. The Ice are so convinced local hockey fans will enjoy seeing the under-20 amateur team play next season, franchise officials are offering a money-back guarantee on season tickets.

PRODUCT DESIGN

Product design is one competitive advantage that is of special interest to sports marketers. It is heavily linked to product quality and the technological environment discussed in Chapter 2. In some cases, product design may even have an impact on the sporting event. For example, the latest technology in golf clubs does allow the average player to improve his or her performance on the course. The same could be said for the new generation of big sweet spot, extra-long tennis racquets. In another example, the official baseball used in the major league games was believed to be "juiced up." In other words, the ball was livelier because of the product design. As a result of this "juiced up" ball, home run production increased, much to the delight of the fans. From a sports marketing perspective, anything that adds excitement and conjecture to a game with public relation problems is welcomed. In the end, what matters is not whether the ball is livelier, but that the game is.

Baseballs are not the only products that are having an impact on the outcome of sporting events, and equipment changes aren't the only way to think about product design or redesign. Baseball is constantly looking for ways to make games shorter and thus more attractive to fans. In a recent rule change, the time a pitcher is allotted to deliver the ball with no runners on base has changed from 20 to 12 seconds. The price for each violation is a ball. It is hoped that this minor product redesign will have a major impact. Historic rule changes that have had a significant impact on the sport product include the designated hitter in baseball, the shot clock in basketball, or (in 1912) when hockey moved from seven to six players on the ice at one time.

Product design is important to sport marketers because it ultimately affects consumers' perceptions of product quality. Moreover, organizations need to monitor the technological environment to keep up with the latest trends that may affect product design. Let us look at this relationship in Figure 7.5.

As you would imagine, the technological environment has a tremendous impact on product design decisions. In almost every sporting good category, sports marketers communicate how their brands are technologically superior to the competition.

The golf equipment industry thrives on the latest technological advances in ball and club design. Bicycle manufacturers stress the technological edge that comes with the latest and greatest construction materials. Tennis racquets are continually moving into the next generation of frame design and racquet length. NordicTrac exercise equipment positions itself as technologically superior to other competing brands. Nike is continually developing new lines of high-tech sports gear in its state-of-the-art Sports Research Lab. Most recently, Nike has introduced the Nike+ wireless system that allows Nike footwear to communicate with an iPod nano for the ultimate personal running and workout experience. "The most common feedback we are receiving from Nike+ users is that the experience has changed the way they approach running," says Brent Scrimshaw, vice president of EMEA Marketing.[32] "Whether it's the instant feedback they hear over their music or the ability to set goals and challenge friends on nikeplus.com, Nike+ is encouraging people who never ran to run, and motivating people who run to run more." In this case, the claim is that product design is actually influencing not only performance, but motivation to perform.

FIGURE 7.5 Relationship Among Product Design, Technology, and Product Quality

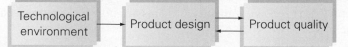

Look Cycle capturing the latest in product design and technology.
Source: Look Cycle USA

The product design of sporting goods, in turn, influences consumer perceptions of product quality. By definition, **product design** includes the aesthetics, style, and function of the product. Two of the eight dimensions of the quality of goods are incorporated in this definition, providing one measure of the interdependency of these two concepts.

The way a good performs, the way it feels, and the beauty of the good are all important aspects of product design. Again, think of the numerous sporting goods that are purchased largely on the basis of these benefits. Consumers purchase golf clubs because of the way they look and feel. Tennis shoes are chosen because of the special functions they perform (cross-trainers, hiking, or basketball) and the way they look (colors and style).

Color has historically been an important factor in the design of almost all licensed merchandise. Recent trends show that in hats, jerseys, and jackets, anything black is "gold." The Oakland Raiders' silver and black are always near the top in NFL merchandise sales regardless of the team's record on the field. The Toronto Blue Jays have even adopted a new logo that incorporates black and moves away from the reds and blues of the past. Although fans associate certain colors with their favorite teams (e.g., Dodger Blue or the Cincinnati Reds), MLB markets licensed products that deviate from the traditional colors. Baby blues, electric oranges, and lime greens are replacing the traditional team colors, and fans seem to be responding. For example, Cleveland (red and navy uniform colors) fans are purchasing jerseys in bright orange, the color of their arch-rival Baltimore Orioles.[33] Examples like these illustrate that color alone may be a motivating factor in the purchase of many sports products. Sports marketers, therefore, must consider color to be critical in product design.

Figure 7.5 also shows that product quality may influence product design to some extent. Sports organizations are continually seeking to improve the levels of product quality. In fact, having high-quality goods and services may be the primary objective of many firms. As such, products will be designed in the highest quality manner with little concern about the costs that will be ultimately passed on to the consumers. Some major league sports organizations (e.g., New York Yankees and Detroit Red Wings) will design their teams to achieve the highest quality levels without cost consideration.

As new technologies continue to emerge, product design will become increasingly important. Organizations with a marketing orientation will incorporate consumer preferences to ensure their needs are being met with respect to product design for new and existing products. What will the future bring with respect to product design, technology, and the need to satisfy consumers? One hint comes to us via the athletic shoe industry. With advances in technology, customized shoes are now being produced for professional athletes. Gone are the days when recreational athletes could wear the same shoes as their professional counterparts. Today's professional athletes are demanding custom fit and high-tech shoes, and weekend athletes will soon require the same. Companies such as Nike are now customizing certain features of their shoes to the mass market under the Nike ID (individualized design) name.

Another perspective on the future of product design is that the design of products will stem from demand and changes in the marketing environment. One such change is the emergence of a viable market for women's sports products. For instance, ski and snowboard companies are now turning their attention to women's products based on a growing number of women hitting the slopes Historically, the only difference in men's and women's ski products was the color, but today there are product design changes that truly address women's needs. Skis for women are softer and lighter. Boots are more cushioned and designed to fit the foot and calf muscles of the female skier. All of these product changes try to capitalize on the marketing environment and satisfy the needs of a growing target market.[34]

Summary

Sport products are defined as goods, services, or any combination of the two that are designed to provide benefits to a sports spectator, participant, or sponsor. Within the field of sports marketing, products are sometimes thought of as bundles of benefits desired by consumers. As discussed in Chapter 1, sports products might include sporting events and their participants, sporting goods, and sports information. The definition of sports products also makes an important distinction between goods and services.

Goods are defined as tangible, physical products that offer benefits to consumers. Conversely, services are intangible, nonphysical products. Most sports products possess the characteristics of both goods and services. For example, a sporting event sells goods (e.g., concessions) and services (e.g., the competition itself). The classification of a sports product as either a good or a service is dependent on four product dimensions: tangibility, standardization and consistency, perishability, and separability. Tangibility refers to the ability to see, feel, and touch the product. In other words, tangibility is the physical dimension of the sports product. Standardization refers to the consistency of the product or the ability of the producer to manufacture a product with little variation over time. One of the unique and complex issues for sports marketers is dealing with the inconsistency of the sports product (i.e., the inability to control the performance of the team or athlete). Perishability is the ability to store or inventory product. Pure services are totally perishable (i.e., you cannot sell a seat after the game has been played), whereas goods are not perishable and can be stored or warehoused. Separability, the final product dimension, refers to the ability to separate the good from the person providing the service. In the case of an athletic event, there is little separation between the provider and the consumer. That is, the event is being produced and consumed simultaneously.

Along with classifying sports products by the four product dimensions, sports products are also categorized based on groupings within the sports organization. Product lines are groups of products that are closely related because they satisfy a class of needs. These products are used together, sold to the same customer groups, distributed through the same types of outlets, or fall within a given price range. The total assortment of product lines is called the product mix. The mix represents all the firm's products. Strategic decisions within the sports organization consider both the product lines and the entire product mix. For instance, an organization may want to add product lines, eliminate product lines, or develop new product lines that are unrelated to existing lines.

Products can also be described on the basis of three interrelated dimensions or characteristics: branding, quality, and design. Branding refers to the product's name, design, symbol, or any combination used by an organization to differentiate products from the competition. Brand names, or elements of the brand that can be spoken, are important considerations for sports products. When choosing a brand name, sports marketers should consider the following: the name should be positive and generate positive feelings, be translatable into an exciting logo, imply the benefits that the sports product delivers, be consistent with the image of the sports product, and be legally and ethically permissible.

The broad purpose of branding is to differentiate your product from the competition. Ultimately, the consumer will (hopefully) establish a pattern of repeat purchases for your brand (i.e., be loyal to your sports product). Before this can happen, sports marketers must guide consumers through a series of steps known as the branding process. The branding process begins by building brand awareness, in which consumers recognize and remember the brand name. Next, the brand image, or the consumers' set of beliefs about a brand, must be established. After the proper brand image is developed, the objective of the branding process is to develop brand equity. Brand equity is the value that the brand contributes to a product in the marketplace. Finally, once the brand exhibits high levels of equity, consumers are prone to become brand loyal, or purchase only your brand. Certainly, sports marketers are interested in establishing high levels of awareness, enhancing brand image, building equity, and developing loyal fans or customers.

One of the important sports product strategies that is contingent upon building a strong brand is licensing. Licensing is defined as a contractual agreement whereby a company may use another company's trademark in exchange for a royalty or fee. The licensing of sports products is experiencing tremendous growth around the world. Advantages to the licensee (the organization purchasing the license or use of the name or trademark) include positive association with the sports entity, enhancing brand awareness, building brand equity, improving distribution and retail relationships, and having the ability to charge higher prices. Disadvantages to the licensee are the possibility of the sports entity experiencing problems (e.g., athlete arrested or team performing poorly or moving). However, the licensor (the sports entity granting the permission) benefits by expanding into new markets, which creates heightened awareness. Yet the licensor may not have tight controls on the quality of the products being licensed under the name.

Quality is another of the important brand characteristics. The two different types of quality that affect brand image, brand equity, and, ultimately, loyalty, are the quality of services and the quality of goods. The quality of services, or service quality, is generally described on the basis of its dimensions. Parasuraman, Berry, and Zeithaml describe service quality as having five distinct dimensions: reliability, assurance, empathy, responsiveness, and tangibles. Reliability refers to the ability to perform a promised service dependably and accurately. Assurance is the knowledge and courtesy of employees and their ability to convey trust and confidence. Empathy is defined as the caring, individualized attention the firm provides its customers. Responsiveness refers to the willingness to help customers and provide prompt service. Tangibles are the physical facilities, equipment, and appearance of the service personnel. Using this framework, sports researchers have designed an instrument called TEAMQUAL to assess the service quality within sporting events.

The quality of goods is based on whether the good conforms to specifications determined during the manufacturing process and the degree to which the good meets or exceeds the consumer's needs. Garvin has conceptualized the quality of goods from the consumer's perspective. He found eight separate dimensions of goods quality, including performance, features, conformity to specifications, reliability, durability, serviceability, aesthetic design, and perceived quality.

Product design is the final characteristic of the "total product." Product design is defined as the aesthetics, style, and function of the product. It is important to sports marketers in that it ultimately affects consumers' perceptions of product quality. For a sporting event, the product design might be thought of as the composition of the team. For sporting goods, product design has largely focused on the development of technologically superior products. In fact, the technological environment is believed to directly influence product design. Product design, in turn, enjoys a reciprocal relationship with product quality. In other words, product design affects perceptions of product quality and may influence product design.

Key Terms

- assurance, p. 222
- brand awareness, p. 210
- brand equity, p. 211
- brand image, p. 210
- brand loyalty, p. 215
- brand mark, p. 208
- brand name, p. 206
- branding, p. 206
- branding process, p. 210
- dimensions of service quality, p. 222
- empathy, p. 222
- goods, p. 200

- idle product capacity, p. 203
- licensing, p. 218
- logo, p. 208
- logotype, p. 208
- perishability, p. 203
- product design, p. 227
- product characteristics, p. 206
- product line, p. 204
- product mix, p. 204
- product quality, p. 224
- product warranties, p. 225
- quality dimensions of goods, p. 224

- reliability, p. 222
- responsiveness, p. 222
- separability, p. 203
- service quality, p. 222
- services, p. 200
- sports product, p. 198
- standardization, p. 202
- tangibility, p. 202
- tangibles, p. 222
- TEAMQUAL, p. 223
- trademark, p. 208

Review Questions

1. Define sports products. Why are sports products sometimes called "bundles of benefits"?
2. Contrast pure goods with pure services, using each of the dimensions of products.
3. Describe the nature of product mix, product lines, and product items. Illustrate these concepts for the following: Converse, Baltimore Orioles, and your local country club.
4. What are the characteristics of the "total product"?
5. Describe branding. What are the guidelines for developing an effective brand name? Why is brand loyalty such an important concept for sports marketers to understand?

6. Define licensing. What are the advantages and disadvantages to the licensee and licensor?
7. Describe service quality and discuss the five dimensions of service quality. Which dimension is most important to you as a spectator of a sporting event? Does this vary by the type of sporting event?
8. Describe product quality and discuss the eight dimensions of product quality. Which dimension is most important to you as a consumer of sporting goods? Does this vary by the type of sporting good?
9. How are product design, product quality, and technology interrelated?

Exercises

1. Think of some sports products to which consumers demonstrate high degrees of brand loyalty. What are these products, and why do you think loyalty is so high? Give your suggestions for measuring brand loyalty.

2. Interview the individuals responsible for licensing and licensing decisions on your campus. Ask them to describe the licensing process and what they believe the advantages are to your school.

3. Construct a survey to measure consumers' perceptions of service quality at a sporting event on campus. Administer the survey to 10 people and summarize the findings. What recommendations might you make to the sports marketing department based on your findings?

4. Go to a sporting goods store and locate three sports products that you believe exhibit high levels of product quality. What are the commonalities among these three products? How do these products rate on the dimensions of product quality described in the chapter?

Internet Exercises

1. Search the Internet for a sports product that stresses product design issues on its Web site. Then locate the Web site of a competitor's sports product. How are these two products positioned relative to each other on their Web sites?

2. Search the Internet for three team nicknames (either college or professional) of which you were previously unaware. Do these team names seem to follow the suggested guidelines for effective brand names?

Endnotes

1. "Introduction to Snowshoeing: A Woman's Guide," http://www.womenssportsfoundation.org/cgi-bin/iowa/sports/article.html?record=162.
2. Shaquille O'Neal, http://cbs.sportsline.com/u/fans/celebrity/shaq; "Athletic Shoes by Shaquille O'Neal Now Available Only at Payless ShoeSource," PR Newswire, *Financial News* (January 14, 2004).
3. Christopher Lovelock, *Services Marketing* (Englewood Cliffs, NJ: Prentice Hall, 1984).
4. Boaz Herzog, "Rising with a Swoosh," *The Sunday Oregonian* (September 21, 2003), D1.
5. Boaz Herzog, "Nike Leaves Critics in the Dust," *Times Picayune* (September 28, 2003), 1.
6. See, for example, Courtland Bovee and John Thill, *Marketing* (New York: McGraw-Hill, 1992), 252.
7. Marcus Nelson, "Want a New Look? There's a Price," *The Palm Beach Post* (October 24, 2003).
8. *The Columbus Crew*, www.thecrew.com.
9. Andrew Lupton, "The NLL Fails to Excel at the Team Name Game," *National Post* (f/k/a *The Financial Post*) (Canada), January 8, 2007, p. S2.
10. Marcus Nelson, "Want a New Look? There's a Price," *The Palm Beach Post* (October 24, 2003).
11. J. Gladden, G. Milne, and W. Sutton. "A Conceptual Framework for Assessing Brand Equity in Division I College Athletics," *Journal of Sports Management,* vol. 12, no. 1 (1998), 1–19.
12. Ray Melick, "Realignment Game Turns Ugly," *Scripps Howard News Service* (January 15, 2004).
13. G. R. Milne and M. A. McDonald, *Sport Marketing: Managing the Exchange Process* (Sudbury, MA: Jones & Bartlett, 1999).
14. Louis E. Boone, C. M. Kochunny, and Dianne Wilkins, "Applying the Brand Equity Concept to Major League Baseball," *Sport Marketing Quarterly,* vol. 4, no. 3 (1995), 33–42.
15. Ibid.
16. John Lombardo, "MLB Makes It 5 Firsts in a Row in Brand Keys Fan Loyalty Survey," *Street and Smith's Sports Business Journal,* vol. 8, no. 10 (August 25–31, 2003), 28.
17. D. F. Mahony, R. Madrigal, and D. Howard, "Using the Psychological Commitment to Team (PCT) Scale to Segment Sport Consumers Based on Loyalty," *Sport Marketing Quarterly,* vol. 9, (2000), 15–25.
18. Sarah Lorge, "The Fan Plan," *Sales and Marketing Management,* vol. 151, no. 5 (May 1999), 11–13; Charles Waltner, "CRM: The New Game in Town for Professional Sports," *Information Week* (August 28, 2000).
19. S. Sleight, *Sponsorship: What Is It and How to Use It* (London: McGraw-Hill, 1989).
20. "*License Magazine* 2006 Annual Industry Report," http://www.licensemag.com/licensemag/data/articlestandard/licensemag/422006/380358/article.pdf.
21. "*License Magazine* 103 Leading Licensing Companies," http://www.licensemag.com/licensemag/data/articlestandard/licensemag/142007/416989/article.pdf.
22. Eddie Baghdikian, "Building the Sports Organization's Merchandise Licensing Program: The Appropriateness, Significance, and Considerations," *Sport Marketing Quarterly,* vol. 5, no. 1 (1996), 35–41.
23. Elliot Harris, "Spitting Image: Ink with DNA Could Put Counterfeiters on Spot at Olympics," *Chicago Sun Times* (June 8, 2000), 133.
24. Robert Thurow, "Busting Bogus Merchandise Peddlers with Logo Cops," *The Wall Street Journal* (October 24, 1997), B1, B14.
25. Rick Burton, "A Case Study on Sports Property Servicing Excellence: National Football League Properties," *Sport Marketing Quarterly,* vol. 5, no. 3 (1996), 23.
26. J. R. Lehtinen and U. Lehtinen, *Service Quality: A Study of Quality Dimensions* (Helsinki: Service Management Institute, 1982).
27. Christian Groonos, "A Service Quality Model and Its Marketing Implications," *European Journal of Marketing,* vol. 18 (1982), 36–44.

28. A. Parasuraman, Valarie Zeithaml, and Len Berry, "A Conceptual Model of Service Quality and Its Implications for Future Research," *Journal of Marketing,* vol. 49 (1985), 41–50.

29. Mark A. McDonald, William A, Sutton, and George R. Milne, "TEAMQUAL: Measuring Service Quality in Professional Team Sports," *Sport Marketing Quarterly,* vol. 4, no. 2 (1995), 9–15.

30. Yong Jae Ko and Donna L. Pastore, "Current Issues and Conceptualizations of Service Quality in the Recreation Sport Industry," *Sport Marketing Quarterly,* vol. 13, no. 3.

31. Jack McCallum, "Going, Going, Gone," *Sports Illustrated,* vol. 84, no. 20 (May 20, 1996), 52.

32. Aaron Reed, "Nike+ Motivates Athletes to 'Run Like You've Never Run Before' in New Commercial" April 20, 2007, SYS-CON Media, http://java.sys-con.com/read/364540.htm.

33. Wendy Bounds and Stefan Fatsis, "Right Here! Get Yer Baseball Cap! Lime Green, Lavender, Baby Blue!" *The Wall Street Journal* (October 13, 1997).

34. "Ski Industry Focusing on Women," sportsbusinessnews. com (January 30, 2004).

CHAPTER

8

MANAGING SPORTS PRODUCTS

After completing this chapter, you should be able to:

- Describe the characteristics of new products from an organizational and consumer perspective.

- Explain the various stages of the new product development process.

- Discuss the phases of the product life cycle and explain how the product life cycle influences marketing strategy.

- Determine the factors that will lead to new product success.

- Discuss the diffusion of innovations and the various types of adopters.

The accompanying article on Ultimate Fighting provides an interesting illustration of a new sports product that is taking off in the North American market. There is obviously nothing new about kickboxing, boxing, wrestling, or even street brawls, but when combined, they create an exciting new sport. The founders of Ultimate Fighting (or mixed martial arts) will have to keep this in mind when executing a marketing strategy for this emerging new sport product.

NEW SPORTS PRODUCTS

Although it might seem as if new products are easy to describe and think about, "new" is a relative term. Think about purchasing season tickets to your favorite college basketball team for the first time. You might consider this a new product even though the tickets have been available for many years. However, consider Bossaball.

Bossaball combines elements of different sports on a pitch of trampolines and bouncy inflatables. The popularity of Xtreme sports, soccer, and volleyball around the globe suggest the time could be right for this new product. There is obviously nothing new about volleyball, soccer, and jumping on a trampoline, but when combined they create an exciting new sport. The founders of Bossaball will have to keep this in mind when developing a marketing strategy for this new sports product. This sports product is new to all spectators who watch and participants involved in the action.

Regardless of how you define "new products," they are critical to the health of any sports organization for two reasons. First, new products are necessary to keep up with changing consumer trends, lifestyles, and tastes. Second, as unsuccessful sports products are dropped from the product mix, new products must be introduced continually to maintain business and long-term growth.

Ultimate Fighting's Rise Creates New Breed of American Brawler

The red-brick gym just a block from the Mississippi River sits tucked among a rundown karaoke bar, a white house straight out of *That '70s Show* and a candy store. From the outside, Champions Fitness Center looks like a small town's small bar, the place flannel-clad John Deere workers go after the second shift, where farmers looking for some fun in the city venture when it's too cold to plant or till.

The only hint that this spot helped spawn a sport that's fast and bloody—a mix of martial arts and wrestling, the kind of no-holds-barred brawl you'd expect at a roadside bar, not featured on television—is a sign that reads, "Miletich Fighting Systems." Inside the cramped gym is a corner room with wrestling mats and guys who wear shirts that say things like "Fighting Solves Everything."

It's here that thousands of young men from around the world have come looking to turn violence into fame. Most arrive with a few dollars, a half-empty suitcase, and a chip on their shoulder, hoping to be just like the 6-foot-8 man who's coming out the front door right now, walking toward the decked-out black Hummer parked on the sidewalk out front, thinking about the seven-figure contract he just signed.

This is Tim Sylvia, a former construction worker who showed up six years ago from Maine to train with Pat Miletich, the famous former ultimate fighting champion whose gym has produced some of the sport's best fighters. "Pat was an idol," Sylvia said. "I came for two weeks to train here. They beat the (heck) out of me. Toward the end of the week, Pat said, 'Stay.' I went home, quit my job, sold both my cars and moved here."

Now he's the Ultimate Fighting Championship heavyweight champion of the world. "I never thought this sport would be that big," he said. "I never thought I'd have this kind of success." That was then. Today, Sylvia owns seven cars, calls Pete Rose a close friend, says Tom Brady wants to meet him, and believes, like a lot of people, that ultimate fighting is about to replace boxing as America's fighting sport.

Miletich is the man who trained him—his ears mushed to a mash of skin, his body bent over from all the abuse he's taken, now a coach of the International Fight League team seen on Spike television and one of the pioneers of the sport. "Our sport is fast, it's exciting, and once you watch the speed going on, you're hooked," Miletich said. "And when you go back to watching boxing, you realize it's boring."

The rules for mixed martial arts are pretty simple. No biting. No hair pulling. No going for the groin or

kidneys. Otherwise, have at it. The sport took off in the 19th century between strongmen who fought until one forced the other to give in. "In the late 1800s into the 1930s, these guys went around beating up the carnival strongman in submission grappling matches," Miletich said. "They had these matches in Minnesota at state fairs in front of hundreds of thousands of people. It was huge. Then boxing came around and knocked it out."

The sport resurfaced in the United States in the 1990s just as boxing began its decline, growing much like Miletich's career: first in backrooms and barrooms, then in dingy rings and cages, sputtering in every small town that would allow an all-out fight. "In 1993 was the first ultimate fighting championship," Miletich said. "From there it started to explode."

By 2002, mixed martial arts events sold out arenas. Spike put it on television. The Ultimate Fighting Championship—which trademarked the term "ultimate fighting," the reason most in the sport now refer to it as mixed martial arts—added a reality television show. The fights were fast, vicious, and bloody. Fighters mixed wrestling, grappling, karate, Thai boxing—anything that can give them an edge in the ring. Matches are normally divided into three rounds—with each round about 4 minutes long. Fighters can win three ways: by forcing their opponent to submit (this often meant breaking arms if the loser refused to give in), by a knockout or technical knockout, or by a decision.

Today, Ultimate Fighting is one of the fastest-growing sports, industry experts say. Among its successes:

- Spike TV now has seven UFC television shows.
- Last October, an Ultimate Fighting Championship fight drew 4.2 million viewers—easily outdrawing Major League Baseball's playoffs on Fox the same night in the male demographic and posting larger numbers than the NBA on ESPN.
- A fight on pay-per-view drew 1.2 million buys, the largest pay-per-view pull for any sport in 2006.

Dino Spencer says he can see the future of fighting sports in America—and it doesn't look good for boxing. "Mixed martial arts is replacing boxing, especially among the younger fans," Spencer said. "In the future, MMA is going to be the big moneymaker for pay-per-view, much bigger than it is now. My guys 50 and older are into boxing, but the younger guys are coming up in MMA."

In an age of video games and instant gratification, mixed martial arts has attracted a certain kind of fan— young, raised on action movies and WWF wrestling.

(Continued)

(*Continued*)

Someone who's looking for competitive violence but thinks boxing moves much too slowly. "In ultimate fighting, you're getting a lot more excitement, more blood, and it's not as restricted," said Gerald Early, the Merle Kling Professor of Modern Letters at Washington University in St. Louis and a well-known boxing expert.

"It makes boxing seem staid and boring and 'something my granddad liked, not something I like.' The UFC is more exciting, the athletes are more colorful, with an image and mystique that boxing doesn't have today," he said. "People are starting to follow them the way they follow their favorite football team."

Source: Bill Reiter, "Ultimate Fighting's Rise Creates New Breed of American Brawler," *The Kansas City Star,* January 28, 2007.

One of the key considerations for any sports organization is to continually improve the products it offers to consumers. New products seek to satisfy the needs of a new market, enhance the quality of an existing product, or extend the number of product choices for current consumers. Before discussing the process for developing new products, let us look at the different types of **new sports products.**

Types of New Products

As noted previously, there is no universally accepted definition of new products. Instead, new products are sometimes described from the viewpoint of the sports organization versus the consumer's perspective. The organization's definition of a new product is based on whether it has ever produced or marketed this particular product in the past. This can be important for organizations trying to understand how the new sports product "fits" with their existing products.

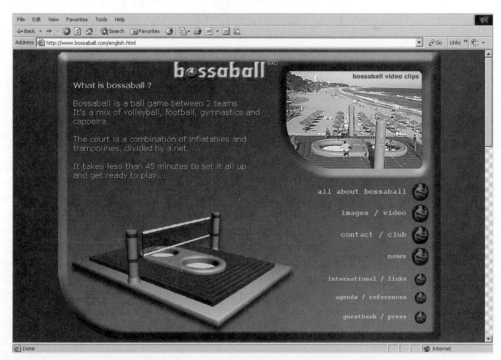

The new sport of Bossaball combines volleyball, football, gymnastics, and capoeira.
Source: Courtesy of Bossaball BuBa.

SPORTS MARKETING HALL OF FAME

Bill Rasmussen

Bill Rasmussen is hardly a household name, but all you have to do is mention four letters—ESPN—and his place in sports marketing history is secured. ESPN's founder developed the 24-hour sports programming channel in the fall of 1979. At that time, Rasmussen was simply looking for a way to broadcast the University of Connecticut basketball games when he happened upon satellite technology.

Today, ESPN reaches more than 93 million households and has more than 5,100 live and/or original hours of sports programming presented annually for more than 65 sports. A second channel, ESPN2, also reaches over 93 million households and has more than 4,800 live and/or original hours of sports programming. ESPN2 also has the distinction of being the fastest network to ever reach 90 million viewers. Combined ESPN has more than 50 business entities, which include ESPN on ABC, six domestic cable television networks (ESPN, ESPN2, ESPN Classic, ESPNEWS, ESPN Deportes, ESPNU), ESPN HD and ESPN2 HD (high-definition simulcast services of ESPN and ESPN2, respectively), ESPN Regional Television, ESPN International (31 international networks and syndication), ESPN Radio, ESPN.com, *ESPN The Magazine,* ESPN Enterprises, and ESPN Zones (sports-themed restaurants). Other new and fast-growing businesses including ESPN360 (broadband), Mobile ESPN (wireless), ESPN On Demand, ESPN Interactive, and ESPN PPV. Amazingly, this media giant continues to expand with all these networks and new products, because of Bill Rasmussen's desire to bring U Conn basketball to the people of Connecticut.

Source: Richard Hoffer, "Bill Rasmussen," *Sports Illustrated* (September 19, 1994), 121; http://www.espnmediazone.com/corp_info/corp_fact_sheet.html.

However, newness from the consumer's perspective is described as any innovation the consumer perceives as meaningful. In other words, the new product could be a minor alteration of an existing product or a product that has never been sold or marketed by any organization. Looking at new products from the consumer's viewpoint helps sports organizations understand the most effective way to market the product. Let us examine the types of new products from the organizational and consumer perspectives in greater detail.

Newness from the Organization's Perspective

New-to-the-World Products   Brand-new sports innovations, such as the first in-line skates, the first sailboard, or the advent of arena football in 1987, all represent new-to-the-world products. These products were new to the organization selling the product as well as to the consumers purchasing or using the product.[1]

Another interesting, **new-to-the-world sports product** is the wireless ballpark. Raley Field, home of the AAA Sacramento River Cats baseball team, has become one of professional sports' most technologically advanced venues. The River Cats were among the first teams to implement wireless Internet access to customers in suites and the exclusive "Solon Club." The stadium is now wired for all fans who are able to operate laptop computers, PDAs, and other wireless devices from their seats for access to up-to-the-minute stats and replays. Additionally, fans can order food or tickets for future games right from their seat.[2]

New Product Category Entries   Sports products that are new to the organization, but not to the world, are referred to as **new product category entries.** For example, IMG, a sports, entertainment, and media company, acquired *Tennis Week Magazine* and its companion online news site, tennisweek.com. Known as the "insider's guide to the game," *Tennis Week* is a leading tennis publication, with a circulation of 60,000 subscribers and a reputation for always going behind court lines to provide the sport's most in-depth reports of industry business as well as locker room chats with its top stars. Tennisweek.com provides instant coverage of the Grand Slams and the ATP and WTA Tours, in addition to major collegiate, junior, and senior events. It reaches millions of visitors annually with up-to-the-minute scores, rankings, earnings, schedules, tournament draws, and camps.

New Balance, known only for its footwear, acquired Brine, Inc., a recognized industry leader in soccer, lacrosse, field hockey, and volleyball. "Brine's history of manufacturing high-performance team sports products will enable us to broaden our offerings at the global level," said Jim Davis, chairman and CEO of New Balance. "Brine's motto, 'Find Your Game,' speaks directly to their long-standing support of game improvement products and programs, and fits in well with New Balance's philosophy of promoting personal athletic achievements."[3]

In another example, the athletic footwear landscape was significantly altered when German-based manufacturer adidas announced it would be acquiring all outstanding shares of Reebok. Under the terms of the deal, adidas will buy Reebok for $3.8 billion. For adidas, the merger strengthens its presence in global athletic footwear, apparel, and hardware markets—allowing for a more competitive vantage point, a more defined brand identity, a wider product offering, and a stronger presence in professional athletics. These products are not new to the sports consumers, but they are new acquisitions for the organizations.

Product Line Extensions Product line extensions refer to new products being added to an existing product line. For instance, the addition of expansion teams in Major League Baseball, or Daiwa's new Dendoh Marine Power power assist fishing reels, precision engineered with Daiwa's unique Power Lever for instant control of winding speed and power, are product line extensions. The Arena Football League 2 is also a product line extension of the original Arena Football League. The league is currently fielding 30 teams across the United States and is entering its eighth season of play as the primary developmental league for the Arena Football League (AFL).

In another example of a product line extension, New Balance footwear launched a new women's volleyball shoe in spring 2007. The WV850 and WV650 shoes are designed to offer the lightweight look and feel of a running shoe, with the support, durability, cushioning, and flexibility of a high-performance volleyball shoe.

Product Improvements Current products that have been modified and improved, such as the new shoe addition to the long line of Jordan Brand called the Air Jordan XX2, retailing at $175, are called product improvements. Another example of a product improvement is the Wilson Hyper Hammer H6 tennis racquet. This improved version of the ever-popular (original) Hammer 6.2 includes the addition of hypercarbon, a new step frame design, and iso-zorb grommet technology. If this new racquet offers benefits that consumers are seeking (more feel and power) and is believed to be improved, then it should be successful.

In another example of a product improvement, any sports team or individual that improves during the off-season can be considered a product improvement. Sometimes this improvement takes place because of trades or purchasing new players, and other times an enhanced product is the result of a new coach or players who are maturing and finally performing to their potential. In either case, product improvements represent an opportunity for sports marketers to promote the improvements (either real or perceived) in product quality.

A final example of a product improvement comes from the Kansas City Royals and their $250 million renovation of Kauffman Stadium. The renovation started in October 2007 with phases being completed over several years. Improvements include a new outfield entertainment area with plazas in both left and right field and fountains in both areas. The right field plaza will house a restaurant and a banquet facility overlooking the stadium's famous fountains, while the left field plaza will house a

Royals Hall of Fame, Kids Zone with interactive game stations, and a "Taste of KC" food court. Both outfield plazas will have rooftop party decks where fans can view the game. The two plazas will be connected by an 800-foot-long Royals "Main Street," featuring the Royals Walk of Fame, highlighting the Royals history.

SPOTLIGHT ON SPORTS MARKETING ETHICS

Outta Sight or Gone Too Far?

Can a middle ground be found in the debate over golf equipment technology improvements? The word fun, or at least the concept, arose in virtually every response to questions about advanced equipment technology and its effect on the golf course, in terms of both design and operation. This held true regardless of the respondent's disposition on the issue and his or her vantage point as a course owner, architect, or equipment manufacturer. If there is one thing everyone agrees on, it is that a healthy dose of fun is crucial to growing the game.

Of course, there is another point of agreement, namely, that longer ball flights will never be scaled back. Choose your analogy—the cat and the bag, the horse and the barn, the genie and the bottle—advanced technology, in some form, is here to stay. "The situation has broken down into two armed camps," is one golf course architect's analogy, "people who love the game of golf and people who love the business of golf." The description captures the fervor of the debate, but oversimplifies the issues. For instance, players—from the 30-handicap hacker to the tour pro—generally want any legal advantage they can get to hit the ball farther. And equipment manufacturers are more than willing to oblige with an array of new drivers and balls released each year "guaranteed" to deliver extra yards.

On the other side, course owners, who generally side with architects in objecting to ever-greater driving distance, focus primarily on the business implications. (The National Golf Course Owners Association's board of directors even went as far recently as officially endorsing a limit on further equipment technology advances.) Thus, as Fred Ridley, president of the United States Golf Association (USGA), noted, "It truly is an issue of balancing the interests of all concerned parties."

Frank Jemsek, owner of Cog Hill Golf Club, in Lemont, Ill., maintains an analysis that accounts for today's sluggish economy by comparing it to Depression-era volume. "In 1934, using five-minute tee-time intervals, we were able to move 941 players around 36 holes. [The facility now has 72 holes.] Although neither the players nor the equipment were as good as they are today, tee-time intervals have gradually spread out to the point that the comparable figure is now more like 700 players per day. In addition, each individual round takes longer."

Besides the day-to-day operations, there are also the broader planning implications of shots that travel farther, especially off the tee. "I haven't done a master plan without being asked about including greater distance," says Rick Jacobson, of Jacobson Golf Course Design, Inc. in Libertyville, Ill. "Nowadays, the standard figure being cited for a golf course is 180 acres, at least, and I've heard of a couple of courses already under construction that will top 8,000 yards. Needless to say, all of this has implications for the acquisition and maintenance components of a project."

"Golf course owners are encountering errant golf ball claims in areas that didn't exist before," says Van Tengberg, an attorney with Foley & Lardner, a firm with expertise in golf-related issues. "It's not a matter of the one bad golfer hitting a horrendously bad shot—a situation that has always existed. But you have golf balls regularly landing in places they didn't before, and that's what requires increased vigilance and sometimes corrective measures. As the joke has it, balls that once landed in some guy's back yard now land in the front yard across the street."

Along with considerations of profitability, there is the question of whether the golf experience has been compromised by advanced equipment technology, even though the course may remain difficult to play. "As someone involved in golf course design," says Brian Silva, a principal in CSM, Inc. of Uxbridge, Mass., "I don't care if guys shoot under par. In fact, on the perfectly conditioned courses of today, I expect it. I'd like to see a player have to use a wider selection of clubs for approach shots than just sand wedge, pitching wedge, or lob wedge. To paraphrase Pete Dye, I'd like players to experience the same thrill Ben Hogan did, hitting a long iron approach to a par 4 green. I just think there's a better type of golf that's more than a driver, followed by an 8-iron or less."

What's more, contrary to the objections of staunch "traditionalists," experimenting with the design and construction of golf clubs and balls has been a part of the game dating back to its origins in Scotland. Clubs and balls have been evolving ever since. "These days, too few players are willing to accept anything but maximum distance," notes Randy Henry, co-founder of Henry-Griffitts, the Hayden Lake, Idaho–based custom clubfitter and manufacturer. "Accuracy be damned. In the main, manufacturers are just answering that call."

(Continued)

(Continued)

Dick De La Cruz, a long-time club designer and president of the Vista, Calif., company that bears his name and produces clubs expressly for amateur players, sounds a similar note. "I'd like to see some excitement put back into the game, and we've proven that adding distance is one way of doing it. The restrictions imposed on club design by the USGA have resulted in a certain 'sameness' in new products. It's not so far-fetched to think that an average high-handicapper who suddenly hit the ball 20 or 30 yards farther would play more."

"With participation flat and a large number of golfers entering and leaving the game every year, I believe we need to do everything we can to make the game more fun through technology," adds Jay Hubbard, vice president of marketing for Tour Edge, the St. Charles, Ill.–based club manufacturer that has specialized in innovative hybrid designs. "And I believe we can do that without making courses obsolete. Yes, players are hitting the ball farther, but this is the result of several factors, and professionals and amateurs are in the same category only insofar as scores haven't come down significantly for either group."

Because the industry is divided when it comes to longer ball flights, it will be a challenge to implement strategies to deal with the changes wrought by advanced equipment technology. During the transition, it would be helpful to keep the following in mind:

- Remember how we got here. Even before the quantum leap in driving distance by tour pros in the 1990s, there was talk of a uniform ball, partly to level the playing field, partly to avoid rendering classic courses obsolete. The idea that ball flights have become excessive across the board—and the urgency attached to that notion—are comparatively recent developments. A USGA-sponsored forum in 1998, for example, showed that the prevailing sentiment of participants favored ongoing, laissez-faire innovation. Although few of those participants were golf course owners, consumer preference has supported such innovation.
- Maintain a sense of proportion. Among the few points of agreement is that the benefits of technology are unattainable to the overwhelming majority of golfers, whose slower swing speeds and marginal swing technique render the issue moot. "The major brand manufacturers devote the majority of their engineering budgets to designing clubs for tour pros," says Steve Divnick, president of DivnickGolf, an equipment manufacturer in Miamisburg, Ohio. "Then they pour millions of dollars more into paying endorsements to those same pros hoping it will convince us average golfers to buy these new sticks." "All it takes is one

guy with a hot ball and a hot driver," Leeke points out, to cause pace-of-play problems. Pace of play has long been a vexing issue in golf course management. Yet many note that whereas longer ball flights may occasionally slow play, they are hardly the source.

- Be creative but don't overcompensate. "The great equalizer to technology is longer rough, well-placed bunkers or hazards and fast, well-manicured greens," says D.J. Flanders, director of golf operations at Kierland Golf Club, a Troon Golf property in Scottsdale, Ariz. "Make the golfers think their way around the golf course and penalize them if they are too aggressive. Find a way to take the driver out of their bag through increased attention to agronomic conditions and force them to hit a greater variety of shots."
- Know your customer. "The problem," says Tim Moraghan, the USGA's tournament agronomist, as well as a single-digit-handicap player, "is that none of us is as good as we think we are." "Those of us involved in golf course architecture have to try to be honest about who we're building courses for," says Silva. "And I would say the vast majority of us are not building courses for this small percentage, this one percent, who are hitting the ball much, much farther. So when we're designing upscale daily-fee golf courses or I'm doing renovation work on a members' course, is it necessary for me to put in a 7,600-yard set of tees? To be honest, more often than not, I don't think it is. Courses that have to be stretched to extreme lengths are for a special purpose and are not the basis for a wide-ranging discussion."

Is help on the way? Ever-longer ball flights may well be "a fad that's in its downward curve," says Marc Solda, president of Florida-based EDH Sports, makers of FlightScope, a portable launch-monitor. Solda's take on the evolution of the game suggests "a refocus on playability, on consistency instead of distance."

"The USGA is on record as saying that we don't think that balls ought to go any farther than they do today," says Dick Rugge, the organization's senior technical director. "Even the balls that are being played on tour are at our test limit. So we don't believe that regular, average players are hitting the ball too far." The movement toward limiting the distances golf balls travel may eventually lead to consensus. Indeed, most golf course owners say they would be content to see advanced technology stopped in its tracks. "I think they ought to ratchet back the golf ball for everybody," says golfing legend Tom Watson. Arnold Palmer agrees. "We need to get into cutting the ball back, slowing it down. How much? Probably 15 to 20 percent would not be ridiculous."

Source: Tom Harack, *Golf Business Magazine,* May 2005, http://www.golfbusinessmagazine.com/pageview.asp?m=5&y=2005&doc=1288.

Repositionings   As defined in Chapter 6, repositioning is changing the image or perception of the sports entity in the minds of consumers in the target market. Sports products such as bowling and billiards are trying to reposition themselves as "yuppie sports activities" by creating trendy and upscale environments in sports facilities that are stereotypically grungy and old-fashioned.[4]

Another repositioning example comes from the city of Chicago as it competes for a chance to bid for the 2016 Summer Olympic Games. World Sport Chicago is the new organization that will try to build on the city's reputation as a sports town by bringing amateur and international events to the city. For example, an exhibition wrestling match will be held between the U.S. National team and the world-champion Russian team. Until the host city is chosen in 2009, Chicago will be trying to reposition itself as a sports mecca and the best site for the Olympic Games.

The most common examples of new products are repositioning and product improvements because of the limited risk involved from the organization's perspective. The rearrangement of existing sports products also has its advantages. For example, this type of new product can be developed more quickly than new-to-the-world or new product category entrants, and it already has an established track record with consumers.

However, new-to-the-world products must undergo more careful research and development because they are new to the organization and to consumers. Moreover, more money must be invested because heavy levels of promotion are necessary to make potential consumers aware of the product. In addition, consumers must learn about the benefits of the new product and how it can help satisfy their needs.

Newness from the Consumer's Perspective

Another way to describe new products is from the perspective of consumers. New products are categorized as discontinuous innovations, dynamically continuous innovations, or continuous innovations.[5]

The new products are categorized on the basis of the degree of behavioral change required by consumers. Behavioral changes refer to differences in the way we use a new product, think about a new product, or the degree of learning required to use a new product. For instance, a new extra-long tennis racquet does not require us to change the way we play tennis or to relearn the sport. However, extensive learning took place for many Americans exposed to soccer for the first time in the 1994 World Cup match and the learning process continues. Similarly, learning will have to occur for the many Americans who will watch cricket or experience the growing sport of lacrosse for the first time. Let us look at the three categories of new products from the consumer's perspective in greater detail.

Discontinuous innovations are somewhat similar to new-to-the-world products in that they represent the most innovative products. In fact, discontinuous innovations are so new and original that they require major learning from the consumer's viewpoint and new consumption and usage patterns. Some of the "extreme sports," such as sky surfing, bungee jumping, and ice climbing, represented discontinuous innovations, but are now becoming more mainstream. New "extremes" such as base jumping, extreme trampolining, wakeskiing, and kite-surfing are also becoming popular.

Many Southerners who have had limited access to ice hockey may view this sport as a discontinuous innovation. Interestingly, a study found that spectator knowledge of hockey was found to be a significant predictor of game attendance and intention to attend hockey games in the future. An equally important finding in the study was that knowledge of hockey may vary based on sociodemographic variables. In other words, the fan's age, gender, educational level, income, and marital status influence the degree of hockey knowledge.[6]

Even distribution patterns for sport have required new consumption and usage patterns and therefore represent discontinuous innovation. Sprint Nextel reached an agreement with Major League Baseball Advanced Media, the sport's Internet wing, to make audio of radio broadcasts available to its subscribers' mobile phones for $5.99 a month. Baseball fans will be able to use their cell phones to take them out to the ballgame.

Dynamically continuous innovations are new products that represent changes and improvements but do not strikingly change buying and usage patterns. For instance, the titanium head and bubble shaft on a golf club or the liquid metal technology aluminum bat are innovations that do not change our swing but do represent significant improvements in equipment (and hopefully our game). When the shot-clock and three-point field goal were added to basketball, changes took place in how the game was played. Coaches, players, and fans were forced to understand and adopt new strategies for basketball. Most basketball enthusiasts believe these dynamically continuous innovations improved the sport.

The latest dynamically continuous innovation from the golf industry, which thrives on new product development, is the mainstream acceptance of the hybrid club. Many low- and high-handicap golfers are replacing their long irons with hybrids—a half iron, half wood alternative to the difficult to hit long irons.

The XOS PlayAction Simulator powered by EA Sports is a dynamically continuous innovation that builds upon EA's engine used to drive EA's top-selling Madden NFL 07 and NCAA Football 07 video games by adding functionality (including customizable playbooks, diagrams, and testing sequences) to better prepare athletes for specific opponents. Additionally, the software includes built-in teaching and reporting tools so coaches can analyze and track the tactical-skill development of their athletes. Instead of simply playing a video game for enjoyment, an athlete can play a game to test and train for upcoming on-field action. For example, a quarterback using the new tool can practice reading a defense, picking up blitzes, and making quick decisions on where to throw the ball, all based on the tendencies of the team he is going to play the upcoming weekend.

Another example of a dynamically continuous innovation is VTV: Varsity Television, the world's first and only 24-hour network exclusively dedicated to teenagers. For the first time ever on national television, viewers can experience the best high school sports in the country. More specifically, VTV will give viewers the opportunity to experience the first high school football superconference, where the best of the best unite on television to compete.[7]

A final example of a dynamically continuous innovation comes from the world of trading cards and technology. Topps, the historic market leader in sports trading cards, has developed a new online division called etopps. "Etopps" is a unique model that works like the stock market, with consumers buying and selling sports cards of specific players online for a one-week period. Working in partnership with eBay, Topps launched this new brand of sports cards in December 2000. These cards are sold exclusively online through individual "IPOs" ("Initial Player Offering"). After a sale, the cards are held in a climate-controlled warehouse unless the buyer requests delivery, and the cards can be traded online without changing hands except in the virtual sense. Certainly, this change represents a new buying behavior for a product (trading cards) that has been on the market for decades.

Continuous innovations represent an ongoing, commonplace change such as the minor alteration of a product or the introduction of an imitation product. A continuous innovation has the least disruptive influence on patterns of usage and consumer behavior. In other words, consumers use the product in the same manner that they have always used the product. Examples of continuous innovations include the addition of expansion teams for leagues such as MLB, the WNBA, or MLS or even expanding the number of games in the season. Another example of a continuous innovation comes to us from the world of sports video game technology. We could debate which new product category best represents a team that has built a new arena and changed its venue or any new sports product, but few new products fall neatly into the three categories. Rather, there is a continuum ranging from minor innovation to major innovation, based on how consumers perceive the new product. Knowing how consumers think and feel about a new product is critical information in developing the most effective marketing strategy. Before we talk more about the factors that make new products successful and spread through the marketplace, let us look at how new products are conceived.

THE NEW PRODUCT DEVELOPMENT PROCESS

Increased competition for sports and entertainment dollars, emergence of new technologies, and ever-changing consumer preferences are just a few of the reasons sports marketers are constantly developing new sports products. As Higgins and Martin point out in their research on managing sport innovations, "Clearly, the list of innovations in sports is extensive and appears to be increasing at a rapid rate. This would suggest that spectators are seeking new and better entertainment and participants are seeking new and better challenges."[8]

Many **new sports products** are conceived without much planning, or happen as a result of chance. For instance, the modern sport of polo was created by British cavalry officers in India who wanted to show off their horsemanship in a more creative way than the parade ground allowed. Although polo represents a sport that was developed by chance, this is more the exception than the rule. More often than not, sports organizations develop new products by using a systematic approach called the **new product development process.** The phases in the new product development process include idea generation, idea screening, and analysis of the concept, developing the sports product, test marketing, and commercialization. Let us briefly explore each phase in the new product development process.

Idea Generation
The first phase of the new product development process is **idea generation.** At this initial phase, any and all ideas for new products are considered. Ideas for new products are generated from many different sources. Employees who work in product development teams, salespeople close to the consumers, consumers of sport, and competitive organizations are just a few of the potential sources of ideas for new sports products.

Naturally, a marketing-oriented sports organization will attempt to communicate with their consumers as much as possible to determine emerging needs. As we discussed in Chapter 3, marketing research plays a valuable role in anticipating the needs of consumers. Moreover, environmental scanning helps sports organizations keep in touch with changes in the marketing environment that might present opportunities for new product development. For instance, in our opening scenario, the entrepreneurs who established Ultimate Fighting understood that the environmental conditions would be conducive to success.

Idea Screening
Once the ideas are generated, the next step of the product development process, **idea screening,** begins. During the idea screening phase, all the new product ideas are evaluated and the poor ones are weeded out. An important consideration in the idea screening process is to examine the "fit" of the product with the organization's goals and consumer demand. The concept of new product fit is consistent with the

TABLE 8.1	New Product Screening Checklist

Rate the new product concept using a 10-point scale. Score 1 if the concept fails the question and 10 if it meets the criterion perfectly.

Relative Advantage

Does the new product offer a cost advantage compared with substitutes?

Does the new product have a value-added feature?

Is your innovation directed at neglected segments of the marketplace?

Compatibility

Is the product compatible with corporate practices, culture, and value systems (i.e., the internal contingencies)?

Is the new product compatible with the market's environment (i.e., the external contingencies)?

Is the new product compatible with current products and services being offered (i.e., product mix)?

Perceived Risk

Note: On the following questions, absence of risk should receive a higher score.

Does the consumer perceive an economic risk in trying the new product?

Does the consumer perceive a physical risk in adopting the new product?

Does the consumer fear the new technology will not perform properly?

Does the product offer a social risk to consumers?

A bottom-line score of 100 (10 points for each question) suggests a new product winner. For most companies, a score of 70 or better signals a "go" decision on the new product concept. A risk-oriented company would probably consider anything that scores 50 or higher. A score of 30 or less signifies a concept that faces many consumer obstacles.

contingency framework, which states that product decisions should consider the external contingencies, the internal contingencies, and the strategic sports marketing process. One formal idea screening tool for analyzing the "fit" of potential products is the new product screening checklist (see Table 8.1).

Sports marketers using some variant of this new product screening checklist would rate potential new product ideas on each item. As Table 8.1 indicates, a score of less than 30 would eliminate the new product from further consideration, whereas a score of 70 or more means the product would be further developed. Obviously, each sports organization must design its own new product screening checklist to meet the demands of its unique marketing environment and organization.

Analysis of the Sports Product Concept or Potential

By the third phase of the new product development process, poor ideas have been eliminated. Now, the process continues as the firm begins to analyze potential new products in terms of how they fit with existing products and how consumers respond to these new products. As new product ideas begin to take shape, marketing research is necessary to understand consumers' perceptions of the new product concepts. One type of marketing research that is commonly conducted during the new product development process is referred to as concept testing.

During concept testing, consumers representative of the target market evaluate written, verbal, and pictorial descriptions of potential products. The objectives of concept testing are to understand the target market's reaction to the proposed product, determine how interested the target market is in the product, and explore the strengths and weaknesses of the proposed product. In some cases, consumers are asked to evaluate slightly different versions of the product so that sports organizations can design the product to meet the needs of consumers.

Concept testing is used to understand consumer reactions to sports such as white water rafting.

The most important reason for conducting a concept test is to estimate the sales potential of the new product. Often, this is done by measuring "intent to buy" responses from tested consumers. Using the results of concept testing, along with secondary data such as demographic trends, sports marketers can decide whether to proceed to the next step of the new product development process, drop the idea, or revise the product concept and reevaluate. Table 8.2 shows a hypothetical concept test for the Beach Soccer World Wide Tour, a new sports product that has been growing around the globe.

TABLE 8.2	Concept Test for the Beach Soccer World Wide Tour

The sport of beach soccer is played on a 30-by-40-yard soft sand surface with five players on each team, including the goalie. There are three periods of 12 minutes each with unlimited player substitutions (as in hockey). In the event of a tie, the game goes into a 3-minute overtime period, followed by sudden-death penalty kicks. Beach Soccer World Wide would feature nation against nation (e.g., United States vs. Italy).

What is your general reaction to beach soccer?

How likely would you be to attend an event if the tour stopped in your city?

   Would definitely attend

   Probably would attend

   Might or might not attend

   Probably would not attend

   Would definitely not attend

What do you like most about this concept of BSWW?

What could be done to improve the concept of BSWW?

Developing the Sports Product

Based on the results of the concept test, design of the product begins in order to conduct further testing. Ideally, if the sports organization is employing a marketing orientation, then the product design and development stem from the consumer's perspective. For instance, Nike began its product design efforts for a new baseball glove by asking 200 college and minor league baseball players what they disliked about their current gloves. Eighteen months and $500,000 later, researchers designed a prototype glove that is lightweight, held together with plastic clips and wire straps, and resembles a white foam rubber clamshell. Nike was hoping this space-age design would not be perceived by baseball purists to be too far afield from traditional models.[9] However, consumers didn't respond favorably and Nike was forced to discontinue the glove line.

In the case of a sporting good, a prototype usually is developed so consumers can get an even better idea of how the product will function and look. Today's superior engineering technology allows manufacturers to develop more realistic prototypes in a shorter period of time. It is common for prototypes to then be sent to select individuals for further testing and refinement. For instance, new golf, tennis, and ski products are routinely sent to club professionals for testing.

Another consideration in **developing the sports product** is making preliminary decisions with respect to the planning phase of the strategic sports marketing process. Potential market selection decisions (segmentation, target markets, and positioning) are considered. Furthermore, packaging, pricing, and distribution decisions are also deliberated. These basic marketing decisions are necessary to begin the next phase of new product development—test marketing.

Test Marketing

In the concept stage of new product development, consumers indicate they would be likely to purchase the new product or service. Now that the product has been designed and developed, it can be offered to consumers on a limited basis to determine actual sales. Test marketing is the final gauge of the new product's success or failure.

Test marketing allows the sports organization to determine consumer response to the product and also provides information that may direct the entire marketing strategy. For instance, test markets can provide valuable information on the most effective packaging, pricing, and other forms of promotion.

The three types of test markets that may be conducted include standardized test markets, controlled test markets, and simulated test markets.[10] In standardized test markets, the product is sold through normal channels of distribution. A controlled test market, also known as a forced-distribution test market, uses an outside agency to secure distribution. As such, the manufacturer of a new product does not have to worry about the acceptance and level of market support from retailers or those carrying the product because the outside agency pays the retailer for the test. A simulated test market uses a tightly controlled simulated retailing environment or purchasing laboratory to determine consumer preferences for new sports products. This type of test market may be especially important in the future as more and more sporting goods and services are being marketed through the Internet.

Whatever type of test market is chosen, it is important to keep several things in mind. First, test marketing delays the introduction of a new sports product and may allow time for the competition to produce a "me-too" or imitation product, thereby negating the test marketer's investment in research and development. Second, costs of test marketing must be considered. It is common for the cost of test marketing to range from $30,000 to $300,000. Third, the results of test marketing may be misleading. Consumers may be anxious to try new sports products and competition may try to influence the sales figures of the tested product by offering heavy discounting and promotion of their own product. Finally, test marketing presents a special challenge for sports marketers because of the intangible nature of many sports services.

Commercialization

The final stage of new product development is **commercialization,** or introduction. The decision has been made at this point to launch full-scale production (for goods) and distribution. If care has been taken at the previous stages of new product development, the new product will successfully meet its objectives. However, even if a systematic approach to new product development is followed, more often than not sports products fail. Just what is it that makes a small portion of new sports products successful while the large majority fail? Let us look at some of the factors that increase the chances of new product success.

New Product Success Factors

The success of any new sports product, such as the NASCAR SpeedParks, depends on a variety of **new product success factors.** First and foremost, successful products must be high quality, create and maintain a positive and distinct brand image, and be designed to consumer specifications. In addition to the characteristics of the product itself, the other marketing mix elements (pricing, distribution, and promotion) play a major role in the success of a new product. Finally, the marketing environment also contributes to the success of a new product. A brief description of these critical success factors is presented in Table 8.3. Let us evaluate how well the new NASCAR SpeedParks perform on each of the critical success factors.

Based on the critical success factors in Table 8.3, would you predict that the NASCAR SpeedParks will be profitable? The NASCAR SpeedParks would seem to perform well on each of the product characteristics. Families can observe others enjoying the SpeedParks and try the sports product once with limited perceived risk. The NASCAR Go-Karts are safe and built for kids, so product complexity is low. With the NASCAR branding, the sophisticated engineering, and the authenticity, the perceived

---

TABLE 8.3   Critical Success Factors for New Products

Product Considerations

- **Trialability**—Can consumers try the product before they make a purchase to reduce the risk?
- **Observability**—Can consumers see the benefits of the product or watch others use the product prior to the purchase?
- **Perceived Complexity**—Does the new product appear to be difficult to understand or use?
- **Relative Advantage**—Does the new product seem better than existing alternatives?
- **Compatibility**—Is the new product consistent with consumers' values and beliefs?

Other Marketing Mix Considerations

- **Pricing**—Do consumers perceive the price to be consistent with the quality of the new product?
- **Promotion**—Are consumers in the target market aware of the product and do they understand the benefits of the product?
- **Distribution**—Is the product being sold in the "right" places and in enough places?

Marketing Environment Considerations

- **Competition**—Are there a large number of competitors in the market?
- **Consumer Tastes**—Does the new product reflect a trend in society?
- **Demographics**—Is the new product being marketed to a segment of the population that is growing?

Source: Courtland L. Bovée and John Thill, *Marketing* (New York: McGraw-Hill, 1992), 307–309.

advantage of these replica cars should be far greater than for "just another Go-Kart." Finally, the SpeedParks are consistent with core values, such as safe and fun entertainment for the entire family.

In addition to the product considerations, other marketing mix considerations have also been well thought out for the NASCAR SpeedParks. Initially, the SpeedParks will be placed in parts of the country known for entertainment (e.g., Myrtle Beach) and the love of NASCAR racing (e.g., Tennessee). Given the signing of Kasey Kahne, Kevin Harvick, Bobby Labonte, and Elliot Sadler, promotion of the SpeedParks should be solid.

The marketing environment also appears to be ready for the growth of the NASCAR SpeedParks. NASCAR is one of the fastest-growing spectator sports in the country and has a huge and loyal fan base. Moreover, there are other Go-Kart tracks, but none with the backing of NASCAR, so competition is limited. In summary, the NASCAR SpeedParks seem to perform well on all the critical success factors, but only time will tell whether this new sports product will run the victory lap.

PRODUCT LIFE CYCLE

From the time a sports product begins the new product development process to the time it is taken off the market, it passes through a series of stages known as the **product life cycle** (PLC). The four distinct stages of the PLC are called introduction, growth, maturity, and decline. As shown in Figure 8.1, the traditional PLC was originally developed by marketers to illustrate how the sales and profits of goods vary over time. However, other sports products, such as athletes, teams, leagues, and events, pass through four distinct phases over time. Regardless of the nature of the sports product, the PLC is a useful tool for developing marketing strategy and then revising this strategy as a product moves through its own unique life cycle. Authors Rick Burton and

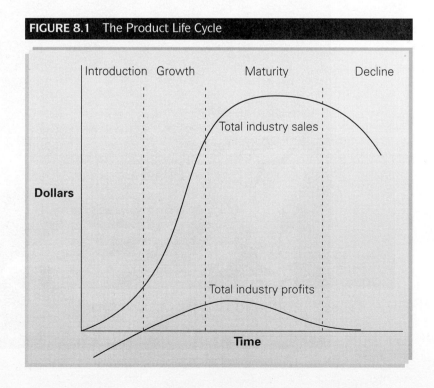

FIGURE 8.1 The Product Life Cycle

Dennis Howard used the product life cycle as a tool to assess the current state of big league sports. Their conclusion was that all four big league sports (baseball, hockey, basketball, and football) have reached either late maturity or decline. The authors speculate that part of the reason for this decline is that professional sports leagues have experienced "player strikes (MLB, August 1994; NHL, September 1995, 2004), player lockout (NBA, July 1998), player free agency and salary demands (all leagues, all the time), various player arrests, rising ticket prices (an annual custom), stadium referendums, franchise movement, and constant legal wrangling." The authors also point out that each league should examine its current position in the marketplace and be prepared to adjust its marketing strategy based on the phase of the product life cycle. As expressed in the article, "despite all the hype and rhetoric, a case can be made that professional sports leagues are marketable brands that require sophisticated marketing plans and an understanding of how the product is perceived, received, and purchased. If a brand is in late maturity or the earliest phases of decline, then new uses, new product features, or new markets must be developed."[11]

The waterbike is an excellent example of a sports product whose life cycle mirrors the shape of the conventional PLC. The waterbike, or personal watercraft, had tremendous growth in the early 1990s. Sales of waterbikes reached their peak in 1995 with 200,000 units sold. However, unit sales have been decreasing since that year. In 2001, U.S. dealers sold 83,000 of the water machines. Sales fell further in 2002, and even James Bond couldn't help the sagging industry as he proudly rode a Sea-Doo in the movie *Die Another Day*.[12] The industry saw sales in 2004 of 79,500 units, and 80,200 were sold in the United States in 2005, indicating some stability in the marketplace.

Industry insiders want to believe the waterbike is in the maturity phase of the PLC and sales have merely reached their plateau. Others, however, contend the industry has developed an image problem because of the safety and pollution

Extending the product life cycle of the waterbike.

issues associated with the activity. In this case, waterbike brands such as JetSki and Sea-Doo may need to find ways to extend the life of their products. Makers of personal watercraft have long been committed to changing the product to be more environmentally friendly, quieter, and safer.

Before we explore the four phases of the PLC, keep several important factors in mind. First, the PLC originally was developed to describe product categories, such as waterbikes or baseball gloves, rather than specific brands, such as Sea-Doo or Mizuno. Second, the product life cycle was designed to monitor the industry sales and profitability of goods rather than services. Third, the traditional shape and length of the product life cycle is generalized. In other words, it is assumed to look the same for all products. In reality, the length of the PLC varies for each sports product. Some products die quickly, some seem to last forever, and others die and are then reborn. Summarizing, sports marketers must carefully consider the unique PLC of each of their products on the market. Let us now explore how the PLC can be used for decision making in the strategic sports marketing process.

Introduction

When a new sports product first enters the marketplace, the introduction phase of the PLC is initiated. New leagues such as the Women's Soccer Initiative and the National Women's Hockey League are excellent examples of sports products being introduced. Another sport product in the introductory phase is Fatheads wall graphics. Fatheads are "sport posters," approximately 6 feet tall by 3 feet wide, printed on thick, high-grade vinyl with a low-tack adhesive that sticks to almost any wall. Additionally, unlike posters of old, Fatheads can be moved from place to place with no loss of adhesion or damage to the wall. These big, bold, colorful graphics have a 3-D look and appear as if the image is jumping off the wall. The Chicago Bears' Rex Grossman, Arizona Cardinals' Matt Leinart, Tennessee Titans' Vince Young, and the Dallas Cowboys Cheerleaders headline Fatheads' latest additions to its National Football League (NFL) wall graphics.

The broad marketing goal of the first phase of the PLC for any sport product is to generate awareness and stimulate trial among those consumers who are willing to try new products. Typically, profits are low because of the high start-up costs associated with getting the product ready to market.

During the introduction phase, pricing of the sports product is determined largely by the type of image that has been determined in the positioning strategy. Generally, one of two broad pricing alternatives is usually chosen during the **introduction** of the product. If the product strategy is to gain widespread consumer trial and market share, a lower price is set. This low pricing strategy is termed penetration pricing. However, a higher priced skimming strategy is sometimes preferred. The advantages of skimming include recouping the early marketing investment and production costs, as well as reinforcing the superior quality usually associated with higher prices.

Distribution of the new product is also highly dependent on the nature of the product. Usually, however, distribution is limited to fewer outlets. That is, there are a small number of places to purchase the product. Incentives are necessary to push the product from the manufacturer to the consumer. Promotion activity is high during the product's introduction to encourage consumers to try the new product. In addition, promotion is designed to provide the consumers with information about the new product and to provide a purchase incentive.

Growth

Sales are usually slow as the new product is introduced. With the onset of the **growth** stage, sales of the product increase. In fact, a rapid increase in sales is the primary characteristic of the growth stage of the PLC. Because industry sales are growing, the broad marketing goal is to build consumer preference for your product and continue to extend the product line. Although competition is usually nonexistent or very weak at introduction, more competitors emerge during the growth phase. Promotion must stress the benefits of your brand over competitive brands.

For example, the sport of lacrosse is currently in the growth stage in the U.S. market. Ten years ago lacrosse was played only in select East Coast cities and considered a sport for prep schools only. Today, an estimated 150,000 men and women play lacrosse in high school and there is an estimated 206 percent growth in the number of high school players over the last decade. The sport should continue to grow at all levels as some 200,000 youth under 15 are playing organized lacrosse.

Another example of a sport product in the growth phase, where more and more competitors are starting to enter the market, is distance measurement devices in golf. The external, environmental factors are ripe for this product's continued growth as the technology develops and golf's governing bodies recognize distance measurement devices as part of the game. "With the recent USGA and R&A rulings that have made GPS distance measurement devices allowable for the game of golf, handheld GPS currently represents one of the fastest growing product sales segments in the golf business," said Scott Lambrecht, CEO of GolfLogix, Inc.[13]

During the growth stage, product differentiation occurs by making minor changes or modifications in the product or service. A premium is placed on gaining more widespread distribution of the product. Manufacturers must secure outlets and distributors at this early phase of the PLC so the product is readily available. Finally, the prices during the growth phase are sometimes reduced in response to a growing number of competitors or held artificially high to enhance perceived quality. Let us look at some of the strategic decisions discussed thus far in the context of the growth of the fantasy sports industry.

Fantasy Sports Craze Attracting Millions of Fans

It's a dream come true for the media business: Some 15 million people laying out more than $1.5 billion on fantasy sports, and marketers spending big to play along.

While fantasy sports were born of paper, pencil and calculator, the preferred venue to trade players and trash-talk is now online, through live drafts, message boards and instant messaging. And those 15 million players who indulge in fantasy sports each year are lucrative targets for advertisers. A University of Mississippi study found most are home-owning men with an average age of 36 who spend an average of 3.8 hours a week managing their teams.

"They've got a high household income, most are married, educated, big spenders," said Eric Bader, senior VP at Media-Vest Digital. "And they spend a lot on fantasy sports."

Some $265 a year, according to Ole Miss data that peg industry growth at a 7% to 10% annual clip.

With an eye on that financial prize, fantasy-sports networks are busy recruiting enthusiasts with a couple different models: subscription-based offerings, like those of Yahoo and CBS Sportsline, and free services, such as

ESPN and Fox Sports/MSN, which sell additional services. This football season, networks are also adding a host of features such as mobile alerts and interactive TV applications.

All are selling advertising, and according to media buyers, the price of entry for advertisers has skyrocketed as fantasy's popularity has grown among marketers seeking engaged audiences. "It's the original great community social-networking product," said Mr. Bader. "Its highly targeted marketing environments are the holy grail if you're looking to find active, like-minded audiences that are mostly male."

While a marketer used to be able to buy into fantasy football with a low six-figure deal, today's main sponsorships command seven figures, with smaller sponsorships running around the half-million mark. It can be a great way for marketers to reach an at-work audience, but as with all social-network advertising, marketers must tread lightly so as not to disrupt the consumer experience.

"The opportunities for marketers don't necessarily align with what the consumer behavior is," said Art Sindlinger, VP-media director at Starcom, suggesting that

(*Continued*)

(*Continued*)

advertising can go unnoticed—or worse, seem intrusive—if it keeps consumers from getting what they want. "It's like having billboards on the autobahn. Users are tearing through multiple page views with a laser focus on what they want to get."

He said networks have had so little trouble selling the packages to advertisers that there was little incentive to move beyond basic offerings of banner ads and sponsored buttons. But this year, they've gotten more creative.

MSN/Fox Sports's fantasy offering, for example, is incorporating its MSN Messenger into live scoring. CBS Sportsline is selling session-based ad units, much like it did for March Madness on Demand, in which a single advertiser follows a user deeper into his or her session on the site. And ESPN is selling cross-platform packages that include fantasy podcasts, three radio shows and a weekly ESPN Original Entertainment show dedicated to the subject. "Fantasy players index higher across all ESPN media, so it's an opportunity for the whole company to benefit," said John Kosner, general manager of ESPN.com.

ESPN will use fantasy to drive adoption of its Mobile ESPN cellular service and its mobile publishing; the others have struck similar deals with carriers. "The reason you subscribe to a sports service on the phone is because you're a fantasy player," said Mr. Kosner. "You want the alerts, injury updates."

For ESPN, a smooth fantasy season is imperative if it hopes to continue to grow the business. Last year glitches in the network caused delays in the draft tool and frustrated players who had switched to the newly free offering. Mr. Kosner said the issues were due to "two separate technical problems" and ESPN stayed out of free fantasy baseball this year in order to devote time to making sure football would work smoothly. "It was a dark day for us," he said.

DirecTV doesn't have its own fantasy league, but is sponsoring ESPN's and has made its NFL Sunday Ticket package, which includes access to every game, fully interactive with fantasy stats and injury updates. One feature, the Red Zone package, automatically switches the channel to a game whenever a team is inside 10 yards of the end zone. And that foreshadowing-fantasy of the future on every screen-has marketers and media buyers really excited.

"Mobile's definitely the next step," said Mr. Bader. "But as soon as true iTV arrives on a wide scale, that's when we'll see great integration between actual games and fantasy activity that isn't just two-screen stuff."

What Are They Playing?
According to the Fantasy Sports Trade Association, more than 16 million American adults participated in fantasy sports leagues in 2006. Here's what they're playing:

Sport	Total*	Pct.
Football	12.8	80
Baseball	4.8	30
Auto racing	4.16	26
Basketball	3.2	20
Hockey	1.92	12
Golf	1.12	7

*In millions.

Source: Abbey Klaassen, "That's Real Money—$1.5B Pouring into Made-Up Leagues," *Advertising Age,* August 7, 2006, p. 4; Eric Page, "Fantasy Sports Craze Attracting Millions of Fans," *The Pantagraph.*

Maturity

Eventually, industry sales begin to stabilize as fewer numbers of new consumers enter the saturated market. As such, the level of competition increases as a greater number of organizations compete for a limited or stable number of consumers. The primary marketing objective at **maturity** is to maintain whatever advantages were captured in growth and offer a greater number of promotions to encourage repeat purchases. Brand strategy shifts from "try me" to "buy one more than you used to." Unfortunately, profitability is also lessened because of the need to reduce prices and offer incentives.

If attempts to maintain sales and market share are unsuccessful in the maturity stage, an organization may try several alternative strategies to extend the PLC before the product begins to decline and eventually die.

One household sport product in the maturity to decline phase of the product life cycle is AstroTurf. In order to extend this dying brand GeneralSports Venue, which recently acquired the rights to the AstroTurf brand, will announce its "re-launch" with a new celebrity spokesman, former pro football quarterback Archie Manning.

AstroTurf was the first synthetic turf used on a sports field when it was installed in the Houston Astrodome in 1966. But the product fell on hard times as rivals made technological advances. GeneralSports plans to spend "several million dollars" over the next few years to promote what it boasts is new-and-improved AstroTurf.[14]

Another excellent illustration of a sport that realized it was rapidly moving toward extinction, decided to take corrective action, and developed and implemented new marketing strategies is badminton. Table 8.4 provides additional suggestions for sports marketers who want to extend the PLC.

Birdies: A Backyard Game Serves Up a New Image

When Gary Yang goes out on weekends, he likes to hang out with his buddies until 3 or 4 a.m.—but he's not exactly partying. Instead, he spends the night smashing shuttles across a net with his racquet. "I don't go clubbing," says Mr. Yang, a 33-year-old sports-equipment salesperson. "I'd rather play badminton."

Mr. Yang is among a growing number of B.C. badminton fans who can't get enough of the sport and often play into the wee hours. Popular among Asians, badminton is now played in almost every community center in Greater Vancouver. To meet growing demand, four new private badminton clubs have sprung up during the past three years in Richmond, a predominantly Asian suburb of Vancouver. The newly opened Richmond Pro Badminton Centre, with 15 courts, is North America's largest private badminton facility.

Mr. Yang says Yumo, which opened in September, 2006, is the place to be on a Saturday night because that's when the high-powered players show up. After sweating through half a dozen sets of doubles, everyone goes out to eat seafood hotpot at a nearby restaurant until 4 a.m. At the Vancouver Racquets Club, each of the 1,300 or so members gets a key to the facility and can play badminton whenever the mood strikes. Few members play at 4 a.m. but plenty start at 6 a.m., while others play well past midnight, says Robert Trepanier, executive director of the non-profit facility. The club's badminton memberships have been full for the past four years and about 35 players are on the waiting list, he says.

The sport is taking off in B.C. schools as well. At the high school level, the number of senior tournaments has doubled to 200 over the past six years, says Mike Charlton, badminton commissioner for B.C. School Sports and a teacher, coach, and vice-principal at J.N. Burnett Secondary School in Richmond. And at the college level, B.C. players swept every gold medal at the 2007 National Badminton Championships, held in Richmond in March.

In China and Taiwan, top badminton players are idolized as national heroes and 24-hour badminton courts are commonplace, says Mr. Yang, who travels to Asia regularly to visit family. Born in Vancouver, Mr. Yang learned the game at age 5 from his Chinese-immigrant parents. But in North America, badminton has yet to shed its image as a lightweight sport. Most people still see it as a backyard game "where you hit and giggle," says Jeff White, executive director of Badminton Canada.

The official game is far from the backyard version, Mr. White explains. Badminton is an intense workout that requires agility, strategy, and excellent hand-eye coordination, he says. It's become a favorite cross-training activity for athletes such as 24-year-old NHL hockey player Duncan Milroy, who was a Canadian badminton champion as a teenager. The sport would draw more players and spectators in North America "if people deemed it hip," Mr. White says.

Next: Speedminton

Badminton officials in British Columbia hope to make their sport hip through a new version of the game, called Speedminton. Although badminton is already wildly popular among members of the city's Asian community, Badminton B.C. wants to attract more players by luring them with Speedminton, which is played outdoors without a net (see www.speedminton.ca). Since last year, when Badminton B.C. started marketing the German-made game in Canada, more than 400 Speedminton kits have been sold in British Columbia.

Endorsed by sexy tennis pro Maria Sharapova, Speedminton is "what beach volleyball was five years ago," says Brock Turner, executive director of Badminton B.C. He points to the success of Vancouver's beach volleyball leagues and the game's popularity on urban shores. Speedminton, played with sturdy racquets and wind-resistant shuttles, has the potential to lure players to indoor badminton, Mr. Turner says. But since the racquet strokes for the new hybrid game are different, Badminton B.C. doesn't recommend it for elite badminton players because it could affect their technique.

Source: Adriana Barton, *The Globe and Mail*, April 26, 2007, L7.

TABLE 8.4	Extending the Product Life Cycle

- Develop new uses for products.
- Develop new product features and refinements (line extensions).
- Increase the existing market.
- Develop new markets.
- Change the marketing mix (e.g., new or more promotions, new or more distribution, increase or decrease price).
- Link product to a trend.

Source: Joel Evans and Barry Berman, *Marketing,* 6th ed. (New York: Macmillan, 1992), 439.

Decline

The marketing goals for the **decline** stage of the PLC are difficult to pinpoint because decisions must be made regarding what to do with a failing product. These decisions are based largely on the competition and how the sports organization chooses to react to the competition.

The distinctive characteristic of the decline phase of the PLC is that sales are steadily diminishing. Several alternative strategies might be considered during the decline phase. One alternative is referred to as deletion. As the name implies, the product is dropped from the organization's product mix. A second alternative, harvesting (or milking), is when the organization retains the sports product but offers little or no marketing support. A final alternative is simply maintaining the product at its current level of marketing support in hope that competitors will withdraw from the market that is already in decline.

Other Life Cycle Considerations

The PLC, although an excellent tool for strategic decision making, is not without limitations. These limitations include generalizing the length of the PLC, applying the PLC to broad product categories only, and using the PLC to analyze "pure" sporting goods only. Each of these potential weaknesses of the PLC model is discussed next.

Length and Shape of the PLC

Figure 8.1 depicted the traditional length and shape of the PLC. However, each product life cycle has its own unique shape and unique length, depending on the product under consideration and the nature of the marketing environment. Several variants of the typical PLC length including the fad PLC, the classic PLC, and the seasonal PLC are shown in Figures 8.2a to 8.2c.

Fad   The **fad** PLC (Figure 8.2a) is characterized by accelerated sales and accelerated acceptance of the product followed by decline stages. Often, sports marketers realize their products will be novelty items that get into the market, make a profit, and then quickly exit. These one-time, short-term offerings would follow the volatile fad cycle. The ABA red, white, and blue basketball followed the fad cycle, as do many products in the golf equipment industry. Other examples of a fad cycle include the bobblehead doll as a sports promotion and retro look jerseys and sports apparel. Fitness and fads seem to go hand in hand. While some exercise routines and machines have endured the test of time to become classics, others come and go in a flash.

High-impact aerobics might have been the first of the more modern fitness fads in the 1970s, followed by the cardio-fitness movement of the 1980s. Then came the incorporation of strength training into workouts, and more recent fads include the indoor cycling program called "spinning" and cardio-kickboxing. The latest and greatest

FIGURE 8.2 Selected Product Life Cycle Patterns

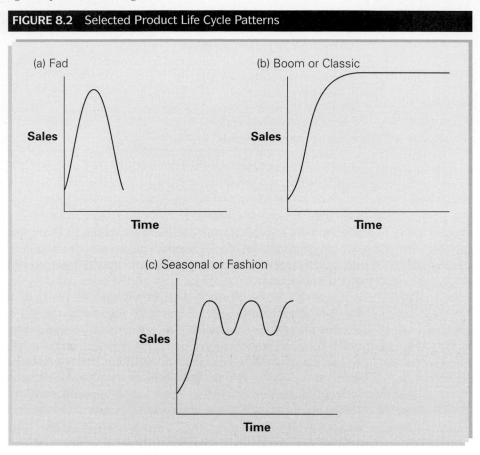

exercise fad links the mind and body in routines such as yoga and tai chi. Who knows what the next fad might bring?

Classic Another variation of the PLC is characterized by a continuous stage of maturity (Figure 9.2b). Season tickets for the Green Bay Packers, Frisbees, baseball gloves and bats, tennis balls, and hockey sticks all represent other examples of the PLC know as the **classic.**

Seasonal The **seasonal** life cycle is found in most sports where the sales of sports products rise and fall with the opening and closing day of the season. To combat the seasonal life cycle, some sports have adopted year-round scheduling. Most auto racing series are run on an 8- to 10-month schedule, giving sponsors almost year-round coverage. Professional tennis has also adopted a continual schedule, but this may not be the best thing for the sport.

When asked what he would do to cure the ills of tennis, former star and current TV analyst John McEnroe did not hesitate before responding, "I would cut the amount of events. Now, there are too many tournaments, so people don't have any idea about what's really important. I would make a schedule that would be like the baseball or basketball season, so we wouldn't go 12 months a year."[15] Somewhat surprisingly, the NBA used the "less-is-more" strategy more than 20 years ago, when the league was plummeting in popularity. David Stern, then a rookie commissioner, significantly cut the number of televised games to increase long-term interest in the sport.

The fad, classic, and seasonal life cycles are three common variants of the traditional PLC. Other products, however, seem to defy all life cycle shapes and lengths. Consider skateboarding. Since its inception in the 1950s, skateboarding has been a fad in nearly every decade. Now, skateboarding seems to be here to stay, according to the National Sporting Goods Association (NSGA). Skateboarding posted an unbelievable growth rate in participation for youth ages seven to 17 from 1995 to 2005. Over that decade, skateboarding participation increased nearly 175 percent and was second only to snowboarding in terms of percentage growth.[16]

The Level of Product

Another consideration for developing marketing strategy based on the PLC is the level of the product. Historically, the PLC was based on total industry sales for an entire product category, such as basketball shoes, bowling balls, mountain bikes, or golf clubs. Although examining the PLC by category is useful, it is also necessary to understand the PLC by product form and product brand.

Product form refers to product variations within the category. For example, titanium woods, metal woods, and "wood" woods represent three variations in product form in the golf club product category. The potential marketing strategies for each of these product forms differ by the stage of the PLC. The titanium woods are in the growth stage, metal woods are in maturity, and traditional woods are near extinction.

In addition to looking at the product category and form, it is also beneficial to examine various brands. Within the titanium wood form, there are a variety of individual brands, such as Titleist 907, Ping G5, and Nike's Non-conforming SasQuatch Sumo Squared Driver. Each of these brands may be in different stages of the PLC. Therefore, sports marketing managers must give full consideration to variations in the PLC, based on the level of the product (category, form, and brand).

Type of Product

The PLC originally was designed to guide strategies for goods. However, the notion of the PLC should be extended to other types of sports products. For instance, individual athletes can be thought of as sports products that move through a life cycle just as products do.

The phenomenal rise and success of Tiger Woods in the professional golf ranks has skyrocketed him out of introduction and into the growth phase of his PLC. The number of products that Woods endorses is rapidly increasing and everyone is aware of his "star" qualities. The Cleveland Cavaliers' star, LeBron James, has emerged and continues in his introductory stage. "King" James signed a $90-million shoe contract with Nike and is still heir apparent to Michael Jordan for his skills both on and off the court. The former Olympic medalist and World Cup champion Bode Miller, who left the U.S. ski team in 2007, is certainly in the decline stage of his individual PLC.

Interestingly, some individual athletes have a unique shape to their PLC. Think about the many professional athletes who have come out of retirement to reintroduce themselves. Mark Spitz attempted to come back to Olympic swimming 20 years after winning seven gold medals in Munich and was no longer able to compete. Jim Palmer, Bjorn Borg, Sugar Ray Leonard, Magic Johnson, and Muhammad Ali all tried to come back after years away from their respective sports and failed miserably. Arnold Palmer, with his incredible staying power, will undoubtedly stay in the maturity phase of his PLC and remain a classic even after playing his last competitive golf tournament. Many aging golfers, such as Tom Jenkins, who won $10.5 million since 1998 on the senior circuit but won only once on the regular PGA

Tour, are experiencing tremendous success on the senior circuit. Unfortunately, many athletes experience a life cycle that is best represented by the fad PLC. For instance, Brian Bosworth (Seattle Seahawks linebacker), Mark "The Bird" Fydrich (Detroit Tigers pitcher), and Buster Douglas (boxing) were all athletes who had short-term success, only to quickly fall into decline for a number of reasons.

Sports teams also can pass through the various phases of the PLC. For instance, the National Basketball Development League awarded a franchise to Fort Wayne in 2007 and it is in the introductory stage of its PLC. The Seattle Supersonics may be in the decline phase, as owner Clay Bennett said the team could leave the state before its arena lease expires in 2010. Likewise, the Penguins were close to leaving Pittsburgh after an impasse in their new arena negotiations. These product examples would each require completely different marketing strategies.

Professional and collegiate sports leagues also pass through the stages of the PLC. Many of the established leagues in the United States are going global and are currently in the introduction phase of their life cycles internationally. Therefore, the leagues have directed their marketing efforts toward making fans aware of them and generating interest. For example, the Chinese market is attracting a lot of attention by major sports leagues in the United States as the accompanying spotlight illustrates.

SPOTLIGHT ON INTERNATIONAL SPORTS MARKETING

NBA Reaches Out to Ever-Growing Basketball Fan Base in China

On the other side of the world, a sleeping giant is rising. Basketball is one of the fastest-growing sports in the world, and nowhere is that more evident than in China, where the sport is more than a century old and where there are enough basketball fans to rival the U.S. population.

The National Basketball Association Development League Albuquerque Thunderbirds ventured by plane, train, bus, and boat to and around China for a pair of exhibition games against the Chinese national team. The Thunderbirds lost both games, but despite the losses, managed to make an impact on Chinese basketball fans, and the games benefited the players, said head coach Michael Cooper.

Cooper, who earned five championship rings with the "Showtime" Lakers and two as head coach of the WNBA's Los Angeles Sparks, is attempting to lead the Thunderbirds to back-to-back D-League championship titles in New Mexico. It was last year's D-League title that brought Cooper and his team to China this year.

"I think part of what was alluring for the Chinese was to have a champion here in China to play their national team," said Kent Partridge, vice president of communication for the NBADL. "Plus, you can't discount

Coop and his success and celebrity with the Lakers. I'm sure that played into it as well." Although this was the first time an NBA D-League team made its way to China for competition, two members of the Thunderbirds were familiar with Chinese basketball after stints in the Chinese Basketball Association. Center Eddy Fobbs and T.J. Cummings spent past seasons playing in the CBA.

National Pride

Chinese audiences weren't as neutral during the Thunderbirds' two recent losses. Although local fans couldn't get enough of the Thunderbirds' athleticism and Cooper's up-tempo coaching style, when it came to the final score, it was all about China's national team getting the victory. "It's nice to have the Thunderbirds here because they are very exciting players, but the Chinese are also very proud of sports and their national team and want to see them win," said Connie Wong of China's NBA offices. "But I also think it's good for the Team China to have the NBA here."

With a total population of 1.3 billion, China is the NBA's second largest basketball market and a country with vast room for expansion. "The Chinese are very passionate and knowledgeable about basketball and the

(Continued)

(Continued)

NBA has a huge fan base in China," said vice president of NBA China Mark Fischer. "We see an extremely bright future for basketball in China."

According to the China Sports Ministry, an estimated 300 million basketball fans live in China. Last year, the CBA had more than 1 million people attend games; more than a quarter billion viewers watched the nationally televised games on TV. "Chinese basketball is waking up fast," said John Kristick, the head of Asia's Infront Sports & Media, which represents the CBA and Team China. "The NBA has been instrumental in helping the sport grow. But history shows that nationalism is a powerful force in sports, so the continued growth of the CBA League and Chinese national team are on course to achieve great things in China for the sport, the fans, and commercial partners."

Traveling Game

While basketball might be one of the fastest-growing sports in China, it's far from the youngest. In 1891, James Naismith modestly invented the sport in Massachusetts by nailing a peach basket to both ends of a YMCA gymnasium. Played almost exclusively as a YMCA sport, basketball migrated into China attached to waves of missionaries who were traveling to the country during the turn of the 19th century. By the 1900s, basketball was rooted in China, making the country the third-oldest basketball nation in the world, after the United States and Canada.

Chinese basketball has come a long way since. Besides its national team, China houses a men's and women's CBA, a university league (modeled after the NCAA), a development league, and a wide range of amateur groups. The linchpin of China's burgeoning basketball scene is Shanghai native Yao Ming. Since coming to the Houston Rockets as the first pick of the 2002 NBA Draft, the 7 1/2-footer has created such a stir throughout

his country that Yao was recently dubbed China's biggest star by *Forbes* magazine.

Yao's NBA performances are featured constantly in Chinese media and he is attached to enough Chinese endorsement deals to make some of his NBA co-stars jealous. "For kids here, Yao is the national hero," said Ip Kam Hung of NBA China. "The NBA was always very famous here in China, but when Yao entered the league, it made an explosion. When Chinese people see Yao, they know that they have a chance to be there. It's not just a foreigner's game and the kids think, 'If Yao can get in, so can I.'"

With Beijing hosting the 2008 Olympics, the pressure for China to perform on a national stage is greater than ever. In preparation for the 2008 games, the CBA even cut short its season by one third of its games. "The biggest goal is 2008," said coach Kazlauskas in Ningbo. "We have small goals to reach before then but we are putting everything towards the Olympics."

As professional leagues in China continue to grow in popularity, so does the country's pool of young basketball talent. NBA scouts are watching a number of young players, none more than 19-year-old, 7-foot Jianlian Yi. Touted as the "next Yao," it was recently announced that the nimble forward will be eligible for the 2007 NBA draft and is expected to be a high first-round pick. "Yi's already got that NBA swagger and he's so quick for a guy his size," said Partridge. "People are going to be keeping a close eye on him."

As more Chinese children grow up playing basketball and the country's leagues continue to develop, the world's most populous country is getting closer to becoming a major player on the international court. "Chinese basketball is more than just Yao Ming," said Kristick. "Team China consists mainly of CBA league players. That shows the potential and the talent among Chinese professional players as they have proven to be competitive on an international basis. There are many superstars like Yao Ming to come."

Source: Eric Lovato Todd, "Spotlight on International Sports Marketing," *Albuquerque Journal,* November 26, 2006, D2.

Each level of sports product must receive careful consideration by sports marketers because of the strategic implications. Sometimes the interaction of athlete, team, and league PLCs can make strategic decisions even more challenging. Take the case of Deron Williams, point guard for the Utah Jazz in the NBA. The Jazz and the NBA could be seen in the maturity phase of the PLC, while Williams is in introduction. What about the case of Barry Zito? Zito is a veteran in Major League Baseball, but needed to be marketed as a new product for the Giants. As complex as this seems, sports marketers must remember not to neglect any of these products. Decisions will be made about the perceived relevance of each of these types of products.

DIFFUSION OF INNOVATIONS

New sports and sports products, or **innovations,** are continually being introduced to consumers and pass through the various stages of the product life cycle as described in the previous section. Initially, the new sport and sports product are purchased or tried by a small number of individuals (roughly 2.5 percent of the marketplace). Then, more and more people begin to try the new product. Consider the "metal wood" in golf. When this innovation was first introduced in the late 1970s, only the boldest "pioneers" of golf were willing to adopt the new technology. Now, only a very small percentage of the golfing population do not carry metal woods in their bags.[17]

The rate at which new sports products spread throughout the marketplace is referred to as the **diffusion of innovation.**[18] The rate of acceptance of a sport innovation is influenced by three factors, which are shown in Figure 8.3. The first factor affecting the rate of diffusion is the characteristics of the new product. These characteristics, such as trialability, observability, perceived complexity, relative advantage, and compatability, were discussed earlier in the chapter in the context of new product factors. The interaction of these factors can accelerate or slow the rate of diffusion. Perceived newness, the second factor that influences the rate of diffusion, refers to the type of new product from the consumer's perspective (continuous, dynamically continuous, and discontinuous innovations). Typically, continuous innovations have a faster rate of acceptance because they require no behavioral change and little disruption for the adopter. The third factor is the nature of the communication network. The rate and way in which information is shared about a new sports product is critical to its success, as well as the speed of acceptance. Most marketers conceptualize the communications network for innovations as a two-step flow of information. In the first step, the initial consumers try a new product or opinion leaders are influenced by mass communication such as advertising, sales promotions, and the Internet. Then, in the second step, opinion leaders use word-of-mouth communication to provide information about the new product to the rest of the target market. Martin and Higgins believe this two-step flow of information is especially important to sports innovations, because "unlike typical consumer purchase decisions, which involve only the individual, recent studies

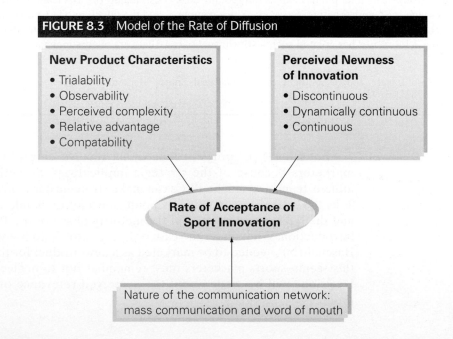

FIGURE 8.3   Model of the Rate of Diffusion

New Product Characteristics
- Trialability
- Observability
- Perceived complexity
- Relative advantage
- Compatability

Perceived Newness of Innovation
- Discontinuous
- Dynamically continuous
- Continuous

Rate of Acceptance of Sport Innovation

Nature of the communication network: mass communication and word of mouth show that of the consumers who attend sporting events, less than 2 percent attend by themselves."[19]

The diffusion of innovations is an important concept for sports marketers to understand because of its strategic implications. Stated simply, the marketer must know the stage of the life cycle and the characteristics of the consumers likely to try the product at any given stage. Let us examine the characteristics of each group as a product spreads throughout the marketplace.

Types of Adopters

There are several **types of adopters. Innovators** represent those consumers who are the first to adopt a new sports product as it enters the marketplace. Because they are the first to adopt, these consumers carry the highest risk associated with the new product. These risks may be social (what will others think of the product?), economic (costs are high and drive up the price), and performance (will the product perform as it was intended?). This younger and usually high-income group of consumers is also known for the high degree of interaction and communication they have with other innovators.

The next group of consumers to adopt a new sports product is the **early adopters.** As with the innovators, this group is also characterized by high social status. It is perhaps the most important group to sports marketers, however, because they carry high degrees of opinion leadership and word-of-mouth influence. As just discussed, these individuals are the key players in communicating the value of new sports products to the majority of consumers.

Once the new sports product has spread past the early stages of the product life cycle, the **early majority** is ready for adoption. This group is above average in social status but more deliberate in their willingness to try new products. In addition, this group is heavily influenced by information provided by the innovators and early adopters.

The **late majority** adopt innovations in the late stages of maturity of the product life cycle. As their name implies, over half (roughly 60 percent) of the market has now purchased or tried the new product before the late majority decide to do so. These individuals are skeptical and have less exposure to mass media.

The final group of adopters is known as **laggards.** These individuals are oriented toward the past and tend to be very traditional in the sports products they choose. They begin to adopt products in the declining stage of the product life cycle. Clearly, prices must be reduced, and promotions encouraging trial and widespread distribution must all be in place for laggards to adopt new products.

Summary

Few sports products are critical to the success of any organization. Newness, however, can be thought of in any number of ways. The organizational perspective on newness depends on whether the firm has marketed the product in the past. From the organizational perspective, new products are categorized as follows: new-to-the-world products, new product category entries, product line extensions, product improvements, and repositionings.

Conversely, newness from the consumer's perspective is based on the consumer's perception of whether the product represents an innovation. From the consumer's perspective, new products are classified as discontinuous innovations, dynamically continuous innovations, or continuous innovations. Discontinuous innovations represent the most innovative new products, whereas continuous innovations are simply improvements or limitation products.

Regardless of how new products are classified, organizations are constantly searching for the next innovation that will help the firm achieve its financial objectives. Rather than leave this to chance, many organizations use a systematic approach called the new product development process. The new product development process consists of the following phases: idea generation, idea screening, analysis of the concept, developing the sports product, test marketing, and commercialization. Idea generation considers any and all ideas for new products from sources such as employees, competitors, and consumers. During the idea screening phase, these new product ideas are screened and the poorer ones are eliminated. To perform this task, organizations sometime use a new product screening checklist. In the third phase, analysis of the sports product concept, marketing research is used to assess consumer reaction to the proposed product. More specifically, concept tests are used to gauge the product's strengths and weaknesses, as well as the consumer's intent to use the new product. Next, a prototype of the new product is designed so that consumers can get an even better idea about the product. In addition, preliminary decisions regarding marketing strategy are established. In the sixth stage, the new product is test marketed. Depending on the product and the market conditions, sports marketers may use either standardized, controlled, or simulated test markets. The final stage of the new product development process is commercialization in which the new product is formally introduced in the marketplace. Whether the product succeeds is a function of a number of factors, such as the product considerations (e.g., trialability and relative advantage), other marketing mix variables (e.g., pricing), and marketing environment considerations (e.g., competition).

As a new product reaches commercialization, it moves through a series of four stages known as the product life cycle (PLC). The PLC is an important marketing concept in that the stage of the life cycle dictates marketing strategy. The four stages of the PLC include introduction, growth, maturity, and decline. At introduction, the marketing goal is to generate awareness of the new sports product. The broad goal of the growth phase is to build consumer preference for the sports product and begin to expand the product line. During maturity, the number of promotions is increased and marketers seek to maintain any competitive advantage they have obtained during

growth. Finally, the product goes through decline, where decisions must be made regarding whether to delete the product or extend the life cycle.

Although each product has a life cycle, the length of that life and the speed at which a product progresses through the four stages is unique for each product. Some sports products grow and decline at a rapid pace. These are known as fads. Other products, which seem to last in maturity forever, are called classics. The most common life cycle for sports products is known as seasonal. Other life cycle considerations are the level of product and the type of product. For example, sports marketers might analyze the life cycle of leagues, teams, and individual athletes, as well as other types of sports products.

The rate of diffusion is the speed at which new products spread throughout the marketplace. The rate of diffusion, or speed of acceptance, is based on three broad factors: new product characteristics (e.g., trialability and observability), perceived newness (e.g., discontinuous innovation), and the nature of the communications network. It is critical that sports marketers monitor the rate of diffusion and understand the characteristics of consumers that try new products as they spread throughout the marketplace.

Innovators are the first group of consumers to try a new product. They are generally younger, have higher incomes, and have a strong tolerance for risk. The next group of consumers to try a sports product are the early adopters. This is a larger group than the innovators and, as such, they are key consumers to target. After the product has passed through the initial stages of the product life cycle, the early majority adopt the product. This group is above average in income, but more deliberate in trying new things. The late majority adopt the product during the late stages of maturity and finally the laggards may try new products. Strategically, sports marketers must adopt a different marketing mix when marketing to each new product adopter group.

Key Terms

- classic, p. 254
- commercialization, p. 246
- continuous innovations, p. 241
- decline, p. 253
- developing the sports product, p. 245
- diffusion of innovation, p. 258
- discontinuous innovations, p. 240
- dynamically continuous innovations, p. 241
- early adopters, p. 259
- early majority, p. 259

- fad, p. 253
- growth, p. 249
- idea generation, p. 242
- idea screening, p. 242
- innovations, p. 258
- innovators, p. 259
- introduction, p. 249
- laggards, p. 259
- late majority, p. 259
- maturity, p. 251
- new product category entries, p. 236

- new product development process, p. 242
- new product success factors, p. 246
- new sports products, p. 242
- new-to-the-world sports product, p. 236
- product form, p. 255
- product life cycle, p. 247
- seasonal, p. 254
- test marketing, p. 245
- types of adopters, p. 259

Review Questions

1. What is meant by a "new sports product"? Describe a "new sports product" from the organization's perspective and from the consumer's perspective.
2. What is the difference between discontinuous, dynamically continuous, and continuous innovations? Provide examples of each to support your answer.
3. Describe, in detail, the new product development process.
4. Why is test marketing so important to sports marketers in the new product development process? What are the three types of test markets? Comment on the advantages and disadvantages of each type of test market.
5. What are the critical success factors for new sports products?
6. Describe the product life cycle concept. Why is the product life cycle so critical to sports marketers? What is it used for? How can the product life cycle be extended?
7. What are some of the variations in the shape of the traditional product life cycle?
8. Define the diffusion of innovations. What are the different types of adopters for innovations? Describe the characteristics of each type of adopter.

Exercises

1. For each of the following sports products, indicate whether you believe they are discontinuous, dynamically continuous, or continuous innovations: WNBA, titanium golf clubs, and skysurfing.
2. Contact the marketing department of three sporting goods manufacturers or sports organizations and conduct a brief interview regarding the new product development process. Does each organization follow the same procedures? Does each organization follow the new product development process discussed in the chapter?
3. In what stage of the product life cycle is Major League Baseball? Support your answer with research.
4. Find an example of a "new sports product." Develop a survey using the critical success factors for new sports products and ask 10 consumers to complete the instrument. Summarize your findings and indicate whether you think the new product will be successful, based on your research.
5. Some people think boxing may be in the decline phase of the product life cycle. Develop a strategy to extend the product life cycle of boxing.

Internet Exercises

1. Search the Internet and find examples of three "new sports products" recently introduced in the marketplace.
2. Find three Internet sites of professional athletes in any sport. In what stage of the product life cycle are these athletes? Support with evidence found on the Internet.
3. Search the Internet for an example of a new sports product that could be classified as a fad. Describe the product and why you think the product is a fad.

Endnotes

1. William Zikmund and Michael d'Amico, *Marketing,* 4th ed. (St. Paul: West, 1993).
2. "Raley Field Pioneers the First Wireless Ballpark; Stadium Launches WiFi—Wireless Technology—Application Throughout Ballpark to Better Serve Fans," *Business Wire* (September 3, 2003).
3. "New Balance Adds Brine to Beef Up Sports Shoes," *The Boston Herald,* August 9, 2006.
4. Mark Glover, "Taking the Cue—New Billiard Parlors Cater to Family Crowds and Aren't Shy About Giving Hustlers the Heave," *The Sacramento Bee* (January 15, 1996), El; "Billiards Growing as a Participant Sport," www.sportlink. com/individual...ng/96billpartstudy/96billpart.html (May 1997).
5. Del Hawkins, Roger Best, and Kenneth Coney, *Consumer Behavior: Building Marketing Strategy,* 7th ed. (New York: McGraw-Hill, 1998), 248–250.
6. James J. Zhang, Dennis W. Smith, Dale G. Pease, and Matthew T. Mahar, "Spectator Knowledge of Hockey as a Significant Predictor of Game Attendance," *Sport Marketing Quarterly,* vol. 5, no. 3 (1996), 41–48.
7. "VTV to Offer High School Football to a National Audience for the First Time Ever," *Business Wire* (September 11, 2003).
8. Susan Higgins and James Martin, "Managing Sport Innovations: A Diffusion Theory Perspective." *Sport Marketing Quarterly,* vol. 5, no. 1 (1996), 43–50.
9. Bill Richards, "Nike Plans to Swoosh into Sports Equipment But It's a Tough Game," *The Wall Street Journal* (January 6, 1998), Al.
10. Gilbert Churchill, *Basic Marketing Research,* 3rd ed. (Fort Worth: Dryden Press, 1996).
11. R. Burton and D. Howard, "Professional Sports Leagues: Marketing Mix Mayhem," *Marketing Management,* vol. 8, no. 1 (1999), 37

12. Dan Hansen, "Personal Watercraft Sales Take Nose Dive. Popularity Wave Crests for Variety of Factors, But Industry Promises Rebound," *Spokesman Review* (June 17, 2003).

13. "GolfLogix and Garmin Enter Consumer Handheld GPS Golf Market; ForeFront to Exclusively Distribute GolfLogix GPS Devices," PR Newswire US, January 25, 2007.

14. David Ranii, "Reclaiming Its Turf; A Raleigh Company That Has the Rights to AstroTurf, the Stuff of Football Legend, Has Big Plans," *The Pantagraph,* April 9, 2007.

15. David Hidgon, "Trim the Season to Grow the Game," *Tennis* (November 1996), 22.

16. National Sporting Goods Association, "2006 Youth Participation in Selected Sports with Comparisons to 1997," http://www.nsga.org/public/pages/index.cfm?pageid=158.

17. James P. Sterba, "Your Golf Shots Fall Short? You Didn't Spend Enough," *The Wall Street Journal* (February 23, 1996), B7.

18. Everett Rogers, *Diffusion of Innovations,* 3rd ed. (New York: Free Press, 1983).

19. B. J. Mullin, S. Hardy, and William Sutton, *Sports Marketing* (Champaign, IL: Human Kinetics Publishers, 1993).

CHAPTER

9 | PROMOTION CONCEPTS

After completing this chapter, you should be able to:

■ Identify the promotion mix tools.

■ Describe the elements of the communication process.

■ Understand the promotion planning model.

■ Compare the advantages and disadvantages of the various promotional mix tools.

■ Understand the importance of integrated marketing communication to sports marketers.

Just ask anyone the first thing that comes to mind when they think of sports marketing, and they are likely to say, "Tiger Woods's Nike advertisements" or "Peyton Manning's endorsement of ESPN, MasterCard, DirecTV, or Sprint, to name a few." As we have discussed, sports marketing is much more than advertisements using star athlete endorsers. It involves developing a sound product or service, pricing it correctly, and making sure it is available to consumers when and where they ask for it. However, the necessary element that links the other marketing mix variables together is promotion.

Typically, the terms *promotion* and *advertising* are used synonymously. **Promotion,** however, includes much more than traditional forms of advertising. It involves all forms of communication to consumers. For many organizations, sports are quickly becoming the most effective and efficient way to communicate with current and potential target markets. The combination of tools available to sports marketers to communicate with the public is known as the promotional mix and consists of the following **promotion mix elements:**

- *Advertising*—A form of one-way mass communication about a product, service, or idea, paid for by an identified sponsor.
- *Personal Selling*—An interactive form of interpersonal communication designed to build customer relationships and produce sales or sports products, services, or ideas.
- *Sales Promotion*—Short-term incentives usually designed to stimulate immediate demand for sports products or services.
- *Public or Community Relations*—Evaluation of public attitudes, identification of areas within the organization in which the sports population may be interested, and building of a good "image" in the community.
- *Sponsorship*—Investing in a sports entity (athlete, league, team, event, and so on) to support overall organizational objectives, marketing goals, and more specific promotional objectives.

Within each of the promotion mix elements are more specialized tools to aid in reaching promotional objectives. For example, sales promotions can take the form of sweepstakes, rebates, coupons, or free samples. Advertising can take place on television, in print, or as stadium signage. Sponsors might communicate through an athlete, a team, or a league. Each of these promotional tools is a viable alternative when considering the most effective promotion mix for a sports organization. Regardless of which tool we choose, the common thread in each element of the promotion mix is communication. Because communication is such an integral part of promotion, let us take a more detailed look at the communications process.

COMMUNICATIONS PROCESS

The communications process is an essential element for all aspects of sports marketing. **Communication** is the process of establishing a commonness of thought between the sender and the receiver. To establish this "oneness" between the sender and the receiver, the sports marketer's message must be transmitted via the complex communications process.

The interactive nature of the communications process allows messages to be transmitted from sports marketer (source) to consumer (receiver) and from consumer (source) to sports marketer (receiver). Traditionally, sports marketers' primary means of communication to consumers has been through the various promotion mix elements (e.g., advertisements, sponsorships, sales promotions, and salespeople). Sports marketers also communicate with consumers via other elements of the marketing mix. For example, the high price of a NASCAR ticket communicates that it is a higher quality event than the more inexpensive Busch Series.

SPORTS MARKETING HALL OF FAME

Bill Veeck

Known as the Promotion King of Baseball, Bill Veeck single-handedly changed the course of sports marketing. Veeck pioneered promotional events that today have become commonplace. For instance, Veeck initiated Ladies Night and Straight-A Night at the ballpark. One of Veeck's most memorable promotions took place on August 19, 1951, when a pinch-hitter was announced in the bottom half of the first inning in a game between the St. Louis Browns and the Detroit Tigers. Over the furious objections of the Detroit manager, Red Rolfe, the batter was declared a legitimate member of the Browns. Bill Veeck, then owner of the Browns, cautioned his pinch-hitter before he left the dugout that "I've got a man in the stands with a high-powered rifle, and if you swing he'll fire."

What was the fuss? Veeck sent in a 3-foot-7-inch midget named Eddie Gaedel to pinch-hit for the Browns. Gaedel was promptly walked on four straight pitches and

removed from the game for a pinch-runner. Gaedel was quoted as saying, "For a minute, I felt like Babe Ruth."

For all his successful promotions, Veeck is also remembered for one that turned sour in the mid-1970s. Called "Disco Demolition Night," the idea of the promotion was for fans to bring their disco albums to the ballpark to be burned in a bonfire. Unfortunately, fans stormed the field, a riot ensued, and the White Sox were forced to forfeit the second game of a doubleheader.

Veeck also instituted a promotion where fans were given signs with "yes" and "no" on them and asked to vote on strategy during a game. The "Grandstand Managers" led the Browns to a 5–3 victory. Promotions such as this led Veeck to be known as a true "fan's fan." He once stated that "every day was Mardi Gras and every fan was king," and "the most beautiful thing in the world is a ballpark filled with people." His marketing and fan orientation forged the way for later marketers of all sports.

Source: Adapted from Bill Veeck, *Veeck as in Wreck: Autobiography of Bill Veeck* (New York: Simon and Schuster, 1962).

In addition to sports marketers communicating with consumers, consumers communicate back to sports marketers through their behavior. Most notably, consumers communicate whether they are satisfied with the sports product by their purchase behavior. In other words, they attend sporting events and purchase sporting goods.

The communications process begins with the source or the sender of the message. The source encodes the message and sends it through one of many potential communications media. Next, the message is decoded by the receiver of the message, and finally feedback is given to the original source of the message. In the ideal world, messages are sent and interpreted exactly as intended. This, however, rarely occurs because of noise and interference.

Figure 9.1 shows a simplified diagram of the communications process. Each box in the figure represents one of the **elements in the communications process.** These elements include the sender, encoding, message, medium, decoding, receiver, feedback, and noise. To maximize communication effectiveness, it is necessary to have a better understanding of each of these elements in the communications process.

Source

The sender or **source** of the message is where the communication process always originates. In sports marketing, the source of messages is usually a star athlete. For example, you might think of Maria Sharapova shooting pictures with her Canon or Arnold Palmer delivering a message on behalf of Pennzoil. Recently *Sports Illustrated* published the 50 top-earning athletes based on their on and off the field income. The top 10 American pitchpeople in 2007 (based on endorsement money only) can be seen in Table 9.1. Interestingly, Tiger also topped the list of athletes to watch as spokespeople in the 21st century. This list also included Peyton Manning and Jeff Gordon.

Although these sources are all individual athletes, there are many other sources of sports marketing messages. The source of a message might also be a group of athletes, a team, or even the league or sports. Additional sources of sports marketing messages are company spokespeople such as John Solheim, the chairman of Ping Golf, or owners such as Mark Cuban of the Dallas Mavericks.

Sources do not always have to be well recognized and famous individuals to be effective. Sports marketers use actors playing the role of common, everyday sports participants to deliver their message from the perspective of the representative consumer of the sports product or service. Other effective sources are inanimate objects, such as the college mascots like the U Mass Minuteman featured in the ESPN ad campaigns. In addition, sports marketers rely on sales personnel to convey the intended message to consumers. Informal sources, such as friends, family, and coworkers, are also sources of marketing information and messages. As we learned in Chapters 4 and 5, reference groups play an important role in influencing purchase behavior and transmitting the marketing message.

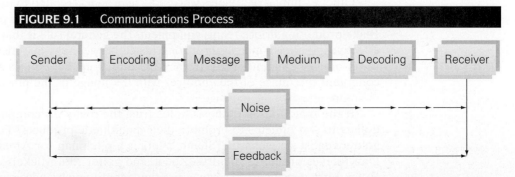

FIGURE 9.1 Communications Process

Source: Michael Solomon, *Consumer Behavior*, 3rd ed. (Upper Saddle River, NJ: Prentice Hall, 1996).

TABLE 9.1 Top Ten American Athlete Endorsers in 2007	
1. Tiger Woods	$100 million
2. Phil Mickelson	47 million
3. LeBron James	25 million
4. Dale Earnhardt Jr.	20 million
5. Michelle Wie	19.5 million
6. Kobe Bryant	16 million
7. Shaquille O'Neal	15 million
8. Jeff Gordon	15 million
9. Peyton Manning	13 million
10. Dwayne Wade	12 million

Whatever the source, it is agreed by researchers that to be effective, the source must be credible. **Credibility** is the source's perceived expertise and trustworthiness. A very persuasive message can be created when a combination of these two factors (expertise and trustworthiness) is present in the source. For a source to be trustworthy, that person must be objective and unbiased. Certain athlete endorsers, such as Arnold Palmer, former coach Mike Ditka, and Michael Jordan, are known for their perceived trustworthiness. We sometimes look to friends and family as information sources because of their objectivity. In fact, word-of-mouth communication is believed to be extremely persuasive because the source of the message has nothing to gain from delivering the message. Additional unbiased sources are those "man-on-the-street" testimonies given by the common consumer. For example, many of us have seen infomercials that use "regular people" to describe how they lost weight or became physically fit by using the latest and greatest fitness equipment.

Source credibility is also enhanced when the sender of the message has perceived expertise. Naturally, an athlete such as Reggie Bush is believed to deliver expert messages when the product being promoted is related to athletics, or more specifically, football. At least this is what adidas is counting on.

Reggie Bush, the USC star running back and Heisman Trophy winner, inked a contract even before the NFL draft. He signed a multiyear endorsement deal with adidas. Bush will promote a line of football and training clothing and launched a new 619 Fly cleat in 2007. "Reggie Bush is one of the most innovative and electrifying athletes in the sport, which makes him the perfect partner to represent our brand and highlight Power Web—the most innovative apparel technology in the game today," according to Eric Liedtke, vice president of marketing at adidas America.[1]

Other examples of athletes who endorse products related to their sport include race car drivers such as Jeff Gordon promoting Chevrolet and tennis players such as James Blake promoting Prince tennis equipment. The general rule is that the message is more effective if there is a match-up, or congruence, between the qualities of the endorser and the product being endorsed. In fact, the **match-up hypothesis** states that the more congruent the image of the endorser with the image of the product being promoted, the more effective the message.[2]

If the match-up hypothesis holds true, then why do companies pay millions of dollars to star athletes to promote their nonathletic products? For example, Olympic gold medalist snowboarder Shaun White is a pitchman for American Express, coach Dan Reeves promotes the drug Zocor, and golfer Phil Mickelson is an endorser for Rolex. First, consumers have an easier time identifying brands associated with celebrity

Arnold Palmer: One of the most credible endorsers ever.

athletes. Second, athletes are used to differentiate competing products that are similar in nature. For instance, most consumers know and associate Derek Jeter with Propel Fitness Water. Jeter's association helps to create and then maintain the desired image of Propel, which in turn differentiates it from other bottled waters on the market.

Encoding

After the source is chosen, encoding takes place. **Encoding** is translating the sender's thoughts or ideas into a message. To ensure effective encoding, the source of the message must make difficult decisions about the message content. Will the receiver understand and comprehend the message as intended? Will the receiver identify with the message?

Consider the slogan "I Am What I Am" used to introduce the new Reebok campaign. The language of this message may be up-to-date and "cool," but it may also be misunderstood or misinterpreted by a large portion of the potential target audience. Likewise, even if the slogan is understood, it may be outdated quickly and seem "unhip" to the receivers of the message. The "I Am What I Am" campaign celebrates contemporary heroes of today's global youth, including music icons, athletes, and entertainers. In the ongoing sneaker wars, Reebok is trying to send the message that it's more inclusive than no. 1 Nike, which gives off a whiff of superathlete exclusivity with its "Just Do It" campaign.

"Every other sporting goods commercial is about buying the shoe to become something you're not. This is about being yourself," Andy Roddick said in a phone interview.[3]

Sources have a variety of tools that they use to encode messages. They can use pictures, logos, words, and other symbols. Symbols and pictures are often used in sports marketing to convey the emotional imagery that words cannot capture. The most effective encoding uses multiple media to get the message across (i.e., visually and verbally); presents information in a clear, organized fashion; and always keeps the receiver in mind.[4]

Message

The next element in the communications process is to develop the **message,** which refers to the exact content of the words and symbols to be transmitted to the receiver. Decisions regarding the characteristics of this message depend on the objective of the

SPOTLIGHT ON SPORTS MARKETING ETHICS

Athlete Dramas, Scandals, Suspensions: How Do Corporations Respond?

Two weeks ago, the Floyd Landis story was one of the most powerful tales of the year—unknown rider with damaged hip extends America's Tour de France winning streak in the footsteps of icon Lance Armstrong.

Within 10 days, his "A" sample showed high levels of testosterone, and his "B" sample "confirms testosterone was taken in an exogenous way," according to the French Anti-Doping Council. Within hours, sponsor Phonax fires Landis; and Barclays Bank (and its subsidiary iShares) rethinks its three-year, $30 million cycling endorsement.

The Amgen Cycling Tour of California (and its five-year, $35 million commitment) seems at risk. T-Mobile fired its two star riders. Liberty Seguros (a division of Liberty Mutual) withdrew its sponsorship of a Spanish cycling team after its director was implicated in a Spanish investigation. Computer Sciences Corp. is reevaluating its corporate support after that team's star, Ivan Basso, was implicated in the French investigation.

Cycling may boast 20 million loyal fans; corporations may now stay 20 million miles away from that sport's athletes.

Cycling is obviously not the only sport that puts corporations at the mercy of volatile athletes and fans. This summer, Nike remade a pair of custom shoes for Buccaneers running back Carnell "Cadillac" Williams after he missed two games last season because of a sprained arch in his right foot. Nike certainly did some backpedaling after the injury was reported. Simultaneously, a *New York Times* report noted that ratings and merchandise revenue for the New York Yankees in Japan have dropped by as much as 25 percent since outfielder Hideki Matsui was placed on the disabled list in May. And Oregon bus driver Allen Heckard sued Nike for $832 million, claiming that being mistaken for Michael Jordan has caused Heckard "substantial discomfort." (Heckard has since dropped the suit.)

Before the World Cup, Zinedine Zidane's every move was chronicled by 15 cameras in the documentary

Zidane: A 21st Century Portrait. A hero in France and for the fans of Real Madrid, his stock fell in one dramatic head butt by Italy's Marco Materazzi in last month's French World Cup Final loss to Italy.

Despite these tales of corporate woe, specific sports spending will rise to $61.6 billion by 2010; and corporate ad spending on sports will exceed $12.4 billion this year alone. Clearly, corporations are investing in sports more than ever before—but are channeling their efforts in unique and diverse ways. The negative impact of Landis and other sports sponsorship debacles will cause corporations to respond in at least six ways.

1. Corporations Will Diversify Their Inventory of Superstar Athlete Spokespersons

Nike remains committed to pay over $1.6 billion for long-term endorsements, growing $192 million from the year before. However, the volume of athlete endorsers will decrease up to 30 percent as corporations become more selective.

Below are the top 10 American athlete endorsers (with annual endorsement income) according to a recent *Sports Illustrated* study:

> Tiger Woods, $87 million; Phil Mickelson, $40 million; LeBron James, $24 million; Andre Agassi, $23 million; Dale Earnhardt, Jr., $20 million; Kobe Bryant, $18 million; Jeff Gordon, $15 million; Shaquille O'Neal, $14 million; Peyton Manning, $11.5 million; Tom Brady, $9 million.

Five of the top 10 come from individual sports; eight of the top 10 play sports without any recent drug or steroid controversy. In fact, 25 of the top 50 endorsers/compensated athletes come from NASCAR, golf, and the NBA (with no recent history of drug or steroid controversies). Look for this diversification trend to continue (potentially bad news for 17 of the top 50 compensated/endorsed athletes— baseball players).

(Continued)

(Continued)

2. Corporations Will Divert Endorsement Money More into Other Forms of Entertainment

The most pervasive trend of the last few years is the merger of sports and entertainment—"Ball-ywood." Fifteen sports-themed motion pictures opened in 2005, with such other notables as *Cars* and *Invincible* coming this year. While $15 billion was spent on ticket purchases for sporting events last year, over $9 billion was spent on movies. This represents an attractive target for Corporate America.

Snoop Dogg pioneered a deal with major league Baseball and its corporate partners—signing an agreement to wear MLB Authentic Apparel during many of his performances on the 32-stop Projekt Revolution tour. The International Licensing Industry Merchandisers Association reported that 43.1 percent of $5.8 billion worth of licensed merchandise was themed around entertainment/TV/movie characters and endorsers. While actors and celebrities have significant personal endorsement risk as well (see Mel Gibson), at least corporations believe that diversifying will minimize the risk of a major marketing campaign tainted by a "superstar gone bad" (see O.J. Simpson).

3. Corporations Will Increase Their Sponsorship Beyond Mainstream Spokespersons and Athletes

In case you haven't noticed, corporate spokespeople are getting younger and younger. Extreme sports led the charge.

Last year, Dylan Oliver, a Louisville, Kentucky skateboarder, signed a major deal with Nice Skateboards—though he was five years old at the time. Mitchie Brusco is in the middle of his deal with Mattel Hot Wheels—begun when he was 12. Nike invests about $15 million a year in amateur youth basketball, adidas spends about $10 million, and Reebok $6 million. And Nike sponsors over 150 high school basketball teams nationally. While substantial risks are involved in "aligning the corporate brand" to young up-and-coming athletes, this diversification model seems to be working.

4. Corporations Will Intensify Their Sponsorship of Other Sports Properties

Corporations now spend over $12 billion sponsoring sports properties. In the future, look for more endorsement money to be funneled into such other creative avenues as naming of facilities. Over $5 billion has been spent by corporations for naming rights to almost 130 arenas, stadiums, performing arts centers, and the like. Witness Whataburger Field in Corpus Christi, Texas, Honda taking over the name of Arrowhead Pond in Anaheim (paying $2.5 million annually for the privilege), the Austrian company Red Bull buying the New York/New Jersey MetroStars this year and renaming the team after the corporation. As more properties become available, look for corporations to continue this trend.

5. Corporations Will Sponsor More International Facilities and Events

The World Cup is always viewed as the preeminent sponsorship opportunity in sports. Over 5.9 billion Internet customers in 54 global markets tuned into World Cup matches. Over 30 billion were said to have watched on traditional television (as opposed to online); 41 percent of the viewers were female.

Soccer's retail war will continue to be significant. Nike doubled its soccer business to over $1 billion in annual sales after signing such stars as Brazil's Ronaldo, Portugal's Luis Figo, and England's Wayne Rooney. adidas/Reebok was said to increase its market share over 37 percent as a consequence of this year's soccer activity.

Multinational corporations may see an opportunity to divert more money into other properties, becoming less reliant on athlete spokesmen. And recently, a ruling by the World Intellectual Property Organization may make it easier for corporations to commit to these long-term international deals. The United Nations agency ruled that ownership of Ronaldinho.com must be handed to Brazil and his Barcelona team because the name is a commercial "trademark" which could be sold. Previously, a Spanish citizen was using the site for his own benefit.

6. Corporations Will Continue to Choose Athletes Based on Performance—with Greater Emphasis on "Emotional Stability" and Character

This may be the most important factor. While superstars burst on the scene in a dramatic way, consistency of performance will always be the biggest factor for long-term corporate success. Corporations will continue to develop contracts that are smaller, shorter, and easier to terminate. Corporations will continue to seek endorsers who are consistent in their on-field performance, but are also minimal risks as far as their character is concerned.

For example, the top three revenue producers for their respective foundations are the following:

Lance Armstrong, $39.9 million; Tiger Woods, $13.4 million; Andre Agassi, $11.6 million.

Predictably, these three are at the top of the endorsement world as well.

Clearly, as the sports and entertainment dollar becomes more competitive, and as the risks of "bad corporate endorsements" continue to skyrocket, corporations will diversify and protect their investments more than ever before.

Source: Rick Horrow, CBS Sportsline, http://cbs.sportsline.com/general/story/9593303/1, August 9, 2006.

promotion, but sports marketers have a wide array of choices. These choices include one- versus two-sided messages, emotional versus rational messages, and comparative versus noncomparative messages.

The **sidedness** of a message is based on the nature of the information presented to the target audience. The messages can be constructed as either one- or two-sided. In a one-sided message, only the positive features of the sports product are described, whereas a two-sided message includes both the benefits and weaknesses of the product.

Another decision regarding the message in the promotion is whether to have an **emotional versus rational appeal.** A rational appeal provides consumers with information about the sports product so they may arrive at a careful, analytical decision, and an emotional appeal attempts to make consumers "feel" a certain way about the sports product. Emotional appeals might include fear, sex, humor, or feelings related to the hard work and competitive nature of sport.

A final message characteristic that may be considered by sports marketers is **comparative messages.** Comparative messages refer to either directly or indirectly comparing your sports product with one or more competitive products in a promotional message. For example, golf ball manufacturers often compare the advantages of their product with competitors' products.

Regardless of the **message characteristics,** the broad objective of promotion is to effectively communicate with consumers. What are some ways to make your sports marketing message more memorable and persuasive? Table 9.2 summarizes a few simple techniques to consider.

Medium

After the message has been formulated, it must be transmitted to receivers through a channel, or communications **medium.** A voice in personal selling, television, radio, stadium signage, billboards, blimps, newspapers, magazines, athletes' uniforms, and even athlete's bodies all serve as media for sports marketing communication. In addition to these more traditional media, new communications channels such as the Internet and the multitude of sports-specific cable programming (e.g., the Golf Channel) are emerging and growing in popularity.

TABLE 9.2	Creating a More Effective Message

- Get the audience aroused.
- Give the audience a reason for listening.
- Use questions to generate involvement.
- Cast the message in terms familiar to your audience and build on points of interest.
- Use thematic organization—tie material together by a theme and present in a logical, irreversible sequence.
- Use subordinate category words—that is, more concrete, specific terms.
- Repeat key points.
- Use rhythm and rhyme.
- Use concrete rather than abstract terms.
- Leave the audience with an incomplete message—something to ponder so they have to make an effort at closure.
- Ask your audience for a conclusion.
- Tell the audience the implications of their conclusion.

Source: James MacLachlan, "Making a Message Memorable and Persuasive," *Journal of Advertising Research*, vol. 23 (December 1983–January 1984), 51–59.

TABLE 9.3	Making Media Decisions

- Cost to reach target audience
- Flexibility of media
- Ability to reach highly specialized, defined audience
- Lifespan of the media
- Nature of the sports product being promoted (e.g., complexity of product)
- Characteristics of the intended target market

Decisions on which medium or media to choose depend largely on the overall promotional objectives. Also, the media decisions must consider the costs to reach the desired target audience, the medium's flexibility, its ability to reach a highly defined audience, its lifespan, the sports product or service complexity, and the characteristics of the intended target market. These media considerations are summarized in Table 9.3. For example, sports marketers attempting to reach the African American market may choose television as a communications medium because this market watches more television than average households. In addition, the African American market watches more WNBA, NBA, and college basketball than the average household (see Table 9.4).[5]

Decoding

The medium carries the message to the receiver, which is where decoding takes place. **Decoding,** performed by the receiver, is the interpretation of the message sent by the source through the channel. Once again, the goal of communication is to establish a common link between sender and receiver. This can only happen if the message is received and interpreted correctly. Even if the message is received by the desired target audience, it may be interpreted differently because of the receiver's personal characteristics and past experience. In addition, the more complex the original message, the less likely it is to be successfully interpreted or decoded. As the accompanying article illustrates, sometimes proper decoding can lead to questionable interpretation of ads.

TABLE 9.4	African American Fan Avidity Index	

Property	Avid fans	Index
NFL	41.6%	169
College football	28.3%	172
NBA	28.1%	314
Olympics	22.3%	97
College basketball	20.6%	204
MLB	18.4%	127
WWE	11.8%	334
NASCAR	10.0%	93
PGA	8.9%	128
WNBA	5.5%	344
MLS	4.9%	211
NHRA	4.5%	148

Note: How to read the data: For example, 41.6 percent of African American men are avid, or the highest level, NFL fans, which is 69 percent more likely than in the general U.S. population. In comparison, 22.3 percent are avid fans of the Olympics, which is 3 percent less likely than in the general population.

SPOTLIGHT ON SPORTS MARKETING ETHICS

Are Hockey Company Ads Crossing the Line?

Experiencing a flat marketplace with little growth over the last few years, hockey companies are getting increasingly creative in their attempts to reach customers. More firms, it seems, are dropping the gloves on edgy and irreverent marketing and communications, but some wonder if they are going too far.

"As marketers, the hockey industry is getting smarter in how to reach the core target audience in a language that they can understand and relate with," said Steve Jones, global brand communications manager for Nike Bauer Hockey, based in Greenland, N.H.

That core market is kids in the 7- to 17-year-old age range, who when not playing hockey are watching videos on YouTube, chatting on MySpace, or involved in some other digital activity.

Just how far some companies will go to gain an edge, however, is a key question.

Nike Bauer, an iconic hockey brand steeped in tradition and authenticity, has spent in the low six figures over the past several months on a comic book–themed grassroots marketing campaign called "Ice Tribe," which includes posters, stickers, and other print and in-ice creative in community rinks in Canada and parts of the United States, including Michigan, Massachusetts and New York. The creative was so popular that kids routinely peeled them off arena walls to take home, with Nike Bauer supplying rinks with replacement creative.

It followed up this initiative with a tongue-in-cheek, soft-goods product line for 2007, with baseball caps featuring such hockey-taunting messaging as "Chirp Wear" and "Top Cheddar," and T-shirts that read "I can see your five-hole."

GongShow Hockey, a small Ottawa, Ontario–based company, is building a loyal following among amateur and even pro players with its "hockey lifestyle" apparel line. The brand, which has recently expanded its distribution in the United States and Europe, has unveiled products with catch phrases such as "Lucky Charm," "Line Brawl," and "Jesus is my backup" that have caught on in the market.

The most aggressive marketing of all, however, comes from Warrior Hockey, of Warren, Mich. Warrior is a newcomer to the business, as it acquired Innovative Hockey, a composite stick manufacturer in California in 2005, and lured away key employees from Easton Hockey to elbow its way into the sport. Warrior is owned by New Balance out of Boston.

Warrior's advertising and product messaging have become increasingly aggressive and controversial. Ads that ran in such publications as *The Hockey News* in 2006 that featured images of pimps have given way to what some say is subliminal marketing, with creative including adolescent boys with erections and slang references to marijuana.

"Warrior is trying to copy what Mission Hockey did in the early roller hockey days," said Chris Malki, president of HockeyGiant.com, a large hockey retailer based in Carlsbad, Calif. "However, that was roller hockey and Mission only used wild colors, not drugs or pimps. This kind of nonsense will not work for ice [hockey] in the long run."

Some of Warrior's recent ad concepts include an image of an open peanut shell, with a peanut in only the right shell, placed alongside one of its sticks. The tag line reads, "What would you give for a Warrior?" implying players would give a "left nut," or their testicle, for a hockey stick.

"We are trying to be different in respect to our equipment advertising and overall branding message," said Neil Wensley, Warrior's director of marketing. "We feel there is a void in the market for a brand for people who also play action sports. We're trying to appeal to them. And for those who don't get it, we don't want them."

There's no question Warrior's strategy is attracting players at both the pro and consumer levels. By the end of the 2006–07 NHL regular season, the company had 158 players using its sticks, or about 22 percent of the NHL market, according to Wensley. That's an 8 percent increase from 2005–06, its first season in the NHL. Easton, the market leader in composite sticks, says it has a 51 percent market share.

"There's really a buzz in our store about the Warrior brand," said Louis Fortin, vice president of sales, purchasing, and marketing of Pro Hockey Life Sporting Goods, Inc., a large Quebec-based hockey retailer.

Warrior's approach, however, is beginning to test the limits of the market. Its new stick for 2007 is called the Kronik, which in some circles is code for marijuana. UrbanDictionary.com, an online slang dictionary, defines "kronik" as "hardcore pot" and "weed." In Warrior's 2007 product catalog, the Kronik creative reads "Get a taste of the bubonic Kronik. Who wants some??!!" Bubonic, on UrbanDictionary.com, is defined as "good marijuana."

"Naming a stick after a pimp or Kronik [marijuana] is absurd and sick," said HockeyGiant's Malki. "I would never let any of my kids use their product."

Wensley said the Kronik name has no hidden meaning at all. "Our thinking was that it makes you a chronic scorer," he said.

(Continued)

(Continued)

Warrior's advertisements have also created a challenge for consumer hockey publications. *The Hockey News* ran an ad featuring a teenage boy looking into a storefront at Warrior sticks, with an excited expression on his face. A closer look reveals the boy has an erection in his pants. *USA Hockey Magazine,* whose circulation is the more than 500,000 member kids and families of USA Hockey, has also had to deal with the issue.

Such market reaction has not caused Warrior to change its advertising approach, Wensley said, though the company has developed a dual-ad strategy. "We always have an 'A' ad and a 'B' ad, since some publications won't allow certain creative to run."

The "erection" ad, for example, did not run in *USA Hockey Magazine* but was replaced by one that featured three boys who weren't showing such arousal.

"It is fair to say that we have rejected advertising content from several vendors over the years and for various reasons. It wouldn't be fair, however, to go into specifics," said Mike Bertsch, senior director of marketing at *USA Hockey*.

"Our intent is not to offend anyone, but to increase the audience for the sport," Wensley said.

"These are the same consumers who do skateboarding and snowboarding, and anything we've done is really tame compared to what you see in [publications that serve those markets], or what's on MTV or YouTube."

Source: Wayne Karl, *Sports Business Journal,* May 21, 2007, p. 9.

Receiver

The **receiver,** or the audience, is the object of the source's message. Usually, the receiver is the sports marketer's well-defined, target audience. However, and as previously mentioned, the receiver's personal characteristics play an important role in whether the message is correctly decoded. For example, consumers' demographic profile (e.g., age, marital status, and gender), psychographic profile (e.g., personality, lifestyle, and values), and even where they live (geographic region) may all affect the interpretation and comprehension of the sports marketing message.

Feedback

To determine whether the message has been received and comprehended, feedback is necessary. **Feedback** is defined as the response a target audience makes to a message. The importance of feedback as an element of the communication process cannot be overlooked. Without feedback, communication would be a one-way street, and the sender of the message would have no means of determining whether the original message should remain unchanged, be modified, or abandoned altogether.

There are several ways for the consumer or target audience to deliver feedback to the source of the message. The target market might provide feedback in the form of a purchase. In other words, if consumers are buying tickets, sporting goods, or other sports products, then the sports marketer's message must be effective. Likewise, if consumers are not willing to purchase the sports product, then feedback is also being provided to the source. Unfortunately, the feedback in this case is that the message is either not being received or being incorrectly interpreted.

When using personal communication media, such as personal selling, feedback is received instantly by verbal and nonverbal means. Consumers will respond favorably by nodding their head in approval, acting interested, or asking intelligent questions. In the case of disinterest or inattention, the source of the message should make adjustments and change the message as it is being delivered to address any perceived problems.

Another common form of feedback comes through changes in attitude about the object of the message. In other words, the consumer's attitude shifts toward a more favorable belief or feeling about the sports product, athlete, team, or sport itself. Generally, the more positive the attitude toward the message, the more positive the consumer's attitude toward the sports product. This should, in turn, lead to increases in future purchases.

One of the many uses of marketing research is to gather feedback from consumers and use this feedback to create or redesign the strategic sports marketing process. The control phase of the strategic marketing process is dedicated to evaluating feedback from consumers and making adjustments to achieve marketing objectives.

Thus far, we have only examined feedback in one direction—from consumer of the product to producer of the product. However, feedback is an interactive process. That is, consumers also receive feedback from the sports organization. Organizations let consumers know they are listening to the "voice of the consumer" by reintroducing new and improved versions of sports products, changing the composition of teams and their coaches, adjusting prices, and even varying their promotional messages.

For example, after a disappointing debut season at their $265 million uptown arena, the Bobcats scrambled to bulk up ticket sales. Paid attendance declined 19.7 percent during the 2005–06 season at Charlotte Bobcats Arena compared with the previous year at Charlotte Coliseum, according to industry experts with access to NBA sales figures. Capacity is 19,026 at the arena; last season, on average, the team sold 9,930 tickets per home date.

The Bobcats announced a 14 percent across-the-board reduction in season ticket prices for 2006–07, including a 38 percent cut in upper-level prices.[6]

Noise

The final element in the communication process is noise. Unfortunately, there is no such thing as perfect communication because of **noise,** or interference, in the communications process. This interference may occur at any point along the channel of communication. For example, the source may be ineffective, the message may be sent through the wrong medium, or there may be too many competing messages, each "fighting" for the limited information-processing capacity of consumers.

When communicating through stadium signage, the obvious source of noise is the game itself. Noise can even be present in the form of ambush marketing techniques, where organizations attempt to confuse consumers and make them believe they are officially affiliated with a sporting event when they are not. An excellent example of how noise can affect the communication process is found in ambush marketing, which will be explored in Chapter 11.

Sports marketers must realize that noise will always be present in the communications process. By gaining a better understanding of the communications process, factors contributing to noise can be examined and eliminated to a large extent.

PROMOTION PLANNING

Armed with a working knowledge of the communications process, the sports marketer is now ready to design an effective promotion plan. Not unlike the strategic marketing process, promotional plans come in all shapes and sizes but all share several common elements. Our **promotional planning** document consists of four basic steps: (1) identifying target market considerations, (2) setting promotional objectives, (3) determining the promotional budget, and (4) developing the promotional mix.

Target Market Considerations

Promotional planning is not done in isolation. Instead, plans must rely heavily on the objectives formulated in the strategic sports marketing process. The first step to promotional planning is identifying **target market considerations.** During the planning phase, target markets have been identified, and promotion planning should reflect these previous decisions. Promotional planning depends largely on who is identified as the primary target audience. One promotional strategy is based on reaching the ultimate consumer of the sports product and is known as a pull strategy. The other strategy identifies channel members as the most important target audience. This strategic direction is termed a push strategy. These two basic strategies are dependent on the chosen target of the promotional efforts and guide subsequent planning. Let us explore the push and pull strategies in greater detail.

Push Strategy

A **push strategy** is so named because of the emphasis on having channel intermediaries "push" the sports product through the channel of distribution to the final consumer. If a push strategy is used, intermediaries such as a *manufacturer* might direct initial promotional efforts at a *wholesaler,* who then promotes the sports product to the retailer. In turn, the *retailers* promote the sports product to the final user. When using a push strategy, you are literally loading goods into the distribution pipeline. The objective is to get as much product as possible into the warehouse or store. Push strategies generally ignore the consumer. A variety of promotion mix elements are still used with a push strategy, although personal selling is more prevalent when promoting to channel members closer to the manufacturer (i.e., wholesalers) than the end users.

Pull Strategy

The target audience for a **pull strategy** is not channel intermediaries but the ultimate consumer. The broad objective of this type of promotional strategy is to stimulate demand for the sports product, so much demand, in fact, that the channel members, such as retailers, are forced to stock their shelves with the sports product. Because the end user, or ultimate consumer, is the desired target for a pull strategy, the promotion mix tends to emphasize advertising rather than personal selling. It is important to note that because sports marketing is based largely on promoting services rather than goods, pull strategies targeting the end user are more prevalent. In pull strategies, your objective is to get consumers to pull the merchandise off the shelf and out the door. For example, Sears Craftsman, through its NASCAR relationships, planned to blitz consumers with discount opportunities for a Father's Day sales push. The official tool of NASCAR and the title sponsor of NASCAR's Truck Series dubbed June 8–10 "Craftsman Weekend at the Races." Coupons good for $10 off a purchase of $50 or more were distributed to fans at 38 races through the NASCAR Whelen All-American Series, a semi-professional and amateur circuit on short tracks throughout the country. Scott Howard, Sears' manager of brand development and sponsorships, said he anticipated distributing about 75,000 coupons at the events. Coupons had to be used by June 17, Father's Day.

In another example, Burger King signed a six-month, seven-figure agreement to become major league Soccer's first official quick-service restaurant. Burger King offered in-store and online promotion of a $100,000 sweepstakes, and also gave away Burger King- and MLS-branded soccer balls and "Have It Your Way" gift cards valued at $2.

Although pull strategies are more common in sports marketing, the most effective promotion planning integrates both push and pull components. For example, marketing giant Procter & Gamble's (P&G) objective was to stimulate consumer demand for its Sunny Delight and Hawaiian Punch brands. To do so, P&G designed a promotion featuring UCLA basketball coach John Wooden and one of his former star players, Bill Walton. The pull strategy offered consumers a Wooden and Walton autographed picture and coin set for $19.95 and proof-of-purchase. The push promotional strategy was directed at Sunny Delight and Hawaiian Punch distributors and retailers who carried the P&G brands. If the "trade" reached their performance goals during the promotion, they earned a framed picture of Walton and Wooden that was autographed and personalized for the distributor.

Promotional Objectives

After target markets have been identified, the next step in the promotion planning process is to define the **promotional objectives.** Broadly, the three goals of promotion are to inform, persuade, and remind target audiences. Consumers must first be made aware of the product and how it might satisfy their needs. The goal of providing information to consumers is usually desired when products are in the introductory phase of the product life cycle (PLC). Once consumers are aware of the sports product, promotional goals then turn to persuasion and convincing the consumer to purchase the product. After initial purchase and satisfaction with a given product, the broad promotional goal is then to remind the consumer of the sports product's availability and perceived benefits.

Informing, persuading, and reminding consumers are the broad objectives of promotion, but the ultimate promotional objective is to induce action. These consumer actions might include volunteering to help with a local 10K race, donating money to the U.S. Olympic Team, purchasing a new pair of in-line skates, or just attending a sporting event they have never seen. Marketers believe promotions guide consumers through a series of steps to reach this ultimate objective—action. This series of steps is known as the hierarchy of effects (also sometimes called the hierarchy of communication effect).

The Hierarchy of Effects

The **hierarchy of effects** is a seven-step process by which consumers are ultimately led to action.[7]

The seven steps include unawareness, awareness, knowledge, liking, preference, conviction, and action. As shown in Figure 9.2, consumers pass through each of these steps before taking action.

- *Unawareness*—During the first step, consumers are not even aware the sports product exists. Obviously, the promotional objective at this stage is to move consumers toward awareness.
- *Awareness*—The promotional objective at this early stage of the hierarchy is to make consumers in the desired target market aware of the new sports product. To reach this objective, a variety of promotional tools are used.
- *Knowledge*—Once consumers are aware of the sports product, they need to gather information about its tangible and intangible benefits. The primary promotional objective at this stage is to provide consumers with the necessary product information. For instance, the NHL.com Web site has a link called Learning Zone, which is designed to give youth players tips on how to play the game. Similarly, major league Baseball has a Baseball Basics link on its Web page targeting international fans of the game. Another example of creating and

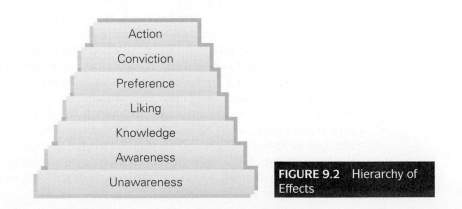

FIGURE 9.2 Hierarchy of Effects

Having greater knowledge of sports such as hockey moves consumers through the hierarchy of effects.

enhancing knowledge is the proliferation of classes called Football 101 targeted toward women and novice fans. Football 101 primers have been held at the Super Bowl XLI Fan Experience and The Ohio State University's homecoming week, and have even been offered in Spanish to Oakland Raider fans. Teams and organizers hope that once the fans become more knowledgeable, they will then move to the next level of the hierarchy—liking.

- *Liking*—Having knowledge and information about a sports product does not necessarily mean the consumer will like it. Generating positive feelings and interest regarding the sports product is the next promotional objective on the hierarchy. The promotion itself cannot cause the consumer to like the product, but research has shown the linkage between attitude toward the promotion (e.g., advertisement) and attitude toward the product.[8] The objective is to create a feeling of good will toward the product via the promotion.

- *Preference*—After consumers begin to like the sports product, the objective is to develop preferences. As such, sports marketers must differentiate their product from the competition through promotion. The sports product's differential advantage may be found in an enhanced image and tangible product features.

- *Conviction*—Moving up the hierarchy of effects, consumers must develop a conviction or intention to take action. Behavioral intention, however, does not guarantee action. Factors such as the consumer's economic condition (i.e., financial situation), changing needs, or availability of new alternatives may inhibit the action from ever taking place. The objective of the conviction step of the hierarchy of effects is to create a desire to act in the mind of the target audience.

• *Action*—The final stage of the hierarchy, and the ultimate objective of any promotion, is to have consumers act. As stated previously, actions may come in a variety of forms, but usually include purchase or attendance.

Theoretically, the hierarchy of effects model states that consumers must pass through each stage in the hierarchy before a decision is made regarding purchase (or other behaviors). Some marketers have argued this is not always the case. Consider, for instance, purchasing season tickets to a professional sport for business purposes. The purchaser does not have to like the sport or team to take action and buy the tickets. Regardless of what the hierarchy of effects proposes to do or not do, the fact remains that it is an excellent tool to use when developing promotional objectives. Knowing where the target audience is on the hierarchy is critical to formulating the proper objectives.

Establishing Promotional Budgets

Total advertising spending in the United States increased 4.1 percent to $149.6 billion in 2006 as compared to 2005.[9]Internet display advertising registered a 17.3 percent increase to $9.76 billion as marketers continued to shift budgets towards targeted, digital media. This represents the highest percentage increase by type of media, while newspaper spending was the only category showing a loss.

In part, this growth has been attributed to a surge in spending for the 2004 Summer Olympic Games NBC estimated that it would generate $1 billion in revenue for Olympic advertisement spots. In fact, over the past several years TV ad expenditures have increased for most sports with tennis and NASCAR experiencing the greatest percentage increases in spending. The NFL is still king, however, with over $2 billion being spent by companies in 2002, according to Nielsen Media Research. As shown in Table 9.5, the companies that lead the way in ad spending for

TABLE 9.5	Top 10 Sports Advertisers (Ranked by Total Sports Ad Spending in 2006)					
		2006 Ad Spending (000s)			Change in Sports Ad Spending	
Rank (2005 rank)	*Company/brand*	*Sports*	*Total*	*% of total ad spending devoted to sports (% in 2005)*	*vs. 2005*	*vs. 2004*
1 (2)	Chevrolet Motor Division	$270,797	$443,089	61.1% (41.5%)	+78.4%	+23.1%
2 (1)	Anheuser-Busch Cos.	$252,468	$326,596	77.3% (61.1%)	+14.7%	−14.0%
3 (99)	AT&T Inc.	$145,125	$295,864	49.1% (47.6%)	+768.4%	+127.3%
4 (3)	Ford Motor Co.	$142,511	$487,070	29.3% (30.1%)	−1.4%	−0.4%
5 (4)	Sprint Nextel Corp.	$142,372	$622,605	22.9% (31.8%)	+21.4%	+10.0%
6 (19)	Visa International	$135,631	$329,932	41.1% (25.5%)	+113.1%	−0.3%
7 (7)	Verizon Communications Inc.	$126,333	$635,801	19.9% (18.1%)	+36.0%	+127.0%
8 (12)	Nissan North American Inc.	$119,842	$331,119	36.2% (22.2%)	+59.1%	+7.8%
9 (13)	McDonald's Corp.	$118,243	$415,411	28.5% (19.2%)	+60.5%	+17.1%
10 (8)	Toyota Motor Sales USA Inc.	$118,232	$344,639	34.3% (26.3%)	+32.9%	+26.7%

sports are makers of beer and cars, with Chevrolet, Anheuser Busch, AT&T, and Ford at the top.

Along with traditional media, an estimated $481 million was spent on online sports advertising last year, according to Nielsen/NetRatings' AdRelevance data, an increase of 9.9 percent over 2005 and 19.7 percent over 2004.

In addition to companies spending huge dollars on sports advertising, teams and leagues are constantly promoting the sport. For instance, the NHL released the poorly reviewed "Game On" campaign after the strike season, MLB is still trying to capture fans with the "I Live for This" campaign, and the NBA is still using the classic "I Love This Game" promotion. In the case of the NHL, increases in advertising were needed to make potential fans more knowledgeable about and able to appreciate hockey. Major league Baseball wanted to stress the passion that their players have for the game and generate the same passion in their fans. In all cases, teams and leagues are advertising to keep up with the tremendous competitive threat of other entertainment choices for the fans.

In theory, the promotional budget of the NHL or the NBA would be determined based on the many objectives set forth by the leagues' marketing strategy. In practice, **promotional budgeting** is an interactive and unscientific process by which the sports marketer determines the amount spent based on maximizing the monies available. Some of the ways promotional budgets may be established include arbitrary allocation, competitive parity, percentage of sales, and the objective and task method.

Arbitrary Allocation

The simplest, yet most unsystematic, approach to determining promotional budgets is called **arbitrary allocation.** Using this method, sports marketers set the budget in isolation of other critical factors. For example, the sports marketer disregards last year's promotional budget and its effectiveness, what competitors are doing, the economy, and current strategic objectives and budgets using some subjective method. The budget is usually determined by allocating all the money the organization can afford. In other words, promotional budgets are established after the organizations' other costs are considered. A sports organization that chooses this approach does not place much emphasis on promotional planning.

Competitive Parity

Setting promotional budgets based on what competitors are spending (**competitive parity**) is often used for certain product categories in sports marketing. For example, the athletic shoe industry closely monitors what the competition is doing in the way of advertising efforts. adidas (annual budget of roughly $50 million), Reebok ($44 million), and K-Swiss ($15 million) must keep pace with Nike's (annual budget of roughly $150 million) promotional spending if they intend to increase market share.

One athletic shoe company that does not follow its competitors' huge promotional spending is New Balance. The New Balance ad budget was $17.3 million in 2005 with revenues of 1.5 billion in 2005 representing steady growth. Instead of using famous athletes, New Balance has paved its success by understanding its primary consumer, the 35- to 59-year-old baby boomer. Rather than paying celebrities to endorse its products, they prefer to invest in research, design, and domestic manufacturing. This unique positioning was illustrated on the New Balance Web page, which stated "N is for mileage, not for image" and ads that explained "N is for Fit."[10]

Percentage of Sales

The **percentage of sales** method of promotional budget allocation is based on determining some standard percentage of promotional spending and applying this proportion to either past or forecasted sales to arrive at the amount to be spent. It is common for the percentage to be used on promotional spending to be derived from some industry standard. For example, the athletic shoe industry typically allocates 5 percent of sales to promotional spending. Therefore, if a new athletic shoe company enters the market and projects sales of $1 million, then they would allocate $50,000 to the promotional budget. Likewise, if Converse totaled $7 million in sales in the previous year, then it might budget $350,000 to next year's promotional budget.

Although the percentage of sales method of budgeting is simple to use, it has a number of shortcomings. First, if percentage of forecast sales is used to arrive at a promotional budget figure, then the sales projections must be made with a certain degree of precision and confidence. If historical sales figures (e.g., last year's) are used, then promotional spending may be either too high or too low. For example, if Converse has a poor year in sales, then the absolute promotional spending would be decreased. This, in turn, could cause sales to slide even further. With sales declining, it may be more appropriate to increase (rather than decrease) promotional spending. A second major shortcoming of using this method is the notion that budget is very loosely, if at all, tied to the promotional objectives.

Objective and Task Method

If arbitrary allocation is the most illogical of the budgeting methods, then objective and task methods could be characterized as the most logical and systematic. The **objective and task method** identifies the promotional objectives, defines the communications tools and tasks needed to meet those objectives, and then adds up the costs of the planned activities.

Although the objective and task method seems the most reasonable, it also assumes the objectives have been determined correctly and the proper promotional mix has been formulated to reach those objectives. For instance, suppose the Vanderbilt University women's basketball team wanted to achieve an attendance increase of 15 percent from the previous season. To this end, the director of marketing for athletics must develop a promotional mix that includes local advertising, related sales promotions, and public relations in an effort to reach all target audiences. Even if the attendance goal is achieved, it is difficult to determine whether the money required to achieve this objective was spent in the most efficient and effective fashion.

Choosing an Integrated Promotional Mix

The final step in building an overall promotional plan is to determine the appropriate promotional mix. As stated earlier, the traditional promotional mix consists of advertising, personal selling, public relations, and sales promotions. The sports marketing manager must determine which aspects of the promotional mix will be best suited to achieve the promotional objectives at the given budget.

In choosing from among the traditional elements, the sports marketer may want to broadly explore the advantages and disadvantages of each promotional tool. For example, personal selling may be the most effective way to promote the sale of personal seat licenses, but it is limited in reaching large audiences. Table 9.6 outlines some of the considerations when deciding on the correct mix of promotional tools.

Although the factors listed in Table 9.6 are important determinants of which promotional tools to use to achieve the desired objectives, there are other considerations. The stage of the life cycle for the sport product, the type of sports product, the characteristics of the target audience, and the current market environment must also be carefully studied. Whatever the promotion mix decision, it is critical that the various elements be integrated carefully.

Promotional planning for sports is becoming increasingly more complex. With the rapid changes in technology, new promotional tools are being used to convey the sports marketer's message. In addition, it is becoming harder and harder to capture the attention

TABLE 9.6 Evaluating the Promotional Mix Elements

	Promotional Tools			
	Advertising	*Personal Selling*	*Sales Promotion*	*Public Relations*
Sender's control over the communication	Low	High	Moderate to low	Moderate to low
Amount of feedback	Little	Much	Little to moderate	Little
Speed of feedback	Delayed	Immediate	Varies	Delayed
Direction of message flow	One way	Two way	One way	One way
Speed in reaching large audiences	Fast	Slow	Fast	Typically fast
Message flexibility	None	Customized	None	Some
Mode of communication	Indirect and impersonal	Direct and face to face	Usually indirect and impersonal	Usually indirect and impersonal

of target audiences and move them along the hierarchy of effects. Because of the growing difficulty in reaching diverse target audiences, the clarity and coordination of integrating all marketing communications into a single theme is more important than ever.

The concept under which a sports organization carefully integrates and coordinates its many promotional mix elements to deliver a unified message about the organization and its products is known as **integrated marketing communications.** Think for a moment about the promotional efforts of the WNBA. The promotional goals are to increase awareness and develop excitement about the league. To accomplish this, the WNBA will combine national advertisements, sponsorships, cable and network broadcast schedules, and tie-ins with the NBA. All of these communications media must deliver a consistent message that produces a uniform image for the league to be successful. Not only must the WNBA deliver an integrated promotional mix, but the league's sponsors and the 13 teams must also transmit a unified message.

The primary advantage of integrating the promotional plan includes more effective and efficient marketing communications. Unfortunately, determining the return on investment (ROI) for an integrated promotion plan is still difficult, if not impossible. Professor Don Schultz has identified four types of information that must be available to begin to measure ROI for integrated communications.[11]

These factors include the following:

- *Identification of Specific Customers*—Identification of specific households, including information on the composition of those households to make inferences.
- *Customer Valuation*—Placing a value on each household based on either annual purchases or lifetime purchases. Without this information on the purchase behavior of the household or individual, the calculation of ROI is of limited value to the marketer.
- *Track Message Delivery*—Understanding what media consumers or households use to make their purchase decisions, and how a household receives information and messages over time. In addition, this involves measuring "brand contacts" or when and where consumers come into contact with the brand.
- *Consumer Response*—To establish the best ROI, behavioral responses are captured. In other words, consumer responses such as attitudes, feelings, and memory are deemed unimportant and purchases, inquiries, and related behaviors (e.g., coupon redemption) are evaluated.

Summary

Promotional planning is one of the most important elements of the sports marketing mix. Promotion involves communicating to all types of sports consumers via one or more of the promotion mix elements. The promotion mix elements include advertising, personal selling, sales promotions, public relations, and sponsorship. Within each of these promotion mix elements are more specialized tools to communicate with consumers of sport. For example, advertising may be developed for print media (e.g., newspapers and magazines) or broadcasts (e.g., radio and television). However, regardless of the promotion mix element that is used by sports marketers, the fundamental process at work is communication.

Communication is an interactive process established between the sender and the receiver of the marketing message via some medium. The process of communication begins with the source or sender of the message. In sports marketing, the source of the message might be an athlete endorser, team members, a sports organization, or even a coach. Sometimes the source of a marketing message can be friends or family. The effectiveness of the source in influencing consumers is based largely on the concept of source credibility. Credibility is typically defined as the expertise and trustworthiness of the source. Other characteristics of the source, such as gender, attractiveness, familiarity, and likeability may also play important roles in determining the source's effectiveness.

After the source of the message is chosen, message encoding occurs. Encoding is defined as translating the sender's thoughts or ideas into a message. The most effective encoding uses multiple ways of getting the message across and always keeps the receiver of the message in mind. Once encoding takes place, the message is more completely developed. Although there are any number of ways of constructing a message, sports marketers commonly choose between emotion (e.g., humor, sex, or fear) and rational (information-based) appeals.

The message, once constructed, must be transmitted to the target audience through any number of media. The traditional media include television, radio, newspapers, magazines, outdoor billboards, and stadium signage. Nontraditional media, such as the Internet, are also emerging as powerful tools for sports marketers. When making decisions about what medium to use, marketers must consider the promotional objectives, cost, ability to reach the targeted audience, and the nature of the message being communicated.

The medium relays the message to the target audience, which is where decoding occurs. Decoding is the interpretation of the message sent by the source through the medium. It is important to understand the characteristics of the target audience to ensure successful translation of the message will occur. Rarely, if ever, will perfect decoding take place because of the presence of noise.

The final elements in the communications model are the receiver and feedback. The message is directed to the receiver, or target audience. Again, depending on the purpose of the communication, the target audience may be spectators, participants, or corporate sponsors. Regardless of the nature of the audience, the sports marketer must understand as much as possible about the characteristics of the group to ensure an effective message is produced. Sports marketers determine the effectiveness of the message through feedback from the target audience.

Understanding the communications process provides us with the basis for developing a sound promotional plan. The promotional planning process includes identifying target market considerations, setting promotional objectives, determining the promotional budget, and developing the promotional mix.

The first step in the promotional planning process is to consider the target market identified in the previous planning phase of the strategic sports marketing process. The two broad target market considerations are the final consumers of the sports product (either spectator or participants) or intermediaries, such as sponsors or distributors of sports products. When communicating to final consumers, a pull strategy is used. Conversely, push strategies are used to promote through intermediaries. After target markets are considered, promotional objectives are defined. Broadly, objectives may include informing, persuading, or reminding the target market. One model that provides a basis for establishing promotional objectives is known as the hierarchy of effects, which states that consumers must pass through a series of stages before ultimately taking action (usually defined as making a purchase decision). The steps of the hierarchy of effects include unawareness, awareness, knowledge, liking, preference, conviction, and action. Once objectives have been formulated, budgets are considered. In the ideal scenario, budgets are linked with the objectives that have been set in the previous phase of the promotion planning process. However, other common approaches to promotional budgeting include arbitrary allocation, competitive parity, and percentage of sales. Most sports organizations use some combination of these methods to arrive at budgets. The final phase in the promotion planning process is to arrive at the optimal promotion mix. The promotion mix includes advertising, personal selling, public relations, sales promotion, and sponsorship. Decisions about the most effective promotion mix must carefully consider the current marketing environment, the sports product being promoted, and the characteristics of the target audience. Ideally, the sports marketer designs an integrated promotion mix that delivers a consistent message about the organization and its products.

Key Terms

- arbitrary allocation, p. 279
- communication, p. 264
- comparative messages, p. 270
- competitive parity, p. 279
- credibility, p. 266
- decoding, p. 271
- elements in the communications process, p. 265
- emotional versus rational appeal, p. 270
- encoding, p. 267
- feedback, p. 273
- hierarchy of effects, p. 276
- integrated marketing communications, p. 281
- match-up hypothesis, p. 266
- medium, p. 270
- message, p. 268
- message characteristics, p. 270
- noise, p. 274
- objective and task method, p. 280
- percentage of sales, p. 279
- promotion, p. 263
- promotion mix elements, p. 263
- promotional budgeting, p. 279
- promotional objectives, p. 276
- promotional planning, p. 274
- pull strategy, p. 275
- push strategy, p. 275
- receiver, p. 273
- sidedness, p. 270
- source, p. 265
- target market considerations, p. 274

Review Questions

1. Define promotion and then discuss each of the promotion mix elements.
2. Describe the elements of the communication process. Why is communication so important for sports marketers? What is the relationship between communication and promotion?
3. Define the source of a sports marketing message and provide some examples of effective sources. What is source credibility? What are the two components of source credibility?
4. What is meant by encoding? Who is responsible for encoding sports marketing messages?
5. Discuss the various message characteristics. What are the simple techniques used to create more effective messages?
6. Why is television considered to be the most powerful medium for sports marketing messages?
7. Define feedback. How is feedback delivered to the source of the message?
8. Outline the basic steps in promotion planning.
9. What is the fundamental difference between a push and a pull strategy?
10. Describe the three broad objectives of any type of promotion. What is the hierarchy of effect, and how is this concept related to promotional objectives?
11. What are the various ways of setting promotional budgets? Comment on the strengths and weaknesses of each.
12. Comment on how you would choose among the various promotion mix tools. Define integrated marketing communication.

Exercises

1. Evaluate the promotional mix used for the marketing of any intercollegiate women's sport at your university. Do you believe the proper blend of promotional tools are being used? What could be done to make the promotional plan more effective for this sport?
2. Find any advertisement for a sports product. Then describe and explain each of the elements in the communications process for that ad. Do the same (i.e., explain the communications process) for the following scenario: A salesperson is trying to sell stadium signage to the marketing director of a local hospital.
3. Conduct an interview with the marketing department of a local sports organization and discuss the role of each of the promotional tools in the organization's promotion mix. In addition, ask about their promotional budgeting process.

4. Describe three television advertisements for sports products that are designed to inform, persuade, and remind consumers. Do you believe the advertisements are effective in reaching their promotional objectives?
5. Locate advertisements for three different sports products. Comment on which response in the hierar- chy of effects you believe each advertisement is trying to elicit from its target audience.
6. Find an example of a comparative advertisement. What do you believe are the advantages and disad- vantages of this type of message?

Internet Exercises

1. Using the Internet, find an example of an adver- tisement for a sports product and a sports-related sales promotion. For each, discuss the targeted audi- ence, the promotional objectives, and the message characteristics.
2. How do organizations get feedback regarding their promotions via the Internet? Find several examples of ways of providing sports marketers with feedback about their promotions.
3. Consider any sports product and find evidence of advertising and sales promotion *not* on the Internet. Then locate the product's promotion on the Internet. Comment on whether or not this organization prac- tices integrated marketing communications.

Endnotes

1. Michael McCarthy, "Investigation Doesn't Curb Endorsement Deals for Bush," *USA Today*, April 26, 2006, 3C.
2. Michael Kamins, "An Investigation into the Match- Up Hypothesis in Celebrity Advertising: When Beauty May Be Only Skin Deep," *Journal of Advertising,* vol. 19, no. 1 (1990), 4–13.
3. Richard Gillis, "The War of Athletes' Feet," The Independent (London), March 6, 2006.
4. Martha Irvin, "If Not on Point, Slang Can Make a Tight Campaign Sound Wack," *The Commercial Appeal* (November 29, 2002), C1.
5. Michael Solomon, *Consumer Behavior,* 3rd ed. (Upper Saddle River, NJ: Prentice Hall, 1996).
6. Erik Spanberg, "Bobcats Unveil New Ticket Plans," *Charlotte Business Journal,* August 25, 2006.
7. Robert Lavidge and Gary Steiner, "A Model for Predictive Measurements of Advertising Effectiveness," *Journal of Marketing,* vol. 24 (1961), 59–62.
8. Rajeev Batra and Michael Ray, "Affective Responses Mediating Acceptance of Advertising," *Journal of Consumer Research*, vol. 13 (September 1986), 236–239; Leon Shiffman and Leslie Kanuk, *Consumer Behavior,* 4th ed. (Upper Saddle River, NJ: Prentice Hall, 1996), 237–239.
9. "TNS Media Intelligence Reports U.S. Advertising Expenditures Increased 4.1 Percent in 2006," http://www.tns-mi.com/news/03132007.htm, March 13, 2007.
10. Peter Grant, "Advertising: New Balance Buys Cable- TV Stake," *Wall Street Journal*, January 18, 2006, B2.
11. Don Schultz, Stanley Tannenbaum, and Robert Lauterborn, *Integrated Marketing Communications: Putting It Together and Making It Work* (Lincolnwood, IL: NTC Publishing Group, 1992); Don Schultz, "Rethinking Marketing and Communications' ROI," *Marketing News* (December 2, 1996), 10; Don Schultz and Paul Wang, "Real World Results," *Marketing Tools* (April–May 1994).

10 PROMOTION MIX ELEMENTS

After completing this chapter, you should be able to:

■ Describe each element of the promotion mix, in detail.

■ Understand the basic process for designing a successful advertising campaign.

■ Discuss emerging forms of promotion.

■ Outline the strategic selling process and explain why sports marketing should use this process.

■ Identify the various forms of promotion.

■ Specify the importance of public or community relations to sports marketers.

The CoActive Marketing Group, one of America's leading marketing agencies, designed a unique sales promotion for Hiram Walker to increase short-term sales of Canadian Club Classic (a 12-year-old whiskey). In this case, the promotion (called a premium) was a baseball card signed by one of four Hall of Fame players, including Willie Stargell, Billy Williams, Ernie Banks, and Brooks Robinson. With each purchase of a 750-ml bottle of Canadian Club Classic, consumers were able to collect one card from the series of cards.

In addition to the end users, Hiram Walker distributors were also involved in the sales promotion. Distributors could win a customized shelf unit to display the set of baseball cards and autographed baseballs. They could win these items for participating in the promotion and selling the idea to their retailers. The prizes motivated distributors to push cases into their retail accounts. By all accounts, the promotion was a huge success. In fact, it was so well received that a second series of cards was issued. To make the sales promotion work, personal selling was needed to secure the baseball legends. Other forms of communication were also necessary to inform the Hiram Walker distributors and consumers about the promotion.

As demonstrated in the Hiram Walker promotion, sports marketers must carefully integrate the promotion mix elements to establish successful promotions to consumers and trade. In Chapter 9, we explored the importance of communication and the basic concepts of promotional planning. This chapter examines each of the **promotional mix elements** in greater detail. By doing so, sports marketers will be in a better position to choose the most effective promotional elements for the construction of the promotional plan. Let us begin by looking at one of the most widely used forms of promotion—advertising.

Stadium signage—one of the first forms of promotion.

ADVERTISING

Advertising remains one of the most visible and important marketing tools available to sports marketers. Although significant changes are taking place in the way sports products and services are advertised, the reasons for advertising remain the same. Advertising creates and maintains brand awareness and brand loyalty. In addition, advertising builds brand image and creates a distinct identity for sports products and services. Most important, advertising directly affects consumer behavior. In other words, it causes us to attend sporting events, buy that new pair of running shoes, or watch the NCAA Women's Basketball tournament on television.

Most of us associate the development of an advertisement with the creative process. As you might imagine, advertising is more than a catchy jingle. To develop an effective advertisement, a systematic process is employed. Some of the steps in this process are very similar to the promotional planning process discussed in Chapter 9. This is not unexpected, as advertising is just another form of communication, or promotional tool, used by sports marketers.

The advertising process is commonly referred to as designing an advertising campaign. An advertising campaign is a series of related advertisements that communicate a common message to the target audience (see Figure 10.1). The advertising campaign (similar to the promotional planning process) is initiated with decisions about the objectives and budget. Next, creative decisions, such as the ad appeal and execution, are developed. Following this, the media strategy is planned and, finally, the advertising campaign is evaluated. Let us explore each of the steps in designing an advertising campaign or the ad process in greater detail.

Advertising Objectives
The first step in any advertising campaign is to examine the broader promotional objectives and marketing goals. The overall objectives of the advertising campaign should, of

FIGURE 10.1 Designing an advertising campaign

course, be consistent with the strategic direction of the sports organization. The specific objectives and budgeting techniques for advertising are much the same as those discussed in Chapter 9. Namely, advertising is designed to inform, persuade, remind, and cause consumers in the target market to take action.[1] In addition to these broad objectives, **advertising objectives** are sometimes categorized as either direct or indirect.

The purpose of **direct objectives** in advertising is to elicit a behavioral response from the target audience. In sports marketing, this behavioral response may be in the form of purchasing tickets to a game, buying sporting goods that were advertised on the Internet, or even volunteering at a local event. Sometimes, an advertisement asks consumers to make multiple behavioral responses—for instance, Dan Wheldon and Danica Patrick are used as spokespeople to urge fans to visit indycar.com and indianapolismotorspeedway.com, tune in to the Indy 500 on ABC Sports, or call a toll-free number for tickets to the event.

Direct advertising objectives can be further categorized into two distinct types: advertising to end users and sales promotion advertising. Both direct response objectives, however, are designed to induce action.

Tennis Warehouse using direct objective.
Source: Tennis Warehouse

Advertising by Sports Organizations to End Users

In this case, the objectives of advertising are not to enhance the perceived image of the event, the team, or the league, but rather to generate immediate response. With this type of objective, the sports marketer is attempting to build immediate sales. As such, the specific objective of advertising to end users is usually stated in terms of increasing sales volume.

Sales Promotion Advertising

It is common for contests, sweepstakes, coupons, and other forms of sales promotions to be advertised via any number of media. As such, the objectives of direct response advertisements are to have consumers participate in the contests and sweepstakes or redeem coupons. Objectives, therefore, are measured in terms of the level of participation in the sales promotion.

Indirect objectives are based on establishing prebehavioral (i.e., prior to action) responses to advertising, that is, accomplishing goals such as increasing awareness, enhancing image, improving attitudes, or educating consumers. These indirect objectives should, in turn, lead to more direct behavioral responses. Consider the ad for Bank of America promoting the fact that they are the "Official Bank of Little League, Minor League, and Major League Baseball." The ad goes on to describe "the long-standing association with baseball that was born out of reaching for higher standards in everything we do." The objective of this advertisement is solely to enhance the image of Bank of America through its connection with baseball, the American pastime. Ultimately, the advertisement's sponsor hopes, these indirect objectives will lead to the behavior response of securing new customers and reminding existing customers to purchase more products and services from Bank of America.

Indirect objectives, such as image enhancement, are always present to some extent in advertising. Sports leagues, such as the NBA, use indirect advertising ("I Love This Game") to generate awareness and interest in the league, whereas individual teams are

Sales promotion advertised on the Web.
Source: Courtesy Upper Deck Company. © 2007 UDC.

more concerned with direct, behavioral objectives (such as the L.A. Dodgers' "Get into the Blue" or the 2007 NBA playoff advertising campaign, "Will You Be Watching When," encouraging fans to watch the games on ESPN).

Advertising Budgeting

As with advertising objectives, budgeting methods for an ad campaign are largely the same as those for other forms of promotion. For example, techniques such as competitive parity, objective and task, and percentage of sales are again relevant to advertising. Whatever the methods used, it is important to remember that **advertising budgeting** should ideally stem from the objectives the advertising is attempting to achieve. However, other factors, such as monies available, competitive activity, and how the sports organization views the effectiveness of advertising, should be kept in mind.

Creative Decisions

After the objectives and the budget have been established, the creative process becomes the focus of the advertising campaign or **creative decisions.** The **creative process** has been defined as generating the ideas and the concept of the advertisement. Advertising and sports marketing agencies hire individuals who possess a great deal of creativity, but even the most innovative people use a systematic process to harness their creativity.

To begin the creative process, most advertising agencies prepare a creative brief. The purpose of any creative brief is to understand clients' communication objectives so the creative process will be maximized. The **creative brief** is a tool used to guide the creative process toward a solution that will serve the interests of the client and their customers. When used properly, the creative brief can be thought of as a marketing-oriented approach to the design of an advertising campaign. Table 10.1 shows a sample of the creative brief .

The three outcomes of the creative process are (1) identifying benefits of the sports product, (2) designing the advertising appeal—what to say, and (3) developing the advertising execution—how to say it. Each of these three elements in the creative decision process is discussed.

Identifying Benefits

Designing a distinctive advertising campaign involves identifying the key benefits of the sports product. We have briefly discussed the importance of understanding benefits in the context of segmenting consumer markets. As defined in Chapter 7, benefits describe why consumers purchase a product or service or what problem the product solves for the consumer. For advertising purposes, describing the benefits or reasons why consumers should buy the sports product is a must. Marketing research is used to understand the benefits desired or perceived by consumers who might use or purchase the sports product.

Advertising Appeals

Understanding benefits and developing **advertising appeals** go hand in hand. Once the desired benefits are uncovered, the advertising appeal is developed around these benefits. In short, the advertising appeal recounts *why* the consumer wants to purchase the sports product. The major advertising appeals used in sports marketing include health, emotion, fear, sex, and pleasure.

Health appeals are becoming prevalent in advertising, as the value placed on health continues to increase in the United States. Obviously, advertisements for the fitness industry and fitness centers capitalize on this growing concern of Americans. One important consideration when using health appeals in advertisements is the demographic profile of the target audience. According to the International Health,

TABLE 10.1   The Creative Brief

"Thinking about the situation is much better than hoping."
Strategic thinking leads to insight, which leads to high-quality execution.

Question: Why do a creative brief?

Answer: Our objective is to help our clients build their business. To do that, we must learn as much as we can so we can best deploy our creative resources to help the client meet their business objectives.

Creative brief elements
1. Project description
2. Target audience description (demographics, psychological data, etc.)
3. Long-term strategy
4. Competitive distinctiveness
5. Desired customer response (1–2 "desires" maximum; e.g., trial, change perception)
6. Mandatory executional elements (1–2 maximum)
7. Known key customer insights

What does the creative brief do?
1. Raises key issues about the business
2. Organizes learning already known about the consumer or business
3. Suggests areas for needed additional learning
4. Can help uncover new insights important to helping the customer
5. Contributes to the creative process

Questions to ask when developing a creative brief
1. Are there proven insights from other products or categories that we could use?
2. Is there a negative perception in category or product that our client's product could refute? Is there a trade-off or compromise that the client's product could eliminate?
3. Are there specific usage habits that could be leveraged into strong executions? How can we breathe creative life into research reports?
4. Is there a potential consumer negative in your principal competitor's strength?
5. Is there a perceived standard of excellence in your category? How does your brand compare with it? Can you create a standard of excellence for your brand?
6. What are the realities of how the client's brand fits their customer's needs? How does this affect the consumer's mindset when considering the alternatives available in the product category?
7. Is there a positive piece of consumer psychology your product can latch onto? Is there an emotional side to the client's brand? How does it interrelate with the practical side?
8. How does the client's consumer perceive their "brand"—not the product—"the brand"?

Source: © 1996 Optimum Group.

Racquet and Sportsclub Association, the strongest growth in health club membership is in the 55+ age range. Over the past 15 years, the defining characteristic of industry change has been the growth in the population of older health club members. In fact, in 2006, more than 20 percent of all health club members were over the age of 55, an increase of over 300 percent since 1990. The demographics of the audience and the health benefits desired from fitness centers should be carefully studied in the advertising process.[2]

A number of **emotional appeals,** such as fear, humor, sex, pleasure, and the drama associated with athletic competition, are also used in sports marketing promotions. One of the unique aspects of sports marketing is the emotional attachment that consumers develop for the sports product. As discussed in Chapter 5, many fans have high levels of involvement and identification with their favorite athletes and teams.[3]

Some fans may even view themselves as part of the team. Recognizing this strong emotional component, many advertisers of sports use emotional appeals. The infamous

"Thrill of victory and agony of defeat" message used for decades for ABC's *Wide World of Sports* opening captures the essence of an emotional appeal. Emotional appeals that allow fans to relive the team's greatest moments and performances of past years are often used to encourage future attendance.

One specific type of emotional appeal is a fear appeal. **Fear appeals** are messages designed to communicate what negative consequences may occur if the sports product or service is not used or is used improperly. Scare tactics are usually inappropriate for sports products and services, but in some product categories, moderate amounts of fear in a message can be effective. Consider, for example, messages concerning exercise equipment or health club membership. Many promotional campaigns are built around consumers' fears of being physically unfit and aging. Even athletic promoters use moderate fear appeals by telling consumers that tickets will be sold out quickly and that they should not wait to purchase their seats. Effective sports marketers identify their sports products as solutions to the common fears of consumers. For example, manufacturers of bike and skateboard helmets are quick to cite the plethora of head injuries that result without the use of proper headgear.

Another emotional appeal is sex. **Sex appeals** rely on the old adage that "sex sells." Typically, marketers who use sex appeals in their messages are selling products that are sexually related, such as perfumes and clothing. This is true also in sports marketing, as demonstrated by Polo Sport fragrance by Ralph Lauren or the Michael Jordan cologne, which made $60 million in sales during its first six months on the market.

In sports marketing, sex appeals are sometimes used, but this is always a delicate and ethical subject. *USA Today*'s Jon Saraceno writes that the LPGA "is largely irrelevant . . . for the vast majority of fans." He believes, however, that sex appeal "still sells. . . . And it would sell a lot more women's golf." Players like Paula Creamer, Cristie Kerr, and Natalie Gulbis "can make a tremendous impact on the LPGA's ability to grow and prosper."[4] In other examples of sex and sport, Olympic gold medalist Amanda Beard, posed in a 2007 issue of *Playboy,* the ATP Masters tournament held in Madrid has been using female models as ball girls since 2004, and ProBeach Volleyball with its bikini-clad players relies heavily on the sex appeal of its players (both male and female) to attract fans. Another sport that is continually flirting with the bounds of sex and sport is women's tennis.

Although it may be hard to argue against sex selling sport in today's society, many think enough is enough.[5] In fact, two researchers showed that women's sports gain

SPOTLIGHT ON SPORTS MARKETING ETHICS

Women's Tennis Cashing In on Sex Appeal

Sharapova. Williams. Williams again. Kournikova. The names are so synonymous with glitz and glamour that they are almost removed entirely from the sport in which the women proved themselves as stalwart competitors. For years, they toiled in a sport that paid women less than men on a regular basis. Now, however, the women have found a way to use their natural appeal and charisma to outpace men in their earnings.

There are those who criticize the "glam appeal" of the women's tennis tour, but women's prizes have traditionally been considerably lower than on the men's tour. The Sony Ericsson WTA Tour will pay out $58.7 million, whereas the men's tour will pay out $80 million. So the women are finding new ways of capitalizing on a marketing product that sells better than their athletic ability: sex.

"I think it's all in the execution," said *Sports Illustrated*'s Jon Wertheim. "In some ways facts are facts and the tour certainly hasn't shied away from playing up the glam factor. But when it starts to undercut the

(Continued)

(Continued)

credibility of the product, it becomes a problem. There are other players that want nothing to do with this."

The proof is in the endorsements. Maria Sharapova recently inked a deal that could be worth as much as $100 million over ten years, according to an article in *Tennis Life* magazine. The Williams sisters, Venus and Serena, make a combined $20 million a year. Anna Kournikova reportedly earns about $12 million a year.

And that's without Kournikova winning a single title. Some pro tour players, however, don't get the treatment that glam personas like Kournikova receive.

"It's been one of these issues that the tour has wrestled with for years now," Wertheim said. "Are they doing this tastefully? I think with a player like Sharapova, she can pull it off. She's a teenager, she's 6'2", she's blonde. Maria Sharapova knows the economics.

"When Lindsay Davenport was at the height of her power, she wasn't making $25 million in off-court income and there's a reason for that."

Wertheim notes that regardless of the off-court endorsements, Venus and Serena Williams are still top competitors.

"The one thing about the Williams sisters," he said, "to their credit, is that they are winning major titles."

The women may be finding that their off-court appeal is drawing big money, but the on-court competitions have been growing in popularity. The TV ratings for women's matches are outpacing the men's. The shorter matches of the women fit better into the television schedules and are easier to show.

At the NASDAQ 100 Open this past spring, women's and men's competitions drew the same number of television viewers. That number, however, was a 50 percent leap up from last year for the women compared to only a 25 percent increase in men's viewership, according to the NASDAQ 100 Web site.

Still, the women have a long way to go. While the Williams sisters generally garner the highest endorsements, which parallel the paydays of marquee stars like basketball players Kobe Bryant and Shaquille O'Neal, they still lag far behind golf's Tiger Woods who, according to ESPN, pulls in $60 million annually from endorsements.

Source: Mark Hoerrner, "Women's Tennis Cashing In on Sex Appeal," Buzzle.com, August 29, 2006, http://www.buzzle.com/editorials/8-29-2006-106944.asp.

nothing from marketing the athletes' looks. Mary Jo Kane and Heather Maxwell showed groups of people photos of sportswomen covering the spectrum from highly athletic to highly sexualized. Their initial findings showed that none of those images motivated men to attend games or buy tickets. Kane and Maxwell's research suggests that selling out women to sexist stereotypes does nothing to advance the cause of women's sports, nor does it serve the bottom line.[6]

Pleasure or fun appeals are designed for those target audiences that participate in sports or watch sports for fun, social interaction, or enjoyment. These advertising appeals should stress the positive relationships that can be developed among family members, friends, or business associates by attending games or participating in sports. A recent advertisement by a major credit card company captured the pleasure of a father taking his son to a baseball game. The essence of the appeal was that, although you might not be able to afford it at the time, you will never be able to replace the priceless moment of taking your child to his or her first ball game. Another classic example of fun appeals is the Budweiser "Whassup" ads. The campaign, featuring four buddies shouting to each other over the phone, specifically targeted young sports fans.

Advertising Execution

The **advertising execution** should answer the appeal that the advertiser is trying to target. In other words, it is not what to say, but how to say it. Let us look at some of the more common executional formats, such as message sidedness, comparative advertisements, slice of life, scientific, and testimonials.

One executional format is whether to construct the message as **one-sided versus two-sided.** A one-sided message conveys only the positive benefits of a sports product or service. Most sports organizations do not want to communicate the negative features of their products or services, but this can have its advantages. Describing the negatives along with the positive can enhance the credibility of the source by making it more trustworthy. In addition, discussing the negative aspects of the sports product can ultimately lower consumers' expectations and lead to more satisfaction. For instance, you rarely hear a coach at any level talk about how unbeatable a team or player is. Rather, the focus is on the weaknesses of the team, which reduces fan (and owner) expectations.

Comparative advertisements, another executional format, contrast one sports product with another. When doing comparative advertisements, sports advertisers stress the advantages of their sports product relative to the competition. For new sports products that possess a significant differential advantage, comparative advertisements can be especially effective. The risk involved with comparative advertisements is that consumers are exposed to your product as well as the competitor's product.

Because of the unique nature of sport, many advertisements are inherently comparative. For example, boxing advertisements touted the "Fight of the Century" between Muhammad Ali and Joe Frazier. In fact, there have been many "Fight of the Century" advertisements that are strikingly similar, comparing two boxers'

Eastern stresses its competitive advantage.
Source: Courtesy of Eastern Sports.

strengths and weaknesses. Other sporting events, such as the made-for-television Skins Game in golf, use a similar comparative format for promoting the events. Many home teams skillfully use comparative advertisements to attract moderately involved fans interested in the success of the local team. These fans are attracted by the allure of the visiting team or one of its star athletes. For instance, many basketball advertisements promote the big-name athletes of the opposing team, rather than highlight their own stars.

Slice-of-life advertisements show a "common" athlete or consumer in a common, everyday situation in which the consumer might be using the advertised sports or nonsports product. For example, Campbell's Chunky Soups features football stars Donovan McNabb and Michael Strahan eating soup prepared by their moms. A slight variation of this style is the **lifestyle advertisements,** wherein the advertisement is intended to portray the lifestyle of the desired target audience. For example, the classic "Just Do It" campaign uses a slice-of-life format that appeals to the participant in each of us. In another slice-of-life example, Zest soap ran a very effective campaign for their product using former football star Ironhead Hayward as their "showering" spokesperson.

Another executional style that is also readily used in sports advertising is called **scientific advertisements.** Advertisers using this style feature the technological superiority of their sports product or use research or scientific studies to support their claims. For instance, many golf ball manufacturers use scientific claims to sell their product. The Srixon UR-X is touted as having the "largest core," which means longer distance. Callaway markets the HX Tour as having "revolutionary hexagonal aerodynamics," and the Titleist Professional ball, which has a core of corn syrup, water, and salts, surrounded by a rubber and plasticlike covering. As Bill Morgan, Titleist's vice president of golf ball research, admits, "A lot of times, chemical words or technical words are talked about in marketing and nobody really knows what they are talking about. But it sounds high tech. There is a little deception there, really."

One of the most prevalent executional styles for sports advertising is the use of **testimonials.** Testimonials are statements about the sports product given by endorsers. These endorsers may be the "common" athlete, professional athletes, teams, coaches and managers, owners, or even inanimate objects, such as mascots. Even retired athletes are making a comeback as popular endorsers, as shown in Table 10.2.

TABLE 10.2	Most Marketable Retired Athletes		
RK Name	Total Points (max: 325)	% Of All Points	% Of 1st-Place Votes
1. Michael Jordan	279	85.8%	73.8%
2. Cal Ripken, Jr.	84	25.8%	3.1%
3. Charles Barkley	60	18.5%	4.6%
4. Jack Nicklaus	59	18.2%	1.5%
5. Lance Armstrong	56	17.2%	4.6%
6. Muhammad Ali	50	15.4%	3.1%
7. Dan Marino	49	15.1%	3.1%
8. Wayne Gretzky	40	12.3%	0.0%
9. Arnold Palmer	39	12.0%	1.5%
10. Andre Agassi	38	11.7%	0.0%

Note: Sports Business Daily asked 65 sports business and media executives, "Who is the most marketable retired athlete in trying to reach North American consumers?"

Why are athlete testimonials so popular among sports advertisers? The answer to this question is the ability of sports celebrities to persuade the target audience and move them toward purchase. Athletes' persuasive power stems from their credibility and, in some cases, attractiveness. **Credibility** refers to the expertise and the trustworthiness of the source of the message. **Expertise** is the knowledge, skill, or special experience possessed by the source about the sports product. Of course, successful athletes who promote products needed to participate in their sport have demonstrable expertise. Examples of the athlete–athletic product match-up include Steve Francis and Sheryl Swoopes—basketball shoe contracts; Tiger Woods, Greg Norman, and Jack Nicklaus—golf equipment; Jeff Gordon and Dale Jarrett—automotive industry; Ken Griffey, Jr. and Mike Piazza—baseball gloves; Martina Navratilova and Juan Carlos—tennis racquets; and Sidney Crosby—hockey equipment. Crosby, the consensus top pick in the National Hockey League draft, is widely anticipated to be the best player to enter the professional ranks in 20 years. Already immensely popular in his native Canada, Crosby's profile is expected to grow in the United States and around the world when his pro career begins. He will be a major

Fred Couples creates a powerful image for the Ashworth Collection.
Source: Courtesy of Ashworth, Inc. www.ashworthinc.com

part of Reebok's marketing strategy. The other dimension of source credibility is **trustworthiness.** This refers to the honesty and believability of the athlete(s) endorser(s). Trustworthiness is an intangible characteristic that is becoming harder and harder for professional athletes to establish. Today's consumers realize athletes with already large salaries are being paid huge sums of money for endorsements. Because of this, the athlete's believability is often suspect. Nevertheless, even some of the highest paid athlete endorsers, such as George Foreman, Arnold Palmer, and Tiger Woods, seem to have established themselves as trustworthy sources of information.

In addition to credibility, another factor that makes athletes successful endorsers is **attractiveness.** Although attractiveness is usually associated with physical beauty, it appears to have another, nonphysical dimension based on personality, lifestyle, and intellect. Attractiveness operates using the process of identification, which means that the target audience identifies with the source (athlete) in some fashion. Gatorade's classic "I wanna be like Mike" campaign, featuring Michael Jordan, is a good example of the identification process. Perhaps an even better example is Nike's "I am Tiger Woods" campaign, where kids of all races and ages were found putting themselves in the shoes of Tiger.

Who will be the most successful and appealing athlete endorsers of the new century? In 2003, a study was conducted by Burns Sports Celebrity Service, Inc. to answer this question. The survey asked more than 2,000 creative directors at national advertising agencies and corporate marketing executives, who hire athletes, to rate the most appealing athlete endorsers. Not surprisingly, the results indicated that the appeal of Tiger Woods continues to grow at an extremely rapid pace. Woods has firmly established himself as one of the top sports celebrity endorsers today, and Burns Sports' president, Bob Williams, believes, "If Tiger Woods takes an aggressive approach accepting endorsements, he could become the first athlete to earn a billion dollars in endorsements. Woods' golf career could last 30 years or more, unlike athletes from other sports whose average career is in the single digits. Hence, the real opportunity to earn a billion dollars from endorsements is within reason for a megastar like Tiger Woods." Other active athletes deemed to be most effective are listed in Table 10.3.

Although athlete endorsers can be extremely effective, there are risks involved. Athletes are costly and may suffer career-threatening injuries or just do foolish things. Here are just a few classic examples of the many athlete endorsers gone bad.

TABLE 10.3   Most Marketable Active Athletes

RK	Name	Total Points (max: 325)	% Of All Points	% Of 1st-Place Votes
1.	Tiger Woods	280	86.2%	69.2%
2.	Peyton Manning	208	64.0%	18.5%
3.	LeBron James	137	42.2%	4.6%
4.	Derek Jeter	78	24.0%	1.5%
5.	Dwayne Wade	62	19.1%	1.5%
6.	Dale Earnhardt, Jr.	48	14.8%	0.0%
7.	Tom Brady	42	12.9%	3.1%
8.	Shaquille O'Neal	30	9.2%	0.0%
9.	Maria Sharapova	11	3.4%	0.0%
t10.	Kobe Bryant	9	2.8%	0.0%
t10.	Brett Favre	9	2.8%	0.0%
t10.	Sidney Crosby	9	2.8%	

Note: Sports Business Daily asked 65 sports business and media executives, "Who is the most marketable active athlete in trying to reach North American consumers?"

The American cyclist Floyd Landis, the would-be heir to Lance Armstrong, appeared before an arbitration panel in California to rebut the charge that his come-from-behind victory in cycling's most celebrated race was a fraud. Landis was stripped of his title as winner of the 2006 Tour de France and placed under a two-year ban from professional racing, following an arbitration panel's 2 to 1 ruling on September 20, 2007. This makes Landis the first winner in the 103-year history of the Tour de France to be stripped of the victor's yellow jersey because of doping. The disastrous toll his case has exacted on cycling's credibility—races canceled for lack of sponsors, a team abandoned by its corporate underwriters, fans staying home—offers a stark picture of what can happen when a sport finally confronts its drug problem in a serious way.[7]

In baseball, U.S. prosecutors have begun to pursue new avenues of investigation after a former New York Mets batboy pleaded guilty to selling performance-enhancing drugs to dozens of major-league players. He is cooperating with authorities.

In addition, a special commission set up by major league Baseball to look into the sport's drug problem asked dozens of players to meet with its investigators and sought medical records from at least two of the game's recent top sluggers, Sammy Sosa and Rafael Palmeiro. The spotlight was not likely to dim as Barry Bonds slugged his way to becoming the all-time home run king, a pursuit that was tarnished as prosecutors investigated whether he lied during grand-jury testimony in a case involving the distribution of steroids to elite athletes. On November 15, 2007, federal prosecutors charged the 43-year-old slugger with perjury and obstruction of justice.[8]

In a scandal of international proportion, the cricketing world was rocked by acclaimed South Africa captain Hanse Cronje's fall from grace in the biggest match-fixing scandal the sport has seen. In 2000 Cronje confessed to accepting about $130,000 (£68,400) from bookmakers for providing them with match information to fix the results of games. He was banned from the sport for life—a devastating blow to the man who achieved iconic status after leading the Proteas, as the South Africa cricket team is known, to victory in 27 Tests—losing 11—and 99 one-day internationals out of 138.

Although scandals typically involve individual athletes, an entire sport can also be involved in unethical, performance enhancing practices. NASCAR officials have been working to even the playing field for years as teams searched for any edge they could find in a sport in which a tenth of a second of extra speed can determine the outcome of a race. Inspections before and after qualifying for the Daytona 500 in 2006 nabbed no fewer than 5 of the 61 teams trying to make the race. One team's crew chief and another team's director were suspended for four races for failing to cover holes in a wheel well, which was seen as giving the teams an unfair aerodynamic advantage. They were also fined $50,000 and assessed a 50-point penalty for the driver and team owner. In the days before taking part in the Great American Race, six teams were penalized for technical violations. The infractions—which ranged from the unintentional (Jeff Gordon's No. 24 Chevrolet was one inch too low after qualifying because of misaligned bolts in the car's rear shocks) to the blatant (Michael Waltrip's No. 55 Toyota was impounded after inspectors found an illegal substance in the engine manifold)—cast a dark cloud on a sport in which cheating has been omnipresent but never consistently targeted.

NASCAR's president, Mike Helton, said: "There is a need for NASCAR to have that same confidence with the fan, with the TV audience, with the car sponsors, with NASCAR sponsors, with the racetracks and all the constituents of the sport to have confidence in NASCAR's way that it handles its sport."[9]

Recently the NFL image has been damaged in a series of off-the-field wrongdoings and arrests of some of its athletes. There have been no fewer than 50 player arrests since the start of 2006, and NFL Commissioner Roger Goodell has instituted the toughest code of conduct in league history. Goodell has shown a willingness to suspend players even before they are convicted in the courts. Goodell stated, "Persons who fail to live up to this standard of conduct are guilty of conduct detrimental and subject to discipline, even where the conduct itself does not result in conviction of a crime." Discipline will include "larger fines and longer suspensions," and for repeat offenders, "the commissioner may impose discipline on an expedited basis for persons who have been assigned a probationary period." The commission also said this about players in trouble, "When that happens, you can be in the wrong place once, twice, maybe three times. But after a certain point, you are reflecting very negatively on the National Football League. It's my job—not law enforcement's job—to protect the National Football League."[10]

Because of the increased risk and incidence of scandal, many sports advertisers are shying away from signing megastar individual athletes to huge contracts and are instead using teams or events as their advertising platform. For instance, Reebok reduced its football endorsement stable from 250 to 150. Baseball endorsers were reduced from 350 to 100, and basketball endorsers were reduced from 100 to 25. Gatorade's vice president of sports marketing, Tom Fox, said it best: "The paradigm in the athlete marketplace has changed. . . . Like a lot of companies, we question the ability of any single athlete to reinforce brand equity to such a huge extent that it would move product off the shelf."[11]

Nonetheless, many companies are still using athletes, and as you might suspect Nike is leading the way. Nike has signed the following stable of athletes to multiyear contracts: NBA stars LeBron James ($90 million), Carmelo Anthony ($15 million), and Kobe Bryant ($45 million); tennis superstar Serena Williams ($40 million); 14-year-old U.S. soccer star Freddy Adu ($1 million); and Canadian world champion hurdler Perdita Felicien ($1 million).[12] Nike estimated its total endorsement commitments for 2006 will be approximately $1.9 billion, an amazing total. How can Nike, and others, reap a return on this huge investment? Table 10.4 presents some general guidelines for using sports celebrities in advertising campaigns.

One promising alternative that reduces the risk of potential problems is to use athletes who are no longer alive. Nike ran a series of 10 commercials using former Green Bay Packer coach Vince Lombardi. Other corporations that have featured departed stars in their ad campaigns include Citibank (Babe Ruth), Microsoft (Lou Gehrig and Jesse Owens), McDonald's, Coca-Cola, Apple Computer, General Mills (Jackie Robinson), and Miller Brewing (Satchel Paige). Dead athletes are more cost effective and scandal-proof and are icons in the world of sports. Ruth was chosen to represent Citibank in an ad campaign—49 years after his death and 62 since his last homer—for similar reasons. "Babe's an American sports icon, instantly recognizable," says Ken Gordon, a Citibank vice president, explaining why Ruth got the nod over contemporary ballplayers.[13]

TABLE 10.4   Guidelines for Using Sports Celebrities as Endorsers

- Sports celebrities are more effective for endorsing sports-related products. The match-up hypothesis again holds true—it does not matter if consumers recognize the athlete if they cannot remember the product that is being endorsed.
- Long-term relationships or associations between the product and the endorser are key—cannot be short-term or one-shot deals to be effective. Examples include Arnold Palmer with Pennzoil and Michael Jordan with Nike.
- Advertisements using athlete endorsers who appear during contests or events in which the athlete is participating are less effective.
- Athletes who are overexposed may lose their credibility and power to influence consumers. Tiger Woods's manager, Hughes Norton of IMG, says that he is planning to limit his association with just five global brands to avoid overexposure.

Source: Adapted from Amy Dyson and Douglas Turco, "The State of Celebrity Endorsement in Sport," *Cyber-Journal of Sport Marketing,* www.cad.gu.edu.au//cjsm/dyson.htm.

Nike Ups Money for Large-Ticket Endorsement Deals

Nike Inc. owes athletes, teams, and leagues $259 million more than the company said it did just three months ago, with overall commitments now exceeding $1.9 billion, according to the company's most recent quarterly report.

Nike is on the hook for $1.901 billion from 2007 on, up from the $1.642 billion the company reported in its July annual report. The increase is the first significant jump in the sneaker and apparel giant's endorsement commitments in nearly three years.

"That's a huge jump," said John Shanley, a sneaker analyst with Susquehanna Financial. "They have been paring down on their endorsement expenses, so it's somewhat surprising, a 16 percent increase. It's intriguing."

Nike spokesman Alan Marks described the revised number as occurring because contracts were signed and bonuses paid to athletes for performance after the annual report went out. That still means the overall commitment has risen, though, whether noted three months ago or last week.

The $1.9 billion level is the most Nike has owed in endorsement obligations since the company first began offering this figure in 2002, the year the Securities and Exchange Commission began requiring companies to make these kinds of disclosures.

The company has been spending lavishly on soccer, and recently cited World Cup marketing expenses as one reason its profit margins were squeezed in the most recent quarter. Marks, however, said World Cup is not the reason the endorsement obligations rose because this figure includes only money committed to 2007 and beyond. He declined to name a single team, athlete, or league that renewed a contract or signed a new one. Nike sponsored eight national teams at the World Cup, including the U.S. and Brazilian squads.

Nike chief executive Mark Parker wrote in his July letter to shareholders that the soccer division in 12 years grew from a $40 million business to a $1.5 billion business. Half the players on the field for the World Cup final wore Nike sneakers.

The company also has been stepping up its involvement in other global sports, recently announcing sponsorship pacts with the national cricket and soccer teams of India. International business now accounts for 40 percent of the company's pretax income.

Typically, the endorsement obligation figure is revealed only in the annual report, which Nike files in July. Nike last revised the number in January 2004, when it raised the then-total from $1.44 billion to $1.63 billion. The company pinned that mid-fiscal-year bump not just on renewals and additions to endorsement contracts, but also foreign exchange rates.

Marks emphasized that the company's key expense is demand creation, which consists of advertising and promotional expenses, including the cost of endorsement contracts.

Source: Daniel Kaplan, *Portland Business Journal,* October 13, 2006.

Media Strategy

As presented in Chapter 9, a medium or channel is the element in the communications process by which the message is transmitted. Traditional mass media, such as newspapers, television, radio, or magazines, are usually thought of as effective ways of carrying advertising messages to the target audience. However, new technologies are creating alternative media. The Internet, for example, represents an emerging medium that must be considered by sports advertisers. Deciding what medium or media to use is just one aspect in developing a comprehensive media strategy. **Media strategy** addresses two basic questions about the channel of communication. First, what medium or media mix (combination of media) will be most effective in reaching the desired target audience? Second, how should this media be scheduled to meet advertising objectives?

Media Decisions or Media Selection

The far-ranging (and growing) number of media choices make selecting the right media a difficult task. Choosing the proper media requires the sports advertiser to be mindful of the creative decisions made earlier in the advertising process. For instance, an emotional appeal—best suited to television—would be difficult to convey using print media. It is also critical that the media planner keep the target market in mind. Understanding the profile of the target market and their media habits is essential to developing an effective advertising campaign.

Every type of media has strengths and weaknesses that must be considered when making advertising placement decisions. Table 10.5 demonstrates selected advantages and disadvantages when choosing among advertising media.

Alternative Forms of Advertising

Because of the advertising clutter present in traditional advertising media, sports marketers are continually evaluating new ways of delivering their message to consumers. Alternative forms of advertising range from the more conventional stadium signage to the most creative media. Consider the following innovative illustrations of alternative forms of advertising: The International Cricket Council has allowed players to sell the top 23 centimeters of their bats for advertising. In Connecticut, 35 public golf courses have signed up for a program that will put advertisements in the bottom of their holes. A convenience store chain's unique branding play via White Sox sponsorship has the start time of the team's home games shifting to 7:11. A company spokesperson calls this a "fun way to insert our name into fans' hearts and minds." This sort of creativity could open up other areas where brands can get involved without impacting the field of play, as well as additional inventory for teams to sell.

Stadium Signage

Stadium signage, or onsite advertising, is back and is an extremely popular form of promotion and sponsorship packages. For some time, nary a sign was found on the

TABLE 10.5	Profiles of Major Media Types	
Medium	*Advantages*	*Limitations*
Internet	Allows messages to be customized; reaches specific market; interactive capabilities	Clutter, audience characteristics, hard-to-measure effectiveness
Newspapers	Flexibility; timeliness; good local market coverage; broad acceptability; high believability	Short life; poor reproduction quality; small pass-along audience
Television	Good mass market coverage; low cost per exposure; combines sight, sound, and motion; appealing to the senses	High absolute costs; high clutter; fleeting exposure; less audience selectivity
Direct mail	High audience selectivity; flexibility; no ad competition within the same medium; allows personalization	Relatively high cost per exposure; "junk mail" image
Radio	Good local acceptance; high geographic and demographic selectivity; low cost	Audio only, fleeting exposure; low attention ("the half-heard" medium); fragmented audiences
Magazines	High geographic and demographic selectivity; credibility and prestige; high-quality reproduction; long life and good pass-along readership	Long advertisement purchase lead time; high cost; no guarantee of position
Outdoor	Flexibility; high repeat exposure; low cost; low message competition; good positional selectivity	Little audience selectivity; creative limitations

Source: Adapted from Philip Kotler and Gary Armstrong, *Marketing: An Introduction,* 4th ed. (Upper Saddle River, NJ: Prentice Hall), 471.

outfield wall of an MLB team or on the boards at an NHL game. Now, stadium signage prevails on every inch of available space. Not unlike other forms of advertising, stadium signage is designed to increase brand or corporate awareness, create a favorable image through associations with the team and sport, change attitudes or maintain favorable attitudes, and ultimately increase the sale of product. The Cubs have struck a three-year sponsorship deal with Under Armour to place two 7-by-12-foot signs on the Wrigley Field outfield doors, the first corporate advertising to be placed among the famed brick-and-ivy outfield wall in the stadium's 93-year history.

One current estimate is that $16.39 billion is spent each year on stadium signage, but this is expected to increase, given the advent of new technologies allowing stadium billboards to be changed and customized for local markets.[14] Although stadium signage can be an effective means of advertising, it can also be costly. For instance, the rotating scorer's and press table stadium signage can cost between $50,000 and $100,000 for NBA games, given the current demand for the space. How is expensive stadium signage sold and justified by sports marketers? First, research has shown that locations considered to be part of the game (e.g., scorer's table or on the ice) are more effective than those locations removed from the action (e.g., scoreboards).[15] Other research found that spectators had improved recognition of and attitudes toward eight courtside advertisers for an NCAA Division I men's basketball team. This finding is, of course, extremely important to sponsors considering the cost and effectiveness of this type of stadium signage.[16]

Coca-Cola creates a positive association with baseball by using stadium signage.
Source: Courtesy of the Coca-Cola Company.

Other Outdoor

A new form of outdoor advertising is also becoming popular at national sporting events. This type of outdoor promotion uses live product demonstrations or characters to attract fans' attention. For example, the U.S. Army staged a live combat reenactment prior to the start of the Charlotte 500 NASCAR race. In another example, Juan Valdez, the very recognizable brand character for Colombian coffee, showed up in the stands of the U.S. Open tennis tournament. Similarly, Ronald McDonald attended the Kentucky Derby and a Chicago Bulls game to promote new products from McDonald's.

In a related fashion, sports marketers sometimes use variations of product placement techniques. Product placement occurs when manufacturers pay to have their products used in television shows, movies, and other entertainment media such as music videos. For instance, *The Best Damn Sports Show Period* on Fox SportsNet incorporates product placement into each show. Each day the hosts eat a dinner from Outback Steakhouse as they discuss the sports news of the day. Gordon and Smith surfboards were prominently featured in the movie *Blue Crush,* written about female surfers; and perhaps the earliest sports product placement was when James Bond, 007, used Slazenger golf balls on the links in the classic *Goldfinger.* In the ultimate product tie-in, the Anaheim Mighty Ducks of the NHL were named after the series of movies created by their then parent company, Disney.

Are these product placements effective? Top-rated TV shows aren't necessarily the best places for product placement. That's the conclusion of a new study of television product placement effectiveness conducted by New York–based Intermedia Advertising Group (IAG), a four-year-old research company whose roots are in measuring the effectiveness and performance of network television commercials.[17] "We both poll viewers and measure the exposure ourselves," IAG co-CEO Alan Gould said. "We code the exposure type, we measure the duration and note factors such as whether the product is embedded into the story line, used as intended, and in the foreground or background."[18] Even though this study seemed to find little support for the effectiveness of product placement, anecdotal evidence shows that product demonstrations seem to work and are certainly popular. Everlast's recent product placement recognition involved its very heavy role in 2005's reality TV show *The Contender.* Name a boxing film and there's a better-than-not chance there's an Everlast appearance: *Requiem for a Heavyweight, Raging Bull, Ali, Cinderella Man, The Hurricane, Million Dollar Baby.* Other sports product placements in recent movies include the following: *Gridiron Gang*—Nike, Puma, Rogers Athletic, Schutt Sports, Spalding; *The Departed*—Adidas; *Invincible*—Adidas; *Talladega Nights*—EA Sports; *Click*—Huffy Bicycle Company; *The Break-Up*—EA Sports, Reebok; and *Failure to Launch*—EA Sports, Nike. The advantages that have been cited for these alternative forms of advertising include:[19]

- **Exposure**—A large number of people go to the movies, rent movies, or could be exposed to a live-product demonstration if they are attending a sporting event or watching television.
- **Attention**—Moviegoers are generally an attentive audience. Sports spectators are also a captive audience when they are waiting for the action to begin.
- **Recall**—Research has shown that audiences have higher levels of next-day recall for products that are placed in movies than for traditional forms of promotion.
- **Source Association**—For product placements, the audience may see familiar and likable stars using the sports product. As such, the product's image may be enhanced through association with the celebrity.

Another alternative form of advertising is using the athlete as a "human billboard."[20] The history of athletes wearing an advertisement can be traced back to the 1960s, when organizations began establishing relationships with stock car drivers. Soon, the practice of drivers wearing patches on their clothing spread to other sports, such as tennis and golf. The use of athletes as advertisers is much more common in individual sports because these individuals have the ability to negotiate and wear whatever they want, as opposed to the tight controls imposed on athletes in team sports by their respective leagues.

Today, the use of athletes as human billboards is part of the integrated marketing communications plan rather than a stand-alone promotion. Fred Couples, Rich Beem, Chris DiMarco, Stuart Appleby, and Steve Flesch of the PGA wear sweaters and shirts, in addition to the other advertisements and promotions they perform for Ashworth. The major appeal of this form of advertising is the natural association (classical conditioning) formed in consumers' minds between the athlete and the organization or product.

How much does it cost sponsors to rent advertising space on an athlete's body? An IndyCar driver's helmet might cost between $50,000 and $250,000, depending on the driver. The precious space on a professional golfer's visor would cost between $250,000 and $500,000. Although these prices may seem outrageous, organizations are willing to pay the price for the exposure and enhanced brand equity.

In addition to these more conventional examples, basketball player Rasheed Wallace was asked by a candy company to tattoo his body for the NBA season. This offer was ultimately rejected as it was thought to potentially violate the NBA Uniform Player contract. Additionally, boxers have started to use their bodies as billboards by tattooing corporate logos on their chest and back. The Nevada State Athletic Commission tried to ban body billboards, but ultimately lost to the state court's ruling protecting boxers' right to free speech.

How big that business can be is something that's still being questioned. A particularly optimistic report from The Yankee Group projects the in-(video)game advertising market rocketing from $56 million in 2006 to $733 million by the end of 2010. Nielsen says it will grow to $1 billion by decade's end. "All the forecasts are overstated, but even

These runners all exemplify the human billboard.

at the low end, it's a healthy business," said Chip Lange, vice president of online commerce at Electronic Arts.[21]

Internet

Another major player in the world of advertising media is the Internet. As discussed in Chapter 2, the Internet has already become a valuable source of sports information for participants and fans. In addition, the Internet is fast becoming the favorite promotional medium for sports marketers. A total user base of over 150 million people exists in the United States alone, and Internet usage is growing globally (as seen in Table 10.6), which is just one advantage to promotion via the Internet.

In addition, the Online Publishing Association recently estimated that U.S. consumers spent $30 million on paid online sports content. Let us take a look at some of the other advantages to promotion via the Internet.

Perhaps the most substantial advantage to using the Internet as a promotional tool is the good fit between the profile of the sports fan and the Internet user. The typical Internet user is described as an entertainment-minded, educated male between 18 and 34 years old. For instance, the demographic profile of espn.com users is 94 percent male, 47 percent single, with 66 percent between the ages of 18 and 34.[22] Sound familiar? These characteristics closely match the traditional sports fan.

A study of online users showed that nearly a third of all Internet users (roughly 50 million people) visited some sort of sport site, with espn.com being the leader. In addition, over 50 percent of all male Internet users between the ages of 25–34 visited a sports site. Slightly older males (35–44) spend the most time surfing sport sites, with an average of 107 minutes spent per visit. Finally, the Internet is the ideal medium to target college sports fans due to greater access and usage rates among students. Generally, the Internet allows the sports advertiser to reach an extremely focused targeted market.[23]

TABLE 10.6	Top 15 Countries by Internet Penetration		
	Jan 2006 (000)	*Jan-2007 (000)*	*Percentage Change*
Worldwide	676,878	746,934	10%
United States	150,897	153,447	2%
China	72,408	86,757	20%
Japan	51,450	53,670	4%
Germany	31,209	32,192	3%
United Kingdom	29,773	30,072	1%
South Korea	24,297	26,350	8%
France	23,712	24,560	4%
India	15,867	21,107	33%
Canada	18,332	20,392	11%
Italy	15,987	18,106	13%
Brazil	12,845	14,964	16%
Spain	12,206	12,710	4%
Russian Federation	10,471	12,707	21%
Netherlands	10,772	11,077	3%
Mexico	8,624	10,149	18%

Note: Excludes traffic from public computers such as Internet cafes or access from mobile phones or PDAs. Unique Visitors age 15+.

Source: comScore World Metrix.

Another distinct advantage of promotion via the Internet is the interactive nature of the medium. Promotions attract the attention of the target audience and then create involvement by having consumers point and click on the information they find of interest. For instance, the major league Soccer site (www.mlsnet.com) has an interactive advertisement for MardiGras paper towels and napkins. A point and click of the mouse will take fans to the Georgia Pacific soccer link, which features the ability to download player screen savers and wallpapers, enter a shootout online contest, and, of course get more information on MardiGras products.

Other advantages of the Internet versus more traditional media include the Internet's ability to be flexible. Web promotions can be updated, and changes can be made almost instantly. This flexibility is a tremendous advantage for sports marketers, who are constantly responding to a changing environment. In fact, the Internet seems to be the perfect tool for sports marketers using the contingency framework for strategic planning.

A final benefit of promotion via the Internet is its cost effectiveness. The Internet provides organizations with a means of promoting sports to consumers around the world at a low cost. The ability to reach a geographically diverse audience at a low cost is one of the primary advantages of Internet promotion.

Although there are many advantages, promotion via the Internet can also pose potential problems. As with other forms of advertising, it is difficult to measure the effectiveness of sports promotion over the Internet. Often, marketers use the "number of hits" as a proxy for effectiveness, but this cannot be used to determine the interest level of the consumer or purchase intent.

Promotional clutter is another difficulty with Internet promotions. As the Internet becomes a more popular advertising medium, more organizations will compete for the audience and its attention. To break through the clutter, sports marketers must design new Internet promotions. Differentiating among Web promotions will become increasingly important in gaining the attention of consumers and developing a unique position for organizations.

The Internet has become a popular medium for all forms of promotion.

The Golf Channel and PGA and LPGA team up for online contests.

A final disadvantage of promotion on the Internet is its inability to reach certain groups of consumers. Although the Internet is a great medium to reach younger, college-educated, computer-literate consumers, it may be extremely inefficient in trying to promote to the mature market or, perhaps, consumers of lower socioeconomic standing.

Although we have looked at some of the pros and cons of promotion via the Internet, the fact remains that the Internet is here to stay. The low costs, ability to target sports fans and participants, and high flexibility far outweigh the disadvantages of this medium. Certainly, sports marketers have accepted the Internet as another important tool in their integrated communications efforts.

Choosing a Specific Medium

Once the medium or media mix is chosen by the sports organization along with the advertising agency, the specific medium must be addressed. In other words, if the advertisement will appear in a magazine, then we must choose which magazine will be most effective. Do we want our advertisement to promote the NHL to appear in *Sports Illustrated, Sporting News Magazine,* the *Hockey News*, or some combination of these specific media? Should we promote Texas Motor Speedway via Internet advertising, text messaging, podcasting, or by more traditional means—television, radio, magazine, and newspaper? To answer this question, we must consider our reach and frequency objectives.

Reach refers to the number of people exposed to an advertisement in a given medium. For the advertiser who wants to generate awareness and reach the largest number of people in the target audience, perhaps *Sports Illustrated,* with a circulation of over 3 million, would be the most effective medium. However, if the target audience is women, then *Sports Illustrated* might be reaching people who are not potential users.

The reach of an advertisement is determined by a number of factors. First, the nature of the media mix influences reach. The general rule is that the greater the number of media used, the greater the reach. For example, if the advertising campaign for the NHL were broadcast on television, printed in magazines, and also appeared on the Internet, reach would be increased. Second, if only one medium is to be used, increasing the number and diversity within this medium will increase the reach. For instance, if cable television were chosen as the sole medium for the NHL campaign, reach would be increased if the commercial were aired on ESPN, Lifetime, and Fox Sports versus ESPN alone. Finally, reach can be enhanced by airing the advertisements during different times of the day or day parts. The advertisement might be shown at night after 9:00 P.M. and also in the morning to reach a greater percentage of the target audience.

Along with reach, another consideration in making specific media decisions is frequency. **Frequency** refers to the number of times the individual or household is exposed to the media vehicle. An important point is that frequency is measured by the number of exposures to the media vehicle rather than the advertisement itself. Just because an advertisement is shown on television during the Super Bowl does not mean that the target audience has seen it. Consumers might change channels, leave the room, or simply become involved in conversation. A study examined this issue using Super Bowl viewers in a bar setting.[24] It found that visual attention levels for the game are similar to attention levels for the advertisements, attention to commercials varies by their location in the cluster of advertisements and time of the game, and that Super Bowl commercials may receive more attention than commercials on other programs.

Media Scheduling

Four basic **media scheduling** alternatives are considered once the medium (e.g., magazines) and specific publications (e.g., *Sports Illustrated*) are chosen. These schedules are called continuous, flighting, pulsing, and seasonal. A **continuous schedule** recognizes that there are no breaks in the demand for the sports product. This is also called steady, or "drip," scheduling. During the advertising period, advertisements are continually run. Most sporting goods and events are seasonal and, therefore, do not require a continuous schedule. Some sporting goods, such as running shoes, have roughly equivalent demand and advertising spending throughout the year.

A **flighting schedule** is another alternative, where advertising expenditures are varied in some months and zero is spent in other months. Consider the case of the Houston Astros. Heavy advertising expenditures are spent in March, April, and May leading up to the season. Reminder-oriented advertising is placed over the course of the rest of the season, and no advertising dollars are spent in the winter months. This type of scheduling is most prevalent in sports marketing due to the seasonal nature of most sports.

A **pulsing schedule** is a variant of the flighting schedule. Ad expenditures may vary greatly, but some level of advertising is always taking place. Although it sounds similar to a flighting schedule, remember that a flighting schedule has some months where zero is spent on advertising.

Personal Selling

Now that we have looked at the advertising process in detail, let us turn to another important element in the promotion mix—personal selling. Personal selling is used in a variety of ways in sports marketing, such as in securing corporate sponsorships, selling luxury suites or boxes in stadiums, and hawking corporate and group ticket sales. In the marketing of sporting goods, the primary applications of personal selling are to get retailers to carry products (push strategy) and consumers to purchase products (pull strategy).

Personal selling represents a unique element in the promotion mix because it involves personal interaction with the target audience rather than mass communication to thousands or millions of consumers. The definition of personal selling reflects this important distinction between personal selling and the other promotion tools. **Personal selling** is a form of person-to-person communication in which a salesperson works with prospective buyers and attempts to influence their purchase needs in the direction of their company's products or services.

All the advantages of personal selling described in Table 10.7 make it an attractive promotional tool, so the ability to use personal selling to develop long-term relationships with consumers is becoming increasingly important to sports marketers. In fact, building long-term relationships with consumers has become one of the critical issues for marketers. More formally, **relationship marketing** is the process of creating, maintaining, and enhancing strong, value-laden relationships with customers and other stakeholders.[25]

As Kotler and Armstrong point out, the key premise of relationship marketing is that building strong economic and social ties with valued customers, distributors, dealers, and suppliers leads to long-term profitable transactions. Many sports organizations are realizing it is cheaper to foster and maintain strong relationships with existing customers than to find new customers or fight the competition for a stagnant consumer base.

Two examples of building relationships with consumers of sport were described in an article entitled "Pursuing Relationships in Professional Sport."[26] In the first example, a promotion was developed by the Pittsburgh Pirates and Giant Eagle Supermarkets. The basic premise of the promotion was that fans could earn discounts and special offers at Pirates games by participating in the Giant Eagle preferred shoppers program. For example, fans with an Advantage Card (given to program participants) were offered discounted ballpark meals for a month, half-price tickets to five games throughout the season, and discounts on Pirates merchandise. The relationship-building program was deemed successful by the Pirates, Giant Eagle, and the fans.

Another relationship-building effort was designed for the fans of the San Diego Padres. The program, called the Compadres Club, rewards fans for attending predetermined numbers of games. In addition, the fans receive frequency points based on player performance. Ultimately, fans can redeem their frequency points for Padres merchandise, posters, and dinners. For example, the top earners receive an authentic baseball bat autographed by a Padres player and presented on the field at a special pregame ceremony. More than 50,000 fans enrolled in the program's initial year, 1996 (it is now up to 200,000 members), and the Padres have gathered a wealth of information on their fans.

Although both the Pirates and the Padres have developed marketing programs to build relationships with fans, the importance of personal selling should not be overlooked. Personal selling was necessary for the Pirates to communicate the benefits of the partnership to Giant Eagle. As a result of selling a successful program to

TABLE 10.7	Benefits of Personal Selling

- Personal selling allows the salesperson to Immediately adapt the message being presented based on feedback received from the target audience.
- Personal selling allows the salesperson to communicate more information to the target audience than other forms of promotion. Moreover, the salesperson can explain complex information.
- Personal selling greatly increases the likelihood of the target audience paying attention to the message. It is difficult for the target audience to escape the message because communication is person to person.
- Personal selling greatly increases the chances of developing a long-term relationship with consumers, due to the frequent person-to-person communication.

CAREER SPOTLIGHT

Kevin Rochlitz, Senior Director, National Partnerships and Sales, Baltimore Ravens

Career Questions

1. How did you get started in the sports industry? What was your first sports industry job?

   I got my start by working as an intern in the University of Wyoming athletic department in promotions and administration. I knew what I wanted to do from the beginning, so I decided to go ahead and volunteer my time, and I got a lot of work experience from it. My father is a basketball coach and I loved the integration between sports and business. My first sports industry job was the assistant marketing director job at Fresno State University. I learned a lot while I was there and it taught me more about selling and the ability to tie in promotions with partners.

2. Can you describe the type of work you are doing right now? What are your job responsibilities? What are the greatest challenges?

   Right now, my main goal is to bring in revenue through a number of channels such as signage, television, radio, print, Internet or converged media, trademarks, and promotional opportunities. I work with all of the retail and national accounts as we try to tie them in together. My overall responsibility is to increase revenue for the team and gain market share with our marks. Since we are a young team, the opportunity to have our logo tied in with promotions is a big help. The greatest challenge for us is that we are between two major markets (Philadelphia and Washington) and both have teams, so the ability to use our

marks outside our area is difficult. Also, the growing popularity of the Internet and all that it can do and trying to get partners to see this can be challenging.

3. Do you foresee any changes in demand in this field in the future? If so, what or how?

   Not really. Right now I think it is going to go in the direction of electronic media, and the more people in this industry have the knowledge of this, the better it will help them.

4. Who or what has influenced you the most in your sports business career?

   I would say my parents as they have taught me to work very hard and things will happen. I love my job and many times I can't believe they pay me to do this. It is a hobby and from the days of working at Wyoming with then Athletic Director Paul Roach, he gave me an opportunity to learn while I was at school, so it was like getting two degrees. Plus one of my old professors at Wyoming, Dr. Brooks Mitchell, who taught me to think outside the box, has been very influential on my career.

5. What advice would you offer students who are considering a career in sports marketing?

   You are going to have to work hard and get involved in a collegiate marketing department and volunteer your time. The experience at this level can be very beneficial and the folks in the athletic department will help you post-graduation.

Giant Eagle, the company increased its Pirates-related marketing budget by roughly 25 percent. The Padres, armed with a database of the demographics and buying habits of its most loyal fans, will use personal selling to secure additional sponsorship and advertising dollars.

The Strategic Selling Process

Now that we have defined personal selling and discussed some of its major advantages, let us examine how the selling process operates in sports marketing. As previously discussed, sports marketers are generally concerned with selling an intangible service versus a tangible good. Most salespeople view the selling of services as a much more difficult process, because the benefits of the sports product are not readily observable or easily communicated to the target audience. It is much easier to sell the new and improved r7 Superquad driver from TaylorMade when the consumer can see the design, feel the weight of the club, and swing the club. In essence, the product sells itself. Contrast this with the sale of a luxury box to a corporation in a stadium that is yet to be built. Selling this sports product is dependent on communicating both the tangible and intangible benefits of the box to the prospective buyer. In addition to the problems associated with selling a service versus a good, the sale of many sports products requires several people to give their approval before the sale is complete. This factor also makes the selling process more complex.

In the ever-changing world of sports marketing, the "good ol' boy" approach to selling is no longer valid. To be more effective and efficient in today's competitive environment, a number of personal selling strategies have been developed. One process, developed by Robert Miller and Stephen Heiman, is called **strategic selling**.[27]

Miller and Heiman suggest the first step in any strategic selling process is performing an analysis of your current position. In this instance, position is described as understanding your personal strengths and weaknesses as well as the opportunities and threats that are present in the selling situation. In essence, the salesperson is constructing a mini-SWOT analysis. Questions regarding how prospective clients feel about you as a salesperson, how they feel about your products and services, who the competition is, and how they are positioned must all be addressed at the initial stages of the strategic selling process.

Good salespeople realize that they must adapt their current position for every account before they can be successful. To change this position, six elements in the strategic selling process must be considered in a systematic and interactive fashion. These elements, which must be understood for successful sales, include buying influences, red flags, response modes, win-results, the sales funnel, and the ideal customer profile. Let us take a brief look at how these elements work together in the strategic selling process.

Buying Influences

A complex sale was earlier defined as one where multiple individuals are involved in the buying process. This is true of large organizations considering a sponsorship proposal or families considering the purchase of exercise equipment for a new workout facility in their home. One of the first steps in the strategic sales process is to identify all the individuals involved in the sale and to determine their buying roles.

Roles are patterns of behavior expected by people in a given position. Miller and Heiman believe there are generally four critical buying roles that must be understood in a complex sale (no matter how many people play these roles). The **economic buying role** is a position that governs final approval to buy and that can say yes to a sale when everyone else says no, and vice versa. The **user buying role** makes judgments about the potential impact of your product or service on their job performance. These individuals will also supervise or use the product, so they want to know "what the product or service will do for them." The **technical buying role** screens out possible suppliers on the basis of meeting a variety of technical specifications that have been determined in advance by the organization. The technical buyers also serve as gatekeepers, who screen out potential suppliers on the basis of failing to meet the stated specifications. Finally, the **coach's role** is to act as a guide for the salesperson making the sale. The coach is a valuable source of information about the organization and can lead you to the other **buying influences**. As Miller and Heiman point out, identifying the individuals playing the various roles is the foundation of the strategic selling process.

Red Flags

Once the individuals have been identified, the next step in the strategic selling process is to look for red flags, or things that can threaten a complex sale. Red flags symbolize those strategic areas that can require further attention to avoid mistakes in positioning. In addition, red flags can be used to capitalize on an area of strength. Some of the red flags that can threaten a complex sale include either missing or uncertain information, uncontacted buying influences, or reorganization. For example, any uncontacted buying influences are considered a threat to the sale. These uncontacted buying influences are analogous to uncovered bases in baseball. Teams cannot be fielded or successful when there is no shortstop or catcher. Likewise, a sale cannot be successful until all the relevant players have been contacted.

Response Modes

After the buyer(s) have been targeted and you have correctly positioned your products or services by identifying red flags, the next step in the strategic selling process is to determine the buyer's reaction to the given sales situation. These varying reactions are categorized in four **response modes.** These modes include the growth mode, trouble mode, even keel mode, and overconfident mode.

The **growth mode** is characterized by organizations who perceive a discrepancy between their current state and their ideal state in terms of some goal (e.g., sales or profits). In other words, the organization needs to produce a higher quality sports product or put more people in the seats in order to grow. In this situation, the probability of a sale is high.

The second response mode is known as the **trouble mode.** When an organization is falling short of expectations, it is in the trouble mode. Here again, there is a discrepancy between the current and ideal states. In the growth mode the organization is going to improve upon an already good situation. However, the trouble mode indicates that the buyer is experiencing difficulties. In either case, the potential for a sale is high.

The **even keel mode** presents a more difficult case for the salesperson. As the name implies, there is no discrepancy between the ideal and current results and, therefore, the likelihood of a sale is low. The probability of a sale can be enhanced if the salesperson can demonstrate that a discrepancy actually exists, the buyer sees growth or trouble coming, or there is pressure from another buying influence.

The final response mode is the **overconfident mode.** Overconfidence is generally the toughest mode to overcome from the salesperson's perspective in that the buyers believe things are too good to be true. Just think about individual athletes or teams who are overconfident. Invariably they lose because of their false sense of superiority. Organizations that are overconfident are resistant to change because they are exceeding their goals (or at least they think so), so sales are difficult. The NFL is one example of a sports league currently at the top in terms of fan popularity, but subject to the overconfident mode. Specifically, off-the-field issues (as noted earlier) may alienate fans and sponsors. Gene Upshaw, the executive director of the NFL Players Association, commented that "I do not want the fans to turn us off because of off-field behavior. It has happened in other sports, and I would not want that to happen to the NFL." In this stage of the strategic sales process, the response mode of the organization should be analyzed. In addition, each of the buying influences should be examined to determine their perception of the current situation. By analyzing the buying influences and their perceptions, the salesperson is in a position to successfully adapt his or her approach to meet the needs of each buying influence and each customer.

Win-Results

Much of sports marketing today is based on the premise of strategic partnerships. The same is true for the strategic sales process. In strategic partnerships, the sales process produces satisfied customers, long-term relationships, repeat business, and good referrals. To achieve these outcomes, the salesperson must look at clients as partners rather than competition that must be beaten.

Miller and Heiman define the **win-results** concept in the strategic selling process as an objective result that gives one or more of the buying influences a personal win. The key to this definition is understanding the importance of both wins and results. A result is the impact of the salesperson's product or service on one or more of the client's business objectives. Results are usually tangible, quantifiable, and affect the entire organization. Wins, however, are the fulfillment of a promise made to oneself. Examples of personal wins for the potential client include gaining recognition within the organization, increasing responsibility and authority, and enhancing self-esteem. It is important to realize that wins are subjective, intangible, and do not benefit all the people in the organization the same way.

The Sales Funnel

The sales funnel is another key element in the strategic sales process. This is a tool used to organize all potential clients, as opposed to developing a means for understanding an individual client. Basically, the **sales funnel** is a model that is used to organize clients so salespeople might organize their efforts in the most efficient and effective manner. After all, allocating time and setting priorities are two of the most challenging tasks in personal selling.

The sales funnel divides clients into three basic levels—above the funnel, in the funnel, and the best few. Potential clients exist above the funnel if data (e.g., a call from the prospective client wanting information or acquiring information from personal sources) suggest there may be a possible fit between the salesperson's products or services and the needs of the potential client. The salesperson's emphasis at this level is to gather information and then develop and qualify prospects.

Potential clients are then filtered to the next level of the sales funnel. If clients are placed in the funnel (rather than above it), then the possibility of a sale has been verified. Verification occurs once a buying influence has been contacted and indicates that the organization is in either a growth or trouble response mode. Remember that these two response modes represent ideal conditions for a sale to occur.

When all the buying influences have been identified, red flags have been eliminated, and win-results have been addressed, sales prospects can be moved from in the funnel to the "best few." At this final level of the sales funnel, the sale is expected to happen roughly 90 percent of the time.

Ideal Customers

The ideal customer concept in strategic selling extends the notion of the sales funnel. In this case, all potential customers outside the funnel are evaluated against the hypothetical "ideal customer." The strategic sales process is based on the belief that every sale is not a good sale. The **ideal customer** profile is constructed to cut down on the unrealistic prospects that should not be in the sales funnel in the first place.

When constructing the ideal customer profile, the salesperson must judge each prospect with respect to organizational demographics, psychographics, and corporate culture. Current prospects can then be evaluated against the ideal customer profile to determine whether additional time and energy should be invested.

Sales Promotions

Another promotion infix element that communicates to large audiences is sales promotions. **Sales promotions** are a variety of short-term, promotional activities that are designed to stimulate immediate product demand. A recent Krispy Kreme sales promotion illustrates how a simple game promotion can affect short-term sales.

The Krispy Kreme promotion allowed each Kansas City Royal fan to redeem his or her ticket stub for a dozen free doughnuts whenever the Royals have 12 or more hits. In the season preceding the promotion, the Royals reached the 12-hit plateau while playing at home just 21 times. By June, the Royals had already reached 10 games with 12 or more hits and fans had turned in about 25,000 stubs for the equivalent of more than 2.1 million doughnuts, a retail value of nearly $1 million. "We never expected this in a million years," said Kelly Lehman, Krispy Kreme's director of marketing for Missouri and Kansas.[28]

The sales promotions used in sports marketing come in all shapes and sizes. Think about some of the sales promotions with which you may be familiar. Examples might include the Bud Bowl; Straight-A Night at the ballpark; coupons for reduced green fees at public golf courses; a sweepstakes to win a free trip to the Super Bowl; a click of the mouse for a special free collector's edition of *Sports Illustrated* from Campbell's Soup; Miller Lite's "make the call for Miller Lite" baseball promotion, which includes banners, display cards, posters, and merchandise; and many other examples.

Minor League Baseball has always been known for its creative sales promotions, and the Pacific Coast League's Portland Beavers provide a number of great examples. Every Thursday the Beavers offer two-dollar beers on Thirsty Thursday, and Wednesdays are Dollar Dog nights, when fans can get a hot dog for a buck. The Beavers have also gained the attention of fans with their "Bark in the Park" promotion, when fans can bring their dogs to the ballpark, and "Two Dead Fat Guys" night in honor of Elvis and Babe Ruth.

As stated in the definition, all forms of sales promotions are designed to increase short-term sales. Additional objectives may include increasing brand awareness, broadening distribution channels, reminding consumers about the offering, or inducing a trial to win new customers. To accomplish these objectives, sports marketers use a variety of sales promotion tools.

When the NHL returned to the ice following a lengthy work stoppage, Molson hired Grand Central Marketing to execute a grassroots promotion that would rekindle excitement among fans and position the brand as the beer of choice for hockey fans. The Molson Goalies program took place in seven NHL cities in the weeks leading up to the start of hockey season. In each market, teams of six brand ambassadors wearing Molson-logoed goalie uniforms made unannounced appearances in high traffic locations, outside stadiums and arenas, and in bars. They entertained consumers with goal scoring contests, hockey trivia questions, and games. Wherever the goalies went, they gave away Molson-branded premiums including T-shirts, hats, stress hockey pucks, inflatable goalie sticks, goalie bags, and jerseys.

The promotion succeeded in its "goal" of reaching hockey fans and closely aligning Molson with the sport. Over the course of the promotion, more than 30,000 premiums were distributed. Not only did the goalies cause a stir among consumers, but the local media also took notice. The goalies appeared on television ten times and their photos were in the newspaper seven times.

In another hockey example, the Syracuse Crunch of the American Hockey League announced the Taco Bell "Crunch Win; Win a Taco" program. When the Syracuse Crunch won a home game during the 2006–07 season, fans could bring their ticket stubs to a participating Taco Bell location for a free seasoned beef taco, courtesy of Taco Bell.

Taco Bell was also involved as MLB's official Quick Service Restaurant, offering a promotion in which fans could post a marriage proposal on the virtual sign behind home plate during a nationally televised game on July 7, 2007. The date was chosen "because of its unique number sequence—07-07-07—and to promote" the restaurant's new 7-layer Crunchwrap. Fans could submit "seven reasons why your significant other would be lucky to marry you." The winner received the televised proposal and a year's supply of Taco Bell food.

Premiums

Premiums are probably the sales promotion technique most associated with traditional sports marketing. **Premiums** are items given away with the sponsor's product as part of the sales promotion. Baseball cards, NASCAR model car replicas, water bottles, hats, refrigerator magnets, posters, and almost anything else imaginable have been given away at sporting events. Although premiums are often given away to spectators at events, they can also be associated with other sporting promotions. For example, *Sports Illustrated* magazine gives away hats, T-shirts, and videos to induce potential consumers to subscribe. In another example, many credit card companies are giving away hats with the logo of the fan's favorite team for applying for a line of credit.

Perhaps the most effective and exciting premium over the past several years has been the bobblehead. The Triple-A Pacific Coast League Portland Beavers, a Padres affiliate, "sent letters to every Bob L. Head they could find" and asked them to submit an essay "explaining why they should be cast as a miniature, head-bobbing figurine." The team narrowed its search to three finalists and the winner had his bobblehead given out to the first 2,000 fans who attended the team's game against the Las Vegas 51s. Who knows what the next premium craze might be in sports?

Although premiums can bring people to games who would not otherwise attend, they can also have negative consequences and must be carefully planned. In the now defunct World Hockey Association (WHA), the Philadelphia Blazers handed out souvenir pucks at the first home game. Unfortunately, the game had to be postponed because the ice was deemed unfit for skating. When the Blazers' Derek Sanderson announced the game cancellation to the crowd at center ice, he was pelted with the pucks.[29] In a similar scenario, the LA Dodgers had to forfeit a game because fans began throwing baseballs (that they had been given) onto the field, endangering players and other fans. The Dodgers can also be used to illustrate the height of premium marketing. In 1984, the Los Angeles Olympic Games created a regionwide craze for pin collecting. Sensing the "legs" of this mania, the Dodgers created six pin-giveaway nights at their stadium. They picked games that would typically have low attendance. The result was that all six of these games sold out on the strength of a $.60 per unit collector's pin!

Giveaways or premiums are a popular promotion technique.

Contests and sweepstakes

Contests and sweepstakes are another sales promotional tool used by sports marketers to generate awareness and interest among consumers. Contests are competitions that award prizes on the basis of contestants' skills and ability, whereas sweepstakes are games of chance or luck. As with any sales promotion, the sports marketing manager must attempt to integrate the contest or sweepstakes with the other promotion mix elements and keep the target market in mind.

One of the classic contests sponsored by the NFL was the punt, pass, and kick competition. In this competition, young athletes competed for a chance to appear on the finals of nationally televised NFL games, making the NFL the winner for promoting youth sports. Other contests have capitalized on the growing popularity of rotisserie sports. Dugout Derby, Pigskin Playoff, and Fairway Golf are all examples of "rotisserie" contests conducted via toll-free numbers where fans could earn prizes for choosing the best fantasy team or athletes. In return, marketers capture a rich database of potential consumers. As sweepstakes become more and more popular, companies are constantly looking for new ways to break through the clutter. Consider this tremendous opportunity for race fans offered by RadioShack and Samsung. They designed the "Call Your Driver" sweepstakes that fans could enter by purchasing any Samsung wireless phone at RadioShack or by requesting an official entry code. Participants "call their driver" by selecting the driver they think will win the Samsung/RadioShack 500 in Fort Worth, Texas. The winning fan and three guests are flown to the Samsung/RadioShack 500 where they spend five nights in a state-of-art RV on the infield of the race, receive passes to tour the pits, and watch the race from the grandstands.

In addition, the grand prize winner receives a RadioShack scanner, race intercom system, and headset, allowing them to listen as pit crews and drivers discuss racing strategies. Afterward, the grand prize winner visits Victory Lane for an experience of a lifetime as the winning driver is presented with the coveted Texas Motor Speedway

Philadelphia Eagles reach out to the community.

"boot" trophy. To top it off, if the driver in Victory Lane is the same one the grand prize winner selected on his or her Call Your Driver sweepstakes entry form, they are presented with a car in the same make and model. Now that's a sweepstakes!

Other sweepstakes are taking advantage of the Internet and its growing audience. For example, Pontiac sponsored a contest in 2004 in which sports fans had a chance to win $10,000 by picking the most winners in the NCAA basketball tournament. The sweepstakes was promoted through the ESPN Web site, and the only information required to win this prize was a name, phone number, and e-mail address. Again, the marketers for Pontiac are collecting a database of potential consumers for their product by running this sales promotion. The typical by-product of this database would be an invitation to visit a dealership, test drive a car, or have information mailed to participants.

Nike Golf and *Golf Digest* offered a "Tee It Up with Tiger Woods" sweepstakes, with 24 winners receiving a trip to play golf with Woods at the Reunion Resort in Orlando.

In yet another example, the Miami Dolphins held a sweepstakes giving fans a chance to win tickets to the game against the Giants at London's Wembley Stadium. New season-ticket holders were automatically entered three times, while other fans could enter at miamidolphins.com. The grand prize included round-trip airfare, hotel accommodations, Royal Box tickets to the game, and passes to NFL pre-parties for four fans.

The NBA Pick Your Play Sweepstakes gave fans a chance to select from one of these NBA fan experience packages:[30]

NBA VIP EXPERIENCE
The winner will receive VIP treatment for two to an NBA game (team of their choice). This prize package includes: round-trip airfare, hotel accommodations, game tickets, and $500 in merchandise from the NBA store.

NBA ABROAD EXPERIENCE
The winner will receive a trip for two to an international preseason game destination in 2007. This prize package includes: round-trip airfare, hotel accommodations, game tickets, behind-the-scenes access, and $250 in merchandise from the NBA store.

NBA MEDIA EXPERIENCE
The winner will be flown to New York City and given a tour through NBATV studios, meet NBATV personalities, receive behind-the-scenes access to a Knicks/Nets game, and $500 in merchandise from the NBA Store.

Sampling

One of the most effective ways of inducing customers to try new products that are being introduced is **sampling.** Unfortunately, it is very difficult to give away a small portion of a sporting event. However, sports have been known to put on exhibitions to give consumers a "taste" for the game. Squash demonstration matches have been held in the middle of New York's Grand Central Station, attracting thousands of fans who would have never otherwise been exposed to the sport. The Olympics, of course, have used demonstration sports since 1904, in sports such as roller hockey and bandy (soccer on ice), to provide a "sample" of the action to spectators. If fan interest is high enough (i.e., attendance), the sport can then become a medal sport in the next Olympiad. In yet another example, one million samples of Nivea for Men were distributed in conjunction with NCAA March Madness. Employees outfitted as referees, cheerleaders, and basketball players distributed the products both on college campuses and in the streets to prospective consumers.

Point-of-Purchase Displays

Point-of-purchase or **P-O-P displays** have long been used by marketers to attract consumers' attention to a particular product or retail display area. These displays or materials, such as brochures, cut-outs, and banners, are most commonly used to communicate price reductions or other special offers to consumers. For instance, tennis racquet manufacturers, such as Prince, design huge tennis racquets, which are then displayed in the storefronts of many tennis retail shops to catch the attention of consumers.

Coupons

Another common sales promotion tool is the coupon. **Coupons** are certificates that generally offer reductions in price for sports products. Coupons may appear in print advertisements, as part of the product's package, inserted within the product packaging, or be mailed to consumers. Although coupons have been found to induce short-term sales, there are disadvantages. For instance, some marketers believe continual coupon use can detract from the image of the product in the minds of consumers. In addition, most coupon redemption is done by consumers who already use the product, therefore limiting the use of coupons to attract new customers.

Public Relations

The final element in the promotional mix that we discuss is public relations. Quite often, public relations gets confused with other promotional mix elements. Public relations is often mistaken for publicity. This is an easy mistake to make because the goals of public relations and publicity are to provide communication that will enhance the image of the sports entity (athlete, team, or league). Before we make a distinction between public relations and publicity, let us define public relations. **Public relations** is the element of the promotional mix that identifies, establishes, and maintains mutually beneficial relationships between the sports organizations and the various publics on which its success or failure depends.

Within the definition of public relations, reference is made to the "various publics" with which the sports organization interacts. Brooks divides these publics into the external publics, which are outside the immediate control of sports marketers, and the internal publics, which are more directly controlled by sports marketers. The external publics include the community (e.g., city and state officials, community members, corporations), sanctioning bodies (e.g., NCAA), intermediary publics (e.g., sports marketing agencies), and competition (e.g., other sports or entertainment choices). The internal publics, such as volunteers, employees, suppliers, athletes, and spectators, are associated with manufacturing, distributing, and consuming the sport itself.

Sports marketers have a variety of public relations tools they can use to communicate with the internal and external publics. The choice of tools depends on the public relations objective, the targeted audience, and how public relations is being integrated into the overall promotional plan. These tools and techniques include generating publicity (news releases or press conferences), participating in community events, producing written materials (annual report or press guides), and even lobbying (personal selling necessary for stadium location decisions).

One of the most important and widely used public relations tools is publicity. Publicity is the generation of news in the broadcast or print media about a sports product. The news about a sports product is most commonly disseminated to the various sports publics through news releases and press conferences. Although public relations efforts are managed by the sports organization, publicity can sometimes come from external sources. As such, publicity might not always enhance the image of the sports product. Because publicity is often outside the control of the sports organization, it is seen as a highly credible source of communication. Information that is coming from "unbiased" sources, such as magazines, newspaper articles, or the televised news, is perceived to be more trustworthy.

In addition to publicity, another powerful public relations tool used to enhance the sports organization's image is **community involvement.** A study was conducted to determine what, if anything, professional sports organizations are doing in the area of community relations. The survey specifically examined the NBA, NHL, NFL, and MLB to determine how they are involved in community relations and how important community relations is to their overall marketing program. All the responding teams indicated they were involved in some sort of community programs, with the most common form of community involvement being (1) sponsoring public programs (e.g., food and toy drives, medical programs and services, auctions, and other fund raisers); (2) requiring time commitment from all of the sports organizations' employees; (3) partially funding programs; and (4) providing personnel at no charge. Interestingly, the study found no differences among the importance of community relations by type of league. In other words, the NBA, NHL, NFL, and MLB are all equally involved in community relations.[31]

Several examples of the community involvement and outreach component of public relations are shown with the Nashville Predators, Philadelphia Eagles, and Pittsburgh Pirates. The Predators players took part in Predators Community Day, a "day of service where nearly every member of the team made an appearance in Middle Tennessee" and interacted with fans at locations including the airport, Supercuts, and Hardee's. The idea was to expand on the normal team participation events by making it a day-long experience."

The Philadelphia Eagles reimburses its employees living in the Philadelphia region and New Jersey who purchase wind energy, making it the first organization to pick up this type of cost for employees. The Eagles presented their Go Green program, which was launched in 2003, during the NFL Business Summit in 2007, as other NFL team representatives shared best practices in the areas of business, marketing, and community relations. "We hope to serve as an example for NFL teams and the corporate sector," said Eagles owner Christina Lurie. "The topic of greening in sports is especially important in cities like Philadelphia with professional teams and sports arenas. Game days have a huge environmental impact considering traffic, trash, energy and material consumption, and water use. They are also opportunities for education and awareness."[32]

The Pittsburgh Pirates continued their community-minded tradition of donating half the ticket sales from a handful of games to such programs as the Boys & Girls Clubs, the United Way of Manatee County, the Manatee Education Foundation, and Wakeland Elementary School, which is located across the street from the Pirate City training complex. Additionally, the organization held a PirateFest street celebration, staged before the game against the Minnesota Twins. The festival featured numerous family activities and free player autographs. Taking another step to cement the bond between team and city, the Pirates increased their charitable efforts. Pitchers Matt Capps and Josh Sharpless and the Pirate Parrot mascot visited children in the pediatric unit of Manatee Memorial Hospital.

The Pirates also held a three-day silent auction inside McKechnie Field that raised almost $8,000 for the Foundation for Dreams Inc., which provides fun, educational, and recreational experiences at Dream Oaks Camp for children with physical and developmental disabilities and serious illnesses. A Sidney Crosby Pittsburgh Penguins hockey jersey drew the top bid of $1,500.

"We want to make sure we're always giving back to the community, since the city of Bradenton and Manatee County have been so generous to us," said Trevor Gooby, the Pirates' director of Florida operations. "As part of our efforts, we try to help a lot of (charitable) groups in Manatee County throughout the course of the year that need items for a silent auction or a golf tournament."[33]

Although community involvement benefits any number of stakeholders in the organization, it is typically more than philanthropy alone. As suggested in the accompanying article, sports entities are reaping the rewards of their good will.

No Charity, No Glory: Teams, Leagues Embrace New Social Consciousness

Why would a team or league care whether the community at large considers it a good citizen? Try ticket sales, revenue, and advertising, which are what drive these organizations.

As the 2004 Cone Corporate Citizenship Study reported, 86 percent of Americans say they are likely to switch from one brand to another of comparable price and quality if that brand is associated with a charitable cause. Seventy-nine percent said they are more likely to buy a product that supports a nonprofit.

Even if those numbers were lower, doesn't that alone make social responsibility a good business decision?

There is another reason: It's the right thing to do. Though the cynic doesn't want to admit it, the truth is, most corporate CEOs and companies want to do the right thing.

Having worked with major league Baseball, the NBA, NFL, NHL, and major league Soccer, I can testify that the people running their community relations departments also care. They care about the charities they support, and they care about the businesses they are part of.

Two of the leagues I worked closest with, MLB and NBA, have been smart enough to make sure community relations is managed from within their commissioner's inner circle. Jacqueline Parkes and Tom Brasuell at MLB report to Tim Brosnan, executive vice president and a key member of Commissioner Bud Selig's inner circle. And at the NBA, Kathy Behrens works closely with Commissioner David Stern to maximize the community relations programs she administers.

These people have a seat at the table because:

- They are very competent.
- They understand how important their work is to the organization's bottom line and have made their case with their commissioners and league leadership.

Thankfully, the commissioners and leagues have listened.

In the course of the work I've done with leagues and teams, I've found there are eight characteristics of those who "got it" versus those who did not. Those who got it:

1. **Incorporated their community relations strategy into their overall business plan.** These initiatives were not one-time promotions or done just because they needed to be seen. They were an integral part of the team or league's overall strategy to meet its goals.
2. **Recognized the strategic importance of philanthropy in their business and put good people in charge of it in their organization.** The days of passing the job off to someone who had been with the team or league for 40 years—yet still needed an office and thus was farmed out to do community relations—are over.
3. **Made their community relations people part of the leadership of the league or team, and often had them report to someone with clout.** For example, the commissioner/president or, at the very least, the senior vice president.
4. **Partnered with charities and other organizations that recognized that the teams and leagues were in the business to make money, not to do charitable work.** This was the hardest one for people who work for charities to grasp.

    At Boys & Girls Clubs, we were successful in our relationships with corporations because we acknowledged and communicated that we understood the business of our partners was not charity. Of course, we also realized that if the business did better, we could then ask for more money.
5. **Chose their charity partners carefully.** The most successful teams and leagues understood that their partners were sub-brands of themselves. What they did and how they were perceived in the community rubbed off on them. And thus they were careful about which charities they chose to work with.

(Continued)

(Continued)

6. **Participated in the process of identifying players to support the team's or league's charitable strategy.** Some leagues have rules about what players are required to do, but the successful teams and leagues work with their players to show them why (beyond their contractual obligations) supporting a cause is important to the success of the team or league, and good for them.

7. **Made sure their leadership was actively involved in community initiatives.** Simply putting your name on some letterhead doesn't mean you're involved, and fans in any town or city can see right through that.

It's when you see the team president not just wielding the hammer for a photo-op, but staying all day to build the house at the Habitat for Humanity site.

8. **Were creative, were always open to new ideas, and were willing to take risks to connect their business goals with philanthropy, giving their fans the enhanced customer experience of seeing the team they love support the causes they care about.** The good news is that now sports teams and leagues, whose primary concern is getting fans in the facilities/fields, are seeing the positive effects (including increased customer loyalty, positive PR, and finding a new audience to market to) that come with doing the right thing. Fans, players, corporate sponsors, charities, and all of the rest of us are also feeling it.

There's no glory without charity.

Source: Kurt Aschermann, "No Charity, No Glory: Teams, Leagues Embrace New Social Consciousness," *Sports Business Journal*, October 16, 2006, p. 30, http://www.sportsbusinessjournal.com/index.cfm?fuseaction= search.show_article&articleId=52285&keyword=community%20relations.

Summary

Chapter 10 focuses on gaining a better understanding of the various promotional mix elements. Advertising is one of the most visible and critical promotional mix elements. Although most of us associate advertising with developing creative slogans and jingles, there is a systematic process for designing effective advertisements. Developing an advertising campaign consists of a series of five interrelated steps, which include formulating objectives, designing an ad budget, making creative decisions, choosing a media strategy, and evaluating the advertisement.

Advertising objectives and budgeting techniques are similar to those discussed in Chapter 9 for the broader promotion planning process. Advertising objectives are sometimes categorized as either direct or indirect. Direct advertising objectives, such as advertising by sports organizations to end users and sales promotion advertising, are designed to stimulate action among consumers of sport. Alternatively, the goal of indirect objectives is to make consumers aware, enhance the image of the sport, or provide information to consumers. After objectives have been determined, budgets for the advertising campaign are considered. Budget techniques, such as competitive parity, objective and task, arbitrary allocation, and percentage of sales, are commonly used by advertisers.

Once the objectives and budget have been established, the creative process is considered. The creative process identifies the ideas and the concept of the advertisement. To develop the concept for the advertisement, benefits of the sports product must be identified; ad appeals (e.g., health, emotional, fear, sex, and pleasure) are designed; and advertising execution decisions (e. g., comparative advertisements, slice of life, and scientific) are made. After creative decisions are crafted, the next phase of the advertising campaign is to design media strategy. Media strategy includes decisions about what medium (e.g., radio, television, and Internet) will be most effective and how to best schedule the chosen media.

Another communications tool that is part of the promotional mix is personal selling. Personal selling is unique in that person-to-person communication is required rather than mass communication. In other words, a salesperson must deliver the message face to face to the intended target audience rather than through some nonpersonal medium (e.g., a magazine). Although there are many advantages to personal selling, perhaps none is greater than the ability to use personal selling to develop long-term relationships with customers.

In today's competitive sports marketing environment, a number of strategies have been developed to maximize personal selling effectiveness. One process, designed by Miller and Heiman, is called the strategic selling process and consists of six elements. The elements, which must be considered for successful selling, include buying influences, red flags, response modes, win-results, the sales funnel, and the ideal customer profile.

Sales promotions are another element in the promotional mix that are designed primarily to stimulate consumer demand for products. One of the most widely used forms of sales promotion in sports marketing includes premiums, or items that are given away with the core product being purchased. In addition, contests and sweepstakes, free samples, point-of-purchase displays, and coupons are forms of sales promotion that often are integrated into the broader promotional mix.

A final promotional mix element considered in Chapter 10 is public, or community, relations. Public relations is the element of the promotional mix that identifies, establishes, and maintains mutually beneficial relationships between the sports organization and the various publics on which its success or failure depends. These publics include the community, sanctioning bodies, intermediary publics, and competition. Other publics include employees, suppliers, participants, and spectators. The tools with which messages are communicated to the various publics include generating publicity, participating in community events, producing written materials such as annual reports and press releases, and lobbying.

Key Terms

- advertising, p. 286
- advertising appeals, p. 289
- advertising budgeting, p. 289
- advertising execution, p. 292
- advertising objectives, p. 287
- attractiveness, p. 296
- buying influences, p. 310
- coach's role, p. 310
- community involvement, p. 318
- comparative advertisements, p. 293
- continuous schedule, p. 307
- coupons, p. 317
- creative brief, p. 289
- creative decisions, p. 289
- creative process, p. 289
- credibility, p. 295
- direct objectives, p. 287
- economic buying role, p. 310
- emotional appeals, p. 290
- even keel mode, p. 311
- expertise, p. 295
- fear appeals, p. 291
- flighting schedule, p. 307
- frequency, p. 307
- growth mode, p. 311
- health appeals, p. 289
- ideal customer, p. 312
- indirect objectives, p. 288
- lifestyle advertisements, p. 294
- media scheduling, p. 307
- media strategy, p. 299
- one-sided versus two-sided, p. 292
- overconfident mode, p. 311
- personal selling, p. 308
- pleasure or fun appeals, p. 292
- P-O-P displays, p. 317
- premiums, p. 314
- promotional mix elements, p. 285
- public relations, p. 317
- pulsing schedule, p. 307
- reach, p. 306
- relationship marketing, p. 308
- response modes, p. 311
- roles, p. 310
- sales funnel, p. 312
- sales promotions, p. 312
- sampling, p. 316
- scientific advertisements, p. 294
- sex appeals, p. 291
- slice-of-life advertisements, p. 294
- stadium signage, p. 300
- strategic selling, p. 310
- sweepstakes and contests, p. 314
- technical buying role, p. 310
- testimonials, p. 294
- trouble mode, p. 311
- trustworthiness, p. 296
- user buying role, p. 310
- win-results, p. 312

Review Questions

1. What are the major steps in developing an advertising campaign?
2. Explain direct advertising objectives versus indirect advertising objectives.
3. Describe the creative decision process. What are the three outcomes of the creative process?
4. Discuss, in detail, the major advertising appeals used by sports marketers. Provide at least one example of each type of advertising appeal.
5. What are the executional formats commonly used in sports marketing advertising?
6. Comment on the advantages and disadvantages of using athlete endorsers in advertising.
7. What two decisions do advertisers make in developing a media strategy? What are the four basic media scheduling alternatives? Provide an example of each type of media scheduling.
8. Discuss the strengths and weaknesses of the alternative forms of advertising available to sports marketers.
9. When is personal selling used by sports marketers? Describe, in detail, the steps in the strategic selling process.
10. Describe the various forms of sales promotion available to sports marketers.

Exercises

1. Design a creative advertising strategy to increase participation in Little League Baseball.
2. Design a survey instrument to assess the source credibility of 10 professional athletes (of your choice) and administer the survey to 10 individuals. Which athletes have the highest levels of credibility, and why?
3. Attend a professional or collegiate sporting event and describe all the forms of advertising you observe. Which forms of advertising do you feel are particularly effective, and why?
4. Visit a sporting goods retailer and describe all the sales promotion tools that you observe. Which forms of sales promotion do you believe are particularly effective, and why?
5. Interview the director or manager of ticket sales for a professional organization or collegiate sports program to determine their sales process. How closely does their sales process follow the strategic selling process outlined in this chapter?
6. Interview the marketing department (or director of community/public relations) from a professional organization or collegiate sports program to determine the extent of their community or public relations efforts. How do sports organizations decide in which community events or activities to participate?

Internet Exercises

1. Using the Internet, find two examples of advertisements for sports products that use indirect objectives and two examples of advertisements that use direct objectives.
2. Find 10 advertisements on the Internet for sports products and describe the executional format for each advertisement. Which type of execution format is most commonly used for Internet advertising?

Endnotes

1. See, for example, Joel Evans and Barry Berman, *Marketing,* 6th ed. (New York: Macmillan, 1994), 610.
2. "U.S. Health Club Membership Reaches 42.7 Million in 2006," International Health, Racquet and Sportsclub Association, April 25, 2007, http://cms.ihrsa. org/IHRSA/viewPage.cfm?pageId=3367.
3. William A. Sutton, Mark A. McDonald, George R. Milne, and John Cimperman, "Creating and Fostering Fan Identification in Professional Sports," *Sport Marketing Quarterly,* vol. 6, no. 1 (1997), 15–22.
4. Jon Saraceno, "Interest in LPGA Is Going Below Par," *USA Today,* March 23, 2007, C2.
5. Kevin Seifert, "Enough Is Enough," *Minneapolis Star Tribune,* April 11, 2007, 3C.
6. Rachel Blount, "Selling Sex and Sports Isn't Working," *Minneapolis Star Tribune,* April 16, 2007.
7. Samuel Abt, "A Sport Without Spectators' Faith," *The International Herald Tribune,* September 22, 2007, p. 2.
8. Christian Red, Teri Thompson, and Michael O'Keeffe, "Feds Unleash a Bonds Blast: Indictment Hits HR King for Lying, Obstruction," *New York Daily News,* November 16, 2007, p. 90.
9. Viv Bernstein, "No More Cutting Corners as NASCAR Seeks a Clean Start," *The New York Times,* February 18, 2007, p. 1.
10. Seifert, Kevin, "Enough is Enough," *Minneapolis Star Tribune,* April 11, 2007, Sport 3C.
11. Terry Lelton, "The Post-Mike Millennium—Gatorade Advertising, *Post*-Michael Jordan," *Brandweek* (January 3, 2000).
12. Rich Thomaselli, "$192 Million: Nike Bets Big on Range of Endorsers," *Advertising Age* (January 5, 2004), 8.
13. Mark Hyman, "Dead Men Don't Screw Up Ad Campaigns," *Business Week* (March 10, 1997), 115.
14. "Stadium Signage," *Sports Business Journal,* http://www.sportsbusinessjournal.com/index.cfm?fuseaction=page.feature&featureId=43.
15. Jay Gladden, "The Ever Expanding Impact of Technology on Sport Marketing, Part II," *Sport Marketing Quarterly,* vol. 5, no. 4 (1996), 9–10.
16. Douglas M. Turco, "The Effects of Courtside Advertising on Product Recognition and Attitude Change," *Sports Marketing Quarterly,* vol. 5, no. 4 (1996), 11–15.
17. Wayne Friedman, "Intermedia Measures Product Placements; Study Shows No Correlation Between Ratings, Effectiveness," *Television Week* (December 15, 2003), 4.
18. Marla Matzer Rose, "Firms Gauge Product Placements," *The Hollywood Reporter* (January 20, 2004).
19. George Belch and Michael Belch, *Advertising and Promotion: An Integrated Marketing Communications Perspective,* 4th ed. (New York: Irwin, McGraw-Hill, 1998), 431–434.
20. Joe Layden, "Human Billboards," *Mark McCormack's Guide to Sports Marketing,* International Sports Marketing Group (1996), 129–136.
21. Terry Lefton, "Will In-Game Advertising Catch Fire?" *Sports Business Journal,* January 15, 2007, p. 19.
22. Masha Geller, "Reaching Young Sports Fans Online," http://www.mediapost.com/dtls_dsp_news.cfm?newsID=198732 (March 13, 2003).

23. Rachel Johns, "Sports Promotion & The Internet," *Cyber-Journal of Sport Marketing,* www.cad.gu.edu.au/market/cv . . . urnal_of_sport_ marketing/htm.

24. Fred Beasley, Matthew Shank, and Rebecca Ball, "Do Super Bowl Viewers Watch the Commercials?" *Sport Marketing Quarterly,* vol. 7, no. 3 (1998), 33–40.

25. Philip Kotler and Gary Armstrong, *Marketing: An Introduction,* 4th ed. (Upper Saddle River, NJ: Prentice Hall, 1997).

26. Sean Brenner, "Pursuing Relationships in Professional Sport," *Sport Marketing Quarterly,* vol. 6, no. 2 (1997), 33–34.

27. Robert Miller and Stephen Heiman, *Strategic Selling* (New York: Warner Books, 1985).

28. Royals' Fans Taking Advantage of Krispy Kreme Promotion," sportsbusinessnews.com (June 23, 2003).

29. Ed Willes, "A Legacy of Slapstick and Slap Shots," *New York Times* (November 30, 1997), 33.

30. "NBA Pick Your Play Sweepstakes," http://www.nba.com/webAction?actionId=surveyInitialize&target=/analysis/nba_start_of_the_season.jsp&surveyId=1316.

31. Denise O'Connell, "Community Relations in Professional Sports Organizations," unpublished master's thesis, The Ohio State University, Columbus, Ohio.

32. "Philadelphia Eagles to Reimburse Employees for Purchasing Wind Energy; During 2007 NFL Business Summit, Eagles Owner Christina Lurie Hopes to Send a Message," *PR Newswire US,* April 11, 2007.

33. Mike Henry, "Pirates Increase Charitable Work: Team Tries to Give Back to Its Spring Home of 38 Years," *The Bradenton Herald,* March 29, 2007.

CHAPTER
11 || SPONSORSHIP PROGRAMS

After completing this chapter, you should be able to:

■ Comment on the growing importance of sports sponsorships as a promotion mix element.

■ Design a sponsorship program.

■ Understand the major sponsorship objectives.

■ Provide examples of the various costs of sponsorship.

■ Identify the levels of the sports event pyramid.

■ Evaluate the effectiveness of sponsorship programs.

GROWTH OF SPONSORSHIP

The opening scenario is just one example of Ford's using sponsorship to help achieve its marketing objectives. A wide variety of organizations are realizing that sports sponsorships are a valuable way to reach new markets and retain an existing customer base. Sponsorships can increase sales, change attitudes, heighten awareness, and build and maintain relationships with consumers. It is no wonder that sponsorships became the promotional tool of choice for sport marketers and continue to grow in importance. Before we turn to the growth of sponsorship as a promotional tool, let us define sponsorship.

In Chapter 9, sponsorships were described as one of the elements in the promotional mix. More specifically, **sponsorship** was defined as investing in a sports entity (athlete, league, team, or event) to support overall organizational objectives, marketing goals, and promotional strategies. The sponsorship investment may come in the form of monetary support and trade. For example, nonrevenue sports have been the biggest winners in the University of Kansas Athletics Department's eight-year, $26.67-million sponsorship deal with adidas.[1] Adidas is sponsoring the university's athletics program to support their marketing objective of increasing awareness of their brand and to associate with a winning NCAA program. Understanding how sponsorship can help achieve marketing goals and organizational objectives is discussed when we look at the construction of a sponsorship plan or program. For now, let us turn our attention to the dramatic growth of sponsorship as a promotional tool.

In our brief discussion of sponsorship, we have alluded to the "dramatic growth" of sponsorship, but just how quickly is sponsorship growing? Review the following facts and figures regarding sponsorship activities:

• Spending on sponsorship was projected to reach $14.93 billion in 2007, a rise of 11.7 percent from 2006, according to sponsorship-research company IEG. In contrast, IEG projected advertising growth in 2007 of just 2.4 percent.

Ford Looks at Sports Sponsorship as a New Way to Connect with the Consumers

Sports sponsorships, such as the ones Ford Motor Company has within NASCAR, are growing in popularity as an effective way to reach consumers. "If you look at the fragmentation in media today—iPods, the Internet, etc.—traditional advertising is becoming less relevant," says Dan O'Toole, director of new products for Nielsen Ventures, a unit of VNU Media Measurement and Information. "That's not to say that it's less effective or that it can't grow sales, but it's becoming less relevant to the average household because they now get a lot of their media from additional sources. Sports sponsorship can start to fill that gap. It's a way to connect with users that general market media cannot hope to attain."

While there is currently no way to quantify the relationship between NASCAR and car sales, says Dan Geist, Fusion marketing manager, Ford is recognizing benefits.

"Our Fusion brand awareness continues to grow," he says. "From that standpoint, you have to attribute it to not only traditional advertising, but increased awareness from venues like NASCAR."

Because a growing number of companies need more concrete ways to measure the return on their investments, AC Nielsen and Nielsen Sports recently developed FANLinks, a service that combines research on consumers' interests in sports with their purchasing actions.

"What FANLinks proposes to do is track how people align to sponsorships and how that affects changes in sales," says O'Toole. "It's really amazing how much sales can grow for a brand that aligns itself with NASCAR. There have been a lot of studies that show that you can't get any better brand recall than NASCAR. It's everywhere. It's done well, and it's done efficiently."

Though FANLinks does not measure car sales, it has unearthed valuable information for other companies such as Unilever, also a NASCAR sponsor. Among a variety of products, Unilever makes Ragu spaghetti sauce.

"What we found is that one out of every 10 race car fans bought Ragu," O'Toole says. "After Unilever became a sponsor of NASCAR, that figure jumped to two out of 10.

"That's an amazing story. It says you're reaching out to a group of consumers who never would've thought about buying in the future, and now suddenly they're changing their purchasing habits. They're excited about NASCAR, and they see this car racing around the track with 'Ragu' all over it, and they say, 'Hey, let's have pasta tonight.' "

Geist believes Ford is on the right track.

"We're really trying to further nameplate awareness," he says. "And NASCAR is the best way for us to get our name out in front of 75 million NASCAR fans each week."

Source: Ford Motor News, December 13, 2006, http://www.prdomain.com/companies/F/FordMotor/newsreleases/2006121438051.htm.

- In 2006, corporations spent an estimated $458 million to sponsor college sports in the United States, according to IEG. Spending was expected to increase to $515 million in 2007.
- North American companies were expected to spend almost $15 billion on sponsorships in 2007, 66 percent of it on sports, according to IEG.
- Sponsorship spending in motor sports was projected to rise 11 percent in 2007 to $3.2 billion, with "the lion's share" going to NASCAR, according to IEG.
- The 2006 Winter Olympics in Turin, Italy generated $725 million in sponsorship revenue, significantly more than the initial projection of $450 million and more than any previous Winter Olympics except the 2002 Games in Salt Lake City, which raised about $840 million (U.S.) in sponsorship.
- Title sponsorships on F1 cars go for about US$29M.
- The International Cricket Council (ICC) has increased the asking price for global cricket sponsorships from $25–$30 million per sponsor now to $60–$70 million per sponsor for the eight years between 2007 and 2015.

Not unlike other forms of promotion, sponsorship marketing is also reaching its saturation point in the marketplace (see Table 11.1 for the official sponsors of NASCAR). Consumers are paying less attention to sports sponsorships as they become more the rule than the exception. Sponsorship clutter is causing businesses to design more systematic sponsorship programs that stand out in the sea of sponsorships. In addition, businesses are fighting the clutter of sponsoring mainstream sports by exploring new sponsorship opportunities

TABLE 11.1   Official Sponsors of NASCAR

Allstate (Official Insurance)

AMD (Official Microprocessor of NASCAR/ The Official Semiconductor Technology of NASCAR)

America Online (Official Internet Service Provider/Instant Messenger/E-Mail)

APlus (Official Convenience Store)

Bank of America (Official Bank, Checking, Savings, Credit/Debit, Mutual Funds and Security Brokerage)

Best Western (Official Hotel)

Budweiser (Official Beer)

Callaway Golf (Official Golf Ball)

Checkers/Rally's (Official Drive-Thru and Official Burger)

Chevrolet (Monte Carlo) (Official Pace Car, Official Passenger Car)

Coca-Cola (Official Non-Alcoholic Beverage of NASCAR)

Combos (Masterfoods) (Official Cheese-Filled)

Craftsman Tools (Official Tools)

Dasani (Official Water)

Daytona USA (Official Attraction)

Diageo (Official Wine)

DirecTV (Official Partner of NASCAR)

Dodge Charger (Official Passenger Car)

Domino's Pizza (Official Pizza Company)

DuPont Performance Coatings (Official Finish)

Duracell (Official Alkaline Battery)

Eastman Kodak (Official Imaging Partner)

Enterprise Rent-A-Car (Official Rent-A-Car Company)

Featherlite—Vantare (Official Trailers and Luxury Coaches)

Ford Trucks (Official Truck)

Freightliner (Official Hauler)

Gillette (Official Shaving Product)

Goodyear (Exclusive Tire Supplier)

Housby (Semitractor Distributor)

Ingersoll-Rand Company (Official Security Partner)

Kellogg's (Official Breakfast Food/Cereal)

M&M'S (Masterfoods) (Official Chocolate of NASCAR)

Minute Maid (Official Juice)

NicoDerm (Proud Sponsor of NASCAR)

Office Depot (Official Office Supply/Products Provider)

Oral B (Official Oral Care Product)

(Continued)

(Continued)

Old Spice (Official Antiperspirant and Deodorant)
Pedigree (Masterfoods) (NASCAR Fans' Best Friend)
POWERade (Official Sports Beverage)
Sirius (Official Satellite Radio Partner of NASCAR)
Sony (Official Consumer Electronics)
Sprint NEXTEL (Official Series Sponsor)
Sunoco (Official Fuel)
The Home Depot (Official Home Improvement Warehouse)
Tissot (Official Timekeeper and Official Watch of NASCAR)
Top-Flite (Official Golf Clubs)
Toyota (Official Partner/Manufacturer)
Tylenol (Official Pain Reliever of NASCAR)
UPS (Official Delivery Service)
USG (Official Partner of NASCAR)
Visa (Official Card)

(e.g., X-Games, women's sports, and Paralympics) and by becoming more creative with existing sponsorship opportunities.

One example of a creative sponsorship approach trying to break through the clutter in a traditional sports medium comes from the world of insurance, as shown in the accompanying article.

In essence, a sports sponsorship program is just another promotion mix element to be considered along with advertising, personal selling, sales promotions, and public

---

Allstate Finds Unique Way to Advertise at Events

Allstate is all about protection, hence the company's proclamation that those who buy insurance from them are in good hands. College football fans have seen the message a lot, thanks to one of Allstate's sponsorship programs.

The company's name and "Good Hands" logo is printed on the field-goal nets at more than 50 schools throughout the country including Georgia Tech, Virginia Tech, Florida State, Wake Forest, and Miami. So the Allstate commercials featuring actor Dennis Haysbert aren't the only advertising the company gets during games.

The nets make for good promotion at the stadiums and on TV since the company's name and logo are clearly seen when a ball is kicked.

"This gave us a nice opportunity to do something in-stadium and really touch the fans at games, but in reality what it did also was give us more broadcast presence at the same time because they show up fabulously from a broadcast prospective," said Tim Fess, project manager for Allstate sponsorship marketing.

Having the nets at so many stadiums makes good business sense for Allstate because the college football market is one of the company's key targets.

"The young adult males that are leaving college and then entering the job market, those are the ones making key lifetime decisions in terms of auto purchases and either renter's insurance or home insurance," Fess said.

Companies are continuously trying to figure out innovative ways to advertise at sporting venues. The field-goal nets have allowed Allstate to score a touchdown in that regard, said Jeff Marks, managing director of Sports Business Ventures.

The Los Angeles-based company is an advisory and investment firm that consults with businesses on what will make money in sports.

"When you're about to go and make an extra point or a field goal, everyone's eyes look at the goal post and look at Allstate, so it's a very unique way of reaching your consumer in the mass media area for brand recognition," Marks said.

Source: Damon Lawrence, *Columbus Ledger-Enquirer,* December 24, 2006.

DLP Products Races into Year Two of Its NASCAR Sponsorship

Over the course of the first sponsorship year, TI saw consumer awareness more than double for DLP HDTV technology among NASCAR fans that attended the races, according to Performance Research, a leading sponsorship measurement research firm. At the end of the 2006 racing season, measurements show that race attendees were almost three times more likely to purchase a DLP HDTV as compared to the beginning of the 2006 racing season. Overall on-air TV network brand exposure for DLP technology was in the top 10 of all competing NASCAR sponsored cars during the entire 2006 season, which placed DLP Products' first-year team in the same league as the top performing veteran sponsored racing teams such as Budweiser and The Home Depot.

"Year one was strong for DLP both on and off the track," said Doug Darrow, brand and marketing manager, DLP Products. "Performance of our #96 DLP HDTV Chevrolet and awareness of the DLP HDTV brand increased with each race. NASCAR fans came to learn that with DLP HDTV they can experience the ultimate in high-definition racing."

Source: PR Newswire US, February 15, 2007.

---

relations. One difference, however, between sponsorship and the other promotion mix elements is that sports marketing relies heavily on developing successful sponsorship programs. In fact, sponsorship programs are so prevalent in sports marketing that the field is sometimes defined in these terms. Since sponsorship is so critical, let's better understand how to develop the most effective sponsorship program.

DESIGNING A SPORTS SPONSORSHIP PROGRAM

Sports sponsorship programs come in all shapes and sizes. Following are just a few examples:

- Denver Public Schools (DPS) is opening its high school sports venues to advertising in a "move expected to generate $400,000 next year and potentially a lot more revenue later," according to James Paton of the *Rocky Mountain News*. The DPS Foundation, which is leading the effort, has "talked with a couple of airlines and a restaurant chain about sponsorships" and is looking at media companies and retailers, "maybe an electronics outfit, as possible partners."
- Adidas begins the first year of its 11-year, $400 million partnership as the official uniform and apparel supplier of the NBA with 15 team sponsorship deals, some of which will include a new "store-within-a-store" concept that will sell both NBA-licensed merchandise and other company apparel.
- Adidas has extended its sponsorship agreement with FIFA for the 2010 and 2014 World Cup finals in a deal worth $351 million.
- Jewel-Osco has signed on as the Bears' official grocery store, in a one-year (plus a one-year option) high-six-figure deal. The grocer, which has 185 stores in the Chicagoland area, gets LED and scoreboard signage at Soldier Field, along with title sponsorship of the Bears' annual winter coat drive, which last year collected more than 18,000 coats. Jewel-Osco will also be the associate sponsor of Bears Family Night and the Bears Backyard Tailgate. The grocery chain will also sell licensed Bears apparel in its stores, beginning around training camp in July. Bears Senior Director of Sales and Marketing Chris Hibbs said pass-through rights for the grocer will be "on a case-by-case basis." This marks the team's latest retail sponsor, a category that can be difficult.

- McDonald's has signed a five-year, $2.5M deal to sponsor Ohio State Univ. (OSU) athletics, according to Barnet Wolf of the *Columbus Dispatch*. The McDonald's brand will replace Wendy's on the scoreboards and other areas in Ohio Stadium and the Value City Arena at the Jerome Schottenstein Center. Also, McDonald's restaurants across central Ohio will sell tickets to OSU's spring football game, marking the first time tickets will be available off campus.

  The PGA Tour has signed Tiffany & Co. to a multiyear sponsorship deal. The company will serve as the official awards and gift provider for the PGA Tour and Champions Tour. Tiffany will also "design and craft the FedEx Cup Trophy."

  The Vancouver Organizing Committee for the 2010 Olympic and Paralympic Winter Games (VANOC) named TransCanada (natural gas) as an official supplier for the Games. Supplier agreements are worth between $3 million and $15 million in cash or in-kind service to the Games organizers, and the TransCanada agreement locks up an association with Canadian Olympic teams for three Games—the 2008 Beijing Olympics, 2010 in Vancouver, and 2012 in London.

  U.S. gold medal–winning skier Ted Ligety has signed a two-year sponsorship deal to compete with Rossignol skis, boots, bindings, and poles.

What do each of these sponsorship examples have in common? First, they were developed as part of an integrated marketing communications approach in which sponsorship is but one element of the promotion mix. In addition, each of the sponsors has carefully chosen the best sponsorship opportunity (with individual athletes, teams, conferences, events, and/or leagues) to meet organizational objectives and marketing goals.

To carefully plan sponsorship programs, a systematic process is being used by an increasing number of organizations. The process for designing a sports sponsorship program is presented in Figure 11.1. Before explaining the process, it is important to remember that sponsorship involves a marketing exchange. The sponsor benefits by receiving the right to associate with the sports entity (e.g., team or event), and the sports entity benefits from either monetary support or product being supplied by the sponsor. Because the marketing exchange involves two parties, the sponsorship process can be explored from the perspective of the sponsor (e.g., Allstate) or the sports entity (e.g., Sugar Bowl). We look at the process from the viewpoint of the sponsor rather than the entity sponsored.

As shown in the model, decisions regarding the sponsorship program are not made in isolation. Rather, the **sponsorship program** is just one element of the broader promotional strategy. It was suggested earlier that all the elements in the promotional mix must be integrated to have the greatest and most effective promotional impact. However, sponsorship decisions influence much more than just promotion. Sponsorship decisions can affect the entire marketing mix, as the accompanying article shows.

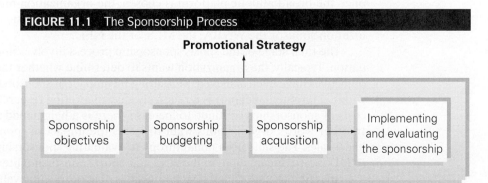

FIGURE 11.1 The Sponsorship Process

Source: Hawkins et al., *Consumer Behavior*, 6th ed. (New York: McGraw-Hill, 1995). Reproduced with permission of the McGraw-Hill Companies.

March to Atlanta: Name of the Game Is Driving Drink Sales

Coke agreed in 2002 to pay an estimated $500 million over 11 years for the right to sponsor the men's basketball tournament and 87 other NCAA college championships, including the Frozen Four hockey tournament and the College World Series. To do that, Atlanta-based Coke has blanketed its hometown with everything from billboards to a giant tournament bracket on the side of the Georgia World Congress Center filled in with faces of fans from each team.

But that's only part of Coke's reach during a 37-day push through Monday's championship game. More than 100 television ads and scores of store-level promotions across the country will combine to put Coke's stamp on one of the biggest events in college sports. In addition to its television ad campaign, the company has tied March Madness to its year-round "MyCokeRewards" frequent drinker program, which has roughly 3.5 million participants, according to Coke's annual report. Fans can turn in points for Final Four–related prizes.

Source: Duane D. Stanford, *The Atlanta Journal-Constitution*, March 30, 2007.

There are two important things to consider before signing a sponsorship agreement: (1) All your organization is getting is the right to be called a sponsor, not a completed sponsorship plan; and (2) you should spend two to three times your sponsorship fee to leverage your relationship as a sponsor—if you do not have the funds to promote, do not buy the sponsorship.

When designing the sponsorship program, the initial decisions are based on sponsorship objectives and budgets. These two elements go hand in hand. Without the money, the most meaningful objectives will never be reached. Alternatively, appropriate objectives must be considered without total regard to cost. If the objectives are sound, senior-level managers will find a way to allocate the necessary monies to sponsorship.

After the objectives and budget have been agreed upon, the specific sports sponsorship opportunity is chosen from the hundreds available. For example, Pepsi receives approximately 500 sponsorship proposals each year, and Pennzoil reports that they receive 200 proposals annually. Others estimate that several corporations receive over 100 sponsorship proposals each week (for an example of proposal guidelines, see Table 11.2). Regardless of the exact number, there are a wealth of sponsorship opportunities available to potential sponsors. Table 11.3 illustrates how the Patriots Showcase Soccer Tournament presents information to potential sponsors.[2]

When choosing from among many sponsorship opportunities, three decisions must be addressed. The first decision is whether to sponsor a local, regional, national, or global event. Second, the organization must choose an athletic platform. For instance, will the organization sponsor an individual athlete, team, league, or stadium? Third, once the broad athletic platform is chosen, the organization must decide on a specific sports entity. For example, if a league is selected as the athletic platform, will the organization sponsor the WNBA, the MLS, or the NFL?

The final stage of the sports sponsorship process involves implementation and evaluation. Typically, the organization wants to determine whether their desired sponsorship objectives have been achieved. Measuring the impact of sponsorship on awareness levels within a targeted audience is a relatively easy marketing research task. However, as the costs of sponsorships continue to increase, there is a heightened sense of accountability. In other words, organizations want to assess the impact of sponsorship on the bottom line—sales. The shift from philanthropy to evaluating sponsorship return on investment (ROI) is also documented in the academic sport sponsorship literature, and new models are emerging to understand the complexities of sponsorship evaluation.[3]

Now that we have a rough idea of how the sponsorship process works, let us explore each stage of the sports sponsorship model in greater detail.

TABLE 11.2   Castrol North America—Sponsorship Criteria Requirements

As you might imagine, we receive a number of requests for a variety of sponsorships from across North America. In order for us to most effectively evaluate each proposal we receive, we have established criteria that will provide us with the pertinent information we need. Including all of the data requested below will improve your chances of a prompt response.

Timeframe:

1. **Submitting a proposal to Castrol North America:** To allow us enough lead-time to line up appropriate resources, your proposal must be submitted at least 6 months prior to the start date of the event/project. We will not consider proposals submitted outside of this timeframe.

2. **Castrol North America Response:** You should expect a reply within 3 months.

What to send and where to send it:

1. **Brief detailed description of sponsorship**

2. **Contract Information**

3. **Fees and Payment Terms/Schedule:** All costs Castrol is expected to pay, including sponsorship fee, Value In Kind, promotional fees, signage, literature, printing costs, creative/production costs, equipment, merchandising, etc.

4. **Direct Onsite Sales Opportunities:** Include a three-year history of Castrol or non-Castrol motor oil product sales as well as projected motor oil product sales over the next three years. If this is a new venue with no previous motor oil related sales, please explain why this is an ideal Do-It-Yourself (DIY) automotive demographic.

5. **Castrol Benefits:** Include items such as TV, radio, and newspaper exposure, Web site visits, complimentary tickets, hospitality, and access to special events at the property and quantity as appropriate.

6. **Product/Category Exclusivity**

7. **Marketing Opportunities:** Onsite and off-site, such as co-sponsor promotional activities, Consumer and Trade promotions available to Castrol, etc.

8. **List of Other Sponsors:** Indicate whether they are potential or committed. Also please indicate historical sponsors and length of association.

9. **Term:** (Annual, two-year, three-year, etc.)

10. **Number of Events per annum**

11. **Attendance:** Annual ticket sales, paid and unpaid, trend history for the last three years, future projections for three years

12. **Demographics:** Include where applicable (i.e., if noticeably different), the following demographics for both attendees *and* the media audience.
    a. age;
    b. gender;
    c. % do it yourself (i.e., change their own oil);
    d. ethnic origin;
    e. income profile; and
    f. any other applicable information

13. **Any Other Pertinent Information**

    Please include as much of this information as possible when sending your proposal to Castrol. Once your proposal is complete, please forward by mail to the address below:

    Sponsorship Department
    Castrol Consumer North America
    1500 Valley Road
    Wayne, NJ, 07470
    USA

We appreciate your interest in Castrol North America as a potential sponsor and look forward to receiving your sponsorship proposal.

Source: www.refresh.castrolusa.com/sponsors/.

TABLE 11.3 Sponsorship Opportunities for the Patriots Showcase Soccer Tournament

About 50 boys and girls select travel teams ranging in age from **under**-14 to **under-19** will compete in Columbia County at the Second Annual 2006 Patriots Showcase Soccer Tournament. Each team will play a minimum of three games during the three days. This will be an event to showcase potential college student athletes to colleges and universities throughout the country. It will also be an **opportunity** to showcase a high level of club soccer to the CSRA. There will be college coaches in attendance from all over the country.

The Marketing Audience

The tournament offers an excellent **opportunity** to capitalize on growing soccer interest. With World Cup 2006 just around the corner and the past results of Women's World Cup '99, men's World Cup '98 and 2002, the 2000 and 2004 Olympics, numerous U.S. National Team and Olympics. The Columbia County portion of the audience makes the tournament an ideal vehicle for product and service marketing just before the Christmas Holiday Season, and for image enhancement with the local community. The tournament is especially well suited for national and regional businesses located or thinking about locating in the CSRA because **sponsorship** demonstrates local support and involvement to participants from this area, but also provides impressions for visitors from other of the sponsor's marketing locations.

The direct audience includes about 2500 boys and girls ranging in age from 6 to **19**; about 250 officials, including coaches, managers, referees and tournament volunteers; and at least 1500 parents, plus siblings and other relatives, friends and fans who attend as spectators. The indirect audience includes readers of tournament publicity in area and community newspapers; soccer coaches and administrators who see the tournament's calendar listings and other promotional material in soccer publications; and parents and others who do not accompany their family's player, but who see the tournament program and other materials both before and after the event

Sponsorship Categories

Principal Name Sponsor

Contribution—$5,000 up

Benefits—

Organization's name on tournament.

- Corporate name will be used in signage, at registration and in printed promotional materials.
- Sponsor may set up its own booth at fields or the tournament headquarters for distribution of promotional materials. Size and location subject to Tournament approval; sponsor to provide booth personnel.
- Full-page advertisement in tournament program; black-and-white camera-ready copy to be provided by sponsor.
- Sponsor may provide promotional materials for inclusion in registration materials distributed to competing teams and players.

Presenting Sponsor

Presenting sponsors will be visibly identified, but not as part of the tournament name.

Contribution—From $2500 up, some or all of which can be offset by suitable contributions-in-kind.

Benefits—

- Sponsor, if it wishes, can select an element of the tournament to sponsor, such as registration, scoreboards, college coach's presentation, or the Saturday night scholarship/Dinner Meeting. Corporate name will be displayed prominently on or with the element as is appropriate.
- Corporate name will be used in signage, at registration and in printed promotional materials.
- Sponsor may set up its own booth at fields or the tournament headquarters for distribution of promotional materials. Size and location subject to Tournament approval; sponsor to provide booth personnel.
- Full-page advertisement in tournament program; black-and-white camera-ready copy to be provided by sponsor.

Sponsor may provide promotional materials for inclusion in registration materials distributed to competing teams and players

Age Group Sponsor

Contribution—$1,000 or $1,500, some or all of which can be offset by suitable contributions-in-kind.

Benefits—

- Sponsor's name will be used to identify one ($1,000) or two ($1,500) age groups, such as U-15 girls or U-**19** boys, in the program, on the trophies, or on other materials concerning the age group.
- Banner to be hung at Patriots Park for Period of One Year
- Random drawing among participants in the relevant age group for any product or service prize the sponsor may care to donate.

(Continued)

(*Continued*)

- Full-page advertisement in tournament program; black-and-white camera-ready copy to be provided by sponsor; ad will be placed adjacent to the schedule for a sponsor age group.
- Sponsor may provide promotional materials for inclusion in registration materials distributed to competing teams and players.

Exclusivity

Principal name and presenting sponsors will be exclusive for their specific product or service category (e.g., grocery, athletic shoe/apparel maker, soccer store, hardware/home center, bank, etc.). This does not apply to age group sponsorships or program advertising.

Program Advertising

The tournament's program book, available to all players and spectators, contains the complete schedule of games, rosters information on all players, directions to all tournament fields and events, the tournament rules, and other useful information.

Full-page advertisements cost $300

Half page advertisements cost $200

Quarter page advertisements cost $100

Business card advertisements cost $50

The advertiser must provide camera-ready black-and-white ad copy. A substantial portion of the revenue from each ad goes to the Columbia County Patriots Club soccer teams that secured the ad. Booster ads from competing teams or their parents are most welcome, and are common at tournaments throughout the country. For more information or to arrange for an ad, contact a Columbia County Patriot soccer player or parent you know, or contact Andrew Hammer at 706–399–4080 or via e-mail to ahyork@aol.com.

Source: http://www.patriotssoccer.org/leagues/2011/graphics/2006%20TournamentSponsorship.doc.

Sponsorship Objectives

The first stage in designing a sponsorship program is to carefully consider the sponsorship objectives. Because sponsorship is just one form of promotion, the **sponsorship objectives** should be linked to the broader promotional planning process and its objectives. The promotional objectives will, in turn, help achieve the marketing goals, which should stem from the objectives of the organization. These important linkages were stated in our definition of sponsorship.

Not unlike advertising objectives, sponsorship objectives can be categorized as either direct or indirect. **Direct sponsorship objectives** have a short-term impact on consumption behavior and focus on increasing sales. **Indirect sponsorship objectives** are those that ultimately lead to the desired goal of enhancing sales. In other words, the sponsor has to generate awareness and create the desired image of the product before consumers purchase the product. The indirect sponsorship objectives include generating awareness, meeting and beating competition, reaching new target markets, building relationships, and improving image.[4]

One of the reasons that sponsoring sporting events has risen in popularity is that sponsorship provides so many benefits to those involved in the partnership. In other words, both the sponsor and the sports entity (event, athlete, or league) gain from this win–win partnership. Let us look at some of the primary objectives of sponsorship from the sponsor's perspective.

Awareness

One of the most basic objectives of any sponsor is to generate **awareness** or raise levels of awareness of its products and services, product lines, or corporate name. Sponsors must understand which level to target (i.e., individual product versus company name) based on the broader promotional or marketing strategy. For a new company or product, sponsorship is an important way to generate widespread awareness in a short period of time.

From the event or sports entity's perspective, having a large corporate sponsor will certainly heighten the awareness of the event. The corporate sponsor will design a promotional program around the event to make consumers aware of the sponsor's relationship with the event. The corporate sponsor will also want to ensure their promotional mix elements are integrated. In other words, advertising, sponsorship of the event, and sales promotion will all work in concert to achieve the desired promotional objectives. However, a study conducted by Hoek, Gendall, Jeffcoat, and Orsman[5] found that sponsorship generated higher levels of awareness than did advertising. In addition, sponsorship led to the association of a wider range of attributes with the brand being promoted than did advertising.

Competition

Another primary objective of sponsorship is to stamp out or meet any competitive threats or **competition**. Many corporate sponsors claim they are not that interested in sponsorship opportunities, but they cannot afford not to do so. In other words, if they do not make the sponsorship investment, their competitors will. Sponsorship is thought of as a preemptive tactic that will reduce competitive threat. For instance, Texaco sponsors virtually every national governing body of U.S. Olympic sports. They promote only a handful of these sports, but their sponsorship of the others effectively keeps other competitors out of any chance of ambushing their Olympic efforts. Another example of competitive threat comes from the fierce rivalry between Pepsi and Coke, including Pepsi's deal with the NFL, snatching that relationship away from Coke, and Coke's turnabout in securing the NCAA, which had been rival Mountain Dew's domain. More recently, Coke's Sprite renewed its long-term deal with the NBA.

In an attempt to gain a competitive edge in the insurance industry, State Farm Insurance signed a three-year deal, at roughly $8 million a year, that would make it major league Baseball's official insurer and garner the title sponsorship to the annual Home Run Derby competition on ESPN—one of the highest-rated sports broadcasts of the summer. While State Farm has long had a presence in women's golf and skating, the MLB deal would continue an aggressive spend in sports for the company, which is trying to grow in the intensely competitive insurance industry.[6]

Unfortunately, a sponsoring company, such as State Farm Insurnacec, can still be harmed by competitors who use ambush marketing tactics. **Ambush marketing** is a planned effort (campaign by an organization) to associate themselves indirectly with an event to gain at least some of the recognition and benefits that are associated with being an official sponsor.[7] One of the earliest examples of ambush marketing at its finest was Nike's 1984 "I Love LA" marketing campaign. Although the company was not an official Olympic sponsor, this campaign inextricably tied Nike to the city and event. Most sports marketers consider this ambush campaign the catalyst for the steady rise in ambush marketing practices.[8]

Today, many examples of ambush marketing exist. However, the Olympic Games seems to be the "sporting event of choice" for ambush marketers. The Atlanta Games are remembered for Nike's aggressive ambush marketing campaign against Reebok, the official Olympic sportswear partner. Nike bought up advertising billboards throughout the city and established "Nike Town" on the edge of the Olympic park. When asked to name brands associated with the Olympics following the games, 22 percent of

Americans named Nike and only 16 percent mentioned Reebok. Consider this 2006 Olympic ambush moment:

> The chief executive of the Vancouver Organizing Committee for the 2010 Winter Olympic Games has used public pressure in order to get Imperial Oil/Esso, a Canadian petroleum company, to modify a marketing campaign which was accused of constituting ambush marketing. Imperial Oil/Esso formulated a "Cheer on Canada/Torino, Italy" campaign which involved a competition with prizes of tickets to attend men's and women's Olympic ice hockey games in Turin. Although the competition did not use any Olympic symbols, by referring to the Olympic Games it created an unauthorized association with the Olympic Games in Turin and with the Canadian Olympic team. Although Imperial Oil/Esso is a sponsor of the national governing body (Hockey Canada) and the national team, it is not a sponsor of either the Olympic Games or the Canadian Olympic team. The company agreed to end the Olympic association in its promotion.[9]

- Do most ambush marketing tactics work for organizations that do not want to pay the cost for official Olympic sponsorship? The answer to this question seems to be an overwhelming yes. Studies have shown that most consumers cannot correctly identify the true Olympic sponsors. Research from the Chartered Institute of Marketing (CIM) revealed that brands that adopted ambush marketing strategies enjoyed more public recognition than the official Olympic sponsors.[10] The study, which questioned 1,000 adults regarding brands associated with the Olympics in an official or nonofficial capacity, found that 33 percent of consumers linked either Adidas or Reebok with the Sydney Games despite the fact that neither were official Olympic partners.
- On the positive side, Coca Cola, an official partner of the Games, achieved the most recognition, with 22 percent of respondents associating the soft drinks brand with the Olympics. However, other sponsors fared less well, with Visa International, Samsung, Panasonic, and IBM all scoring less than 5 percent in terms of public recognition. In the case of Visa, this lack of awareness was put into even more perspective by the fact that its main rival, American Express, scored higher recognition despite not being an official sponsor.
- Because ambush marketing tactics are effective and consumers do not really care (only 20 percent of consumers said that they were angered by corporations engaging in ambush marketing), it appears that there is no end in sight for this highly competitive tactic. However, harsh preventive measures are taking place to protect the investments of the actual sponsors of the Olympic Games. As the accompanying article indicates, the 2012 London Olympic Games are already addressing the issue.

Arguably the most effective means for organizers of sporting events to block out unauthorized advertising is to negotiate deals with stadium owners (which may be, for example, cities, sports clubs, or operating companies), which allow organizers to fully control advertising on the premises. For example, the organizer may demand the stadium to be handed over as a clean site, so that the stadium would have to be cleared of all advertising by unofficial sponsors. The organizer may also require the stadium to be renamed for the time of the event and control access to the stadium grounds, including the airspace above. By cleverly designing the general terms and conditions of ticket sales, organizers can even impose dress codes on the spectators, enabling the exclusion of those wearing shirts or caps which display the logos of nonsponsors.

SPOTLIGHT ON SPORTS MARKETING ETHICS

Protecting Sport Sponsors from Ambush Marketing

While the UK's athletes are battling for medals in Turin, another Olympic tussle is taking place closer to home, in the Westminster corridors of power. But this battle will have a commercial, and not sporting, outcome.

The London Olympics Bill is designed to curb the advertising phenomenon known as ambush marketing before the summer games take place in the capital in 2012. The bill is wending its way through Parliament as the government and the British Olympic Association (BOA) seek to ensure that sponsors get full value for money.

The BOA says the bill is needed to protect the integrity of its sponsorship deals, but the UK advertising industry says the proposed act's strictures are draconian and that business may suffer. It wants proposals on the restriction of certain words surrounding the games amended.

Getting "Connected"

Depending on your standpoint, ambush marketing is either clever and inventive advertising, or a means of cunningly reaping the benefits of a major sporting event—without paying any official sponsorship monies. Dictionaries describe it as a strategy whereby brands attach themselves to major sporting events without paying sponsorship fees, while at the same time creating a sense that they are somehow connected to the tournament.

Previous examples have included campaigns by sportswear maker Nike at both Olympic and World Cup events, and by beer-makers trying to intrude on legitimate sponsor territory by getting branded items into stadiums. In Germany, the venue for this year's football World Cup, firms outside the official 15 FIFA partners and six suppliers are using ploys to associate themselves in the public mind with the event.

Aircraft "Ambassadors"

National airline Lufthansa has put football decals on the nosecones of 40 of its aircraft.

To the casual viewer it may seem the airline is an official sponsor of World Cup 2006, but Emirates is in fact the official airline of the FIFA tournament. "The Lufthansa aircraft with the football nose will act as football's ambassadors inviting all to enjoy their stay here," says Lufthansa, associating itself with the tournament but avoiding any official connection. And electrical retailer MediaMarkt is proclaiming "We Will Be the Champions" (Wir Wollen Den Titel), and that it provides a "Gold" service on prices.

However, if the UK government and British Olympic Association get their way, expressions such as "Gold" could be forbidden for advertisers when the games come to London. The government is aware of the boost the games could give the UK economy and is doing everything to ensure big sponsors will be attracted and not have their rights packages diluted by the ambushers. Hence the current bill, which makes a list of Olympic-related words and images prohibited for use by nonsponsors.

Forbidden Words

Existing legislation already prohibits the use of distinctive "marks" like the Olympic rings, but now words like gold, silver, and bronze could be on the banned list. The proposed new legislation covers goods, packaging, advertising, and other unauthorized uses. The International Olympic Committee (IOC) has an Olympics Partners Programme, which gives big names like Coca-Cola, McDonald's, and Visa exclusive marketing rights.

The London organizing committee estimates up to 40 percent of its operating budget will come from sponsorship, hence the determination to tackle anything that might diminish sponsor revenues.

One tactic used in the past by ambushers—strategically placed billboards near stadiums—has been tackled by the London organizers securing first rights on nearly all major city boards at the time of the games.

British Olympic Association lawyer Sara Friend says: "Ambush marketing should be seen as working against

Proposed Protection
The words Olympic, Olympiad, and Olympian
Olympic rings, Team GB, and British Olympic Association logo
Words London 2012, London's bid logo, and derivatives of London2012.com
The 2012 Games logo and mascots (not designed yet)
Olympic motto "Citius, Altius, Fortius/Faster, Higher, Stronger"
The British Paralympic Association and team logos
Other banned words may soon include games, medals, gold, silver, bronze, 2012, sponsor, summer

(Continued)

(Continued)

the interests of official rights package holders. We acknowledge there has to be a balance between the interest of sponsors and rights holders, and in allowing clever and creative advertising and marketing. But the BOA is not government funded and money for funding comes either through the IOC's partner programs, or our own domestic sponsor programs. Therefore we need to protect the rights that partners receive for backing Team GB. And it is incredibly important to protect the Team GB identity."

She said that at major events run by global bodies like the IOC, FIFA, and cricket's ICC, it was not unreasonable for host nations to put in place "legislative protection." "We have no problems with creative advertising—but well thought-out attempts to ride on the back, and goodwill, of an event can be potentially damaging to sponsorship agreements."

"Too Far"

But Christopher Hackford, legal manager at the Institute of Practitioners in Advertising, says: "Sponsorship should be protected, but we think the existing law in the UK is sufficient to protect sponsors. There are already safeguards covering copyright, trademarks, passing-off, and misleading advertising, as well as the Olympic Symbols Protection Act. The Olympics Bill takes this protection potentially too far."

The IPA has written to all 646 Members of Parliament to advise them of its concern, and says the proposed new law is "too broad and disproportionate." "The position is clearly an unfair limitation of commercial expression," Mr Hackford says. "Such radical and disproportionate legislation does not benefit anyone, it gives unparalleled power to event holders, which pushes up the price of sponsorship and prevents ordinary smaller businesses from benefiting at all from major national events."

Source: Bill Wilson, "Protecting Sport Sponsors from Ambush," *BBC News*, http://news.bbc.co.uk/1/hi/business/4719368.stm.

For example, during a 2006 World Cup game in Germany, some Dutch supporters wearing orange trousers displaying the logo of a beer company that was not an official sponsor were refused entry. The plucky Dutch, having purchased expensive tickets and keen to see their team play, took off their clothes and attended the game in their underwear. Notably, at the next Holland game, the same Dutch brewer also gave out orange boxer shorts. These too displayed the brewer's logo. In a stadium of at least 50,000 spectators, many of whom were wearing orange, one wonders who would even notice the offending logo. Even if some people did, it is difficult to see what damage the official sponsor suffers.[11]

Reaching Target Markets

Reaching new target markets is another primary objective of sponsorship programs. One of the unique features and benefits of sponsorship as a promotional medium is its ability to reach people who are attracted to sports entities because they share a common interest. Therefore, sporting events represent a natural forum for psychographic segmentation of consumers, that is, reaching consumers with similar activities, interests, and opinions (AIOs). Sue Tougas, assistant vice president of corporate communications at Mass Mutual, sums up their worldwide sponsorship of the U.S. Open Tennis event by saying, "Viewership and audience attendance for the U.S. Open continues to be among the largest in professional sports, and the demographics of tennis fit precisely with our target consumer audience."[12] "It really reaches our demographic group," she said of tennis, describing that sector as having household income above $100,000 and being between 34 and 65 years of age. She also cited brand exposure as an important ingredient in agreeing to the new deal.

Lauded as the world's premier big-wave surf event, the 2007 Mavericks Surf Contest presented by Ask.com was earmarked as the season's most anticipated big-wave surf occurrence. "Ask.com is excited to be an integral part of the preeminent big-wave surfing event, and, as a leading search engine, to be the official go-to source for information for all things Mavericks," said Greg Ott, vice president of marketing for Ask.com. A quick search for Mavericks Surf Contest on Ask.com gave fans quick access to webcasts and viewing locations, videos, bios on the surfers, and the history of the event. In addition, using Ask.com and Ask.com Mobile, fans could find Mavericks images, news, maps, walking and driving directions, blogs, and other information.

Starwood Hotels & Resorts and Special Olympics signed a three-year global partnership with Starwood Hotels as the exclusive hotel sponsor of Special Olympics and the 2007 Special Olympics World Summer Games in Shanghai, China. The sponsorship included financial and in-kind support from Starwood. In addition, Starwood broadcast Special Olympics public service announcements on its internal television channel in its hotels. In addition to some 7,000 athletes, the Games drew 40,000 volunteers, 3,500 event officials, and thousands of families, spectators, and journalists from every region of the world. Before the Games, Steven J. Heyer, chief executive officer for Starwood Hotels and an active member of the board of directors of Special Olympics, Inc., said, "This unique global sponsorship will help increase public awareness of the Special Olympics, enhance our corporate social responsibility mission, and further strengthen our brand presence in important travel markets and diverse local communities."[13]

Consider the following examples of how sponsors have attempted to reach new and sometimes difficult-to-capture audiences: The X-Games represent a perfect opportunity to reach Generation Xers, a target market that is "difficult to reach through traditional media." Another target market that has been neglected includes the millions of disabled Americans. With the growth of the Paralympic Games and programs such as Sporting Chance, which provide opportunities for people with disabilities to participate in sports, marketers are now addressing this market. Begun in 1960 as an event "parallel" to the Olympics, the Paralympics have blossomed into a major competition of their own. The Paralympic Games are a multisport, multidisability competition of elite, world-class athletes held approximately two weeks after the regular Olympics in the same host city.

Disabled athletes compete in Paralympic games.

Source: U.S. Paralympics is a division of U.S. Olympic Committee. Copyright © U.S. Paralympics. All rights reserved.

Just consider some of the impressive numbers expected three years from now when the cities of Whistler and Vancouver, Canada, will host the Paralympics, which is expected to bring up to 1,300 athletes and team officials from 40 countries for the 10-day event in March. In all, there will be 56 medal events. About 1,300 media are expected to cover the events, many of which will be televised. More than 1.4 billion people around the world watched the Paralympic events in Torino, Italy. In fact, the Paralympic Games are the second largest sporting event in the world after the Olympic Games.[14]

Perhaps the fastest growing target market for many marketers interested in sports sponsorship opportunities is women, and the growth of women's sports is taking place at all levels. More and more women are participating in sports and watching sports, which has created opportunities for equipment and apparel manufacturers as well as for broadcast media. In addition, marketing to women through the athletic medium has become an interesting and valuable tool for corporate America. In short, women are becoming the target market of choice for sports marketers.

Although women are growing in importance to sports marketers, relatively little is known about the sponsorship decisions relative to women's sport. What are the women's sports that are experiencing the most sponsorship growth? As seen in Table 11.4, at the collegiate level, soccer, golf, lacrosse, cross country, and softball have all grown in sponsorship spending at a rate of over 100 percent in the last 25 years. Additionally, only two sports (field hockey and gymnastics) have shown a decrease in spending.

A study by Nancy Lough and Dick Irwin was designed to better understand corporate sponsorship of women's sport.[15] The study questioned whether corporate sport sponsorship decision makers differ with respect to why they sponsor women's sport versus more "traditional" sponsorship opportunities. The authors found that corporate decision makers are more concerned with meeting objectives related to image building and increasing target market awareness, as opposed to building sales and market share. Summarized results of the research are shown in Table 11.5.

Relationship Marketing

As discussed in Chapter 10, **relationship marketing**, building long-term relationships with customers, is one of the most important issues for sports marketers in today's competitive marketing environment. Building relationships with clients or putting the principles of relationship marketing to work is another sponsorship objective.

TABLE 11.4	NCAA Women's Sports Sponsorship Growth
Sport	*% Growth Over 25 Years*
Soccer	1041%
Golf	286%
Lacrosse	151%
Cross country	125%
Softball	119%
Outdoor track	65%
Volleyball	63%
Basketball	45%
Tennis	44%
Swimming	41%
Field hockey	−4%
Gymnastics	−35%

TABLE 11.5	Importance of Corporate Sport Sponsorship Objective by Sport Sponsorship Type	
Mean ratings (1–7)		
Objective	*General*	*Women's*
Increase sales/market share	5.94	5.72
Increase target market awareness	5.88	5.89
Enhance general company image	5.81	5.94
Increase public awareness of company	5.56	5.53
Demonstrate community involvement	4.75	4.88
Build trade relations	4.50	4.29
Build trade good will	4.31	4.24
Demonstrate social responsibility	4.19	4.57
Block/preempt the competition	4.19	4.00
Enhance employee relations	3.76	3.78
Demonstrate corporate philanthropy	3.13	3.71

Corporate hospitality managers see to it that sponsors are given ample space to "wine and dine" current or perspective clients.

Companies began throwing more lavish sports-related parties at the Super Bowl during the mid-1980s. David M. Carter of The Sports Business Group, a Los Angeles–based sports consulting firm, says the demand for corporate sports hospitality has grown "exponentially" since then. "As sports' fan base has shifted from the everyday fan to the corporate fan, these events have increasingly catered to fans who are there to conduct business-to-business marketing," Carter says. These companies are trying to generate new business and keep current clients as well.

When Bank of America became the sponsor of the BAC Colonial Tournament, the company wanted to create a touring hospitality program that would further enhance the bank's "Higher Standards" brand statement and give them a fitting opportunity to socialize with a large number of current and prospective customers.

"Banking is done at the local level so we use hospitality as a one-to-one relationship building opportunity and a very key part of our marketing mix," said David Jessey, senior vice president of sponsorship marketing for Bank of America. "Hospitality is more than a sign or a commercial. It is a higher standards experience that the guest actively takes part in."

The result was Hogan's Alley, an environment that resembled more of a leather-clad country club than simply a tent serving hot dogs and cold beverages. The area included a library filled with golf magazines and books on legendary golfer Ben Hogan, a conversation area, a large bar and dining area and cocktail tables.

To measure the business impact of Hogan's Alley and determine the tangible results of its investment from their attendees after their experience, Bank of America established a database for all their guests. The company offered high-end door prizes for guests who completed detailed surveys querying them about the event and their banking activities. According to company research, Bank of America determined that 96 percent of attendees were satisfied with the experience, 73 percent said it was the best corporate hospitality they had ever experienced, and 84 percent said it strengthened their relationship with the bank. More than 88 percent of attendees stated that they were more likely to consider using the bank because of the experience.

Very few academic studies have explored company attitudes toward corporate hospitality or the effectiveness of this activity, but recently Bennett looked at this growing sports marketing function. He found that two-thirds of the companies he surveyed believed that "highly formal" procedures were applied to the management of corporate hospitality and that one-third of the expenses were incorporated into marketing budgets. Additionally, two-thirds of the companies responding to the survey said that the decision on choice of events for corporate hospitality was based on "the in-house assessment of the goodness of the match between corporate hospitality activities and specific clients." Two-thirds of the companies felt that corporate hospitality was a vital element of the marketing mix and even if faced with a recession would not cut their budget in this area. Finally, companies stated that the greatest benefit of corporate hospitality activities was retaining profitable customers.[16]

How much are organizations willing to pay to retain and gain customers? Here's just a glimpse at the prices for hospitality areas at the 2008 U.S. Open, hosted at Torrey Pines. Incidentally, all of these areas sold out:[17]

Where: The Grille-Lodge-operated restaurant near the South's first tee and 18th green
Highlights: Seats 90; 150 weekly ticket packages, with option to purchase 100 more; 75 preferred parking passes; pre-Open outing for 12
Cost: $575,000, not including food and beverage

Where: Charles Reiffel Room—Room adjacent to South's 18th hole
Highlights: Seats 120; 150 weekly ticket packages, with option to buy 50 more; 75 preferred parking passes; pre-Open outing for 12
Cost: $550,000

Where: Gamble Suite—Room in the Lodge
Highlights: Seats 70; 100 weekly ticket packages, with option to buy 74 more; 50 preferred parking passes; pre-Open outing for eight
Cost: $350,000, not including food and beverage

Where: Charles Fries Room—Room in the Lodge
Highlights: Seats 60; 100 weekly ticket packages, with option to buy 25 more; 50 preferred parking passes; pre-Open outing for eight
Cost: $325,000, not including food and beverage

Although corporate sponsors and their clients live and die by the relationships they forge, the community is another public with which sponsors want to build relationships. Many corporate sponsors believe returning something to the community is an important part of sponsoring a sporting event. With the 2007 Shell Houston Open, the PGA Tour regular golf tournaments passed $800 million in total charity contributions since 1938. Combined with charitable donations from the Champions and Nationwide events, more than $1.1 billion has been generated for charities over the history of the PGA Tour.

At the Shell Houston Open, charity contributions focused on local youth-related charities. More than 14 Super Bowl stadiums could be filled with children who have benefited from these charities through the Shell Houston Open.

"Over the past 15 years, Shell Oil and the Houston Golf Association have made it a top priority to generate more than $42 million for hundreds of youth-related charities through the Shell Houston Open," noted Kevin Ilges, director of U.S. Social Responsibility and Business Support at Shell Oil Company. "It is estimated that more than a million children have benefited by the cooperative efforts of Shell Oil, the Houston Golf Association, and the Shell Houston Open Charity Partners during that time."[18]

Image Building

Perhaps the most important reason for sponsorship of a sports entity at any level is to maintain or build an image. **Image building** is a two-way street for both the sponsoring organization and the sports entity. The sponsoring organization associates itself and/or its brands with the positive images generated by the unique personality of the sporting event. Ferrand and Pagés describe the process of finding a congruence between event and sponsor as "looking for the perfect wedding."[19] The researchers also point out that "any action toward sponsoring an event should begin with an analysis of the common and unique attributes of the event and the brand or product."

Gillette is the presenting sponsor of Father's Day for MLB. Why? Tim Brosnan, executive vice president, business, for major league Baseball, stated, "We both have an intense commitment to men's health and prostate cancer awareness. We're working with them on an initiative around Father's Day where we get the message out that one in six men will be diagnosed with prostate cancer. We're having a little fun with it and changing from the seventh-inning stretch to the sixth-inning stretch [around the holiday]. Gillette has been with us since 1937. That relationship is, we believe, the longest *sports* partnership ever."[20]

Consider an event like the Summer Extreme Games (X-Games), which possess a well-defined image that includes characteristics such as aggressiveness, hip, cool, no fear, and no rules. The image of extreme sports such as skysurfing, street luge, or the adventure race will certainly "rub off" or become associated with the sponsoring organization. Taco Bell, Nike, and Mountain Dew will take on the characteristics of the extreme sports, and the image of their products will be maintained or enhanced. "Sponsorship is an opportunity to directly touch consumers and be true to the lifestyle of the brand," explains Chris Fuentes, VP-marketing at Nautica. "It lets you have a conversation with consumers."

In Chapter 9, the **match-up hypothesis** was described as the more congruent the image of the endorser with the image of the product being promoted, the more effective the message. This simple principle also holds true for sponsorship. However, the image of the sports entity (remember, this may be an event, individual athlete, group of athletes, or team) should be congruent with the actual or desired image of the sponsor's organization or the product being sponsored. In Figure 11.2, we can see how the image of Taco Bell has shifted toward the X-Games and how the image of the X-Games also shifts toward the sponsor.

Sometimes the "match up" between sponsor and sports entity is not seen as appropriate. For example, Anheuser-Busch's $40 million sponsorship of the 2006 World Cup turned out to be a bad match between sponsor, event, and target audience, as described in the accompanying article.

In another alcohol-related example, full-page ads in college newspapers called on university leaders, athletic conferences, and the NCAA to "stop the madness" by banning alcohol marketing from college sports. The ads, tied to March Madness and sponsored by the American Medical Association, ran in college papers in six cities in advance of the NCAA men's basketball tournament: in the *Chronicle of Higher Education* and student newspapers at Georgia Tech, University of Iowa, University of Wisconsin, Indiana University, University of Mississippi, and DePaul University.

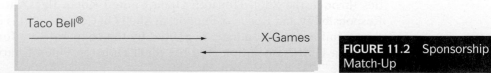

Taco Bell®

X-Games

FIGURE 11.2 Sponsorship Match-Up

BUD KICKS UP WORLD CUP BREW-HAHA

Budweiser beer may be royalty in American bars, but it's getting no respect in the land of Oktoberfest.

As one of seven U.S. sponsors at this summer's World Cup in Germany, Anheuser-Busch paid $40 million for "pouring rights" at 12 stadiums across Germany, something Germans and tourists have had trouble swallowing.

Simply put, Germans hate Budweiser. Weeks before the inaugural games kicked off the Cup, Germans were furious at the prospect of having to drink what they refer to as "dishwater" at stadiums. Germans even set up a Web site with an image of an American eagle vomiting beer to lampoon the American brewer and express their disgust.

"Human dignity is inviolable," reads the Web site, quoting the German constitution. The Web site goes on to call Budweiser "an insult to all true beer lovers" and an "insult to your tongue."

Soccer's governing body—the Federation Internationale de Football, or FIFA—did little to improve Budweiser's standing when it forced thousands of Dutch fans to watch the first round Holland–Ivory Coast game in their underwear. Close to a quarter million Dutch fans have purchased orange-colored shorts to support their team, shorts that carry the logo of the Dutch beer, Bavaria.

In a contentious move to protect Budweiser's rights, FIFA officials forced Dutch supporters to remove their shorts.

"It's ridiculous," said Sjoerd Schreurs, a Dutch fan quoted by *The Guardian* in London. "I took my trousers off. I managed to chuck them over the fence to some friends. But another official spotted them and took them away."

The World Cup is a marketer's dream. More than a billion people watched the 2002 World Cup final between Brazil and Germany. FIFA says 32 billion cumulative viewers will watch this year's month-long tournament, with an estimated audience of 350 million for each match—numbers that dwarf the 95 million viewers worldwide who watched the 2006 Super Bowl.

These titanic international audiences are the reason companies will spend $1 billion in advertising before the tournament's end. Budweiser is expected to spend $70 million in advertising and marketing, more than it spends on the Super Bowl and the Olympics.

"For us it's the No. 1 beer consumer event in the world," said Tony Ponturo, vice president for global media and sports marketing at Anheuser-Busch. Ponturo pointed out that Anheuser-Busch has been a World Cup sponsor since 1986 and that it markets heavily at the event, whether it's held in France, Korea, or Germany.

But denting the German market has been a royal pain for Budweiser. A Beer Purity Law established in 1516—it limits beer ingredients to yeast, water, barley, and hops—was watered down in the late 1980s, allowing the sale of Budweiser through a loophole for import beers (rice is a key ingredient in Budweiser). Various legal challenges kept Budweiser out of Germany until 1996. Even then, Budweiser could only be sold as "Anheuser-Busch Bud," so it would not be confused with the popular Czech beer Budweiser Budvar.

In an effort to appease German drinkers, Budweiser made a deal to allow the German-made Bitburger beer to be sold in stadiums, albeit in unmarked cups. Ponturo said Budweiser is outselling Bitburger at a 70 to 30 percent rate.

Ponturo pointed to an extremely competitive beer market in Germany, where there are over 1,200 breweries, and where Budweiser represents less than 1 percent of market share in Germany.

"It's difficult for even German beers to grow in certain areas of Germany because there are so many local beers," said Ponturo. "There are so many options, and they take pride in that."

Source: Alfonso Serrano F., http://www.cbsnews.com/stories/2006/06/27/world/main1754277.shtml, June 27, 2006.

"The truly insane thing about March basketball is all the money universities get from alcohol advertising," the ads read. An illustration showed cheering sports fans holding signs reading: "Stop the Madness." The ad claimed that the alcohol industry spent more than $52 million to advertise its products during televised college sports in a recent year. Spokesman Bob Williams said the NCAA limits alcohol ads to one minute per hour of broadcast, won't allow ads for hard liquor, and encourages "responsibility themes and messages" in the ads.[21]

Philip Morris USA and Philip Morris International (both subsidiaries of Altria) claim they are changed, responsible companies that do not market to kids and are concerned about the health risks of their products. But the companies' actions tell a different story. In the latest example, Philip Morris International is the only tobacco company that continues to sponsor Formula One auto races, which exposes spectators and tens of millions of television viewers worldwide—including millions of children—to the name, logo, and red-and-white colors of the company's best-selling Marlboro cigarettes. Arguably, no responsible company would continue to associate deadly and addictive cigarettes with the excitement and glamour of auto racing, thereby increasing their appeal to children.

Sales Increases

The eventual objective for nearly all organizations involved in sponsorship programs is **sales increases**. Although sometimes there is an indirect route to sales (i.e., the hierarchy of effects model of promotional objectives, which states that awareness must come before action or sales), the major objective of sponsorship is to increase the bottom line. Organizations certainly would not spend millions of dollars to lend their names to stadiums or events if they did not feel comfortable about the return on investment. Likewise, the events are developed, in some cases (e.g., the Skins Game and the World's Strongest Man Competition), for the sole purpose of making a profit. Without sponsorship, the event would lose the ability to do so.

It is clear that when organizations are considering a sponsorship program, the first step is to determine the organizational objectives and marketing goals that might be achieved most effectively through sponsorship. However, the primary motivation for organizations participating in sports sponsorships is still unclear. Historically, organizations entered into sponsorships to create awareness and enhance the image of their brands, product lines, or corporations. Three studies examining the primary reasons for engaging in sponsorship found increasing awareness and enhancing company image to be the most important objectives. More recently, studies have shown that increasing sales and market share are the primary motives of sponsorship (see Table 11.6).

Regardless of the relative importance of the various sponsorship objectives, organizations must carefully evaluate how the sponsorship will help them achieve their own unique marketing objectives. Along with examining the sponsorship objectives,

TABLE 11.6	Importance of Sponsorship Objectives
Objectives	*Mean Importance Rating*
Increase sales and market share	6.14
Increase target market awareness	6.07
Enhance general public awareness	5.88
Enhance general company image	5.47
Enhance trade relations	4.60
Enhance trade goodwill	4.55
Involve community	4.48
Alter public perception	4.15
Enhance employee relations	3.84
Block competition	3.68
Develop social responsibility	3.13
Develop corporate philanthropy	3.12

Source: Doug Morris and Richard L. Irwin, "The Data-Driven Approach to Sponsorship Acquisition," *Sport Marketing Quarterly*, vol. 5, no. 2 (1996), 9. Reprinted with permission of Fitness Information Technology, Inc., Publishers.

the organization must find a sponsorship opportunity that fits within the existing promotion budget. Let us look briefly at the basic budgeting considerations, the next step in the sponsorship model.

Sponsorship Budgeting

As with the promotional budget, determining the **sponsorship budgeting methods** includes competitive parity, arbitrary allocation, percentage of sales, and the objective and task method. Because the fundamentals of these budgeting methods have already been discussed, let us examine the sponsorship budgeting process at several organizations.

The only generality to be made about the budgeting process is that decision making varies widely based on the size of the company and its history and commitment to the practice of sponsorship.[22] Larger organizations that have used sponsorship as a form of communication for many years tend to have highly complex structures and those new to sponsorship tend to keep it simpler.

Consider, for example, the budgeting process at Anheuser-Busch. Anheuser-Busch's budgeting process begins with determining the corporate-wide marketing budget. This is usually anywhere from 3 to 5 percent of the previous year's sales (percentage of sales method discussed in Chapter 10). The total budget is then divided among the company's 32 brands, with Budweiser, the flagship brand, receiving the largest share of the budget. The final decision on budget allocation is made by two high-level management teams, who receive and review potential sponsorships. The first team looks at how the managers plan on supporting their sponsorships with additional promotional mix elements such as point-of-sale merchandising. The second team hears the brand managers present their case and defend their budget.

Although Anheuser-Busch's budgeting process represents a more complex and structured approach, Marriott uses a simpler technique. Marriott, a relative newcomer to sports sponsorship, leaves the whole business to its corporation's hotel and time-share properties. The same practice holds true for Philip Morris, where managers of individual brands like Virginia Slims decide which sponsorship opportunities to pursue and how much money to allocate.

Once specific budgets are allocated, the organization must look for sponsorship opportunities that will meet objectives and still be affordable. To accommodate budgetary constraints, most sports entities offer different levels of sponsorship over a range of sponsorship fees. One example of the cost of sponsorship and the tangible benefits received by the sponsor is the McDonald's LPGA Championship (see Table 11.7). The professional golf tournament attracts slightly more men (60 percent) than women (40 percent), with more than half of the spectators between 45–64 years old and over half having an average household income of over $100,000. Sponsorship packages are presented in the following areas: hospitality, executive, on-course signage, advertising, and visibility.

It is important to note that the sponsorship fee is not the only expense that should be considered. As Brant Wansley of BrandMarketing Services, Ltd., points out, "Buying the rights [to the sponsorship] is one thing, capitalizing on them to get a good return on investment is another. . . . Purchasing a sponsorship is like buying an expensive sports car. In addition to the initial cost, you must invest in the maintenance of the car to ensure its performance."[23] Sponsorship must be integrated with other forms of promotion to maximize its effectiveness. Rod Taylor, senior vice president of the CoActive Marketing Group, adds, "The only thing that you get as a sponsor is a piece of paper saying you've paid to belong. It is up to you as the marketer to convince consumers that you do, in fact, belong!" Bill Chipps, of the IEG Sponsorship Report, says that "the rule of thumb is that for every dollar a company spends on a rights fee, to maximize the sponsorship, they spend another $2 to $3 on leverage."

TABLE 11.7   Sponsorship Opportunities: McDonald's LPGA Championship

Executive Sponsorships

Platinum $48,000
　4 Pro-Am Spots
　3 Nights Lodging at Hotel Included
　8 Sponsor Badges
　1 Preferred Parking Pass
　100 Good-Any-One-Day Tickets
　Exclusive use of hospitality tent for one day, with
　　4 preferred parking passes for that day
　Name on Sponsor Board
　Name in Tournament Program

Gold $24,000
　2 Pro-Am Spots
　3 Nights Lodging at Hotel Included
　6 Sponsor Badges
　1 Preferred Parking Pass
　75 Good-Any-One-Day Tickets
　Name on Sponsor Board
　Name in Tournament Program

Silver $13,000
　1 Pro-Am Spot
　3 Nights Lodging at Hotel Included
　2 Sponsor Badges
　1 Preferred Parking Pass
　25 Good-Any-One-Day Tickets
　Name on Sponsor Board
　Name in Tournament Program

On Course Signage

Caddie Jackets $32,000
Corporate name prominently displayed on each Caddie Jacket
　1 Pro-Am Spot
　3 Nights Lodging at Hotel Included
　6 Sponsor Badges
　1 Preferred Parking Pass
　75 Good-Any-One-Day Tickets
　Name on Sponsor Board
　Name in Tournament Program

Standards $27,000
Standards follow every group keeping galleries updated on players' scores. Corporate name prominently displayed on standards.
　1 Pro-Am Spot
　3 Nights Lodging at Hotel Included
　6 Sponsor Badges
　1 Preferred Parking Pass
　50 Good-Any-One-Day Tickets
　Name on Sponsor Board
　Name in Tournament Program

Main Scoreboard $27,000
Corporate name prominently displayed on main scoreboard located behind clubhouse
　1 Pro-Am Spot
　3 Nights Lodging at Hotel Included
　6 Sponsor Badges
　1 Preferred Parking Pass
　50 Good-Any-One-Day Tickets
　Name on Sponsor Board
　Name in Tournament Program

Cart Signs $27,000
Corporate name and logo on Pro-Am & Am-Am Cart Signs
　1 Pro-Am Spot
　3 Nights Lodging at Hotel Included
　6 Sponsor Badges
　1 Preferred Parking Pass
　50 Good-Any-One-Day Tickets
　Name on Sponsor Board
　Name in Tournament Program

(Continued)

(*Continued*)

On Course Signage (*Continued*)

Green Signs $22,000
Corporate name on Green Signs during Pro-Am
- 1 Pro-Am Spot
- 3 Nights Lodging at Hotel Included
- 6 Sponsor Badges
- 1 Preferred Parking Pass
- 50 Good-Any-One-Day Tickets
- Name on Sponsor Board
- Name in Tournament Program

Pairing Sheet Boxes $22,000
Corporate name displayed on Pairing Sheet Boxes throughout the course
- 1 Pro-Am Spot
- 3 Nights Lodging at Hotel Included
- 6 Sponsor Badges
- 1 Preferred Parking Pass
- 50 Good-Any-One-Day Tickets
- Name on Sponsor Board
- Name in Tournament Program

Champions' Board $22,000
Corporate name prominently displayed on Champions' Board
- 1 Pro-Am Spot
- 3 Nights Lodging at Hotel Included
- 6 Sponsor Badges
- 1 Preferred Parking Pass
- 50 Good-Any-One-Day Tickets
- Name on Sponsor Board
- Name in Tournament Program

Chipping Green $15,000
Driving Range $15,000
Putting Green $18,000
Corporate name prominently displayed on sign at location
- 1 Pro-Am Spot
- 3 Nights Lodging at Hotel Included
- 4 Sponsor Badges
- 1 Preferred Parking Pass
- 25 Good-Any-One-Day Tickets
- Name on Sponsor Board
- Name in Tournament Program

Leader Board or Status Board $15,000
Corporate name prominently displayed on manual Leader Board or Status Board
- 1 Pro-Am Spot
- 3 Nights Lodging at Hotel Included
- 4 Sponsor Badges
- 1 Preferred Parking Pass
- 25 Good-Any-One-Day Tickets
- Name on Sponsor Board
- Name in Tournament Program

Tee Sign $14,000
Corporate name prominently displayed on Tee Sign
- 1 Pro-Am Spot
- 3 Nights Lodging at Hotel Included
- 3 Sponsor Badges
- 1 Preferred Parking Pass
- 25 Good-Any-One-Day Tickets
- Name on Sponsor Board
- Name in Tournament Program

"Quiet Please" Paddles $20,000
Corporate name displayed on marshals' paddles during tournament
- 1 Pro-Am Spot
- 3 Nights Lodging at Hotel Included
- 4 Sponsor Badges
- 1 Preferred Parking Pass
- 25 Good-Any-One-Day Tickets
- Name on Sponsor Board
- Name in Tournament Program

Course Map $17,000
Corporate name prominently displayed on Course Map
- 1 Pro-Am Spot
- 3 Nights Lodging at Hotel Included
- 4 Sponsor Badges
- 1 Preferred Parking Pass
- 25 Good-Any-One-Day Tickets
- Name on Sponsor Board
- Name in Tournament Program

Ecology Containers $17,000
Corporate name prominently displayed on each Ecology Container
- 1 Pro-Am Spot
- 3 Nights Lodging at Hotel Included
- 4 Sponsor Badges
- 1 Preferred Parking Pass
- 25 Good-Any-One-Day Tickets
- Name on Sponsor Board
- Name in Tournament Program

Source: Courtesy McDonald's/LPGA. www.mcdslpgachampionship.com/.

The average sponsor spends $1.90 to leverage its deals for every $1 it pays in rights fees, according to the seventh annual IEG/Performance Research Sponsorship Decision-Makers Survey. That amount equals the highest ratio in the survey's history, achieved in 2003 before dropping to 1.3-to-1 in 2004 and recovering to 1.7-to-1 in 2006. A rise in the number of sponsors spending 3-to-1 or higher on activation caused the increase; nearly 23 percent of sponsors reported their leveraging spending would be at least three times their rights fees. When it comes to spending on those fees, 44 percent of respondents said their budgets would stay the same for 2006, while 38 percent would increase spending and 18 percent would spend less.[24]

An excellent example of an organization leveraging its Olympic sponsorship is Anheuser-Busch. In addition to print and broadcast advertisements, Anheuser-Busch produced commemorative Olympic cans and accompanying P-O-P displays to stimulate sales at the retail level. Bob Lachky, group vice president of Budweiser brands at Anheuser Busch, says, "When you can drill [sponsorship] all the way through every element of the marketing mix—from advertising all the way through point-of-sale . . . and if you can get something that looks seamless from top bottom, you're going to have a successful promotion."[25]

Choosing the Sponsorship Opportunity

Once sponsorship objectives have been carefully studied and financial resources have been allocated, organizations must make decisions regarding the appropriate sponsorship opportunity. Whatever the choices, thoughtful consideration must be given to the potential opportunities.

Choosing the most effective sponsorship opportunity for your organization necessitates a detailed decision-making process. Several researchers have examined the organizational decision-making process in attempts to understand the evaluation and selection of sponsorship opportunities. A conceptual model of the corporate decision-making process of **sport sponsorship acquisition** developed by Arthur, Scott, and Woods is shown in Figure 11.3.

The process begins with the acquisition of sponsorship proposals. Generally, this is a reactive process in which organizations receive a multitude of sponsorship possibilities from sports entities wanting to secure sponsors. Within the sponsorship proposal, potential sponsors commonly look for the following information to assist in decision making:

- Fan attendance and demographic profile of fans at the event
- Cost or cost per number of people reached
- Length of contract
- Media coverage
- Value-added promotions
- Sponsorship benefits

After the proposals have been acquired, the next step is to form the buying center. The buying center is the group of individuals within the organization responsible for **sponsorship evaluation** and choice. The buying center usually consists of four to five individuals who each play a unique role in the purchase. Typically, these roles are described as gatekeepers, influencers, decision makers, and purchasers. These roles were previously discussed in the context of personal selling. You will recall that one of the sales activities was to identify the individuals within the organization who performed these roles. Similarly, the sponsorship requester must learn who these individuals are before submitting the proposal. Hopefully, the proposal can then be tailored to meet the unique needs of the individuals who comprise the buying center.

FIGURE 11.3 Sport Sponsorship Acquisition Model

Source: Reprinted by permission from D. Arthur, D. Scott, and T. Woods. "A Conceptual Model of the Corporate Decision-Making Process of Sport Sponsorship Acquisition," *Journal of Sport Management*, vol. 11, no. 3 (1997), 229.

Gatekeepers control the flow of information to the other members of the buying center. They are able to pass on the relevant proposals to other group members and act as an initial filtering device. The **influencers** are individuals who can impact the decision-making process. These individuals often have information regarding the sports entity that is requesting the sponsorship. The influencers have acquired this information through contacts they have in the community or industry. The **decision maker** is the individual within the buying center that has the ultimate responsibility to accept or reject proposals. In our earlier examples, describing the budgeting process for Phillip Morris, the brand managers were the ultimate decision makers in the sponsorship acquisition process. Finally, the **purchasers** are responsible for negotiating contracts and formally carrying out the terms of the sponsorship.

The composition of the buying center, in terms of the number of individuals and the interaction between these individuals, is a function of the type of sponsorship decision. The buying grid refers to the organization's previous experience and involvement in sponsorship purchases. If this is the first time the organization has engaged in sport sponsorship, then more information will be needed from the sponsorship requester. In addition, the buying center will have additional members with greater interaction. However, if the sponsorship is simply being renewed (also known as a straight sponsorship rebuy), the buying center will play a less significant role in the decision-making process.

The next step in the sponsorship acquisition model is to make the purchase decision. Typically, it takes an organization three to six weeks to make a final sponsorship decision. While this may seem slow, purchasing a sponsorship is a complex decision that requires the coordination and interaction of all the members in the buying center.

The purchase decision consists of three interrelated steps. In the first step, the organization must consider the desired scope of the sponsorship (e.g., international versus local). To do this, a simple scheme for categorizing sponsorship opportunities has been developed, called the Sport Event Pyramid. The second interrelated step requires the organization to select the appropriate athletic platform for the sponsorship. Does the organization want to sponsor an event, a team, a league, or an individual athlete? Finally, after the organization has chosen the scope of sponsorship and the athletic platform, it specifies the particular sports entity. After the final decision is made, a quick audit can be conducted to determine whether the organization has made the appropriate choice of sponsorship. Let us examine the three steps in the purchase decision-making process in greater detail.

Determining the Scope of the Sponsorship

The first step in the purchase decision phase of sponsorship acquisition is to determine the desired scope of the sponsorship. David Shani and Dennis Sandler have developed a way to categorize various sponsorship opportunities called the **Sports Event Pyramid**.[26] The Sports Event Pyramid is an excellent first step in reducing the number of sponsorship proposals to a smaller subset.

The Sports Event Pyramid consists of five levels: global events, international events, national events, regional events, and local events. Each level of the Sports Event Pyramid classifies events on the basis of the width and depth of interest in the event. Shani and Sandler describe the width as the geographic reach of the event via the various communications media, and the depth of the event refers to the level of interest among consumers.

Global events are at the apex of the pyramid. As the name implies, global events have the broadest coverage and are covered extensively around the world. In addition to their wide coverage, global events generate a great deal of interest among consumers. Shani and Sandler suggest that the World Cup and the Olympic Games are the only examples of truly global events. Corporations that want to position themselves in the global market should be prepared to pay top dollar for sponsorship of these events due to the tremendous reach and interest in the events.

International events are the next level in the hierarchy. For any event to be considered international in scope, it might (1) have a high level of interest in a broad, but not global, geographic region, or (2) be truly global in scope but have a lower level of interest in some of the countries reached. Examples of international events include Wimbledon, European Cup Soccer, America's Cup (yachting), the Rugby Union World Cup, and the Pan-American Games. Sponsoring these types of events is useful for corporations that have more narrowly targeted global markets.

Little League World Series—an international event.

Source: Copyright © 2003 Little League. All rights reserved.

Extremely high interest levels among consumers in a single country or two countries is categorized in the Sports Event Pyramid as a **national event.** National events, such as the World Series, the NCAA Final Four, and the Super Bowl, attract huge audiences in the United States.

Regional events have a narrow geographic focus and are also characterized by high interest levels within the region. The Big East conference tournament in basketball and the Boston Marathon are considered good examples of regional events.

In the lowest level of the pyramid are **local events.** Local events have the narrowest geographic focus, such as a city or community, and attract a small segment of consumers that have a high level of interest in the event. High school sports, local races, and golf scrambles are examples of local events.

The primary purpose of the pyramid is to have marketers first develop an understanding of what level of sponsorship is consistent with corporate sponsorship objectives and budgets. Next, the corporation can decide which specific sporting events at the correct level present the best match. The organization may start small and choose to sponsor local events at the beginning. The larger the organization gets, the more likely it will be involved in sponsorship at each of the five levels of the pyramid. For example, Coca-Cola is deeply involved in sponsorships at all five levels.

Although the Sports Event Pyramid is a great tool for marketers developing a sponsorship program, it does have some potential flaws. First, the local events are shown at the base of the pyramid. To some, this may imply the broadest geographic focus whereas, in fact, the local events have the most narrow focus. Second, it may be extremely difficult to categorize certain events. For example, the Super Bowl is cited as a national event that, by definition, has a one- or two-country focus with a high level of interest. The Super Bowl, of course, is broadcast in hundreds of countries, but may have limited interest levels in most. Therefore, it is uncertain as to whether the event should be categorized as a national event, an international event, or both.

Determining the Athletic Platform

After the general level of sponsorship reach is considered via the sponsorship pyramid, a more specific sponsorship issue must be considered, namely, choosing the appropriate athletic platform. Professor Christine Brooks defines the **athletic platform** for sponsorship as being either the team, the sport, the event, or the athlete.[27] In addition, choice of athletic platform could be further subdivided on the basis of level of competition. For instance, common levels of competition include professional, collegiate, high school, and recreational.

The choice of athletic platform (or, in some instances, platforms) is based on sponsorship objectives, budget, and geographic scope. More specifically, when selecting the athletic platform, several factors should be considered.

- What is the sponsorship budget? What type of athletic platform is feasible given the budget?
- What is the desired geographic scope? How does the athletic platform complement the choice made in the sports sponsorship pyramid?
- How does the athletic platform complement the sponsorship objectives?

Let us take a closer look at each of the broad choices of athletic platform for sponsorship. These include athletes, teams, sports/leagues, and events.

Athletes   We have previously examined the opportunities and risks of athletes as endorsers in Chapters 9 and 10. To summarize, athletes can have tremendous credibility with the target audience and can create an immediate association with a product in the consumer's mind. For example, NASCAR fans talk about Ward Burton

Marketers Are Joining the Varsity

Athletes, if they are talented, train hard, and get a break or two, can climb the sports ladder from high school to college to the pros. Madison Avenue, sensing a lucrative opportunity, is heading the other way.

Decades after marketers began selling products by capitalizing on consumer interest in professional teams, then college teams, they are becoming big boosters of high school sports. Big media companies are getting into the market as well, in part by offering high school competitors a taste of the exposure that is typically lavished on college and pro athletes. In March, the CSTV Networks division of the CBS Corporation—the "CS" stands for college sports—acquired MaxPreps, which operates a Web site (maxpreps.com) and has more than a million high school athletes in its database. Last month, CSTV began creating video-on-demand television channels under the MaxPreps brand carrying high school sports programming. Another media giant, the Time Inc. division of Time Warner, formed an alliance in December with Takkle, which operates a social-networking Web site for high school athletes (takkle.com). Visitors to the site can nominate students for the familiar "Face in the Crowd" feature in *Sports Illustrated* magazine.

"High school kids are more sophisticated than a generation ago," said Mark Ford, president and publisher of *Sports Illustrated* in New York, "and brands like Nike and Gatorade are on this, reaching athletes at a much earlier stage than they previously have."

The goal is to gain favor with student athletes and also their coaches, teachers and principals—not to mention their fans, friends, and families. "Energy for student athletes, and the moms who keep up with them" is, for instance, the theme of advertisements for EAS AdvantEDGE nutritional bars and shakes, sold by Abbott Laboratories.

High school athletes buy all the obvious products—sneakers, gear, sports beverages—along with general items like grooming aids, magazines, and video games. Many high schoolers shop for the family while their parents work, so they may be buying groceries along with items for themselves. Students can also influence the purchasing choices of their parents in important categories like cars, cell phones, and computers.

For example, in 2005 Allstate Insurance started coordinating a program for local agents "to demonstrate their support of high school athletes," said Lisa Cochrane, vice president for integrated marketing communications at Allstate in Northbrook, Ill. Today, the brand is present in more than 700 high schools where agents sponsor teams and make donations to athletic departments.

"In many, many communities, high school athletics is one of the premier events," Ms. Cochrane said, adding: "Teenagers themselves are not big customers for insurance, but their parents are. And they will be, in the future."

The trend is also visible in the popular culture, as two TV series—*Friday Night Lights* on NBC and *One Tree Hill* on CW—are centered on high school teams that play football and basketball, respectively. Both have attracted sponsors willing to pay to weave their brands into plot lines; among them are Applebee's restaurants, Cingular Wireless, and Secret deodorant.

"We've spent more than 30 years building our relationships with customers," said Jeff Webb, chief executive at Varsity Brands in Memphis, which specializes in goods and services for high school cheerleading and dance teams. "In the last 10 years, our programs with consumer marketers have expanded dramatically."

Companies like Bic, S. C. Johnson & Son, Nike, PepsiCo, and Playtex Products work with Varsity Brands, which sends 300 field representatives to high schools across the country to give away product samples and coupons and operates cheerleader camps that draw about 280,000 high school students each year.

"They're trying to find unique ways to reach the teen audience," Mr. Webb said of marketers, adding that cheerleaders and other student athletes are especially attractive because "they're visible, they're leaders and they're influential."

The ardor among advertisers to go back to high school coincides with the rising national attention to junior sports. Examples include the basketball star LeBron James appearing on the cover of *Sports Illustrated* when he was still in high school, coverage of high school sports tournaments and all-star games in mainstream media, and programming on CSTV devoted to "Generation Next" high school football and basketball players (and which colleges might recruit them).

One reason that high school is getting its own chapter in the sports-marketing playbook is the large number of athletically inclined students in grades 9 through 12. Call them Millennials, Generation Y, or baby boom babies, the 7.2 million children who played sports in high school during the 2005–06 school year, as estimated by the National Federation of State High School Associations, represent a target market that has grown 80 percent since the 1971–72 school year.

"We're seeing sports becoming increasingly important for young girls as more and more of them are being empowered through athletics," said Lela Coffey, associate North American marketing director for the Tampax brand of feminine hygiene products owned by Procter & Gamble in Cincinnati.

(Continued)

(Continued)

Another reason that advertisers are crowding high school gymnasiums is their newfound ability to use the Internet, in the form of social-networking Web sites, to unite what had been diffused audiences.

"Technology allows you for the first time to aggregate small, fragmented communities in one place and try to reach the athletes themselves," said Brian Bedol, president and chief executive of CSTV Networks. "It's a very different approach from fan-based college and pro sports."

The eagerness among marketers to clamber down the sports ladder worries those who are concerned with the intensifying presence of marketing in the American culture. "Youths are overwhelmed with commercial messages," said Robert Weissman, managing director at Commercial Alert in Washington, a nonprofit advocacy organization that decries what it considers to be creeping commercialization.

"To the extent possible, schools should be a haven from those pressures," he added. Most marketers turning their attention to athletes in high schools already "are linked up with sponsorships at the professional level and the college level," Mr. Weissman said, "so they get to exploit the kids on the cheap." And by sponsoring local teams, advertisers "get the benefit of seeming to be part of the community," he added, even when they are not.

Needless to say, the companies involved with high school sports describe themselves as sensitive to the potential pitfalls. "We don't want to be too intrusive," said David Birnbaum, chief executive at Takkle in New York, which is owned by investors that include Greycroft Partners and the Wasserman Media Group. For instance, no ads appear on the takkle.com home page, Mr. Birnbaum said, because "it's not just about the dollars."

And although "I'm not going to say we wouldn't" ever accept sponsors that peddle products like candy or soft drinks, he added, the intent is to run "the ads that the athletes want to see, that speak to their passion and engage them the way they want to be engaged." (When Varsity Brands works for PepsiCo, employees distribute Propel Fitness Water to high school cheerleaders rather than soda.)

As Under Armour, the maker of athletic apparel, completes plans for a campaign carrying the theme "Team Girl," the inclusion of high school athletes with their college counterparts is being handled carefully, said Steve Battista, vice president for brand marketing in Baltimore. Female high school athletes were assembled in focus groups to gather opinions, he added, which led to changes in marketing approaches. For example, "we've had a women's campaign featuring Heather Mitts, a women's soccer star, on her own, not with the rest of her team," Mr. Battista said, "but the girls said they want to see her with her team."

As CSTV adds MaxPreps to its operations, Mr. Bedol of CSTV said, "often it comes down to judgment calls" when determining how to speak to students younger than the college students. "We need to be vigilant," he added, "and make sure we're responding to the needs of our audience, not just to the needs of our marketers."

What about going even younger? "I don't think we're looking to go into middle school or younger," Mr. Bedol said. At the cheerleader camps that Varsity Brands operates, however, Mr. Webb said, about 25,000 students who attend each year are from junior high and middle schools.

Source: Stuart Elliott, "Marketers Are Joining the Varsity," http://www.nytimes.com/2007/06/11/business/media/11adcol.html?pagewanted=1&_r=1. June 11, 2007.

driving the "NetZero HighSpeed " car or Tony Stewart driving the "Home Depot" car. Interestingly, when it comes to athletes as sponsors, golfers have always been at the head of the pack. In fact, most believe the entire sports marketing industry was built on the backs of professional golfers, such as Arnold Palmer, Jack Nicholas, and Gary Player. Of course, Tiger Woods is now carrying the flag with appearance fees, earnings, and endorsement deals worth an estimated $100 million in 2006, making him the world's best paid athlete. While Tiger has remained squeaky clean to this point in his career, the problem, however, is that individual athletes can perform poorly or be seen as troublemakers.

One athlete that is always surrounded by controversy and seems to exemplify the bad boy image is Falcons QB Michael Vick. In March 2005 a woman named Sonya Elliot filed a civil lawsuit against Vick alleging that she contracted genital herpes from Vick and that he failed to inform her that he had the disease. Elliot further alleged that Vick had visited clinics under the alias "Ron Mexico" to get treatments and thus he knew of his condition. After a Falcons loss to the New Orleans Saints in the Georgia

Dome on November 26, 2006, Vick made an obscene gesture at Atlanta fans, holding up two middle fingers. In yet another incident, Vick surrendered a water bottle to security at Miami International Airport. Due to Vick's reluctance to leave the bottle behind, it was later retrieved from a trash receptacle. The bottle was found to have a hidden compartment that contained a small amount of dark particulate and a pungent aroma closely associated with marijuana. On April 24, 2007, Vick was scheduled to lobby on Capitol Hill, hoping to persuade lawmakers to increase funding for afterschool programs. Vick missed a connecting flight in Atlanta and failed to show for his morning appearance.[28] In his most publicized and scandalous act yet, Vick pleaded guilty to a federal dogfighting conspiracy charge on August 27, 2007, in U.S. District Court. He could face up to 5 years in prison, but most suspect he will serve 12 to 18 months. Whether his football career will ever be regained remains to be seen. Additionally, he is losing millions of dollars in endorsements and salary.[29] Vick previously had deals with Nike, Coca-Cola's Powerade, Kraft, and AirTran, but those agreements have lapsed amid a string of off-the-field incidents.

Teams   Teams at any level of competition (Little League, high school, college, and professional) can serve as the athletic platform. 7-Eleven Stores presents an excellent example of an organization that has chosen to focus on professional sports teams as its athletic platform.

7-Eleven Hopes to Win Over Sports-Loving Customers with Major Team Sponsorships and Integrated Marketing

The world's largest convenience store chain has signed multi-year sponsorship agreements with 18 professional sports organizations and venues, including teams with the National Football League (NFL), major league Baseball (MLB), and National Basketball Association (NBA). In addition to its ongoing sponsorship of Indy Racing League (IRL) Team 7-Eleven driver Tony Kanaan of Andretti Green Racing, 7-Eleven has added events at the Texas Motor Speedway and in St. Petersburg, Fla., to its motor sports portfolio.

Financial terms of the agreements are not disclosed, but Jim Andrews, senior vice president with Chicago-based sponsorship firm IEG, said the 7-Eleven sponsorship is certainly one of the most comprehensive initiatives recently announced. "The geographic scope of the program and the interaction with fans demonstrate that 7-Eleven realizes how sports sponsorship provides value and is a great way to connect with customers," Andrews said. While customized by market, every sponsorship agreement is built around radio and television advertising, venue signage, coupon distribution at events for proprietary 7-Eleven fresh-food products and beverages, and a 7-Eleven presence on the team Web sites.

"7-Eleven customers are sports fans, and vice versa," said Doug Foster, 7-Eleven vice president of marketing. "We reach them on their way to and from work and during their lunch hour. Now we want to join them when they play or enjoy leisure activities. The teams recognize the commonality and benefits as well. Not only will we have visibility at their venues, but we also will ensure that each team has opportunities to reach their fans through our stores."

Promotional activities vary by market and also include elements like halftime or game-night contests; special "7-Eleven Day" games; street team sponsorships; store appearances by players, cheerleaders, or mascots; pep rallies and tailgate parties; team charity participation; distribution of exclusive premium prizes and products with 7-Eleven and team logos; and in-store distribution of pocket-size team schedules. Foster said the sports activities allow the company to better integrate its marketing and public relations initiatives locally, such as advertising or donations to local charitable organizations.

Sponsorship agreements and highlights of each include:

NFL
- Chicago Bears—Serve 7-Eleven Exclusive Blend coffee at Soldier field; store appearances by Bears alumni players like linebacker Otis Wilson; donation to Bears Care team charity.
- Dallas Cowboys—Players and cheerleaders store appearances; "Cowboys on Tour" mobile vehicle at stores.

(Continued)

(Continued)

- Denver Broncos—Sampling-coupon giveaway tables at games; alumni players and cheerleaders store appearances.
- Philadelphia Eagles—Pep rallies at stores with cheerleaders, mascot, and alumni appearances; giveaways for three VIP tailgate parties; game ticket giveaways.
- Washington Redskins—Training camp participation; "tailgate parties" at stores; "Watch & Win" in-store promotion.
- New England Patriots—7-Eleven in-game activities for all home games.
- Seattle Seahawks—Sponsorship of "Tee Hawk of the Week," in which winners will receive a customized "12" jersey and a 7-Eleven Tee Hawk of the Week football.
- Oakland Raiders—Designated "7-Eleven Fan Zone" seating section; two "7-Eleven" days of game sponsorship; title sponsor of the Oakland Raiders' weekly show, *Raiders Report*.

NBA

- Dallas Mavericks—7-Eleven Lucky Dice Roll at half- or quarter-time with winners receiving 7-Eleven products; title sponsor of Mavs' Street Team and store appearances.
- Chicago Bulls—7-Eleven Lucky Dice Roll; distribution of Bulls' pocket-size schedules.
- Miami Heat—Sponsor of Miami Heat Family Festival; presenting sponsor of Miami Heat Xtreme Team; interactive 7-Eleven fan event.
- Los Angeles Lakers—Distribution of Lakers pocket schedules; halftime contests; 7-Eleven Night at the Lakers.

MLB

- New York Yankees—Consumer Sweepstakes Program; 7-Eleven promotional day at Yankee Stadium.
- Chicago White Sox—7:11 P.M. start time for home games; 7-Eleven Fireworks Night; donation to White Sox charities.
- Chicago Cubs—"Step Up to Home Plate" event at Sunday home games; "Score 7 or 11 & Win" promotion in which fans win prize if Cubs score either 7 or

11 runs during home games; 7-Eleven Day at Wrigley Field; $100 donation to Cubs Care Charity for every double a Cubs player hits during a home game; pocket calendar giveaways.

"I believe we've had a very successful 'draft' for our customers by signing with these top teams in America, and can look forward to continuing to win our customers' loyalty in the years to come," Foster said. Our research shows that one of the top ways our core customers spend their leisure time is attending or watching sports events. I can't think of a better way to reach them than to support their hometown team and favorite pastime. These local sports sponsorships reflect 7-Eleven's Retailer Initiative strategy that focuses on merchandising and developing new fresh foods to meet taste preferences of various regions of the country where we have stores." 7-Eleven also can get coupons into the hands of hungry and thirsty fans, redeemable for free products like its made-fresh-and-delivered-daily deli sandwiches, proprietary coffee, cappuccino, and hot chocolate beverages.

Additionally, 7-Eleven will continue its relationship with AGR as the primary sponsor for the entry driven by 2004 IndyCar Series champion Tony Kanaan. 7-Eleven has sponsored the No. 11 driver for the past four IRL seasons.

Beyond the Team 7-Eleven sponsorship, 7-Eleven signed a multi-year agreement in 2006 to be the "Official Convenience Store" of the Texas Motor Speedway and headline sponsor of November's qualifying day events leading up to the Busch Series and Nextel Chase weekend races. In Florida, 7-Eleven has signed an agreement to be a sponsor of the Honda Grand Prix race in late March on the streets of St. Petersburg. The company again will be involved with extreme sports as a media sponsor when the X Games competition airs on ABC Network in 2007 through 2009.

"We invite our suppliers and business partners to consider working with us to provide even more value for consumers through these kinds of promotions," Foster said. "7-Eleven is in a unique position to be there 24/7 when the customer wants a cold beverage or a great-tasting snack when rooting for their hometown team—whether at the ballpark, stadium, arena, or in the comfort of their own home."

Source: "MVC-Store: 7-Eleven Hopes to Win Over Sports-Loving Customers with Major Team Sponsorships and Integrated Marketing," *PR Newswire US*, January 17, 2007.

The accompanying 7-Eleven example illustrates that sponsorship is typically associated with professional teams, but college athletic departments also rely heavily on sponsorship partnerships.

The marketing of collegiate sports has skyrocketed in recent years. For example, advertisers are lining up to take their shots during the National Collegiate Athletic Association's March basketball tournament. Spending may exceed half a billion dollars

Sponsorship of teams can occur at any level of competition.

for the men's tournament. A report by TNS Media Intelligence estimates that advertisers have spent $2.73 billion on commercials during the tournament in the last seven years. Over that time, the average cost of an ad during the championship game has been $1.2 million—more than a 30-second spot during the World Series or the NBA finals. The Collegiate Licensing Company, which represents more than 200 colleges, universities, bowl games, athletic conferences, the Heisman Trophy, and the NCAA, including the Men's and Women's Final Four, the College World Series, and all NCAA championships, estimates the licensed collegiate market at around $3 billion in retail sales annually, including both apparel and non-apparel sales.[30] Add to that the multimillion-dollar television contracts and deals that most university coaches have with Nike, Reebok, and Adidas, and college athletics is a huge business (see Table 11.8 for a list of universities with the highest revenues from licensed merchandise sales).

Becoming the official outfitter for a university's athletic teams has become especially lucrative for colleges and has given sponsors great exposure. For instance, the University of North Carolina recently extended an eight-year, $28.3 million contract with Nike to fuel the growth of the university's athletic program. Nike will provide North Carolina's athletic department with the following: (1) $18 million in footwear, apparel, and equipment; (2) $200,000 annually, of which half will go to the North

TABLE 11.8	University Merchandise Sales Leaders in 2006
Top Universities	
1. Texas	
2. Notre Dame	
3. Georgia	
4. Michigan	
5. Florida	
6. Alabama	
7. Penn State	
8. Tennessee	
9. North Carolina	
10. Oklahoma	

Carolina general fund and half will go to an academic and athletic excellence fund; (3) $100,000 annually to the Chancellor's Academic Enhancement Fund; (4) up to $175,000 funding for each of five foreign exhibition trips for men's and women's basketball teams and the women's soccer team.[31]

Sport or League   In addition to sponsoring teams, some companies choose to sponsor sports or leagues. One example of this is Procter & Gamble (P&G) and the WNBA. P&G, hoping to attract female audiences, has agreed to a multiyear deal with the league that will include the marketing of brands such as Secret, Head and Shoulders, Herbal Essences, Cascade, Swiffer, Cheer, and Joy. The agreement also allows P&G to leverage their sponsorship through advertising, cross-promotion activities, and team sponsorships, teaming up with the WNBA and its nationwide mobile fitness initiative, the WNBA Be Fit Tour, which promotes the importance of health, fitness, and self-confidence to teens and women through interactive activities and positive messages. Craisins and the WNBA are also conducting supermarket sweepstakes in several markets, allowing customers to submit an entry form found on the supermarket Craisins display for a chance to win a shot at $50,000. One advantage to sponsoring women's sports and the WNBA is that there is less sponsorship clutter. Fewer companies are sponsoring women's sports or leagues, and those that do are creating a unique position and differentiating themselves.

"WNBA marketing partners love the fact that we have direct contact with their target demographics of families and young women," said Donna Orender, commissioner at the WNBA, New York. "Craisins, for example, told us they had double-digit sales increases last season in WNBA cities." [32]

Anheuser-Busch is a corporation that has chosen an integrated approach in sponsoring a number of sports or leagues. Anheuser-Busch became the official beer of Major League Baseball in 1996 and became the official beer of the NBA in 1998.

The A10 corporate partner program.

Source: Copyright © 2002–2003, The Atlantic 10 Conference. All rights reserved.

Bud Light began its sponsorship of Team Seebold in 1982, sponsors the ChampBoat Racing Series team, and became a founding partner of the Professional Bull Riders in 1993. Budweiser and Bud Light are the official beer sponsors of 28 NFL teams and the exclusive alcohol and nonalcohol malt-based beverage sponsor of the Super Bowl. Bud Light also signed on as the official beer of the NHL in 1988 and currently sponsors 21 domestic teams. It has been the official alcoholic beverage of major league Lacrosse since the league started in 2001, and has sponsored the sport since 2004. Current surfer sponsorships include Serena Brooke, Bron Heussenstamm, Sean Moody, and Benji Weatherly. The AVP Tour named Bud Light its official beer of the tour in 2000.

The "Ben Hogan Tour" was established in 1990 as a breeding ground for golf professionals who have not cracked the PGA. In 1993, Nike sponsored the tour, followed by Buy.com, which ended its sponsorship in 2002. Currently, the tour is sponsored by Nationwide, which signed a five-year agreement beginning in 2003. Although the Nationwide Tour was initially thought of as the "minor league" of professional golf, it has become a viable tour in and of itself. Nationwide Insurance signed a five-year extension with the PGA Tour worth nearly $50 million to remain title sponsor of what is effectively golf's top minor league circuit. The 32-event tournament series hits secondary markets (Wichita, Rochester, Chattanooga, Omaha, and Scranton, among others), but company executives say the grassroots marketing and hospitality (pro-ams and VIP passes) provide ample benefit.

In addition, Nationwide cares more about the frequency of events and national TV coverage on The Golf Channel, not to mention alliances with the PGA Tour's other properties. The top 25 players on the Nationwide Tour advance to the PGA Tour, providing an endless source of potential references as a player's career advances. Nationwide's recognition among golf fans increased to 80 percent from 56 percent from the inception of the tour sponsorship five years ago, according to internal research.

Nike has thrown itself into the sponsorship of soccer. By agreeing to pay the U.S. Soccer Federation $120 million over eight years, Nike has boosted U.S. soccer into the big leagues. Nike aspires to dominate the world's most popular sport and capture the largest share of the billions being spent on soccer shoes and apparel. The company has gone from $40 million in sales to $1.5 billion in just 12 years. Nike spent some $100 million on the 2006 World Cup (compared with Adidas' $200 million). The sneaker manufacturer has offered the German soccer federation about $778 million over an eight-year period to switch from current sponsor—and Nike's archrival—Adidas AG and start wearing Nike swooshed uniforms. Lately, leagues have been trying to organize themselves to become more attractive to sponsors. MLS is structured as a single entity, which means that each team owner has a financial stake in the league. This is different from the other professional sports leagues, which consist of individual franchise owners. This structure decreases the opportunity for ambush marketing and offers organizations an integrated sponsorship and licensing program.[33]

The MLS was not the first league to think about how best to serve the interests of sponsors. NFL Properties was designed in 1963 primarily to meet and beat the competition posed by major league Baseball. The league, in attempting to offer a competitive advantage to sponsors, built a system whereby potential sponsors receive collective and individual team rights. That is, sponsors can create opportunities or promotions that feature all NFL teams and local teams in a local market.[34]

Sponsors choose to use the power of the league and its recognizable league logo and, therefore, support all the teams. From the sponsors' perspective, this represents easy and less expensive one-stop shopping. As Burton points out, "If an NFL corporate partner had to design individual local contracts to secure key markets, the collective local team fees would quickly surpass the single sponsorship fee." By allowing sponsors the opportunity to receive collective team rights, the league gains enhanced exposure. As an example, Motorola, Inc., and the National Football League announced a five-year contract extension through the 2011 season. Motorola, one of two sponsors that have an on-field presence, will work with the NFL to develop and implement game-changing communication innovations. Motorola will also expand from a national to a global NFL partner, enabling the two organizations to test technology solutions in the NFL Europe League. The company will continue to be the NFL's exclusive telecommunications hardware sponsor, both at the league level and with all 32 NFL teams.

Events   An athletic platform that is most commonly associated with sports marketing is the event. Examples of sporting events sponsorship are plentiful, as are the opportunities to sponsor sporting events. In fact, sometimes the number of events far outweighs the number of potential corporate sponsors. For example, the city of Winnipeg staged two national and international sporting events over the space of 16 months. In a city that ranks as the eighth largest in Canada and has a population of only 680,000, the challenge was to find enough corporate sponsors. In response to this challenge, event organizers were forced to be more creative in designing sponsorship packages that appeal to organizations of all sizes.[35]

The advantages to using an event as an athletic platform are similar to those benefits gained by using other athletic platforms. For instance, the event will hopefully increase awareness and enhance the image of the sponsor. In addition, consumers have a forum in which to use and purchase the sponsor's products. Lexus offered a swing simulator at its vehicle display tent that lets fans take shots on a computer-generated Oakmont course, while AmEx hosted an interactive area open to all ticket holders at the 2007 U.S. Open.

In another example, Seattle Mariner fans received magnetic season schedules and product samples courtesy of Oberto Sausage Co.

As with the other athletic platforms, one of the primary disadvantages of using events as the athletic platform is sponsorship clutter. In other words, sponsors are competing with other sponsors for the attention of the target audience. One popular way to combat this clutter is to become the title sponsor of an event. Every college football bowl game now has a title sponsor, with the exception of the Rose Bowl—and this too has changed. In 1999 the Rose Bowl added a sponsor's tag line. More formally, this is called a presenting sponsor (i.e., the Rose Bowl presented by Citi).

Choosing the Specific Athletic Platform

The choice of a particular athletic platform follows the selection of the general platform. At this stage of the sponsorship process, the organization makes a decision regarding the exact athlete(s), team, event, or sports entity. For instance, if the organization decides to sponsor a professional women's tennis player, who will be chosen—Serena Williams, Martina Hingis, or Maria Sharapova? As with the previous decisions regarding sponsorship, the choice of a specific sponsor is based largely on finding the right "fit" for the organization and its products

A recent trend is for sports marketers to ensure and control the fit by manufacturing their own sporting events. For example, Nike has created a new division to create and acquire global sporting events. By creating their own events, Nike will be able to control every aspect of how each event is marketed. Moreover, Nike will be able to develop events that are the perfect fit for their multiple target markets.[36] Other organizations, such as Honda, are pursuing a similar strategy. They have put pressure on their advertising agency to develop sporting events that will be the ideal match for the Honda target market.

Once the decision regarding the general level of sponsorship and the specific athletic platform have been addressed, it may be useful to review carefully the choice(s)

of sponsorship before taking the final step. To do so, Brant Wansley of BrandMarketing Service, Ltd. offers the following suggestions for choosing a sponsorship:[37]

- Does the sponsorship offer the right positioning?
- Does the sponsorship provide a link to the brand image?
- Is the sponsorship hard for competitors to copy?
- Does the sponsorship target the right audience?
- Does the sponsorship appeal to the target audiences' lifestyle, personality, and values?
- How does the sponsorship dovetail into current corporate goals and strategies?
- Can the sponsorship be used for hospitality to court important potential and current customers?
- Is there a way to involve employees in the sponsorship?
- How will you measure the impact of the sponsorship?
- Can you afford the sponsorship?
- How easy will it be to plan the sponsorship year after year?
- Does the sponsorship complement your current promotion mix?

SPONSORSHIP IMPLEMENTATION AND EVALUATION

Once the sponsorship decisions are finalized, plans are put into action and then evaluated to determine their effectiveness. Do sponsorships really work? The findings to this million-dollar question are somewhat mixed. In Chapter 13, we discuss the techniques organizations use to determine whether the sponsorship has met their objectives. For now, let us look at the results of several studies that were conducted to determine consumer response to sponsorship. In a poll conducted by Performance Research, more than half of the respondents indicated they would be "not very likely" or "not at all likely" to purchase a company's products because it was an Olympic sponsor.[38] Surveys by Performance Research have found that if given the choice between two similar products, 72 percent of NASCAR fans would purchase the product of a NASCAR sponsor. Fans are three times as likely as nonfans to try to purchase NASCAR sponsors' products and services. That so-called "loyalty rate" compares with about 35 percent for the NFL and baseball, and 40 percent for the NBA. The only groups that have loyalty rates close to NASCAR's are nonprofits and the performing arts, both in the 60 percent range, according to the firm's data.

Most studies report that sponsorship is having a positive impact on their organizations. For example, Visa reported that since its affiliation with the Olympic Games, its market share in the United States increased by one-third, but the number of consumers who considered it the best overall card doubled to 61 percent.[39] Delta Air Lines also increased awareness levels from 38 percent to 70 percent due to its Olympic sponsorship. A recent study by the International Olympic Committee found that 22 percent of respondents would be more likely to buy a product if it were an Olympic sponsor's product.[40] In another study, roughly 60 percent of consumers indicated that they "try to buy a company's product if they support the Olympic Games.[41] In addition, 57 percent of consumers around the world agreed that "they look favorably towards a company if it is associated with the Olympics."

However, some researchers found that the majority of consumers say sponsorship makes no difference to them and their purchase behavior. For example, Quester and Lardinoit conducted a study and found that Olympic sponsors could not expect to find higher levels of brand recognition or loyalty.[42] Additionally, a study by Pitts and Slattery found that over 60 percent of respondents said they would not be more likely to purchase a product just because they knew it was a sponsor's product.[43] One potential reason for

TABLE 11.9	Why Sponsorships Fail

No Budget for Activation—Be prepared to spend several times your rights fees to leverage the property.

Not Long-Term—One-year commitments generally don't work. It takes time to build the association.

No Measurable Objectives—Must have internal agreement on sponsorship goals.

Too Brand-Centric—Sponsorship should be based on the needs of consumers, not brands.

Overlook Ambush and Due Diligence—Knowing what you are not getting as important as what you are getting.

Too Much Competition for Trade Participation—When products sold through the same distribution channel sponsor the same property, the impact is diluted.

Failure to Excite the Sales Chain—A sponsorship program will not work unless the concept is sold throughout the entire distribution channel.

Insufficient Staffing—Additional staffing is needed to meet the time demands of sponsoring an event.

Buying at the Wrong Level—Higher sponsorship levels equate to more benefits. Make sure you are reaping all the benefits or buy at a lower level.

No Local Extensions—National brands must create localized execution overlays for a sponsorship to truly reach their audiences.

No Communication of Added Value—For maximum impact, sponsors must be viewed as bringing something to the event. The activity should be "provided by" the brand rather than "sponsored by" it.

these less than encouraging findings is the amount of sponsorship clutter. For example, Ohio-based Wendy's, which had been an OSU sponsor for "more than two decades," decided to drop its sponsorship with the school "under pressure from activist investors to reduce costs and improve its financial performance."[44] The company has also ended its sponsorships of the Blue Jackets and a local LPGA tournament.

Other reasons that sponsorships are dropped or fail are highlighted in Table 11.9.

Summary

The element of the promotional mix that is linked with sports marketing to the highest degree is sponsorship. A sponsorship is an investment in a sports entity (athlete, league, team, or event) to support overall organizational goals, marketing objectives, and/or promotional objectives. Sports sponsorships are growing in popularity as a promotional tool for sports and nonsports products (and organizations). For example, an estimated $4.56 billion was spent on sports sponsorships in 1998. Because so much emphasis is placed on sponsorship, an organization must understand how to develop the most effective sponsorship program.

The systematic process for designing a sponsorship program consists of four sequential steps, which include setting sponsorship objectives, determining the sponsorship budget, acquiring a sponsorship, and implementing and evaluating the sponsorship. Because sponsorship is one of the promotional mix elements, it is important to remember the relationship it has with the broader promotional strategy. As suggested in Chapters 9 and 10 all the elements of the promotional mix must be integrated to achieve maximum effectiveness.

The sponsorship process begins by setting objectives. These objectives, not unlike advertising objectives, can be categorized as either direct or indirect. Direct sponsorship objectives focus on stimulating consumer demand for the sponsoring organization and its products. The sponsoring company benefits by attaching their product to the sports entity. The sports entity also benefits by increased exposure given by the sponsor. As such, both parties in the sponsorship agreement benefit through the association. Indirect objectives may also be set for the sponsorship program. These objectives include generating awareness, meeting and beating the competition, reaching new target markets (e.g., disabled) or specialized target markets (e.g., mature market), building relationships with customers, and enhancing the company's image.

After objectives have been formulated, the sponsorship budget is considered. The techniques for

setting sponsorship budgets are also in accord with the promotional budgeting methods discussed in the previous chapter. Generally, sponsorship of sporting events is not an inexpensive proposition—especially given the threat of ambush marketing. Ambush marketing is the planned effort by an organization to associate themselves indirectly with an event to gain at least some of the recognition and benefits that are associated with being an official sponsor. In past years, the Olympics have been a playground for ambush marketing techniques. For example, Nike, not an official sponsor of the 1996 Summer Olympics, constructed a building overlooking the Olympic Park to associate themselves with the festivities of the Olympic Games. Today, more stringent policing and regulation of ambush marketing is occurring by the sporting event organizers to protect the heavy financial outlay of official sponsors.

The third step of the sponsorship process is to choose the sponsorship opportunity, or acquire the sponsorship. This means making decisions about the scope of the sponsorship, choosing the general athletic platform, and then choosing the specific athletic platform. The scope of the sponsorship refers to the geographic reach of the sports entity, as well as the interest in the entity. Shani and Sandler describe the scope of athletic events using a tool called the Sports Event Pyramid. The Sports Event Pyramid is a hierarchy of events based on geographic scope and level of interest among spectators. The five-tiered hierarchy ranges from international events, such as the Olympic Games, to local events, such as a Little League tournament in your community. Once the scope of the sponsorship has been chosen, the athletic platform must be determined. The athletic platform for a sponsorship is generally a team, sport, event, or athlete. In addition, the athletic platform could be further categorized on the basis of level of competition (i.e., professional, collegiate, high school, or recreational). Decisions regarding the choice of athletic platform should be linked to the objectives set in the previous stages of sponsorship planning. After choosing the general athletic platform, the potential sponsor must select the specific platform. For example, if a collegiate sporting event is to be the general platform, then the specific athletic platform may be the Rose Bowl, the Championship Game of the Final Four, or a regular season baseball game against an in-state rival.

The final phase of the sponsorship process is to implement and evaluate the sponsorship plans. Organizing a sponsorship and integrating a sponsorship program with the other promotional mix elements requires careful coordination. Once the sponsorship plan is put into action, the most critical question for decision makers is, "Did the program deliver or have we met our sponsorship objectives?" The implementation and evaluation of the strategic sports marketing process and, more specifically, sponsorships are considered in Chapter 13.

Key Terms

- ambush marketing, p. 333
- athletic platform, p. 351
- awareness, p. 333
- competition, p. 334
- decision maker, p. 349
- direct sponsorship objectives, p. 333
- gatekeepers, p. 349
- global events, p. 350
- image building, p. 342
- indirect sponsorship objectives, p. 333
- influencers, p. 349
- international events, p. 350
- local events, p. 350
- national event, p. 351
- match-up hypothesis, p. 342
- purchasers, p. 349
- reaching new target markets, p. 337
- regional events, p. 350
- relationship marketing, p. 339
- sales increases, p. 344
- sponsorship, p. 324
- sponsorship budgeting methods, p. 345
- sponsorship evaluation, p. 349
- sponsorship objectives, p. 333
- sponsorship program, p. 329
- sport sponsorship acquisition, p. 348
- sports event pyramid, p. 350

Review Questions

1. Define sponsorship and discuss how sponsorship is used as a promotional mix tool by sports marketers. Provide evidence to support the growth of sports sponsorships worldwide.
2. Outline the steps for designing a sports sponsorship program.
3. Discuss, in detail, the major objectives of sports sponsorship from the perspective of the sponsoring organization.
4. What is ambush marketing, and why is it such a threat to legitimate sponsors? What defense would you take against ambush marketing tactics as a sports marketer?
5. In your opinion, why are sports sponsorships so successful in reaching a specific target market?
6. How are sponsorship budgets established within an organization?

7. Describe the various levels of the sponsorship pyramid. What is the Sports Event Pyramid used for, and what are some potential problems with the pyramid?
8. Define an athletic platform. In determining what athletic platform to use for a sponsorship, what factors should be considered?

9. What questions or issues might an organization raise when choosing among sponsorship opportunities?
10. Describe the different ways that sports sponsorships might be evaluated. Which evaluation tool is the most effective?

Exercises

1. Design a proposed sponsorship plan for a local youth athletic association.
2. Provide five examples of extremely good or effective match-ups between sporting events and their sponsors. In addition, suggest five examples of extremely poor or ineffective match-ups between sporting events and their sponsors.
3. Find at least one example of sponsorship for each of the following athletic platforms: individual athlete, team, and league.

4. Contact an organization that sponsors any sport or sporting event and discuss how sponsorship decisions are made and by whom. Also, ask about how the organization evaluates sponsorship.
5. Design a survey to determine the influence of NASCAR sponsorships on consumers' purchase behaviors. Ask 10 consumers to complete the survey and summarize the findings. Suggest how NASCAR might use these findings.

Internet Exercises

1. Search the Internet and find an example of a sponsorship opportunity at each level of the Sports Event Pyramid.
2. Locate at least three sports marketing companies on the Internet that specialize in the marketing of

sponsorship opportunities. What products or services are these organizations offering potential clients?

Endnotes

1. "Adidas Contract Provides More Than Nike," *The University Daily Kansan*, November 26, 2007, http://www.kansan.com/stories/2007/mar/06/contract/?news.
2. Patriot Soccer, http://www.patriotssoccer.org/leagues/2011/graphics/2006%20TournamentSponsorship.doc.
3. David Stotlar, "Sponsorship Evaluation: Moving from Theory to Practice," *Sport Marketing Quarterly*, vol. 13, no. 1 (2004), 61–64.
4. See, for example, Nigel Pope, "Overview of Current Sponsorship Thought," www.cad.gu.edu.au/cjsm/pope21.htm; R. Abratt, B. Clayton, and L. Pitt, "Corporate Objectives in Sports Sponsorship," *International Journal of Advertising*, vol. 6 (1987), 299–311; Christine Brooks, *Sports Marketing: Competitive Business Strategies for Sports* (Englewood Cliffs, NJ: Prentice Hall, 1994).
5. Janet Hoek, Philip Gendall, Michelle Jeffcoat, and David Orsman, "Sponsorship and Advertising: A Comparison of Their Effects," *Journal of Marketing Communications* (1997), 21–32.
6. "Major League Baseball Properties Announces State Farm as 'Official Insurance Company of major league Baseball,'" June 29, 2007, http://mlb.mlb.com/news/press_releases/press_release.jsp?ymd=20070629&content_id=2055865&vkey=pr_mlb&fext=.jsp&c_id=mlb&partnered=rss_mlb.
7. D. M. Sandler and D. Shani, "Ambush Marketing: Who Gets the Gold?" *Journal of Advertising Research*, vol. 29 (1989), 9–14.
8. *Atlanta Constitution Journal* (December 29, 1995). www.atlantagames.com/WEB/oly/getcoke2.html.
9. Jeff Lee, "Trademark Law to Protect the Olympics: Ambush Marketing," *Vancouver Sun*, March 6, 2007, p. 14.
10. "Brands Set Sponsor Ambush," *Sports Marketing* (November 2000), 2.
11. Luke Harding and Drew Culf, "Ambush Marketing: The New World Cup Rule: Take Off Your Trousers, They're Offending Our Sponsor," *The Guardian* (London), June 19, 2006.
12. "MassMutual Signs New Five-Year Deal for US Open Sponsorship; Expanded Relationship Includes New US Open Series," (March 1, 2004), prnewswire.com.
13. "Starwood Hotels & Resorts Announces Exclusive Global Hotel Partnership with Special Olympics" (December 14, 2006), http://www.starwoodhotels.com/westin/about/news/news_release_detail.html?obj_id=0900c7b98071c432.

14. Clare Ogilvie, "Countdown to 2010; 2010 a Turning Point for Paralympics: Event Will Make Heroes Just as the Olympics Does," *The Vancouver Province* (British Columbia), March 12, 2007, A6.

15. Nancy Lough and Richard Irwin, "A Comparative Analysis of Sponsorship Objectives for U.S. Women's Sport and Traditional Sport Sponsorship," *Sport Marketing Quarterly,* vol. 10, no. 4 (2001), 202–211.

16. Roger Bennett, "Corporate Hospitality: Executive Indulgence or Vital Corporate Communications Weapon," *Corporate Communications: An International Journal*, vol. 8, no. 4 (2003), 229–240.

17. Tod Leonard, "Partying Venues Largely Sold Out at Torrey Pines," *Union-Tribune,* May 8, 2007.

18. "Shell Houston Open Helps PGA Tour Reach $800 Million in Charity Contributions, While Helping a Million Children in the Gulf Coast Region," PR Newswire US, April 2, 2007.

19. Alain Ferrand and Monique Pagés, "Image Sponsoring: A Methodology to Match Event and Sponsor," *Journal of Sport Management*, vol. 10, no. 3 (July 1996), 278–291.

20. "Gillette and Major League Baseball Team Up to Take On Prostate Cancer," http://www.gillettepcc.org/pdfs/Gillette-MLB%20Press%20Release%20-%20FINAL%206.6.06.pdf.

21. Jennifer C. Kerr, "Consumer Group Wants College Sports to Nix the Beer Ads," *Associated Press* (November 12, 2003).

22. Roger Williams, "Making the Decision and Paying for It," *Mark McCormack's Guide to Sports Marketing*, International Sports Marketing Group (1996), 166–168.

23. Brant Wamsley, "Best Practices Will Help Sponsorships Succeed," *Marketing News* (September 1, 1997), 8.

24. "What Sponsors Want: Latest IEG Survey Findings," http://www.sponsorship.com/IEG-Insights/Content/IEG-Insights-Article.aspx? id=1&redirect=/IEG-Insights/What-Sponsors-Want —Latest-IEG-Survey-Findings.aspx.

25. "Scoring with Sports Fans," *Beverage Industry* (November 1996), 46, 48, 49.

26. David Shani and Dennis Sandler, "Climbing the Sports Event Pyramid," *Marketing News* (August 26, 1996), 6.

27. Christine Brooks, *Sports Marketing* (Benjamin-Cummings, 1994).

28. Jeremy Mullman, "Is Nike Next? ATA Drops Scandal-Prone Vick; Football Pitchman Faces Indictment for His Alleged Role in Dog-Fighting Ring," *Advertising Age,* June 4, 2007, p. 6.

29. Veronica Gorley Chufo, "Vick's Dog Act—NFL Star Faces Five Years' Jail," *The Courier Mail* (Australia), October 1, 2007.

30. Caroline Kennedy, "Selling School Spirit; Say Hurrah for Collegiate Licensed Product, a Growing Category That Taps Team Loyalty and Alumni Pride," *Gifts and Decorative Accessories*, June 1, 2007.

31. "Nike Swoosh Expands in $28.3 Million Contract," *North Carolina General Alumni Association On-Line* (October 16, 2001).

32. "Ocean Spray Craisins Team Up with the WNBA," June 21, 2006, http://www.craisins.com/news/pr/pressrelease98.aspx.

33. "A Look Back at the First Two Years of MLS," www.mlsnet.com/aboum/#The Structure.

34. Rick Burton, "A Case Study on Sports Property Servicing Excellence: National Football League Properties," *Sport Marketing Quarterly*, vol. 5, no. 3 (1996), 23–30.

35. Nancy Boomer, "Winnipeg's Next Flood," www.marketingmag.ca/Content/1.98/special.html.

36. Jeff Jenson, "Nike Creates New Division to Stage Global Events," *Advertising Age* (September 30, 1996), 2.

37. Brant Wamsley, "Best Practices Will Help Sponsorships Succeed," *Marketing News* (September 1, 1997), 8.

38. Howard Schlossberg, *Sports Marketing* (Cambridge, MA: Blackwell Publishers, 1996).

39. Carol Emert, "Olympic Seal of Approval," *The San Francisco Chronicle* (September 2, 2000), D1.

40. Pascale Quester and Thierry Lardinoit, "Sponsors' Impact on Attitude and Purchase Intentions: Longitudinal Study of the 2000 Olympic Games," December 2001, http://130.195.95.71:8081/WWW/ANZMAC2001/home.htm.

41. Stuart Elliott, "After $5 Billion Is Bet, Marketers Are Racing to Be Noticed Amid the Clutter of the Summer Games," *The New York Times* (July 16, 1996), D6.

42. Pascale Quester and Thierry Lardinoit, "Sponsors' Impact on Attitude and Purchase Intentions: Longitudinal Study of the 2000 Olympic Games— December 2001," http://130.195.95.71:8081/WWW/ANZMAC2001/home.htm.

43. Brenda Pitts and Jennifer Slattery, "An Examination of the Effects of Time on Sponsorship Awareness Levels," *Sport Marketing Quarterly*, vol. 13, no. 1 (2004), 43–54.

44. "McDonald's to Sponsor Ohio State Athletics," March 13, 2007, http://www.bizjournals.com/columbus/stories/2007/03/12/daily9.html?from_msnbc=1.

CHAPTER

12

PRICING CONCEPTS AND STRATEGIES

After completing this chapter, you should be able to:

■ Explain the relationship among price, value, and benefits.

■ Understand the relationship between price and the other marketing mix elements.

■ Describe how costs and organizational objectives affect pricing decisions.

■ Explain how the competitive environment influences pricing decisions.

■ Describe how and when price adjustments should be made in the final stage of pricing.

If you were an executive of a sports franchise, what price would you charge your fans? What factors would you consider when making your pricing decision in a continually changing marketing environment? How would you estimate the demand for tickets? Will the financial benefit of increasing prices offset the negative fan relations?

In this chapter, we explore the subjective nature of pricing sports products. More specifically, we consider how factors such as consumer demand, organizational objectives, competition, and technology impact pricing. Also, we examine how pricing interacts with the other elements of the marketing mix and how effective pricing adjustments are made. Let us begin by developing a basic understanding of pricing.

WHAT IS PRICE?

Price is a statement of value for a sports product. For example, the money we pay for being entertained by the Boston Celtics is price. The money that we pay for shorts featuring the Notre Dame logo is price. The money we pay for a personal seat license, which gives us the right to purchase a season ticket, is price. The money we pay on tuition to the Dave Pelz Scoring Game Golf School is price. In all these examples, the price paid is a function of the value placed on the sports product by consumers.

The essence of pricing is the exchange process discussed in Chapter 1. Price is simply a way to quantify the value of the objects being exchanged. Typically, money is exchanged for the sports product. We pay $26 in exchange for admission to the sporting event. However, the object of value that is being exchanged does not always have to be

To some, golf lessons may be priceless.

money. For instance, Play It Again Sports, a new and used sporting goods retailer, allows consumers to trade their previously owned sports equipment for the store's used or new equipment. This form of pricing is more commonly referred to as barter or trade. It is common for kids who exchange baseball cards to use this form of trade. Many golf courses hire retirees and pay them very low wages in exchange for free rounds of golf.

Regardless of how pricing is defined, value is the central tenet of pricing. The value placed on a ticket to a sporting event is based on the relationship of the perceived benefits to the price paid. Stated simply,

$$\text{Value} = \frac{\text{Perceived benefits of sports product}}{\text{Price of sports product}}$$

The perceived benefits of the sports product, or what the product does for the user, are based on its tangible and intangible features. The tangible benefits are important in determining price because these are the features of the product that a consumer can actually see, touch, or feel. For example, the comfort of the seats, the quality of the concessions, and the appearance of the stadium are all tangible aspects of a sporting event. The intangible benefits of going to a sporting event may include spending time with friends and family, feelings of association with the team when they win (e.g., BIRGing), or "being seen" at the game.[1]

The perceived benefit of attending a St. Louis Cardinals game is a subjective experience based on each individual's perception of the event, the sport, and the team. One consumer may pay a huge amount to see the game because of the perceived benefits of the product (mostly intangible), whereas another consumer may attend the game only if given a ticket. In either case, the perceived benefits either meet or exceed the price, resulting in "perceived value."

For the high-involvement sports fan, the Cardinals ticket represents a chance to be able to tell his grandchildren that he saw the 2001 Rookie of the Year and 2005 MVP, Albert Pujols. To the no- or low-involvement individual, the same game may appear to be a complete waste of time. Again, it is important to recognize that the value placed on attending the sporting event is unique to each individual, even though they are consuming the same product (in this case, the Cardinals game). As researcher Valerie Zeithaml points out, "What constitutes value—even in a single product category—appears to be highly personal and idiosyncratic."[2]

Using a different example, a Reggie Jackson rookie baseball card in mint condition may be priced at $600. A collector or baseball enthusiast may see this as a value because the perceived benefits outweigh the price. However, the noncollector (or the mom or dad who threw our cards away) may perceive the card as having barely more value than the cost of the paper on which it is printed.

In yet another example, professional sports franchises are assigned monetary values based on tangibles such as gate receipts, media revenues, venue revenues (e.g., concessions, stadium advertising, and naming), players' costs, and operating expenses. Further consideration in the value of a professional sports franchise is brand equity, a highly intangible characteristic. Table 12.1 provides a list of the franchises having the highest values in each sport and the respective percentage change from the previous year.

The combination of revenue growth and investments in new, revenue-rich ballparks (the St. Louis Cardinals moved into their new home in the 2006 season, while the Mets, Yankees, Minnesota Twins, and Washington Nationals should all be in new stadiums by 2010) fueled a 15 percent increase in MLB average team values, to an average of $431 million.[3] The average NFL team is worth $898 million, 211 percent more than when *Forbes* began calculating team values eight years ago. The average hockey team is now worth approximately $180 million and makes an operating profit, while NBA teams are worth $353 million and growing at a rapid pace.[4]

Two important points emerge from the previous examples of value. First, value varies greatly from consumer to consumer because the perceived benefits of any sports product will depend on personal experience. Second, pricing is based on perceived value and perceived benefits. As such, consumers' subjective perceptions of the sports product's benefits and image are fundamental to setting the right price. In this case, image really is everything.

All too often, price is equated incorrectly with the objective costs of producing the sports product. Because many sports products are intangible services, setting prices based on the costs of producing the product alone becomes problematic. For instance, how do you quantify the cost of spending time with your friends at a sporting event or having the television rights to broadcast NFL games?

How do sports organizations provide a quality experience for fans so they feel they are getting their money's worth? Many event promoters believe the solution

TABLE 12.1   Top Professional Sports Franchise Values

Major League Baseball	*Current in millions*	*1-Year Change*
Yankees	$1200	+17%
Mets	$736	+22%
Red Sox	$724	+17%
National Football League	*Current in millions*	*1-Year Change*
Redskins	$1432	+13%
Patriots	$1176	+13%
Cowboys	$1173	+10%
National Basketball Assoc.	*Current in millions*	*1-Year Change*
Knicks	$592	+9%
Lakers	$568	+7%
Mavericks	$463	+15%
National Hockey League	*Current in millions*	*2-Year Change*
Maple Leafs	$332	+18%
Rangers	$306	+9%
Red Wings	$258	+4%

is to add more value via interactive experiences for the fan. For example, the Indy Racing League (IRL) has added a Fan Experience allowing racing fans to compete on the simulated Indy Racing Challenge, change tires at the Indy Racing League Pit Stop Challenge, purchase merchandise at the Racing Gear tent, or visit the kid-friendly Indy Racing Kids area. The Fan Experience has reached some 1.6 million fans. Bill Long, vice president of marketing for the IRL, believes "this is the largest traveling fan exhibit of any sports property in terms of numbers of locations and event days, as we made over 600 appearances this year."[5] In a similar vein, the NCAA created Hoops City for the men's and the women's Final Four. The interactive experience gives basketball fans a chance to participate in a number of hoop skills contests, get autographs, and share the excitement of the national championship.[6]

The stadium experience has also been jazzed up to enhance value. One of the best examples of in-arena experiences was at the Miami Sol, where kids under 12 formed a human "Sol train" and paraded around the court during intermissions to a bongo beat. They were able to set foot on the court and provide audience entertainment. Kids who attended the game were selected from the audience before the game and instructed on their involvement in the action. Small, in-seat video screens are also becoming popular at stadiums and arenas that want to offer the ultimate balance between watching the action live and on TV. Each seat is equipped with a video monitor that can offer game replays, other cable TV networks, stock market updates, and online service.[7]

The ultimate question is whether these "extras" create value and add benefits for the fans. SMRI research has found that nine out of ten fans attend sporting events out of a love for the game or team. So are these extras creating real fans or trying to buy their way into fans' hearts? Do stadiums and arenas pay more for the interactive fan elements and end up receiving much less in the end—a fan that attends for the extras, not for the love of sports, the competitive element, the rivalry, the action; in other words—the game?

THE DETERMINANTS OF PRICING

Now that we have discussed the core concept of price, let us look at some of the factors that affect the pricing decisions of sporting marketers. Pricing decisions can be influenced by internal and external factors, much in the same way that the contingency framework for sports marketing contains both internal and external considerations. **Internal factors,** which are controlled by the organization, include the other marketing mix elements, costs, and organizational objectives. **External (or environmental) factors** that influence pricing are beyond the control of the organization. These include consumer demand, competition, legal issues, the economy, and technology. Figure 12.1 illustrates the influence of the internal and external forces on pricing decisions. Let us look at each of these forces in greater detail.

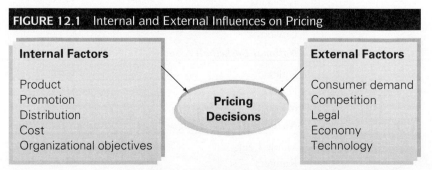

FIGURE 12.1 Internal and External Influences on Pricing

Internal Factors	Pricing Decisions	External Factors
Product		Consumer demand
Promotion		Competition
Distribution		Legal
Cost		Economy
Organizational objectives		Technology

Source: Gary Armstrong and Philip Kotler, *Marketing: An Introduction,* 7th ed. © 2005. (Reprinted by permission of Pearson Education, Inc. Upper Saddle River, NJ.)

SPORTS MARKETING HALL OF FAME

Pete Rozelle

Pete Rozelle led the National Football League for nearly three decades, helping it survive bidding wars with three rival leagues and three players' strikes, before retiring unexpectedly in 1989.

Rozelle's pioneering sports marketing accomplishments include Monday Night Football and the Super Bowl, which blossomed into America's most-watched sporting event. The "Father of the Super Bowl" put the NFL on television just about everywhere and transformed the way Americans spend Sunday afternoons.

Rozelle arrived at about the same time as the rival American Football League, a development that created competition for players and television ratings. In 1962, Rozelle negotiated a $9.3 million television contract with CBS, a deal that earned him reelection as commissioner and a $10,000 bonus that pushed his salary to $60,000. By 1966, the two warring leagues, weary of the battle for player talent, merged, creating a single professional football league, with Rozelle as commissioner. The merger also produced a world championship game, which would eventually come to be known as the Super Bowl.

It was Rozelle who brought sports into 10 figures when he negotiated a landmark five-year, $2.1 billion contract with television's three major networks in 1982. Then he expanded to cable, selling a Sunday night series to ESPN in 1986. The current television contract, for which Rozelle set the groundwork, gets $1.58 billion for four years from Fox alone, more than 2,000 times what Rozelle got in his first contract with CBS in 1962.

Along with these accomplishments, Rozelle's biggest contribution may have been introducing revenue sharing in pro football 30 years before it created havoc in other sports. Doing so allowed teams in minor markets like Green Bay to equally share TV revenues—the biggest part of the NFL pie—with teams in New York, Chicago, and Los Angeles.

Rozelle is also credited, along with Roone Arledge, for creating Monday Night Football, now the nation's longest-running sports series. Because the NFL had an agreement not to televise on Friday night or Saturday in competition with high school and college football, he decided Monday night would be the obvious time to showcase a single game nationally. Overall, Rozelle's impact was as much social as it was financial. He changed the nation's leisure habits and lifestyle by making Sunday afternoons and Monday nights sacred during football seasons.

Source: "Innovator Rozelle Dies at 70," *Cincinnati Enquirer* (December 7, 1996), C1, C5.

Internal Factors

Other Marketing Mix Variables

Price is the element of the marketing mix that has been called a "pressure point" for consumers. That is, price can make or break a consumer's decision to purchase a sports product. Although price is critical, the other **marketing mix variables** must be carefully considered when determining the price of a sports product. Pricing must be consistent with product, distribution, and promotional planning. For marketing goals to be reached, all the marketing mix elements must work in concert with one another.

How is price connected to other marketing mix variables? Let us begin by examining the relationship between price and promotional planning. Each of the promotional mix elements discussed in Chapter 9 (advertising, public relations, personal selling, sales promotions, and sponsorships) is related to price. Broadly, the promotion function communicates the price of the sports product to consumers. For example, advertisements often inform consumers about the price of a sports product. In comparative advertisements, the price of a sports product versus its competition may be the central focus of the message.

Many forms of sales promotion are directly related to price. For example, price reductions are price discounts designed to encourage immediate purchase of the sports product. Coupons and rebates are simply another way for consumers to get money back from the original purchase price. Moreover, premiums are sometimes offered for reduced prices (or for free) to build long-term relationships with consumers. For instance, kids can join the Pittsburg Pirates Bucaroos Kids Club for just $15 dollars for the entire season. For this, kids receive the following benefits: Official Bucaroos VIK (Very Important Kid) membership card that gets them special offers from the Pirates and Pirates corporate partners; official Bucaroos T-shirt; two vouchers for any Sunday–Thursday home game (excluding Opening Day and Skyblast); subscription to the *Bucaroos Newsletter*; invitation to a pregame autograph and photo session with Pirates players; front-of-the-line privileges during Kids-Run-the-Bases; and inclusion in the lottery to be a part of Kids-Take-the-Field.

The relationship between pricing and promotion also extends to personal selling. Depending on the sports product, sales personnel sometimes negotiate prices. Although not the case for most sports products, some prices are negotiable. The sale of boats, golf clubs, squash lessons, scalped tickets, and luxury boxes each represents an example of a sports product that has the potential for flexible pricing.

The public relations component of the promotional mix is also related to pricing in several ways. First, publicity and public relations personnel often stress the value of their ticket prices to potential consumers. For example, the Phoenix Coyotes public relations department may provide fans information about how the Coyotes have the lowest cost in the NHL for a family of four to attend a game. The Kansas City Royals may emphasize that they have the lowest average ticket prices in baseball, compared with other major league sports and teams.

Second, public relations are important in the launch of a new sports product. Media releases that alert the public to the features of the new product, as well as the pricing, are an important aspect of creating awareness. In addition, sources not only inside but also outside of the sports organization play roles in providing information about changes to the product. For instance, when a professional sports team raises its ticket price, you can bet that the story will generate "negative public relations."

A final link between price and promotion is the cost of the promotion itself. The price of running a promotion may influence potential consumers. The price of a Super Bowl advertisement (a record $2.6 million for a 30-second spot in 2007), upon becoming public knowledge, may shape consumers' expectations and perceptions of not only the advertisement, but also the product and the company. Consumers' expectations for advertisements featured during the Super Bowl are generally higher because of the hype and the advertisement's high price tag. At the same time, the high levels of free publicity generated by Super Bowl advertisements, both prior to and after the event itself, can offset the exorbitant expense and render the advertisements cost effective.

The distribution element of the marketing mix is also related to pricing. The price of a sports product is certainly dictated (in part) by the choice of distribution channel(s). In a traditional channel (manufacturer of the sporting good to wholesaler to retailer to consumer), the costs of covering the various functions of the channel members are reflected in the ultimate price charged to consumers. In a more nontraditional channel, such as purchasing a product over the Internet, prices are generally reduced. For example, the Callaway FT-5 Tour driver may cost $500 in a golf specialty store but is sold for hundreds of dollars less via the Internet.

The retailer is also a common member of the distribution channel that shapes pricing decisions. More specifically, the type of retailer selling the sporting good or facility where the sporting event takes place will affect price perceptions. For instance, consumers expect to pay more for golf equipment in a country club pro shop than they do at a local golf discount outlet. Likewise, consumers who attend a football game at Dallas' new Cowboy Stadium (to open in 2009) expect to pay higher ticket prices for the state-of-the-art facility than do consumers at an aging facility such as Arrowhead Stadium in Kansas City (built in 1972). A concern facing professional sports is that the new sports palaces being built around the country may drive the common fan out of professional sports markets.

A final element of the marketing mix related to price is the sports product itself. The price of attending a sporting event is related to expectations of service quality. The higher the ticket price being purchased, the higher fan expectations of customer service. Likewise, the higher the price of the sporting good, the higher the consumer expectations of product quality. In this way, price is used to signal quality to consumers, especially to those who have little or no previous experience using the sports product.

Pricing is also used to differentiate product lines within the sports organization. An organization will offer product lines with different price ranges to attract different target markets. For example, Converse still offers a canvas basketball shoe at a low price for traditionalists who prefer canvas over the more popular—and more expensive—leather style.

The product life cycle also suggests the strength of the price–product relationship. As illustrated in Chapter 8, pricing strategies vary throughout the stages of the product life cycle. For example, during the introductory phase, products are typically priced either low to gain widespread acceptance or high to appeal to a specific target market and to signal quality. Product prices are slashed during the decline phase of the life cycle to eliminate inventory and related overhead costs.

The design of sports products is the final factor that demonstrates the close relationship between product and price. Product design and pricing are interdependent. Sometimes, product design is altered during the manufacturing process to achieve a target price. For instance, a number of championship teams have dramatically dropped payroll in the year following winning the championship, causing fan dissatisfaction and poor performance on the field or court. In this case, the product design refers to the quality of the team; the manufacturing process is the team's performance on the field. Unfortunately, the team and its fans may suffer from this move to achieve target price. Other times, prices must be adjusted (usually upward) to achieve the desired product design. New York Yankees owner George Steinbrenner has historically spent large sums of money to build a winning team (with a record high payroll of $195 million in 2007), with success as the team has appeared in the World Series Championships six times between 1996 and 2003.

Research has been conducted to examine the relationship between team payroll and team performance in Major League Baseball from 1985 to 2002. The results indicate that the relationship has changed over time. Unlike the early years, there is now a much clearer relationship between payroll and performance. Specifically, in the latter part of the 1990s and continuing into the 21st century, the greater the team payroll and the more equally this payroll is distributed among team members, the better the on-field performance of the team. This is a problem of particular concern because of the growing disparity in team payrolls, which, in turn, affects the competitive balance of the sport.[8] Clearly, price is closely associated with the rest of the marketing mix. Usually, there are two ways of coordinating the element of price with the rest of the marketing mix variables: nonprice and price competition. Let us look at these two distinctly different pricing strategies in greater detail.

Nonprice versus Price Competition

Nonprice competition is defined as creating a unique sports product through the packaging, product design, promotion, distribution, or any marketing variable other than price. This approach permits a firm to charge higher prices than its competitors because its product has achieved a competitive advantage. In turn, consumers are often willing to pay more for these products because the perceived benefits derived from the product are believed to be greater. Nevertheless, an element of risk is attached to using this nonprice competition approach.

Consider a commodity like a golf ball. Bridgestone may adopt a nonprice competition strategy for its brand of golf balls (Precept) by featuring the packaging, the product design, or something other than price. This can be a risky strategy for Bridgestone. What if consumers fail to recognize the superiority of the Precept golf ball? They may instead purchase a competitor's lower-priced golf ball that offers the same benefits.

When adopting the distinctly different **price competition** strategy, sellers primarily stimulate consumer demand by offering consumers lower prices. For example, minor league franchises successfully use price competition to attract dissatisfied fans unable or unwilling to spend large sums of money to attend major league sporting events. In response to a price competition strategy, and to offset its own higher ticket costs, a major league franchise is likely to stress the greater intangible benefits associated with attending its more prestigious events. These benefits include the higher quality of competition, the more exciting atmosphere, and the greater athletic abilities of the stars.

Costs

Costs are those factors associated with producing, promoting, and distributing the sports product. Consider the cost of owning a minor league hockey franchise. To produce the competition or event, players are necessary. These players require salaries and equipment in order to perform. In addition, these players require support personnel such as coaches, trainers, equipment managers, and so on. Also, these players need a place to play, which includes the costs of rent, utilities, cleaning, and maintenance. These represent some of the basic costs for producing a hockey game. However, they do not tell the entire story.

In addition to these core costs, other costs can include advertising, game promotions, and the salaries of front-office personnel (secretaries, general managers, and scouts). Team transportation is another cost. All these costs, or the **total cost** of owning a minor league hockey franchise, can be expressed as the sum of the variable and fixed costs, as shown:

$$TC = FC + VC$$

where TC = total cost
   FC = fixed cost
   VC = variable costs

Fixed costs are the sum of the producer's expenses that are stable and do not change with the quantity of the product consumed. Almost all costs associated with the minor league hockey team in the preceding example would be considered fixed. For example, rent on the arena, salaries, and transportation are all fixed costs. They do not vary at all with the amount of the product consumed (or in this case the team's attendance). The bulk of the game promotions are determined prior to the season and, as a result, are also considered fixed costs.

Variable costs are the sum of the producer's expenses that vary and change as a result of the quantity of the product being consumed. Advertising may represent a variable cost for the minor league hockey franchise. If advertising expenditures increase from one month to the next because the team is doing poorly at the box office, then the dollar amount spent varies. Similarly, advertising could represent a variable cost if additional advertising or promotions are used because attendance is higher than expected.

Although an athletic team experiences very few variable costs in the total cost equation, a manufacturer of pure sporting goods would encounter a significantly greater number of variable costs. Usually, variable costs for manufacturing a sporting good range between 60 and 90 percent of the total costs. For example, the cost of the packaging and materials for producing the good varies by the number of units sold.

Costs are considered an internal factor that influences the pricing decision because they are largely under the control of the sports organization. The minor league hockey team management makes decisions on player salaries, how much money to spend on advertising and promoting the team, and how the team travels. These costs loom large in the sport franchise because they affect the prices charged to the fans.

Obviously, the most visible and controversial costs incurred by professional sports organizations are player salaries. The Spotlight on Sports Marketing Ethics box discusses whether any athletes are worth the huge payday they are receiving.

SPOTLIGHT ON SPORTS MARKETING ETHICS

Astronomical Athlete Salaries: Are They Worth It?

It is a great day to take in a ball game, do not you think? With our hustling, bustling jaunt through the economy, we probably deserve a relaxing afternoon of hot dogs and peanuts with my favorite baseball team—the Shady Valley Primadonnas. Of course, the hot dogs and peanuts are overpriced, and you might need a second mortgage on your house to buy the ticket, but the expense is worth watching the finest athletes in the world display their world-class athletic abilities. We might even coax an autograph from the Primadonnas' all-star centerfielder—Harold "Hair Doo" Dueterman.

Are These Guys Worth It?
Although we thoroughly enjoy the game—the Primadonnas come from behind to win in the bottom of the ninth—our favorite player, Hair Doo, strikes out four times and commits an error in center field. This raises a really, really important question in the grand scheme of the universe: Is Hair Doo worth his $10 gadzillion salary? Should Hair Doo get 100 times the salary of an average, overworked, underappreciated member of the third estate?

Hair Doo's salary really raises another more general question: Why does anyone get paid what they get paid? Any questions we ask about Hair Doo Dueterman's salary could also be asked about the wage of any average, overworked underappreciated member of the third estate—Hair Doo's numbers just happen to be bigger. Because wages and salaries are nothing more than prices, the best place to look for answers is the market.

The Market Says Yes!
Let us first ponder the supply side of the market. Hair Doo performs his athletic prowess before thousands of adoring fans—supplies his labor—because he is willing and able to take on his designated duties for a mere $10 gadzillion. If Hair Doo was not willing and able to play baseball for $10 gadzillion, then he would do something else.

Hair Doo's willingness and ability to play our nation's pastime depends on his opportunity cost of other activities, such as deep sea diving, coal mining, ballet dancing, or game show hosting. By selecting baseball,

(Continued)

(*Continued*)

Hair Doo has given up a paycheck plus any other job-related satisfaction that could have been had from those pursuits. He has decided that his $10 gadzillion salary and the nonmonetary enjoyment of playing baseball outweigh his next best alternative. We should have little problem with this decision by Hair Doo, because we all make a similar choice. We pursue a job or career that gives us the most benefits.

But . . . (this is a good place for a dramatic pause) . . . someone also must be willing to pay Hair Doo Dueterman $10 gadzillion to do what he does so well. This is the demand side of the process, which we affectionately call the market. It deserves a little more thought.

The someone who's willing to pay Hair Doo's enormous salary, the guy who signs Hair Doo's paycheck, is the owner of Shady Valley Primadonnas—D. J. Goodluck. You might remember D. J.'s grandfather from Fact 3, "Our Unfair Lives," a wheat farmer on the Kansas plains who had the good fortune of homesteading 160 acres with a BIG pool of crude oil beneath. (The Goodlucks still visit the toilet each morning in a new Cadillac. They did, however, sell their ownership in Houston, Texas, and bought South Carolina.)

Why on earth would D. J. and his Shady Valley Primadonnas baseball organization pay Hair Doo this astronomical $10 gadzillion salary? D. J. must have a pretty good reason. Let us consider D. J.'s position.

Hair Doo's statistics are pretty impressive. In the past five years, he has led the league in umpire arguments, souvenir foul balls for adoring fans, product endorsements for nonbaseball-related items, and instigation of bench-clearing fights. All these have made Hair Doo an all-star, number-one fan attraction.

While Hair Doo may or may not help the Shady Valley Primadonnas win the championship, he does pack fans into the stands. And he has packed fans into the stands for the past five years.

Fans in the stands translates into tickets for the Shady Valley Primadonnas, national television broadcasts, and revenue for D. J. Goodluck. D. J. is willing to pay Hair Doo $10 gadzillion to perform his derring-do, because Hair Doo generates at least $10 gadzillion in revenue for the team. If Hair Doo failed to generate revenue equal to or greater than his $10 gadzillion salary, then D. J. would trade him to the Oak Town Sludge Puppies (the perennial last-place cellar-dwellers in the league), send him to the minor leagues, or just release him from the team.

The bottom line on Hair Doo's salary is the same for any average, overworked, underappreciated member of the third estate—an employer is willing and able to pay a wage up to the employee's contribution to production. If

your job is making $20 worth of Hot Mamma Fudge Bananarama Sundaes each day, then your boss—Hot Mamma Fudge—would be willing to pay you $20 per day.

Many Are Worth Even More

As entertainers, athletes are paid for fan satisfaction. The more fans who want to see an athlete perform, the more an athlete is paid. In fact, most athletes—even those who make gadzillions of dollars for each flubbed fly ball, dropped pass, and missed free throw—probably deserve even higher salaries. The reason is competition. The degree of competition on each side of the market can make the price too high or too low. If suppliers have little or no competition, then the price tends to be too high. If buyers have little or no competition, then the price tends to be too low.

In the market for athletes, competition is usually less on the demand side than on the supply side. The supply of athletes tends to be pretty darn competitive. Of course, Hair Doo is an all-star player, but he faces competition from hundreds of others who can argue with umpires and hit foul balls into the stands.

The demand side, however, is less competitive. In most cases, a particular team, like the Shady Valley Primadonnas, has exclusive rights to a player. They can trade those rights to another team, like the Oak Town Sludge Puppies, but the two teams usually do not compete with each other for a player's services. There are a few circumstances—one example is "free agency"—where two or more teams try to hire the same player, but that is the exception rather than the rule.

With little competition among buyers, the price tends to be on the low side. This means that Hair Doo Dueterman's $10 gadzillion salary could be even higher. It means that the Shady Valley Primadonnas probably get more, much more, than $10 gadzillion from ticket sales and television revenue. It means that D. J. Goodluck would probably be willing and able to pay more, much more, than $10 gadzillion for Hair Doo Dueterman's athletic services. The only way to find out how much Hair Doo is worth to the Shady Valley Primadonnas is to force them to compete for Hair Doo's services with other teams.

This is a good place to insert a little note on the three estates. Most owners of professional sports teams, almost by definition if not by heritage, tend to be full-fledged members of the second estate. The players, in contrast, usually spring from the ranks of the third. The idea that one team owns the "rights" of a player stems from the perverse, although changing notion, that the third estate exists for little reason other than to provide second-class servants for the first two estates.

(*Continued*)

(*Continued*)

Colleges Are Worse

If professional athletes who get gadzillions of dollars to play are underpaid, how do college athletes, who get almost nothing, compare? It depends on the sport.

Big-time college sports, especially football and basketball, are highly profitable entertainment industries. Millions of spectators spend tons of money each year for entertainment provided by their favorite college teams. Star college athletes can pack the fans into the stands as well as star professional athletes. With packed stands come overflowing bank accounts for the colleges.

What do the athletes get out of this? What are their "salaries"? Being amateurs, college athletes are not paid an "official" salary. They are, however, compensated for their efforts with a college education, including tuition, books, living accommodations, and a small monthly stipend. Although a college education is not small potatoes—$100,000-plus at many places—this compensation tends to fall far short of the revenue generated for the school. The bottom line is that big-time college athletes, like the pros, are usually underpaid.

The reason is very similar to that of the professional athletes. College athletics have limited competition among the "employers" but a great deal of competition among the "employees." Many more high-school athletes hope to play big-time college ball than ever realize that dream. While different colleges may try to hire—oops, I mean recruit—the same athlete, the collegiate governing bodies, most notably the National Collegiate Athletic Association, limit the degree of competition and fix the "wage" athletes can receive. You often hear about the NCAA penalizing a college because it went "too far" in its recruiting efforts. This translates into the charge that a college paid an athlete "too much" to play, such as new cars, bogus summer jobs with high wages, and cash payments from alumni.

Underpayment is most often a problem for big-time football and basketball revenue-generating sports. Athletes in sports with less spectator interest, such as tennis, gymnastics, or lacrosse, actually may be overpaid based on their contribution to their colleges' entertainment revenue.

Here's a tip to keep in mind in the high- priced world of athletics: Athletes are paid based on their contribution to fan satisfaction. If you think athletes are paid too much, then do not contribute to their salaries by attending games or watching them on television. If, however, you enjoy their performance and are willing to pay the price of admission, then worry not about their pay.

Source: Orley Amos, "Those Astronomical Athlete Salaries," *A Pedestrian Guide.* www.amos.bus.okstate.edu/guide/ISO2.html. Courtesy of Orley M. Amos Jr.

Whether you agree or disagree with escalating player contracts, there is no dispute that the increasing cost of player salaries has been passed on, in part, to the fans. Table 12.2 shows an example of the Fan Cost Index (FCI) for the NHL. The FCI represents the total dollar amount that a family of four would have to pay to attend a home game. This total cost includes the price of four tickets, two small beers, four sodas, four hot dogs, parking, two game programs, and two twill caps. The other costs indicate the pricing of one unit. In other words, the cost of one beer at the LA Kings game is $7.25.

Although cost is usually considered to be an internal, controllable factor for organizations, it can have an uncontrollable component. For instance, the league may impose a minimum salary level for a player that is beyond the control of the individual team or owner. The costs of raw materials for producing sporting goods may rise, representing a cost increase that is beyond the control of the manufacturer. Players' unions for professional teams may set minimum standards for travel that are not under the individual team's control. All these examples describe the uncontrollable side of costs that must be continually monitored by the sports marketer.

Organizational Objectives

The costs associated with producing a good or service are just one factor in determining the final price. Cost considerations may determine the "price floor" for the sport product. In other words, what will be the minimum price that an organization might charge to cover the cost of producing the sports product? Covering costs, however,

TABLE 12.2 An Example of the Fan Cost Index (FCI) for the NBA

Team	Avg. Ticket	% Change	Prem. Avg. Ticket	Ticket Rank	Beer	(oz.)	Soda	(oz.)	Hot Dog	Parking	Program	Cap	FCI	% Change
Montreal[2]	$56.82	5.6%	$99.74	2	$4.94	16	$3.16	14	$2.96	$18.02	$3.83	$22.48	$332.27	5.6%
Boston	$56.44	6.40%	$77.50	3	$6.00	16	$3.00	14	$4.00	$18.00	$4.00	$18.00	$327.77	6.0%
New Jersey	$54.67	0.0%	$0.00	5	$7.00	16	$3.50	16	$3.75	$10.00	$5.00	$23.00	$327.66	5.8%
Vancouver[2]	$58.96	3.9%	$120.00	1	$6.31	16	$3.60	20	$3.38	$18.02	$2.70	$12.61	$325.00	2.8%
Philadelphia[3]	$55.66	5.50%	$169.80	4	$5.75	12	$3.75	24	$3.75	$10.00	$5.00	$16.00	$314.15	4.0%
Minnesota	$51.37	2.5%	$90.00	7	$5.75	20	$3.50	20	$3.25	$10.00	$2.00	$18.00	$293.98	3.9%
New York Rangers*	$45.83	2.7%	$141.67	12	$5.75	20	$3.00	24	$3.50	$20.00	$10.00	$12.00	$284.83	1.7%
Edmonton[2]	$51.76	12.4%	$118.33	6	$5.86	16	$2.98	16	$3.38	$4.51	$3.60	$13.52	$283.65	8.7%
Calgary[2]	$47.35	9.2%	$102.56	9	$6.08	20	$3.15	20	$3.60	$9.01	$4.51	$18.01	$282.60	8.1%
Los angeles	$45.98	4.9%	$105.24	10	$7.25	16	$3.50	16	$3.75	$10.00	$5.00	$12.00	$271.42	3.3%
Florida	$44.28	29.1%	$105.17	13	$6.50	20	$4.00	20	$4.25	$12.00	n/a	$18.00	$271.12	20.6%
Toronto[2]	$49.23	-0.80%	$154.59	8	$4.51	14	$2.25	20	$2.48	$13.52	$2.25	$13.52	$271.07	-0.60%
Ottawa[2]	$45.95	5.10%	$89.78	11	$4.66	14	$3.16	20	$2.96	$7.90	n/a	$20.72	$266.93	3.70%
Atlanta	$43.54	4.50%	$93.42	17	$5.75	20	$2.00	14	$3.75	$10.00	$8.00	$15.99	$266.64	2.90%
Tampa Bay	$44.27	0.0%	$81.90	14	$6.00	12	$3.50	12	$4.00	$10.00	n/a	$18.00	$265.09	0.0%
Detroit	$43.13	0.0%	$58.58	18	$5.00	16	$2.00	12	$3.00	$15.00	$7.00	$15.00	$261.51	0.0%
League average	$43.13	3.70%	$95.59	-	$5.55	17	$3.04	17	$3.42	$11.06	$3.36	$15.43	$258.08	3.20%
New York Islanders	$44.01	0.0%	$97.92	16	$5.50	20	$3.00	14	$5.00	$6.75	n/a	$15.00	$255.77	0.0%
Columbus	$44.08	4.90%	$93.27	15	$6.00	20	$3.00	16	$3.00	$7.00	n/a	$12.00	$243.31	4.60%
Nashville	$40.78	9.20%	$86.47	19	$5.25	16	$3.00	16	$4.25	$10.00	n/a	$15.00	$242.63	7.90%
Colorado	$38.48	0.0%	$112.45	20	$6.00	16	$3.75	16	$3.75	$10.00	$5.00	$9.99	$235.91	0.0%
Dallas	$36.36	6.20%	$106.13	24	$4.00	16	$2.75	15	$4.00	$12.00	$5.00	$14.99	$232.41	4.20%
Washington	$38.15	0.0%	$94.82	21	$4.50	16	$2.50	16	$2.50	$15.00	$5.00	$12.00	$230.61	0.0%

(Continued)

TABLE 12.2 An Example of the Fan Cost Index (FCI) for the NBA (Continued)

Team	Avg. Ticket	% Change	Prem. Avg. Ticket	Ticket Rank	Beer	(oz.)	Soda	(oz.)	Hot Dog	Parking	Program	Cap	FCI	% Change
Chicago	$34.88	0.0%	$71.72	25	$5.00	16	$3.00	16	$3.00	$16.00	$5.00	$13.00	$225.52	0.0%
San jose	$33.00	0.0%	$76.92	26	$4.50	16	$2.50	16	$3.75	$13.00	$5.00	$15.00	$219.02	0.0%
Carolina	$37.91	45.0%	$81.34	22	$5.00	16	$2.75	20	$3.00	$7.00	$1.00	$12.00	$217.62	27.60%
Pittsburgh	$36.61	0.0%	$100.99	23	$5.25	21	$2.50	16	$2.50	$10.00	n/a	$15.00	$216.96	0.0%
Anaheim	$30.32	0.0%	$88.34	27	$6.25	16	$3.50	16	$3.50	$12.00	n/a	$18.00	$210.77	2.40%
St. Louis[4]	$28.23	-29.30%	$96.58	29	$5.25	14	$3.50	12	$3.50	$10.00	$5.00	$12.99	$197.39	-16.80%
Buffalo	$30.07	1.30%	$65.05	28	$5.00	22	$2.00	12	$2.00	$7.00	$5.00	$12.00	$187.29	0.0%
Phoenix	$25.41	-7.20%	$87.54	30	$6.00	16	$3.00	16	$3.00	n/a	$2.00	$20.00	$181.62	-8.50%

*Prices listed as reported on team's Web site.

[1] Superscript figures beside the beer and soda prices denote the ounces of the beverage.

[2] All prices are converted to USD at the exchange rate of $1CAD=$0.901USD or $1USD=$1.091CAD.

[3] The Philadelphia Flyers have children's pricing for one category. The FCI is calculated with two tickets at $55.41.

[4] The St. Louis Blues re-classified its plaza seating section as premium. Season tickets in that area now include free entrance to the Scotttrade Center private dining area.

Source: Average ticket price represents a weighted average of season ticket prices for general and club-level seats, determined by factoring the tickets in each price range as a percentage of the total number of seats in each stadium. Luxury suite sales are excluded from the survey. Season-ticket pricing is used for any team that offers some or all tickets at lower prices for customers who buy season tickets. Costs were determined by telephone calls with representatives of the teams, venues, and concessionaires. Faxes were sent to verify the information supplied. Identical questions were asked in all interviews. http://www.teammarketing.com/fci.cfm?page=fci_nhl_06-07.cfm

may be insufficient from the organization's perspective. This depends largely on the organization's objectives. As we have stressed throughout this text, marketing mix decisions—including pricing—must consider the broader marketing goals. Effective marketing goals should be consistent with the organizational objectives.

There are four categories of **organizational objectives** that influence pricing decisions. These include income, sales, competition, and social concerns. **Income objectives** include achieving maximum profits or simply organizational survival. In the long term, all professional sports organizations are concerned with maximizing their profits and having good returns on investment. Alternatively, amateur athletic events and associations are in sports not necessarily to maximize profits but to "stay afloat." Their organizational objectives center around providing athletes with a place to compete and covering costs.

Sales objectives are concerned with maintaining or enhancing market share and encouraging sales growth. If increasing sales is the basic organizational objective, then a sporting goods manufacturer or team may want to set lower prices to encourage more purchases by existing consumers. In addition, setting lower prices or offering price discounts may encourage new groups of consumers to try the sports product. By doing so, the team may increase fan identification and, ultimately, fan loyalty. This will, in turn, lead to repeat purchases.

Another broad organizational objective may be to compete in a given sports market. An organization may want to meet competition, avoid competition, or even undercut competitive pricing. These **competitive objectives** are directly linked to final pricing decisions. Traditionally, professional sports franchises are the "only game in town," so competitive threats are less likely to dictate pricing than they would in other industries.

A final organizational objective that influences pricing is referred to as a **social concern.** Many sports organizations, particularly amateur athletic associations, determine the pricing of their sporting events based on social concerns. For example, consider a local road race through downtown St. Louis on St. Patrick's Day. The organizational objective of this race is to encourage as many people as possible to participate in the community and the festivities of the day. As such, the cost to enter the race is minimal and designed only to offset the expense of having the event.

Regardless of which organizational objective is established, each has a large role in setting prices for sports products. In practice, more than one objective is typically set by the sports organization. However, prices can be determined more efficiently and effectively if the organization clearly understands its objectives. Let us look at an example of how the MLS mission statement provides a direction for pricing.

Major League Soccer's mission statement is:

> To create a profitable Division I professional outdoor soccer league with players and teams that are competitive on an international level, and to provide affordable family entertainment. MLS brings the spirit and intensity of the world's most popular sport to the United States. Featuring competitive ticket prices and family oriented promotions such as "Soccer Celebration" at the stadium, MLS appeals to the children who play and the families who support soccer. MLS players are also involved with a variety of community events.

As indicated in the mission statement, MLS is concerned with profitability for its league and teams. Moreover, the pricing of MLS games should be affordable so families who support soccer will be financially able to purchase tickets, reflecting a social concern. Finally, the mission statement reflects the competitive nature of pricing. The interaction of the organizational objectives of the MLS should exert a great influence on the price that fans pay to see U.S. professional soccer.

External Factors

Thus far, we have described the internal, or controllable, determinants of pricing and factors believed to be under the control of the sports marketer. The uncontrollable or **external factors** also play an important role in pricing decisions. The uncontrollable factors that influence pricing include consumer demand, competition, legal issues, the economy, and technology. Let us turn our discussion to each of these major, external factors.

CAREER SPOTLIGHT

Don Schumacher: President, Don Schumacher and Associates, and Executive Director, National Association of Sports Commissions

Career Questions

1. How did you get started in the sports industry? What was your first sports industry job?

I got started by answering my telephone when the chairman of Taft Broadcasting called to say he needed to see me in his office! When I arrived, I was informed that the general manager of the College Football Hall of Fame had just been terminated. He went on to say I would move my office to the Hall of Fame, assume the duties of the general manager, and continue with my other assignment as director of sponsorships and promotions for all of Taft Broadcasting's theme parks. What made things very interesting was the fact that Galbreath Field, a 10,000-seat football stadium, was opening in just 48 hours with a college game in the afternoon and a high school game that evening. I knew nothing about stadium operations, but that changed in two days. During the next three years I started work on projects with the NCAA and the Ohio High School Athletic Association, which led to a number of high school playoff games and the Division III National Football Championship (Amos Alonzo Stagg Bowl) being played at Galbreath Field. These projects led me to become president of a major arena, and then to my own sports marketing company.

2. Can you describe the type of work you are doing right now? What are your job responsibilities? What are the greatest challenges?

Now, 25 years later, I own my own sports marketing, management, and consulting company. We manage the National Association of Sports Commissions (NASC), own and promote our own events through DSA Prep Sports, and I consult with cities throughout the United States. Our specialty is conducting market analysis to assist cities in obtaining more sports events. We also consult on new sports facilities, especially in motor sports.

3. Do you foresee any changes in demand in this field in the future? If so, what or how?

I believe that no matter how reliant we may become on new technology, personal relationships and personal references will continue to determine the amount of success anyone will have in our industry.

4. Who or what has influenced you the most in your sports business career?

The single most influential experiences I have had relate to the satisfaction gained by doing a good job preparing for an event. And I will never tire of delivering another report to a consulting client.

5. What advice would you offer students who are considering a career in sports marketing?

A career in sports marketing is a career in selling. You must want to sell . . . ideas, products, and yourself . . . every day.

Consumer Demand

One of the most critical factors in determining the price of a sports product is **consumer demand.** Demand is the quantity of a sports product that consumers are willing to purchase at a given price. Generally, consumers are more likely to purchase products at a lower price than a higher price. More formally, economists refer to this principle as the **law of demand.** To better understand the nature of the law of demand and its impact on any given sports product, let us examine the price elasticity of demand.

Price elasticity explains consumer reactions to changes in price. **Price elasticity** or **price inelasticity** measures the extent to which consumer purchasing patterns are sensitive to fluctuations in price. For example, if the St. Louis Cardinals raise their bleacher ticket prices from $12.00 to $16.00, will the demand for seats decline? Similarly, if the ticket prices are reduced by a given amount, will the demand increase?

Mathematically, price elasticity is stated as

$$e = \frac{DQ/Q}{DP/P}$$

where e = price elasticity
DQ/Q = percentage change in the quantity demanded
DP/P = percentage change in the price

Consumer price elasticity may be described in one of three ways: elastic demand, inelastic demand, or unitary demand. **Inelastic demand** states that changes in price have little or no impact on sales. In the previous example, demand probably would have been inelastic, because even relatively large increases in the ticket prices would have had little impact on the number of fans attending each game. If demand is inelastic, then e is less than or equal to 1 (see Figure 12.2a). Because of the great demand for tickets, the Green Bay Packers, who have been sold out on season tickets since 1960, could probably raise their minimum ticket price to $300 and still sell out all their games.

Elastic demand refers to small changes in price producing large changes in quantity demanded. For example, if the average price of a ticket to an Orlando Magic game is reduced from $45.00 to $37.00, and if the number of units sold increases dramatically, then demand is considered elastic, because e is greater than 1 (see Figure 12.2b).

Finally, **unitary demand** is defined as a situation where price changes are offset exactly by changes in demand. In other words, price and demand are perfectly related. A small change in price produces an equally small change in the number of units sold. Similarly, a large change in price causes an equally large change in the number of units sold. In a situation where demand is unitary, e is equal to 1 (see Figure 12.2c).

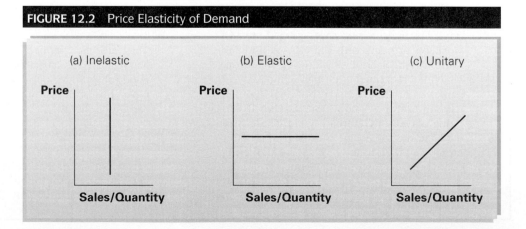

FIGURE 12.2 Price Elasticity of Demand

(a) Inelastic
Price
Sales/Quantity

(b) Elastic
Price
Sales/Quantity

(c) Unitary
Price
Sales/Quantity

Estimating Demand

The basic notion of demand allows sports marketers to explore the relationship between price and the amount of sports product that is sold. In practice, a sports marketer cannot continually change the price of a product and then determine the impact of this price change. Rather, the sports marketer must develop estimates of demand. The three basic factors that are used in **estimating demand** are consumer trends and tastes, availability of substitute sports products, and the consumer's income. Let us briefly explore the three demand factors.

Consumer Tastes

Consumer tastes play an influential role in estimating demand. Consumer demand for football is at an all-time high, which influences ticket prices (and the price of rights to televise football). Similarly, paintball games, water skiing, and weight lifting are the hottest participant sports (measured by percentage change in participation rates), according to the National Sporting Goods Association (see Table 12.3). The increased demand for these "popular" sports will also affect pricing of equipment to consumers.

With sophisticated statistical techniques, sports marketers can understand what, when, and how factors are influencing consumer tastes and the likelihood of purchasing products. For example, demand for a new design of in-line skates in any given market may be expressed as a function of a number of factors other than price. These factors can include the number of consumers currently participating in this recreational activity, the desire of recreational skaters to have more technologically advanced skates, the amount that the new skates have been advertised or promoted, or the availability of the skates.

Marketing research (as discussed in Chapter 3) allows us to estimate demand for new and existing sports products. Firms conduct research to determine consumers' past purchase behavior and the likelihood of their buying a new product. In addition, businesses rely on environmental scanning to monitor changes in the demographic profile of a market, changes in technology, shifts in popular culture, and other issues that may affect the size or tastes of the consumer market.

Environmental scanning and marketing research assist sports marketers in understanding what consumers expect and are willing to pay for sports products. Let us look at how consumers evaluate price (see Figure 12.3).

TABLE 12.3	2006 Participation—Ranked by Percent Change	
Sport	*Total*	*Percent Change*
Skiing (cross country)	2.6	36.7%
Football (tackle)	11.9	19.7%
Cheerleading	3.8	15.6%
Workout at club	36.9	6.5%
Boating, motor/power	29.3	6.2%
Hockey (ice)	2.6	6.0%
Camping (vacation/overnight)	48.6	5.7%
Hiking	31.0	4.0%
Exercise walking	87.5	1.7%
Backpack/wilderness camp	13.3	0.4%

Note: Participated more than once (in millions). Seven years of age and older.
http://www.nsga.org/public/pages/index.cfm?pageid=150

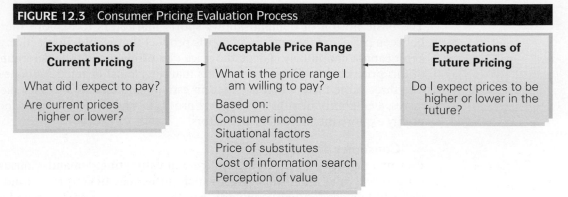

FIGURE 12.3   Consumer Pricing Evaluation Process

Expectations of Current Pricing

What did I expect to pay?

Are current prices higher or lower?

Acceptable Price Range

What is the price range I am willing to pay?

Based on:
Consumer income
Situational factors
Price of substitutes
Cost of information search
Perception of value

Expectations of Future Pricing

Do I expect prices to be higher or lower in the future?

In the **consumer pricing evaluation process,** acceptable price ranges are determined by consumers' expectations. These expectations are influenced by communicating with other consumers (i.e., word of mouth), promotions or advertising, and, to some extent, past experience in purchasing the products. If the gap between expectations and the actual price is too large, a problem arises for the sports organization. If prices are much higher than expected, the consumer will be much less likely to purchase. However, if prices are much lower, then the quality of the sports product may be called into question.

The sport of professional boxing provides an excellent example of the role past experience plays in determining an acceptable price range for consumers. Fan satisfaction with professional boxing has reached an all-time low because of the short length of heavyweight fights and the heavyweight prices paid by pay-per-view (PPV) customers to watch these fights. To combat this problem of short telecasts, Cablevision introduced a controversial pricing strategy. Consumers who wanted to view the historic title fight between Evander Holyfield and Mike Tyson paid a $10-a-round price with a $50 cap.

This innovative strategy apparently sparked a 200 percent jump in sales in Cablevision's 1.9 million PPV homes (a PPV record). Equally important, the product quality was not called into question. Cablevision paid a flat fee (roughly $4 million) for the rights to the fight, and the boxers did not receive any additional money based on the fight's length.[9]

Along with previous experience with pricing, expectations of future pricing also influence the acceptable range of prices a consumer is willing to pay. For example, when an innovative sports product, such as the Quik Change Dumbbell System, is in the introductory phase of the product life cycle, little competition exists and start-up costs are high. Most consumers would expect the price of this product to drop over time, and some may be willing to wait for this to occur. However, sports fans may expect prices to continually rise in the future and purchase the new product immediately rather than waiting for the inevitable higher prices.

Along with expectations of current and future prices, a number of other individual consumer judgments will also play a role in determining the acceptable price range for any given sports product. As shown in Figure 12.3, these variables include consumer income, situational factors, price of substitutes, cost of information search, and perceptions of value.

Consumer income, one of the three demand factors, refers to the consumer's ability to pay the price. Generally, the higher the consumer's income, the wider the range of acceptable prices. For example, a sports fan who has an annual income of $100,000 might perceive a $10 increase in ticket prices as still within his or her price range. However, the same $10 increase in price may be unaffordable to the fan earning

$30,000 per year. Significantly, both fans may find the increase in ticket prices unacceptable, but only the latter finds it unaffordable.

The **situational factors** that may affect a consumer's acceptable range of prices include the presence or absence of time, the usage situation, and social factors. Consider the following situations and how each might affect the price you would be willing to pay. First, you are getting ready for a much anticipated round of golf when you discover you only have one ball left in your bag. Typically, you purchase golf balls at your local discount store for roughly $6 a sleeve (package of three). Given the situation (absence of time), you are forced to "cough up" $12 at the pro shop for the three balls needed to get you through the round. This absence of time to shop for less expensive golf balls caused the acceptable price range to double in this situation.

The next scenario illustrates how your usage situation influences the range of acceptable prices. Imagine you are purchasing a new set of golf clubs that will be used only once or twice a month at the local public course. In this situation, the acceptable price range for this set of clubs might be from $200 to $300. It is likely that you may even purchase less expensive, previously owned clubs. However, if you are planning to use the clubs once or twice a week and are more concerned about their quality and your image, the acceptable range of prices would increase.

The final situation places you in the position of purchasing tickets for the 3M Performance 400 NASCAR race. The cost of purchasing one ticket is approximately $105. You are not a huge NASCAR fan and the thought of spending $105 for a ticket seems disagreeable. However, a group of your best friends are attending the event and encourage you to "go along for the ride." You agree and purchase the ticket because of the social situational influence.

Another interesting social situational influence is referred to as the "mob effect." The **mob effect** (or the crowd effect) describes a situation in which consumers believe it is socially desirable to attend "special" sporting events, such as the NBA Finals, bowl games, or the World Series. Because these events constitute unique situations that can never be duplicated, consumers are willing to pay more than usual for the "right" to be a part of the mob (or crowd).

An additional consumer determinant of acceptable prices is the **expected price range of substitute products.** The prices of competitive products will have a major influence on what you deem acceptable. If a sports organization's pricing becomes out-of-line (higher) versus competition, then consumers will no longer pay the price.

The **cost of information search** also determines what a consumer considers acceptable. A consumer wanting to purchase a series of tennis lessons has a relatively low cost of information search because information is easily obtained from friends or by calling various tennis professionals. In this case, the cost of the search is less than the benefit of finding the best value. Interestingly, in purchasing a sports product, the cost of information search may be negligible because fans may find the search itself to be intriguing.

Finally, as discussed previously, **perception of value** will dictate acceptable price ranges for sports products. Remember, perceptions of value will vary from individual to individual and are based on the perceived benefits. The greater the perceived benefits of the sports product, the higher the range of acceptable prices. Most people would consider $400 an outrageous price to attend a single pro football game. However, that cost might look like the bargain of a lifetime if that single game were the Super Bowl.

Availability of Substitute Products   Another demand factor, other than price alone, that may affect demand is the **availability of substitute products.** Generally, as the number of substitute products for any given sports product increases, demand for the product will decrease. Consider the case of almost any professional sports franchise and substitute products. Typically, there is no substitute product for the professional sports team. Therefore, demand remains relatively unchanged, even when ticket prices are increased (in other words, demand is highly inelastic). For example, there is no substitute product for the St. Louis Cardinals, although baseball is played in St. Louis at the collegiate, high school, and amateur levels. However, consumers may choose to spend their sports dollars on purchasing televised broadcasts of the Cardinals, rather than pay the price increase.

Consumer income   The final demand factor that influences the consumer's ability to purchase the sports product is the consumer's income. Simply stated, the more income a consumer realizes, the higher the demand for various sports products. This "income-related" demand factor is related to the cost of the sports product under consideration. That is, the higher the cost of the sports product, the more "consumer income" matters. Consider the case of San Antonio Spurs courtside seats that are priced at $2,250 per seat. For this "paltry" sum, fans get a small TV display and as much food and drink as they can ingest. Obviously, these are not seats that most middle-income consumers would be able to afford.[10]

The potential consumer's personal income and ability to purchase products is also highly related to the state of the economy, in general. The economy is one of the "other external factors" that influences pricing, which is discussed in the next section.

Economy

The current economic cycle, or **economy,** also influences pricing decisions. A recessionary period, for instance, is characterized by reduced economic activity. During these times, there is a reduced demand for goods and services. In addition, unemployment rates are typically higher. Although this sounds grim for consumers and sports fans, imaginative sports marketers might be able to take advantage of these slowdowns in the economy by holding or slightly reducing prices, while stressing the continued value of the sports product.

Periods of inflation also require a pricing review. During inflationary periods, the cost of inputs (e.g., supplies or raw materials) necessary to produce the sports product will rise and ultimately increase prices to consumers. Rather than increase prices, sports marketers may adopt a cost reduction strategy during inflation. Such a strategy necessitates reducing or stabilizing costs of producing the product so consumer prices need not be increased.

Whatever the phase of the economic cycle, it is important to understand the direct relationship between pricing and the economy. In the preceding discussion, prices were adjusted due to changes in the economy. The prices set by manufacturers and sports organizations equally have a tremendous impact on the demand for these products and services and, in turn, affect the economy.

Competition

As stated earlier, **competition** is one of the most critical factors in determining prices. Every sports organization must closely monitor the pricing structure of competing firms to successfully implement prices for its own products. One key to understanding the relationship between price and competition is exploring the sports organization's competitive environment. These four competitive environments include pure monopolies, oligopoly, monopolistic competition, and pure competition.

Most professional sports organizations operate in a pure monopoly, which means they are the only seller who sets the price for a unique product. With the exception of New York, Chicago, and California, there are few areas large enough to support two professional sports franchises in the same sport (e.g., the Cubs and White Sox). As such, most professional sports are free to manipulate prices as they want. The same would hold true for many college athletic programs, where college sports may be "the only show in town."

An oligopoly is where a small number of firms control a market. Conditions for an oligopoly exist when no one seller controls the market, but each of the few sellers has an impact on the market. In the sports industry, an example of an oligopoly is the sports news networks where ESPN and Fox have dominant control over the market.

In the case of many sporting goods, monopolistic competition is the norm. There are dozens of brands with identical products to sell. This competitive environment requires both price competition and nonprice competition. For example, all tennis balls are designed the same, but the many different brands compete based on lower prices and/or other marketing mix elements (promotions, product image, and sponsorships). The same holds true for golf balls, basketballs, and so on.

Pure competition is a market structure that has so many competitors that none can singularly influence the market price. The market conditions that must exist for pure competition include homogeneous products and ease of entry into the market. Although pure competition exists in industries selling uniform commodities such as agricultural products, it does not exist in the sports industry.

Legal Issues

In addition to the other external factors, sports marketers must consider **legal issues,** such as constraints imposed on pricing. Several key laws that affect sports marketers were presented in Chapter 2. Table 12.4 presents U.S. legislation that specifically affects the pricing of sports products.

One of the most notable legal issues that the sports industry has been wrestling with for years is the secondary ticket market, or as it is more commonly known, ticket scalping (see the accompanying article).

Technology

Without a doubt, all sports products are becoming more and more technologically advanced. The trend toward **technology** can have an indirect or direct influence on pricing decisions. Experience tells us that greater technology costs money. The high cost of research and development, as well as the higher costs for production and materials, drive up the price of the sports product. For example, if our stadiums are equipped with miniscreen monitors at every seat, the consumer would be expected to pay the price for this technology in the form of higher ticket prices. In this case, an advance in technology has a direct impact on the pricing.

Although technology and higher prices are typically believed to go hand in hand, technology does not always have to increase pricing. For example, a consumer may be able to buy a King Cobra titanium driver for $299 using electronic commerce (in other words, purchasing it through the Internet). The same driver may cost $125 more if purchased in a traditional retail outlet. In this case, technology is having an indirect influence on pricing, happily reducing the price of goods to consumers.

TABLE 12.4	Laws Influencing the Pricing of Sports Products

- **Sherman Act, 1890**—Establishes legality of restraint/price of trade and fixing. It also restricts the practice of predatory pricing to drive competition from the marketplace through pricing.
- **Clayton Act, 1914**—Restricts price discrimination.
- **Robinson-Patman Act, 1936**—Limits the ability of firms to sell the same product at different prices to different customers.
- **Wheeler-Lea Act, 1938**—Ensures pricing practices are not deceiving to consumers.
- **Consumer Goods Pricing Act, 1975**—Eliminates some control over retail pricing by wholesalers and manufacturers. It allows retailers to establish final retail prices in most instances.

Ticket Scalping Comes Out of the Shadows

The days of seeking out ticket-scalpers in the shadows, ducking into alleys, and dodging police for that elusive Yankees–Red Sox seat are fading fast. New York is poised this week to become the latest state to ease or eliminate decades-old restrictions on scalping. For the first time, it would become entirely legal in the state for average fans to scalp their seats on the Internet. And, for better or worse, they could sell those tickets at whatever price the market is willing to bear.

The state assembly approved the changes Tuesday. The Senate is expected to follow suit, and Gov. Eliot Spitzer could sign the measure by Friday, when the state's old anti-scalping law expires.

"If you have something to sell, you should be able to sell it for what it is truly worth," said Sean Pate, spokesman for the online ticket broker StubHub Inc., which lobbied hard for the change. StubHub is owned by eBay Inc. Some old regulations would stay in place. Scalpers would still be banned from selling tickets within 1,500 feet of large arenas, like Madison Square Garden and Yankee Stadium, and within 500 feet of smaller venues. Large-volume brokers would still need to get a license, too.

It's those brokers who have Russ Haven of the New York Public Interest Research Group worried. Haven argues that lifting the price caps will only prompt greedy opportunists to snap up every available seat, and then jack up prices.

"I think this is a bum deal for consumers," Haven said. "As it is, seats to popular events are often selling for 10 times their face price. It may be that there will be some portion of tickets that go for less than face value, but that's not what they're all banking on," he said of the brokers and ticket agencies pushing for change.

Other states have also reconsidered anti-scalping laws. Minnesota tossed its old anti-scalping laws this spring. The state previously allowed tickets to be resold only at face value. A bill that would ease Missouri's ban on selling tickets to sporting events at more than face value passed the legislature and is now before the governor. Illinois and Florida also recently did away with old anti-scalping rules, and bills to ease restrictions are under discussion in Massachusetts and Connecticut.

The shift has been propelled in part by the explosion of Internet ticket sales that has made it nearly impossible for states to enforce price caps. New York's old rule limiting a seller's profits to no more than 45 percent over face value has been widely ignored online.

But perhaps the biggest change was a switch in business strategy by some of the sports and entertainment companies that previously fought scalping the hardest: Realizing that a multibillion-dollar market was being left untapped, a growing number of teams and theaters have been entering the secondary ticket market themselves.

The NCAA signed a deal last year to resell tournament tickets through RazorGator.com. The NBA and some NFL teams have made Ticketmaster their official reseller under an agreement that gives teams a percentage of the profit when a seat is resold. "There is obviously a business opportunity here for us," said Ticketmaster vice president Joseph Freeman.

Yet to be seen is how much control sports teams, theaters, and concert halls will retain over the tickets being resold. Some have pushed for legislation that would limit reselling to venue-approved brokerages, in part to cut down on the possibility of fraud.

Both the New York Yankees and their archrival the Boston Red Sox recently made a practice of cracking down on season ticket holders caught selling their unwanted seats on the Internet, in violation of team policy. New York's new rules, if signed in their current form, would actually ban New York sports teams from taking such punitive action.

"My feeling is, if I have a ticket, and I can't go to a ballgame, I should certainly have a right to give it to my brother or my cousin—and if they want to pay me for it, why should I have to go through the Yankees to do it?" state Sen. Dean G. Skelos said.

Source: David B. Caruso, Associated Press, May 31, 2007, http://www.breitbart.com/ article.php?id=D8PFBEU80&show_article=1&cat=0.

Another example is the Philadelphia Phillies' "loaded ticket," which has proved so successful that the club has expanded the program at Citizens Bank Park, and other teams are planning to adapt it at their own facilities.[11] The Phillies launched the loaded ticket, a ballpark admission with credit toward concessions and merchandise built into a bar code, when they opened their ballpark in 2004. Ticket holders for 350 Diamond Club seats behind home plate pay an extra $30 a seat and get $30 worth of stored value they can spend without reaching for their wallets. The club now has added 900 left-field seats to the program and eventually wants to include the entire park.

The cost of investing in the technology used with loaded tickets has kept many teams from using the concept. The Baltimore Ravens are one of the few using stored-value tickets, offering them to club-seat holders at M&T Bank Stadium. Other organizations using or considering stored-credit tickets include the Air Force Academy, Boston Red Sox, Cleveland Indians, Philadelphia Flyers, and 76ers. The numbers will continue to grow.

PRICE ADJUSTMENTS

As we discussed in the preceding sections, initial prices are determined by a variety of internal and external issues that are continually changing with new market conditions. For instance, more or less competition may provide the impetus for price changes. Also, **price adjustments** may be made to stimulate demand for sports products when

---

Would Teams Dare Change How Season Tickets Are Priced?

Will the changing landscape of technology trigger a fundamental shift in pricing philosophy? Should it?

Matt Marolda, CEO of StratBridge, a software company that analyzes ticket sales and customer data, said Web-based technologies have laid the foundation for what he calls "dynamic" pricing for sports ticketing. And not just when tickets are resold on the secondary market. Marolda thinks such market-based pricing could affect even season tickets. In his vision, prices for each game in a season-ticket package would move up or down throughout the season, based on team success, the opponent, or other market forces.

"The notion that ticket prices should be rigid from some arbitrary date going forward, that seems a little artificial," Marolda said. "There is an awful lot of value that gets lost in the upside." He points to Yankees–Red Sox games as being, perhaps, underpriced by the teams at the start of the season.

Some teams already sell single-game tickets at differing prices, but such "variable pricing" is set at the start of the season. For example, this past season, a Buffalo Sabres club ticket against the Toronto Maple Leafs sold for $150; against the lesser Nashville Predators it was $72. But, for season-ticket holders willing to make an investment in the entire season, the club ticket for all games cost $69. Also, some teams offer plans in which consumers wanting tickets to the most desirable games have to purchase tickets for one or a few less-desirable dates.

Some people in the ticketing industry say Marolda's proposal for dynamic pricing for season-ticket holders is off base. "It's outright dangerous for teams," said Frank Luby of Simon-Kucher & Partners, an international firm that has consulted the Toronto Blue Jays on ticketing.

Luby said that a set value on a game ticket in a season-ticket bundle is "essentially a hedge. The team is protecting itself from a big downside. Of course, you're sacrificing some upside that may be there. But the dream that [Marolda] is trying to sell is you have a breakout season. . . . The fact that this is all technologically possible is beyond the point. If you turn the market loose on [season tickets] you're inviting disaster."

Marolda acknowledges that sales and retention of the season-ticket holder are core strategies for teams. "Season-ticket holders as we know them are probably not going anywhere soon," he said. "This base of recurring, predictable revenue is pretty tantalizing."

Of course, the burgeoning secondary market via StubHub, eBay, and teams' own Web sites encourages auctions for hot tickets, and many of those on the resale market come from season-ticket holders. Teams see the prices their tickets fetch on the secondary market and are looking for ways to get a piece of the action.

In Marolda's brainstorming, the seasonlong customer would buy "rights" and contribute to a prepaid "account," rather than purchase tickets for every home game. The rights could include discounts on some games and perks, such as parking or concessions discounts, he said. As pricing fluctuated, the seasonlong customer would purchase tickets and draw down on his account. Transactions would be Web-based.

It may sound far-fetched, but in the ever-changing world of ticketing, "never say never," said Chad Estis, the Cleveland Cavaliers' chief marketing officer. "A few years ago variable pricing and teams endorsing the secondary market were widely scoffed at. My, has that changed."

Source: Jay Weiner, *Sports Business Journal*, June 18, 2007, p. 25, http://www.sportsbusinessjournal.com/index.cfm?fuseaction=search. show_article&articleId=55517&keyword=Would%20teams%20dare%20change%20how%20season%20tickets%20are%20priced?

sales expectations are not currently being met. Finally, prices might be adjusted to help meet the objectives that have been developed. The next section explores some of the ways in which price adjustments are implemented by sports marketers, and as the accompanying article illustrates, there may be new approaches to pricing of traditionally priced products, like season ticket packages.

Price Increases and Reductions

As with most things in sports marketing, prices are dynamic and decisions are continually being made about whether prices should be increased or decreased based on a number of internal and external factors.

Price increases represent an important adjustment made to established prices. In recent years, many sports organizations have had to increase prices for a variety of reasons, even though consumers, retailers, and employees discourage such actions. One of the primary reasons for increasing prices is to keep up with cost inflation. In other words, as the cost of materials or of running a sports organization increases, prices must be increased to achieve the same profit objectives. Another reason for implementing a price increase is because there is excess demand for the sports product. For example, if thousands of fans join the season-ticket waiting list in the week that a Hall of Fame coach returns to a team, then slight increases to these ticket prices may be acceptable.

A winning season may have a huge impact on the decision to raise prices. For the fourth consecutive year, the Chicago Bears are raising ticket prices after gaining a trip to the Super Bowl in 2007. The increase is for all except the most expensive seats in Soldier Field, according to a report in the *Chicago Sun-Times*. Non-club-level seats, which make up about 85 percent of the stadium, will cost $65–$104 a game, while club seats will cost $235–$340, according to the report

Because of the negative consequences of raising prices, sports organizations may consider potential alternatives to straight price increases. These alternatives include eliminating any planned price reductions, lessening the number of product features, or unbundling items formerly "bundled" into a low price.

If there are no viable alternatives to increasing prices, it is important to communicate these changes to fans and consumers in a straightforward fashion to avoid potential negative consequences. Remember, much of pricing is based on consumer psychology. If fans or consumers of sporting goods are told why prices are being increased, they may believe price increases are justified.

Typically, **price reductions** are efforts to enhance sales and achieve greater market share by directly lowering the original price. In addition to the direct reductions in price, rebates or bundling products are other types of price breaks commonly employed. After raising season-ticket prices, the St. Louis Blues lowered them for the 2007–08 season. The Charlotte Bobcats reduced some season ticket prices for their fourth season, the second time in as many years the team lowered prices to stimulate demand. On the court, the Bobcats have been successful by the standards of NBA expansion teams. But the team still has poor attendance, averaging 15,421 fans per home game—27th out of 30 teams in the NBA.

The Diamondbacks expected to spend about $60 million for their 2007 product but announced a reduction in ticket prices for 29,577 seats at Chase Field. The price won't change on another 13,623. The average decrease was 5.3 percent, the team said in a letter to season-ticket holders. "It's a strong statement to our fans that we are committed to them," D-Backs president Derrick Hall said. "We need to increase our season ticket fan base." The D-Backs drew 2,091,685 in 2006, the second-lowest figure in team history but an increase from the previous season. They averaged 25,823 per game in 2006—406 more than in 2005.

Although teams commonly reduce or increase prices after the season, sports organizations rarely reduce or increase the price charged to consumers during the course of the season to stimulate demand. It is much more common, however, for marketers of sporting goods to reduce and increase prices. Simply said, the Los Angeles Dodgers will probably never have an end-of-the-season sale of tickets. You will, however, be able to find any number of sales of baseball equipment at the end of the summer.

Whatever the form of price reductions, they are frequently risky for sports organizations for a number of reasons. First, consumers may associate multiple price reductions with inferior product quality. Second, consumers may associate price reductions with price gouging (always selling products at a discount so the initial price must be unreasonably high). Third, price reductions may wake a sleeping dog and cause competition to counter with its own price decreases. Finally, frequent price changes make it more difficult for the consumer to establish a frame of reference for the true price of sports products. If tennis balls regularly sell for $4.99 for a package of three, and I conduct three sales over the season that offer the balls for $2.99, then what is the perceived "real" price?

An important concept when making price adjustments (either up or down) is known as the **just noticeable difference (JND).**[12] The just noticeable difference is the point at which consumers detect a difference between two stimuli. In pricing, the two stimuli are the original price and the adjusted price. In other words, do consumers perceive (notice) a difference when prices are increased or decreased? The following examples illustrate the importance of the just noticeable difference.

Dick's Sporting Goods may sell Wilson softball gloves at a regular price of $49.99 (note the psychological price strategy of odd pricing being used). With softball season right around the corner, Dick's decides to reduce prices and sell the gloves for $44.99. Does this $5 reduction surpass the difference threshold? In other words, does the consumer believe there is a noticeable difference between the regular price and the sale price? If not, then the price reduction will not be successful at stimulating demand.

Suppose that because of the increasing cost of raw materials needed to produce the gloves, the price has to be increased from $49.99 to $54.99. Again, the sports marketer has to determine whether consumers will notice this increase in price. If not, then the price increase may not have negative consequences for the sale of Wilson softball gloves.

Price Discounts

Combined with straight price decreases, **price discounts** are other incentives offered to buyers to stimulate demand or reward behaviors that are favorable to the seller. The two major types of price discounts that are common in sports marketing are quantity discounts and seasonal discounts.

Quantity discounts reward buyers for purchasing large quantities of a sports product. This type of discounting may occur at all different levels of the channel of distribution. Using the previous softball glove example, Wilson may offer a quantity discount to Dick's Sporting Goods for sending in a large purchase order. Consumers hope that Dick's Sporting Goods will pass the savings on to them in the form of price reductions. The purchase of group ticket sales is another common example of quantity discounts in sports marketing.

Seasonal discounts are also prevalent in sports marketing because of the nature of sports. Most sports have defined seasons observed by both participants and spectators. Seasonal discounts are intended to stimulate demand in off-peak periods. For example, ski equipment may be discounted in the summer months to encourage consumer demand and increase traffic in skiing specialty stores. Ski resorts also frequently offer seasonal deals. For instance, the Hunter Mountain Ski Resort in New York offers a Value Pass from March 1 through the next season. For $229 you get unlimited skiing seven days a week at five different resorts for the rest of the season.[13]

Ski resorts may use seasonal discounting.

In addition to sporting goods, seasonal discounts are often offered for ticket prices to sporting events. The former Kroger Senior Classic (Champions Tour golf) event provided discounts for customers purchasing tickets in advance during the winter months for this summer event. The Holiday Badge promotion allowed consumers to purchase an all-week ground badge for $55 and get the second one free.

Summary

The pricing of sports products is becoming an increasingly important element of the sports marketing mix. Price is a statement of value for a sports product, and understanding consumers' perceptions of value is a critical determinant of pricing. Value is defined as the sum of the perceived benefits of the sports product minus the sum of the perceived costs. The perceived benefits of the sports product, or what the product does for the user, are based on its tangible and intangible features. Each consumer's perception of value is based on his or her own unique set of experiences with the sports product.

A variety of factors influences the pricing decisions for any sports product. Similar to the internal and external contingencies that affect the strategic sports marketing process, pricing influences can be categorized as internal or external factors. Internal factors are those under the control of the sports organization, such as the other marketing mix elements, cost, and organizational objectives. External factors are those factors beyond the control of the sports organization that influence pricing. These include consumer demand, competition, legal issues, the economy, and technology.

Marketing mix elements other than price must be carefully considered when determining the price of the sports product. Promotional mix elements (e.g., advertising and sales promotions) often communicate the price (or price reductions) of the sports product to consumers. The channel of distribution that is selected influences the price of sports products. For instance, consumers expect to pay higher prices (and are charged higher prices) when purchasing tennis equipment from a pro shop versus directly from the manufacturer. Product decisions are also highly related to pricing. Simply, price is used to signal product quality. Generally, the higher the price that is charged, the greater the perceived quality of the product.

Two distinct pricing strategies that emerge based on the emphasis of marketing mix elements are price and nonprice competition. As the name suggests, nonprice competition tries to establish demand for the sports product using the marketing mix elements other than price. Price competition, however, attempts to stimulate demand by offering lower prices.

In addition to other marketing mix variables, costs play a major role in pricing decisions. Costs are those factors that are associated with producing, promoting, and distributing the sports product. The total cost of producing and marketing a sports product is equal to the sum of the total fixed costs and the total variable costs. The fixed costs, such as players' salaries, do not change with the quantity of the product consumed, whereas variable costs change as a result of the quantity of the product being consumed. Today, the costs of running a professional sports franchise are skyrocketing because of players' salaries.

A final internal factor that influences pricing is organizational objectives. The four types of pricing objectives include income, sales, competitive, and social objectives. Typically, a combination of these four objectives is used to guide pricing decisions.

External factors, which are beyond the control of the organization, include consumer demand, competition, legal issues, the economy, and technology. Demand is the quantity of a sports product that consumers are willing to purchase at a given price. Price elasticity measures the extent to which consumer purchasing patterns are sensitive to fluctuations in price. For some sports products, such as a ticket to the Super Bowl, demand is relatively inelastic, which means that changes in price have little impact on game attendance. However, when demand is elastic, small changes in price may produce large changes in quantity demanded. Sports marketers try to estimate the demand for products by examining consumer trends and tastes, determining the number of substitute products, and looking at the income of the target market.

One of the most critical factors in determining pricing for sports products is to examine the prices charged for similar products by competing firms. Most professional sports franchises operate in a monopolistic environment in which no direct competitors exist. Because of this market condition, the price of attending professional sporting events is continually increasing. In fact, many "average" fans believe they are being priced out of the market and can no longer afford the cost of admission. In addition to competition, laws influence the pricing structure for sports products. For example, the Sherman Act was designed to protect freedom of competition, thereby freeing prices to fluctuate subject to market forces. The phase of the economic cycle is another important consideration in pricing. During periods of inflation, prices may rise to cover the higher costs, and during periods of recession, prices may be lowered. Finally, advances in technology are related to pricing decisions. Typically, consumers are willing to, and expect to, pay more for "high-tech" sports products. However, this is not always the case, as sometimes technological change can reduce pricing by facilitating marketing of the sports product.

Once the price of the sports product has been determined, adjustments are constantly necessary as market conditions, such as consumer demand, change. Price reductions or increases are used to reach pricing objectives that have been determined. Generally, price reductions are used to help achieve sales and market share objectives, whereas increases are used to keep up with rising costs. Regardless of whether adjustments are made to raise prices or lower prices, an important consideration in pricing is the concept known as the JND, or just noticeable difference. The JND is the point at which consumers can detect a "noticeable" difference between two stimuli—the initial price and the adjusted price. Depending on the rationale for price adjustments, sports marketers sometimes want the change to be above the difference threshold (i.e., consumers will notice the difference) and sometimes it will be below the difference threshold (i.e., consumers will not notice the difference).

Key Terms

- availability of substitute products, p. 383
- competition, p. 384
- competitive objectives, p. 378
- consumer demand, p. 380
- consumer income, p. 382
- consumer pricing evaluation process, p. 382
- consumer tastes, p. 381
- cost of information search, p. 383
- costs, p. 372
- economy, p. 384

- elastic demand, p. 380
- estimating demand, p. 381
- expected price range of substitute products, p. 383
- external (or environmental) factors, p. 368
- fixed costs, p. 372
- income objectives, p. 378
- inelastic demand, p. 380
- internal factors, p. 368
- just noticeable difference (JND), p. 389

- law of demand, p. 380
- legal issues, p. 385
- marketing mix variables, p. 369
- mob effect, p. 383
- nonprice competition, p. 372
- organizational objectives, p. 378
- perception of value, p. 383
- price, p. 365
- price adjustments, p. 387
- price discounts, p. 389
- price increases, p. 388
- price reductions, p. 388

Review Questions

1. Define price, perceived value, and perceived benefits. What is the relationship among price, value, and benefits?
2. Discuss the advantages and disadvantages of personal seat licenses from the consumer's perspective and the sports organization's perspective.
3. Outline the internal and external factors that affect pricing decisions. What is the primary difference between the internal and external factors?
4. Provide examples of how the marketing mix variables (other than price) influence pricing decisions.
5. Define fixed costs and variable costs and then provide several examples of each type of cost in operating a sports franchise. Do you believe costs should be considered controllable or uncontrollable factors with respect to pricing?
6. What are the four organizational objectives, and how does each influence pricing? Which organizational objective has the greatest impact on pricing?
7. What is meant by the law of consumer demand? Explain the difference between elastic and inelastic demand.
8. Describe, in detail, how sports marketers estimate the demand for new and existing sports products. What are the three demand factors, and which do you believe is the most critical in estimating demand?
9. What laws have a direct impact on pricing? Briefly describe each law.
10. How do advances in technology influence pricing? How does the economy influence pricing decisions?
11. Describe the different types of competitive environments. Why is competition considered one of the most critical factors influencing pricing?
12. What are the risks associated with reducing the price of sports products? Describe two common types of price discounting.

Exercises

1. Interview five consumers and ask them, "If a new athletic complex was built for your college or university basketball team, would you be willing to pay higher seat prices?" Summarize your results and discuss the findings in terms of perceived value and perceived benefits.
2. Interview five consumers and ask them to describe a sports product they consider to be of extremely high value and one they consider to be of extremely poor value. Why do they feel this way?
3. Find two examples of sports products you consider to compete solely on the basis of price. Provide support for your answer.
4. For any professional sports franchise, provide examples of how the rest of its marketing mix is consistent with its pricing.
5. Provide two examples of sports organizations that have (either in whole or in part) a social concern pricing objective.
6. Interview five people to determine whether demand could be characterized as elastic or inelastic for the following sports products: season tickets to your favorite basketball team's games, golf lessons from Greg Norman, and Nike Air Jordans.
7. Provide examples of how technology has increased the ticket prices of professional sporting events. Support your examples from a cost perspective.
8. Interview the organizer of a local or neighborhood road race (e.g., 5K or 10K) and determine the costs of staging such an event. Categorize the costs as either fixed or variable. Assess the role of cost in the price of the entry fee for participants.

Internet Exercises

1. Using the Internet, find three examples of promotions for sport products that provide consumers with pricing information.
2. Find an example of a sports product that is being sold via the Internet for a lower price than offered via other outlets. How much cheaper is the sports product? What does the consumer have to give up to purchase the product at a lower price over the Internet?
3. Using the Internet, find an example of price bundling sports products.
4. Using the Internet, find an example of product line pricing for the pricing of a sponsorship package (i.e., sponsorship levels at different prices).
5. Searching the Internet, find an example of a sports product that uses prestige pricing. Comment on the construction of the Web site itself. Is it consistent with the prestige pricing?

Endnotes

1. See, for example, R. B. Cialdini, R. J. Borden, A. Thorne, M. R. Walker, S. Freeman, and L. R. Sloan, "Basking in Reflected Glory: Three (Football) Field Studies," *Journal of Personality and Social Psychology,* no. 34 (1976), 366–375.

2. Valerie Zeithaml, "Consumer Perceptions of Price, Quality, and Value: A Means-End Chain Model and Synthesis of Evidence," *Journal of Marketing,* vol. 52 (July 1988), 2–21.

3. Kurt Badenhausen, Michael K. Ozanian, and Christina Settimi, "Baseball's Big Bucks," April 19, 2007, http://www.forbes.com/2007/04/19/baseball-team-valuations-07mlb-cz_kb_0419 baseballintro.html.

4. Kurt Badenhausen, Michael K. Ozanian, and Maya Roney, "The Business of Football," August 31, 2006, http://www.forbes.com/lists/2006/30/06nfl_NFL-Team-Valuations_land.html.

5. Tom Savage, "IRL Fan Experience Reaches Fans Nationwide," indyracing.com; http://irl.autoracing sport.com/2003_novnews/irl_1113_fan_experience.html.

6. "2004 NCAA Hoop City and March Madness Heading to San Antonio and New Orleans," http://www.hostcommunications.com/0,6032,1_1410_0_52107,00.html.

7. Kathleen Davis, "Val-pac: Assessing the Value in Attending Sporting Events," August 10, 2000, FoxSportsBiz.com.

8. Frederick Wiseman and Sangit Chatterjee, "Team Payroll and Team Performance in major league Baseball: 1985-2002," *Economics Bulletin,* vol. 1, no. 2 (2003), 1-10.

9. Rudy Martzke, "SET Expects Pay-Per-View Recordbreaker," *USA Today* (November 8, 1996), 2C.

10. Johnny Ludden, "Spurs Mailbag: For Right Price, Watch Parker Hog Ball up Close," *Express-News*, December 5, 2006, http://www.mysanantonio.com/sports/basketball/nba/spurs/stories/MYSA12042006.WEBspursmailbag.en.510d1de9.html.

11. Don Muret, "More Teams Gearing Up to Offer Option of Stored-Credit Tickets," SportsBusinessJournal.com, July 9, 2007.

12. See, for example, John Mowen and Michael Minor, *Consumer Behavior,* 5th ed. (Upper Saddle River, NJ: Prentice Hall, 1998).

13. "Hit Slopes on the Cheap," *The New York Post* (February 26, 2004), 61.

IMPLEMENTING AND CONTROLLING THE STRATEGIC SPORTS MARKETING PROCESS

13

IMPLEMENTING AND CONTROLLING THE STRATEGIC SPORTS MARKETING PROCESS

After completing this chapter, you should be able to

- Describe how the implementation phase of the strategic sports marketing process "fits" with the planning phase.

- Explain the organizational design elements that affect the implementation phase.

- Identify the general competencies and the most important skills that effective sports marketing managers possess.

- Describe the basic characteristics of total quality marketing (TQM) programs and how TQM might be implemented in sports organizations.

- Identify some of the guidelines for designing reward systems.

- Define strategic control and how the control phase of the strategic sports marketing process "fits" with the implementation phase.

- Explain the differences among planning assumption control, process control, and contingency control.

The opening scenario presents an excellent example of how sports organizations operate in uncertain and changing conditions. Moreover, sports organizations must consider the internal and external environments and formulate a plan that achieves a "fit" with these environments. The strategic sports marketing process is ultimately directed toward the achievement of the organization's mission, goals, and objectives. The contingency theory of sports marketing suggests that there are a variety of marketing plans that can achieve these goals. However, not all these plans are equally effective. Likewise, organizations have a variety of ways to implement and control the strategic sports marketing plan they have developed, all of which are not equally useful for putting the plan into action. Thus, sports marketers should allocate the time and effort necessary to develop a program that will lead to the desired outcomes and most effectively implement and control the planning process.

The remainder of this chapter looks at the last two phases of the strategic marketing process—implementation and control. We begin by examining a model of the

NHRA Owners Fire Up Marketing Plan

The new owners of the NHRA Pro Racing division didn't shy away from comparisons to the NASCAR model last week while announcing their $121 million acquisition. HD Partners Acquisition Corp., a group of former DirecTV executives who raised $150 million from investors to pursue a sports entertainment property, acknowledged a desire to emulate NASCAR's marketing success by filling more sponsorship categories and increasing the NHRA's licensing revenue.

The first step likely will include expansion of the Powerade Series' 23-race schedule with an eye on moving into Canada and/or Mexico in the not-too-distant future. In the next three to five years, the NHRA hopes to add at least three new events, possibly more. HD Partners said it will use the excess capital of about $30 million to pursue other acquisitions that would be ancillary to NHRA Pro Racing.

"NASCAR did not become what it is today because the racing evolved. They've been driving around in circles for 50 years," said Eddy Hartenstein, CEO of HD Partners and the former president of DirecTV. "It grew because of how they marketed the sport. That's our opportunity."

With the acquisition, the NHRA Pro Racing division will break away into a separate entity from the association's amateur side, which consists of 80,000 members and 35,000 licensed competitors. HD Partners bought all of the assets that go with the Powerade Series, including the contract with ESPN that goes through 2011, a perpetual license to the NHRA brand, sponsorship and licensing rights, media rights, merchandise rights related to the brand and four tracks, as well as a long-term lease to a fifth. HD Partners paid $100 million in cash, $9.5 million in HDP common stock, and assumed $11.5 million in NHRA debt. The money was paid to the NHRA, which maintains sanctioning duties, such as safety.

The NHRA is a nonprofit organization, but the sale means the Powerade Series will go public as part of HD Partners. The essential benefit to the move is that the NHRA will no longer have to reinvest its profits from the Powerade Series into the amateur side of the association.

Under the old model, the NHRA had experienced revenue growth in recent years, going from $82 million in 2004 to $93 million in 2006. Nearly half of that revenue comes from admissions, a revenue line that grew from $41 million to $46 million from 2004 to 2006.

The NHRA's sponsorship and licensing revenue remains underdeveloped, though, and those are areas Hartenstein and his team will target, he said. Hartenstein cited categories such as wireless, satellite TV, consumer-packaged goods, big-box electronics, and quick-service restaurants as obvious areas for growth. NHRA's nonendemic partners include UPS, Brut, Budweiser, U.S. Army, AAA, Oakley, and Motel 6. He also said that NASCAR-branded products generated license fees of more than $300 million in 2005, pointing out another opportunity for the NHRA to have revenue surge. NHRA showed revenue of $7 million last year in royalties.

The series will revamp and relaunch its licensing efforts, offer more merchandise through its Web site, NHRA.com, and establish a presence in retail outlets. The series also will relaunch NHRA.com. "As a property, the NHRA has been very successful in an under-the-radar way," said Tim Frost, a financial analyst and consultant in motorsports. "This is going to raise a lot of eyebrows."

Source: Michael Smith, *Sports Business Journal,* June 4, 2007, p. 8, http://www.sportsbusinessjournal.com/index.cfm?fuseaction=search.show_article&articleId=55367&keyword=NHRA%20owners%20fire%20up%20marketing%20plan.

implementation process and the organizational design elements that facilitate or impede the execution of the marketing plan. Then, we shift our focus to the control phase and look at some of the common forms of strategic control.

IMPLEMENTATION

Implementation can be described as putting strategy into action or executing the plan. As illustrated in the opening scenario, NHRA's dream of growing as large as its racing counterpart, NASCAR, can be achieved with proper planning. However, none of these plans matter unless the NHRA continually monitors the implementation process to make sure plans are being carried out in the correct manner.

To successfully manage the implementation process, the sports marketer must consider a number of organizational design elements. These organizational design elements include communication, staffing, skills, coordination, rewards, information, creativity, and budgeting. Implementation must begin with **communication.** Effective communication requires a leadership style that allows and encourages an understanding of the marketing plan by all members of the sports marketing team. A second critical element involves **staffing** and developing the **skills** in those people who are responsible for carrying out the plan. These people must also be placed within the organization so they can work together to implement the plan, thus a third critical design element is **coordination. Rewards** that are congruent to the plan can provide the motivation and incentives necessary for people to work effectively toward the achievement of the goals and objectives outlined within the plan. **Information** must be available to those people who will carry out the plans so effective decisions can be made throughout the implementation phase. Effective work environments also allow for and encourage **creativity** from individuals who are expected to find ways to carry out the strategic marketing plan. Finally, a supportive **budgeting** system is critical to the successful achievement of strategic goals and objectives. These seven organizational design elements of implementation and their relationship to the strategic sports marketing process are outlined in Figure 13.1.

Each of these seven elements must be carefully considered within the strategic marketing process by the sports marketing manager. The implementation design must be appropriate for the plan. In other words, a "fit" between the planning phase and the implementation phase is required. Thus, a change in the strategic marketing plan of a sports organization could lead to the need to make changes in one or more of these design elements. As you read the accompanying article on the demise of the XFL, think about what design elements could have been changed to save the league.

FIGURE 13.1   Implementation Phase of the Strategic Sports Marketing Process

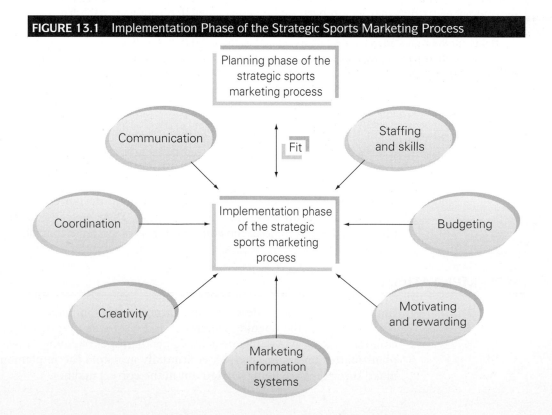

XFL: What Went Wrong?

After plunging into the sports arena with unparalleled fanfare and first-day success, the XFL closed its initial season with a whimper. If this were a wrestling match, it would have been stopped. XFL President Basil Devito acknowledged as much before the title game. "The biggest mistake was starting too quickly," he said. "In Week 1, we were not prepared either from a football or television production side. Following the season, we will be moving forward with what the new shape of the XFL will be. We have to improve it."

Attendance averaged 23,410 a game in the regular season, 17 percent above initial projections. But this is a made-for-TV league, and the TV audience dwindled. The XFL produced some interesting images, using cameramen on the field, cameras over the field, and shooting from other unconventional angles. But while cinematography can enhance the viewers' enjoyment of the game, it means little if there are no viewers. The season average for the XFL was 3.3. Only 2.5 percent of the homes with television sets in the nation's 49 largest markets tuned in, according to Nielsen Media Research. That was the story of the made-for-television league from Week 2 onward.

In February, when the league started, the World Wrestling Foundation's Vince McMahon had ventured that his latest promotion would dazzle the public with "real football" and teach the "pantywaist" NFL a thing or two along the way. "We know how to listen and we know what the people want," McMahon had said. "This league isn't just going to survive. It's going to thrive. . . . We'd have to be blithering idiots for this not to succeed."

Midway through the first, and perhaps last XFL season, New York/New Jersey Hitmen Coach Rusty Tillman was asked to assess the quality of play in his league compared with what he saw in more than 30 years of playing and coaching in the NFL. "We've got some great kids out here really busting their butts," Tillman said. "But here's the biggest problem. The quarterbacks pretty much stink, and the receivers pretty much stink. Basically, it's still football, and it's getting better every week. These kids try real hard, but it is what it is."

"The quality of play is decent," said Mike Keller, director of football operations for the new league. "We knew it wouldn't be the NFL. We were always looking for the best players who were not in the NFL. Sure we're struggling at quarterback, like everyone does. But our games have been fairly compelling and many of them are very close."

Where did the league go wrong? Tony Ponturo is vice president of media and sports marketing at Anheuser-Busch and was ranked by *The Sporting News* among the top 10 most powerful people in sports last year because of the vast amount of advertising money he and his associates spend on sporting events. He blames much of the league's demise on McMahon.

"He personally may have been his own worst enemy," Ponturo said from his St. Louis office, pointing out that McMahon already had a sullied reputation in the media because he used many distasteful tactics in his wrestling shows. "If he was John Doe starting with lower expectations (and less negative press), things might have been different."

The league started with a roar as curiosity seekers were lured by what XFL officials said was the biggest promotional effort ever directed at a start-up league. Many weeks of commercials aired during WWF and NBC programming, and the campaign seemed to work. According to Nielsen, the first telecast was seen in 9.5 percent of the nation's homes with a TV, far above projections.

Only 2.4 percent of the homes with TVs tuned in for the rest of NBC's regular-season telecasts. Advertisers had been guaranteed a 4.5 rating, which was reached only once in the final nine weeks, so the network gave away free commercials to offset the shortfall.

Another problem with the league may have been a lack of marketing planning. The XFL elected to use mostly no-name players instead of stocking up with high-priced National Football League-caliber talent. It played games that were nothing like the offense-dominated contests that made the AFL the only successful start-up pro football league in the past 50 years.

Ponturo also said the XFL erred by rushing into things. It failed to do enough test marketing and enough training sessions for players, who went to camp only about a month before the first game and played no formal exhibition contests. He compared it to Anheuser-Busch rolling out a new brand but failing to introduce it in test markets—a small geographical proving ground to get feedback—before going national. "It's one thing to fail in a rollout market," he said. "But when you go full bore without testing, you pay the consequences."

Sources: Kevin Modesti, "First XFL Season Is History; TV Viewers Ignored It, but League Had Its Fans." *Star Tribune* (April 23, 2001), 12C; Leonard Shapiro, "The XFL: 'It's Not Very Good Football'; Started with a Bang, Ending with . . ." *The Washington Post* (April 18, 2001), D10; Dan Caesar, "XFL Seems Destined to Exit NBC, as Sex Didn't Sell; A-B Marketing Exec Says League Misread Audience and Was Poorly Planned," *St. Louis Post-Dispatch* (April 25, 2001), D1.

Communication

Effective communication is critical to the successful implementation of the strategic sports marketing plan. Before we discuss the issues involved in effective communication, we must understand the importance of having a leader who is committed to the strategic sports marketing plan. Without such commitment, the best communication efforts will be ineffective. The values of the marketing leader not only affect the strategic sports marketing process, but also the way the plan will be implemented. Strategy leadership requires a "champion," someone who believes so strongly in the strategic marketing plan that he or she can share the "what," "why," and "how" with those who will be responsible for its implementation.

The commitment of the leader to the plan usually dictates the level of commitment among those who will carry it out. In addition, different strategies require different skills, even among leaders. Therefore, when strategy changes, a change in leadership often follows. That relationship may also be reversed. A change in leadership will often lead to a change, or at least an adjustment, to the strategy. In fact, because of the close relationship between strategy and leadership, it is sometimes necessary to bring in outside sports marketers to implement a changed or new strategy. Organizations will also often bring in someone new when they believe a new marketing strategy is needed to enhance performance.

Just how important is communication? The results of a recent study indicate that when selecting a new commissioner/CEO to run a major sports property, being able to effectively communicate and manage the media was deemed "extremely important" by 81 percent of the respondents.[1] Certainly, the LPGA had this in mind when they hired their new commissioner, Carolyn Bivens. The LPGA's first female commissioner came to the job after four years as president of a media consulting firm in Los Angeles. Unfortunately, Bivens got off on the wrong foot with the media at the first tournament of the year, the SBS Open at Turtle Bay. Without warning, media representatives showing up to cover the tournament were told they must agree to restrictive regulations concerning who controlled the images and stories from the tournaments. Rather than sign, the Associated Press walked out, as did two weekly magazines that cover the LPGA, *Golf World* and *Golf Week*.[2]

As discussed in the LPGA example, organizational leadership sets the tone for communication within the sports organization. Communication may be formal or informal and may use a number of different channels. For example, some organizations may require that all communications be written and meetings be scheduled and documented. Other organizational leaders may have an informal, open-door policy and allow for more "spur of the moment" meetings and "hallway" discussions. Either policy

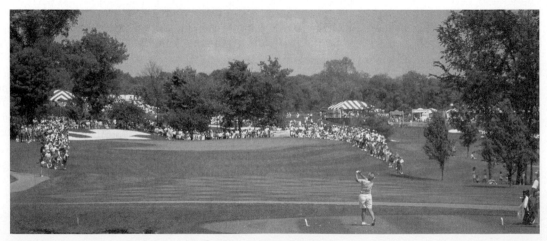

The LPGA is growing under strong leadership.

can be effective when it comes to implementing strategy within the sports organization, as long as the necessary information is clearly and accurately communicated.

Strategy was once considered a "top-down" only process where those who had a "big-picture" view of the organization were considered the best candidates for formulating strategy. This often led to huge communication requirements as organizational leaders attempted to inform those who had to carry out the strategy about not only the strategy, but also the rationale for strategic choices made by the top management. Experience has shown that the communication process is easier when those who are expected to implement the plan are involved throughout the process. Thus, involving the entire sports marketing team throughout the strategic sports marketing process can usually be more effective than attempting to communicate the plan after it has been developed.

Even when everyone responsible for implementing the plan is involved in its development, strategic sports marketing plans should be communicated often. Due to the contingent nature of the strategic sports marketing process, plans and circumstances can change, and people can forget the original plan and the basic premise on which the plan was formulated. Employees can learn about or be reminded about the content and purpose of the plans in a variety of ways. This information can be communicated in regularly scheduled meetings or at gatherings where the strategic plan is the primary agenda item. Printed material can also be useful. Some sports organizations may give employees desk items, such as calendars or paperweights, with keywords that remind them of the strategy. They may even program screen savers on computers with words that will remind employees of the strategic thrust of the marketing plan. Promotional literature that can be displayed around the office or sent to employees through e-mail is also useful. In essence, sports marketing organizations that can provide daily reminders of the strategy are more likely to keep everyone involved on the same strategic path. Many forms of internal promotion can be used to achieve this goal.

Communication with groups and individuals outside the marketing department is also important. Many such individuals and groups, both within the organization and outside the organization, have a stake in the marketing strategy and can have an impact on the implementation of the plan, and so it is important to inform other departments within the sports organization who affect or are affected by the strategy or the strategic marketing direction. For example, many teams and leagues are in the process of trying to develop long-term relationships with their fans. One of the ways to build these relationships is to allow fans more access and contact with the players. At the collegiate level, Xavier University Women's Basketball Team has implemented a Kid's Club. Young Musketeer fans are sent a handwritten note by a member of the team inviting them to a pregame pizza party. This creative plan can only be executed by communicating its importance to coaches and members of the XU team.

On the professional front, many teams hold an annual fan appreciation day to enhance fan relations. The Orlando Magic, for example, hold an annual fan appreciation night. Highlighting Fan Appreciation Night is a jersey presentation to 15 randomly selected Magic season ticket holders and 15 community partners, who each receive an authentic jersey from a Magic player following the game. The night also includes a number of activities centered around the fans, including pregame festivities, in-game activities, and giveaways. In addition, the first 10,000 fans receive Cheer Cards. Taking it one step further, the Memphis Grizzlies have developed a Fan Advisory Board. The board, consisting of 40 avid fans, has a voice in how to improve the Grizzlies experience. Of course, the ownership hopes this will help curb a slide in season-ticket sales too. All of these activities contribute to strengthening the team–fan relationship, but as shown in Table 13.1, the Magic aren't even among the top fifteen in professional sports.

As with internal promotion, external promotion and communication of the strategic sports marketing plan can take many forms. Some channels for these communications

TABLE 13.1	Stadium Experience Rankings of Professional Sports Teams

1. Minnesota Wild
2. Green Bay Packers
3. Pittsburgh Pirates
4. Dallas Mavericks
5. San Francisco Giants
6. Columbus Blue Jackets
7. Chicago Cubs
8. Seattle Seahawks
9. St. Louis Cardinals
10. Seattle Mariners
11. Detroit Pistons
12. Milwaukee Brewers
13. Houston Astros
14. San Antonio Spurs
15. Cleveland Indians

Stadium experience: Friendliness of environment; quality of game-day promotions.

Source: http://sports.espn.go.com/chat/sportsnation/franchiseRanks?sort=fanrel_rank&marketId=all&sport=all&year=2007.

include Web sites, annual reports, mailers, marketing specialties such as calendars, or meetings. Again, the key to effectively communicating to outside or inside groups is committed and competent leadership. It is with this leadership and effective communication efforts that the foundation for successful implementation of the strategic sports marketing plan is provided.

Staffing and Skills

As we just discussed, it is critical to the success of the strategic sports marketing plan to have a leader who can "champion" and communicate the strategy. As important as the leader is to effective implementation, it is equally important to have a staff that cares about and is capable of implementing the strategy. A group of individuals must be assembled who have the appropriate mix of backgrounds, experiences, know-how, beliefs, values, work and managerial styles, and personalities.

It is important to consider strategy prior to hiring and training new employees and in retraining those who are already with the marketing team. This is especially vital in

SPORTS MARKETING HALL OF FAME

Gary Davidson

Gary Davidson was once called the man who has had the greatest impact on professional sports in America. A former lawyer, Davidson founded and served as president of the American Basketball Association (ABA), the World Hockey Association (WHL), and the World Football League (WFL) in the late 1960s and early 1970s.

These leagues, of course, offered alternatives for professional athletes that would have never existed otherwise. By breaking the virtual monopoly held on talent by the existing NBA, NHL, and NFL franchises, Davidson attracted stars such as Wayne Gretzky, Bobby Hull, "Dr. J." Julius Erving, and Rick Barry to play in his rebel leagues. Davidson and his leagues are also credited with

some major rule changes that subsequently were adopted by the existing professional leagues. For instance, the three-point shot was created to add excitement to the ABA and has changed the entire course of modern basketball.

In addition to his ambush marketing tactics, Gary Davidson broadened the scope of professional sports. He placed professional franchises in cities that were previously considered too small to support major league sports. For example, San Antonio and Indianapolis were two of his original ABA teams that are now successful NBA franchises. Davidson's leagues have benefited the fans, the players, and major league sports.

Source: Steve Rushin, "Gary Davidson," *Sports Illustrated* (September 19, 1994), 145.

managerial or other key positions. However, staffing for the implementation of strategic sports marketing plans must go much deeper into the organizational ranks. In fact, putting together an effective marketing team is one of the cornerstones of the implementation process.

A few studies have examined the relationship between types of strategy and staff characteristics. One study of corporate executives and their perceptions regarding the relationship between managerial characteristics and strategy offered two interesting findings.[3] First, experience and exposure to a particular type of strategy has been viewed by corporate executives as being essential for managers. Previous experience and exposure to a strategy can provide an opportunity for these experienced individuals to provide important input into the implementation of the plan. However, the second finding suggests that a "perfect match" between managerial characteristics and strategy is likely to result in an overcommitment to a particular strategy. In other words, managers may not be able to change strategic direction when contingencies change if they are perfectly matched in education, training, experience, and personality to one particular strategy. These findings may be particularly relevant for sports organizations. Because sports organizations operate in changing, uncertain, and unpredictable environments where the internal and external contingencies can change frequently, staffing must consider the capacity for change among employees.

To develop a staff capable of implementing the strategy, three categories of characteristics must be considered: education, training, and ability; experience and previous track record; and personality and temperament. With any team-building activity, it is important to consider the compatibility of the individuals who will work together to implement the strategic sports plan.

Just what skills are necessary to land and keep your dream job in sports marketing? The answer to this question is best addressed in two parts. First, what knowledge is required for an individual to be successful in all sports management positions? In other

Sports careers on the Web.
Source: Copyright © 2004. Work in Sports L.L.C. All rights reserved.

words, what are the foundation skills for a successful career? Second, what are the marketing-specific core competencies of the sports marketing manager?

In addressing the first question, the general competencies necessary for all sports marketing management careers include being able to:[4]

- Direct the work effort of people or groups of people.
- Interrelate with the community.
- Negotiate to arrive at a solution to a problem.
- Function within a specified budget.
- Use supervision techniques.
- Evaluate the results of your decisions in light of work objectives.
- Self-evaluate employees' job performance.
- Use problem-solving techniques.
- Interpret basic statistical data.
- Speak before large audiences.
- Apply the knowledge of the history and evolution of sport into the structure of today's society.
- Appreciate the psychological factors that pertain to an athlete's performance and attitude on the playing field.

These general skills are required of all sports marketing managers to some extent, but what about more specific marketing skills? This question was posed to sports marketing professionals employed in sports marketing firms, amateur sports organizations, professional sports organization, and college athletics. The results of this study are presented in Table 13.2.

TABLE 13.2   Most Important Skills for Sports Marketing Managers

Presented in rank order where 1 is the most important skill and 20 is the least important skill.

1. Establish a positive image for your sporting organization.
2. Achieve sponsors' promotional goals.
3. Stimulate ticket sales.
4. Maximize media exposure for events, athletes, and sponsors.
5. Acquire sponsors through personal contacts.
6. Maintain good relations with community, authorities, and partners.
7. Acquire sponsors by formal presentations.
8. Develop special promotions.
9. Improve budget construction.
10. Negotiate promotion contracts.
11. Evaluate sports marketing opportunities and performance.
12. Design and coordinate content of events.
13. Coordinate press coverage of events.
14. Create contracts.
15. Provide corporate hospitality of events.
16. Build public image and awareness of athletes.
17. Schedule events and facilities.
18. Establish event safety factors.
19. Build rapport with editors, reporters, and other media reps.
20. Buy and resell media rights.

Source: Peter Smolianov and David Shilbury, "An Investigation of Sport Marketing Competencies," *Sport Marketing Quarterly*, vol. 5, no. 4 (1996), 27–36. Reprinted with permission of Fitness Information Technology, Inc., Publishers.

Remember, changes in strategy may lead to modification of the staff and skill base. Thus, employee training and retraining is often an important part of the implementation process. As strategy is developed and the implementation plan formulated, sports marketers must consider not only new staffing needs, but also new skill needs. Training and retraining programs should be designed and included in the implementation plans so the staff is prepared to implement the new or modified strategy. Until all the staff and skills are in place, it is unlikely that the sports organization can proceed with the successful implementation of the marketing plan.

Coordination

Successful implementation of the marketing plan depends not only on capable and committed leadership who can effectively communicate internally and externally and a staff with the necessary skills, but also on the effective organization of those people and their tasks. Structure helps to define the key activities and the manner in which they will be coordinated to achieve the strategy. A fit between strategy and structure has been shown to be critical to the successful achievement of strategy and the performance of organizations. According to one important study of organizations, when a new strategy was chosen, a decline in performance was observed and administrative problems occurred until a new method of organizing people and activities was put into place. Once the new method was implemented, organizational performance began to improve, and the strategy was more likely to be achieved.[5] Thus, the strategic marketing plan must dictate how people and tasks are organized.

CAREER SPOTLIGHT

Stu Eversole, District Athletic Director, Lakota Local Schools

Career Questions

1. How did you get started in the sports industry? What was your first sports industry job?

   My career in the sports industry probably had its roots in coaching. As the head football coach in one of Ohio's larger high schools, my charge was to manage a sports program on various levels from the junior high through the varsity level. This management charge included personnel, budgeting, scheduling, and a large measure of public relations, all of which served as a solid training ground for me in my current position as district director of athletics for Lakota Local Schools.

2. Can you describe the type of work you are doing right now? What are your job responsibilities?

   My current duties as district director of athletics for Lakota Schools are heavily impacted by various aspects of athletic finance as well as scheduling, in-service building athletic adminis-

trators, athletic Internet responsibilities, district sports medicine coordination, transportation budgeting, as well as some of the public relation issues associated with interscholastic athletics. The area that seems to percolate to the top is that of athletic finance, which can be broken down into the broad topics of budgeting for eight separate athletic departments, sports marketing for the district, sport fundraising coordination, and centralized purchasing.

3. What are the greatest challenges?

   One of the biggest challenges of this position is the responsibility for districtwide balance between Lakota East and Lakota West in a multitude of areas. In a two high school district where all the junior highs are aligned to either East or West and the freshman athletic program is also divided between East and West, one of our most important issues is balance. Some of these facets of balance would include budgets, schedules, coaching

(Continued)

(*Continued*)

staff equity, facilities, and issues that arise in the area of intra-district student transfers.

Another challenge specific to Lakota Schools would be dealing with a consistent and constant population growth rate that continues to strain the district funding. With state funding to public education being what it is, public school systems of growth find themselves returning to the voters for operational dollars. The athletic spinoff from this public funding challenge is that extracurricular programming many times takes a back seat to the funding necessary for educating every student during the regular school day. Diminished funding for extracurricular activities leaves the athletic administration searching for additional sources of revenue to maintain programming quality.

4. Do you foresee any changes in demand in this field in the future? If so, what or how?

Changes that I see on the horizon for individuals in my particular position would be the ever increasing need for a blended athletic knowledge base that includes an emphasis on athletic finance and budget management training.

5. Who or what has influenced you the most in your sports business career?

I have been influenced in my current position by fellow athletic directors who have been willing to serve as mentors for specific issues. I have also been fortunate to be housed in the same central office complex with our district treasurer and business manager who have both been very helpful in supporting my initiatives.

6. What advice would you offer students who are considering a career in sports marketing?

My advice to students looking to move into this field would be that they need to understand that the hours are long, rewards are often not tangible, and a thick skin would be an asset. As far as a training experience, I would wholeheartedly recommend some type of mentoring or shadowing program as part of graduate or undergraduate training. I also think it would be beneficial to have an understanding of the interpersonal aspects of working with groups of people in building consensus as well as having skills in conflict mediation.

One way of coordinating people and tasks in a sports organization is by practicing **Total Quality Management (TQM).** Quality improvement programs and practices have become an important and powerful tool for organizations, including sports organizations.[6] Nearly all major corporations and industries in the United States have adopted some type of quality initiative to meet competitive challenges. Traditionally, TQM programs have been focused on manufacturing quality. To manufacturers of sporting goods, quality is likely to mean an excellent consistency of goods and deliveries made by their suppliers. In a manufacturing environment, TQM has been primarily concerned with both the counting and reduction of defects and reducing the cycle time taken to complete any given process.

Even though TQM philosophies originally were used in manufacturing companies, a large number (69 percent) of service organizations are also using the principles of TQM. Although the nature of services is vastly different from those of manufactured products (see Chapter 7), Roberts and Sergesketter argue that the fundamental quality issues are similar.[7] A service organization, like a manufacturing organization, must concentrate on the reduction of defects and cycle times for important processes. As such, the philosophies of TQM are just as applicable for sports services as they are for manufacturing.

Although TQM represents a quality philosophy, there is little agreement as to what TQM (or quality) actually is and how best to manage the TQM process in an organization.[8] Evans and Lindsay define TQM as an integrative management concept for continuously improving the quality of goods and services delivered through the participation of all levels and functions of the organization.[9] In addition, TQM is described as incorporating design, control, and quality improvement, with the customer as the driving force behind the process.

Although the definitions of TQM may vary on the basis of wording and relative emphasis, all quality improvement programs share a common set of features or characteristics.[10] These characteristics include, but are not limited to, the following:

1. *Customer-Driven Quality*—Quality is defined by customers, and all TQM practices are implemented to please the customer.
2. *Visible Leadership*—Top management is responsible for leading the quality charge and places quality above all else.
3. *Data-Driven Processes*—All TQM processes are driven by data collection, use of measurement, and the scientific method.
4. *Continuous Improvement Philosophy*—It is always possible to do a better job, and continual, small changes in improvement are just as critical as an occasional major breakthrough.

Rewards

As we discussed previously, the execution of strategy ultimately depends on individual members of the organization. Effective communication, staffing, skill development and enhancement, and coordination are vital to implementation efforts and should be planned for and considered throughout the strategic sports marketing process. Another critical component in the design of an implementation plan is to provide for motivating and rewarding behavior that is strategy supportive. Thus, a reward system is a key ingredient in effective strategy implementation.

There is no one "correct" reward system. From a strategic perspective, rewards must be aligned with the strategy; therefore, the best reward system is contingent upon the strategic circumstances. These rewards and incentives represent another choice for management. Thus, reward systems will reflect the beliefs and values of the individuals who design them. However, to successfully motivate desired behavior, reward systems must consider the needs, values, and beliefs of those who will be motivated by and receiving the rewards.

Management can choose from several types of motivators, which can be classified on the basis of three types of criteria. Motivators can be positive or negative, monetary or nonmonetary, and long run or short run. Some examples include compensation (salary or commission), bonuses, raises, stock options, benefits, promotions, demotions, recognition, praise, criticism, more (or less) responsibility, performance appraisals, and fear or tension.

Experience has shown that positive rewards tend to motivate best in most circumstances; however, negative motivators are also frequently used by organizations. Many organizations assume that only financial motivators will lead to desired behaviors. However, many organizations have obtained great success with nonfinancial rewards. Typically, a combination of both provides optimal results. Timing is also an important consideration in motivating performance with reward systems. Rewards systems should be based on both short- and long-term achievements so that employees can receive both immediate feedback and yet be motivated to strive for the longer term strategic goals.

In an interesting twist, some sports owners would like to link their teams' on-field performance to salaries. David Gill, chief executive of Manchester United, English football's biggest brand, said he "would like to see players' salaries more variable, where they win rewards if we are winning." His model is not new to some industry executives, like bankers, but sports is arguably different. Athletes risk injury and the end of their career every time they run out to play, and also have a short career span. Unsurprisingly, the sports stars prefer a guaranteed salary to a performance-related payout.[11]

In summary, reward systems are critical to the successful achievement of the strategic sports marketing plan. To be effective, these systems must motivate behavior that "fits" with and ensures adequate attention to the strategic plan. Although reward systems are contingent upon the internal and external contingencies and the specific

TABLE 13.3	Guidelines for Designing Reward Systems

1. Rewards must be tightly linked to the strategic plan.
2. Use variable incentives and make them part of the compensation plan for everyone involved in strategy execution.
3. Rewards should be linked to outcomes that the individual can personally effect.
4. Performance and relationship to the success of the strategy should be rewarded rather than the position held by the individual.
5. Be sensitive to the discrepancies between top and bottom of the organization.
6. Give everyone the opportunity to be rewarded.
7. Being fair and open can lead to more effective reward systems.
8. Reward success generously—make the reward enough to matter and motivate.
9. Do not underestimate the value of nonfinancial rewards.
10. Be willing and open to adapting the reward system to people and situation changes.

Source: John Pearce and Richard Robinson, *Formulation, Implementation, and Control of Competitive Strategy,* 5th ed. (Boston: Irwin, 1994).

circumstances around which a sports marketing group must operate, there are some important general guidelines for developing effective reward systems (see Table 13.3).

Information

Accurate information is an essential guide for decision making and action, and necessary for all phases of the strategic sports marketing process. Execution of the sports marketing plan depends on effective information systems. These systems should provide the necessary information but should not offer more than is needed to give a reliable picture of issues critical to the implementation of the strategy.

Reports of information must be timely. The flow of information should be simple, including all the critical data being reported only to the people who need it. In other words, reports do not necessarily need wide distribution.

To aid strategy implementation, information reports should be designed to make it easy to flag variances from the strategic plan. In designing these reports, the critical questions to ask are as follows:

1. Who is going to need this information?
2. For what purpose will they need it?
3. When do they need it?

The NHL provides an example of a sports organization that enhanced their ability to implement marketing strategy through an information system.[12] One of the organizational objectives of the NHL was to make better use of emerging technologies. NHL Commissioner Gary Bettman believes "everything is connected to everything else" and that the league needs to be a leader in the use of technology to achieve its goals. Toward this end, the NHL has implemented a program called NHL-ICE (Interactive Cyber Enterprises), which has developed information systems for the media, fans, coaches, and players. The NHL-ICE programs also includes the design and content of the NHL Web site, implementing a real-time scoring system that captures statistics for every hockey game, and integrating network computing solutions into the marketing of the league's products and services.

The NBA's Detroit Pistons also present another fine example of information driving strategies. The Pistons have implemented ePrize's Intelligent Promotion Platform (IPP), a proprietary interactive marketing technology used via the Internet. The primary feature of the IPP includes customizing content so that fans can enjoy special offers, coupons, and game experiences based on their registration information and past consumption behaviors. In addition, the IPP allows the Pistons to learn more about their fans by creating a fan profile through an interactive survey. The system seems to be paying off as the Pistons have increased ticket sales by more than $500,000 in the past two years.[13]

The Portland Trail Blazers understand the importance of information sharing among their stakeholders. They are the first NBA franchise to create their own social networking site, the latest experiment as teams increasingly market to users of blogs, message boards, and other community fan sites. The Blazers launched iamatrailblazersfan.com, their first team-run social networking site. Since the mid-February 2007 launch, more than 3,000 people have registered to participate on the site, and team officials hope it will assist their grassroots marketing efforts while increasing fan communication.

"If you are pushing information via e-mail and only 20 percent of fans open up the e-mail, then you want to find a way to spread news about the team in a fast and effective way," said Dan Harbison, Internet marketing manager for the Blazers. "Others can leverage sites such as MySpace, but we are not able to sell tickets or sponsors through it so we are looking at what we see as benefits of our own [social network]."[14]

Creativity

The design of the strategic sports marketing plan's implementation phase is concerned with putting in place an effective system for executing marketing programs that will lead to the achievement of goals and objectives developed by the organization. The premise of this book is that the changing and uncertain environments in which sports organizations operate often require the need to adjust or change plans based on changing internal and external contingencies. Innovative plans and processes are vital to finding a fit with those contingencies. Thus, innovation, in the context of the strategic sports marketing process, is concerned with converting ideas and opportunities into a more effective or efficient system.

The **creative process** is the source of those ideas and, therefore, becomes an important component in the successful formulation and implementation of strategic sports marketing plans. Without creative endeavors, innovation is unlikely, if not impossible. An increase in creative efforts should likewise lead to an increase in innovative plans and processes.

When we talk about creativity, it is important to consider both the creative process and the people who engage in that process. The creative process can be learned and used by virtually anyone. However, some people have more experience with being creative and more confidence in their ability to be creative than others.

Many organizations can encourage creativity in their employees. This process of creating and innovating within an organization has been referred to as intrapreneurship, or corporate entrepreneurship. Intrapreneurial efforts have become popular as organizations have acknowledged the value of innovation in changing and uncertain environments. The watchword of today's businesses, sports organizations included, is change. As we discussed, innovation is vital to an organization's ability to change and adapt to internal and external contingencies. There are two general steps that can lead to an increase in the number of creative efforts and the resulting innovations: education and training regarding the creative process, and establishing an organizational culture and internal environment that encourages creativity.

The Creative Process

Although creativity is usually associated with promotion, it is important for all elements of the marketing mix. To be competitive, sports organizations must be creative in their pricing, in developing new products and services, and in getting new sports products to the consumer. The first step in increasing creative efforts within a sports organization is educating employees about the creative process. Creativity is a capability that can be learned and practiced. It is a distinctive way of looking at the world and involves seeking relationships between things that others have not seen.

Although they are referred to by different names, there are four commonly agreed-upon steps in the creative process. They are knowledge accumulation, incubation, idea generation, and evaluation and implementation.

The *knowledge accumulation phase* is an often overlooked, but absolutely vital, stage in the process of creating. Extensive exploration and investigation must precede successful creations. Because creations are simply putting together two existing ideas or tangibles in a new way, it is necessary to have an understanding of a variety of related and unrelated topics. This information gathering provides the creator with many different perspectives on the subject under consideration. Information can be gathered through reading, communication with other people, travel, and journal keeping. Simply devoting time to natural curiosities can be useful in this stage. The key is that the more the creator can learn about a broad range of topics, the more there is to choose from as the new creation is being developed.

In phase two, *the incubation period,* the creative individual allows his or her subconscious to mull over the information gathered in the previous stage by engaging in other activities. The creative effort is dropped for other pursuits. Routine activities, play, rest, and relaxation can often induce the incubation process. "Getting away" from the creative endeavor allows the subconscious mind to consider all the information gathered.

Often, when the creator least expects it, solutions will come. The next stage, *idea generation,* is the stage that is often portrayed as the "light bulb" coming on in one's mind. The opportunity for this has been set, however, in the first two phases. As the body rests from the research and exploration, the subconscious mind sees the creative opportunity or the "light."

The last stage, *evaluation and implementation,* is often the most difficult. It requires a great deal of self-discipline and perseverance to evaluate the idea and determine whether it will lead to a useful innovation. Following through with that implementation is even more challenging. This is especially true because those individuals who are able to generate creative ideas are often not the ones who can turn those ideas into innovations. Creators may fail numerous times as they attempt to implement creative efforts. And as the accompanying article illustrates, sometimes the innovative ideas that do reach the marketplace aren't the most welcomed.

Do-Overs: NBA Ball Hardly First Sports Innovation to Be Recalled

NBA players like Jason Kidd and Steve Nash must be pretty relieved to be getting their lacerated hands on the old NBA basketball when it gets resurrected from the dead Jan. 1. Still, even though the new ball didn't stick (literally—many players complained that it was too slippery), the NBA has a lot of company in the sports world when it comes to hitting Ctrl+Z for "undo." Basketball's version of New Coke is just the latest of many short-lived sports innovations that have had their proverbial cups of coffee before being widely ridiculed and sent back from whence they came.

Some bad ideas, like O.J.'s *If I Did It* fiasco and putting ads on baseball uniforms and bases, were shot down so quickly that they never even made it past the planning stage. Others, like the designated hitter and having Terrell Owens write a children's book (about sharing, no less) are still around. But today we're only talking about the product recalls, the ideas that saw the light of day for a brief moment before getting rejected like a Nate Robinson jump shot. In order of ascending crapulence, here's a countdown of the best of the worst.

Celebrities as Sportscasters: Rush Limbaugh made it three whole weeks on *Sunday NFL Countdown* before his insensitive comments led to his resignation. Dennis Miller, on the other hand, said nothing wrong but his obscure pop culture references made the MNF audience feel more confused than Karen Mistal in *Cannibal Women*

(Continued)

(Continued)

in the *Avocado Jungle of Death*. Well, at least we can be thankful that the comedians-in-the-booth experiment stopped there and we were spared seeing, say, Henny Youngman doing color commentary: "I just flew in from Miami, and boy, do the Dolphins suck. But take the Lions—please! I told my doctor, 'Doctor, it hurts when I go like this.' He said, 'You must be Donovan McNabb.'"

Instant Replay: I have no problem with leagues using instant replay to correct on-field calls by officials. But it would be nice if they could settle on some rules and stick to them for a while. Instant replay has been tried, changed, outlawed, and tried again so often that it should be on this list three or four times.

The Fisherman Logo: The idea wasn't so bad in theory: to represent the New York Islanders, a logo featuring a fictitious islander portrayed as a grizzled old fisherman holding a hockey stick. Unfortunately, the team must have hired the same model whose portrait graced the packaging for Gorton's fish, a resemblance not lost on the thousands of opposing fans who taunted the visiting Isles with chants of, "We want fish sticks!" The fish sticks logo went back into the freezer less than a year later.

Charlie Finley: The former owner of the Kansas City and then Oakland A's pioneered several short-lived "innovations," including such winners as using grazing sheep to cut the grass beyond the outfield wall. Finley is also responsible for introducing orange baseballs, which he thought would be easier to see than white balls. Tried in a few exhibition games in 1973, umpires and fans praised the improved visibility but hitters found it too hard to pick up the spin, and the orange balls were never heard from again. Finley's most hare-brained scheme, though, was the mechanical rabbit named Harvey that he had built to pop out of its underground lair near the backstop when beckoned and deliver fresh baseballs to the home plate umpire. Eventually the A's took Elmer Fudd's advice and killed the wabbit after the 1969 season.

The XFL: It's hard to say what killed the heavily hyped XFL after just one season. It might have been the low quality of play, or the constant and drastic rule changes during the season, or the concern that with WWE's Vince McMahon at the wheel the games might be fixed or even scripted, or the relative tameness it needed to hold onto because games were broadcast on network TV, or the high percentage of injuries during the ill-conceived scramble for the ball in lieu of a coin toss, or the bad grammar of Rod "He Hate Me" Smart, or the accidental effect of the highly touted "no fair catch" rule actually making punt returns less exciting, or the awkward,

Abbott-and-Costello-but-without-the-comedy pairing of Jesse Ventura and Fred Roggin in the broadcast booth.

Glowing Hockey Puck: Like so many of the monumental failures listed here, it started with a reasonable idea. Casual hockey fans complained that the puck was hard to follow during televised games, so when Fox started broadcasting NHL games their engineers developed FoxTrax, a normal puck with an electronic chip inserted that made the puck glow on screen and gave it a sort of comet's tail as it moved quickly across the ice. But when the "glow puck" debuted at the 1996 NHL All-Star Game, die-hards ridiculed it as distracting and unecessary. After all, you'd have to be blinder than an NBA referee not to be able to see a black puck on a white rink. FoxTrax survived through the 1998 Stanley Cup Finals, but was mercifully euthanized thereafter. That didn't stop the mockery, though, as Fox's glowing puck was derided on Canadian TV and by hockey fans everywhere.

The Olympic Triplecast: "You know how nobody really watches the Olympics anymore? Well what if, instead of broadcasting them over network television so people can ignore them for free, we put them on three different pay-per-view channels and charged people $95–$170? Then they'd definitely watch, right?" I don't know the name of the NBC executive who made that proposal to the top brass before the 1992 Summer Olympics, but I'm guessing it was "Mud." The idea was such a dramatic failure that NBC essentially abandoned the pay format halfway through the Games and started broadcasting several-hour blocks of it for free on CNBC.

Disco Demolition Night: The Chicago White Sox' 1979 promotion to destroy disco albums between games of a doubleheader attracted a crowd that was more interested in the destruction than in the ballgames. Many of the 50,000 disco haters in attendance spent the first game climbing stadium walls and fences and throwing vinyl records onto the field. And when it finally came time for the official demolition, things only got worse. The explosives used to detonate the huge mound of records on the field tore up the outfield grass as thousands of fans stormed the field to cause further mayhem. Riot police were called in to clear out the crowds, 39 people were arrested, and the Sox were forced to forfeit the second game and then postpone several others because the field remained unplayable for days.

As bad as all these failed "advances" were, a ball that actually injures the players has to take the top honor as worst sports innovation of all time. If necessity is the mother of invention, then this ball's father must have been one seriously unsavory character. Or at least a grizzled old fisherman.

Source: Adam Hofstetter, December 20, 2006, http://sportsillustrated.cnn.com/2006/writers/adam_hofstetter/ 12/14/uncommon.sense/?cnn=yes.

Encouraging Intrapreneurship

Creative efforts and the innovations within organizations are a function of both individual and organizational factors. Entrepreneurial employees add value to the organization and enhance implementation by finding creative ways to achieve the strategic plan. However, these efforts can flourish only if organizational features foster creativity. To encourage an intrapreneurial environment, staff members must be rewarded for entrepreneurial thinking and must be allowed and even encouraged to take risks. Failure and mistakes must be allowed and even valued as a means to creative and innovative expression.

The key to successfully creating a climate that encourages creativity and innovation is to understand the components of such an atmosphere. Those components include management support, worker autonomy, rewards, time availability, and flexible organizational boundaries. To understand these components, consider the following guidelines used at 3M Company:[15]

- *Do Not Kill a Project*—If an idea does not seem to find a home in one of 3M's divisions at first, 3M staff members can devote 15 percent of their time to prove it is workable. In addition, grant money is often provided for these pursuits.
- *Tolerate Failure and Encourage Risk*—Divisions at 3M have goals of 25–30 percent of sales from products introduced within the last five years.
- *Keep Divisions Small*—This will encourage teamwork and close relationships.
- *Motivate Champions*—Financial and nonfinancial rewards are tied to creative output.
- *Stay Close to the Customer*—Frequent contact with the customer can offer opportunities to brainstorm new ideas with them.
- *Share the Wealth*—Innovations, when developed, belong to everyone.

Sports marketers are always looking for new and innovative approaches to all elements of the marketing mix. On the promotion side, for instance, the Chicago Cubs designed a simple, yet effective, promotion linked to the game. Instead of using the old landline technology, the Cubs manager now uses a secure Motorola phone to communicate with the bullpen. Motorola benefits from the increased exposure to fans at the park and on televised games. On the product side, Sportsline's HydraCoach bills itself as the world's first "intelligent water bottle." You enter your weight and activity level, and then indicators on the side of the unit tell you whether you are meeting your "personal hydration goal." One area of innovation in sports facility design is going green. The Cleveland Indians and Green Energy Ohio installed a new solar electric system at Jacobs Field, the first American League ballpark to go solar. The Washington Nationals' new ballpark has what its architect, HOK Sport, says is the first "green roof" at a big league sports facility. The Chesapeake Bay Foundation, an environmental nonprofit, gave a $101,670 grant to the D.C. Sports and Entertainment Commission to cover the cost of planting grass and other plants on top of a 6,300-square-foot waterproof surface above a concession stand in left field.

In other examples, for the first time in the history of any major North American professional sports league, a league-wide uniform innovation has been established. The National Hockey League and Reebok partnered to create a technologically advanced uniform for players called the Rbk EDGE Uniform System,[16] and University of New Mexico officials are offering youth tickets, which cost only $8 per game or $99 per season, to those ages 3 to 18, with seats available in bench rows 1–10 and in the mezzanine.

Budgeting

Budgets are often used as a means of controlling organizational plans. However, the budgeting process can be an important part of the implementation plan if budget development is closely linked to the sports marketing strategy. In fact, the allocation of financial resources can either promote or impede the strategic implementation process.

Marketers within the sports organization must typically deal with two types of budgetary tasks. First, they must obtain the resources necessary for the marketing group to achieve the marketing plan goals. Second, they must make allocation decisions among the marketing activities and functions. These two types of activities require working with individuals and groups internal and external to the sports marketing function.

To develop strategy-supportive budgets, those individuals responsible should have a clear understanding of how to use the financial resources of the organization most effectively to encourage the implementation of the sports marketing strategy. In general, strategy-supportive activities should receive priority budgeting. Depriving strategy-supportive areas of the funds necessary to operate effectively can undermine the implementation process. However, overallocation of funds wastes resources and decreases organizational performance.

In addition, just like the rest of the strategic sports marketing process, the budgeting process is subject to changing and often unpredictable contingencies that may necessitate changes in the marketing budget. A change in strategy nearly always calls for budget reallocation. Thus, those individuals who are responsible for developing budgets must be willing to shift resources when strategy changes.

CONTROL

In the uncertain and changing environments in which sports organizations operate, it is critical to consider four questions throughout the strategic sports marketing process.

1. Are the assumptions on which the strategic marketing plan was developed still true?
2. Are there any unexpected changes in the internal or external environment that will affect our plan?
3. Is the marketing strategy being implemented as planned?
4. Are the results produced by the strategy the ones that were intended?

These questions are considered the basis of strategic control and the fundamental issues to be considered in the **control** phase of the strategic sports planning process model. **Strategic control** is defined as the critical evaluation of plans, activities, and results—thereby providing information for future action. As illustrated in Figure 13.2, the control phase of the model is the third step to be considered. However, it is important to note that the arrows allow for "feedforward." In other words, even though control is the third phase of the model, we consider it as we develop earlier phases of the process. Once the initial plan is developed, the assumptions on which the plan was developed and the internal and external contingencies must be examined and monitored. As the implementation process is set in place and as the plan is executed, strategic control reviews the process as well as the outcomes. Variances from the original assumptions, plans, and processes are noted and changes are made as needed.

The three types of strategic control that sports marketers must consider are planning assumptions control, process control, and contingency control. The following sections outline each of these three types of control.

Planning Assumptions Control

As we have discussed throughout this text, it is vital to understand internal and external contingencies and formulate strategic sports marketing plans that establish a fit with those contingencies. During the planning phase, it is often necessary to make assumptions concerning future events or contingencies about which we do not have

FIGURE 13.2 Control Phase of the Strategic Sports Marketing Process

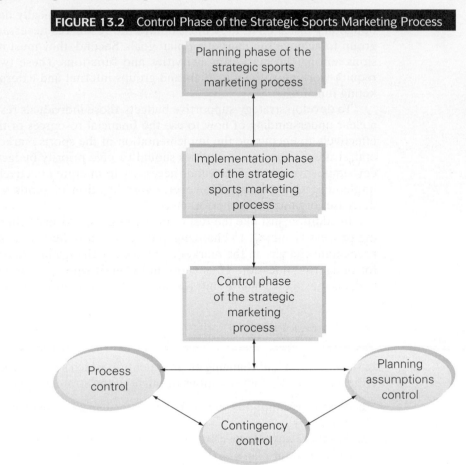

complete information. In addition, individual planners may perceive and interpret data differently. In other words, the strategic sports marketing plan is based on a number of situation-specific premises and assumptions. This level of control attempts to monitor the continuing validity of these assumptions. Thus, in **planning assumptions control,** the sports marketer asks the question: "Are the premises or assumptions used to develop the marketing plan still valid?" To fully evaluate the responses to this question, the assumptions used during the development of the marketing plan must be listed. This step is vital to the success of this control mechanism so those individuals who are responsible can monitor them throughout the process.

A good example of planning assumptions control at work was when Presbyterian College, in an effort to gain greater exposure while competing at a higher level of athletics, joined the Big South Conference for the 2007–08 school year. Big South members compete at the NCAA Division I-AA level in football and at the Division I-A level in all other sports. Another example of a planning control assumption no longer being valid was the marketing of the home run king Barry Bonds. Corporations such as MasterCard that market through Bonds had to seriously rethink their plans when Bonds was accused of steroid use and now has been indicted on perjury and obstruction of justice charges.

Because of the complexity of the decision-making process, it may be impossible to monitor all the assumptions or premises used to formulate the strategic sports marketing plan. Therefore, it is often practical not only to list the premises, but also to prioritize them based on those that may most likely effect a change in the marketing plan.

Although all assumptions should be considered in this form of control, two categories of premises are most likely to be of concern to the sports marketer: external environmental factors and sports industry factors. As we discussed earlier, strategic sports marketing plans are usually based on key premises about many of these variables. Some examples of external environmental factors include technology, inflation, interest rates, regulation, and demographic and social changes. The relevant sports industry in which a sports organization operates is also usually a key premise aspect in designing a marketing plan. Competitors, suppliers, league regulations, and leadership are among the industry-specific issues that need to be considered when identifying the critical assumptions used to develop the strategic plan.

Monitoring the premises or assumptions used to develop the strategic sports marketing plan is vital to the control phase of the strategic sports marketing process, but it is not sufficient. In other words, this form of control does not measure how well the actual plan is progressing, nor is it able to take into account the aspects of the internal and external environment that could not be detected during the planning phase when the premises were developed. Thus, effective control must consider two additional forms of evaluation: process control and contingency control.

Process Control

Process control monitors the process to determine whether it is unfolding as expected and as desired. This type of control measures and evaluates the effects of actions that have already been taken in an effort to execute the plan.

Because of changes in premises and contingencies, the realized strategic marketing plan is often not the intended strategic marketing plan. Changes and modifications to the plan usually occur as a result of the process control activities carried out by marketers. In other words, during this stage of control, sports marketers attempt to review the plan and the implementation process to determine whether both remain appropriate to the contingencies. Either the marketing plan or the implementation process put in place to execute the plan may not proceed as intended. These variances may lead to a need to change the plan or the process or both. Thus, the key question asked by this form of control is: "Should either the strategic plan or the implementation process be changed in light of events and actions that have occurred during the implementation of the plan?" It is important to note that to change or modify the marketing plan or implementation process is not necessarily a decision to avoid. The benefit of this form of control is that sports marketers can minimize the allocation of resources into a strategic plan or implementation process that is not leading to achievement of the objectives and goals they deem important.

To answer the preceding question, two measures are typically used: *monitoring strategic thrusts* and *reviewing milestones*. As we discussed earlier, the strategic sports marketing plan is a means of achieving strategic and financial organizational goals and marketing objectives. An important part of evaluating the plan and process is to review the achievement of these objectives and goals during the execution of the plan. Because objectives are not time specific or time bound (as discussed in Chapter 2), strategic thrusts can be examined to evaluate progress in the direction of strategic and financial objectives. On the other hand, reviewing milestones typically examines achievement of marketing objectives. Let us look at each of these two forms of process control more closely.

Monitoring Strategic Thrusts

Monitoring strategic thrusts attempts to evaluate or monitor the strategic direction of the plan. As a part of the overall strategic plan, smaller projects are usually planned that will lead to the achievement of the planned strategy. Successful pursuit of these smaller projects can provide evidence that the strategic thrust is the intended one.

However, if these projects are getting lost to other "nonstrategic" projects, it could mean that the overall strategy is not progressing as planned.

One strategic thrust of special interest to sports organizations and organizations marketing their products through sports is, of course, sponsorship. Determining the effectiveness of a sponsorship program is becoming increasingly more important as the costs of sponsorship continue to rise. A Turnkey Sports Poll was conducted with 400 senior-level sports industry executives to understand just how important measurement can be to the sponsorship package. Half of those surveyed indicated that the fact that "certain sponsors are paying closer attention to measuring return on investment" is "good for sports." Additionally, nearly 60 percent of the executives indicated that in the last three years spending on consumer research was either "up slightly" or "up significantly."[17]

Just how, then, do we measure or determine whether we are seeing a return on our marketing investment? Lesa Ukman, president of IEG Chicago, which publishes the IEG sponsorship report, believes sponsorship return can be measured. Ukman stresses the following regarding sponsorship measures:[18]

> Sponsorship return can be measured. The key lies in defining objectives, establishing a presponsorship benchmark against which to measure, and maintaining consistent levels of advertising and promotion so that it is possible to isolate the effect of sponsorship.
>
> The lack of a universal yardstick for measuring sponsorship is a problem, but it is also an opportunity. The problem is that sponsorships often are dropped, not because they don't have measurement value, but because no one has actually measured the value.
>
> The lack of a single, standardized measurement is also an opportunity because it means sponsors can tailor their measurement systems to gauge their specific objectives.

Teams, Sponsors and Agencies All Share ROI Accountability

If you can't measure it, you can't manage it. Whether you live by that statement or consider it outdated, you have certainly felt the movement toward an era of accountability. Despite the fact that "sponsorship ROI" is fast supplanting "activation" as the industry's favorite buzzword, the reality is that smart measurement is still not taking place.

Virtually every agency claims measurement capabilities exist in-house, but few actually have the resources at hand. Even fewer follow through on their promises to include measurement as a key component to their programs. The same could be said for the teams and leagues. But who can blame them? They deliver what clients demand.

Ultimately, the blame falls on sponsors for not holding their agencies and sponsorship properties accountable and demanding cooperation. The sobering reality is that far too few investments (10 percent to 30 percent, according to most industry experts) are measured. Of those that are measured, simple marketing metrics or the return on objectives accounts for more than half of what is labeled "return on investment."

The future of sponsorship ROI lies in the hands of the proactive marketers who will preempt calls from their boss or client to measure results. These early adopters will presumably make a name for themselves in the marketplace by asking the hard questions today and understanding the boomerang effects of sponsorship. They also will force the hand of those around them to accept a higher standard of success, one judged by measurable results.

Several sponsors and agencies are indeed setting the bar higher. Their impact in the marketplace has already been felt. One needs only to look at the most respected and efficient marketers to know who is tracking results.

Sponsors such as Bank of America and General Motors know exactly how much profit is derived from each investment. Leading-edge agencies such as Engage Marketing distinguish themselves from other agencies through their commitment to measuring results.

(Continued)

(Continued)

"At Engage, we are committed to providing a superior value to our clients, and a major component of that value is our commitment and confidence in measuring what we deliver," said Kevin Adler, founder and chief solutions officer. "Every proposal that leaves our office has budget specifically allocated to measurement."

Regardless of the stage a current organization is in, the writing is on the wall. The attraction and retention of sponsorship dollars without measurable results will go from difficult to nearly impossible over the next decade. The good news is that accurate measurement for sponsors is within reach and affordable. One to three percent of a sponsorship budget should be set aside for measurement and research.

As an example, the Class AAA Sacramento River Cats recently commissioned a sponsorship ROI study for less than $20,000 that helped retain one of their largest marketing partners. Even without a budget available for outsourcing research, any property can take a few simple steps to proactively track measurable results. A team, for example, should always gather the key indicators for program success from their sponsors.

Whether it is lead generation, the trial of a new service, or interacting with the product, a simple metric of

Methods to Measure ROI
In house: • Track sales leads generated. • Track the number and identity of prospects hosted at events. • Ask for the sponsor's average contribution margin or lifetime customer value and use it to estimate the profit driven by the sponsorship. **Outsourced:** • Conduct a study measuring intent to buy, shifts in brand perception or other variables valued by the sponsor. • Measure shifts in market share within the fan base.

success reveals the sponsor's ultimate goal. Knowing a client's ultimate goal and managing its investment to meet that goal should be every marketer's primary objective.

The current call to arms for sports marketers is measurement. The benefits of being proactive are numerous, and the door is closing on the opportunity to act early. Take action today and set the wheels in motion for your organization.

Source: AJ Maestas, founder and president of Navigate Marketing, an agency specializing in measurement, research, and sponsorship ROI; http://www.sportsbusinessjournal.com/index.cfm?fuseaction=search.show_article&articleId=55583&keyword=Teams,%20sponsors%20and%20agencies%20all%20share%20ROI%20accountability.

Although there are no universal measures, here are a few of the more popular ways of measuring sponsorship effectiveness against the objectives of awareness and exposure, sales, attitude change, and enhancing channel-of-distribution relationships:

- Number of stories and mentions in popular media, such as newspapers, televised shows, and magazines, serve as a measure of exposure. For example, John Hancock Financial Services measures the impact of its football bowl sponsorship using this method. In one year, approximately 21 binders of newspaper clippings were collected at an estimated advertising equivalency of $1 million.[19]

  Awareness is also assessed through "media equivalencies," that is, determining how much "free" time the sponsor has accumulated through television coverage. For example, Joyce Julius and Associates has estimated that Louisville-based Yum Brands earned almost $2.7 million in exposure in its debut as the first presenting sponsor of the Kentucky Derby.

  While the measurement of brand exposure has historically used human observation, new companies like Margaux Matrix are testing electronic tools to perform the same operation more accurately.[20] Not all researchers are sold on the notion of media equivalencies. In fact, public relations firm Jeffries-Fox's most recent study conclusions led to the official Institute for Public Relations (IPR) position that "The IPR Commission does not endorse Ad Value Equivalencies as a measurement tool."[21]

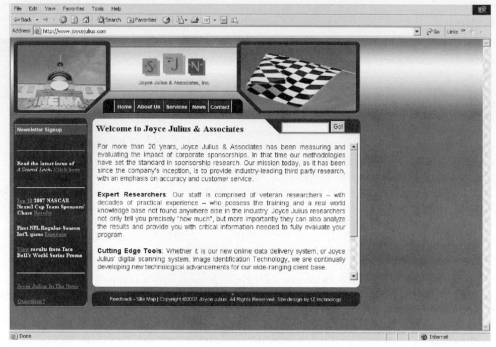

Sponsorship ROI evaluation.

Source: Used by permission of Joyce Julius & Associates, www.joycejulius.com. All rights reserved.

- Sales figures for products and services can be examined both prior to (pre) and after (post) the event to estimate the potential impact of the sponsorship. Other methods of tracking sales include looking at sales for the sponsorship period versus the same time period in prior years or measuring sales in the immediate area versus national sales. In addition, sales might be tied directly to the sponsored event. For example, discounts for products might be offered with proof of attending the event (show ticket stub); therefore, the number of redemptions might be tracked. Of course, many other factors, such as competitive reaction and additional sales promotions, will influence the sales figures.

     One final variation of measuring the impact of sales is to involve the sales force in tracking the value of leads and contacts generated through sponsorship.

- To assess consumer attitudes toward various products and services, as well as the sponsored event, research is conducted in the form of surveys or in-depth interviews. This primary market research is used to gauge the image of the event and its sponsors, attitudes that consumers have toward the event and its sponsors, and awareness of events and sponsors' products and services.

When determining the impact of sponsorship on channels of distribution, it is common practice to track the number of outlets carrying the given product before and after the sponsored event. In addition, sponsors may want to assess the number of retailers or dealers participating in a program versus previous promotions. Finally, companies may measure incremental display at the point of purchase in retail outlets.

For example, Kraft General Food's primary objective for sponsorship of a NASCAR team for Country Time Drink Mix was to enhance distribution in the Southeast and in-store merchandising nationally. To this end, Kraft created a

Sponsors such as Jaguar and Castrol must design controls to
evaluate sponsorship effectiveness.

promotion in which consumers who had a proof of purchase could get to ride in a
race car simulator. The simulator ride offer increased sales 66 percent in the
Southeast and generated more than 40 incremental case displays at each retail stop
nationwide.[22]

Milestone Review

The second form of process control is **milestone review.** Marketing managers at sports
organizations usually establish milestones that will be reached during the execution of
the marketing plan. These milestones may be critical events, major allocations,
achievements, or even the passage of a certain amount of time. As these milestones are
reviewed on a continuous basis, an evaluation of the advisability of continuing with the
plan and the process is afforded.

Financial Analysis

Financial information can be used to understand and control the process of strategic
marketing plan implementation; that is, to perform **financial analyses.** It is important
for any sports organization to have a good accounting system. In terms of process control, the accounting system can provide the following:

- A ready comparison of present financial performance with past performance,
  industry standards, and budgeted goals
- Reports and financial statements that can be used to make appropriate strategic
  decisions
- A way of collecting and processing information that can be used in the strategic
  sports marketing process

Two important components of a good accounting system are the *income statement*
and *balance sheet.* Income statements provide a summary of operating performance.
These documents summarize both money coming into and going out of the sports organization and the marketing department or division. Because income statements are a
good measure of customer satisfaction and operating efficiency, they should be prepared frequently—at least every three months, if not monthly. Balance sheets provide a
summary of the financial health of the sports organization at a distinct point in time.

TABLE 13.4A	Rich Creek Rockers Income Statement	

Income Statement for the Year Ended December 31, 2006

Revenues:		
Single game admissions	$ 140,000	
Season ticket holders	275,000	
Concessions	250,000	
Advertising revenue	95,000	760,000
Expenses:		
Cost of concessions sold	100,000	
Salary expense—players	235,000	
Salary and wages—staff	130,000	
Rent	150,000	615,000
Profits before taxes		145,000
Income tax		33,000
Income after taxes		$ 112,000

TABLE 13.4B	Rich Creek Rockers Balance Sheet	

Balance Sheet at December 31, 2006

Assets		Liabilities and Owner's Equity	
Cash	$10,000	Accounts payable	$20,000
Accounts receivables	82,000	Capital stock	50,000
Equipment	40,000	Retained earnings	62,000
Total assets	$132,000	Total liabilities and owner's equity	$132,000

The balance sheet provides the sports marketer with a summary of what the organization is worth; what has been invested in assets, such as inventories, land, and equipment; how the assets were financed; and who has claims against the assets. Tables 13.4A and 13.4B provide simple examples of the information typically found on income statements and balance sheets.

One of the more useful methods of financial analysis for control purposes is known as **ratio analysis.** Financial ratios are computed from income statements and balance sheets. These ratios can tell the sports marketing manager a lot about the progress and success of the strategic sports marketing plan. In other words, using financial ratios can help a sports marketing manager assess whether the marketing strategy continues to provide an appropriate fit with internal and external contingencies. There are several types of financial ratios that can be categorized as follows:

- *Profitability Ratios*—Provide an indication of how profitable the organization or division is during a period of time.
- *Liquidity Ratios*—Indicate the ability of the organization to pay off short-term obligations without selling off assets.
- *Leverage Ratios*—Measure the extent to which creditors finance the organization.
- *Activity Ratios*—Measure the sales productivity and utilization of assets.
- *Other Ratios*—Determine such things as return to owners in dividends, the percentage of profits paid out in dividends, and discretionary funds.

TABLE 13.5   Summary of Selected Key Financial Ratios

Ratio	Calculation	Question(s) Answered
Gross profit margin	$\dfrac{\text{Sales} - \text{Cost of goods sold}}{\text{Sales}}$	What is the total margin available to cover operating expenses and provide profit?
Net profit margin	$\dfrac{\text{Profits after taxes}}{\text{Sales}}$	Are profits high enough given the level of sales? Are we operating efficiently?
Return on total assets	$\dfrac{\text{Profits after taxes}}{\text{Sales}}$	How wisely has management employed assets?
Asset turnover	$\dfrac{\text{Sales}}{\text{Average total assets}}$	How well are assets being used to generate sales revenue?
Current ratio	$\dfrac{\text{Current Assets}}{\text{Current liabilities}}$	Does our organization have enough cash or other liquid assets to cover short-term obligations?
Debt-to-assets load	$\dfrac{\text{Total debt}}{\text{Total assets}}$	Is the organization's debt excessive?
Inventory turnover	$\dfrac{\text{Cost of goods sold}}{\text{Average inventory}}$	Is too much cash tied up in inventories?
Accounts receivables turnover	$\dfrac{\text{Annual credit sales}}{\text{Accounts receivables}}$	What is the average length of time it takes our firm to collect for sales made on credit?

Table 13.5 lists some of the more commonly used ratios, how each is calculated, and what each can tell the sports marketing manager. Examples of how these ratios are applied and interpreted are shown in Table 13.6.

Contingency Control

The third form of control, **contingency control,** is based on the assumption that sports marketers operate in an uncertain and unpredictable environment and that the changing nature of the internal and external environments may lead to the need to reassess strategic choices. Although it is included as a part of the control phase, this form of control should be of concern throughout the strategic sports marketing process.

The goal of contingency control is to constantly scan the relevant environments for internal and external contingencies that could affect the marketing planning process. Unlike planning assumptions control, the goal here is to remain unfocused so any unanticipated events will not be missed. In other words, the "big picture" is of most concern in this phase of control. The primary question to be addressed here is: "How can we protect our marketing strategy from unexpected events or crises that could affect our ability to pursue the chosen strategic direction?" Attempts to control without a prestructured list of variables of concern may not seem to make sense at first. However, it is easier to understand this form of control if one thinks in terms of how a crisis usually occurs. The daily events leading up to an unpredicted event lead to a focus in the form of a crisis. Previously unimportant or unnoticed events become more problematic until an actual crisis requires some action. Learning to notice and interpret signals thus becomes an important way to circumvent crises. Thus, the goal of contingency control is to learn to notice these signals and to have a plan of action in place to cope with a crisis if it occurs.

TABLE 13.6	Examples of Financial Ratios

Net profit margin $\dfrac{112,000}{760,000} = 14.7\%$

Interpretation—Approximately 15 percent of sales is yielding profits. This percentage should be compared with industry (similar sports organizations) averages and examined over a period of several years. Declining or subpar percent could mean expenses are too high, prices are too low, or both.

Return on assets $\dfrac{112,000}{132,000} = 84.8\%$

Interpretation—This is a measure of the productivity of the assets in the sports organization. Once again, this number should be compared with similar sports organizations and examined over several years. If this number is declining, it may indicate that assets are not being used as effectively or efficiently as they were in previous years.

Inventory turnover $\dfrac{2,500,000}{100,000} = 25$ times

Interpretation—Inventory turnover is a measure of the number of times inventory is sold during a period of time. Assuming an average inventory of $100,000 (beginning inventory + ending inventory/2) the inventory (in this example, concessions) was sold 25 times. If this number is higher than the average for this type of sports organization, then ordering costs may be too high and stockouts may be occurring. If the number is lower, it may mean too much inventory is being stored, tying up money unnecessarily, and the products (in this case, food) may lack freshness.

Sports scandals and crises are not infrequent. Anyone who reads a newspaper sports section has observed situations that could lead to a public relations nightmare for a sports organization or individual athlete. More research is now being conducted on better understand the defining characteristics of scandal and attempting to quantify the magnitude of a specific scandal. Hughes and Shank found that media and corporate sponsors generally identified four consistent characteristics that make an event in athletics scandalous or not. These characteristics included an action that was either illegal or unethical, involved multiple parties over a sustained period of time, and whose impact affected the integrity of the sport with which they are associated.[23]

Recently *USA Today* published the top 25 sports scandals of all time. Table 13.7. presents the top ten scandals.[24]

Although crises such as these are unpredictable, it is useful to plan so the chosen response can be not only faster, but also more effective. A **crisis plan** should include the following:[25]

- Well-defined organizational response strategies
- Specific procedures that will lead to more efficient and effective response
- Steps that will deal effectively with potential media impact and will enhance image
- Efficient ways to deal with a variety of problems that could occur

Moreover, sports organizations may benefit from an informal and a formal crisis response plan. The key is that any crisis plan should offer priorities for proactive and reactive response under a variety of circumstances. It should have the capacity to both alert and calm people during an unexpected event that could have the potential for major consequences.

TABLE 13.7   Top 10 Sports Scandals

1. **Pete Rose**

   Baseball's all-time hits leader spent a lifetime as Charlie Hustle, in the good sense, but betting on the game as manager of the Cincinnati Reds cast that nickname in a different light.

2. **BALCO/steroids**

   In baseball it's difficult to think of the bulging home run records of the late 1990s and early 21st century without wondering how many would have been set without chemical enhancement.

3. **Ben Johnson**

   The 100 meters flew by in 9.79 seconds, a world record, but three days later the Canadian was stripped of the gold medal when he tested positive for an anabolic steroid in the 1988 Summer Olympics in Seoul. Carl Lewis was awarded the gold, and his 9.92 seconds became the world record.

4. **Tonya/Nancy**

   Forever linked, captivating a nation, the skating lives of Tonya Harding and Nancy Kerrigan diverged when Harding's camp, with her knowledge, carried out a plot to injure Kerrigan before the 1994 U.S. Figure Skating Championships.

5. **Olympic bribery**

   The seedy underbelly of hosting one of the most recognized international events was exposed when leaders of the 2002 Salt Lake City Olympic Committee were charged with bribing to secure the bid. The two main figures were acquitted; reforms came in the bid process.

6. **O.J.**

   An American sports icon, O.J. Simpson was accused of killing his ex-wife and her friend in June 1994 in Brentwood, California. The 1995 criminal trial ended in acquittal, but a subsequent civil suit found Simpson liable for compensatory damages.

7. **Skating judging**

   Into the subjective world of judging landed accusations of a fix in pairs skating in the 2002 Winter Games. Canadians Jamie Sale and David Pelletier skated flawlessly but lost the gold to Russians Elena Berezhnaya and Anton Sikharulidze, who had a major error. A French judge said she was "pressured" to vote for them. The result: two golds.

8. **Mike Tyson**

   From heavyweight champion of the world to being led away in handcuffs. The ups and downs of Tyson's life got no lower than when the boxer was sentenced to six years in prison for raping a Miss Black America contestant in 1991. Tyson, who denied the charge, served three years.

9. **SMU football**

   The NCAA leveled its first "death penalty" in 1987, citing "long-term abuses and a pattern of purposeful violations" of rules, such as a banned booster paying thousands to recruits. The team did not play in 1987. SMU canceled the 1988 season because of penalties.

10. **Danny Almonte**

    What could be more perfect than a perfect game in the Little League World Series? Except it was not perfect. Dominican Republic birth records revealed Almonte was 14, past the Little League limit of 12, when he pitched in 2001 for the Rolando Paulino All-Stars of the Bronx, New York. Third place? Forfeited.

Summary

Implementing and controlling the strategic sports marketing process is the emphasis of Chapter 13. After the planning phase of the strategic marketing process is completed, the implementation and control phases are considered. Implementation is described as an action step where strategic marketing plans are executed. Without the proper execution, the best plans in the world would be useless. To facilitate the implementation process, seven organizational design elements must be addressed. The organizational design elements include communication, staffing and skills, coordination, rewards, information, creativity, and budgeting. To begin, the organization must effectively communicate the plan and its rationale to all the members of the sports marketing team who will play a role in executing the plan. In terms of staffing and skills, there must be enough people and they must have the necessary skills and expertise to successfully implement the strategic marketing plan. Research has shown that the skills deemed most important for sports marketing managers include establishing a positive image for your sports organization, achieving sponsors' promotional goals, stimulating ticket sales, maximizing media exposure for events, athletes, and sponsors, and acquiring sponsors through personal contacts.

Coordination is another of the organizational design elements that influences implementation. Coordination involves determining the best structure for the organization to achieve the desired strategy. Research has shown the importance of good fit between structure and successful implementation. One way of coordinating people and tasks that has received considerable attention over the last decade is through total quality management (TQM). TQM philosophies are based on aligning the organizational structure to best meet the needs of the customers.

Another important organizational design element that affects implementation is the rewards structure of the sports organization. With proper pay and incentives, employees may be motivated to carry out the strategic plan. Some guidelines for designing effective rewards systems include linking rewards to the strategic plan, using a variety of incentives: link performance with rewards, give everyone the opportunity to be rewarded, and be willing to adapt the rewards system.

Information is one of the most essential elements of effective implementation. To aid in the gathering and dissemination of information for strategic decision making, organizations must design information systems. Before gathering information, consider who is going to need this information, for what purpose is the information needed, and when do they need it?

Fostering creativity, another organizational design element, is yet another important aspect of implementation. Creativity and innovation within the organization is called intrapreneurship or corporate entrepreneurship and is developed through education and training. To enhance employee creativity the creative process, consisting of four steps, is used by organizations. These steps include knowledge accumulation, idea generation, evaluation, and implementation. Efforts to encourage intrapreneurship are also enhanced by creating an organizational environment that cultivates such thinking.

The final organizational design element that has a direct impact on implementation is budgeting. Without proper monies, the strategic sports marketing plan cannot be properly implemented or carried out. Budgets must be secured for all marketing efforts within the larger organization. Once these monies are obtained, they must then be allocated within marketing to achieve specific marketing goals that have been prioritized.

After plans have been implemented, the control phase of the strategic sports marketing process is considered. Strategic control is defined as the critical evaluation of plans, activities, and results, thereby providing information for future action. In other words, the control phase explores how well the plan is meeting objectives and makes suggestions for adapting the plan to achieve the desired results. Three types of strategic control considered by sports marketers include planning assumptions control, process control, and contingency control.

Planning assumptions control asks whether the premises or assumptions used to develop the marketing plan are still valid. Two categories of assumptions that should receive special consideration from sports marketers are those concerned with the external contingencies and the sports industry. Because plans are typically developed by carefully considering the external environment and the sports industry, assumptions with respect to these two issues are critical.

Process control considers whether the plan and processes used to carry out the plan are being executed as desired. The key issue addressed by process control is whether the planning or implementation processes should be altered in light of events and actions that have occurred during the implementation of the plan. To make decisions about whether plans or the implementation process should be changed, sports organizations review milestones that have been set or monitor strategic thrusts. Milestones such as financial performance are more specific objectives that can be examined, while strategic thrust evaluates whether the organization is moving toward its intended goals.

Key Terms

- activity ratios, p. 420
- budgeting, p. 398
- communication, p. 398
- contingency control, p. 421
- control, p. 413
- coordination, p. 398
- creative process, p. 409
- creativity, p. 398
- crisis plan, p. 422

- financial analyses, p. 419
- implementation, p. 398
- information, p. 398
- leverage ratios, p. 420
- liquidity ratios, p. 420
- milestone review, p. 419
- monitoring strategic thrusts, p. 415
- planning assumptions control, p. 414

- process control, p. 415
- profitability ratios, p. 420
- ratio analysis, p. 420
- rewards, p. 398
- staffing and skills, p. 398
- strategic control, p. 413
- total quality management (TQM), p. 406

Review Questions

1. What are the organizational design elements that must be managed for effective implementation?
2. Why must there be a fit between the planning and implementation phases of the strategic sports marketing process?
3. What are some of the common ways of communicating with groups both inside and outside the sports organization?
4. What are the marketing-specific core competencies of the sports marketing manager?
5. Define TQM. What are the common characteristics of any TQM program? Why is it important for sports organizations to practice a TQM philosophy?
6. What are the guidelines for designing rewards systems?
7. What is intrapreneurship? What are the four steps in the creative process? How can sports organizations encourage intrapreneurship?
8. Define strategic control. What are the three types of strategic control that sports marketers must consider?
9. What two measures are typically used during process control?
10. How can we evaluate sponsorship effectiveness?
11. Describe the different financial ratios that can be calculated to assess whether a sports organization's financial objectives are being met.
12. What are the fundamental components of a crisis plan?

Exercises

1. Describe three sports organizations that have a strong leader who communicates well outside the sports organization. What are the common characteristics of these leaders, and why do these leaders communicate effectively?
2. How does the training that you are receiving complement the marketing-specific skills required of sports marketing managers?
3. Locate the organizational charts for the marketing department of two professional sports organizations. How will this structure facilitate or impede the implementation of their strategic marketing effort?
4. Design a rewards system to encourage intrapreneurship.
5. Discuss the last three major "crises" in sport (at any level). How did the organizations or individuals handle these crises?
6. Discuss how being the quarterback of a football team is similar to being a marketer responsible for implementing and controlling the strategic sports marketing process.
7. Interview three marketing managers who are responsible for sponsorship decisions in their organization. Determine how each evaluates the effectiveness of their sponsorship.

Internet Exercises

1. Browse the Web site of the Sporting Goods Manufacturers Association (www.sgma.com) and discuss how the information found on this site might be useful for developing a strategic marketing plan for the new IBL.
2. Find two Web sites that would provide sports marketing managers with information about whether their planning assumptions regarding the demographics of the U.S. population remain valid.
3. Find examples of three nonsports organizations that advertise on ESPN's Web site (www.espn.com). How might these companies evaluate the effectiveness of their Web-based advertising?

Endnotes

1. Turnkey Sports Poll, *Sports Business Journal,* November 13, 2006, p. 26, http://www.sportsbusinessjournal.com/index.cfm?fuseaction=search.show_article&articleId=52785&keyword=selecting%20a%20new%20commissioner/CEO.

2. Joe Logan, "LPGA's First Female Commissioner Rides Out Bumpy Start," *Buffalo News* (New York), July 20, 2006, D1.

3. A. K. Gupta and V. Govindarajan, "Build, Hold or Harvest: Converting Strategic Intentions into Reality," *Journal of Business Strategy* (Winter 1984), 41.

4. Peter Smolianov and Dr. David Shilbury, "An Investigation of Sport Marketing Competencies," *Sport Marketing Quarterly,* vol. 5, no. 4 (1996), 27–36.

5. A. D. Chandler, *Strategy and Structure* (Cambridge, MA: MIT Press, 1963).

6. L. Marlene Mawson, "Total Quality Management: Perspectives for Sport Managers," *Journal of Sport Management,* vol. 7 (1993), 101–106.

7. Harry Roberts and Bernard Sergesketter, *Quality Is Personal* (New York: Free Press, 1993).

8. George Easton and Sherry Jarrel, "The Effects of Total Quality Management on Corporate Performance: An Empirical Investigation," *Journal of Business,* vol. 71, no. 2, 253–261.

9. James Evans and William Lindsay, *The Management and Control of Quality,* 2nd ed. (St. Paul, MN: West, 1993).

10. Ibid.

11. "Pay for Performances: Why Footballers Are Not Remunerated Like Investment Bankers," *Financial Times* (London), January 27, p. 10.

12. "NHL Teams with IBM to Promote and Enhance Hockey Through New Alliance, NHL-ICE," www.issc2.boulder.ibm.com/telmedia/prnhl996.htm; "NHL-ICE: A Virtual Power Play," www.domino.www.ibm.com/ebusine...s/35E438D34E58CD4A852651E00639D54.

13. "Technology Driving the Pistons," http://www.sportandtechnology.com/news.php?pageId=0135#5.

14. John Lombardo, "Blazers First with Social Networking Site," *Sport Business Journal,* March 5, 2007, p. 3.

15. Russell Mitchell, "Masters of Innovation," *Business Week* (April 10, 1989), 58–63.

16. "Reebok and NHL to Unveil New Technologically Advanced Uniform System."

17. Noah Liberman, "Agencies Roll Out New Measurement Tools as Sponsors Seek to Justify Their Investments," *Sports Business Journal,* September 26, 2005, p. 23.

18. Lesa Ulkman, "Evaluating ROI of a Sponsorship Program," *Marketing News* (August 26, 1996), 5.

19. "And Now a Word from Our Sponsors." *Marketing Tools* (June 1995); www.demographics.com/publications/mt/95_mt/9506_mt/mt169.htm; John Burnett, Anil Menon, and Denise Scott, "Sports Marketing: A New Ball Game with Old Rules," *Journal of Advertising Research* (September–October 1993), 21–38.

20. "Sponsorship: Keeping an Eye on the Ball," *Marketing Week* (October 30, 2003), 43.

21. "Institute for Public Relations Releases First-Ever Guidelines for Measuring Importance of Internet Audience," *U.S. Newswire* (February 17, 2004).

22. Lesa Ulkman, "Evaluating ROI of a Sponsorship Program," *Marketing News* (August 26, 1996), 5.

23. S. Hughes and M. D. Shank, "Defining Scandal in Sport: Media and Corporate Sponsor Perspectives," *Sport Marketing Quarterly,* vol. 14, no. 4 (2005), 207–216.

24. Rachel Shuster, "Top 25 Sports Scandals," *USA Today,* July 9, 2007, B6.

25. "Defining Crisis and Crisis Planning," www.sports.mediachallenge.com\crisis\index.html#feature.

Appendix A

CAREER OPPORTUNITIES IN SPORTS MARKETING

Many of us have dreamed of becoming a professional athlete. Unfortunately, reality sets in rather quickly. We discover that we cannot throw a 90-mile-per-hour fastball or even touch the rim—much less slam-dunk. However, there are many other opportunities for careers in sports. In fact, there are a wide variety of sports careers in sports marketing. In this appendix, we will explore some of the career options in sports marketing and present some interview and resumé writing tips for landing that dream job. Finally, we will examine some additional sources of information on careers in sports marketing.

Before we look at some of the career alternatives in sports marketing, it is useful to think about how the concepts discussed in this text can be useful in your job search. As you know, the strategic marketing process begins by conducting a SWOT analysis. You should build a SWOT into your career planning. First, ask questions about your own strengths and weaknesses. You can be sure the organizations you interview with will be asking similar questions. Next, try to identify the opportunities that exist in the marketplace. What sports are hot? Where are the growth areas in sports marketing?

The next step of your strategic career search should be to gather information and conduct research on prospective employers. Research could be conducted by talking to people within the organization to gain a better understanding of the culture. In addition, observation might take place both before and certainly during the interview.

Next, you need to consider your target market. Do not apply for all of the sports marketing jobs in the world. Target the job opportunities based on location, type of position, and how the position or organization fits with your current and potential strengths. You also need to position yourself. Remember, careers in sports marketing are in demand and you need to find a way to market yourself and stand out from the competition.

The marketing mix variables also should be considered in your job search. The product, in this case, is you. You are the bundle of benefits that is being offered to the prospective organization. You should also enter into the strategic career search with some understanding of price. What is the value you attach to the service and expertise that you will provide? Are the salary and benefits package being offered a satisfactory exchange?

Your resumé, cover letter, interviewing skills, and ability to sell you are the elements of the promotion mix. These elements communicate something about you to prospective employers. Finally, the place element of the marketing mix is the location in which you are willing to work.

From this brief discussion, you can begin to understand that finding the right job for yourself in sports marketing can be done in a systematic, organized fashion. By using the basic principles of the strategic marketing process, you will be in a better position to land your dream job. Let us turn our attention to some of the job opportunities that exist in the field of sports marketing.

Job Opportunities in Sports Marketing

There are a wide variety of jobs in sports marketing that may be of interest to you. Here are just a few of the opportunities that exist. As you look through this section, pay attention to the sample advertisements and the qualifications that are stressed for each position. In addition, remember not to suffer from marketing myopia when you look for your first job. Have a broad perspective and think of your first job as an entrée into the sports industry.

Internships

Nearly 70 percent of sports marketing executives began their careers interning for a sports organization, and 90 percent of sports organizations offer some type of internship. Many sports marketing students believe they will secure high-paying, glamorous, executive-level positions upon completion of their degree. The truth is, jobs in sports marketing are so competitive that internships are usually the only route to gaining the experience needed for a permanent position. By working as an intern, you become familiar with the organization and learn about the sports industry. In turn, the organization learns about you and reduces its risk in hiring you for a permanent position.

Sample Advertisements

- **Sales and Marketing Manager**—Interns will assist the marketing department in the following areas: sponsorship fulfillment, lead qualification, sampling/couponing programs, health and fitness expo at the Los Angeles Convention Center, and race day festival. Must be hardworking, detail-oriented, friendly, energetic, computer-literate, and have good communication skills. Hours would be flexible to fit interns' schedule.

- **Marketing Intern**—We have an opening for a sports marketing intern to assist in marketing programs designed to facilitate the growth of our products and services. Ideal person should have a sports marketing or sports management background. Computer, organization, and strong communication skills are essential. Internet experience preferred.

Facilities Management

Whatever the sport, there must be a place to play. From brand-new multimillion-dollar sports complexes such as Nationals Stadium in Washington, D.C. to community centers used for recreational sports, facilities management is an important function. Although facilities management positions are more managerial in nature, they do include a strong marketing emphasis. For example, facilities managers are expected to perform public and community relations tasks, as well as have a strong promotion management background. Two of the largest facility management companies in the United States that you may want to explore are Global Spectrum (www.global-spectrum.com) and SMG (www.smgworld.com).

Sample Advertisements

- **Advertising and Public Relations Manager**—Opportunity for a creative, energetic, hands-on individual to develop and implement advertising and PR programs for an established golf course facility. Minimum of five years' experience in advertising, design, broadcast production, and media planning. Desktop experience a must. Internet experience a plus. Must be able to maximize preestablished budgets.
- **Facility Manager**—The Special Events Center is seeking candidates for the position of facility manager. Candidates should be sales and marketing driven with experience in event planning, marketing and promotions, and facility management. Bachelor's degree with three years' related experience required. Primary liaison between users and facility staff. Provide leadership in event planning, onsite event management, and customer service.

Professional Services

As the sports industry grows, the need for more and more business professionals in all areas is increasing. Today, sports careers are automatically associated with being a sports agent because of the Jerry McGuire "show me the money" phenomenon. However, professional services are also needed in sports law, advertising, accounting, information systems, marketing research, finance, and sports medicine. Having the appropriate educational background before attempting to secure sports industry experience is a must. Salaries for professional services positions vary greatly depending on the job type and responsibilities.

Sample Advertisements

- **Director of Special Olympics**—Seeking persons with excellent communication, fund raising, and management skills. Special Olympics is a year-round program of sports training and competition for children and adults with intellectual disabilities. Responsibilities include planning and organizing competitive events, training programs, public awareness campaigns, and fund-raising activities. Candidates for position must possess excellent communication and fund-raising skills as well as administrative, organizational, and volunteer management experience. Previous Special Olympics experience not required, but helpful.
- **Global Advertising/Merchandising Manager**—Multinational manufacturer of cycling components. Responsible for leading the creation and execution of global advertising; athlete and event sponsorship; media planning and communication; global product merchandising; global cost center management. This position requires an analytical thinker with excellent leadership and execution skills. A successful candidate is an MBA who has in-depth knowledge of ad strategy, planning, and production.

Health and Fitness Services

As the sports-participant market continues to grow, so will jobs in the health and fitness segment of the sports industry. Numerous jobs are available in management and sales for health clubs. Additionally, health and fitness counseling or instruction (personal trainer or aerobics instruction) represents another viable job market in health and fitness. Careers in sports training and sports medicine are also increasing. In addition to working for sports organizations as a trainer or physical therapist, a number of sports medicine clinics (usually affiliated with hospitals) are targeting the recreational participant and creating a host of new jobs in the prevention or rehabilitation of sports injuries.

Sample Advertisements

- **Director of Campus Recreation**—Major responsibilities: provide opportunities to enhance participant fitness, personal skills, and enjoyment for a variety of student recreational activities; supervise, coordinate, and evaluate the activities of the department; prepare operating and capital expenditure budgets; develop goals, objectives, policies, and procedures; and perform personnel administration within the department. Qualifications: Master's degree and three years' experience in recreation or a similar field, two years' experience in administrative position, and current CPR and first aid certification required.
- **Fitness Club Operations Director**—Oversee all pool and tennis associates. Duties include hiring, training, supervising, and reviewing the performance of staff; administering weekly payroll; designing employees

work schedules; and overseeing maintenance/cleanliness of facilities and inventory. Bachelor's degree; minimum two years' experience in athletic club/resort and one year in club management; basic knowledge of tennis, fitness and aquatics; excellent communication skills. Sales and marketing experience, with a strong member services background and experience developing/implementing member retention programs preferred.

Sports Associations

Nearly every sport has a governing body or association that is responsible for maintaining the integrity and furthering the efforts of the sport and its constituents. Examples of sports associations include Federation International Football Association (FIFA), National Sporting Goods Association (NSGA), United States Tennis Association (USTA), and the National Thoroughbred Racing Association (NTRA). Each sports association has executive directors, membership coordinators, and other jobs to help satisfy the members' needs.

Sample Advertisements

- **U.S. Tennis Association**—Assist director of marketing in sponsorship, donations, and ad sales. Professional tournament operations for one tournament and booth promotions at all Northern California tournaments.
- **Research Associate**—A nonprofit golf association. Duties include survey research, statistical analysis, report writing, and database management. Knowledge of SAS and related bachelor's degree a must. Proficiency required in mapping, spreadsheet, and word processing software. Position requires demonstrated experience in technical writing and good verbal communication skills. Knowledge of the golf industry a plus. Entry-level position.

Professional Teams and Leagues

Along with being a sports agent, the types of jobs most commonly associated with sports marketing are in the professional sports industry segment. Working as the director of marketing for one of the "big four" sports leagues (NBA, MLB, NHL, or NFL) or one of the major league teams requires extensive experience with a minor league franchise or college athletic program and a master's degree. Job responsibilities include sales, designing advertising campaigns to generate interest in the team, and supervision of game promotions and public relations.

Sample Advertisements

- **Assistant Marketing Director**—Develops season ticket campaign strategies, negotiates advertising and media tradeouts, directs promotion coordinator, sales representative. Master's degree preferred; bachelor's degree required, preferably in marketing. Excellent communication skills a must. Should have extensive experience in working with corporate sponsors and developing a client base to support athletic sales.
- **Advertising Sales**—Major sports league seeks account executive to sell print advertising for event publications. The ideal candidate will possess two to four years' consumer or trade publication sales experience; excellent written and verbal communication skills; a proven track record of increasing sales volume; the ability to work in a fast-paced environment; and the flexibility to travel.

College Athletic Programs

If your ultimate career objective is to secure a position with a professional team or league, college athletic departments are a great place to start. Nearly all Division I and Division II athletic programs have marketing, sales, and public relations functions. In fact, most of the larger Division I programs have an entire marketing department that is larger than most minor league franchises.

Sample Advertisements

- **Coordinator of the Goal Club**—Responsibilities include identifying, cultivating, soliciting, and stewarding donors together with managing special events and direct mail programs. Candidates must possess a bachelor's degree and two or three years of fund-raising experience.
- **Athletic Recruiting Coordinator**—Responsibilities include developing and organizing a vigorous recruiting program for eight sports within the guidelines of NCAA III, represent the athletics department at college fairs, and coordinate all recruiting activities with the admissions department.

Sporting Goods Industry

Sporting goods is a $60+ billion industry that is growing and presents career choices in all of the more traditional marketing or retailing functions. Opportunities include working for sporting goods manufacturers' (e.g., Nike, Adidas, Callaway, or Wilson) or retailers such as Dick's, Sports Authority, or Footlocker.

Sample Advertisements

- **Associate Buyer**—Lady Foot Locker is looking for a professional. To qualify you will need chain store buying experience. Sporting goods exposure a plus.
- **General Manager/Catalog Division**—An outdoor recreation equipment retailer in the burgeoning backpacking/mountaineering/climbing industry is looking for a hands-on GM with full responsibility for its fast-growing catalog division. Responsibilities include bottom-line profitability, strategic planning/execution, financial planning, marketing, prospecting, circulation and database management,

catalog development and production, purchasing and inventory control, and systems coordination. Qualifications include five-plus years' management in a mail-order operation.

Event Planning and Marketing

Rather than work for a specific team or league, some sports marketers pursue a career in events marketing. Major sporting events such as the World Series, All-Star games, or the Olympics do not happen without the careful planning of an events management organization. The largest and most well-known events management company is the International Management Group (IMG) (www.imgworld.com) with offices worldwide. Event marketers are responsible for promoting the event and selling and marketing sponsorships for the event.

Sample Advertisements

- **Event Management Leader**—A service management association serving the bowling industry. Candidates will have a bachelor's degree in business or hotel management along with a proven track record of professional event production.
- **Event Planner**—National sports marketing firm organizing sports leagues and special events for young professionals is seeking an entry-level candidate to assist with operations and promotions of sports leagues, parties, and special events. Should be sports minded, extremely outgoing, and organized for this very hands-on position.

Researching Companies

The previous section gives you a good idea of the types of job opportunities in sports marketing. Having considered your options, it is now time to get serious about finding that first job that will launch an exciting career. You will soon send out cover letters and resumés tailored to each position and organization. If they are not, the prospective employer will sense you have not done your homework. Your research efforts should include the following types of information: age of the organization, services or product lines, competitors within the industry, growth patterns of the organization and of the industry, reputation and corporate culture, number of employees, and financial situation.

Today, most of the organizational information can be obtained quickly and easily via the Internet. Other popular sources of industry and company information include the following: *Team Marketing Report's Inside the Ownership of Professional Sports Teams, Million Dollar Directory* (Dun & Bradstreet), *Standard and Poor's Register,* and *Ward's Business Directory of U.S. Private and Public Companies.*

Cover Letters and Resumés

Once you have researched prospective employers, you are ready to communicate with the organizations that you wish to pursue. Let us look at how to construct simple, yet persuasive, cover letters and resumés. Remember, these documents are within your complete control (think of this as an internal contingency); use this to your advantage and present yourself in the best possible light. Let us begin with the fundamentals of cover letter preparation.

Cover Letters

The major objective of any cover letter is to pique the interest of the prospective employer. First impressions are everything and the cover letter is the employer's first glimpse of you. There are a few basic guidelines that you can follow to make your cover letters more effective.

In the first paragraph, state the letter's purpose and how you found out about the position. Follow this with an overview of your most impressive job-related attributes such as skills, knowledge, and expertise. Obviously, the attributes you choose should relate to the position in mind. The third part of the cover letter should stem from all the research previously gathered on the organization. Show off your knowledge of the company and their current needs. Finally, let the organization know how you can help solve their current needs. Stress the fit between your background and values and the organization's culture.

Resumés

Now that your cover letter has been constructed, you are ready to begin work on an effective resumé. Here are seven tips for writing a resumé that are guaranteed to tell your story.

1. **Be Thorough**—A good resumé should give the employer an indication of your potential based on your previous accomplishments. Include things such as job-related skills, previous work experience, educational background, volunteer experiences, special achievements, and personal data.

   Activities that you might deem to be unimportant could provide a great deal of insight into your ability to succeed on the job. For example, how about the student that has coached a Little League team throughout his or her collegiate career? Some candidates might view this as totally unrelated to the job. However, wise candidates will see how this activity could be used to demonstrate unique aspects of their personality such as patience, leadership, and good organizational skills.

2. **Be Creative**—Most students are under the false impression that there is a right way and a wrong way to organize their resumé. In fact, most career development centers use a boilerplate format making every student's resumé standard and neglecting the job and the industry.

   All resumés should include topical areas such as job objectives, skills, knowledge, accomplishments, personal data, education, employment history, observations of superiors, and awards. Organizing and writing these sections is limited only by your imagination.

The most important thing to remember is that the format should reflect both you and the job you are seeking.

3. **Use Quotations**—A powerful tool that is not widely used in resumé preparation is the use of quotations. These quotes can be found in old performance evaluations or letters of recommendation. Here is an example of a quote that was used to reinforce the strength of an application.

> "Mr. Gamble has contributed in a positive manner to the success of the athletic department at WPU by organizing and implementing an effective game day promotional plan."
> —Melissa Luekke, promotions manager, athletic department, WPU.

Quotes like this can provide further evidence of your abilities while relieving you of having to toot your own horn.

4. **Make the Resumé Visually Appealing**—Looks are everything. In one study, 60 percent of employers indicated that they formed an opinion about the candidate on the basis of the resumé's appearance. The resumé that looks good will be given more consideration than one that does not. The resumé that is badly written and produced will be tossed, regardless of the applicant's qualifications. A few things to think about when designing your resumé include length (keep it to one page), paper (high-quality stock in white or off-white), spelling, grammar, and neatness (any error is unacceptable).

5. **Include a Career Objective**—Most employers consider the career objective to be the most important part of the resumé. Why? A specific career objective indicates that you know what you want in a job. This type of goal-directed behavior is what employers want to see in a candidate.

On the other hand, some resumé preparation experts strongly disagree with this line of reasoning. They argue that by placing an objective on your resumé, you are limiting the potential position. In other words, if you leave your options open, the employer will direct your resumé to the job that best suits your qualifications.

The best advice is to have multiple resumés prepared and ready to go with multiple career objectives. Most people have multiple career interests and do not have to settle for just one job. If you are truly practicing target marketing, you should have several different resumés ready. You should try to make the career objective sound like the description of the job you are targeting. Here is a sample career objective for a student who wishes to pursue a public/community relations position at a major university or professional sports franchise:

Public Relations Assistant—Interested in copy writing, editing, writing speeches and news releases, photography, graphics, etc. Desire experience on organization's internal and external publications. Good writing and speaking skills with communications background should assist in advancement to a management position within the athletic department of a major university or professional sports organization.

6. **Honesty Is the Best Policy**—Employers are checking prospective candidates' qualifications more than ever before, due to a wave of people falsifying their credentials. Obviously, deceiving the employer about what you have done, or what you are able to do, is no way to start a positive relationship.

7. **Spread the Word**—You should seek feedback and constructive criticism about your resumé by showing it to everyone you know. Ask for comments from other students, your professors, and career development specialists at school. In addition, you should circulate it among people in the sports industry. Resumé writing is a dynamic process that requires constant changes and improvement.

Interviewing

Most jobs in sports marketing require a high degree of interpersonal communication; therefore, the interview becomes a place to showcase your talents. Each person should have his or her own interview style, but here are some tips that should assist all job candidates with their interviewing skills.

1. **Be Mentally Prepared**—As with athletes, mental preparation is the name of the game for job seekers. Most job candidates do not come to the interview fully prepared. To get ready, you should have thoroughly researched the sports organization. Next, you need to learn as much as possible about the person or people who will be conducting the interview. Being mentally prepared means being able to ask intelligent questions. Naturally, the types of questions you ask will vary by the position of the interviewer. Here are just a few of the potential questions that you might ask of the personnel manager or human resource representative:

- What do employees like best about the company? What do employees like least about the company?
- How large is the department in which the opening exists? How is it organized?
- Why is this position open?
- How much travel would normally be expected?
- What type of training program does a new employee receive? What type of professional development programs are offered? Who conducts them?
- How often are performance reviews given and how are they conducted?

- How are raises and promotions determined? What is the salary range of the position?
- What are the employee benefits offered by the company?

Possible questions for your potential supervisor include:

- What are the major responsibilities of the department?
- What are the major responsibilities of the job?
- What would the new employee be expected to accomplish in the first six months or year of the job?
- What are the special projects now ongoing in the department? What are some that are coming in the future?
- How much contact with management is there? How much exposure?
- What is the path to management in this department? How long does it typically take to get there, and how long do people typically stay there?

Here are some questions that might be asked of would-be colleagues:

- What do you like most or least about working in this company? What do you like most or least about working in this department?
- Describe a typical workday.
- Do you feel free to express your ideas and concerns? Does everyone in this department?
- What are the possibilities here for professional growth and promotion?
- How much interaction is there with supervisors, colleagues, external customers? How much independent work is there?
- How long have you been with the company? How does it compare with other companies where you have worked?

2. **Be Physically Prepared**—Image is important to all organizations, and a large part of the image that you project is largely a function of your physical appearance. In other words, if you look the part, the chances of getting the job increase exponentially. The key to dressing for an interview is not only to be professionally dressed, but to convey an image that is consistent with the company and the position. An interview is not the time to redefine the meaning of professional dress. Make sure you feel comfortable in the clothes that you choose to wear to the interview. If you look good and feel good, you will undoubtedly convey these positive feelings throughout the interview.

3. **Practice Makes Perfect**—Many marketing experts have discussed the similarities between finding a job and personal selling. When you are job hunting, you are, in essence, marketing or selling yourself. If you were selling a product, you would strive to become as familiar as possible with that product. You would not only learn the positive features and benefits of the product, but understand the limitations of the product. In this case, you have to know everything the interviewer could conceivably ask about you. This should not be difficult, but you have to be prepared. The best way to prepare is through practice and repetition, so that you feel confident answering questions about yourself.

The following is a list of questions regarding school, work, and personal experiences that are often asked during the interview. The more you have thought about these questions prior to the interview, the better your responses. Questions pertaining to school experiences might include:

- Which courses did you like most? Why?
- Which courses did you like least? Why?
- Why did you choose your particular major?
- Why did you choose to go to the school you attended? What did you like most or least about this school?
- If you could start college again, what would you do differently?

Questions pertaining to work experiences might include:

- What did you like most or least about the job?
- What did you like most or least about your immediate supervisor?
- Why did you leave the job?
- What were your major accomplishments during this job?
- Of all the jobs you have had, which did you like the most and why? Of all the supervisors you have had, which did you like the most and why?

Questions pertaining to personal experiences might include:

- Of all the things that you have done, what would you consider to be your greatest accomplishment and why?
- What do you consider to be your major strengths? What do you consider to be your major weaknesses?
- What kind of person do you have the most difficulty dealing with? Assuming that you had to work with such a person, how would you do it?
- What do you think are the most valuable skills you would bring to the position for which you are applying?
- What are your short-term goals (within the next five years), and what are your long-term goals?

4. **Maintaining a Proper Balance**—A good interviewee will know when to talk and when to listen. Your job is to present a complete picture of yourself without dominating the conversation. The best strategy for success is adapting to the interviewer and following his or her lead. When you are answering questions, do not let your mouth get ahead of your mind. Take a

moment to think and construct your answers before rushing into a vague and senseless reply.

5. **The Interview Process Does Not End with the Interview**—After the interview be sure to write a letter expressing your thanks and desire for future consideration. It is a good idea to mention something in the body of the letter that will trigger the memory of the interviewer. Look for unique things that happened or were said during the interview and write about these. Too often, students neglect writing this simple letter and lose the opportunity to present their professionalism one more time.

Where to Look for Additional Information

Sports Career Books

Aspatore Books. *Career Insights: Presidents/GMs from the NFL, MLB, NHL and MLS on Achieving Personal and Professional Success: Landing a Job with a Sports Team* Boston: Aspatore Books, 2004).

Field, Shelly. *Career Opportunities in the Sports Industry* (Checkmark Books, 2004).

Fischer, David. *The 50 Coolest Jobs in Sports: Who Got Them, What They Do, and How Can You Get One!* (New York: Arco, 1997).

Floyd, Patricia A., and Allen, Beverly. *Careers in Health, Physical Education, and Sports* Ohio: Brooks/Cole 2003).

Heitzmann, William Ray. *Opportunities in Sports and Fitness Careers* (McGraw-Hill/Contemporary Books, 2003).

Holzhauer, Tom. *Sports Career Tips for Teens* (Bloomington, IN: AuthorHouse, 2006).

Menard, Valerie. *Careers in Sport* (Hockessin, DE: Mitchell Lane Publishers, 2001).

Stein, Mel. *How to Be a Sports Agent* (Oldcastle Publishing, 2006).

Sports Career Web sites

careerplanning.about.com/od/occupations/a/sports_industry.htm
www.jobsinsports.com/
www.jobs4sports.com/
www.onlinesports.com/pages/jobs.html
www.scottishsport.co.uk/business/jobs.htm
www.sgma.com/jobbankdisplaylistings.cfm
www.sportscareers.com
www.sportscareerfinder.com/
www.sportsdiversityrecruiting.com/
www.sportsmanagementworldwide.com/sportsjobstraining.asp
www.teammarketing.com/jobs.cfm
www.teamworkonline.com/
www.usgolfjobs.com/
www.wiscfoundation.org/
www.womensportsjobs.com/
www.workinsports.com/

General Career Preparation Books

Bennett, Scott. *The Elements of Resume Style: Essential Rules and Eye-Opening Advice for Writing Resumes and Cover Letters That Work* (AMACOM/American Management Association, 2005).

Hansen, Katherine, and Hansen, Randall. *Dynamic Cover Letters Revised* (Ten Speed Press, 2001).

Kador, John. *201 Best Questions to Ask on Your Interview* (McGraw-Hill, 2002).

Rosenberg, Arthur, and Hizer, David. *The Resume Handbook: How to Write Outstanding Resumes & Cover Letters for Every Situation* (Adams Media Corporation, 2003).

Whitcomb, Susan Britton. *Resume Magic: Trade Secrets of a Professional Resume Writer*, 3rd ed. (St. Paul, MN: JIST Publishing, 2006).

Appendix B

SPORTS MARKETING SITES OF INTEREST ON THE INTERNET

Category	URL	Annotation
Professional Sports	www.nba.com	Official site of the NBA
	www.nhl.com	Official site of the NHL
	www.nfl.com	Official site of the NFL
	www.mlb.com	Official site of MLB
	www.mlsnet.com	Official site of MLS
	www.wnba.com	Official site of the WNBA
	www.pga.com	Official site of PGA
	www.lpga.com	Official site of the LPGA
	www.nascar.com	Official site of NASCAR
	www.pba.org	Official site of PBA
	www.apttour.com	Official site of ATP
	www.minorleaguebaseball.com	Official site of Minor League Baseball
	www.formula1.com	Formula One Racing
	www.theahl.com	Official site of the AHL
International Sports	www.sportcal.com	Database of International Sports
	www.ausport.gov.au	Australian Sports Directory
	www.ismhome.com	Institute of Sport Management
	www.olympic.org	International Olympics Committee
	www.nbcolymics.com NBC	Olympic coverage
	www.paralympic.org	Paralympic information
	www.ontariohockeyleague.com	Official site of the OHL
	www.cfl.ca	Official site of the CFL
	www.uefa.com	Official site of UEFA
Sports Media	www.espn.go.com	ESPN
	www.cnsi.com	CNN and Sports Illustrated
	www.sportingnews.com	The Sporting News
	www.sportsnetwork.com	Sportsnetwork sports
Women in Sports	www.womenssportsfoundation.org	Women's Sports Foundation
	www.womenssportsnet.com	Women's Sports
	www.womenssportscareers.com	Women's Sports Careers
	www.aahperd.org/nagws	National Assoc. of Women in Sports
Careers in Sports	careerplanning.about.com/od/ occupations/a/sports_industry.htm	Job opportunities
	www.sportsmanagementworldwide. com/sportsjobstraining.asp	Job opportunities
	www.scottishsport.co.uk/business/ jobs.htm	Job opportunities
	www.workinsports.com/	Job opportunities
	www.teamworkonline.com/	Job opportunities
	www.wiscfoundation.org/	Job opportunities

Category	URL	Annotation
	www.sportscareers.com	Job opportunities
	www.sportsdiversityrecruiting.com/	Job opportunities
	www.womensportsjobs.com/	Job opportunities
	www.sportscareerfinder.com/	Job opportunities
	www.jobsinsports.com/	Job opportunities
	www.jobs4sports.com/	Job opportunities
	www.usgolfjobs.com/	Job opportunities
	www.sgma.com/jobbankdisplay listings.cfm	Job opportunities
	www.onlinesports.com/pages/jobs.html	Job opportunities
	www.teammarketing.com/jobs.cfm	Job opportunities
Sporting Goods Industry Info	www.sgma.com	Sporting Goods Manufacturing Assoc.
	www.americansportsdata.com	Sporting Goods Research
	www.sportinggoodsresearch.com	Sporting Goods Research
	www.nsga.org	National Sporting Goods Assoc.
	www.esports-report.com	E-Commerce in Sports
College Sports	www.ncaa.com	Official site of NCAA
Sports Marketing Industry info and Research	www.teammarketing.com	General Sports Marketing Info
	www.sportbusinessdaily.com	General Sports Marketing Info
	www.cjsm.com	Cyber Journal of Sports Marketing
	www.nasss.org	North American Society for Sociology of Sport
	www.sportseconomics.com	Sports Economics Info
	www.sportsbusinessjournal.com	The Sports Business Journal
	www.sportsbusinessnews.com	Sports Business News
	www.nassm.org	North American Society of Sport Management
	www.joycejulius.com	Joyce Julius Sponsorship
	www.sbrnet.com	Sport Business Research
Other Sports	www.soccerlinks.net	Soccer links
	www.flakezine.com	Snowboarding
	www.usa-gymnastics.org/links	Gymnastics
	www.churchilldowns.com	Horse racing
	www.thoroughbredtimes.com	Horse racing
	www.baseball-links.com	Baseball links
	www.baseballprospectus.com	Baseball
	www.tennis.com	Tennis links
	www.golflink.com	Golf links
	www.tenpin.org	Bowling links
	www.hockeyzoneplus.com	Hockey news and information
Indices	www.el.com/elinks/sports	Index for general sports links
	www.sports.yahoo.com	Index for general sports
	www.refdesk.com/sports.html	Index for general sports
	www.sportslinkcentral.com	Index for general sports
Educational Opportunities	www.nassm.com/InfoAbout/Sport MgmtPrograms	Colleges offering sports business

Glossary

activity ratios   Measure the sales productivity and utilization of assets.

advertising   Creating and maintaining brand awareness and brand loyalty.

advertising appeals   Telling why the consumer wants to purchase the sports product.

advertising budgeting   Budgeting methods stemming from the objectives the advertising is attempting to achieve.

advertising execution   The format of the advertising.

advertising objectives   Direct or indirect actions designed to inform, persuade, remind, and cause consumers in the target market to take action.

aesthetic value   One of Wann's 8 basic motives for watching sport: to appreciate the beauty of the performance and the pleasure of the art form.

affective component   The part of attitude based on feelings or emotional reactions.

agent   Intermediary whose primary responsibility is leveraging athletes' worth or determining their bargaining power.

AIO dimensions   Statements describing consumers' activities, interests, and opinions.

amateur sporting event   Sporting competition for athletes who do not receive compensation for playing the sport.

ambush marketing   A planned effort by an organization to associate itself indirectly with an event to gain some of the recognition and benefits associated with being an official sponsor.

antecedent states   Temporary physiological and mood states that a sports consumer brings to the participant situation.

arbitrary allocation   Setting a promotional budget without regard to other critical factors; allocating all the money the organization can afford.

assurance   The knowledge and courtesy of employees and their ability to convey trust and confidence.

athletic platform   For sponsorship, the choice of team, sport, event, athlete, or level of competition.

attitudes   Learned thoughts, feelings, and behaviors toward a given object.

attractiveness   Characteristics of personality, lifestyle, and intellect of the source (athlete) that lead the target audience to identify with him or her in some fashion.

availability of substitute products   As the number of substitute products increases, demand for the product will decrease.

awareness   Consumers' knowledge of a company's products and services, product lines, or corporate name.

behavioral component   The part of attitude based on actions.

behavioral learning   Concerned with how various stimuli elicit certain responses (feelings or behaviors) within an individual.

behavioral segmentation   Grouping consumers based on how much they purchase, how often they purchase, and how loyal they are to a product or service.

benefits   The goods or services consumers derive from a product.

benefits segmentation   Describing why consumers purchase a product or service or what problem the product or service solves for consumers.

brand awareness   Making consumers in the target market recognize and remember the brand name.

brand equity   The value that the brand contributes to a product in the marketplace.

brand image   Consumers' set of beliefs about a brand, which shape attitudes.

brand loyalty   A consistent preference or repeat purchase of one brand over all others in a product category.

brand mark   The element of a brand that cannot be spoken.

brand name   The element of the brand that can be vocalized.

branding   A name, design, symbol, or any combination that a sports organization or individual athlete uses to help differentiate its products from the competition.

branding process   Establishing brand awareness; developing and managing brand image; developing brand equity; and sustaining brand loyalty.

budgeting   Obtaining the resources necessary to achieve the marketing plan goals, and making allocation decisions among the marketing activities and functions.

buying influences   The various roles of individuals involved in the buying process.

classic   Type of product life cycle characterized by continuous stage of maturity.

coach's role   Acting as a guide for the salesperson making the sale.

cognitive component The part of attitude concerned with beliefs.

cognitive dissonance Experiencing doubts or anxiety about the wisdom of a decision.

cognitive learning Concerned with the ability to solve problems and use observation as a form of learning.

commercialization Final phase of the new product development process in which full-scale production and distribution of the product begins.

communication Allowing and encouraging an understanding of the marketing plan by all members of the marketing team; also, the process of establishing a commonness of thought between the sender and the receiver.

community involvement Community activities in which the sports organization sponsors public programs, requires time commitments from its employees, partially funds programs, provides personnel at no charge, and so on.

comparative advertisements Contrasting one sports product with another.

comparative messages Directly or indirectly comparing a sports product with one or more competing products in the promotional message.

competition The attempt all organizations make to serve similar customers; also, a threat that is thought to be reduced by sponsorship.

competitive objectives Those that are directly linked to final pricing decisions.

competitive parity Setting a promotional budget based on what competitors are spending.

concomitant variation The extent to which a cause and an effect vary together.

consumer demand The quantity of a sports product that consumers are willing to purchase at a given price.

consumer income Consumers' ability to pay the price of the product.

consumer pricing evaluation process Using consumers' expectations to determine acceptable price ranges.

consumer socialization Learning the skills, knowledge, and attitudes necessary to be a consumer.

consumer tastes Trends and desires of consumers.

contingency control Scanning the relevant environments for internal and external contingencies that could affect the marketing plan.

contingency framework for strategic sports marketing A model for predicting and strategically aligning the marketing process with internal and external contingencies.

continuous innovations Ongoing, commonplace changes such as minor alterations of a product or introduction of an imitation product.

continuous schedule Continually running the advertisement during the advertising period without any breaks.

control Phase of the strategic sports planning process model.

control phase The phase of the strategic sports marketing process of evaluating the response to plans to determine their effectiveness.

convenience sampling techniques Choosing sample data collection units that are easy to reach but may not be representative of the population of interest.

coordination The effective organization of people and their tasks to implement the marketing plan.

cost of information search Affects a consumer's determination of the acceptable price of a product.

costs Factors associated with producing, promoting, and distributing the sports product.

coupons Certificates that offer reductions in price to induce sales.

creative brief Tool used to guide the creative process toward a solution to serve the interests of the client and the customers.

creative decisions The advertising campaign.

creative process The source of innovative ideas; knowledge accumulation, incubation, idea generation, and evaluation and implementation; also, generating the ideas and concepts of the advertising.

creativity A distinctive way of looking at the world, seeking relationships between things that others have not seen.

credibility A source's perceived expertise and trustworthiness.

crisis plan Well-defined organizational procedures and strategies to deal with problems that could occur.

cross-sectional studies Surveys that describe the characteristics of a sample at one point in time.

cultural values Widely held beliefs that affirm what is desirable by members of a society.

culture The set of learned values, beliefs, language, traditions, and symbols shared by members of a society and passed down from generation to generation.

data collection techniques Methods of collecting information about a population of interest.

decision maker In the buying center, the person with the ultimate responsibility to accept or reject proposals.

decision-making process Problem recognition; information search; evaluation of alternatives; participation; and postparticipation evaluation.

decline Stage of product life cycle when sales are diminishing.

decoding The interpretation by the receiver of the message sent by the source.

demographic environment Population trends such as total number of consumers, age, ethnic background, geographic dispersion, and so on.

demographic factors Variables such as population, age, gender, education, occupation, ethnic background.

demographic segmentation Grouping consumers on the basis of demographic variables such as age, gender, ethnic background, or family life cycle.

dependent variable The variable to be explained, predicted, or measured.

developing the sports product Phase of the new product development process in which basic marketing decisions are made.

diffusion of innovation The rate at which new sports products spread throughout the marketplace.

dimensions of service quality Reliability, assurance, empathy, responsiveness, and tangibles.

direct competition Competition between sellers producing similar products and services.

direct objectives Designed to elicit a behavioral response from the target audience.

direct sponsorship objectives Objectives that have a short-term impact on consumption behavior and focus on increasing sales.

discontinuous innovations Products that are so new and original that they require major learning by consumers and new consumption and usage patterns.

diversion from everyday life One of Wann's 8 basic motives for watching sport: to "get away from it all."

dynamically continuous innovations New products that represent changes and improvements but do not strikingly change buying and usage patterns.

early adopters Consumers who adopt a new sports product after innovators and communicate its value to others.

early majority Consumers who adopt a sports product after being influenced by innovators and early adopters.

economic activity The flow of goods and services between producers and consumers.

economic buying role A position that governs final approval to buy and that can approve a sale even when others say no, and vice versa.

economic factors Controllable (such as the price of tickets) and uncontrollable (such as average income) factors that affect game attendance.

economic value One of Wann's 8 basic motives for watching sport: the potential for economic gains from gambling on sporting events.

economy The current economic cycle, which influences pricing decisions.

elastic demand The principle that small changes in price will produce large changes in quantity sold.

elements in the communications process Sender, encoding, message, medium, decoding, receiver, feedback, and noise.

emotional appeals Using such emotions as fear, humor, pleasure, or identification with a team or athlete in advertising.

emotional versus rational appeal Attempting to make consumers feel a certain way about a product, or providing information so consumers can make an analytical decision.

empathy The caring, individualized attention a firm provides to its customers.

encoding Translating the sender's thoughts or ideas into a message.

entertainment value One of Wann's 8 basic motives for watching sport: sports as a form of entertainment.

environmental scanning A firm's attempt to continually acquire information on events occurring outside the organization so it can identify and interpret potential trends.

esteem According to Maslow, the need for recognition and status.

estimating demand Studying consumer tastes, availability of substitute products, and consumers' income to determine the relationship between price and the amount of product sold.

ethnic background A type of market segmentation that groups consumers on the basis of having a common race, religion, or nationality.

eustress One of Wann's 8 basic motives for watching sport: because it is enjoyable and exciting to the senses.

evaluation of alternatives Considering and judging the acceptability of a range of criteria.

evaluative criteria The features and characteristics that a decision maker looks for.

even keel mode Characterized by a buyer that is experiencing no discrepancy between the current and ideal states.

evoked set Alternatives given the greatest consideration by a decision maker.

exchange A marketing transaction in which the buyer gives something of value to the seller in return for goods and services.

expected price range of substitute products The prices of competitive products have a major influence on what consumers deem an acceptable price.

experiential source An external information source.

experimentation Research in which one or more variables are manipulated while others are held constant; the results are then measured.

expertise The knowledge, skill, or special experience possessed by the source of a message.

extensive problem solving (or extended problem solving) Comprehensive information search and evaluation of many alternatives on many attributes.

external (or environmental) factors Factors beyond the control of the organization that influence pricing decisions, such as consumer demand, competition, legal issues, the economy, and technology.

external contingencies All influences outside the organization that can affect its strategic marketing process.

external source A personal, marketing, or experiential source of information.

facility aesthetics The exterior and interior appearance of a stadium, which can play a role in fan satisfaction and attendance.

fad Type of product life cycle characterized by accelerated sales and acceptance of the product by consumers followed by decline.

family influence The influence of family members on decisions.

family life cycle The concept describing how individuals progress through various life stages.

family ties One of Wann's 8 basic motives for watching sport: to foster family togetherness.

fan identification The personal commitment and emotional involvement customers have with a sports organization.

fan motivation factors Reasons why individuals are sports fans or sports consumers.

fear appeals Telling what negative consequences may occur if the sports product or service is not used or is used improperly.

feedback The response of a target audience to a message.

financial analysis Comparing present with past financial performance, and collecting and processing financial information that can be used to make strategic decisions.

fixed costs The sum of the producer's expenses that are stable and do not change with the quantity of the product consumed.

flighting schedule Advertising expenditures vary in some months and zero is spent in other months.

focus group A moderately structured discussion session with 8 to 10 people.

frequency The number of times an individual or household is exposed to the media vehicle.

game attractiveness A situational factor that varies from game to game; its perceived quality based on the skill level of participants.

gatekeepers In the buying center, those who control the flow of information to other members.

geodemographic segmentation Grouping consumers by combining geographic and demographic characteristics.

geographic segmentation Grouping consumers on the basis of local, regional, national, or international characteristics.

global events At the top of the Sports Event Pyramid; events that have the broadest international coverage and generate a great deal of interest among consumers.

goal A short-term purpose that is measurable and challenging, yet attainable and time specific.

goods Tangible, physical products that offer benefits to consumers.

growth Stage of product life cycle when sales increase.

growth mode Characterized by a buyer wanting to improve an already good situation.

habitual problem solving (or routinized problem solving) Limited information search and evaluation of alternatives; a decision becomes a habit or routine.

health appeals Telling why purchasing the product will be beneficial to consumers' health.

hierarchy of effects Steps of leading consumers to purchase the product: unawareness, awareness, knowledge, liking, preference, conviction, action.

idea generation Initial phase of the new product development process: consideration of any and all ideas.

idea screening Phase of the new product development process in which ideas are evaluated on how well they fit the organization's goals and consumer demand.

ideal customer A hypothetical customer model against which all potential customers can be evaluated to determine where salespeople should invest time and energy.

idle product capacity "Down time" in which a service provider is available but there is no demand.

image building A sponsoring organization associates itself and/or its brands with the positive images generated by the unique personality of the sporting event.

implementation Putting strategy into action; executing the plan.

implementation phase Phase of the strategic sports marketing process of deciding who will carry out the plans, when the plans will be executed, and how the plans will be executed.

income objectives Concerned with achieving maximum profits or simply organizational survival.

independent variable The variable that can be manipulated or altered in some way.

indirect competition Sports marketers' competition with all other forms of entertainment for the consumers' dollar.

indirect objectives Establishing prebehavioral responses to advertising that should lead to direct behavioral responses.

indirect sponsorship objectives Objectives that ultimately lead to the desired goal of enhancing sales: generating awareness, beating competition, reaching new target markets, building relationships, and improving image.

inelastic demand The principle that changes in price will have little or no impact on sales.

influencers In the buying center, those who can affect the decision-making process.

information Accurate information is essential for decision making and necessary in all phases of the strategic sports marketing process.

information search Seeking relevant information to resolve a problem.

innovations New sports or sports products.

innovators Consumers who are the first to adopt a new sports product as it enters the marketplace.

integrated marketing communications How a sports organization integrates and coordinates its promotional mix elements to deliver a unified message.

internal contingencies All influences within the organization that can affect its strategic marketing process.

internal factors Factors controlled by the organization, including other marketing mix elements, costs, and organizational objectives, which influence pricing decisions.

internal source Information recalled from memory, based on previous experience.

international events The second level of the Sports Event Pyramid; events that have a high level of interest in a broad but not global geographic region, or that are global in scope but have a lower level of interest in some of the countries reached.

introduction Initial stage of product life cycle when product is introduced in the marketplace.

judgment sample Study participants chosen subjectively based on the researcher's judgment that they will best fit the purpose of the study.

just noticeable difference (JND) The point at which consumers detect a difference between the original price and the adjusted price.

laggards Consumers who adopt a sports product in its declining stage.

late majority Consumers who adopt a sports product in its late stages of maturity.

law of demand The principle that consumers are more likely to purchase products at a lower price than a higher price.

layout accessibility Referring to whether spectators can move freely about a stadium.

learning A relatively permanent change in response tendency due to the effects of experience.

legal issues Factors such as legislation that affect pricing.

leverage ratios Measure the extent to which creditors finance the organization.

licensing A contractual agreement whereby a company may use another company's trademark in exchange for a royalty or fee; also, a practice whereby a sports marketer contracts with other companies to use a brand name, logo, symbol, or characters.

lifestyle advertisements Portraying the lifestyle of the desired target audience.

limited problem solving Internal and sometimes limited external information search and evaluation of a small number of alternatives on few criteria.

liquidity ratios Indicate the organization's ability to pay short-term obligations without selling assets.

local events The lowest level of the Sports Event Pyramid; events that have the narrowest geographic focus and attract a small segment of consumers who have a high level of interest.

logo *See* brand mark.

logotype *See* brand mark.

longitudinal study A study conducted over time in which several measurements are made.

love and belonging According to Maslow, the social need to be a respected part of a group.

macroeconomic elements The big picture, such as the national income.

majority fallacy Assuming that the largest group of consumers should always be selected as the target market.

market niche A very homogeneous group of consumers as reflected by their unique need.

market segmentation Identifying groups of consumers based on their common needs.

market selection decisions Decisions made to segment markets, choose targeted consumers, and position the sports product against the competition. These decisions that dictate the direction of the marketing mix.

marketing environment The competitive forces to be assessed in the strategic sports marketing process.

marketing mix Integrating sports products, pricing, promotion, and place to meet identified sport consumer needs.

marketing mix variables Factors that must be considered when determining the price of a sports product.

marketing myopia The practice of defining a business in terms of goods and services rather than in terms of the benefits sought by customers.

marketing orientation Understanding consumers' wants and needs and providing a product that meets those needs while achieving the organization's objectives.

marketing research The systematic process of collecting, analyzing, and reporting information to enhance decision making throughout the strategic sports marketing process.

marketing sources Information from advertisements, sales personnel, brochures, Web sites, and so on.

Maslow's hierarchy of needs A theory of human motivation based on classification of needs.

match-up hypothesis The more congruent the image of the endorser with the image of the product, the more effective the message.

mature adults, age 55-plus The mature market, about 21 percent of the U.S. population.

maturity Stage of product life cycle when sales stabilize.

media scheduling Continuous, flighting, pulsing, or seasonal types of advertising schedules.

media strategy Determining what medium or media mix will be most effective in reaching the desired target audience, and how this media should be schedules to meet advertising objectives.

medium A communications channel, such as television, radio, newspapers, signage, billboards, Web sites, and so on.

message The exact content of the words and symbols to be transmitted to the receiver.

message characteristics The attributes of the promotional message.

methodology Description of how a study is conducted.

microeconomic elements Smaller elements of the big picture, such as consumer income level.

milestone review Evaluating critical events, major allocations, achievements, or the passage of a certain amount of time as part of process control.

mob effect Also called the crowd effect; a situation in which consumers believe it is socially desirable to attend "special" sporting events, such as the World Series, and therefore they are willing to pay more than usual to be part of the crowd.

model of participant consumption behavior Model that tries to understand how consumers arrive at their decisions.

monitoring strategic thrusts Evaluating the strategic direction of the marketing plan.

motivation An internal force that directs behavior toward the fulfillment of needs.

national events In the Sports Event Pyramid, events that have an extremely high level of interest among consumers in a single country or two countries.

need for affiliation Fans' need to feel connected to the community and to identify with the team.

new product category entries Products that are new to the organization but not to the world.

new product development process Idea generation, idea screening, analysis of the concept, development of the product, test marketing, and commercialization.

new product success factors Characteristics of the product, the marketing mix, and the marketing environment that contribute to the success of the product.

new sports products Created because of competition for sports and entertainment dollars, emergence of new technologies, or changing consumer preferences; products that seek to satisfy the needs of a new market, enhance the quality of an existing product, or extend the number of product choices for current consumers.

new-to-the-world sports product A brand-new innovation that is new to the organization selling the product as well as to consumers purchasing or using the product.

niche marketing The process of carving out a relatively tiny part of a market that has a very special need not currently being filled.

noise Interference in the communications process.

nonprice competition Creating a unique sports product through the packaging, product design, promotion, distribution, or any marketing variable other than price.

nonprobability sampling The researcher chooses sample units subjectively so there is no way of ensuring that the sample represents the population of interest.

objective and task method Identifying promotional objectives, defining the communications tools and tasks needed to meet those objectives, and then adding up the costs of the planned activities.

objectives The long-range purposes of the organization that are not quantified or limited to a time period.

one-sided versus two-sided Messages that convey either just the positive or both the positive and negative features of the product.

organizational culture The shared values and assumptions of organizational members that shape an identity and establish preferred behaviors.

organizational objectives Factors that influence pricing decisions: income, sales, competition, and social concerns.

organizational strategies The means by which the organization achieves its objectives and marketing goals.

organized sporting events Sporting competitions that are sanctioned and controlled by an authority such as a league, association, or sanctioning body.

overconfident mode Characterized by a buyer that believes it is already exceeding its goals.

participant consumption behavior Actions performed when searching for, participating in, and evaluating the activities believed to satisfy needs.

participants Those who take part in a sport.

perceived risk The potential threats inherent in making the wrong decision.

percentage of sales Determining a standard percentage of promotional spending and applying this proportion to past or forecasted sales to arrive at the amount to be spent.

perception The complex process of selecting, organizing, and interpreting stimuli.

perception of value The acceptable price ranges for sports products, which varies from person to person and is based on perceived benefits.

perceptual maps Created through advanced marketing research techniques to examine product positioning.

perishability The ability to store or inventory "pure goods," whereby services are lost if not consumed.

personal selling A form of person-to-person communication in which a salesperson works with prospective buyers and attempts to influence their purchase needs in the direction of the company's products.

personal source Information from friends and family.

personal training Products that are produced to benefit participants in sports at all levels, including fitness centers, health services, sports camps, and instruction.

personality The set of consistent responses an individual makes to the environment.

physical environment Natural resources and other characteristics of the natural world that have an impact on sports marketing.

physical surroundings The location, weather, and physical aspects of the participation environment.

physiological needs According to Maslow, the biological needs to eat, drink, and meet other physiological needs, such as have some level of physical activity.

planning assumptions control Monitoring the validity of the assumptions used to develop the marketing plan.

planning phase Phase of the strategic sports marketing process of understanding sports consumers through marketing research and identifying their wants and needs.

pleasure or fun appeals Directed at target audiences that participate in or watch sports for fun, social interaction, or enjoyment.

political, legal, and regulatory environment Legal and political issues that affect sports and sports marketing.

P-O-P displays Point-of-purchase displays to attract consumers' attention to a product or retail display area.

positioning Fixing a sports entity in the minds of consumers in the target market.

postparticipation evaluation Evaluation of a decision after making it and participation has begun.

premiums Items given away with the sponsor's product as part of the sales promotion.

pretest A "trial run" for a questionnaire to determine if there are any problems in interpreting the questions.

price A statement of value for a sports product.

price adjustments Changing the price of a product to stimulate demand.

price competition Stimulating consumer demand by offering lower prices.

price discounts Incentives offered to buyers to stimulate demand or reward behaviors favorable to the seller.

price elasticity A measure of the extent to which consumer purchasing patterns are sensitive to fluctuations in price.

price increases Raising established prices to keep up with inflation or if there is excess demand for the product.

price inelasticity *See* price elasticity.

price reductions Efforts to enhance sales and achieve greater market share by lowering the original price.

primary data Information gathered for a specific research question.

primary reference group Those people, such as friends and coworkers, who have frequent contact with us and have the power to influence our decisions.

probability sampling Objective procedures in which sample units have a known and nonzero chance of being selected for a study and the accuracy of the results can be estimated.

problem definition Specifying the information needed to assist in either solving problems or identifying opportunities.

problem recognition The result of a discrepancy between a desired state and an actual state important enough to activate the decision-making process.

process control Measuring and evaluating the effects of actions that have already been taken to execute the marketing plan.

producers and intermediaries The manufacturers of sports products or the organizations that perform some function in the marketing of sports products.

product characteristics The important attributes or characteristics that, when taken together, create the total product.

product design The aesthetics, style, and function of a product.

product form Product variations within a category.

product life cycle Introduction, growth, maturity, and decline.

product line A group of products that are closely related because they satisfy a class of needs, are used together, are sold to the same customer groups, are distributed through the same type of outlets, or fall within a given price range.

product mix The total assortment of product lines that a sports organization sells.

product quality Consumers' perception of the performance, features, reliability, conformance, durability, serviceability, aesthetics, and perceived quality of a product.

product warranties Statements indicating the liability of the manufacturer for problems with the product.

professional sports Sporting competitions in which athletes receive compensation, commonly classified as major or minor league status.

profitability ratios Indicate how profitable the organization is during a period of time.

projective techniques Methods that allow respondents to project their feelings, beliefs, or motivations onto a relatively neutral stimulus.

promotion All forms of communication to consumers.

promotion mix elements The combination of tools available to sports marketers to communicate with the public: advertising, personal selling, sales promotion, public or community relations, and sponsorship.

promotional budgeting Determining the amount to spend on promotion based on maximizing the monies available.

promotional objectives Informing, persuading, and reminding the target audience.

promotional planning Identifying target market considerations; setting promotional objectives; determining the promotional budget; and developing the promotional mix.

psychographic segmentation Grouping consumers on the basis of a common lifestyle preference and personality.

psychological or internal factors Basic factors such as personality, motivation, learning, and perception that are unique to each individual and guide decision making.

public relations The element of the promotional mix that identifies, establishes, and maintains mutually beneficial relationships between the sports organization and the various publics on which its success or failure depends.

pull strategy Stimulating demand by consumers for the product so that channel members will provide it.

pulsing schedule Advertising expenditures may vary greatly, but some level of advertising is always taking place.

purchasers In the buying center, those responsible for negotiating contracts and formally carrying out the terms of the sponsorship.

push strategy Emphasizing channel intermediaries "pushing" the product through the channel of distribution to the final consumer.

quality dimension of goods A measure of how well a sporting goods product conforms to specifications and performs its function.

quantity discounts Rewarding buyers for purchasing large quantities of a product.

questionnaire design Specifying information requirements, deciding the method of administration, determining the content of questions, determining the form of response, deciding on question wording, designing the order of questions, designing the physical characteristics of the questionnaire, and modifying it according to pretest results.

quota sampling Choosing sample units on the basis of some control characteristic or characteristics of interest.

ratio analysis Computing financial ratios from income statements and balance sheets to evaluate the success of the marketing plan.

reach The number of people exposed to an advertisement in a given medium.

reaching new target markets A primary objective of sponsorship programs.

receiver The audience or object of a source's message.

reference groups Individuals who influence the information, attitudes, and behaviors of other group members.

regional events In the Sports Event Pyramid, events that have a narrow geographic focus but high interest levels in the region.

relationship marketing The process of creating, maintaining, and enhancing strong, value-laden relationships with customers and other stakeholders.

reliability The ability to perform promised service dependably and accurately.

reposition To change the image or perception of the sports entity in the minds of consumers in the target market.

research design The framework for a study that collects and analyzes data.

research objectives The various types of information needed to address a problem or opportunity.

research problem statement Definition of the problem to be solved or opportunity to be identified.

research proposal A written blueprint describing all the information needed to conduct and control a study.

response modes The various reactions of buyers in a sales situation.

responsiveness The willingness to help customers and provide prompt service.

rewards As part of an implementation plan, used to motivate behavior that supports the strategy.

roles Patterns of behavior expected by people in a given position.

safety needs According to Maslow, the need to be physically safe and to remain healthy.

sales funnel A model of organizing clients so that salespeople can allocate their efforts in the most efficient and effective manner.

sales objectives Concerned with maintaining or enhancing market share and encouraging sales growth.

sales promotions A variety of short-term promotional activities designed to stimulate immediate product demand.

sample A subset of the population of interest from which data are gathered to estimate some characteristic of the population.

sampling Inducing customers to try new products by giving away a product or putting on an exhibition game.

scientific advertisements Featuring the technological superiority of the advertised product or using research or scientific studies to support these claims.

scoreboard quality A dimension of the stadium that is sometimes seen as the focal point of the interior.

seasonal Type of product life cycle characterized by rise and fall of sales according to opening and closing dates of the sports season.

seasonal discounts Intended to stimulate demand in off-peak periods.

seating comfort Perceived comfort of the seating and the spacing of the seats relative to each other in a stadium.

secondary data Data that were collected earlier than when a study is conducted but that are still related to the research question.

selective attention A consumer's focus on a specific marketing stimulus based on personal needs and attitudes.

selective interpretation Consumers perceive things in ways that are consistent with their existing attitudes and values.

selective retention The tendency to remember only certain information.

self-actualization According to Maslow, the individual's need to fulfill personal life goals.

self-esteem enhancement One of Wann's 8 basic motives for watching sport: to enhance or maintain self-esteem through associating with a winning team.

separability The ability to separate the quality of a good from the quality of a service.

service quality The physical, interactive, and corporate dimensions of a product.

services Intangible, nonphysical products that offer benefits to consumers.

sex appeals Type of emotional appeal used in advertising.

sidedness Based on the nature of the information presented to the target audience; only positive features of the product, or both benefits and weaknesses.

signage A factor of the sportscape that affects spectators' enjoyment of the game experience.

simplified model of the consumer–supplier relationship A model of the sports industry consisting of three major elements: consumers, products, and suppliers of the products.

simulated test market Nontraditional test market approach in which respondents participate in a series of activities in a laboratory environment.

situational factors Factors that may affect a consumer's acceptable range of prices: presence or absence of time, usage situation, and social factors.

situational factors Temporary factors within a particular time or place that influence the participation decision-making process.

slice-of-life advertisements Showing an athlete or consumer in an everyday situation in which the consumer might be using the advertised product.

social class The homogeneous division of people in a society sharing similar values, lifestyles, and behaviors that can be hierarchically categorized.

social concerns A type of organizational objective that influences pricing.

social learning Watching others and learning from their actions.

social surroundings The effect of others on a participant during participation in an event.

socialization Learning the skills, knowledge, and attitudes necessary for participation.

socializing agents Direct and indirect influences on children.

socioeconomic segmentation Grouping consumers on the basis of social class and income.

sociological or external factors Influences outside an individual that affect the decision-making process.

source   Sender of a message; beginning of the communication process.

space allocation   A factor of the sportscape that affects spectators' enjoyment of the game experience.

spectators   Consumers who derive benefit from observing a sporting event.

sponsorship   Investing in a sports entity to support overall organizational objectives, marketing goals, and promotional strategies.

sponsorship budgeting methods   Determining competitive parity, arbitrary allocation, percentage of sales, and the objective and task method.

sponsorship evaluation   Process of determining the sponsorship decision by the buying center in the organization.

sponsorship objectives   Direct or indirect objectives linked to the promotional planning process.

sponsorship program   One element of the promotional strategy.

sport   A physical activity or entertainment.

sport involvement   the perceived interest in and personal importance of sports to an individual.

sport sponsorship acquisition   Model of the corporate sponsorship decision-making process by Arthur, Scott, and Woods.

sporting event   The primary product of the sports industry—the competition.

sporting goods   Tangible products that are manufactured, distributed, and marketed within the sports industry.

sports equipment manufacturers   Responsible for producing and sometimes marketing the sports equipment used by consumers.

Sports Event Pyramid   Shani and Sandler's model of categorizing various sponsorship opportunities.

sports information   News, statistics, schedules, and stories about sports.

sports involvement   The perceived interest in and personal importance of sports to an individual participating in a sport.

sports marketing   Applying marketing principles and processes to sports products and nonsports products associated with sports.

sports marketing mix   The coordinated set of product and service strategies, pricing decisions, and distribution issues that sports organizations use to meet marketing objectives and satisfy consumers' needs.

sports marketing research   *See* marketing research.

sports product   A good, a service, or any combination of the two designed to provide benefits to a sports spectator, participant, or sponsor.

sports product map   The intersection of the dimensions of goods–services and body–mind.

sports sponsorship   Exchanging money or product for the right to associate a name or product with a sporting event.

sportscape   The physical surroundings of the stadium that affect spectators' desire to stay at the stadium and to return to the stadium to watch future games.

stadium access   Issues such as availability of parking, ease of entering and exiting the parking areas, and location of parking relative to the stadium.

stadium factors   Variables such as newness of the stadium, stadium access, aesthetics of the stadium, seat comfort, and cleanliness of the stadium, which are all positively related to game attendance.

stadium signage   Onsite advertising.

staffing and skills   Having a leader who can champion and communicate the marketing strategy and a staff that cares about and can implement the strategy.

standardization   Receiving the same level of quality over repeat purchases.

strategic control   The critical evaluation of plans, activities, and results, providing information for future action.

strategic selling   A personal selling strategy that takes into account buying influences, red flags, response modes, win-results, the sales funnel, and the ideal customer profile.

strategic sports marketing process   The process of planning, implementing, and controlling marketing efforts to meet organizational goals and satisfy consumers' needs.

strategic windows   Limited periods of time during which the characteristics of a market and the competencies of a firm fit together and reduce the risks of a market opportunity.

sweepstakes and contests   Sales promotional tools; games of chance or luck and competitions that award prizes on the basis of contestants' skills and ability.

tangibility   The ability to see, feel, and touch the product.

tangibles   The physical facilities, equipment, and appearance of the service personnel.

target market considerations   Identifying the target market and planning promotions to reach that specific market.

target marketing   Choosing the market segment(s) that will allow an organization to most efficiently and effectively attain its marketing goals.

task definition   The reasons that occasion the need to participate in a sport, which affect the decision-making process.

TEAMQUAL   A survey instrument used to evaluate spectators' perceptions of service quality for an NBA team.

technical buying role   Screening potential suppliers on the basis of meeting or failing to meet a variety of technical specifications that have been determined in advance.

technology   A rapidly changing environmental influence on sports marketing; it can have an indirect or direct influence on pricing decisions.

test marketing   Phase of the new product development process in which a new product or service is offered to consumers in one or more limited geographic areas to determine their response and to gain information to direct the marketing strategy.

testimonials   Statements about the sports product given by endorsers.

time   A situational influence on the decision-making process.

Total Quality Management (TQM) An integrative management concept for continuously improving the quality of goods and services at all levels of the organization.

trademark Identifies that a sports organization has legally registered its brand name or brand mark and prevents others from using it.

trouble mode Characterized by a buyer experiencing difficulties.

trustworthiness The honesty and believability of the athlete endorser.

types of adopters Various groups of consumers likely to try a product at any given stage.

unitary demand The situation when price changes are offset exactly by changes in demand; price and demand are perfectly related.

unorganized sports The sporting activities people engage in that are not sanctioned or controlled by some external authority.

user buying role Making judgments about the potential impact of the product on job performance.

values Widely held beliefs that affirm what is desirable in a culture.

variable costs The sum of the producer's expenses that vary and change as a result of the quantity of the product being consumed.

vision An organization's long-term road map that creates its purpose and identity.

win-results In the strategic selling process, an objective result that gives one or more of the buying influences a personal win.

Photo Credits

Chapter 1
11 Ken Karp/Pearson Education/PH College; **20** National Baseball Hall of Fame and Museum

Chapter 2
36 Andy Clark Reuters/Corbis/Bettmann; **57** Guy Drayton/ Dorling Kindersley Media Library

Chapter 3
86 Getty Images, Inc.—PhotoDisc; **89** Alliance Research, Inc.

Chapter 4
107 Getty Images, Inc.—PhotoDisc; **109** Ed Bock/ CORBIS/Corbis/Bettmann; **118** Getty Images, Inc.— PhotoDisc; **130** Andy Crawford/Dorling Kindersley Media Library; **132** Getty Images, Inc.—PhotoDisc

Chapter 5
139 AP Wide World Photos; **141** Getty Images, Inc.— PhotoDisc

Chapter 6
169 Kevin Fleming/Corbis/Bettmann; **179** Getty Images, Inc.—PhotoDisc

Chapter 7
199 Getty Images, Inc.—PhotoDisc; Pearson Education Corporate Digital Archive

Chapter 8
244 Getty Images, Inc.—PhotoDisc

Chapter 9
277 AP Wide World Photos

Chapter 10
286 AP Wide World Photos; **303** AP Wide World Photos; **314** Getty Images

Chapter 11
356 Larry Fleming/Pearson Education/PH College

Chapter 12
366 Aldo Torelli/Getty Images Inc.—Stone Allstock; **390** Getty Images Inc.—PhotoDisc

Chapter 13
400 Jack Stohlman/LPGA Ladies Professional Golf Association; **419** AP Wide World Photos

Index